THE
ILLUSTRATED
ENCYCLOPAEDIA
—— OF ——
WALKING &
BACKPACKING

by Hugh Westacott

The Oxford Illustrated Press

For Joan, my lovely Texas rose.

ISBN 0 946609 81 0

Published by: The Oxford Illustrated Press, Haynes Publishing Group, Sparkford, Nr Yeovil, Somerset BA22 7JJ, England

Printed in England by: J.H. Haynes & Co Limited, Sparkford, Nr Yeovil, Somerset

British Library Cataloguing in Publication Data:
Westacott, H.D. (Hugh Douglas) *1932-*
    The illustrated encyclopaedia of walking.
    1. Recreations : Walking
    I. Title
    796.51

    ISBN 0-946609-81-0

Library of Congress Catalog Card Number:
90-84878

By the same author

Footpaths and Bridleways in Buckinghamshire No.1: Winslow Area, Footpath Publications, 1974.
Footpaths and Bridleways in Buckinghamshire No.2: Buckingham Area, Footpath Publications, 1975.
Walks around Buckingham and Winslow, Footpath Publications, 1976.
A Practical Guide to Walking the Devon South Coast Path, Footpath Publications, 1976.
Walks and Rides on Dartmoor, Footpath Publications, 1977.
A Practical Guide to Walking the Ridgeway Path, Footpath Publications, 4th Ed., 1978.
Discovering Walking, Shire Publications, 1979.
A Practical Guide to Walking the Dorset Coast Path, Footpath Publications, 1982.
The Devon South Coast Path (with Mark Richards), Penguin Books, 1982.
The Dorset Coast Path (with Mark Richards), Penguin Books, 1982.
The Ridgeway Path (with Mark Richards), Penguin Books, 1982.
The Brecon Beacons National Park (with Mark Richards), Penguin Books, 1983.
Dartmoor for Walkers and Riders (with Mark Richards), Penguin Books, 1983.
The North Downs Way (with Mark Richards), Penguin Books, 1983.
The Somerset and North Devon Coast Path (with Mark Richards), Penguin Books, 1983.
The Walker's Handbook, Oxford Illustrated Press, 3rd Ed., 1989.
Walking; an Annotated Bibliography, Footpath Publications, 1990.

CONTENTS

List of figures and illustrations   **iii**
Acknowledgements   **iv**
Introduction   **5**
Entries   **7**
Appendix of useful addresses   **165**
Index   **170**

LIST OF FIGURES

Figure 1: Aiming off   **8**
Figure 2: Attack point   **11**
Figure 3: Bench mark   **17**
Figure 4: Silva compass   **31**
Figure 5: How to stay on course   **31**
Figure 6: Plotting a course from the map   **32**
Figure 7: Making a fix   **32**
Figure 8: Model of hill showing contour lines   **33**
Figure 9: Typical contour shapes   **33**
Figure 10: Counting contours   **33**
Figure 11: Cornice   **34**
Figure 12: Crampons   **38**
Figure 13: Map of European international long-distance paths   **46**
Figure 14: Grid reference   **58**
Figure 15: Ice axe   **65**
Figure 16: Braking with an ice axe   **65**
Figure 17: Magnetic variation   **89**
Figure 18: Correcting for magnetic variation   **89**
Figure 19: Naismith's formula   **100**
Figure 20: National grid   **100**
Figure 21: Resections showing position of 'cocked hat'   **120**
Figure 22: Methods of crossing rivers   **122**
Figure 23: Romer   **123**
Figure 24: Route card   **123**
Figure 25: Scenic divisions of Scotland   **127**
Figure 26: Construction of sleeping bags   **131**
Figure 27: Snow shelters   **133**
Figure 28: Spiral search   **139**
Figure 29: Sweep search   **144**
Figure 30: Tranter's variations to Naismith's rule   **149**
Figure 31: Triangulation pillar   **150**
Figure 32: Directional waymarks   **156**
Figure 33: Non-directional waymark used on national trails by the Countryside
           Commission   **156**
Figure 34: Non-directional waymark used on national trails by the Countryside
           Commission for Scotland   **156**
Figure 35: Wind-chill scale   **159**
Figure 36: Map showing national parks, areas of outstanding natural beauty,
           national scenic areas, heritage coasts, national trails and other official
           long-distance paths   **163**

ACKNOWLEDGEMENTS

Most of the research for this book has been done in libraries, and I should like to express my appreciation to the Trustees of the British Library, and the Trustees of the Maddux Library of Trinity University, San Antonio, Texas for permission to use their extensive collections, and to the staff of both institutions for their assistance. I am also grateful to **Alan Mattingly**, Director of the **Ramblers' Association** for permission to use the Association's library, and to the librarian, Janice Samuel, for her help and advice.

A great many people have provided me with information and assistance essential to the writing of this book. My first duty is to thank my old friend **Walt Unsworth** of Cicerone Press whose splendid and scholarly book, *The Encyclopaedia of Mountaineering*, provided the inspiration to write this companion volume for walkers. Remarkably few subject entries occur in both books, and those that do are usually treated from different aspects. I have consulted Walt on several matters and he has always responded promptly with sage advice, although we are not yet entirely agreed on the definition of a **mountain**. Special thanks are also due to another friend, **Hamish M. Brown**, who not only lent me books from his library (greater love hath no bibliophile!), but offered advice and steered me into **paths** that I had not navigated before. I am particularly grateful to the **Long Distance Paths Advisory Service** for permission to use their database of **long-distance paths**.

Others who have provided information include Mrs Valerie Green of Chester City Library; Mr L. G. Meadowcroft of the **Peak and Northern Footpaths Society**; Mr E. Baker of the **Manchester Pedestrian Club**; the staff of the **Countryside Commission**; **Roger Smith**, Gerry Thompson of the **Camping & Outdoor Leisure Association**; the writer **Harry Griffin**; my erstwhile colleague Sylvia Pybus of Sheffield City Library; Mrs A. Heap of Leeds City Library; George Watkins, librarian of the **Fell and Rock Club**; Mr J. R. Elliott of Plymouth Library; Mr W. Bryant of the **Forest Ram-blers' Club**; **Hilary Bradt** of Bradt Publications; Miss P. A. Poppy, Mrs Wendy Fellingham and Mr K. W. Foster of the **Ordnance Survey**; **Roly Smith** of the **Peak National Park**; Andrew Dalby of the **Ramblers' Association**; Mr M. Maguire of Exeter Library; my old friend Roy Field, now County Librarian of Shropshire; Mrs J. Radford of Derbyshire County Library; Mr J. Brian Rhodes of the **Rucksack Club**; Peter Brown and the staff of Palmers Green Library; Mike Ellison and Jeff Vinter of the **Railway Ramblers**; and Mr R Sykes of the Sheffield Clarion Ramblers. Information has also been supplied by the secretaries of the organisations listed in the Appendix.

The greatest debt is owed to my dear wife, Joan, for her help, interest and encouragement, and especially for releasing her house-husband from some of his domestic and child-rearing duties that enabled him to research and write this book.

INTRODUCTION

The purpose of this book is to provide, in encyclopaedic form, a succinct distillation, suitable for expert and novice alike, of information about all aspects of walking and **backpacking**. It covers not only techniques and places to visit, but also the history of walking and its personalities (which are often surprisingly difficult to trace from other sources). If you want to know what the recommendations of the **Scott Committee** were, what **trespass** is, or what to look for when buying a **rucksack**, you will find the information in these pages. Similarly, although it is well known that **William Wordsworth** was an enthusiastic walker all his life, most of us have only the haziest understanding of the influence that he had on popularising pedestrian tours, and no conception at all of the large number of accounts of walking tours that were published in the eighteenth and nineteenth centuries. *The Illustrated Encyclopaedia of Walking and Backpacking* attempts to record as many of these accounts as I have been able to trace. My researches will also result in a detailed history of walking for pleasure, and a major series that will reissue some of the best accounts of early walking tours.

Each entry in the *Encyclopaedia* has been written on the assumption that the reader is without knowledge of the subject. The term is defined or described, and where appropriate, the historical background is given together with references to books where the subject may be pursued further. The reader is normally referred to the Appendix for addresses of organisations etc mentioned in the entries. An exception is made in the case of foreign countries where all addresses are given in the main entry to prevent the reader having to refer constantly to different parts of the Appendix.

The *Encyclopaedia* is arranged in one alphabetical sequence, but entries may be classified into the following main subject areas:

1 *Techniques* There are entries for such subjects as **backpacking**, **river crossing**, **scrambling** etc.

2 *Equipment* There are entries under such headings as **boots**, **compass**, **gaiters**, rucksack, **tent** etc. and non-technical descriptions of the properties of materials such as **Gore-Tex**, **Sympatex**, **wool** etc.

3 *Maps*, *mapping and* **navigation** There are entries under such headings as **aiming off**, **attack points**, **bench marks**, **contours**, **Landranger Maps**, **Ordnance Survey**, **scale**, **surveying** etc.

4 *Hazards* These include **avalanches**, **benightment**, **ice**, **lightning** etc.

5 *Places* Entries for places have been compiled on the following principles. In general, there are no entries for individual geographical features such as summits or **mountain** ranges in the British Isles, unless they are important for other reasons. Thus, there are entries for **Kinder Scout** and the **Pennines**, but not for the Rhinogs, Ben Nevis or Crossfell.

In **England** and **Wales** there are entries for every **national park**, **area of outstanding natural beauty**, and **national trail**. In **Scotland** there are entries for official **long-distance paths** and the names of the generally accepted regions that define walking areas (eg **Central Highlands**), all of which are listed in the entry for Scotland.

Northern Ireland and **Eire** are treated in the same way as Scotland. Wherever the term 'Ireland' is used, it refers either to events that occurred before the partition of the country brought about by the Government of Ireland Act, 1920, or to something that is applicable to both countries.

Other countries have brief entries which outline the main walking opportunities and list addresses from where further information may be obtained. In addition, there are entries for important mountain ranges that cross more than one country, and for which English-language guidebooks exist.

There are also definitions of some topographical terms and features such as **edge**, **hanging valley**, **lochan**, **mountain**, **tarn** etc.

6 *Persons* Entries for persons have been compiled on the following principles:
They must have walked primarily for pleasure and recreation, or have influenced walking by example, their deeds and work, by some political role, or by their writings. I have omitted pilgrims and explorers, even though many of them travelled on foot and probably enjoyed their experiences, as their inclusion would be spreading the net too wide, and the prime purpose of their travels was not for recreation. With some regret, I have also omitted individuals such as Peter Lockie and Gordon Davidson of Berghaus, Mike Parsons of Karrimor International, Bob Saunders of Robert Saunders, and Nick Brown of Nikwax who have designed excellent products for walkers.

a) Pre 1900
I have tried to include everybody who wrote books published in English about walking in the British Isles, as well as all Britons and a selection of north Americans who have written books about walking abroad. There are also entries for a few foreigners (eg **John Muir**) whose influence has extended to Britain. A few writers (eg **Edward Ward** and **William Kemp**) do not qualify according to the strict application of these criteria, but their works are so entertaining that I had to include them. There are also entries for all famous English-speaking people who are known to have walked for pleasure. This last group has caused me some heart-searching as it is inherently perverse to describe persons of the stature of **William Wordsworth**, **Samuel Taylor Coleridge**, Queen **Victoria**, **Edward VII** and Sir **Leslie Stephen** solely in terms of their contribution to walking. In such cases I have indicated their main sphere of importance. I have been very impressed with the quality of much of the material written during this period, and have included extracts from particularly interesting writers to give a flavour of their work and their attitude to walking.

It should be noted that before the coming of the motor car, most pedestrians used roads because they had a relatively good surface and avoided steep gradients, the fastest traffic they carried never exceeded sixteen kilometres per hour, and maps and accommodation were readily available. These factors, together with the absence of gates and **stiles**, permitted the covering of long distances at a very fast pace. Pedestrian tourists usually only took to **footpaths** when they could hire a guide.

b) Post 1900
The general principles outlined above apply, but I have had to be much more selective because of the quantity of material available. I have excluded the authors of worthless and ephemeral material (eg the lady novelist who wrote a book about walking in the nineteen thirties which stated that **maps** published by the Ordnance Survey had a **scale** of two inches to the mile, and that weight could be saved when **backpacking** by using a twig instead of a toothbrush). It has been necessary to be selective in describing those who occupied positions of power and influence in the walking world, and in general I have favoured those who wrote about the subject.

Contemporary writers and personalities have also been included with the majority of entries compiled from information supplied by themselves. Those who did not respond to my request for information have, in most cases, been omitted.

7 Legislation There are entries for important parliamentary acts and government reports (eg. **National Parks and Access to the Countryside Act, 1949** and the **Gosling Committee**) affecting walking, as well as for subjects controlled by legislation such as **bulls** and **ploughing**.

8 Organisations Clubs and societies that have influenced walking are included, and if they are extant their current address is given in the Appendix.

9 Serials Commercially published periodicals and magazines have entries, and if extant their address is given in the Appendix. A surprising number of walking and camping magazines were published in the years between the two world wars.

The entries are for the most part factual and neutral in tone, although I have, in a few instances, followed the example set by Dr Johnson in his *Dictionary*, and let my feelings show. Quite apart from being a useful and informative addition to the literature of walking and backpacking, the book should prove to be an entertaining bedside book for those who enjoy browsing through encyclopaedias of their favourite recreation. I am aware that I must have overlooked persons and subjects worthy of inclusion and welcome suggestions for additional entries in future editions of the book. Correspondence should be addressed to me in care of the publisher.

How to use this book
Both the entries and the index are arranged alphabetically on the 'nothing before something' principle rather than 'letter by letter' (ie **Mountain Walking Training Board** comes *before* **Mountaineer**). Words in **bold type** are cross-referenced and have an entry of their own. As with all encyclopaedias, *the index should be consulted first*. Here all references to the subject are listed and the page number of the main entry given in **bold type**. The index has been compiled very carefully; it is extremely detailed and contains references to material that does not have a main entry including place names and the authors and titles of books mentioned in the text. In a very few instances, the title of a book is underlined which indicates that I have not read it, but only seen it listed in some reasonably authoritative source. Here is an example of a typical index reference and main entry:

In the index under 'Chubb, Sir Lawrence' the following page numbers are given **28,** 48, 51, 102, 107. Page **28** is in **bold type** and here will be found the main entry:

Chubb, Sir **Lawrence** [Wensley] (1873-1948) The first Secretary of the **National Trust** (1895-6), from 1896-1948 the Secretary of the

Commons, Open Spaces and **Footpaths** Preservation Society (now the **Open Spaces Society**), joint founder of the **Federation of Rambling Clubs**, and a member of the **Forest Ramblers**. Chubb was the foremost authority on the complex problems of commons and **rights of way** and was frequently consulted by government departments and local authorities. He had the reputation of being a skilful and tactful negotiator, but was severely criticised by **Tom Stephenson** and the **Ramblers' Association** for what they felt was his behind-the-scenes sell-out to landowners' interests in private negotiations during the passage through the House of Commons of the **Access to the Mountains Act, 1939**. Chubb was the author of numerous articles and also a **footpath guide** entitled *Over the Sussex Downs*, 1935.

That part of his name in **bold type** is the name under which he wrote or was generally known, and the remainder of his full name is given in square brackets. Then follows the years of his birth and death in parentheses, and a description of his work and contribution to walking. The words in **bold type** have an entry of their own, thus for example, it is possible to look up the **Forest Ramblers**. Note that for consistency, cross-references are made for words that appear in book titles, and for both the singular and plural forms, although most entries actually appear in the singular. Chubb's book *Over the Sussex Downs* is underlined to indicate that I have not read it. Finally, in order to ensure that all the information about Chubb in the book has been exhausted, check the index references that are in plain type. An unfamiliar term in plain type should be checked in the index to discover whether it is defined in another entry.

A

Access The term used to describe the right to roam at will away from **rights of way** on uncultivated land. It is usually, though not universally, understood to apply to **mountain** and **moorland** beyond the limits of cultivation and **enclosure**. There is no legal right to roam at will on mountain and moorland, although the custom is hallowed by tradition in **Scotland**, and in some parts of **England** and **Wales**. In some instances, **access agreements** have been negotiated, but there are still large tracts of wild country in **England** and **Wales** where the walker is likely to be challenged if he departs from the **right of way**. The situation has been eased since the enactment of the **National Parks and Access to the Countryside Act, 1949**, but even now, with the passing of the **Wildlife and Countryside Act, 1981** and the **Countryside (Scotland) Act, 1967** there is no general right of access enshrined in law. Before legislation was enacted there was tremendous pressure for access to be granted to the grouse moors of **Kinder Scout**, and before the war organised mass trespassing took place.

It should be clearly understood that pasture is *not* uncultivated land; grass is a valuable crop.

Access agreements Agreements negotiated between landowners, local authorities and **national parks** that allow the public to use **permissive paths** across private land. In some cases the agreement allows the public to wander at will in **open country**.

Access to the Mountains Act, 1939 A number of parliamentary bills were introduced between 1884 and 1939 in an attempt to give the public greater **access** to **mountains** and **moorland**. The first was introduced after the **Macrae** case by **James Bryce**, MP for South Aberdeen, which was intended to grant the right of **access** to all uncultivated moorlands and mountains in **Scotland**, but it was defeated. In 1888, 1892 and 1898, Bryce made further attempts to introduce bills on the subject, but they were all defeated. His brother Annan Bryce introduced similar bills in 1900, 1906, 1908 and 1909, and nine more Bills were introduced before the outbreak of war. In 1939 the Access to the Mountains Act received the Royal Assent, but it was a very poor thing and many walkers regarded it as

worse than useless. In **England** and **Wales** the **National Parks and Access to the Countryside Act, 1949** enabled many disputed **paths** to be placed on the **definitive map** and greatly increased the opportunities for the public to enjoy mountains and moorland.

The best account of the history of the Access to the Mountains Act will be found in *Forbidden Land; the Struggle for Access to Mountain and Moorland*, by **Tom Stephenson** and edited by Ann Holt, Manchester University Press, 1989.

Acclimatisation The term used to describe the process of adapting the body to high altitudes. The amount of oxygen in the air decreases as height is gained which results in deeper and quicker breathing, increased heartbeat rate, and thickening of the blood . The effect varies markedly between individuals, but most walkers will probably notice a slight change in their breathing patterns at altitudes in excess of 3000 metres. Anyone venturing above this height should be aware of the problems of acclimatisation and allow time for their bodies to adjust. In extreme cases the walker may suffer from **mountain** sickness (also known as altitude sickness) which is characterised by headaches, nausea, loss of appetite, and sleeplessness. The final stage is pulmonary oedema and cerebral oedema in which water is not evacuated from the body and collects in the lungs and brain. This condition is frequently fatal unless oxygen and diuretics are administered and the patient is transferred to lower ground. Walkers are unlikely to suffer any ill effects among European mountains, but should be aware of the dangers when **trekking** in the **Andes** and the **Himalayas**. Further information may be found in *The Medical Handbook for **Mountaineers*** by Peter Steele, Constable, 2nd Ed., 1988.

Adventure and Environmental Awareness Group This organisation, founded in 1984, aims to encourage awareness, understanding and concern for the natural environment amongst those involved with education and recreation. It holds workshops and conferences, publishes discussion papers and develops links with outdoor leaders and environmentalists. *(For address see Appendix.)*

Agassiz, Louis A captain in the Royal Navy and Royal Marines and author of *A Journey to **Switzerland*** *and Pedestrian Tours in that Coun-*

try, 1833. He went by diligence with his wife, daughter and her governess, two infants, and two servants to Lausanne, and then went on four solitary pedestrian tours. The first half of the book describes the journey to Lausanne in which the gallant officer distinguished himself by resourcefully repulsing the attempts of coachmen and waiters to cheat him. The second half describes his walking tours in which he often used **footpaths**. The book is quite well written with good descriptions of scenery and the life of the countryside.

Aikin, Arthur (1773-1854) Chemist, scientific writer, friend of Joseph Priestley and author of *Journal of a Tour through North **Wales*** *and Part of Shropshire with Observations in Mineralogy and other Branches of Natural History,* 1797. The tour took place with his brother and a friend from 25th July to 22nd August 1796. During the course of their journey they ascended Snowdon and Cadair Idris. The author states his purpose thus: '*Mineralogy being one of the chief objects of this tour, it was necessary to perform it on foot; and from experience of its advantages over any other mode of travelling in this mountainous country, I would warmly recommend it to all whose strength will allow them to make use of it. On foot, a man feels perfectly at ease and independent; he may deviate from the road to climb any **mountain**, or descend to any torrent that attracts his notice; whereas on horseback in many cases this is impossible, and several of the most striking scenes can only be visited on foot.*

'*A **map** and **compass** are articles of the first necessity in traversing a country where the inhabitants are so thinly scattered, and the roads frequently so obscure that the course of the streams is generally the surest direction. The map that we made use of is a large nine sheet one published about three years ago by the late Mr Evans; it was painted on canvas, and folded up into single sheets for the convenience of carriage. Of this map it is not easy to speak too highly. Every turning of the road, every winding of every rivulet, is laid down with the most scrupulous exactness, and the plan of every mountain is given with such minute accuracy, that a person conversant with the forms of mountains may, by a bare inspection of the map, distinctly trace the course of the primitive, secondary, and limestone ridges through the whole of North Wales. Of this map an impression has lately been published of the reduced size of a single sheet, which will answer the purposes of most travellers as well as the larger one.*'

Aiming off A technique, originally developed in **orienteering**, used in **navigation** by walkers when traversing pathless countryside, or in poor visibility for finding a small object (eg a **stile**, a footbridge, or a junction of

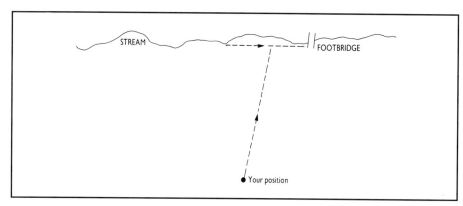

STREAM   FOOTBRIDGE

● Your position

Figure 1: Aiming off.

paths) in a linear feature (eg a wall, a fence, a river, a path etc) that crosses the route. Even an expert navigator walking on a **bearing** can only be accurate to within plus or minus 4° which, over 2 kilometres, amounts to an error of approximately 250 metres (see figure 1). Thus, when the linear feature was reached, the navigator would not know whether the object lay to his left or right. The secret of finding the object lies in selecting a bearing that the navigator knows will bring him on one side of the object of his search. Then he has only to make the appropriate turn to be certain of finding it.

Aiton, John (1797-1863) Doctor of Divinity, writer on religious subjects and the author of the pseudonymous *Eight Weeks in Germany; Comprising Narrative Descriptions and Directions for Economical Tourists* by 'The **Pedestrian**', 1842. Note that this tour was undertaken before the modern state of **Germany** was created, when 'Germany' denoted a geographical area with a cultural identity, rather than a country. Roughly half the book is taken up with an account of his journey by sea, train and coach to Scharnitz in the Austrian Tyrol where his walk commenced. His normal method of travel was to rise at dawn, walk sixteen or nineteen kilometres before breakfast, continue for a similar distance before lunch, and then to hire a conveyance in which he rode until the late afternoon, then he would continue walking until dinner. In this way he was able to cover sixty-five or eighty kilometres in a day. He climbed several **mountains** and visited the salt mines at Durrenberg, Salzburg, the Falls of Traun, Linz, Vienna, Prague, Toplitz, Kulm, Dresden, Leipzig, Berlin, Potsdam, Magdeburg and Hamburg from whence he returned by steamship to **England**.

The book is detailed enough to serve as a guidebook but there is no mention of **maps**. The author gives methods of travel, and advice on how to behave, in considerable detail. He took an umbrella, a **mackintosh** and a **knapsack** containing '*a complete change of apparel of a rather more gentlemanly cut and cast, coat, waistcoat and trowsers, a finer pair of shoes, with linens, flannels, and worsted* **socks**, *a portable dressing case, a small piece of soap; and in fact, every article requisite to a gentleman's comfort*'. Aiton gives vivid descriptions of the scenery and the customs of the countries through which he passed.

Allison, Lincoln (1952-) An outdoor journalist who described a series of walks which were published in *New Society* and the *Countryman* and collected as *A Journey Quite Different*, Manchester University Press, 1987. These essays are more than conventional accounts of walks as they contain a certain amount of social criticism.

Alpine Club The most prestigious mountaineering club in Britain which was founded in 1857 and was the model on which many national climbing clubs were based. It is first and foremost a climbing club although many of its members, such as Sir **Leslie Stephen**, were enthusiastic walkers, too.

The Club publishes *Alpine Journal* which was once issued quarterly but now appears annually. It is the successor to *Peaks, Passes and Glaciers*, a collection of papers issued in three volumes in 1859 and 1862. *Alpine Journal* is an invaluable source for the history of mountaineering, and to a much lesser extent, **mountain** walking, and the sustained quality of its writing, especially the earlier volumes, makes it a delight to read. The Club's library, which in certain circumstances may be used by non-members, contains an important collection of mountaineering literature. (*For address see Appendix.*)

Alps The highest and most extensive **mountain** range in Europe with a splendid network of **footpaths** that provide wonderful walking at all grades of difficulty. The Alps stretch in a huge arc from the Ligurian Alps on the Mediterranean coast in eastern **Italy**, through southeast **France**, encompass most of **Switzerland**, pass through the southern tip of **Germany**, include most of **Austria**, and end in Yugoslavia. Mont Blanc in **France** is the highest peak (4807 metres) and there are another 63 summits exceeding 4000 metres. There are numerous **glaciers** and many of the peaks are covered in permanent **snow**. Many peaks are accessible to walkers competent in the use of **ice axe** and **crampons**. English-language **footpath guides** are listed under each individual country.

Note that the term 'alp' is derived from the name given by the Swiss to the pastures on the side of the mountains, and only later applied by visitors to the actual mountain.

Early Alpine pedestrians include **Louis Agassiz**, **William Conway**, **J. J. Cowell**, **William Coxe**, **James Forbes**, **H. D Inglis**, **William Liddiard**, **W. W. Moore**, **John Ruskin**, **Thomas Noon Talfourd**, **Bayard Taylor**, **John Tyndall**, **Edward Whymper**, and **Alfred Wills**.

Andes A huge **mountain** range that extends for 6500 kilometres along the western seaboard of south America from Venezuela in the north through Columbia, Ecuador, Peru, Bolivia, Chile to Tierra del Fuego in Argentina in the south. There are several peaks rising to more than 6000 metres, including Aconcagua (6960 metres) in Argentina which is the highest summit in the western world. The most popular country for trekkers and **backpackers** is Peru, especially the Cordillera Blanca in the north which has several **long-distance paths** including the Inca **Trail**. Chile and Argentina have superb **national parks** which have waymarked trails. Sherpa Expeditions and Exodus Expeditions organise **treks** to the Andes (*for addresses see Appendix*).
Guides to Walking
Bradt, Hilary, ***Backpacking** and Trekking in Peru and Bolivia*, Bradt Publications, 5th Ed., 1989.
Bradt, Hilary, and others, *No Frills Guide to Backpacking in Venezuela*, Bradt Publications, 1989.

Brod, Charles, *Apus and Incas; A Cultural Walking and Trekking Guide to Cuzco*, Bradt Publications, 2nd Ed., 1987.

Hargreaves, Clare, Editor, *Backpacking in Chile and Argentina*, Bradt Publications, 2nd Ed., 1989.

Rachowiecki, Rob, *Climbing and Hiking in Ecuador*, Bradt Publications, 1989.

Anglesey An **area of outstanding natural beauty**, designated in 1966, which covers 215 square kilometres of this island off the coast of North **Wales**, forming part of the county of Gwynedd. The scenery may be described as a low plateau with a few isolated **hills** rising to just over 200 metres and containing a number of shallow valleys. The coastline is particularly attractive with a series of crescent-shaped bays and rocky headlands. There are fine views across to the **mountains** of Snowdonia, and the island has numerous prehistoric remains. (See figure 36 for a **map** showing the location of all AONBs in the United Kingdom.)
Maps
1:50000 **Landranger** sheet 114.
1:25000 **Pathfinder** sheets P733 (SH29/39/49), P734 (SH28/38), P735 (SH48/58), P750 (SH27/37), P751 (SH47/57), P752 (SH67), P768 (SH36/46), P769 (SH56).
Footpath Guide
Sale, Richard, *Best Walks in North Wales*, Constable, 1988.

Anorak Originally a weatherproof jacket with a hood attached made from skin or cloth used by Eskimos. It was first introduced into the United Kingdom as a waterproof hip-length garment with a hood, a short chest zip to allow the garment to be pulled over the head, a drawstring at the waist, and very often a kangaroo pocket across the chest. In the course of time the definition has become modified and is now often applied loosely to any hooded hip-length garment. Good quality waterproof anoraks designed for use in upland areas are suitable for use as shell **clothing**. The essential difference between an anorak and a **cagoule** is in the length of the skirt. In north America an anorak is usually called a parka.

Anthologies of walking A number of collections of accounts of walks have been published this century. They usually include actual walks as well as fictional accounts that appear in literature, but in order to include a sufficient number, some have stretched their brief to the utmost limit.

Bibliography
Baker, Ernest A., and Ross, Francis Edward, *The Voice of the **Mountains***, 1905.
Belloc, Hilaire, *The **Footpath** Way; an Anthology for Walkers*, 1911.
Macdonald, Hugh, *On Foot; an Anthology*, Oxford University Press, 1942.
Taplin, Kim, *The English **Path***, Boydell Press, 1979.

Antrim Coast and Glens An **area of outstanding natural beauty** in **Northern Ireland**, stretching from Larne to Ballycastle. It has a long coastline of black and white cliffs with a hinterland of high rough **moorland**, broken by beautiful **glens**, that provides excellent walking on heather and short grass. The northern tip joins the **Causeway Coast** AONB. (See figure 36 for a **map** showing the location of all AONBs in the United Kingdom.)

Maps 1:50000 **Ordnance Survey of Northern Ireland** sheets 5, 8, 9
Footpath Guides
Hamill, James, *North Ulster Walks Guide*, Appletree Press, 1988.
Rogers, R., *Irish Walks Guides North East; Down and Antrim*, Gill & Macmillan, 1980.

Aquatex A proprietary waterproof **poromeric fabric**, suitable for use in shell **clothing**, manufactured by Phipps-Faire Ltd. It uses a micro-porous membrane laminated to the shell fabric.

Areas of Outstanding Natural Beauty In **England** and **Wales**, under the provisions of the **National Parks and Access to the Countryside Act, 1949**, the Secretary of State for the Environment has the power to declare regions where the landscape is of outstanding value to be Areas of Outstanding

The Malvern Hills is just one of the 38 Areas of Outstanding Natural Beauty in Britain (photo © Ramblers' Association).

Natural Beauty (AONBs). Since 1968 the Secretary of State has been advised by the **Countryside Commission**. The designation confers on local authority planners the duty of ensuring that any development is sympathetic, and each AONB has a Joint Advisory Committee made up of representatives of local authorities and amenity groups.

Detailed descriptions of every AONB together with **maps**, the names of organisations forming the Joint Advisory Committee, and much other useful information is contained in *Directory of Areas of Outstanding Natural Beauty* published by the Countryside Commission, 1989 (it is in loose-leaf form and additional pages will be issued as new AONBs are designated). Information about a particular AONB may also be obtained from one of the county councils included in the designation. Maps published by the **Ordnance Survey** do not show the boundaries of AONBs (except as insets on the 1:250000 series), but they are delineated on the Royal Automobile Club *Regional Maps* series (1:190080). Several maps showing the boundaries of AONBs are available from the Publications Department of the Countryside Commission. These include monochrome dyeline or diazo prints of each AONB overprinted on outline editions of either 1:25000, 1:50000 or 1:63360 maps published by the Ordnance Survey, a 1:625000 and a 1:1250000 monochrome map published by the Ordnance Survey overprinted to show all **national parks**, areas of outstanding natural beauty, **long-distance paths**, **heritage coasts**, country parks and picnic sites, and a 1:2750000 coloured map showing all protected areas in the United kingdom.

The following list of the 38 AONBs designated as at 1st January, 1990 cover approximately 13% of the land in England and Wales: **Anglesey**, **Arnside and Silverdale**, **Cannock Chase**, **Chichester Harbour**, **Chilterns**, **Clwydian Range**, **Cornwall**, **Cotswolds**, **Cranborne Chase and West Wiltshire Downs**, **Dedham Vale**, **Dorset**, **East Devon**, **East Hampshire**, **Forest of Bowland**, **Gower**, **High Weald**, **Howardian Hills**, **Isle of Wight**, **Isles of Scilly**, **Kent Downs**, **Lincolnshire Wolds**, **Lleyn**, **Malvern Hills**, **Mendip Hills**, **Norfolk Coast**, **North Devon**, **North Pennines**, **North Wessex Downs**, **Northumberland Coast**, **Quantock Hills**, **Shropshire Hills**, **Solway Coast**, **South Devon**, **South Hampshire Coast**, **Suffolk Coast and Heaths**, **Surrey Hills**, **Sussex Downs**, and

Wye Valley. Other areas being considered for designation are the Berwyn **Mountains**, the Blackdown **Hills**, the Nidderdale Moors, and the Tamar and Tavy Valleys.

In **Northern Ireland**, under the provisions of the Amenity Lands Act, 1965 and the Nature Conservation and Amenity Lands Order (Northern Ireland), 1985 the following Areas of Outstanding Natural Beauty have been designated by the Department of the Environment for Northern Ireland (*for address see Appendix*): **Antrim Coast and Glens**, **Causeway Coast**, **Lagan Valley**, **Lecale Coast**, **Mourne**, **North Derry**, **South Armagh**, **Sperrin**, and **Strangford Lough**,

There are no areas of outstanding natural beauty in **Scotland** because there is no relevant legislation, although in certain respects **national scenic areas** fulfil a similar purpose.

Figure 36 is a map showing the approximate location of all AONBs in the United Kingdom.

Arête From the French meaning an ear of corn, a fish-bone or spine, and now used by walkers and **mountaineers** to describe a steep-sided rocky ridge. From a distance an arête often looks intimidating and the walker can be forgiven for wondering whether the crossing will be possible without the use of a rope. In practice, most arêtes prove to be wider than anticipated, and can be crossed easily in good conditions by experienced walkers. Occasionally, as in the Cuillins on **Skye** and on Tryfan in the **Snowdonia National Park**, there are needles, teeth or buttresses on the arête which provide serious obstacles that may require the use of **scrambling** or even rock-climbing skills. Among the best known British arêtes are Striding Edge in the **Lake District National Park** and Carn Mor Dearg on the northern flank of Ben Nevis, both of which can be crossed by competent walkers; Crib Goch in the **Snowdonia National Park** and Aonach Eagach, **Glen** Coe require scrambling skills; and the magnificent eleven-kilometre arête that links eleven **mountains** in the Black Cuillin of Skye is only fully accessible to competent climbers, although walkers with good scrambling skills can walk sections of the route. It should be noted that arêtes should only be attempted by walkers when conditions are good. In foul weather, and especially when covered in **ice** and **snow**, they are formidable obstacles that require the climbing skills of experienced **mountaineers**.

Arnside and Silverdale An **area of outstanding natural beauty**, designated by the Secretary of State for the Environment on the advice of the **Countryside Commission** in 1972, situated on the north-east shore of Morecambe Bay on the southern tip of the **Lake District National Park** in the counties of Cumbria and Lancashire. It is limestone country with **hills** up to 150 metres high giving splendid views over Morecambe Bay and to the **mountains** of the Lake District. The particular charm of this 75 square kilometre AONB lies in its miniature landscape. (See figure 36 for a **map** showing the location of all AONBs in the United Kingdom.)
Maps
1:50000 **Landranger** sheet 97.
1:25000 **Pathfinder** sheets P627 (SD48/58), P636 (SD37/47), P637 (SD57).
Footpath Guide
Evans, R. Brian, *Walks in the Silverdale/Arnside AONB*, Cicerone Press, 1986.

Ashton, Steve (ie John Harold Stephen Ashton 1954-) Walker, climber, photographer, outdoor journalist and author of several books on walking, climbing and the outdoors. He has worked in the outdoor retail trade and as an outdoor pursuits instructor.
Publications about Walking
Scrambles in Snowdonia, Cicerone Press, 1980.
Ridges *of Snowdonia*, Cicerone Press, 1985.
Hill Walking and **Scrambling**, Crowood Press, 1987.
Hill Walking in Snowdonia, Cicerone Press, 1988.
Also contributed to: Edwards, Mike and Anne-Marie, Editors, *The Family Outdoor Book*, Arcady Books, 1984.
Wilson, Ken, and **Gilbert, Richard**, *Wild Walks;* **Mountain**, **Moorland** and *Coastal Walks in Britain and Ireland*, Diadem books, 1988.
Reynolds, Kev, Editor, *The Mountains of Europe*, Oxford Illustrated Press, 1989.

Association for the Protection of Rural Scotland Founded in 1926, this Association aims to help keep rural Scotland a desirable place. It encourages appropriate development to keep people in jobs and advises on planning matters, restores and records historic bridges, and gives environmental improvement and building awards. It publishes a newsletter and **Rights of Way** *in Scotland: a Directory of Sources of Information* (the latter publication is a most useful guide to the registers and records kept by local authorities). (*For address see Appendix*.)

Association of Countryside Rangers The Association was founded in 1966 and is now one of the most representative bodies of countryside management staff in Britain. It seeks to promote good professional practice in the **ranger** service and provides a forum for the exchange of ideas and common problems. Membership is open to rangers and wardens employed in **national parks**, **areas of outstanding natural beauty**, nature reserves, **heritage coasts**, country parks, the **National Trust**, the urban fringe and the wider countryside. Its official journal is *The Ranger*. (*For address see Appendix.*)

Association of Heads of Outdoor Centres The Association (formerly the Association of Wardens of **Mountain** Centres) is the professional body that looks after the interests of heads of outdoor centres. It aims to encourage all-round personal development through residential experience and the use of the outdoors; and to develop, establish and maintain good safe practice in outdoor activities. (*For address see Appendix.*)

Association of Mountaineering Instructors The organisation, founded in 1990, that looks after the interests of the five hundred instructors who have registered with the **British Mountaineering Council** or the Scottish Mountain Leader Training Board since the introduction of the Mountaineering Instructor's Certificate. (*For address see Appendix*).

Association of National Park Officers The Association is the professional body that looks after the interests of **national park** officers. It aims to promote the study and understanding of national parks in **England** and **Wales**, their conservation and effective management, and is the professional association of national park officers. (*For address see Appendix.*)

Atlas Mountains A significant **mountain** range in northwest Africa that runs for 1600 kilometres across Algeria, Tunisia, and Morocco. The main area of interest to walkers is the High Atlas in Morocco which forms a barrier between the desert south and the rest of the country. Djbel Toubkal, 4176 metres, to the south of Marrakech is the highest summit in north Africa. There are good opportunities for **trekking**, either with a group, or independently, with the most popular destinations being Asni and Imlil, from where walks and **treks** can be made at all seasons of the year, and the Toubkal **Trail**. In summer, treks over the high **passes** are made with mules. **Maps** are difficult to obtain but those for Toubkal are stocked by Cordee and Edward Stanford Ltd. Tour companies that organise treks to the Atlas include Explore Worldwide, Sherpa Expeditions, and Exodus. (*The addresses of map retailers and tour companies will be found in the Appendix.*)

Guides to Walking

Brown, Hamish M., *The Great Walking Adventure*, Oxford Illustrated Press, 1986.

Crowther, Geoff, and Finlay, Hugh, *Morocco, Algeria and Tunisia; a Travel Survival Kit*, Lonely Planet, 1989.

Ellingham, Mark, and McVeigh, Shaun, *The Rough Guide to Morocco*, Harrap in association with Colombus, 1988.

Smith, Karl, *The Atlas Mountains*, Cicerone Press, 1989.

Attack point A useful technique used in **navigation**, pioneered in the sport of **orienteering**, which involves aiming for a large object (the attack point) located near a small object which is the ultimate objective. For example, the navigator has to find, in poor visibility, a small **mountain** refuge 3 kilometres distant by walking on a compass **bearing**. Even an expert cannot navigate with an error of less than plus or minus 4° which, over 3 kilometres, amounts to approximately 400 metres (see figure 2) so it is necessary to find a large object nearby (tarn, plantation etc)

Figure 2: Attack point.

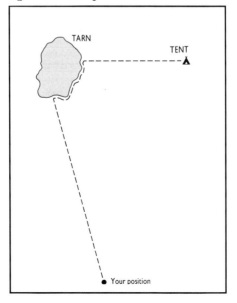

which can be reached in confidence. In the example shown in figure 2 there is a large conifer plantation located one kilometre from the **hut** and the navigator will make for this attack point in the first instance. Then a new bearing will be taken from the plantation to the refuge, and by using a combination of **pace counting** and a **spiral search** the refuge will be found. If an error is made, the navigator can return to the attack point and try again. If a journey of several kilometres has to be undertaken in poor visibility, it is helpful to identify a sequence of attack points and navigate from one to the other. This method usually involves a longer journey but almost always saves time, and obviates the risk of getting lost.

Austen, Jane (1775-1817) A novelist who chronicled the minutiae of English middle-class country life in a series of unsurpassed comedies of manners. She led an unexceptional life as the unmarried daughter of a clergyman, and her main pleasures were reading, writing, and walking in the countryside around Bath, and Steventon and Chawton in Hampshire. Her novels contain many references to country walks.

A useful and interesting **footpath guide** that explores her limited world is *In the Steps of Jane Austen; Town and Country Walks* by Anne-Marie Edwards, Arcady Books, 2nd Ed., 1985.

Austin, Alexander Berry The author of a charming book *In Your Stride*, 1931 which describes the author's walks built round the theme of the months of the year. It is not a **footpath guide**.

Australia The scenery and climate of Australia is very varied but it includes large areas of arid country and several **mountain** ranges. The emptiness of Australia, sixteen million people in a country almost as large as the **United States**, could hardly provide a greater contrast to our over-crowded island. There are several **long-distance paths** including the Great North Walk (250 kilometres through New South Wales from Sydney Harbour to Newcastle); the Hume and Hovel Track (600 kilometres from the Murray River through Victoria to Melbourne); and the Australian National **Trail**, which claims to be the world's longest continuous designated **path** (5000 kilometres from Cooktown, Queensland to Healesville, Victoria).

Backpacking is known in Australia as bushwalking and requires skills unknown to the

Denuded hills in Queenstown, Tasmania (photo © Australian Tourist Commission).

British **backpacker**, including the ability to read signs that denote the presence of underground water. There is no national organisation of bushwalkers but a number operate at state level and these have been listed below together with the state addresses of the **National Parks** and Wildlife Service.

A useful publisher of **footpath guides** is the Hill of Content Publishing Company Pty Ltd, 86 Bourke Street, Melbourne, Victoria 3000.

Useful Addresses
Australian Tourist Commission, Heathcote House, 20 Savile Row, London W1X 1AP. Tel. 071-434-4371.
Australian High Commission, Australia House, The Strand, London WC2B 4LA. Tel. 071-379-4334.

The reference library is open to the public and contains a collection of books and materials about Australia, including the Australian National Bibliography which is a useful source of information about footpath guides.
*National **Map** Survey*: Division of National Mapping, PO Box 31, Belconnen, ACT 2616.
National Survey Maps: 1:50000 (in progress).

Maps and guides are available from the following state addresses:
New South Wales: National Parks and Wildlife Service, Bridge Street, Hurstville, NSW 2220.
New South Wales Federation of Bushwalking Clubs, GPO Box 2090, Sydney, NSW 2001.
Queensland: National Parks and Wildlife Service, MLC Centre, 239 George Street, Brisbane, Qld 4000.
Queensland Federation of Bushwalking Clubs, GPO Box 1573, Brisbane, Qld 40001.
South Australia: National Parks and Wildlife Service, 55 Grenfell Street, Adelaide, SA 5000.
Adelaide Bushwalkers Inc, PO Box 178, Unley, SA 5061.
Tasmania: National Parks and Wildlife Service, 134 Manquarie, Hobart, Tas 7000.
Hobart Walking Club, GPO Box 753 H, Hobart, Tas 70001.
Victoria: National Parks and Wildlife Service, 240 Victoria Parade, East Melbourne, Vic 3002.
Federation of Victorian Walking Clubs, GPO Box 815F, Melbourne, Vic 3001.
Western Australia: National Parks and Wildlife

Service, 50 Hayman Road, Como WA 6152.
Footpath Guides
Chapman, John, and Monica, *Bushwalking in Australia*, Lonely Planet (distributed in the UK by Roger Lascelles), 1988.
Thomas, Tyrone, T., *50 Walks in the Grampians*, Hill of Content, 3rd Ed., 1986.
Groom, Tony, and Gynther, Trevor, *100 Walks in South Queensland*, Hill of Content, 1980.
Thomas, Tyrone, T., *100 Walks in Tasmania*, Hill of Content, 2nd Ed., 1985.
Thomas, Tyrone, T., *100 Walks in New South Wales*, Hill of Content, 3rd Ed., 1988.
Thomas, Tyrone, T., *120 Walks in Victoria*, Hill of Content, 5th Ed., 1989.
Thomas, Tyrone, T., *20 Best Walks in Australia*, Hill of Content, 1989.

Austria Most of Austria is mountainous and therefore offers exceptionally fine opportunities for walking. Routes are well-signposted and waymarked, and there is a choice of grades to suit every kind of walker from the ambler to the alpinist.
Useful Addresses
Austrian National Tourist Office, 30 St George

A family enjoy a walk at Seefeld, Austria (photo © Austria Tourist Board).

Street, London W1R 9FA. Tel. 071-629-0461.
Ramblers' Organisation: The Austrian **Alpine Club**, 13 Longcroft House, Fretherne Road, Welwyn Garden City, Herts AL8 6PQ. Tel. Welwyn Garden (0707) 324835 or 331133 ext 27. NB this is the UK branch of Österreichischer Alpenverein.
Official Survey **Maps**: Österreichischer Karte 1:50000 in four editions of which the standard edition shows **footpaths.**
Other Maps: Kompass Wanderkarte 1:50000 show footpaths graded according to degree of difficulty, and **huts.**
Alpenverein Walking Maps cover the mountainous areas on a scale of 1:25000 and show footpaths.
Guide to Walking
Evans, Craig, *On Foot through Europe: a* **Trail** *Guide to Austria,* **Switzerland** *and* **Leichtenstein**, Quill, 1982.
Footpath Guides
Caselli, G., and Sugden, K., *Ancient Pathways in the* **Alps**, George Philip, 1988.
Davies, Cecil, **Mountain** *Walking in Austria*, Cicerone Press, 1986.

Hurdle, Jonathan, *Walking Austria's Alps: Hut to Hut*, Cordee, 1988.
Proctor, Alan, *The Kalkalpen Traverse; a Long Distance Walk in the Limestone Alps of Austria*, Cicerone Press, 1986.
Speakman, Fleur and Colin, *Walking in the Salzkammergut*, Cicerone Press, 1990.
Spencer, Brian, *Walking in the Alps*, Moorland Publishing Co., 1983.
 Spencer, Brian, *Walking in Austria*, Moorland Publishing Co., 1988.
Spring, Ira, and Edwards, Harvey, *100 Hikes in the Alps*, Cordee, 1979.

Avalanche An avalanche is a mass of falling rock, **snow** or **ice**, or a combination of all three. In Britain, most avalanches are caused by ice and snow melting on steep slopes, or fresh snow being disturbed by walkers and climbers. Most British avalanches are comparatively minor affairs when compared with Alpine avalanches, and rarely involve damage to property. Nevertheless, even in Britain, and especially **Scotland**, avalanches are a serious **hazard** that claim a number of victims every

year, and those who enjoy walking in winter in the upland areas should be aware of the dangers.

The causes of avalanches are extremely complex and depend upon the structure of the snowflake, the temperature of the ground and surrounding air, wind speed, turbulence, humidity and **lapse rate**. Snowflakes are unstable and the structure is liable to **metamorphism** which, in certain conditions, can result in an avalanche. Avalanches are most likely to occur immediately after heavy snowfalls on slopes with an angle of 30°-45°, although they can occur on slopes of 20°-60°, (they do not normally occur on steeper slopes because the angle prevents snow accumulating). The best way of avoiding avalanches, which are often set off by human activity, is to avoid snow-covered slopes as much as possible, and to keep to **ridges**.
Bibliography
Daffern, Tony, *Avalanche Safety; for Skiers and Climbers*, Diadem, 1983.
Fraser, Colin, *Avalanche and Snow Safety*, John Murray, 1978.
Lachappelle, Edward R., *The ABC of Avalanche Safety*, Cordee, 1979.

Ayton, Richard (1786-1823) Dramatist, miscellaneous writer and the author of the first two volumes of *A Voyage Round Great Britain Undertaken in the Summer of 1813, and Commencing from the Land's End*, **Cornwall**, *with a Series of Views, Illustrations of the Character and Prominent Features of the Coast Drawn and Engraved by* **William Daniell** *A.R.A.*, 8 volumes, 1814-26.

B

Backpacker One who practises the craft and skill of **backpacking**. It is a north American term that has been adopted in Britain and has now entirely superseded the indigenous term 'tramp camper'. **Thomas de Quincey** was the first person who walked for pleasure known to have used a **tent**, and can thus lay claim to being the first backpacker.

Backpackers' Club The Club, founded in 1972 by Eric Gurney, aims to ensure continual rights of **access** to meadow, **mountain**, woodland, moor and shore; to campaign for, and aid provision of, sections of public

footpath and rights of **access** to these; to encourage, by example and instructions, the full use of the established **long-distance footpaths**, **national parks** and open areas; to campaign and aid the establishment of further similar areas in this country and in the European continent; and to encourage and aid the development of lightweight camping, walking and camping equipment. (*For address see Appendix.*)

Backpacking A north American word, now universally adopted in the United Kingdom superseding the indigenous term tramp-camping, to describe the craft and skill of walking and carrying on the back all the essentials for living, including food, cooking equipment, shelter and **clothing**. A person on a walking tour who relies on overnight accommodation is *not* a **backpacker**. The earliest references to Britons using **tents** on walking tours were made by **Thomas de Quincey** in 1802, and **John Wilson** in 1815.

Backpackers require the high quality **boots** and clothing used by serious walkers, a light-weight tent, **stove**, **sleeping bag** and

*Above: Three lightweight tents suitable for backpackers (photo © **Camping and Walking**). Below: A selection of backpacking stoves (photo © **Camping and Walking**).*

a suitable backpack or **rucksack** to carry them in. Every attempt should be made to keep the weight of the load as light as possible consistent with comfort and safety. As a rule of thumb guide, a summer outfit should not normally exceed 15 kilograms, and a winter outfit should not normally exceed 19 kilograms. Listed below are typical backpacking outfits together with the approximate weight of each item. It does not include those items that are being worn, but only those that are actually carried in the rucksack. Most walkers find that carrying a fully-loaded backpack reduces their normal average daily mileage by about two-thirds. A solo backpacker has to carry everything himself, but a party can reduce the weight carried by each individual by sharing such common items as a tent and cooking equipment.

Summer Outfit	Approx weight in grams
Rucksack	1500
Tent	1500
Sleeping bag	1100
Insulating mat	250
Butane stove	180
Butane fuel cartridge	500
Canteen	300
Cutlery	100
Panhandle	30
Cup	30
Nylon scourer	25
2-litre water carrier	60
Washing-up bowl	60
Water-sterilising tablets	24
Matches	30
3 pairs of **socks**	225
2 pairs of underpants	120
1 light woollen sweater	350
2 cotton shirts	300
Pyjamas (long-johns and thermal sweater)	300
Lightweight trousers	300
Trainers	500
Toilet kit	400
Pertex towel	100
Torch	120
Survival bag	100
Food for 3 days	2500
Water	1000
First aid kit	150
Sundries (pen, paper, toilet tissue, J-cloths, plastic bags etc)	1000
Weight of packed rucksack	13154

Equipment not carried in the rucksack: clasp knife, whistle, **compass, map** & **footpath guide**, camera, binoculars, miniature radio, and sunglasses.

Winter Outfit	Approx weight in grams
Rucksack	1500
Mountain tent	3500
Four-season sleeping bag	2500
Insulating mat	250
Petrol stove	750
Fuel	600
Canteen	300
Cutlery	100
Panhandle	30
Cup	30
Nylon scourer	25
2-litre water carrier	60
Washing-up bowl	60
Water-sterilising tablets	24
Matches	30
3 pairs of **stockings**	225
Thermal underwear	500
2 woollen sweaters	1000
Pyjamas (long-johns and thermal sweater)	300
Lightweight trousers	300
Trainers	500
Toilet kit	400
Pertex towel	100
Torch	120
Survival bag	100
Food for 3 days	2500
Water	1000
First aid kit	150
Candles	180
Ice axe	1500
Crampons	500
Sundries (pen, paper, toilet tissue, J-cloths, plastic bags etc)	1000
Weight of packed rucksack	20134

Equipment not carried in the rucksack: clasp knife, whistle, Silva compass, map and footpath guide, camera, binoculars, miniature radio, and **snow** goggles.

Apart from the heavier pack carried, the winter backpacker will carry extra weight in the form of winter-weight boots, **breeches**, sweater and shirt, and will also wear **gloves**, overmitts, and a **balaclava**.

The two best books on backpacking are *The Backpacker's Manual* by **Cameron McNeish**, Oxford Illustrated Press, 1984, and *Wild Country Camping* by **Kevin Walker**, Constable, 1989. *The Outdoor Companion* by **Rob Hunter**, Constable, 1979 and *Winter Skills*, Constable, 1982 by the same author are also useful.

Baddeley, M[ountford] **J**[ohn] **B**[yrde] (1843-1906) Schoolmaster, conservationist, writer and editor. Baddeley was attracted to what is now the **Lake District National Park** at an early age, spent most of his life exploring it on foot, and probably nobody, with the exception of **William Wordsworth** and **A. Wainwright**, has done more to popularise it. He walked extensively and thought nothing of covering 60 kilometres in a day, he formed a corps of voluntary wardens to report on the condition of Lakeland **paths**, and was associated with the Lake District Defence Society. But he is best known for the aptly named series of *Thorough Guides* that he edited with C. S. Ward which was published by Ward Lock in 20 numbered volumes. Baddeley was the author of the following guides in the series: 1. *The Lake District*; 2. *Highlands of **Scotland** as far as Stornaway, Lochinver and Lairg*; 4. *Peak District*; 5. ***Northern Highlands** & Islands*; 7. **South Devon** & South **Cornwall**; 8. *North **Wales** (Part 1)*; 9. *North Wales (Part 2)*; 10. *South Wales & Wye District of Monmouthshire*; 11. *Scotland Part 3—Lowlands*; 12. *Ireland Part 1—Northern Counties*; 15. *Yorkshire (Part 1)*; 16. *Yorkshire (Part 2)*; 18. *Bath & Bristol & 40 Miles Around*; 19. *Orkney & Shetland*. The most famous volume in the series was *The Lake District* which was first published in 1880, went through many editions, and remained in print until the Second World War. The 'Introduction' includes useful information about the history of walking and climbing in the Lake District, and the book contains many suggestions for walking expeditions. His dry, precise style is now out of fashion.

Baines, Sir Edward (1800-1890) Member of Parliament, proprietor of *The Leeds Mercury*, and author of *A Companion to the Lakes of Cumberland, Westmorland and Lancashire; in a Descriptive Account of a Family Tour and Excursions on Horseback and on Foot, with a New, Copious and Correct Itinerary*, 1829. A delightful account of a charming family, two ladies and two gentlemen, who toured the Lake District, mostly by carriage and boat, but occasionally making excursions on foot '. . . *if considered to be not too fatiguing for the ladies* . . .' Sometimes the author went off on his own and described some of the major mountains. 'The *EXCURSIONS ON HORSEBACK* and the two *EXCURSIONS ON FOOT* are faithful descriptions of journeys performed by the Author, and they will be found to contain much useful information for those who may travel in either of these methods.

'The *FOUR PARTS* together contain a full

description of all the principal Routes and Excursions at the Lakes; including a particular account of the ascents *of Skiddaw, Helvellyn, Scawfell Pikes, Great Gavel* [Gable] *Bowfell, Langdale Pikes, Hill* [Ill] *Bell, High Street and several other mountains.*' The book is a pleasant mixture of personal reminiscence and guidebook and proved so popular that by 1834 it had run to three editions.

Baker, Ernest A[lbert] (1869-1941) Librarian, bibliographer, lexicographer, prolific author of books about literature and mountaineering, and member of the **Rucksack Club**. He was of that generation that did not make a clear distinction between **mountain** walking and climbing, and his books describe numerous walks and climbs in **Scotland** and what are now the **Lake District National Park**, **Snowdonia National Park**, the **Peak National Park** and the **Pennines**. His books are well-written with good descriptions of scenery, and he has the gift of making small adventures interesting. His publications include the following titles about walking and mountaineering *Moors, Crags and Caves of the High Peak*, 1903; *The Highlands*, 1923; *On Foot in the Highlands*, 1932 (2nd Ed., 1933); *The British Highlands with Rope and Rucksack*, 1933 (new edition with an Introduction by **A. Harry Griffin**, 1973). He also wrote *The Forbidden Land*, 1924 which is an impassioned plea for **access** to the upland areas of Britain, and in collaboration with Francis Edward Ross *The Voice of the Mountains*, 1905 which is an interesting anthology of mountaineering literature.

Balaclava A hat named after the famous battle in the Crimean War which is worn by walkers in cold weather. It is usually made of **wool** or **fibrepile**, and protects the ears, neck and mouth as well as the head. In milder conditions the sides are usually rolled up and the balaclava is worn on the top of the head like a conventional woolly hat.

Barclay, Captain [ie Captain Robert Barclay Allardyce] (1779-1854) A Scottish soldier and landowner and one of the most remarkable exponents of **pedestrianism**. He was an indefatigable walker all his life and thought nothing of walking one hundred and sixty kilometres to purchase cattle for his farms. But he was most famous for his exploits as a 'ped'. In 1796 he won his first wager for 100 guineas by walking '*six miles within the hour, fair heel and toe*' and later covered 70 miles in 14 hours

Captain Barclay, the famous 'ped' (photo © British Library).

beating Ferguson, the celebrated walking clerk, by several miles. But the climax of his career came in 1808 when he undertook to walk for a wager of 1000 guineas, 1000 miles in 1000 successive hours, which meant that he had to walk just one mile in each of the twenty-four hours for a period of 42 days. Despite a great deal of suffering he won the wager completing the final mile in 22 minutes.

Barry, William Whittaker (18--?-1875) Barrister and author of two pseudonymous books describing his walking tours. *A Walking Tour around Ireland in 1865* by 'An Englishman', 1867 is an account of his anti-clockwise walk around the Irish coast commencing at Belfast. He started his journey on 10th August 1865 and finished on 17th October of the same year. He records his daily itinerary which ranges from six and a half kilometres (Ballyshannon to Bundoran) to sixty kilometres (Waterford to Wexford). For route-finding he used a **map** by Wyld and *Murray's Handbook*. Barry had an eye for a pretty girl and writes well and entertainingly, though he had no adventures of note.

'*My work professes to give a strictly original account or description of Ireland as it appeared to—I hope I may say—an intelligent and well-informed Englishman. I have also endeavoured to be impartial. With regard to my opportunities for observation, these may be briefly summed up. I spent nearly ten weeks in Ireland, visited more or less twenty out of the thirty-two counties, and walked upwards of a thousand miles.*'

Following the success of this book he wrote an account of an earlier tour made in 1863 from 1st September to 6th October entitled *A Walking Tour in Normandy*, 1868. This work is similar to the one noted above but he does not seem to have enjoyed it so much.

Beck A term used in some parts of the north of **England**, especially Lancashire, Yorkshire, South Durham and Cumbria to describe streams and brooks, in particular, those with stony beds and a rugged course. The synonym **burn** is used only in **Scotland**, Northumberland and north Durham, and the dividing line is the **ridge** of **hills** between the rivers Wear and Tees which runs from Burnhope Seat (**grid reference** NY 788376), south of Alston, eastwards to Pawlaw Pike (grid reference NZ 008322), north of Middleton-in-Teesdale. Streams that flow north of this line are called burns, and those that flow southwards are becks.

Belgium A small country containing a great variety of scenery including extensive forests and charming towns and villages. The best area for walking is in the south-east of the country, in the Ardennes, where the highest land rises to 683 metres.
Useful Addresses
Belgian National Tourist Office, 38 Dover Street, London W1X 3RB. Tel. 071-499-5379
Ramblers' Organisation: Comité National Belge des Sentiers de Grande Randonnée, Boîte Postale 10, Liège 4000.
*National **Map** Survey*: Institut Géographique Militaire, Abbaye de la Cambre 13, Bruxelles 1050.
Official Survey Maps: Carte Topographique de Base de Belgique 1:50000. Carte Topographique de Belgique 1:25000. **Footpaths** are marked on both series.
Guide to Walking
Evans, Craig, *On Foot through Europe: a **Trail** Guide to **France** and the Benelux Countries*, Quill, 1982.

Belloc, [Joseph Pierre] **Hilaire** (1870-1953) Poet, essayist, polemicist, historian, critic, travel-writer, man of letters and author of over one hundred books. In 1890 he went to America,

Hilaire Belloc wrote four books on walking (photo © National Portrait Gallery).

ostensibly to stay with cousins in Philadelphia, but in reality to visit Elodie Hogan who resided in Napa, near San Francisco, California and who was later to become his wife. Belloc had no money and walked most of the way from Philadelphia to Napa following roads and railway tracks. He earned money by gambling in saloons and making sketches which he sold in return for lodging. Episodes from this epic and romantic three-month walk are recalled in his letters, and in *The Contract* (1923). He wrote four other books about walking, *The Old Road* (1904) in which he 'rediscovers' the **Pilgrims' Way**, the route supposedly taken by medieval pilgrims travelling from the shrine of St Swithin, Winchester to that of St Thomas à Becket at Canterbury. Modern research has vitiated most of his ideas about the Pilgrims' Way; the route, which is followed for part of its length by the **North Downs Way**, is a prehistoric **trackway**, and in any case, pilgrims travelling between the shrines were more likely to have used the much better roads via London, or gone by sea from Southampton to Dover. Even better known, and a minor classic, is *The Path to Rome* (1902) a discursive account of a month's walk from Toul, in **France**, to Rome in which he comments freely on European history, culture and religion. In *The Pyrénées* (1909) he wrote a less literary and much more conventional guide, designed to introduce walkers to the region, in which he gives advice on practical matters such as **clothing** and equipment. His masterpiece is another book about walking. *The Four Men* (1911) is an account of a solitary walk across Sussex at the end of October 1902. His three companions, Grizzlebeard, the Poet, and the Sailor are all aspects of his own

personality, and the book is a hymn of praise to **England** in general, and Sussex in particular. During this walk he wrote the delightful poem *Duncton* **Hill**. Belloc also compiled an **anthology of walking** *The* **Footpath** *Way* (1911).

The best biography of Belloc is *Hilaire Belloc* by A. N. Wilson, Hamish Hamilton, 1984.

Belvedere A term derived from the Italian *bel* 'beautiful' and *vedere* 'sight'—hence beautiful view. It is rarely used in the United Kingdom, but is sometimes applied by English-speaking walkers to describe vantage points in Alpine countries. A belvedere lies below the summit of the **mountain**, and is an attractive grassy area which forms a natural viewing platform that encourages the pedestrian to linger and enjoy the prospect of mountains framing the valley.

Bench mark A small arrow-head with a line below engraved by the **Ordnance Survey** that indicates a known height that may be used for local surveying purposes. Bench marks (see figure 3) may be found on the sides of buildings, especially churches, the abutments of bridges, milestones, and even stone gateposts. They are shown only on the 1:1250 (50 inches to the mile) and 1:2500 (25 inches to the mile) **maps**, and unlike **triangulation stations**, are of no practical importance to walkers. There is a system of continuous replacement of bench marks because hundreds are lost every year through building development. During the Second World War, when milestones were removed to confuse any invading army, many thousands were lost overnight.

Figure 3: Bench mark.

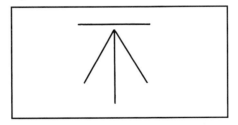

Benightment The condition of being stranded after dark in **mountain** or **moorland** regions. It usually happens because the walker has become lost, injured or has miscalculated the time necessary to complete the walk. The action to be taken depends on the

physical condition of the walker, the weather, the terrain and how well the **path** is defined. If there is a good moon and the path is well-defined the walker should proceed with caution, but if conditions make it unsuitable, it may be wiser to make an emergency **bivouac** and wait till daylight, or until found by the **mountain rescue** team alerted by friends, family or by the police finding an unattended vehicle in the car park.

Bennett, G[eorge] **J**[ohn] (1800-1879) An actor and the author of *A Pedestrian Tour through North* **Wales** *Performed in 1837*. Bennett started his walk from Shrewsbury. Between Chirk and Llangollen he walked along the canal towpath, visited Plas Newydd, which he was shown round by the gardener, and climbed Dynas Bran. He continued to Bala and Dolgellau and ascended Carreg y Saeth in the Rhinogs on horseback. The author gives brief descriptions of towns and scenery, noted down the music of songs, recorded tales and legends, and wrote some self-conscious verse. The appendix contains the routes for ascending Snowdon given by Thomas Pennant and **William Bingley**. The book is quite well-written, but lacks shape, leaving the reader with the impression that the author could not sustain the enthusiasm with which he started his tour.

Bergschrund A German term, meaning mountain **crevasse**, used to describe the crevasse that separates a snowfield from a **glacier**. Bergschrunds constantly, but imperceptibly, change shape according to the season and the movement of the glacier. Sometimes they are formidable obstacles, especially if double or triple bergschrunds have formed, that can only be surmounted by using ice-climbing techniques, but in many instances they may be crossed without special equipment.

Berry, Geoffrey [Victor] (1912-1988) Local government officer, environmentalist, naturalist, photographer, and enthusiastic **hill walker**. From 1966-76 he was the secretary of the **Friends of the Lake District**, and was consulting secretary from 1976 until his death, and he also served as a committee member of the **National Trust**, the **Youth Hostels Association**, the **Ramblers' Association** and the **Council for National Parks**. In 1976 he was awarded an OBE for his work for conservation. He wrote numerous articles about walking and conservation, and was the author of *Across Northern **Hills***, Westmorland Gazette, 1975 which describes a number of **long-distance paths**.

Bingley, W[illiam] (1774-1823) Sometime curate at Christchurch, Hampshire, minister of Fitzroy Chapel, Charlotte Street, London and prolific author. In 1798, when an undergraduate at Cambridge, he took a coach to Chester and spent the long vacation walking in North **Wales**. He published an account of his tour under the title *A Tour Round North Wales Performed during the Year 1798* which was published in 1800 and ran to three editions. '*My mode of travelling was chiefly on foot, but sometimes I took horses, and at other times proceeded in carriages, as I found convenient. The former, notwithstanding all the objections that have been made against it, will I am confident, upon the whole, be found the most useful, if health and strength are not wanting. To a naturalist, it is evidently so, since by this means, he is enabled to examine the whole country as he goes along; and when he sees occasion, he can also strike out of the road, amongst the **mountains** or morasses, in a manner completely independent of all those obstacles that inevitably attend the bringing of carriages or horses . . .*' On **maps** he says '*Evans's smaller map of North Wales (the price of this map is eighteen shillings) which is the correctest map I have ever travelled by, will be found a most useful companion. The roads in this have been laid down with so much accuracy, that, wherever the traveller may have occasion to find fault, it will be more than probable that some change has taken place since the survey was taken. A small pocket **compass**, amongst the mountains, will be almost as necessary as the map . . .*' With the arrogance of youth he does not hesitate to make statements about **Richard Warner** that border on the libellous '*. . . I have, as will be found upon perusal, interspersed them but little, either with reflecti.ns or incidental stories; indeed of the latter, I ought candidly to confess, that I met with very few which I thought worth recording. Two late tourists Mr Pratt and Mr Warner, if they have not introduced the novelist too often in their works, (which, by the way, I shrewdly suspect they have) were infinitely more fortunate in meeting with adventures than I was . . .*'

He ascended Glyder Vawr with a guide, but climbed Snowdon unguided in the company '*of a clergyman of the neighbourhood*'. He recommends going from '*. . . Caernarvon to Dolbadarn Castle, and then turning to the right, go by the waterfall, Caunant Mawr, up the mountain to a vale called Cwm Brwynog, and proceeding along the **ridge**, south west of, and immediately over the Vale of Llanberis, he will come within sight of a black, and almost perpendicular rock, with a small lake at its bottom,*

called Clogwyn Du'r Arddu. This he will leave a quarter of a mile on his right, and then ascending the steep called Llechwedd y Re, he must direct his course south west to the well (a place sufficiently known by the guides) from where he will find it about a mile to the highest peak of Snowdon, called Yr Wyddfa, the conspicuous . . .' Bingley did not follow his own advice but climbed the face of the precipice from the foot of Clogwyn Du'r Arddu, and badly frightened, managed to reach the top.

He also climbed Snowdon by several other routes. From Llanberis he went via Ffynnon Frech, Llyn Llwydan, Llyn y Cwm Glas and Bwlch Glas; from Betws y Coed he went via Bwlch Cwm Brwynog and Llyn Fynnon y Gwas; and from Beddgelert he was guided by the village schoolmaster via Clawdd Coch. He also climbed Cadair Idris.

Although particularly interested in botany and bird-life, Bingley had a real feeling for mountain scenery and described the changing patterns of light, with which every sensitive mountaineer is familiar, very well.

It should be noted that *North Wales; Including its Scenery, Antiquities, Customs, and some Sketches of its Natural History, Delineated from Two Excursions through all the Interesting Parts of that Country during the Summers of 1798 and 1801*, published in 1804 is an expanded edition of the earlier work. A third edition, revised by his son W. R. Bingley, '*with corrections and additions made during excursions in the year 1838*' appeared posthumously in 1839. The revisions include corrections required by the new road system, and the construction of the Menai and Conwy bridges.

Birtles, Geoff[rey Brent} (1947-) Journalist and climber. In 1976 he founded a climbing magazine *Crags*, and in 1982 founded and edited *High* which is now the official journal of the **British Mountaineering Council**.

Bivouac A term used by climbers to describe an overnight stop on a long **mountain** climb where conditions make it impossible to pitch a **tent**. In order to stay warm, the climber pulls on all his spare **clothing**, wriggles into a **survival bag** (colloquially known as a bivvy bag) or plastic sack. Walkers rarely bivouac in the climbing sense because modern tents are so light in weight that the saving in weight is not worth the discomfort involved. However, all who walk in upland areas should carry a plastic bivvy sack or survival bag to provide protection from the elements in the event of accident or **benightment**.

Blenkinsop, Arthur (1911-79) A Labour Member of Parliament who was a keen **hillwalker** and supported moves in Parliament to gain better **access** to the countryside. He was president of the **Ramblers' Association** 1956-8.

Blister The most common ailment among walkers is caused by friction between **boots**, **socks** and the skin of the foot made tender by heat and perspiration. Constant chafing causes fluid to form under the surface with a characteristic swelling covered with whitish skin. To prevent blisters forming all footwear should fit well and the boots should be well broken in by wearing them for a series of short walks before using them on a longer expedition. **Backpackers** are particularly prone to blisters because the weight of the **rucksack** causes the feet to expand inside the boots. The first indication of the start of a blister is the formation of a 'hot spot' which can be prevented from developing by covering with a dressing such as a Band-aid. Once a blister has formed, it should be lanced with a needle sterilised in a match flame, the fluid gently squeezed out with a tissue and a corn pad applied so that the affected area is contained within the hole. This will both relieve the pressure and protect the tender area. Some who regularly suffer from blisters in a particular spot apply dressings before they start walking.

Bob Graham 24 Hour Club A club, formed in 1971, with the following aims:
1 To specify and define the 42 summits traversed by **Bob Graham**.
2 To provide intending qualifying members with all details and relevant information.
3 To encourage intending qualifying members with all details and relevant information.
4 To record in detail all registered attempts.

Membership is open to all who have completed the route on foot within 24 hours, starting and finishing at the Moot Hall, Keswick, and also to those who have completed the Round but included additional peaks. The person who holds the record for the Round (currently Joss Naylor) is the president of the Club. 620 men and 33 women were members of the Club at the end of 1989. Further information about the Bob Graham Round may be found in *42 Peaks; the Story of the Bob Graham Round* by **Roger Smith** published by the Bob Graham 24 Hour Club. *(For address see Appendix.)*

Bog-trotting Eric Byne and Geoffrey Sutton state in *High Peak; the Story of Walking and Climbing in the Peak District* published by Secker & Warburg in 1966, that the term bog-trot was first used at the beginning of the century to describe '. . . *a fast-moving walking expedition across the high peaty plateaux and **moorlands** of the Peak and **Pennines**. . . '*. It seems to have been invented by Cecil Dawson, a Manchester cotton merchant, who was known to his fellow bog-trotters Mac Forrester, Tom Arnfield, Harry Lees, Jack Capper and Billy Thornber, who were members of his informal club, 'the 94th', as the 'Colonel'. Dawson devised such famous bog-trots as the Marsden to Edale Walk in 1902, and the Colne to Buxton Walk in 1904. These were the forerunners of several similar **challenge walks** including the Colne to Rowsley Walk (Fred Heardman, J. F. Burton and H. Garrard in 1926) and the Tan Hill to the Cat and Fiddle Walk (1952). Dawson also pioneered the use of gym shoes for bog-trotting in the years 1906-7. These early bog-trotters discovered that if the **groughs** and **hags** of what is now the **Peak National Park** were covered at speed, there was less likelihood of sinking very far into the bog.

The expression now tends to be applied derisively to any walk that involves crossing large areas of boggy country.

Booth, Derrick (19-- -) International oil journalist, outdoor journalist and indefatigable **backpacker** who has walked extensively in Britain and many parts of the world. More than any other writer he was responsible for introducing American **backpacking** techniques and equipment into Britain, thus revolutionising the British backpacking scene. His book *The Backpacker's Handbook*, Hale, 1972 (2nd Ed., 1979 published by Letts) has now largely been superseded, but in its time it was one of the most important books on the subject. He was also the co-author, with Robin Adshead, of *Backpacking*, Oxford Illustrated Press, 1974.

Boots The traditional and preferred footwear for serious walkers, although there is nothing inherently wrong with wearing stout **shoes**, running shoes or even wellingtons, except in mountainous country.

Many of the myths repeated in generations of books about walking have now been exploded. Boots do not provide support for the ankles to any significant degree, and the only real advantage they have over shoes is that the higher cuff gives more protection in wet con-

ditions underfoot, and also protects the sensitive ankle-bone from painful knocks when walking among boulders.

Modern walking boots are much lighter and more comfortable than they were ten years ago, and often of more sophisticated construction with the more expensive models having such refinements as breathable waterproof linings made of **Gore-Tex** or **Sympatex**, **speed lacing** and **footbeds** made of **Sorbothane**. It is also possible to obtain both detachable linings and socks made of Gore-Tex to keep the feet dry. Most boots are constructed of leather although some models combine **Cordura** and leather though these are more difficult to waterproof satisfactorily, take longer to dry when wet and are more suited to dry climates. Soles are manufactured from a special form of hard moulded rubber marketed under a number of brand names of which the first and most famous was **Vibram**.

Wear two pairs of thick **socks** when buying boots and ensure that the fit is sufficiently large as the feet tend to swell when hot. Most boots are made in only one width for each size and walkers with broad feet often find it more comfortable to start lacing their boots at the third or fourth eyelet to give their feet room to expand.

Boots should be cleaned with cold water and a washing-up brush, and then stuffed with paper and allowed to dry in a cool place well away from direct heat, before being lightly dressed with a proprietary waterproofing and leather preservative such as Nikwax.

Boreens The name given to narrow lanes in Ireland which is derived from the Erse *bothar*, 'a road' and the suffix *een* meaning 'little'. They are often used to link sections of **long-distance paths** and make for fast, easy walking.

Borrow, George (1803-81) Novelist, traveller and linguist. Borrow had a flamboyant personality, was immensely strong and enjoyed walking all his life. In 1832, he walked the 180 kilometres from Norwich to London in 27 hours to attend an interview at the Bible Society which resulted in his missionary efforts in Russia and **Spain**. In 1853, when he was in more comfortable circumstances, he embarked on a series of walking tours of the British Isles, which included a walk to Land's End, and the famous walking tour of **Wales**. This latter tour he described in *Wild Wales; its People, Language and Scenery*, 1864 which, with its vivid descrip-

George Borrow whose walking tour of Wales was brilliantly described in Wild Wales; its People, Language and Scenery, *1864 (photo © National Portrait Gallery).*

tion of scenery and local characters, must rank among the best accounts of a walking expedition ever written. In 1855 he tramped about the **Isle of Man**, and in 1857 went on another walking tour of Wales. The following year he went on an extended walking tour of **Scotland** and got as far as Orkney and the Shetlands. He went to Ireland in 1860 and 1868, and in the latter year visited Scotland again. In 1868 he walked through Sussex and Hampshire, but after the death of his wife in the following year he confined himself to wanderings near his home.

Bothy A simple shelter, found mainly in the upland areas of Britain, especially **Scotland** and the north of **England**, for the use of walkers and climbers. They are usually deserted mine or farm buildings, or crofts, but very occasionally they are purpose-built like the one at Yearning Saddle on the **Pennine Way**. They normally lack any facilities although occasionally they may be stocked with emergency supplies of **food**. The organisation that makes itself responsible for the care and upkeep of many bothies is the **Mountain Bothy Association**.

Boyd, Donald The author of two excellent books on walking, *On Foot in Yorkshire*, 1932, and *Walking in the **Pennines*** (with **Patrick Monkhouse**), 1937.

Boyes, Malcolm [David] (1942-) Author of a number of guidebooks and articles for the outdoor press. For twelve years he was a member of the Scarborough and District Search and Rescue Team, and devised a number of **long-distance paths** across the **North York Moors National Park**, including the North York Moors Crosses Walk, the **Cleveland Way** Missing Link, the Captain Cook Memorial Walk and the Falcon Flyer, as a way of raising funds for the organisation.

Publications

The Crosses Walk, Dalesman 2nd Ed., 1974.

Guide to the Cleveland Way and the Missing Link, Constable, 1977.

North York Moors A to Z, Dalesman, 1979.

Yorkshire Coast A to Z, Dalesman, 1980.

Walking in Rosedale and Farndale, Dalesman, 2nd Ed., 1983.

Thornton-le-Dale, Dalesman, 3rd Ed., 1983.

Countryside Walks around Scarborough, Dalesman, 1983.

Walks in the James Herriot Country, Dalesman, 2nd Ed., 1985.

Great Walks: North York Moors (with Hazel Chester), Ward Lock, 1988.

Walking the Cleveland Way and Missing Link, Cicerone Press, 1988.

Exploring the Lake District, Dalesman, 5th Ed., 1988.

Exploring the North York Moors, Dalesman, 6th Ed., 1989.

Bradt, Hilary (neé Cross 1941-) Writer, publisher and author of several pioneering walk

Hilary Bradt, publisher and author of guides to Africa and central and southern America.

ing and **backpacking** guides to Africa and central and south America. She leads **treks** in the **Andes** for travel companies, and has her own publishing company, Bradt Publications, (formerly Bradt Enterprises), that specialises in publishing and distributing guides to unusual destinations.

Publications

Backpacking in Peru and Bolivia, Bradt Publications, 5th Ed., 1989.

Backpacking in Mexico and Central America, Bradt Publications, 3rd Ed., 1990.

Backpacking in Venezuela, Colombia and Ecuador (with George Bradt), Bradt Enterprises, 1979.

Backpacking in Chile and Argentina, Bradt Publications, 2nd Ed., 1989.

Backpacking in North America (with George Bradt), Bradt Enterprises, 1979.

Backpacker's Africa, Bradt Publications, 3rd Ed., 1989.

Let's Walk There! Eastern England, Javelin Books, 1987.

Also contributed to

Cleare, **John**, Editor, *Trekking; Great Walks of the World*, Unwin Hyman, 1988.

Brecon Beacons National Park This park was established in 1957 and covers an area of 1344 square kilometres bordered by the towns of Hay-on-Wye, Abergavenny, Brynamman, Llandeilo, Llandovery and Brecon. The most characteristic feature is the flat-topped **mountains** which rise to a height of 886 metres, and over which it is possible to walk for miles without descending below 600 metres. By way of contrast, the 50 kilometres of towpath of the Monmouthshire and Brecon Canal can be walked by those who fancy less strenuous exercise. There are numerous sites of archaeological interest, three national nature reserves, and at Agen Allwed, the most extensive cave system yet discovered in the United Kingdom. (See figure 36) for a map showing the location of all **national parks** in the United Kingdom.)

(For addresses of National Park Headquarters and Information Centres see Appendix.)

Official Guidebook

Thomas, Roger, *Brecon Beacons*, Webb & Bower in association with Michael Joseph, 1987.

Maps

1:50000 **Landranger** sheets 159, 160, 161.

1:25000 **Outdoor Leisure Maps** 11 (Brecon Beacons—Central), 12 (Brecon Beacons—Western), 13 (Brecon Beacons—Eastern).

Footpath Guides

Barber, Chris, *Exploring the Brecon Beacons, Black Mountains and Waterfall Country; a Walker's Guide*,

Regional Publications, 2nd. Rev. Ed., 1985.

Poucher, W. A., *The Welsh Peaks*, Constable, 9th Rev. Ed., 1987.

Thomas, Roger, *Great Walks; Brecon Beacons and Pembrokeshire Coast*, Ward Lock, 1989. **Walker, Kevin**, *Mountain Walking in the Crickhowell Area*, Heritage Guides, 1986.

Walker, Kevin, Mountain Walking in the Brecon Beacons, Heritage Guides, 1986.

Walker, Kevin, Family Walking in the Crickhowell Area, Heritage Guides, 1986.

Walker, Kevin, The Ascent of Table Mountain, Heritage Guides, 1986.

Breeches The preferred walking garment to cover the legs and lower trunk of both men and women (although some ladies prefer **tweed** skirts or culottes), except in warm weather when shorts may be substituted. The best designed breeches are self supporting and also have belt loops, are secured neatly at the knee by buckles or velcro, are reinforced at the seat and and the knee, and have two rear pockets and two side pockets that can be closed with zips, buttons or velcro (there is much to be said in favour of the old-fashioned button for flies and pocket flaps because they are easily replaced—an important consideration when on a long march in remote areas). Most modern breeches are either made from a synthetic stretch material such as **Helenca** that is warm when wet and absorbs little water, **needlecord** or **corduroy**. These two latter materials absorb a lot of water and do not remain warm when wet. The current fashion is for tightly-fitting breeches made from a synthetic stretch material and it is now becoming increasingly difficult to find traditional loose-fitting tweed breeches that last for years and which many walkers still prefer. The Hebden Cord Company (for address see Appendix) will supply by mail order made-to-measure and ready-to-wear breeches and skirts in modern and traditional designs and materials.

Brew-up A colloquialism used to describe a short rest taken for the purpose of making of a hot drink and eating a snack. The essence of the term is that the drink is made on a **stove**, and not carried in a thermos flask.

Bridges, George Wilson (17--?-18--?) The author of *Alpine Sketches Comprised in a Short Tour through Parts of Holland, Flanders, **France**, Savoy, **Switzerland** and **Germany** during the Summer of 1814*, which was published anonymously 'by a Member of the University of Oxford' in 1814. He travelled mostly by diligence and coach, but also climbed a number of **mountains** to which he made the conventional reactions of the time. The book is not very well written, but he gives good descriptions of the way of life of the country people.

Bridleway A **path** over which the public have the right to ride or lead a horse. In the post-war years, bridleways have received statutory definitions. In **England** and **Wales** a bridleway is defined by the **Wildlife and Countryside Act, 1981** as '*A highway over which the public have the following, but no other, rights of way, that is to say, a right of way on foot and a right of way on horseback or leading a horse, with or without a right to drive animals of any description along the highway.*' (Note that the **Countryside Act, 1968** Section 30 allows the riding of bicycles on bridleways providing that they give way to horse-riders and pedestrians. The local authority has the power to make bye-laws prohibiting the riding of bicycles on any particular highway).

In **Scotland**, a bridleway is defined in the **Countryside (Scotland) Act, 1967** and the **Town and Country Planning (Scotland) Act, 1972** as '*A way on which the public have the following but no other rights of way, that is to say, a right of way on foot and a right of way on horseback or leading a horse with or without a right to drive animals of any description along that way.*'

English and Welsh bridleways are depicted on 1:126720, 1:63360, 1:50000 and 1:25000 **maps** published by the **Ordnance Survey**.

British Activity Holiday Association BAHA was founded in 1986 after public concern had been expressed about the standard of leadership and supervision among operators in the outdoor leisure holiday industry. It aims to maintain standards of safety, instruction and quality of activity and special interest holidays; to provide a network for the exchange of ideas and information on activity and special interest holidays; to manage any matters of common concern to the membership; to focus public attention on the aims and benefits of the Association; to encourage communication and co-operation between related bodies in the field of activity and special interest holidays; and to act generally as a professional association for its members. BAHA publishes a newsletter, *Code of Practice*, and a *List of Members*. *(For address see Appendix.)*

British Association of Mountain Guides Formerly known as the Association of British

Mountain Guides, founded in 1975, the BAMG is the professional association of those guides who have passed the exacting standards of the Association and been awarded the British Guide's Carnet and the International Guide's Carnet which is a qualification recognised throughout the mountaineering world. British Mountain Guides will, for a fee, lead and instruct individuals and groups in all mountaineering activities from **hill-walking** to winter ascents of the major Alpine peaks. *(For address see Appendix.)*

British Mountaineering Council Founded in 1944 to foster and promote the interests of British **mountaineers** and mountaineering in the United Kingdom and overseas and jointly with the **Mountaineering Council of Scotland** is the representative body of British mountaineers. Full membership is open to mountaineering clubs and organisations whose principal objects are mountaineering, and associate membership is open to bodies that do not qualify for full membership, and to individuals. Its official journal is ***High***. *(For address see Appendix.)*

British Textile Technology Group Formerly known as the Wira (Wool Industries Research Association) Technology Group, BTTG is an organisation financed by textile companies to provide research, consultancy and testing for the textile industry. Many manufacturers of textiles designed for the outdoor market submit their products for independent testing under laboratory conditions to the Group. There are 254 standard tests available which cover such properties as flammability, abrasion resistance, burst strength, permeability, **pilling**, seam failure, tear strength, thermal resistance and water repellency. *(For address see Appendix).*

British Trust for Conservation Volunteers The Trust, founded in 1959, exists to involve people of all ages in practical conservation work including **footpath** improvement, bridge-building, and the repair of stone walls. The Trust organises residential courses and working holidays in which practical skills can be learned and put to good use. It publishes a journal, *The Conserver*, and a series of practical handbooks covering such subjects as dry stone walling, fencing, hedging etc. Of particular interest to walkers is *Footpaths* by Elizabeth Agate published in 1983 and generally accepted as the standard work on footpath management. *(For address see Appendix.)*

The Broads A 288-square kilometre region of watery landscape in Norfolk and Suffolk lying to the east of Norwich that contains 200 kilometres of lock-free navigation. A 'broad' is a lake-like expanse of water formed by the flooding of medieval **peat** workings. The rivers Bure, Waveney and Yare, and their tributaries the Ant, Chet and Thurne link the forty or so broads, making it a paradise for inland sailors.

The status of the Broads is unique. It was not designated a **National Park** by the **National Parks and Access to the Countryside Act, 1949**, but in 1978 the local councils in the Broads area, with encouragement from the **Countryside Commission**, set up the Broads Authority to manage the Broads and to reduce pollution and other environmental damage. As a result of pressure from the Countryside Commission, the **Council for National Parks**, local councils, and the original Broads Authority, Parliament enacted the Broads Act in 1988 which established a new Broads Authority with responsibility for managing the area, and granting it national park status in everything except name.

The Broads contain a network of **rights of way** but the area is unlikely to appeal to walkers and **backpackers** as much as the other British national parks which are all situated in upland areas (see figure 336 for a map showing the location of all national parks in the United Kingdom). *(For addresses of the Headquarters of the Broads Authority and Information Centres see Appendix.)*

Maps
1:50000 **Landranger** sheet 134.
1:25000 **Pathfinder** sheets P862 (TG 22/32), P863 (TG 42), P883 (TG 21/31), P884 (TG 41/51), P903 (TG 20/30), P904 (TG 40/50), P924 (TM 29/39), P925 (TM 49/59).

Footpath Guide
Le Surf, Jeanne, *Explore the Broads*, Bartholomew, 1987.

Brocken spectre The greatly magnified shadows of human figures cast by the sun's rays on a bank of cloud or **mist**. Brocken spectres are most likely to occur when traversing an **arête**, such as Crib Goch in **Snowdonia National Park**, in the morning when the valley is filled with low cloud or thick mist. The name is derived from the Brocken (1142 metres), the highest peak in the Harz Mountains in Germany, where the phenomenon is common and was first described. If a coloured ring appears round the shadow, it is known as a **glory**.

Brontë sisters Anne (1820-49), Charlotte (1816-55), and Emily (1818-48) were all fond of walking. From their home in Haworth, West Yorkshire they explored the surrounding **Pennine** moors on foot. One of their favourite walks was from Haworth Parsonage along the Sladen **Beck** to the waterfall that now bears their name. Charlotte records that Emily, in particular, loved the wild **moorland** scenery which figures so prominently in her poetry and in her great novel. 'Wuthering Heights' is generally supposed to be based on Top Withens, now a ruin, and 'Thrushcross Grange', the home of the Lintons, is generally held to be Ponden Hall. Both places lie a short distance from each other on the **Pennine Way**, and Ponden Hall has a camp-site, a bunkhouse, accommodation, and offers refreshment to Pennine **wayfarers**.

Brown, Alfred J[ohn] (1894-1969) A textile agent, broadcaster, journalist, author and hotelier who wrote a series of articles about walking for the *Yorkshire Post*. He wrote two excellent and popular walking guides *Tramping in Yorkshire; North & East*, 1932, and **Moorland** *Tramping in West Yorkshire*, 1931 which were reissued in updated form as *Striding through Yorkshire* in 1938, with a revised edition in 1943. Brown also wrote the first official guide to the **North York Moors National Park** as well as a number of popular books unrelated to walking, including novels, published under the pen-name Julian Laverack.

Brown, Alice (1857-1948) An American novelist and author of *By Oak and Thorn*, 1886 which is an account of her walking tour of **England**. She believed that *'to walk is to truly live'* and quickly learned that after walking all day *'you seem to be walking still—even in sleep.'* Her book, although interesting, does not contain much detail about walking.

Brown, Charles Armitage (1786-1842) The friend and biographer of **John Keats** with whom he made a walking expedition to **Scotland** in 1818. Brown also mentions the tour in his letters, and then, many years after the event, wrote a series of articles about it which were published in the *Plymouth & Devonport Weekly Journal Nos 146-7* of 1st—22nd October, 1840. He also wrote *A Walk from Siena to Rome* which originally appeared in the *New Monthly Magazine*, 1825, Part II, pages 463-9, and reprinted in *Some Letters & Miscellanea of Charles Brown, the Friend of* **Keats** *and Thomas Richards,*

The Brontë sisters; all three sisters enjoyed moorland walks (photo © National Portrait Gallery).

edited by Maurice Buxton Foreman and published by the Oxford University Press in 1937.

Brown, Hamish M[acmillan] (1934-) Formerly a teacher and advisor in outdoor education but now a professional **mountaineer**, freelance writer about outdoor activities, poet, author of short stories, guide, lecturer, photographer and broadcaster. He is one of the foremost authorities on walking in **Scotland** and Morocco, and one of the few contemporary outdoor journalists who writes really well. In 1974 he became the first person to climb all the **Munros** in one expedition, and has also climbed all the **Corbetts**, **Donalds** and most of the major **mountains** of the British Isles. In 1979, he walked from John O'Groats to Land's End (see **Land's End to John O'Groats**) linking the **county summits** en route, and in 1980, he devised the **Ultimate Challenge**.

Publications about Walking
Hamish's Mountain Walk, Gollancz, 1978 (Paladin, 1980).
Hamish's Groat's End Walk, Gollancz, 1981 (Paladin, 1983).
Eye to the **Hills**, Pettycur Publishing, 1982.
Time Gentlemen, Aberdeen University Press, 1983.

Hamish Brown, well-known writer on Scotland and Morocco in particular (photo © Hamish Brown).

Munro's Tables of the 3000-feet Mountains of Scotland and other Tables of Lesser Heights, (with J. C. Donaldson), Scottish Mountaineering Trust, 1984.

The Great Walking Adventure, Oxford Illustrated Press, 1986.

Travels, Scotsman Publications, 1986.

Hamish Brown's Scotland, Aberdeen University Press, 1988.

Climbing the Corbetts; Scotland's 2500ft Summits, Gollancz, 1988.

The Island of Rhum, Cicerone Press, 2nd Ed., 1988.

Great Walks, Scotland, (with R. H. Owan and R. Hearns), Ward Lock, 1989.

Scotland Coast to Coast; a Long Distance Walk from Glenshiel to Arbroath, Thorsons, 1990.

Also contributed to

Smith, Roger, Editor, *Outdoor Scotland*, **Scottish Youth Hostels Association**, 1981.

Smith, Roger, Editor, *Walking in Scotland*, Spurbooks, 1981.

Wilson, Ken and **Gilbert, Richard**, compilors, *Classic Walks*, Diadem, 1982.

Brown, Hamish M., Editor, *Poems of the Scottish Hills*, Aberdeen University Press, 1982.

Brown, Hamish M., and Berry, Martyn, Editors, *Speak to the Hills*, Aberdeen University Press, 1985.

Bennet, D., *The Munros*, **Scottish Mountaineering Club**, 1985.

Unsworth, Walt, Editor, *Classic Walks of the World*, Oxford Illustrated Press, 1985.

Smith, Roger, Editor, *The Winding **Trail***, Paladin, 1986.

Unsworth, Walt, Editor, *Classic Walks in Europe*, Oxford Illustrated Press, 1987.

Wilson, Ken and Gilbert, Richard, Compilers, *Wild Walks*, Diadem, 1988.

Bryce, James (1838—1922) Politician and keen walker and **mountaineer**. He was elected liberal Member of Parliament in 1880 and introduced an **Access to the Mountains Bill** in 1884, 1888 and 1892, but it was not until 1939 that a bill on this subject was enacted. He was appointed British Ambassador in Washington in 1907, and entered the House of Lords as Lord Bryce of Dechmont in 1914.

Budworth, Joseph (1756-1815) A military man and miscellaneous writer who wrote much of the *Gentleman's Magazine* under the pseudonym 'Rambler'. He was the author of *A Fortnight's **Ramble** to the Lakes in Westmorland, Lancashire and Cumberland*, by 'A Rambler', 1792, which, much to the author's surprise ran to three editions. He went by ship from Margate to London and then by coach to Leeds and Kendal. He was rowed across several of the lakes and climbed Helm Crag (which he described as devoid of **paths** so it must have

been quite a scramble) near Ambleside, Coniston Old Man, Helvellyn from Ambleside (a round trip of 48 kilometres!), and Skiddaw. He frequently used paths.

Budworth had a lively, enquiring mind and gives good descriptions of scenery, local customs, farming, and the people he met. He had a sense of humour and obviously enjoyed his experiences. The book contains some of his high-minded, but dull, verse. The *Preface* to the second edition gives a flavour of his enthusiasm '*We were exactly one fortnight with constant fair weather, during which we walked upwards of two hundred and forty miles, besides boat and chaise conveyance, and what with admiring the wonders around us, writing them down, or storing them in my memory for an early morning's pen, I can truly say, I enjoyed a noble hurry of imagination, and that I had not time to be idle.*'

Budworth changed his name to Palmer on the death of his wife's brother when he inherited his estates in 1811.

Bull The name given to the male of all bovine animals but applied especially to cattle. All bulls must be treated by walkers as dangerous animals and treated with circumspection. Unfortunately, the law allows, under certain conditions, for bulls to be pastured in fields crossed by **rights of way**. Under section 59 of the **Wildlife and Countryside Act 1981** and section 44 (1) of the **Countryside (Scotland) Act, 1967**, **farmers** may pasture beef breed bulls that are accompanied by cows or heifers in fields crossed by rights of way. However, it is illegal to pasture bulls more than ten months old of a recognised dairy breed such as Ayrshire, British Friesian, British Holstein, Dairy Shorthorn, Guernsey, Jersey, and Kerry in fields crossed by rights of way.

Bunyan, John (1628-1688) Tinker, puritan preacher and the author of the religious and literary classic *The Pilgrim's Progress* as well as several lesser-known works. His life was spent in the countryside around Bedford which he got to know intimately by walking in pursuit of his trade and preaching activities. He was greatly troubled by religious doubts, and whether he would be numbered among the saved and enjoy the spiritual delights of heaven. His spiritual autobiography, *Grace Abounding to the Chief of Sinners*, contains many references to escaping to the fields in order to assuage his troubled spirit by walking and reading his bible. Many of the places mentioned in *The Pilgrim's Progress* have been identified with features in the Bedfordshire landscape.

Burn A term used in **Scotland**, Northumberland and north Durham to describe streams and brooks, in particular, those with stony beds and a rugged course. The synonym **beck** is used only in Lancashire, Yorkshire, Cumbria and south Durham. The dividing line is the **ridge** of **hills** between the rivers Wear and Tees which run from Burnhope Seat (**grid reference** NY 788376), south of Alston, eastwards to Pawlaw Pike (grid reference NZ 008322), north of Middleton-in-Teesdale. Streams that flow north of this line are called burns and those that flow southwards are becks.

Burritt, Elihu (1810–1879) Known as 'the learned blacksmith', Burritt was a self-taught American, early pacifist and internationalist, who was sometime **United States** consul in Birmingham, and walked extensively in Great Britain during the years 1863-4. He described his adventures in three delightful books *A Walk from London to John O'Groats* 1864; *A Walk from London to Land's End and Back* 1865; and *Walks in the Black Country and its Green Borderlands*, 1868. His '*leading motive . . . was originally to see and note the agricultural system, aspects and industries of Great Britain, and to collect information that might be useful to American **farmers**, the general reader, not specially interested in these matters, will find other topics in the work that may contribute to his entertainment.*' His books include much topographical and historical information.

Burroughs, John (1837-1921) American naturalist, author and friend of Walt Whitman. In his youth he walked extensively in the Catskill Mountains in upstate New York, and later in life camped and rode with **John Muir** and Teddy Roosevelt in the Yellowstone **National Park** which he described in *Camping with Roosevelt*, 1907. He also wrote a polished essay *The Exhilarations of the Road*.

Butterfield, Irvine (1936-) **Mountain** photographer, journalist and the author of a number of unusual books about walking. His most important work is undoubtedly *The High Mountains of Britain and Ireland* which gives detailed instructions for climbing every summit over 3000 feet (914 metres) in the British Isles. It is also unusual in that the route descriptions have also been published separately as a **footpath guide** in *The High Mountains Companion*. *Publications about Walking*

Dibidil; a Hebridean Adventure, published by the author, 1970.

A Survey of Shelters in Remote Mountain Areas of the Scottish Highlands, published by the author, 1979.

In the Footsteps of the Fugitive Prince; a Portfolio of Colour Slides Illustrating the Wanderings of Bonnie Prince Charlie after the Battle of Culloden, published by the author, 1980.
The High Mountains of Britain and Ireland, Diadem, 1986.
The High Mountains Companion, Diadem, 1987.

Byway open to all traffic A type of **right of way**, often referred to colloquially as a BOAT, found in **England** and **Wales**. It is defined in the **Wildlife and Countryside Act, 1981** as '*a **highway** over which the public have a right of way for vehicular and all other kinds of traffic, but is used by the public mainly for the purpose for which **footpaths** and **bridleways** are so used.*' Under the terms of earlier legislation, byways open to all traffic were known as **roads used as public paths** (RUPPS).

There was a time when byways open to all traffic were used almost exclusively by walkers, riders and the occasional farm vehicle, but the increasing use of off-road vehicles by the general public has caused considerable alarm among conservationists and walkers about the amount of damage being done to such routes.

The **Byways and Bridleway Trust** is the organisation that protects the interests of users of byways.

Byways and Bridleway Trust The Trust is an organisation that strives to keep open byways and **bridleways** for everyone, including **trail**-riders. It monitors all modification orders pertaining to **byways open to all traffic** and bridleways and works to ensure that **definitive maps** are accurate. It publishes a journal, *Byway and Bridleway*. (*For address see Appendix*.)
P181/Walkers Encyclopaedia/SP/Section C
pages 35 to 54/44

C

Cagoule The name is derived from the hooded sleeveless garment worn by French monks, but nowadays the term is used to describe a waterproof thigh-length jacket with a hood attached. The essential difference between a cagoule, often referred to colloquially as a 'cag', and an **anorak** lies in the length of the skirt. Good quality cagoules designed for use in upland country form an essential item of shell **clothing**.

Cairn A term, derived from the Gaelic *carn* meaning 'a heap of stones', used to describe the numerous piles of stones erected on upland **paths** and **mountain** summits. They have been built for a number of reasons. Those found on paths have usually been constructed to assist in route-finding, especially in bad weather, following in the tradition of the medieval monks who sometimes erected crosses to assist travellers find their way across the wild, inhospitable wastes of what is now the **Dartmoor National Park** and the **North York Moors National Park**. Cairns found on summits were often built out of sheer exuberance by walkers and climbers who fell into the habit of adding another stone to the pile to celebrate their ascent. A few examples have been built as memorials and have a plaque attached. Some of the more popular peaks have so many cairns that the overall effect is unsightly, and it is now considered environmentally unsound to add any more stones to them. Cairns vary greatly in size; some are enormous and must weigh several tons, whilst others consist of no more than half a dozen small stones strategically sited on boulders to mark the way.

Cairngorm Club One of the oldest and most venerable of Scottish walking and climbing clubs. It was founded in 1887 by two walkers who met at the Shelter Stone at the head of Loch Avon in the **Cairngorms**. *The Cairngorm Club* by Sheila Murray, published by the Club in 1987 relates its history. (*For address see Appendix*.)

Cairngorms Although containing some of the highest land in the United Kingdom, the Cairngorms, which lie on the eastern side of **Scotland** between the rivers Dee and Spey, are not so dramatic as other **mountain** ranges in Scotland. This is because they are plateaux that have been eroded into mountains, often giving an unexciting slope on one side with magnificent **corries** and walls of cliff on the other side. There is splendid **hill-walking** on Cairn Toul (1272 metres), Braeriach (1264 metres) and Ben Macdui (1289 metres), and the Lairig Ghru, an ancient **pass**, makes an interesting route for anyone who wishes to avoid the high tops.

The Cairngorms have a significantly lower rainfall than other mountainous regions of Scotland which even on the highest mountains does not exceed 150 centimetres per year. Extremes of temperature are more likely in this region, and the Cairngorms are often warmer

in summer than other parts of Scotland and significantly colder in winter with high winds and a great deal of snow. (See figure 25 for **map** on showing the major scenic divisions of Scotland.)
Maps
1:50000 **Landranger** sheets 278, 28, 29, 36, 37, 43, 44.
1:63360 **Tourist Map** of the Cairngorms.
1:25000 **Outdoor Leisure Map** 3 Aviemore and the Cairngorms.
Guidebook
Watson, Adam, *The Cairngorms*, West Col, Rev. Ed., 1975.
Footpath Guides
Cairngorm Passes Path Map, **Scottish Rights of Way Society Ltd.**, 1980.
Hallewall, Richard, *Walk Royal Deeside and North East Scotland*, Bartholomew, 1989.
MacInnes, Hamish, *Highland Walks Vol. 4: Cairngorms and Royal Deeside*, Hodder & Stoughton, 1988.

Camping and Caravanning Club The Club was founded in 1901, when it was known as the Camping Club, and claims to be the world's oldest camping and caravanning club. It aims to promote the knowledge, love and care of the countryside through camping and kindred activities. The Club owns or manages 85 full facility camping and caravanning sites, and licences a further 2000 minimum facility 'Hideaway' sites. It has special interest groups, including some devoted to walking and lightweight camping, and it organises walking holidays from some of the Club sites. It publishes a journal, *Camping and Caravanning*, as well as guides to sites, and leaflets giving advice and information on camping and caravanning. (*For address see Appendix*.)

Camping and Outdoor Leisure Association (COLA) The body that looks after the interests of manufacturers, distributors and retailers of outdoor equipment and **clothing**. It was founded in 1960 as the Camping Trade Association of Great Britain Ltd, and changed to its present name in 1976. COLA organises an annual trade exhibition in November at Harrogate which is the most important British showcase for manufacturers and distributors of walking, mountaineering and camping products. The exhibition is not open to the general public, but is widely reported in the outdoor press. COLA publishes a journal, *COLA News*, and has an arbitration and conciliation service that may be used by anyone who has a complaint about a product or serv ice supplied by a member. *(For address see Appendix.)*

Camping & Walking A monthly magazine, founded in 1961 as *Camping*, and incorporating *Camping, Camping & Trailer* and *Popular Camping and Autocamping*. Even though each issue contains articles on subjects not directly connected with walking, it is, nevertheless, an interesting magazine. It is written in a popular style with a strong family flavour, and occasionally publishes an outstandingly good article. *(For address see Appendix.)*

Canada Canada is the second largest country in the world with a population of only 23 million people. It contains vast areas of wilderness, and the Canadian Rockies is one of the most beautiful **mountain** ranges in the world. **Hiking**, as it is universally known throughout north America, is very popular but there is no local **footpath** network, and it is usually necessary to visit a state or **national park** to enjoy walking.

Useful Addresses
Canadian Government Office of Tourism, Canada House, Trafalgar Square, London SW1Y 5BJ. Tel. 071-629-9492.
The Government Office of Tourism maintains a reference library which may be used by the public by appointment. Two useful bibliographies that may be consulted there are *The Subject Guide to Canadian Books in Print and Canadiana: the Canadian National Bibliography.*
National **Map** *Survey:* Department of Energy, Mines and Resources, Surveys, Mapping and Cartographic Information, 615 Booth Street, Ottawa, Ontario K1A OE9.
Official Survey Maps:
1:125000
1:50000
1:25000

Guides to Walking
Bradt, George and **Hilary**, ***Backpacking** in North America; the Great Outdoors*, Bradt Enterprises, 1979. (Even though it was published some time ago and some of the addresses will be out of date, it is still very useful. North Americans take backpacking very seriously and have developed philosophical theories about which visitors should have at least some knowledge.)
Katz, Elliott, *The Complete Guide to Backpacking in Canada*, Doubleday, 1985.
Footpath Guides
Ambrosi, Joey, *Hiking Alberta's Southwest*, Douglas & McIntyre, 1984.
Cousins, Jean and Robinson, Heather, *Easy Hiking around Vancouver*, Douglas & McIntyre, 1980.
Daffern, Gillean, *Kanaski's Country* **Trail** *Guide*, **Rocky Mountain** Books, 1985.
Fairley, Bruce, and Culbert, Dick, *A Guide to*

As there is no local path network in Canada, it is often necessary to walk in one of the national parks (photo © Tourism Canada Photo).

Hiking and Climbing in Southwestern British Columbia, Soules, 1986.

Harris, Bob, *The Best of B. C.'s Hiking **Trails**; Twenty Great Hikes*, Special Interest, 1986.

Macaree, David and Mary, *109 Walks in British Columbia's Lower Mainland*, Douglas & McIntyre, 1983.

Macaree, David and Mary, *103 Hikes in Southwestern British Columbia*, Douglas & McIntyre, 1980.

Patton, Brian, and Robinson, Bart, *Canadian Rockies Trail Guide*, Summer Thought, New Ed., 1989 (distributed in the UK by Cordee).

Roberge, Claude, *Hiking Garibaldi Park and Whistler*, Douglas & McIntyre, 1983.

Robertson, Doug, *The Best Hiking in Ontario*, Hurtig, 1984.

Russell, Elizabeth and others, *Waterton and Northern **Glacier** Trails for Hikers and Riders*, Waterton, 1984.

Stewart, Colin, Editor, *Hiking Trails of Nova Scotia*, Canadian Hostelling, 5th Ed., 1984.

Waddell, Jane, Editor, *Hiking Trails I:, Victoria and Vicinity*, Outdoor Club of Victoria, Rev. Ed., 1987.

Waddell, Jane, Editor, *Hiking Trails II: Vancouver Island, Area from Kokilah River Park to Mount Arrowsmith*, Outdoor Club of Victoria, 5th Ed., 1982.

Waddell, Jane, Editor, *Hiking Trails III : Central and Northern Vancouver Island Including Hiking Routes of Strathcona Park*, Outdoor Club of Victoria, 5th Ed., 1982.

Canal walking There is a dense network of canals in **England**, and to a lesser extent in **Wales** and **Scotland**, most of which are now owned by British Waterways who permit the use of the towpaths by walkers. Towpaths offer easy, fast walking with no route-finding problems, often through unspoiled scenery with an abundance of aquatic wildlife. The architecture associated with canals, such as locks, lock-keepers' cottages, warehouses, tunnels, aqueducts and bridges, is often aesthetically pleasing. Even in large cities, canals can provide interesting, and often surprisingly rural routes into open country (the Regent's Canal from Paddington Basin to the Thames is remarkably attractive and passes through the London Zoo).

Individual canal guides are too numerous to list, but mention must be made of the excellent **Ordnance Survey** *Guide to the Waterways* Vol. 1 *South*; Vol. 2 *Central*; Vol. 3 *North*; and the companion volumes *The River Thames* (which includes the Wey Navigation and the

The Leeds and Liverpool canal. Towpaths offer easy, fast walking with no route-finding problems (photo © Hugh Westacott).

Basingstoke Canal), and *The **Broads** and Fens* published by Robert Nicholson in revised editions in 1989, that cover all the canals in England and Wales. *The Ordnance Survey Inland Waterways **Map** of Great Britain*, also published by Robert Nicholson, shows all the navigable waterways in Great Britain and is useful for planning canal and river walks.

Cannock Chase An **area of outstanding natural beauty**, designated in 1958, covering 68 square kilometres near Stafford. It is one of the traditional lungs of the Black Country with a landscape made up of bracken-clad heathland and woods broken by attractive valleys. There are **access agreements** for the wilder parts of the Chase, and some of it is free from vehicular traffic and specially reserved for walkers and riders. (See figure 36) for a **map** showing the location of all AONBs in the United Kingdom.)
Maps
1:50000 **Landranger** sheet 127, 128.
1:25000 **Pathfinder** sheets P850 (SJ82/92), P851 (SK02/12), P871 (SJ81/91), P872 (SK01/11).
Footpath Guide
Merrill, John N., *Short Walks in the Staffordshire **Moorlands***, JNM Publications, 1986.

Carlyle, Thomas (1795-1881) Historian, essayist, and literary and social critic known as 'the Sage of Chelsea'. He was born at Ecclefechan, near Dumfries, and in his youth was fond of walking in the **hills** around his home. In his *Reminiscences*, published posthumously in 1887, he describes how, in 1817, he walked with four friends from Kirkcaldy to the Trossachs and Loch Lomond. They covered 35 kilometres on the first day arriving at their destination at 2 a.m. as they did not start until the evening. He also walked with his friend Edward Irving from Peebles to Moffat, almost entirely on **paths**, and mentions several places that are now on the route of the **Southern Upland Way**. In 1820, also with Irving, he set out from Paisley to walk to Dumfries. Irving went only part of the way with him and on the last day, Carlyle left Muirkirk alone at 4 a.m. and arrived in Dumfries at 8 p.m. having walked 87 kilometres '. . . *the longest walk I ever made in one day . . .*'. In 1882, J. A. Froude compiled *Reminiscences of my Irish Journey in 1849*, from Carlyle's journal. These are actually notes, and although nothing Carlyle wrote could be described as dull, they lack his customary polish, and in any case, he only walked if transport was not available.

Causeway Coast An **area of outstanding natural beauty** in **Northern Ireland** that stretches from Ballycastle, where it joins the **Antrim Coast and Glens** AONB, to just east of Portrush. It includes the Giant's Causeway and Rathlin Island. (See figure 36 for a **map** showing the location of all AONBs in the United Kingdom.)
Maps
1:50000 **Ordnance Survey of Northern Ireland** sheets 4, 5.
Footpath Guides
Hamill, James, *North Ulster Walks Guide*, Appletree Press, 1988.
Rogers, R., *Irish Walks Guides North East; Down and Antrim*, Gill & Macmillan, 1980.

Central Highlands The Central Highlands of **Scotland** are situated largely in Inverness-shire and Argyll between the **Western Highlands** and the **Cairngorms**. The boundary of the region is formed in the south by Bridge of Orchy, Dalmally and Connel; on the western side by Loch Linnhe and the Great **Glen**; on the north from Whitebridge to Aviemore; and on the east from Aviemore southwards to Dalnacardoch, Kinloch Rannoch and along the railway line to Bridge of Orchy.

The whole area is mountainous and includes Ben Nevis, at 1321 metres the highest peak in the British Isles, as well as several other peaks more than 1200 metres high. There is a good network of **paths**, it is possible to walk for miles without crossing a road, and there are a number of superb **ridge** walks. Ben Nevis itself is a splendid viewpoint and in summer can be climbed easily from Fort William or Glen Nevis, but in winter, however, it can be very hazardous. Until the beginning of the century there was an hotel and observatory on the summit. Walkers must be prepared for plenty of rain in the Central Highlands. Records from the observatory show that on Ben Nevis in 1898, no less than 610 centimetres of rain fell, and in December 1900, 122 centimetres of rain was recorded for the month. (See figure 25 for **map** on showing the major scenic divisions of Scotland.)
Maps
1:50000 **Landranger** sheets 41, 42, 49, 50, 51.
1:66360 **Tourist Map** of Ben Nevis and **Glen** Coe.
Guidebook
Hodgkiss, Peter, *The Central Highlands*, **Scottish Mountaineering Club**, 1984.
Footpath Guides

Hallewall, Richard, *Walk Loch Ness and the River Spey*, Bartholomew, 1987.
Hallewall, Richard, *Walk Oban, Mill and Lochaber*, Bartholomew, 1988.
MacInnes, Hamish, *Highland Walks Vol 1: Ben Lui to the Falls of Glomach*, Hodder and Stoughton, 1984.
*Principal **Rights of Way** in the West Central Highlands: Path Map*, **Scottish Rights of Way Society Ltd**, 1983.
Williams, Noel, *Walks in Lochaber*, Cicerone Press, 1989.

Challenge walk A walk in which there is some element of competition, or a requirement to reach a particular goal, sometimes within a given time. Challenge walks are so diverse that they are difficult to classify. In some, eg the Chiltern Marathon, the competitor has to complete a given course and distance within a specified time, and if successful, receives a certificate. Others, especially those involving **peak-bagging**, may be done at any time, and at the walker's convenience. Some, such as the **Land's End to John O'Groats** and the **Ultimate Challenge** involve walking considerable distances. The generally accepted governing body for most challenge walks is the **Long Distance Walkers' Association**, although each event has its own organisation and rules. The best sources of information about challenge walks are *the Long Distance Walker's Handbook* by Barbara Blatchford, A. & C. Black, 2nd Ed., 1990, and *The Strider*, the journal of the Long Distance Walkers' Association.

Channel Islands This group of beautiful islands comprising Guernsey, Jersey, Alderney and Sark as well as some smaller islands, are situated nearer **France** than **England.** They contain much attractive countryside with a network of **rights of way**. The Channel Islands are responsible for their own mapping although the **Ordnance Survey** has published a 1:25000 **map** of Jersey.
Useful Addresses
States of Guernsey Tourist Board, PO Box 23, White Rock, Guernsey, CI. Tel. 0481-26611.
States of Jersey Tourism Department, Weighbridge, Jersey, CI. Tel. 0534-7800.
Footpath Guides
Barber, Alan, *Walks with a Car in Guernsey*, Bailiwick Publications, 1984.
Bois, F. de L., *Jersey Walks for Motorists*, Warne, 1979.

Chesterton, Keith (1935-) An early member

of the **Long Distance Walkers' Association** and the creator of the London Countryway, an unofficial **long-distance path** that encircles London. He also wrote the guide to the route *The London Countryway*, Constable, 1978.

Chichester Harbour An **area of outstanding natural beauty,** designated in 1964, containing 75 square kilometres of harbour and estuary around Chichester and Emsworth in West Sussex and Hampshire. This is a sailing centre, and although the salt marshes are very attractive, it is not primarily a walking area.

Maps
1:50000 **Landranger** sheet 197.
1:25000: **Pathfinder** sheets P1304 (SU60/70), P1305 (SU80/90), P1323 (SZ89).

Chilterns An **area of outstanding natural beauty**, designated in 1965, covering 800 square kilometres of chalk hills stretching in a broad band through the counties of Oxfordshire, Buckinghamshire, Hertfordshire and Bedfordshire from Goring-on-Thames, where it links with the **North Wessex Downs** AONB, to Luton. It is very popular with Londoners as it is so easy to reach by public transport. The Chilterns contain some excellent walking country with well-defined paths, and this AONB is famous for its attractive and stately beech woods and lovely villages. (See figure 36 for a **map** showing the location of all AONBs in the United Kingdom.)

Maps
1:50000 **Landranger** sheets 165, 166, 175, 176.
1:25000 **Pathfinder** sheets P1048 (TL03/13), P1072 (TL02/12), P1094 (SP81/91), P1095 (TL01/11), P1117 (SP60/70), P1118 (SP80/90), P1119 (TL00/10), P1138 (SU89/99), P1139 (TQ09/19), P1155 (SU48/58), P1156 (SU68/78) P1157 (SU88/98), P1171 (SU47/57), P1172 (SU67/77), P1173 (SU87/97), P1187 (SU46/56), P1188 (SU66/76).

Footpath Guides
Pigram, Ron, *Discovering Walks in the Chilterns*, Shire Publications, 1983.
Chiltern Society, *1:25000 Footpath Maps*, Shire Publications, 1986.
1. *High Wycombe and Marlow*
2. *Henley and Nettlebed*
3. *Wendover and Princes Risborough*
4. *Henley and Caversham*
5. *Sarratt and Chipperfield*
6. *Amersham and the Penn Country*
7. *West Wycombe and Princes Risborough*
8. *Chartridge and Cholesbury*
9. *The Oxfordshire Escarpment*
10. *Ewelme and District*
11. *The Hambleden Valley*
12. *The Hughenden Valley and Great Missenden*
13. *Beaconsfield and District*
14. *Stokenchurch and Chinnor*
15. *Crowmarsh and Gifford*
16. *Goring and Mapledurham*
17. *Chesham and Berkhamsted*
18. *Tring and Wendover*

Chlorofibre A synthetic material available in various weights, used in underwear, that has the property of **wicking** moisture away from the skin (**vapour transmission**) leaving the body feeling dry. It needs frequent washing to keep it sweet-smelling.

Chubb, Sir Lawrence [Wensley] (1873-1948) The first Secretary of the **National Trust** (1895-6), from 1896-1948 the Secretary of the **Commons**, Open Spaces and **Footpaths** Preservation Society (now the **Open Spaces Society**), joint founder of the **Federation of Rambling Clubs**, and a member of the **Forest Ramblers**. Chubb was the foremost authority on the complex problems of commons and **rights of way** and was frequently consulted by government departments and local authorities. He had the reputation of being a skilful and tactful negotiator, but was severely criticised by **Tom Stephenson** and the **Ramblers' Association** for what they felt was his behind-the-scenes sell-out to landowners' interests in private negotiations during the passage through the House of Commons of the **Access to the Mountains Act, 1939**. Chubb was the author of numerous articles and also a **footpath guide** entitled <u>Over the Sussex Downs,</u> 1935.

Cirque A French word, derived from the Latin 'circus' meaning 'ring', that is used by **mountaineers** to describe a semi-circular ring of **mountains** that form a natural amphitheatre at the head of a valley. It is similar to the Welsh '**cwm**' and the Scottish '**corrie**', although it is usually applied only to European mountains on a grander scale than those found in the United Kingdom. A fine example is the Cirque de Gavarnie in the **Pyrénées**.

Claude glass A small black convex glass, named after the French painter Claude Lorraine who was reputed to have used one, that was carried by tourists and artists for reflecting landscapes and outdoor scenes in miniature. The idea was to hold the glass in your hand, with your back to the view, and see the tonal values reflected in the glass. In this way the eye was not distracted by detail or colour. Many of the tourists who sought the picturesque carried one, and **Thomas Gray** in his *Journal* mentions using a Claude glass on one of his walking tours.

Cleare, John (1936-) Climber, walker, lecturer, film-maker and the outstanding British **mountain** photographer of the post-war years. He has made numerous expeditions to the **Himalaya**, was a member of the 1971 Everest expedition., and has contributed accounts of these and other adventures to both the national and the outdoor press. Although best known as a climber, photographer and film-maker, with such titles as *The Matterhorn Centenary* 1965, *The Old Man of Hoy* 1967, and *The Eiger Sanction* 1974, he believes that '**Hill-walking** . . . *is the quintessential craft from which all other mountain sports are born* . . .' He has also founded Mountain Camera, a large picture library much used by writers and publishers.
Publications about Walking
*John Cleare's Fifty Best **Hill** Walks in Britain*, Webb & Bower in association with the **Ordnance Survey**, 1988.
Walking; the Great Views (with **Roland Smith**), David & Charles, 1991.
Also contributed to
Cleare, John, Editor, **Trekking**; *Great Walks of the World*, Unwin Hyman, 1988.

*John Cleare is an outstanding mountain photographer (photo © **John Cleare**).*

Cleveland Way A **national trail** designated by the **Countryside Commission** and opened in 1969, that starts at Helmsley (**grid reference** SE 611839) on the edge of the **North York Moors National Park**, and runs for 175 kilometres around three sides of the park to finish at Crook Ness (grid reference TA 026936), near Filey on the coast. The scenery includes **moorland** and magnificent sea cliffs. There is an 81-kilometre unofficial extension, known as the Cleveland Way Missing Link, that runs from Scarborough to Helmsley and turns part of the Cleveland Way into a circular walk. (See figure 36 for a **map** showing the location of all national trails and official **long-distance paths** in the United Kingdom.)

Youth Hostels
Helmsley, Osmotherley, Westerdale Hall, Saltburn, Whitby, Boggle Hole and Scarborough.
Maps
1:50000 **Landranger** sheets 93, 94, 99, 100, 101.
1:25000 **Outdoor Leisure Maps** North York Moors 26 (Western area), 27 (Eastern area).
Footpath Guides
Boyes, Malcolm, *Walking the Cleveland Way and the Missing Link*, Cicerone Press, 1989.
Hannon, Paul, *Cleveland Way Companion*, Hillside Publications, 1986.
Merrill, John, *The Cleveland Way*, JNM Publications, 1989.
Sampson, Ian, *Cleveland Way*, Aurum Press in association with the Countryside Commission and the **Ordnance Survey**, 1989.

Climaguard A synthetic microfibre fabric, manufactured by Rotofil of Switzerland, which, when woven, forms a windproof and water-repellent material that breathes (water vapour transmission). It is used for jackets.

Climber & Hill Walker A monthly magazine, founded in 1962 as *The Climber*, currently edited by **Cameron McNeish** and published by Holmes McDougall Ltd. Written for experts, it concentrates on climbing and to a lesser extent on **hill walking**. It contains good, well-illustrated articles, news items, and reviews of guides, books and equipment. When edited by **Walt Unsworth**, it was for a time the official journal of the **British Mountaineering Council**. *(For address see Appendix.)*

Clothing The purpose of clothing is to keep the walker dry and at a reasonable temperature. Clothing should be comfortable, allowing the walker to move easily and without restriction, and should be versatile so that the wearer can control his body temperature by removing or adding garments. Clothing is usually classified into the following groups:
Shell clothing: waterproof outer garments such as **anoraks**, **cagoules**, over-trousers and **gaiters** that are designed to protect the wearer from the wet.
Outerwear: garments such as jackets that are designed primarily to protect the walker from the cold rather than the wet, and worn over midwear and under shell clothing.
Midwear: clothing such as sweaters, shirts and breeches designed to keep the wearer at a comfortable temperature. According to accepted wisdom it is better to have several thin layers of midwear, rather than one heavy garment, as the layer principle allows the walker to control his temperature more precisely.
Underwear: clothing that is worn next to the skin and underneath midwear. The best materials for underwear are **silk**, **wool**, **chlorofibre**, **Dunova** and **polypropylene** which will **wick** perspiration and water-vapour away from the body, leaving the skin dry at all times.

Clough The local name given to steep-sided ravines and valleys found in the **Peak National Park**.

Clwydian Hills A long, narrow **area of outstanding natural beauty**, designated by the Secretary of State for the Environment on the advice of the **Countryside Commission** in 1985, of 156 square kilometres stretching south from Prestatyn, Clwyd to the A525. The hills rise to 500 metres, and the final part of **Offa's Dyke Path** passes through this lovely, unspoiled region of Wales. (See figure 36 for a **map** showing the location of all AONBs in the United Kingdom.)
Maps
1:50000 **Landranger** sheets 116,117.
1:25000 **Pathfinder** sheets P737 (SJ08/18), P755 (SJ07/17), P772 (SJ06/16), P773 (SJ26/36), P788 (SJ05/15), P789 (SJ25/35), P805 (SJ04/14).
Footpath Guide
Sale, Richard, *Best Walks in North* **Wales**, Constable, 1988.

Cochrane, John Dundas (1780-1825) Naval officer and grandson of the 8th Earl of Dundonald. During his naval career, in which he reached the rank of captain, he twice walked with six hundred seamen from Quebec to Lake Ontario. In 1819 he walked through **France**, **Spain** and **Portugal** but no details of this journey are known. The Royal Navy did not require him for active service and consequently he was on half pay. He submitted a scheme to the Admiralty to make a solitary exploration of the Niger, but this was rejected. In a fit of pique he resolved to walk round the world *'to trace the shores of the Polar Sea along America by land as Captain Parry is now attempting to do by sea . . .'* He set out from Dieppe in February 1821 and reached St Petersburg (present-day Leningrad) after walking 2500 kilometres in 83 days. Here he was well received by the Tsar who offered him every assistance. He walked another 2000 kilometres to Topolsk in western Siberia, and from then on, through the courtesy of the authorities, travelled by coach or on horseback. He had numerous adventures, was robbed three times, he married in Kamchatka and returned to St Petersburg in June 1823. He described his adventures in *Narrative of a Pedestrian Journey through Russia and Siberian Tartary*, 1824 which was so popular that it ran to a fourth edition by 1829. The work was bitterly attacked by a critic in *The Quarterly Review* who impugned the honour of Mrs Cochrane, which brought a dignified reply from her husband in later editions.

Coleridge, Samuel Taylor (1772-1834) Poet, essayist, critic, man of letters and with **William Wordsworth** the main architect of the **romantic movement** in **England**. According to Thomas Carlyle he was '. . . *a fat, flabby, incurvated personage, at once short, rotund, and relaxed . . . He never straightens his knee-joints. He stoops with his fat, ill-shapen shoulders, and in walking does not tread, but shovel and slide . . . .'* Nevertheless, Coleridge was a strong walker who thought nothing of covering 65 kilometres in a day, and he undertook several walking tours before his addiction to opium ruined his health. According to **William Hazlitt**, Coleridge often composed poetry whilst walking. In the summer of 1794 he walked with his friend and fellow Cambridge undergraduate, **Joseph Hucks**, who wrote a book about their adventures, put their clothes in *'a wallet or knapsack'* and walked from Oxford to north **Wales**. During this arduous 960-kilometre tour they spent much time discussing Coleridge's ideas for founding a pantisocracy or utopia in Virginia. Coleridge's account of this expedition can be found in his letters.

A walk that changed the whole course of English literature began in November 1797

Samuel Taylor Coleridge undertook several walking tours before his addiction to opium ruined his health (photo © National Portrait Gallery).

when Coleridge walked with William and **Dorothy Wordsworth** along the Somerset coast, now part of the **South West Coast Path**, from Alfoxenden, via Watchet to Minehead, and back through Dulverton, where the idea for the poem *The Ancient Mariner* was discussed. At first it was to be a joint effort between the two poets, but was then left to Coleridge to complete, and was included in *Lyrical Ballads*, published in 1798, which is generally regarded as the seminal work that triggered the **romantic movement** in English literature.

In 1799 he made his first visit to what is now the **Lake District National Park** in the company of John and William Wordsworth, and spent three weeks walking some of the best routes in Cumberland and Westmorland. In August, 1802 he spent a week walking alone in the Lake District and recorded his experiences in letters to friends. In 1803, he and the Wordsworths undertook a carriage tour to the Scottish Highlands, but the friends fell out and Coleridge left them at Loch Lomond and walked alone to Edinburgh

via Inverness, covering 423 kilometres in eight days. In 1828 he went with William Wordsworth, who was accompanied by his daughter Dora, on a walking tour of the Rhine and Meuse. During the course of this tour they met **Thomas Grattan** who describes walking with them in his reminiscences *Beaten* **Paths** *and Those who have Trod Them*, 1862.

Collett, Anthony The author of *Country* **Rambles** *Round London; with Precise Directions for Fifty Routes and Descriptions of Features of Interest*, 1912. This is a detailed, well-written guide with **maps** by Stanford in a pocket in the rear cover. It also gives train times and contains succinct descriptions of scenery, and literary and historical associations.

Collins, Martin (1941-) Formerly a college lecturer in art and design but now a full-time writer, journalist and photographer. He is the author of numerous guidebooks and contributes articles to the national and outdoor press.
Publications about Walking
GR5: Walking the French **Alps**, Cicerone Press, 1984.
Alta Via: High Walks in the Dolomites, Cicerone Press, 1986.
Walking in Northern **France**, Moorland Publishing Co., 1987.

Martin Collins, prolific author and photographer of walking books (photo © Martin Collins).

North York Moors: Walks in the **National Park**, Cicerone Press, 1987.
Laughs along the **Pennine Way**, Cicerone Press, 1987. (A book of cartoons.)
Chamonix Mont Blanc: a Walker's Guide, Cicerone Press, 1989.
South West Way: A Walker's Guide to the Coast **Path**, 2 vols, Cicerone Press, 1989.
Classic Coastal Walks of Britain, Oxford Illustrated Press, 1990.
Classic Walks on the **North York Moors**, Oxford Illustrated Press, 1990.
Also contributed to
Unsworth, Walt, Editor, *Classic Walks of the World*, Oxford Illustrated Press, 1990.
Unsworth, Walt, Editor, *Classic Walks in Europe*, Oxford Illustrated Press, 1987.

Collins, [William] Wilkie (1824-89) English novelist, friend of **Charles Dickens** and author of *The Woman in White* and *The Moonstone*. He walked around **Cornwall** in the summer of 1850 with his friend Henry C. Brandling, and described their adventures, including a vivid account of a visit to the Botallack tin mine, in **Rambles** *beyond Railways* 1851 (in those days the southwesterly terminus was Plymouth). The work was reissued in 1982.

Combe From the Old English meaning a deep hollow or valley, especially on the flank of a hill. In **England** the term, often used as a suffix, has slightly different connotations according to locality. In the Lake District it means much the same as a **corrie** in **Scotland**, or a **cwm** in **Wales**, but in the south, and especially in Devonshire, it means a wooded valley. Variant spellings are comb, coomb and coombe.

Comeraghs A **mountain** range situated in the south-east of **Eire** in County Waterford. Their main features are the splendid **corries** and the flat, plateau-like summits. They extend westward to meet the Knockmealdowns which are much less rugged and offer somewhat easier walking. The highest peak is Fauscoum (779 metres).
Maps
Irish Ordnance Survey 1:63360 sheets 167, 177, 178. 1:126720 sheet 22.
Footpath Guides
Martindale, Frank, *Irish Walks Guides South East: Tipperary and Waterford*, Gill & Macmillan, 1979.

Common Land in private ownership over which certain people, known as commoners, have particular rights. It has its origins in the manorial system of feudal times whereby the lord of the manor allowed his tenants to graze their animals and gather wood etc on his land. In the course of time these privileges became enforceable rights, and such lands became known as common land because the tenants shared the rights in common. The **Enclosure** Acts of the eighteenth and nineteenth centuries divided the commons into smaller fields but did not extinguish the commoners' rights. Note that commons are not necessarily open to the general public, although there is sometimes a general right to air and exercise, and only certain persons can claim commoners' rights. The traditional rights of commons are estovers (the taking of wood), pannage (the feeding of pigs on acorns and beech mast), pasture (grazing of animals), piscary (fishing), turbary (the taking of **peat** and turf for fuel), and common in the soil (the taking of stone and gravel for building). Under the Commons Registration Act, 1965, all commons and their rights had to be registered or the rights were extinguished. The organisation that concerns itself with the protection of commons is the **Open Spaces Society** *(for address see Appendix)*.

Compass An instrument used in the first instance for establishing the position of **magnetic north**, and an essential complement to a **map** for accurate **navigation**. Virtually all compasses used by walkers and in **orienteering** are based on the design pioneered by the Silva Company of Sweden which incorporates a protractor in the compass housing allowing the user to take **bearings** and plot courses without orientating the map. The orienteering compass may be used in the following ways:
1 *To assist in staying on course in poor visibility* (see figure 5). Before the weather closes in the direction-of-travel arrow should be pointed at the objective, and the compass housing turned until the arrow on the base plate is lined up with the north end of the compass needle. When the objective of the journey can no longer be seen it will be possible to reach it by keeping the arrow on the base plate, and the north needle, lined up, and then following the direction-of-travel arrow.
2 *Plotting a course from the map* (see figure 6). Place the base plate of the compass along the line of the route to be followed. Without moving the base plate, turn the compass housing until the arrow points towards the north end of the map and is exactly parallel to the north-south **grid lines**, and then add the **magnetic variation**. The compass should be removed from the map and held in front of

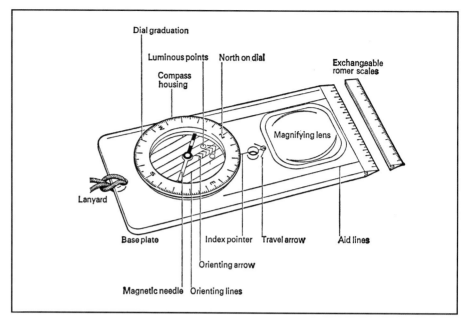

Figure 4: Silva compass.

Figure 5: Staying on course.

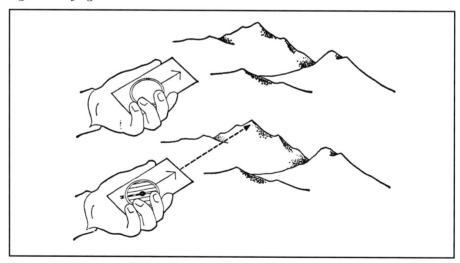

the user who should then turn his body until the red arrow in the compass housing lines up with the north-facing needle. Follow the direction-of-travel arrow.
3 *Making a fix* (see figure 7). Assuming that a **path** is being followed, the easiest way of establishing your exact position is to select a known prominent landmark that can be identified both on the ground and on the map. Point

the direction-of-travel arrow at it and turn the compass housing so that the arrow on the base lines up with the north-facing needle. Subtract the magnetic variation and place the base plate of the compass on the map with the straight edge touching the landmark from where the **bearing** was taken. Without altering the position of the compass housing, turn the base plate on the map until the arrow on the base

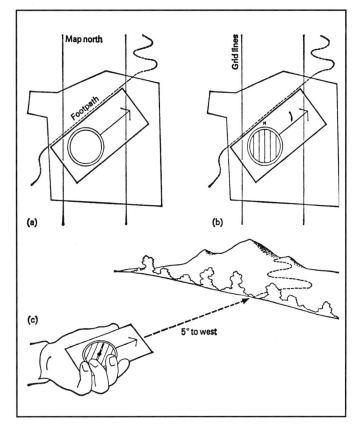

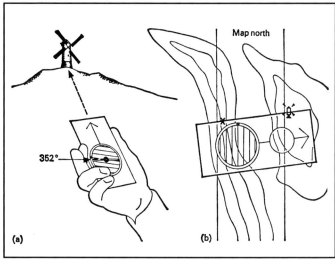

Figure 7 (above): Making a fix.

Figure 6 (left): Plotting a course from the map.

plate points to the north and is exactly parallel to the north-south grid lines. Draw a line along the base plate from the landmark, and the place where it intersects with the path is the position. A more sophisticated version of this technique is known as a **resection**.

Compton, Thomas (17--?—18--?) A civilian member of staff of the Corps of Military Surveyors and Draftsmen who was seconded to the Royal Military Academy as an assistant drawing-master for ground (the Corps of Military Surveyors and Draftsmen was part of the Ordnance Board which was also responsible for the **Ordnance Survey**). He joined the Academy in 1806 and seems to have been made redundant in 1820. He is the author of an account of two walking tours undertaken in 1814 and 1815 entitled *The Northern Cambrian* **Mountains***; or a Tour through North* **Wales***, Describing the Scenery and General Characters of that Romantic Country, and Embellished with a Series of Highly-finished Coloured Views, Engraved from Original Drawings*, 1817. This is a prosaic account made interesting because the author gives precise instructions for following the route, often on **paths**, in the manner of a

modern **footpath guide** and reflecting his training as a surveyor. The book is also unusual in that it is beautifully illustrated with aquatints. He had a sanguine attitude to route-finding *'It may be mentioned, that the Tours were performed on foot, without ever having recourse to a guide: a method which cannot be too strongly recommended, as no other possesses the same advantages for viewing the scenery; and the difficulties occasionally encountered for want of a guide, always lead to a more intimate knowledge of the country'.*

Condensation Water formed by water vapour coming into contact with a cold surface. The human body is constantly excreting water vapour through the pores of the skin. Water vapour will pass unchecked through porous fabrics into the atmosphere, but if it meets an impermeable barrier, such as **nylon** coated with conventional **polyurethane**, it will collect on the inner surface and turn into tiny droplets of water. If this condensation is unable to escape, porous clothes, such as shirts and sweaters, will gradually absorb it and the wearer will be conscious that he is getting damp. Condensation can be prevented, or at least markedly reduced, by using a *poromeric* or

hydrophyllic material that encourages **water vapour transmission**.

Connemara Mountains A group of **mountains** in County Galway in the far west of **Eire**. They include the Twelve Bens and the Maumturks and offer some of the finest walking in the country.
Maps
Irish Ordnance Survey 1:63360 sheets 83, 84, 93, 94. 1:126720 sheets 10, 11.
Footpath Guides
Lynam, Joss *and* Robinson, Tim, *The Mountains of Connemara: Guidebook and Map*, Folding Landscapes, 1988. (Distributed in the UK by Cordee.)
Robinson, Tim, *Connemara: Map and Guide*, Folding Landscapes, 1988. (Distributed in the UK by Cordee.)
Whilde, T., *Irish Walks Guides West; Clare, Galway and Mayo*, Gill and Macmillan, 1979.

Contour lines The lines found on most topographical **maps** that are used to indicate relief by means of **contours**.

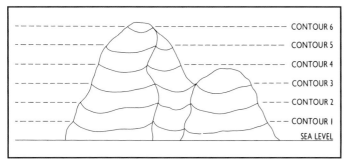

Figure 8: Model of a hill showing contour lines.

Figure 9: Typical contour shapes.

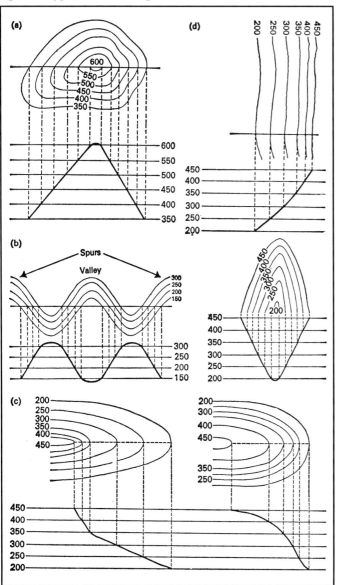

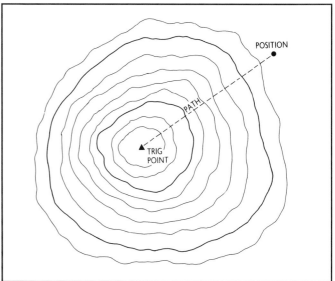

Figure 10: Counting contours.

Contouring The technique of traversing a hillside or mountainside whilst staying at the same height. The term is derived from **contours** because the walker follows an imaginary **contour line**.

Contours A method of depicting the three dimensional shape (length, width and height) of the earth's surface on a two dimensional (length and width) **map** by the use of lines drawn at uniform heights eg 200 metres, 210 metres, 220 metres etc. The system has been adopted by the **Ordnance Survey** and by most other national surveys for their larger scale maps.

Figure 8 shows a **hill** with contours sketched in. Imagine that the three-dimensional model is made of **ice** and that the contours are made of thin wire. If it were possible to melt the ice without disturbing the relative position of the wire contours, they would sink to the base-board on which the model stands and look exactly like the contours of a map (see figure 9). The shape of hills and valleys can be reconstructed by projecting the contours as shown.

The height of contour lines on maps published by the Ordnance Survey is shown only at intervals, and it is often necessary to trace the line of the contour for some distance to establish the height. Unless the heights are traced it is sometimes difficult to decide whether the contours indicate a hill or a valley

33

because the patterns are the same as can be seen by comparing figures 8 and 9. However, if a stream is shown it *must* be a valley, and if there is no stream it is likely to be a hill, although it could be a dry valley. If in doubt it is essential to trace the contour lines to check the heights. The figures indicating the height of contour lines on maps published by the Ordnance Survey *always* read *up* the slope, so if the figures on the contours can be read you must be looking up the slope.

As every fifth contour is shown as a thicker line, the quickest way of calculating height gained is to establish the contour interval from the map key, count the thicker contour lines and multiply by the distance between the thick lines. Then count the number of thin lines at each end, multiply these by the contour interval and add to the figure obtained from the thick lines.

Example Figure 10 shows contours taken from the 1:25000 map. According to the key the distance between thick contour lines is 25 metres and there is a 5 metre interval between the thin lines. Therefore the height is

2 thick lines x 25 = 50 metres
3 thin lines x 5 = 15 metres
———
Height gained   65 metres

Conway, William Martin, Baron Conway of Allington (1856-1937) Art collector, critic **mountaineer**, and **Sunday Tramp**. Like many of his generation who explored the **Alps** in the latter half of the nineteenth century, he enjoyed both walking and climbing for his real passion was for the **mountains** themselves. In his *Alps from End to End*, 1895 he describes a 1600-kilometre walk and climbing expedition that took him 86 days—21 for writing and 65 on the march. He went with his friend A. E. Fitzgerald, two Alpine guides and two Ghurkas, commencing at the Colle di Tenda, near Turin, and finishing at Lend in **Austria**. Conway and the Ghurkas wore turbans and puttees (the turban of one of the Ghurkas was so large that during a storm they formed a **tent** from it and all four sheltered underneath). He also explored and climbed in Spitzbergen, the **Andes** and the **Himalaya**, and was President of the **Alpine Club** 1902-4. He wrote several other books including *Mountain Memories; a Pilgrimage of Romance*, 1920.

Cooper, Arthur Nevile (1850-1943) Vicar of Filey from 1880-1935, canon of York Minster, and long-distance walker. Canon Cooper,

who liked to style himself 'the walking parson', first conceived a love of walking when he was a curate at Chester-le-Street and had to walk long distances to conduct services in that scattered parish. In the nineteenth century, life in a country vicarage was very leisurely, the hard work was often done by the curates, and Cooper was able to indulge in his passion for walking long distances. He enjoyed rude health, which he attributed to walking, and tried to persuade others to adopt the practice by extensive writing and lecturing on the subject. He lived to be ninety-three. Despite his enthusiasm, he was an unimaginative man, and his method of selecting a route was to draw a line with a ruler on a school atlas between the start and finish, and to follow it as closely as possible. He had a number of unusual encounters, and his books make fascinating reading, although it is sometimes difficult to understand how, or why, he chose his destinations. His longest walks were to Rome (1887 and 1914); to Budapest (1890); To Venice (1900); to Monte Carlo (1903); to Barcelona (1904); to Copenhagen (1905); to Stockholm (1906); to Pompeii (1907); to the Carpathians (1909); to Lourdes (1910); to Vienna (1912); to Berlin (1913); and to Madrid (1920). He also walked extensively in the British Isles. Cooper described his walks, adventures and philosophy in *A Walk to Rome*, 1887; *The Tramps of the Walking Parson*, 1905; *With **Knapsack** and Notebook*, 1906; *Quaint Talks about Long Walks*, 1907; *A Tramp's Schooling*, 1909; *Walking as Education*, 1910; and *Tales of my Tramps*, 1913.

Corbett The name given to Scottish **mountains** of more than 2500 feet (762 metres) and under 3000 feet (914 metres) with a re-ascent of at least 500 feet (152 metres) on all sides. The list, currently containing 223 summits, which is of interest to those who enjoy **peakbagging**, was first compiled by J. Rooke Corbett. A complete list of Corbetts, together with a list of **Munros** and **Donalds** will be found in *Munro's Tables of the 3000-feet Mountains of Scotland and other Tables of Lesser Heights* edited and revised by J. C. Donaldson and **Hamish M. Brown**, **Scottish Mountaineering Club** District Guide Books, Scottish Mountaineering Trust, 1984. An account of climbing all the Corbetts may be found in *Climbing the Corbetts; Scotland's 2500ft Summits* by Hamish M. Brown, Gollancz, 1988.

Cordura A special weave of rugged and abrasive-resistant **nylon**, developed by Du

Pont, that is similar in appearance to **cotton duck** and is ideal for use in **gaiters** and **rucksacks**. It is often coated with **polyurethane** to make it waterproof.

Corduroy A cut-weft pile **cotton** fabric in which the cut fibres form the surface of the material from which it gets its characteristic ridge and furrow texture. It is soft to the touch and will absorb large quantities of water which makes it feel cold and unpleasant, and it takes a long time to dry. It was once a popular material for **breeches**. Needlecord is a finer version of corduroy. Both corduroy and needlecord can be made water repellent by coating with silicones, or by applying one of the proprietary waterproofing agents such as Technix.

Cornice A bank or projection of **snow** that overhangs a **ridge**, **arête** or **corrie** (see figure 11). Cornices are formed by the action of the wind, and are extremely dangerous because there is nothing to support them. If trodden on, both cornice and walker will be hurled down the mountainside. Cornices, which may not be obvious, should be avoided by walking on the windward side of the ridge. They can also be dangerous to those walking below the ridge on which they are formed. In thaw conditions they may collapse without warning, engulf anyone below, and even start an **avalanche**.

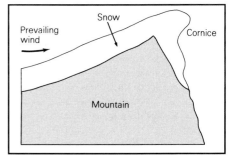

Figure 11: Cornice.

Cornwall An **area of outstanding natural beauty** part of which was designated in 1959 and the remainder in 1983. It does not cover the whole county, as its name suggests, because the designated area includes only the glorious coastline, which contains some of the finest coastal scenery in England, plus Bodmin Moor. Unfortunately, much of the rest of the county outside the designated area of 2122 square

kilometres is dull and spoiled by ribbon development, mining and china clay workings. (See figure 36 for a **map** showing the location of all AONBs in the United Kingdom.)
Maps
1:50000 **Landranger** sheets 190, 200, 201, 203, 204.
1:25000 **Pathfinder** sheets P1310 (SX19), P1311 (SX29/39), P1325 (SX08/18), P1326 (SX28/38), P1337 (SW87/97), P1338 (SX07/17), P1339 (SX27/37), P1346 (SW86/96), P1347 (SX06/16), P1348 (SX26/36), P1352 (SW75), P1354 (SX05/15), P1355 (SX25/35), P1356 (SX45/55), P1359 (SW54/64), P1360 (SW74/84), P1361 (SW94/SX04), P1364 (SW33/43), P1366 (SW83), P1368 (SW32/42), P1369 (SW52/62), P1370 (SW72), P1372 (SW61/71).
Footpath Guides
Smith, Eleanor, *Cornish Coastal Walks for Motorists; 30 Circular Walks for Motorists*, Warne, 1983.
Vage, Donald, *Walking Cornwall*, Devon Books, 1987.
Ward, Ken, *Land's End & the Lizard*, Jarrold, 1986.

Corrie A Scottish term, from the Gaelic 'coire' meaning a cauldron, used to describe a large hollow on a mountainside, often formed by a hanging valley or by the action of **glaciers**. The English equivalent is a **combe,** and in **Wales** it is a **cwm.**

Coryate, Thomas (1577?—1612) 'The Peregrine of Odcombe' or 'the Odcombian legge-stretcher' as he variously described himself was one of the earliest of the literary pedestrians. He was born at Odcombe, Somerset and educated at Westminster School and Gloucester Hall, Oxford where he became a considerable classical scholar. He was friendly with **Ben Jonson** and became a courtier where he played the buffoon and was the butt of many jokes. In 1608 he travelled on horseback and by coach across **France** to **Italy** where his money ran out and he had to return home from Venice, via the Rhine, on foot. He described his adventures in *Coryate's Crudities Hastily Gobbled up in Five Months Travels in France, Italy etc w*hich was edited by Ben Jonson and published in 1611. It is an extraordinary work of 800 pages of which about 100 are panegyric verses. It is both an accurate guidebook and a commentary on the social customs of the countries he visited, as well as an account of his own adventures and the unusual sights he

witnessed. In 1611 he embarked on his travels again and walked through **Greece**, Palestine, Persia to India, where he was received by the Great Mogul. He died of 'a flux', which was probably dysentery, whilst in India, and the news of his death was relayed to England by the trading community. The best modern edition of *Crudities* was published in 1905.

Cotswolds An **area of outstanding natural beauty** containing much excellent walking country, designated in 1965, covering the counties of Gloucestershire, Hereford and Worcester, Oxfordshire, Avon and Wiltshire, and bounded by Bath, Cheltenham and Cirencester. The 1507 square kilometres contains **hills** of limestone and sandstone from which the buildings of the exceptionally beautiful villages have been constructed. (See figure 36 for a **map** showing the location of all AONBs in the United Kingdom.)
Maps
1:63360 Cotswold **Tourist Map.**
1:50000 **Landranger** sheets 150, 151, 163, 164, 172, 173.
1:25000 **Pathfinder** sheets P1019 (SO84/94), P1020 (SP04/14), P1042 (SO83/93), P1043 (SP03/13), P1044 (SP23/33), P1066 (SO82/92), P1067 (SP02/12), P1068 (SP22/32), P1089 (SO81/91), P1090 (SP01/11), P1091 (SP21/31), P1110 (SP20/30), P1113 (SO80/90), P1114 (SP00/10), P1117 (SO60/70), P1132 (ST69/79), P1133 (ST89/99), P1151 (ST68/78), P1152 (ST88/98), P1167 (ST67/77), P1168 (ST87/97), P1183 (ST66/76).
Footpath Guides
Airey, John, *Cotswolds Walks with a Point*, Foulsham, 1986.
Hargreaves, Harry, *Cotswold **Rambles***, Thornhill Press, 1983.
Hargreaves, Harry, *Second Book of Cotswold Rambles*, Thornhill Press, 1985.
Kershaw, R. and Robson, B., *Discovering Walks in the Cotswolds*, Shire Publications, 3rd. Rev. Ed., 1983.
Richards, Mark, *Country Walks around Stow-on-the-Wold*, Walx Publications, 1988.
Richards, Mark, *Country Walks around Chipping Norton*, Walx Publications, 1988.
Richards, Mark, *Country Walks around Burford*, *Walx Publications,* 1989.

Cotton A natural fibre that can be woven into a variety of cloths such as corduroy, **cotton duck**, **gaberdine**, **moleskin**, needlecord, **polycotton**, **Stormbeta**, and **Ventile** used

in outdoor **clothing**. Cotton breathes and will absorb water and perspiration which makes it suitable for underclothes, although when wet, it loses its warmth and becomes unpleasantly cold and clammy. It can be made water-repellent by coating with silicones, or by applying one of the proprietary waterproofing agents such as Technix. It can also be used in shell clothing if made completely waterproof by applying paraffin wax (it will then lose the capacity to breathe and **condensation** will form on the inside of the garment).

Cotton duck A tough, hard-wearing material made from **cotton** and once widely used in the manufacture of **rucksacks** and **gaiters**. It has now been superseded by **nylon**, **Cordura**, and **KS100.**

Couloir A French word, meaning 'corridor' or 'passage', that has been widely adopted by British **mountaineers** to describe a gully or steep **gorge** on a mountainside. Couloirs often provide relatively easy access to summits, but they must be treated warily as they are often the natural route for **stonefalls** and **avalanches**.

Council for National Parks The Council exists to protect and promote the **national parks** of **England** and **Wales**, and the Norfolk and Suffolk **Broads**. It is a charity established more than fifty years ago and now has 45 member organisations representing over three million supporters of **national parks**. Individuals can support the Council's work by becoming a Friend of National Parks. It publishes a journal, *Tarn and Tor*, as well as *Fifty Years for National Parks*, *Know Your National Parks* and various reports and conference proceedings on matters relating to national parks. *(For address see Appendix.)*

Council for the Protection of Rural England The CPRE was founded in 1926 to protect all that is worthwhile in the English countryside. It recognises that changes must take place, but where they do they should be for the better. The Council has branches in all counties, and concerns itself with new housing and industrial development, power stations, overhead transmission lines, new reservoirs and the extraction of water from rivers and lakes, sand and gravel workings, limestone quarrying and opencast coal-mining, the felling and planting of trees, the siting of new roads, especially motorways, and the use of land by government departments. Whenever necessary, the CPRE co-operates with other amenity bodies and lobbies MPs, briefs counsel for public enquiries, and offers advice to government departments and planning authorities. It publishes a journal, *Countryside Campaigner. (For address see Appendix.)*

Council for the Protection of Rural Wales (Cymdethas Diogelu Cymru Wledig) The CPRW is the country's leading independent countryside conservation pressure group. Established in 1928, it plays a vital role in defending the whole of the Welsh coast and countryside. The Council protects the Welsh landscape from insensitive development, and fights for a prosperous and healthy countryside that balances a wide range of needs. It monitors central government and Welsh Office proposals as well as the work of statutory agencies, and acts as an environmental watchdog, contributing well researched views on planning issues. It publishes a journal, *Rural **Wales** (Cymry Wledig). (For address see Appendix.)*

Country and Travel A magazine launched in 1950, published by Ramblers' Association Services (the commercial arm of the Ramblers' Association) and edited by **Tom Stephenson**, that was intended both to make money for the Ramblers' Association, and to promote walking as the best way of seeing the countryside. It had a list of distinguished contributors and was well-received by the public, but failed to get sufficient advertising revenue. The first issues appeared monthly, then it became a quarterly, and it folded after only a few issues. It was one of several similar magazines aimed at countrygoers which were published at about this time, reflecting the hunger for contact with the eternal verities of the countryside after the rigours of war. Most of them can best be described as a cross between *The Countryman* and a downmarket version of *Country Life.*

Country Code A code of conduct for those visiting the countryside that is now promoted by the **Countryside Commission**. The history of the Country Code is lost in the sands of time, but it is known that an early version was used by the **Youth Hostels Association** immediately after the Second World War, and was being printed on membership cards by 1948. Section 86 (1) of the **National Parks and Access to the Countryside Act, 1949** called for *'The preparation and publication of a code of conduct for the guidance of persons visiting the coun-*

tryside...' A sub-committee of the **National Parks Commission** drafted the first official Country Code in 1950, and it was published in 1951. In March 1978, the **Countryside Commission** decided to review the Country Code and set up a study group of interested organisations which published a consultation paper. After further deliberations the Countryside Commission approved the following version which, at the time of writing, is the official Country Code:

1 *Enjoy the countryside and respect its life and work.*
2 *Guard against all risks of fire.*
3 *Fasten all gates.*
4 *Keep your **dogs** under close control*
5 *Keep to public **paths** across farmland.*
6 *Use gates and **stiles** to cross fences, hedges and walls.*
7 *Leave livestock, crops and machinery alone.*
8 *Take your litter home.*
9 *Protect wild life, wild plants and trees.*
10 *Take special care on country roads.*
11 *Make no unnecessary noise.*

The Country Code surfers from the ambiguities and vagueness inherent in all succinct codes of conduct that are so easily learned parrot-fashion. For example, if *'Fasten all gates'* is intended to mean 'close all gates', then the instruction is incorrect because gates are sometimes deliberately left open by **farmers** as part of their system of farm management. *'Keep to public paths across farmland'* implies that it is permissible to walk anywhere in **open country**, although in most parts of **England** and **Wales**, the walker commits a **trespass** if he deviates from the **right of way**, unless an **access agreement** has been negotiated.

Country Walking A magazine, published by EMAP of Peterborough, that first appeared in 1986 which currently has the largest circulation of any commercially published walking magazine in Britain. It is popular in style and aimed at the family rambler interested in all aspects of the countryside. *(For address see Appendix.)*

Countrygoer Books The title of a series of books, uniform in style and magazine-like format, that appeared in the immediate postwar years. Each book was devoted to a particular outdoor theme, eg ***National Parks***, and contained contributions from distinguished authors. The editorial board was formed by **C. E. M. Joad**, Francis Ritchie, Joan Spence and Cyril Moore. No. 20, published in 1950,

seems to have been the last in the series.

Countryside Act, 1968 An important Act that affected **England** and **Wales** and made the first amendments to the **National Parks and Access to the Countryside Act, 1949**. The *Preamble* to the Act states its purpose as *'An Act to enlarge the functions of the Commission established under the National Parks and Access to the Countryside Act, 1949, to confer new powers to local authorities and other bodies for the conservation and enhancement of natural beauty for the benefit of those resorting to the countryside, and to make other provision for the matters dealt with in the Act of 1949 and generally as respects the countryside, and to amend the law about trees and woodlands, and **footpaths** and **bridleways**, and other public **paths**.'* The Act replaced the **National Parks** Commission with the **Countryside Commission** and gave it responsibility for all countryside matters in **England** and **Wales**; it gave local authorities the power to establish country parks; the signposting of **rights of way** became mandatory; it made minor amendments to the **ploughing** of rights of way; **roads used as public paths** were to be reclassified; traffic regulation orders could be made in national parks, **areas of outstanding natural beauty**, and to **long-distance paths**; and it gave landowners the right to claim 25% of the cost of maintaining gates and **stiles** from the highway authority.

Countryside Commission A statutory agency that cares for the countryside of **England** and **Wales** and helps people to enjoy it. The Commission was established under the terms of the **Countryside Act, 1968** as the successor to the **National Parks** Commission but with wider responsibilities, and has been an independent agency since 1982 with an annual grant from the Department of the Environment. It is an advisory and promotional body, working in partnership with others such as local authorities, public agencies, voluntary bodies, **farmers**, landowners and private individuals, and providing grants and advice for projects which conserve the natural beauty of the countryside and make it more accessible for public enjoyment. To enable people to enjoy the countryside on foot, the Commission establishes **national trails**, which pass through some of the wildest and finest scenery, and it also supports the development of regional routes, as well as encouraging local authorities to open up **rights of way** and local **paths**. It acts as the government's advisor on countryside matters, and it has special responsibility for designating national parks, **areas of outstanding natural beauty** and defining **heritage coasts**.

The Commission maintains an excellent library, open to the public by appointment, of British and foreign books and serials, and publishes two journals, *Countryside Commission News* and *National Parks Today*, as well as a newsletter *Enjoying the Countryside. (For address see Appendix.)*

Countryside Commission for Scotland

The Commission was established under the **Countryside (Scotland) Act, 1967** and is an autonomous government agency financed by an annual grant from the Scottish Development Department. The Commission's duties are to conserve and enhance the Scottish landscape; to develop and improve public **access** into the countryside and improve facilities for its enjoyment including the provision of **long-distance paths**; to have regard for the need for economic and social development in the countryside; to advise the Secretary of State for **Scotland**, planning authorities, the **Forestry Commission** and other agencies on development in the countryside; to increase public understanding and awareness and promote the best use of the countryside; and to develop and update a factual base from which sound policies can be developed through research and review. The Commission publishes a journal, *Scotland's* **Countryside**, and a wide range of material on such subjects as the law and tradition of access, countryside conservation for **farmers**, information sheets and educational leaflets. *(For address see Appendix.)*

Countryside (Scotland) Act, 1967

The most important single piece of legislation affecting **Scotland's** countryside. It established the **Countryside Commission for Scotland**, and gave local planning authorities the general statutory duty to *'keep clear and free from obstruction or encroachment any public right of way which is wholly or partly in their area'*, as well as the right to create, divert and extinguish public **paths**. It also made provision for the pasturing of **bulls** in fields crossed by rights of way, misleading notices, **ploughing**, the creation of **national scenic areas** and **long-distance paths**.

County summits of the British Isles

The following list of county summits, with **grid references**, is provided for those interested in **peak-bagging** and **challenge walks**. Walkers should be aware that many of these summits are on private land with no **access** along a **right of way**.

English counties Avon: East Harptree (264 metres) ST 5653; Bedfordshire: Dunstable Downs (243 metres) TL 0019; Berkshire: Walbury Hill; known locally as Inkpen Beacon (297 metres) SU 3761; Buckinghamshire: Wendover Woods (267 metres) SP 8908; Cambridgeshire: Great Chishill (146 metres) TL 4238; Cheshire: Shining Tor (559 metres) SJ 9973; Cleveland: Gisborough Moor (329 metres) NZ 6312; Cornwall: Brown Willy (420 metres) SX 1579; Cumbria: Scafell Pike (978 metres) NY 2107; Derbyshire: Kinder Scout (636 metres) SK 0887; Devon: High Willhays (621 metres) SX 5889; Dorset: Pilsdon Pen (277 metres) ST 4101; Durham: Mickle **Fell** (790 metres) NY 8024; East Sussex: Ditchling Beacon (248 metres) TQ 3313; Essex: Oldfield Grove; Langley (147 metres) TL 4436; Gloucestershire: Cleeve Cloud (330 metres) SO 9924; Greater London: Westerham Heights (247 metres) TQ 4356; Greater Manchester: Featherbed Moss (541 metres) SE 0401; Hampshire: Pilot Hill (286 metres) SU 3960; Hereford & Worcester: Black **Mountains** (703 metres) SO 2535; Hertfordshire: Hastoe (244 metres) SP 9109; Humberside: Cot Nab (246 metres) SE 8256; **Isles of Scilly**: St Mary's (51 metres) SV 9112; **Isle of Wight**: St Boniface Down (239 metres) SZ 5678; Kent: Westerham Hill (251 metres) TQ 4356; Lancashire: Gragareth (627 metres) SD 6879; Leicestershire: Bardon Hill (279 metres) SK 4513; Lincolnshire: Normanby-le-Wold (168 metres) TF 1296; Merseyside: Billinge Hill (180 metres) SD 5201; Norfolk: Roman Camp Beacon; Sheringham (105 metres) TG 1841; Northamptonshire: Arbury Hill (224 metres) SP 5358; Northumberland: The Cheviot (815 metres) NT 9020; North Yorkshire: Whernside (736 metres) SD 7381; Nottinghamshire: Herrod's Hill (202 metres) SK 4659; Oxfordshire: Whitehorse Hill (261 metres) SU 3086; Salop: Brown Clee Hill (540 metres) SO 5986; Somerset: Dunkery Beacon (520 metres) SS 8941; South Yorkshire: Margery Hill (546 metres) SK 1895; Staffordshire: Oliver Hill (513 metres) SK 0267; Suffolk: Rede (128 metres) TL 7855; Surrey: Leith Hill (294 metres) TQ 1343; Tyne & Wear: near Chopwell (259 metres) NZ 1059; Warwickshire: Ilmington Downs: (260 metres) SP 1842; West Midlands: Turner's Hill (269 metres) SO 9688; West Sussex: Black Down Hill (280 metres) SU 9129; West Yorkshire: Black Hill: (582 metres) SE 0704; Wiltshire: Milk Hill (294 metres) SU 1064 and Tan Hill (294 metres) SU 0864.

Welsh counties Clwyd: Moel Sych (827 metres) SK 0631; Dyfed: near Fan Foel (773 metres) SN 8222; Gwent: Chwarel-y-Fan (679 metres) SO 2529; Gwynedd: Snowdon (1085 metres) SH 6154; Mid-Glamorgan: Carn Foesen (584 metres) SN 9003; Powys: Pen-y-Fan (886 metres) SO 0121; South Glamorgan: Pant-glas (264 metres) ST 1985; West Glamorgan: Cefnffordd (600 metres) SN 9003.

Scottish regions Borders: Broad Law (840 metres) NT 1423; Central: Ben More (1174 metres) NN4324; Dumfries & Galloway: Merrick (844 metres) NX 4285; Fife: West Lomond (522 metres) NO 1906; Grampian: Ben Macdui (1309 metres) NN 9898; Highlands: Ben Nevis (1344 metres) NN 1671; Lothian: Blackhope Scar (651 metres) NT 3148; Orkney: Ward Hill; Hoy (479 metres) HY 2202; Shetland: Ronas Hill; Mainland (450 metres) HU 3083; Strathclyde: Bidean nam Bian (1150 metres) NN 1454; Tayside: Ben Lawers (1214 metres) NN 6341; Western Isles: Clisham; Harris (799 metres) NB 1507.

Northern Ireland *counties* Antrim: Trostan (551 metres) D17234; Armagh: Slieve Gullion (575 metres) J0220; Down: Slieve Donard (850 metres) J3527; Fermanagh/Cavan border: Cuilcagh (664 metres) H1228; Londonderry: Sawel (680 metres) H6197; Tyrone: Mullaghclogha (634 metres) H5595.

Isle of Man Snaefell (621 metres) SC 3988.

Channel Islands near Les Platons; Jersey (134 metres) 652556.

Republic of Ireland counties Carlow/Wexford border: Mount Leinster (796 metres) H1228; Cavan/Fermanagh border: Cuilcagh (664 metres) H1228; Clare: Glennagalliagh (533 metres) R6475; Cork: Knockboy (707 Metres) W0062; Donegal: Errigal (752 metres) B9290; Dublin: Kippure (754 metres) 01115; Galway: Benbaun (730 metres) L7853; Kerry: Carrauntoohil (1041 metres) V8084; Kildare: Dunmurry Hill (234 metres) N7117; Kilkenny: Brandon Hill (519 metres) S6940; Laoise/Offaly border: Arderin (529 metres) S2398; Leitrim/Sligo border: SE of Truskmore (632 metres) G7647; Limerick/Tipperary border: Galtymore Mountain (920 metres) R8723; Longford: Corn Hill (279 metres) N1884; Louth: Slieve Foy (590 metres) J1612; Mayo: Mweelrea (819 metres) L7966; Meath: Slieve Na Galliagh (278 metres) N5877; Monaghan: Mullyash (320 metres) Offaly/Laoise border: Arderin (529 metres) S2398; H8725;

Roscommon: Slieve Bawn (263 metres) M9574; Sligo: Truskmore (646 metres) G7547; Tippery/Limerick border: Galtymore Mountain (920 metres) R8723; Waterford: Knockmealdown (795 metres) S0508; Westmeath: Mullaghmeen (261 metres) N4679; Wicklow: Lugnaquillia (926 metres) T0391.

Cowell, J. J. Author of *Graian **Alps** and Mount Iseran, an Account of a Walking Exploration of the **Mountains*** on the Franco-Italian Border which appeared in *Notes of Travel in 1860* compiled and edited by **Francis Galton**.

Cox, Jack (ie John Roberts Cox) A journalist and author who was sometime editor of the *Boy's Own Paper*, and also wrote under the pseudonym of David Roberts. In the post-war years he wrote a number of books about walking and camping including *Camping*, 1952; *Camping for All*, 1953; *The Outdoor Book*, 1954; *Camp and **Trek***, 1956; and *The **Hike** Book*, 1960 (2nd Ed., 1965). These titles were quite useful until superseded by the popularisation of American **backpacking** techniques in the United Kingdom by **Derrick Booth**.

Coxe, William (1747-1828) Scholar, historian, sometime archdeacon of Wiltshire, and traveller who made a series of journeys in Europe with the object of providing accurate information about the constitution, law, cus-

William Coxe who recorded details of his walks in Travels in Switzerland, 1789 *(photo © National Portrait Gallery).*

toms and economy of the countries visited. Among his books only *Travels in **Switzerland** in a Series of Letters to William Melmoth Esq*, 3 vols 1789 (4th Ed., 1801) records accounts of walks, and was based on visits made in 1779, 1785 and 1787, although the letters were written in 1787. He did not set out with the intention of making a walking tour, but circumstances compelled him to cover some of the more remote areas on foot. He had an engaging character and there is something very appealing about this stout little clergyman having to gird his loins to take gamely to **mountain tracks**. He obviously enjoyed the experience as this extract describing his crossing of the Mer de Glace from Montenvers above Chamonix in the **Alps** shows:

'*After we had sufficiently refreshed ourselves, we prepared for our adventure across the **ice***. *We had each of us a long pole spiked with iron; and, in order to secure us as much as possible from slipping, the guides fastened to our shoes **crampons***, *or small bars of iron, provided with four small spikes of the same metal . . . We began our walk with great slowness and deliberation, but gradually gaining courage and confidence as we advanced, we soon found that we could safely pass along those places, where the ascent and descent were not very considerable, much faster even than when walking at the rate of our common pace: in other parts we leapt over the clefts, and slid down the steeper descents. In one place, where we descended and stepped across an opening upon a narrow ridge of ice scarcely three inches broad, we were obliged to tread with peculiar caution: for on each side were chasms of great depth. We walked some paces sideways along this **ridge***; *stept across the chasm into a little hollow, which the guides contrived on purpose for our feet; and got up an ascent by means of small holes which we made with the spikes of our poles.*'

In an interesting aside, which gives a revealing glimpse of the state of topographical knowledge at the time, he expresses the conviction that Mont Blanc is higher than any mountain in Asia or Africa. He believes Mont Blanc to be 15,562 feet as computed by Sir George Schuckborough (it is actually 15,767

feet). He pours scorn on a certain Father Kircher '. . . *who took the elevations of mountains by the uncertain method of measuring their shadows . . .*' and calculated the height of Aetna as 25,600 feet (it is 10,899 feet), the Peak of Teneriffe as 64,000 feet (Mount Teneriffe, also known as Mount Teide, is 12,198 feet), Mount Athos as 128,000 feet (it is 6668 feet), and Lariffa, Egypt as 179,200 feet! (Lariffa is not mentioned in modern gazetteers. The highest mountain in Egypt is Gebel Katherine which is 8659 feet high.)

An appendix lists his itinerary, with distances, of all his Swiss tours, and there is a **map** of the country. It is interesting to note that neither Zermatt nor the Matterhorn are mentioned in the text or shown on the map, and he appears to be unaware of their existence.

Crag-fast The condition of being trapped on a crag and unable to move. It is most likely to occur when **scrambling** beyond the limits of your ability, but it can also be caused by a change in weather conditions that turns an easy scramble into a serious rock climb. The only remedy is to attract attention, if necessary by using the **international mountain distress signal**, and wait to be rescued by the **mountain rescue** team, or a friendly climber with the necessary equipment.

Crampons Pointed metal devices that are strapped to the sole of the **boot** to provide better grip on **snow** and **ice**. They are of considerable antiquity and are known to have been used at least 2500 years ago in the Iron Age. Crampons is a French word, first known to have been used in 1490, derived from the Low German 'cramp', hence 'cramp iron'; the original British terms 'claws' and 'climbing irons' are now obsolete.

Crampons usually consist of ten or twelve spikes on a frame that can be adjusted for length, which is then secured to the sole of the boot by webbing straps secured round the

Figure 12: Crampons.

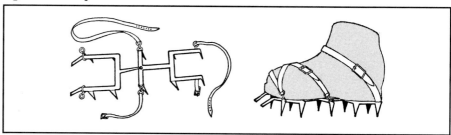

upper (see figure 12). There are usually two forward-facing spikes to assist grip on steep slopes. The frame must fit securely round the sole which may necessitate bending it to provide a snug grip. Soft snow tends to collect in a ball under the crampon, but this can be prevented by fitting a piece of polythene sheeting under the crampon allowing the spikes to protrude. Sometimes snowballs can be dislodged by tapping the side of the boot with an **ice axe**. Care must always be used when wearing crampons as the steel spikes can easily tear **clothing** and inflict nasty injuries. Some walkers, who only need crampons occasionally, use instep crampons which are smaller and attach to the instep of the boot, but they cannot be used for climbing steep snow slopes.

Cranborne Chase and West Wiltshire Downs An **area of outstanding natural beauty** that was designated by the Secretary of State for the Environment on the advice of the **Countryside Commission** in 1983. It covers 960 square kilometres of Wiltshire, but also includes parts of Dorset, Hampshire and Somerset, and is bounded by Frome, Salisbury, Wimborne Minster and Shaftesbury. The western edge joins the **Dorset** AONB. The AONB includes a delightful mixture of **downland** and rolling wooded hills with charming villages and small towns. (See figure 36) for a **map** showing the location of all AONBs in the United Kingdom.)

Maps
1:50000 **Landranger** sheets 183, 184, 194, 195.
1:25000 **Pathfinder** sheets P1219 (ST64/74), P1220 (ST84/94), P1221 (SU04/14), P1239 (ST63/73), P1240 (ST83/93), P1241 (SU03/13), P1261 (ST82/92), P1262 (SU02/12), P1281 (ST81/91), P1282 (SU01/11), P1300 (ST80/90), P1301 (SU00/10).

Footpath Guide
Jones, Roger, Wiltshire *Rambles*, Countryside Books, 1987.

Crevasse The term used to describe a crack in a **glacier**. In summer, when the glacier is dry, crevasses are easy to see and can usually be jumped, but when covered with snow they are often invisible and walkers must be roped for safety, and the surface of the glacier must be probed with an **ice axe**. Crevasses are often depicted on Alpine **maps**, although these are not accurate plottings but indications of areas where they are known to occur. The

crevasse that separates the glacier from the snowfield is known as a **bergschrund**.

Crossing, William (1847-1928) Miscellaneous writer, antiquarian and enthusiast for what is now the **Dartmoor National Park**. He spent most of his life exploring Dartmoor and wrote extensively about its history, topography, customs, traditions and **paths**. His most important work is *Guide to Dartmoor; a Topographical Description of the Forests and Commons*, first published in 1909 with a second edition in 1912, and subsequently reissued, with an Introduction by **Brian Le Messurier**, by David & Charles in 1965.

Crossing knew Dartmoor intimately, and probably better than any man before or since, but his books, though invaluable, should be treated with caution when he is dealing with archaeological features. The *Guide to Dartmoor* contains, among other things, a complete account of every **moorland** path and track. Crossing wrote several other books about Dartmoor of which *Amid Devonia's* **Alps**, 1888 (reissued by David & Charles in 1974 and edited by Brian Le Messurier), and *Gems in a Granite Setting, 1905*, deal with walking.

Cwm The Welsh form of the English **combe** and the Scottish **corrie** to signify a **hanging valley** or glaciated hollow in the side of a **mountain**.

Cyclone A proprietary waterproof **poromeric fabric** manufactured by Carrington Performance Fabrics. It has a shell that is coated with a **poromeric** polymer and is then bonded to a layer of **nylon** and is suitable for use in shell **clothing**.
P181 Walkers Encyclopedia/SP/Section D/44

D

Daniell, William (1769–1837) Landscape painter, Royal Academician and illustrator and co-author with **Richard Ayton** of *A Voyage Round Great Britain Undertaken in the Summer of 1813, and Commencing from the Land's End, Cornwall, with a Series of Views, Illustrations of the Character and Prominent Features of the Coast Drawn and Engraved by William Daniell A.R.A.*, 8 volumes, 1814-26. This monumental work, undertaken during the summer months of 1813-23, was planned to illustrate the coastline from the sea, but the authors sometimes found that stormy weather prevented the use of a boat and so considerable stretches were

covered on foot and horseback. Richard Ayton and Daniell had a disagreement over the future of the project after the publication of the second volume and Daniell completed the subsequent volumes alone. The work contains many beautiful aquatints and is very well written (it is not immediately obvious to the reader that two authors are responsible for the text).

As well as describing the coastline, the work contains accounts of their journey and details of the topography, land use and customs. The following extract, written by William Daniell, recounts his twenty-four kilometre tramp from Stornaway, on the Isle of Lewis in the Hebrides, and gives an indication of the heroic nature of the project. *'On the following day, Friday 10th July, although the weather was very unpromising, this pedestrian journey was resumed, and a guide was procured for the purpose of traversing the extensive tract of* **moorland** *between this place and the northern extremity of the isle. In no part of this summer's excursion, nor indeed at any remembered period since the commencement of the voyage, has there occurred a day of such fatigue and discomfort. There was a dense drizzling rain, usually called a Scotch* **mist**, *throughout nearly the whole way (* **path** *indeed there was none), which lay over an expanse of quaggy* **peat**, *mostly ankle deep in wet, intersected by frequent ravines and gullies both narrow and abroad, requiring an equally frequent interruption of the regular travelling pace, ambulatory variations of striding, skipping, and leaping-variations, which in their recurrence afforded no very perceptible relief to the uniform drudgery of walking . . .'*

Dartmoor National Park This **national park** covers an area of 945 square kilometres in central and south Devonshire between Exeter and Plymouth. It was established in 1951 and is the only piece of really wild country left in southern **England**. Much of Dartmoor lies 300 metres above sea level with High Willhays reaching 621 metres. Its many outcrops of granite, known as **tors**, have been eroded by the wind into strange shapes, and in some places the huge granite blocks have been shattered into 'clitters' by the action of **snow** and **ice**. Dartmoor is particularly rich in prehistoric remains and there are many relics of the tin-mining industry.

On a warm summer's day with the roads jammed by the cars of holidaymakers it is difficult to imagine the very real dangers of Dartmoor, but the **paths** and **tracks** over the moors are not always clearly defined, and there are large areas of **featherbed** bog (Foxtor Mires, near Whiteworks, is usually considered to be the 'Grimpen Mires' of Conan Doyle's

The Hound of the Baskervilles). Moreover, **mists** can form very quickly and catch the unwary which can be a very frightening experience. Unfortunately, the army uses a large area of the northern part of the moor for training exercises and artillery practice. Red flags are flown when firing is taking place and information about dates and times of firing can be obtained from National Park information centres and local post offices.

A curious feature of walking on Dartmoor is the 'letterbox' craze. The walker buys a card which gives him the **grid references** of the letterboxes, and a space to record their discovery. Letterboxes are usually old ammunition cases secreted among rocks, or in some other hiding place, and contain a rubber stamp which the walker uses to mark his card. The object is to fill the card with as many stamps as possible. (See figure 36 for a **map** showing the location of all national parks in the United Kingdom.) (*For addresses of National Park Headquarters and Information Centres see Appendix.*)
National Park Newspaper
Dartmoor Visitor
Official Guidebook
Weir, John, Editor, *Dartmoor*, Webb & Bower in association with Michael Joseph, 1987.
Maps
1:63360 **Tourist Map** of Dartmoor.
1:50000 **Landranger** sheets 191, 201, 202.
1:25000 **Outdoor Leisure Map** 28 *Dartmoor.*
Footpath Guides
Walks booklets compiled and published by the Dartmoor National Park:
    No 1: Moreton Hampstead / Manaton / Lustleigh
    No 2: Southwest Dartmoor
    No 3: The Dart Valley
    No 4: Haytor and Area
Earle, John, *Walking on Dartmoor*, Cicerone Press, 1987.
Starkey, F. H., *Exploring Dartmoor*, published by the author at High Orchard, Haytor Vale, Newton Abbot, Devon TQ13 9EP, 1981.
Starkey, F. H., *Exploring Dartmoor Again*, published by the author at High Orchard, Haytor Vale, Newton Abbot, Devon TQ13 9EP, 2nd Rev. Ed., 1988.

David-Neel, Alexandra An intrepid French lady who made many journeys on foot between 1911-24 in China, Nepal and Tibet, and claimed to be the first white woman to visit the forbidden city of Lhasa. She described this journey, in which she disguised herself as a man, in *My Journey to Lhasa*, 1927. An account of her life and adventures may be found in *Spinsters Abroad; Victorian Lady Explorers* by Dea Birkett, Blackwell, 1989.

Davies, Hunter (1936-) Writer, broadcaster and author of several books about walking who believes that *'Walking is easy. It's one foot in front of the other. Everything else written about walking is Show Business.'*
Publications about Walking
A Walk along the Wall, Weidenfeld & Nicolson, 1974.
A Walk around the Lakes, Weidenfeld & Nicolson, 1979.
A Walk along the **Tracks**, Weidenfeld & Nicolson, 1982.
A Walk around London's Parks, Hamish Hamilton, 1983.

Hunter Davies, writer and broadcaster (photo © BBC).

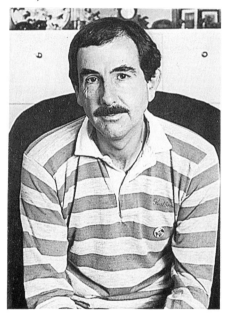

Davies, W[illiam] **H**[enry] (1871-1940) A Welsh poet, writer and traveller who is probably best known for the couplet
'What is this life, if full of care
We have no time to stand and stare?'
In 1893 he went to the **United States** and tramped and begged his way round the country covering thousands of kilometres on foot and by riding freight cars, and later recording these adventures in *The Autobiography of a Supertramp*, 1908. On his way to the Klondike, he fell from a train and his leg was severed, but he returned to **Wales** and started walking again supporting himself by peddling and singing hymns in the street. He also wrote two novels that are largely autobiographical *The True Traveller*, 1912 and *The Adventures of Johnny Walker, Tramp*, 1926.

De Quincey, Thomas (1785-1859) Essayist and critic, author of the *Confessions of an English Opium Eater*, and one of the greatest of English prose writers. Like all those associated with the **Lake Poets** he was an enthusiastic walker all his life. In his youth he walked for pleasure, but after he became addicted to opium he often walked as many as twenty-two kilometres in a day in an effort to counter the soporific effects of the drug. In 1801, at the age of sixteen, he resolved to run away from school and walk to what is now the **Lake District National Park** to meet his idol **William Wordsworth**, but he changed his mind and went to north **Wales** instead. In two days he walked the sixty-one kilometres from Manchester to Chester where he persuaded his mother to finance his venture. It was on this walk, described many years later in his autobiography *Confessions of an English Opium Eater*, 1822, that in order to husband his resources, he made himself a **tent**; and this seems to be the earliest known reference to **backpacking**. *'I did, however, for some weeks try the plan of carrying a canvas tent manufactured by myself, and not larger than an ordinary umbrella, but to pitch this securely I found difficult; and on windy days it became a troublesome companion . . . And I counted, on the whole, that in a fortnight I spent nine nights abroad.'* He visited Wales on foot three years later but little is known of this tour.

From 1809-20 he lived at Grasmere in the Lake District and frequently walked with the Wordsworths, **Coleridge** and especially with **John Wilson** with whom he was on particularly intimate terms. For a short period he edited the *Westmorland Gazette*. On his return to London, he became close to **Charles** and Mary **Lamb**, and then removed to Edinburgh in 1828 where he spent the rest of his life. As he grew older, he became almost obsessive about the virtues of pedestrian exercise, and once, after being confined to bed for several weeks with a liver complaint, he rebuilt his strength by walking round his garden. He calculated that it was '. . . *forty-four yards in circuit, so that forty rounds were required for one mile* . . .' so he set himself a task and '. . . *had within ninety days walked one thousand miles. And so far I triumphed.'*

Dedham Vale An **area of outstanding natural beauty** covering 72 square kilometres of the Constable country between Manningtree in Essex and Wayland in Suffolk. It is full of picturesque villages and has a 'typically English' pastoral landscape. (See figure 36 for a **map** showing the location of all AONBs in the United Kingdom.)

Maps
1:50000 **Landranger** sheets 155, 168, 169. 1:25000 **Pathfinder** sheets P1030 (TM04/14), P1031 (TM24/34), P1052 (TL83/93), P1053 (TM03/13), P1054 (TM23/33).

Footpath Guides
Andrews, John, *Discovering Walks in Suffolk*, Shire Publications, 1982.
Pratt, Jean and Geoff, *Suffolk Rambles*, Countryside Books, 1987.

Definitive map The **map** kept by all local authorities in **England** and **Wales** that shows all public **paths** within their jurisdiction. If a path is shown on the definitive map that is conclusive evidence in law that it is a **right of way** at the time the map was made, and may only be diverted or extinguished by due legal process. The **National Parks and Access to the Countryside Act, 1949** laid upon county councils a statutory duty to compile and publish definitive maps showing all public paths on a **scale** not less than 1:25000. The county council normally invited each parish council to survey the paths in its parish, and from this information the draft map was compiled and published.

Interested parties could object to the inclusion or omission of paths on the draft map, and these disputes were settled by negotiation or public enquiries. The provisional map was then published incorporating these decisions. A period of 28 days was allowed for objections to the provisional map, and these were settled either by negotiation or, if agreement could not be reached, by a judge at the Quarter Sessions. The definitive map was then published.

Denmark The smallest of the Scandinavian countries, consists of some five hundred islands, of which about one hundred are inhabited. The scenery is a pleasant combination of rolling **hills**, forests and lakes. Local tourist offices in Denmark have a large selection of leaflets giving details of walks in their areas, and the Dansk Skovforening (Danish Forestry Commission — see below) publishes numerous walks leaflets. In common with other European countries, the Danes have a tradition of massed-start long-distance walks or marches that are organised by Dansk Marchforbund

(Danish March Association — see below). Another organisation that arranges walks throughout the year, and publishes an annual calendar, is the Dansk Gangforbund (see below).

Useful Addresses
The Danish Tourist Board, Sceptre House, 169/173 Regent Street, London W1R 8PY. Tel. 071-734-2637.
Ramblers' Organisations: Dansk Vandrelaug, Kultorvet 7, DK 1175, Copenhagen K.
Dansk Gangforbund, Indraettens Hus, 2605 Brondby Strand.
Dansk Marchforbund, Solsikkevej 105, 8700 Horsens.
Forestry Commission: Dansk Skovforening, Direktoratet for Statsskovbruget, Strandvejen 863, 2930 Klampenborg.
*National **Map** Survey:* Geodaetisk Institut, Riggsdagsgarden 7, DK1218, Copenhagen K.
Official Survey Maps: Kort over Danmark 1:50000 and 1:25000 (both series show **paths**).
Walking Guide
Evans, Craig, *On Foot through Europe: a **Trail** Guide to Scandinavia*, Quill, 1982.

Derry, John the author of a series of articles in the *Sheffield Daily Independent* about walking in Derbyshire. In 1904, they were published as a book which, according to the title-page, was called *Walks near Sheffield* but it is more usually known as *Across the Derbyshire Moors* which is the title given on the wrapper. This important little book had a great influence on walking in what is now the **Peak National Park**, and the 26th and last edition was published by the *Telegraph & Star* as late as 1952.

Dickens, Charles [John Huffham] (1812–70) Author of some of the finest and most popular novels in the English language. Dickens was fond of walking all his life and there are many references to walking in his novels (eg *Nicholas Nickleby* and *Pickwick Papers*). His favourite walking areas were the streets of London and the surroundings of his home at Gad's Hill, 3 kilometres NW of Rochester, Kent.

A surprising number of walking guides based on the topography of his novels were published within a few years of Dickens' death. They include *In Kent with Charles Dickens*, 1880 by Thomas Frost which tells the story of a walking tour through Kent visiting and describing some of the scenes found in the novels. *A Week's Tramp in Dickens-land together with Personal Reminiscences of the Inimitable 'Boz' therein Collected* by William R Hughes was published in 1891 and describes a week's walking tour in Kent,

preceded by a tour of London, undertaken in 1888 in which the author interviews a number of people who knew Dickens. Robert Allbut wrote a **footpath guide** entitled *London **Rambles** 'en Zigzag'* in 1886 which describes a number of walks in London and includes an excursion to Chatham, Rochester and Gad's Hill. This was later expanded and revised as *Rambles in Dickens' Land*, 1990. Mention must also be made of *A Dickens Atlas; including Twelve Walks in London with Charles Dickens* which was published in a limited edition of 300 by the Hatton Garden Press in 1923. It contains detailed descriptions of the walks with both specially drawn modern **maps** and historical maps.

The best biography of the novelist is *Dickens* by Peter Ackroyd published in 1990 by Sinclair-Stevenson.

Diversions and extinguishments A method of legally amending the **path** network. It is necessary from time to time for **rights of way** to be diverted or extinguished, either to allow development to take place, or for the land to be used more efficiently. In **England** and **Wales** it is essential that any attempt to divert or extinguish a right of way without authority should be vigorously opposed, otherwise the path network will be impaired, the changes will not appear on **maps**, and a great deal of ill-will and confusion will be caused.

In **Scotland**, under common law, a right of way may be deemed to be extinguished if the public have acquiesced and have not used the route for a period of at least twenty years. A landowner can usually make minor changes to the route of a path, although there may be objections if the diversions were made in a heavily walked area, and the changes were considered to be unreasonable. Under the provisions of the **Countryside (Scotland) Act, 1967**, rights of way may also be diverted or extinguished by due legal process.

Dodd A dialect word, first recorded in 1878, peculiar to the Lake District and used to describe a rounded summit or eminence.

Dogs A quadruped of the genus *canis* that is reputed to be man's best friend. There are many who recognise the value of these animals on farms, as companions to the elderly and lonely, and as aids to the blind, but who deplore the damage done to our environment by their constant fouling of our cities, towns and public playgrounds, and by causing blindness, and sometimes death and injury to children.

Statute law makes no mention of dogs on **rights of way**, but the judgement *R v Matthias* (1861) held that a landowner in **England** and **Wales** could remove from a public **path** '. . . *anything . . . except such things as are usual accompaniments of a large class of foot passengers, being so small and light, as neither to be a nuisance to other passengers nor injurious to the soil.*' Although this particular case was about a perambulator the principle enunciated would seem to apply to dogs. Section 1 (2) (c) of the Dogs (Protection of Livestock) Act, 1953 forbids the owner of a dog to allow it to be at large in a field or **enclosure** where there are sheep (maximum penalty £200). Section 1 (2) of the same Act makes it an offence to allow a dog to attack or chase livestock, and section 9 of the Animals Act, 1971 gives **farmers** the right to shoot dogs found chasing livestock.

Donald A term, named after Percy Donald who first compiled the list, used to describe a summit in the Lowlands of **Scotland** which is at least 2000 feet (610 metres) high. A complete list of the 87 **hills** and 138 tops that comprise all the Donalds, which is of interest to those who enjoy **peak-bagging**, together with the **Munros** and **Corbetts**, may be found in *Munro's Tables of the 3000-feet Mountains* of Scotland and other Tables of Lesser Heights edited and revised by J. C. Donaldson and **Hamish M. Brown**, Scottish Mountaineering Club District Guide Books, Scottish Mountaineering Trust, 1984.

Donegal A mountainous area in the far north of **Eire** that is one of the country's favourite regions for walking and mountaineering.

Maps
Irish Ordnance Survey 1:63360 sheets 1, 2, 3, 4, 5, 6, 9, 10, 11, 15, 16, 17, 22, 23, 24, 32. 1:126720 sheets 1, 3.

Footpath Guide
Simms, P., and Foley, G., *Irish Walks Guides North West; Donegal, Sligo, Armagh, Derry, Tyrone and Fermanagh*, Gill & Macmillan, 1979.

Dorset An **area of outstanding natural beauty** covering more than one-third of the county, including nearly the whole of the coastline, amounting to 1036 square kilometres, that was designated in 1959. At its eastern extremity it links with the **Cranborne Chase and West Wiltshire Downs** AONB. Apart from the splendid coastal and **downland** scenery, the area contains extensive prehistoric remains,

including Maiden Castle. (See figure 36 for a **map** showing the location of all AONBs in the United Kingdom.)

Maps
1:50000 **Landranger** sheets 193, 194, 195. 1:25000 **Pathfinder** sheets P1281 (ST81/91), P1297 (ST20/30), P1298 (ST40/50), P1299 (ST60/70), P1300 (ST80/90), P1316 (SY29/39), P1317 (SY49/59), P1318 (SY69/79), P1319 (SY89/99), P1331 (SY58), P1332 (SY68/78), P1334 (SZ08), P1343 (SY67/77) plus **Outdoor Leisure Map** 15 *Purbeck.*

Footpath Guides
Edwards, Anne-Marie, *In the Steps of Thomas Hardy*, (this is the third edition of *Discovering Hardy's Wessex*).
Legg, Rodney, *Hardy Country Walks; 22 Walks of Moderate Length through the Heart of* **Thomas Hardy's** *Dorset*, Dorset Publishing Co., 1984.
Legg, Rodney, *Purbeck Walks; 21 Country Walks on Public* **Paths** *on the Isle of Purbeck*, Dorset Publishing Co., 1983.
Legg, Rodney, *Walks in Dorset's Hardy Country*, Dorset Publishing Co., 1987.
Legg, Rodney, *Walks in West Dorset; 20 Walks of Moderate Length along Public Paths through Superb Scenery*, Dorset Publishing Co., 1986.
Shurlock, Barry, *Dorset* **Rambles**; *10 Country Walks around Dorset*, Countryside Books, 1987.

Dower, John [Gordon] (1900-47) An architect, civil servant and sometime president of the **Ramblers' Association**. He is best known as the author of the influential *National Parks in England and Wales*, 1945 [Cmd 6628] that is usually referred to as the **Dower Report**. The headquarters of the **Countryside Commission** is named John Dower House.

John Dower, author of the Dower Report (photo © Countryside Commission).

Dower Report The colloquial name of *National Parks in England and Wales*, 1945 [Cmd 6628] which was the first government discussion paper to make recommendations for national parks and **access** to the countryside.

This influential report, written by **John Dower**, defined the concept of, and suggested locations for, national parks, and also recommended the establishment of **long-distance paths**, and unrestricted access, with certain exceptions, to **open country**. This last recommendation is the only one that has yet to be enacted by legislation. The report's proposals were considered in detail by the **Hobhouse Committee** and formed the basis of later legislation in the **National Parks and Access to the Countryside Act, 1949**.

Downland The term used to describe the characteristic rolling chalk **hills** of southern **England** which usually range in height from 150 to 300 metres. Traditional downland was largely treeless, except in parts of West Sussex, and used for grazing sheep, but in the years since the Second World War, vast areas have been ploughed for growing cereals. In downland country there are often **footpaths** that follow the crest of the hills for miles, as well as many **long-distance paths** including the **North Downs Way**, the **South Downs Way** and the **Ridgeway Path**. The word 'down' is derived from the Old English 'dun, duna' which means a hill.

Drove road There is no legal definition of the term, but drove roads may be described as routes regularly used by drovers. Droving, the transporting of animals on the hoof, was practised for hundreds of years until it died out, almost overnight, with the coming of the railways in the nineteenth century. Before railways and refrigeration, the only way to supply large towns with fresh meat was to drive the animals from their breeding place, which might be as far away as **Wales** or **Scotland**, and slaughter them on arrival at the market. Over the years recognised droving routes became established, especially after the introduction of the turnpikes when it became necessary to select routes that would avoid tolls. Many of the fine **green roads** (eg Mastiles Lane and the Hambleton Drove Road) found in Yorkshire and elsewhere are relics of the trade, and make excellent walking routes. Sometimes such routes are marked on old **maps** as 'driftways'. The best book on the subject is *The Drovers* by K. J. Bonser, Macmillan, 1970.

Duerden, Frank (1932-) Former polytechnic lecturer and now an outdoor journalist, writer, broadcaster and lecturer on countryside topics. He is the author of one of the best 'how to' books on walking yet published, and also the series editor for Ward Lock's *Great Walks*.
Publications
Rambling *Complete*, Kaye & Ward, 1978 (this was reissued in paperback as *The Complete Rambler*, Granada, 1980).
Adventure Walking for Young People, Kaye & Ward, 1980.
Great Walks: North **Wales**, Ward Lock, Rev. Ed., 1989.
Great Walks: Yorkshire Dales, Ward Lock, Rev. Ed., 1990.
Best Walks in the Lake District, Constable, 1986.
Best Walks in the Peak District, Constable, 1988.

Frank Duerden, author of several walking books (photo © Frank Duerden).

Dunova A synthetic **acrylic** fibre, made by Bayer of Germany, which is similar in feel to **cotton** and used in underwear. It has an inner absorbent fibre surrounded by a non-absorbent, porous sheath. Moisture is wicked from the skin by capillary action (**vapour transmission**) leaving the body feeling dry.

Duvet clothing Quilted clothing for extreme conditions in which the **insulation** is provided by a loose material such as **down**, **Hollofil** or **Quallofil**. Other kinds of insulated garments are made from **wadding**.

E

Earle, John [Dekker] (1929-) Walker, climber, film-maker, **mountaineer** and author of articles and guidebooks. He has walked, climbed, led expeditions and made films for the BBC in the **Alps**, Tierra del Fuego, Patagonia, Baffin Island, the Sahara, and the **Himalaya** as well as a series of walks on **Dartmoor**, the **Southwest Coast Path**, Bodmin and rivers in the southwest. He is the founder and warden of the Dartmoor Expedition Centre (*for address see Appendix*) which includes courses approved by the **Mountain Walking Leader Training Board**.
Publications
Walking on Dartmoor, Cicerone Press, 1987.
Walking on Exmoor, Cicerone Press, 1990.

East Devon An **area of outstanding natural beauty** bordering the western edge of the **Dorset** AONB, designated in 1963, and covering 267 square kilometres. It runs westward as far as Exmouth and inland as far as Honiton, although small areas around Seaton, Beer and Sidmouth are excluded. The area contains some fine coastal scenery, through which part of the **South West Coast Path** runs, including some of the magnificent red sandstone cliffs so typical of Devon. Inland are found charming villages and lovely rolling farmland. (See figure 36 for a **map** showing the location of all AONBs in the United Kingdom.)
Maps
1:50000 **Landranger** sheets 192, 193.
1:25000 **Pathfinder** sheets P1296 (ST00/10), P1297 (ST20/30), P1315 (SY09/19), P1316 (SY29/39), P1330 (SY08/18).
Footpath Guides
Clarke, Nigel J., *West Dorset and East Devon Walks and Local Attractions*, published by the author at 3 Russell House, Lyme Close, Lyme Regis, Dorset DT7 3DE, 1982.
Stoker, Hugh, *East Devon Walks*, Mill House Publications, 1984.

East Hampshire An **area of outstanding natural beauty** covering a triangular area of 391 square kilometres of rolling farmland on the Hampshire/Sussex borders between Winchester and Petersfield where it links with both the **Sussex Downs** and **Surrey Hills** AONBs. Apart from the fine **downland** scenery, the area contains Hambledon, the birthplace of modern cricket, and Butser Hill

Farm, near Petersfield, which is an Iron-Age farm that is run just as the original **farmers** tilled the ground. (See figure 36 for a **map** showing the location of all AONBs in the United Kingdom.)
Maps
1:50000 **Landranger** sheets 185, 186, 196, 197.
1:25000 **Pathfinder** sheets P1244 (SU63/73), P1264 (SU42/52), P1265 (SU62/72), P1285 (SU61/71).
Footpath Guide
Parker, Brenda, *Walks in East Hampshire*, Paul Cave Publications, Rev. Ed., 1981.

Easting The term used, along with **northing**, to describe half of a **grid reference**. To avoid error, always establish the easting before the northing.

Edge A local term used particularly in the **Peak National Park** and the **Pennines** to describe an outcrop of rock forming a vertical face on a **ridge** or plateau.

Edging The practice of crossing steep slopes by pressing the soles of the **boots** sideways into the slope to get a better grip.

Edward VII (1841-1910) King of Great Britain and Ireland and Emperor of India. Both his mother Queen **Victoria**, and his father, Albert, the Prince Consort, enjoyed walking but were only reluctantly persuaded to allow Edward, the Prince of Wales to undertake a walking tour as part of his education. In 1856, accompanied by his tutor, Frederick Gibbs, and Colonel Cavendish he started from Wimborne Minster, Dorset and walked through Swanage, Wareham, Dorchester, Bridport and Charmouth to Honiton. He was travelling under the pseudonym Baron Renfrew, but the story leaked out and the tour was abandoned at Honiton.

In 1857 the experiment was repeated in what is now the **Lake District National Park** when, accompanied by Gibbs, Cavendish, a doctor and four Etonians of his own age, Charles Wood, William Henry Gladstone, George Cadogan and Frederick Stanley, he visited Bowness and Grasmere and climbed Helvellyn. The Prince, away from the baleful parental influence, became quite high-spirited and he and Cadogan chased some sheep into Windermere, an act of folly that earned them a well-deserved scolding from the shepherd's wife. In the same year he visited Chamonix and was guided over the **Glacier** des Boissons by **Albert Smith**. Later the Prince walked over the Grosse Scheidegg pass.

In 1858 he spent two weeks with his tutor in the south of Ireland visiting Killarney, Bandon, Bantry and Skibhereen. It is not certain that he walked, but he is known to have experimented with a velocipede. This is the last occasion that he is known to have covered any distance by his own efforts, and henceforward 'Tum-Tum's' pleasures were confined to the more conventional regal entertainments of eating, drinking, gambling, killing little birds, horse-racing, and adultery.

Accounts of these tours may be found in the hagiographic official biography, *King Edward VII* by Sir Sidney Lee, Macmillan, 2 Vols, 1925-7, and also in an article entitled *A Royal Ramble* by **W. S. Tysoe** in *Ramblers' News* No 28, Winter 1957-8.

Eire A thinly populated country with comparatively few field **paths** or **mountain** tracks, but with a maze of country lanes that carry very little traffic. Much of the countryside near the coast is mountainous, with some peaks exceeding 900 metres. Although there are not many paths in the mountains, anyone proficient in the use of **map** and **compass** can virtually roam at will in glorious, uncultivated countryside. The best walking areas are the **Comeraghs**, the **Connemara Mountains**, **Donegal**, the **Galty Mountains**, **Kerry and West Cork**, the **Nephins and North Mayo Highlands**, **Sligo and Leitrim**, and the **Wicklow Mountains**.

A number of **long-distance paths** have been established and more are planned which will ultimately provide a continuous walking route all around Ireland. The **Kerry Way**, **Kildare Way**, **Munster Way**, **Sli Chorca Dhuibhne Way**, **Slieve Bloom Way**, and **South Leinster Way** are already open. They are waymarked and utilise field paths, mountain, farm and forest tracks, **boreens**, drove roads, butter roads and coffin roads.

The Irish Ordnance Survey has mapped the country completely on a scale of 1:126720 (1/2 inch to the mile) based on a survey made in the late 1970s and early 1980s. Most of the country, except the border areas, are covered by the 1:63360 Black Outline series based on the 1899-1900 survey, and there are four coloured 1:63360 District Maps covering Dublin, Killarney and Wicklow. There are plans for a 1:50000 series but the only one currently available is for Macgillacuddy's Reeks. Some paths and **tracks** are shown on all Ordnance Survey maps mentioned above, but they are not necessarily **rights of way**. Edward Stanford Ltd (*for address see Appendix*) carries stocks of Irish Ordnance Survey maps.

The Irish Tourist Board (*for address see Appendix*) publishes *Walking Ireland—Only the Best* an informative leaflet containing a folding map, useful addresses and much helpful advice.

Elitism A weasel-word sometimes used as a term of abuse against those who make value judgements (eg that Bach was a better musician than the Beatles, and that Evelyn Waugh was a more accomplished writer than Jackie Collins). In walking circles it is applied to those who shun crowds and walk alone, and particularly to those rare souls who wish to keep unspoiled countryside and delicate environments unsullied by the tramp of the masses. The proposal, submitted in 1987, to build a footbridge over the Fords of Avon, in a remote area of the **Cairngorms**, to replace the stepping stones illustrates the point well. Some amenity bodies favoured the idea to give easier access and make the difficult crossing of the river Avon safer. The so-called elitists opposed it on the grounds that walkers must expect **hazards** in wild, remote and ecologically sensitive areas, and if they lacked the skill to cross the **burn**, they probably should not be walking in such difficult country. The elitists won. Many Scottish walkers object to too easy access being provided to remote areas by the provision of footbridges, **waymarks** and **footpath** signs. I am proud to be a humble elitist.

Enclosure A term which has two meanings.
1 A parcel of land surrounded by hedges, walls or fences; a field. Countryside that contains fields is known as enclosed land, and throughout the United Kingdom the walker is required to keep to **rights of way** in such areas. In **England** and **Wales** there are some areas beyond the limits of enclosed land where **access** is permitted and it is possible to roam at will away from rights of way. In **Scotland** and **Northern Ireland**, by custom and tradition it is usually permissible to wander anywhere on unenclosed land providing that sporting interests are respected.
2 The act of enclosing which involved dividing the large open fields, so characteristic of medieval farming, into smaller parcels of land contained by hedges, walls or fences. The movement gathered pace in the eighteenth and nineteenth centuries with the enactment of the Enclosure Acts. It was during this period that many disputes arose over the enclosure of **commons**, with effects that reverberate to the present day.

England Despite having a population of 45 million packed into such a tiny area, there is still a great deal of unspoiled countryside in which to walk. England is blessed with a particularly dense network of **rights of way** making it easy to explore the countryside on foot. Almost any part of England, outside the main conurbations, contains some good walking country, but in the intensively farmed areas, the walker is likely to experience problems with **obstructions** and **ploughing** because many **farmers** and landowners fail to comply with the law and have no respect for rights of way. The best walking areas are to be found in the **national parks** and **areas of outstanding natural beauty**. There are also **national trails** and many other **long-distance paths**.

English 3000s The collective name given to Scafell Pike 3210 feet (979 metres), Scafell 3162 feet (964 metres), Helvellyn 3118 feet (951 metres), and Skiddaw 3053 feet (931 metres) which are the only four summits in **England** that exceed 3000 feet (914 metres). They are sometimes incorrectly called 'English 3000ers', but this term should only be applied to those who climb the English 3000s. They are all in the **Lake District National Park**, and are of particular interest to those who enjoy **peak-bagging**. Information on how to ascend all peaks exceeding 3000 feet in the British Isles can be found in *The High **Mountains** of Britain and Ireland; a Guide for Mountain Walkers*, by **Irvine Butterfield**, Diadem, 1986.

English Tourist Board The Board was established under the terms of the Development of Tourism Act, 1969, and aims to stimulate the development of English tourism by encouraging the British to take holidays in **England**; and by the provision and improvement of facilities for tourists in England. It is required to develop and market tourism in close co-operation with Regional and National Tourist Boards, the British Tourist Authority, local authorities and public sector organisations and the private sector; to advise government and public bodies on all matters concerning tourism in England; to maximise tourism's contribution to the economy through the creation of wealth and jobs; to enhance the image of England as a tourism destination by all appropriate means, including undertaking and encouraging innovative marketing; to encourage and stimulate the successful development of tourism products of a high standard, which offer good value for money; to bring greater recognition to tourism as an industry for investment, employment and economic development, by providing information, and where appropriate, advice and financial support; to produce and disseminate information on tourism to the trade and the consumer; to research trends in tourism and consumer requirements to show marketing and development needs and opportunities and evaluate past performance, future prospects and the impact of tourism; to improve the industry's status and performance by encouraging and stimulating the adoption of up-to-date business methods and appropriate technology and the provision of education and training programmes; and to ensure that England's unique character and heritage is recognised and protected through the sensitive management of tourism.

The ETB maintains a network of Tourist Information Centres throughout the country that can offer assistance and advice. Many of them will make provisional reservations through the Local Bed-Booking and Book-a-Bed Ahead services. Publications include *England Holidays, Where to Stay, Activity and Hobby Holidays, Let's Go!* etc. Many of the Regional Tourist Boards publish guides, pamphlets and lists of accommodation. (*For addresses of the head office and the Regional Tourist Boards see Appendix.*)

English 2000s Those summits in **England** that exceed 2000 feet (610 metres) and thus can lay claim to be considered **mountains** (they are sometimes incorrectly called 'English 2000ers', but this term should only be applied to those who climb the English 2000s). The list was first compiled by W. T. Elmslie and further compilations may be found in *The Mountains of England and* **Wales**; *Tables of Mountains of Two Thousand Feet and more in Altitude* by Nick Wright, Gaston's Alpine Books/West Col Productions, 1973 and *The Mountains of England and Wales* by John and Anne Nuttall, *Part 1: Wales,* 1990, *Part 2:England,* 1991, published by Cicerone Press.

Entrant A proprietary synthetic waterproof **poromeric** fabric, manufactured by Toray Industries for use in **shell clothing**, that uses a micro-porous coating applied to the inside of **nylon** twill.

Erosion of paths The destruction of the **path** surface by wind, rain, over-grazing and walkers' **boots**. Many paths in the most popu-

Popular paths such as the Pennine Way are now suffering badly from erosion (photo © Peak National Park).

lar walking areas of the country, such as the **Yorkshire Dales National Park** and the **Lake District National Park**, are now seriously eroded and cannot cope with the amount of traffic they have to bear. It is not a new phenomenon, but has got immeasurably worse during the walking explosion of the last twenty years, and wide, ugly scars have appeared at places like Esk Hause, Penyghent and on considerable sections of the **Pennine Way**. Various solutions, including duckboards over boggy

areas, step-cutting on steep sections, and rebuilding the path with rocks, are being tried, but the underlying principle must be that the surface should be restored in a form sufficiently strong to withstand the traffic that it has to bear. At first the results may look out of keeping, but they soon tone in with the surroundings and after a few years the worst of the scars have healed. An outstandingly successful example is Malham Cove, in the Yorkshire Dales National Park, where the new path is a great improvement on the old, ugly eroded scar, and stands up remarkably well to the many thousands of visitors every year. Some of our best-known paths (eg Mastiles Lane and the Miners' Track to Snowdon) were originally built as **drove roads** or mineral ways and supported

much heavier traffic than they do now. Many still have the original surface that copes very well with walkers' boots.

Escarpment A steep slope or inland cliff found particularly in the chalk country of

southern **England**. The steeper slope is known as the scarp and the more gradual incline is called the dip.

European international long-distance paths The **European Ramblers' Associ-**

Figure 13: European long-distance paths.

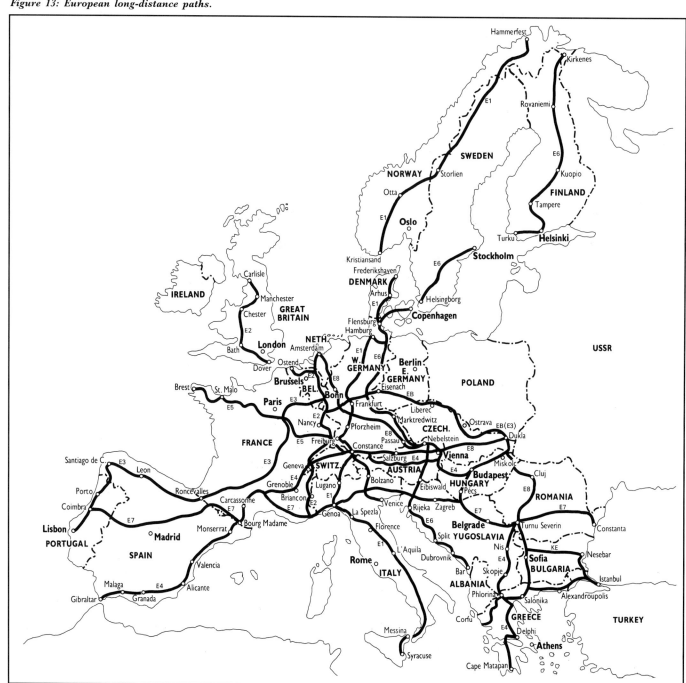

ation (Europäische Wandervereinigung e. V. or Association Européenne de Randonnée Pédestre – *(for address see Appendix)* has established eight international **long-distance paths** in western Europe. In most cases they have been created by providing links between existing national long-distance paths. International long-distance paths also exist in eastern Europe and it is likely that the political changes of 1989–90 will result in routes that run the length and breadth of the continent. The following international routes exist in western Europe:

E1: North Sea—Mediterranean. 2800 kilometres from Flensburg, **West Germany** via Hamburg, Frankfurt, Constance, Lugano, Genoa to Florence, **Italy**. Extensions to Hammerfest, **Norway** and Syracuse, Sicily are planned.

E2: North Sea—Mediterranean. 2600 kilometres from Ostend, **Belgium** or the Hook of Holland via Liège, Echternach, Grand Ballon, Nyon, Chamonix to Nice, **France**. An extension to Carlisle is planned.

E3: Atlantic Ocean—Forest of Bohemia. 2600 kilometres from Roncevalles, France via Le Puy, Paris, Bouillon, Echternach, Fulda, Coburg to Marktredwitz, Germany. An extension to Lisbon, **Portugal** is planned.

E4: Pyrénées—Lake Balaton. 3500 kilometres from Montserrat, **Spain** via Carcassonne, Grenoble, Chasseral, Constance, Bregenz, Sonthofen, Salzburg, Vienna, Koszeg to Budapest, Hungary. An extension to Mount Olympus, **Greece** is planned.

E5: Lake Constance—Adriatic Sea. 600 kilometres from Constance, Germany via Bregenz, Sonthofen, Bolzano, Verona to Venice, Italy. An extension to Brittany is planned.

E6: Baltic Sea—Adriatic Sea. 2800 kilometres from Copenhagen, **Denmark** via Lubeck, Coburg, Marktredwitz, Nebelstein, Mariazell, Eibiswald to Rijeka, Yugoslavia. An extension to Greece is planned.

E7: Atlantic Ocean—Slovenia. 3500 kilometres from Lisbon, Portugal, via Madrid, Lourdes, Carcassonne, Nice, Genoa, Lake Garda, Skopje Loka to Kumrovec, Yugoslavia. (This route is still in the planning stage, but already there are suggestions that it should be extended to the Black Sea.)

E8: North Sea—Carpathians. 2200 kilometres from Amsterdam, **Holland** via Aachen, Bonn, Coblenz, Worms, Rothenburg, Pasau, Vienna to Hainburg, **Austria**. An extension to Tokay, Hungary is planned.

A leaflet *Europäische Fernwanderwege* giving details of the routes together with addresses from where further information may be obtained is available from the **European Ramblers' Association** as can a **map** showing all the E-**paths**. German-language guides to routes E1—E6 inclusive may be obtained from the same source.

European Ramblers' Association The ERA (Europäische Wandervereinigung e. V. or Association Européenne de Randonnée Pédestre) was founded by a German walker, Georg Fahrbach in 1969. The **Ramblers' Association** and the Countrywide Holidays Association became members in 1971, and it now has a membership of 40 major walking organisations representing 2,500,000 walkers from 20 European countries. The Association has created a number of **European international long-distance paths**. The aims of the Association are:
1   The furtherance of rambling and **mountain**-climbing activities.
2   Concern and care for the countryside.
3   The protection of nature and the environment.
4   The creation of European long distance trans-frontier **footpaths** (the E-**paths**) and other international paths.
5   The greater understanding of the peoples of Europe, one with another.
(For address see Appendix.)

Evans, John (17--?-1812) A London schoolmaster who wrote two accounts of walking tours in **Wales** in which his main interest was the identification of botanical specimens. *A Tour through Part of North Wales in the year 1798, and at Other Times Principally Undertaken with a View to Botanical Researches in that Alpine Country Interspersed with Observations on its Scenery, Agriculture, Manufactures, Customs, History and Antiquities*, 1800. The book is dedicated to Thomas Pennant, and he frequently comments on Pennant's observations, but it is a very dull account full of tendentious moralising. He climbed Cadair Idris, but bad weather prevented him from ascending Snowdon. He sometimes used **footpaths** with the help of guides, and he mentions that a cottage in 'Bedd-kelert' had a sign outside proclaiming that 'The guide to Snowdon lives here'. The book ran to three editions.

Letters Written During a Tour through South Wales, in the Year 1803, and at other Times; Containing Views of the History, Antiquities, and Customs of that Part of the Principality; and Interspersed with Observations on its Scenery, Agriculture, Botany, *Mineralogy, Trade and Manufactures*, 1804. There is not much description of walking, and only part of the tour was made on foot. It contains a good description of the process for manufacturing iron.

Evans, John (1814-76) Publisher and bookseller from Ludlow, Shropshire, and the author of *Evans' Handbook to Ludlow: with Rides and Rambles round Ludlow to the Extent of Ten Miles, Compiled by an Old Inhabitant*, 1861. The book contains a history and description of Ludlow, and a quite detailed route-guide to fourteen walks, largely on **footpaths**, in the environs of the town.

Evans, Thomas (17--?-18--?) Author of *Walks through* **Wales**; *Containing a Topographical and Statistical Description of the Principality to which is Prefixed a Copious Travelling Guide Exhibiting the Direct and Principal Cross Roads, Inns, Distances of Stage, and Noblemen and Gentlemens' Seats*, 2nd edition 1815 (the date of the first edition is not known). The title suggests that this work was written for pedestrians, and it gives instructions on how to climb Snowdon, but is actually a very detailed and comprehensive road book suitable for any kind of tourist.

Exmoor National Park The second smallest **national park** in Britain covers 686 square kilometres and was established in 1954. It stretches along the coast from Combe Martin to Minehead, and goes inland as far as Dulverton. The scenery is mostly **moorland** intersected by deep wooded valleys known as **combes**, and there are magnificent cliffs along the coast. Much of Exmoor lies above 300 metres, and the highest point is Dunkery Beacon (559 metres). Exmoor probably offers some of the easiest walking in any of the national parks. (See figure 36 for a **map** showing the location of all national parks in the United Kingdom.) *(For addresses of National Park Headquarters and Information Centres see Appendix.)*
Official Guidebook
Court, Glyn, *Exmoor*, Webb & Bower in association with Michael Joseph, 1987.
National Park Newspaper
The Exmoor Visitor
Maps
1:63360 **Tourist Map** of Exmoor.
1:50000 **Landranger** sheets 180, 181.
1:25000 **Pathfinder** sheets P1213 (SS44/54), P1214 (SS64/74), P1215 (SS84/94), P1216 (ST04/14), P1234 (SS63/73), P1235 (SS83/93), P1236 (ST03/13), P1256 (SS82/92).

Footpath Guides
Butler, David, *Exmoor Walks for Motorists*, Warne, 1979.
Walks guides compiled and published by the Exmoor National Park:

Suggested Walks and **Bridleways**: *North Devon (Combe Martin, Woody Bay, Lynton, Lynmouth, Malmsmead and Brendon* **Common***).*

Walks from County Gate.

Waymarked Walks 1: (Dunster, Minehead, Brendon Hill, Luxborough, Roadwater).

Waymarked Walks 2: (Porlock, Oare, Dunkery, Malmsmead, Exford, Simonsbath).

Waymarked Walks 3: (Dulverton, Winsford Hill, Tarr Steps, Anstey Common, Haddeo Valley).
P181/Walkers Encyclopedia/SP/F-section/44

F

Farmers A group of persons, who may be either landowners or tenants, engaged in producing food. The good husbandry of countless generations of farmers was largely responsible for the astonishing beauty of the British countryside which probably reached its apogee around the turn of the century. In the postwar years, farmers have been encouraged by grants and subsidies from successive governments to increase yields so that we now produce more food than we can consume. Most farmers are delightfully friendly and engaging individuals, but collectively the farming community has systematically stolen our **rights of way** by making them unusable by **ploughing**, and by placing **obstructions** across them. A survey carried out by the **Countryside Commission** in 1989 concluded that 18% of the **footpath** network in **England** and **Wales** was unusable and that on an average four-kilometre route, walkers had a 71% chance of finding the **path** obstructed or illegally ploughed. Farmers have so poisoned and polluted the soil and rivers with herbicides, pesticides and nitrates that it will cost millions of pounds to eradicate them from the environment. Modern farming methods have destroyed much of our fauna and flora, and seriously impaired the beauty of the countryside.

The dawning of the green revolution is forcing the National Farmers' Union onto the defensive, but it still has the effrontery to suggest that many rights of way are no longer needed, conveniently ignoring the fact that many of them are unusable because they are illegally ploughed and obstructed. The Countryside Commission has launched a campaign to make every right of way walkable by the year 2000. If it achieves its aim it will have stopped fifty years of systematic defiance of the law.

Fearon, Henry [Bridges] The author of a series of very popular weekly articles, each featuring a country walk, that were published under the pseudonym 'Fieldfare' in the [London] *Evening News* during the immediate post-war years. Many of them were published in book form by the newspaper.
Tramping round London; Forty-one Walks in London's Country, 1933.
Thirty Walks with Fieldfare, 1948.
More Walks with Fieldfare, 1949.
New Walks with Fieldfare, 1951.
Walking again with Fieldfare, 1952.
20 Walks in Berkshire, 1955.
20 Walks in Buckinghamshire, 1955.
20 Walks in Essex, 1955.
20 Walks in Hertfordshire, 1955.
20 Walks in Kent, 1955.
20 Walks in Surrey, 1955.
Round Walks in the Home Counties, 1956.
Country Walks around London, 1967.

Fearon was also the author of a series of essays about walking and related subjects *Mark my Footsteps* published under his real name in 1955.

Featherbed A term used to describe extensive tracts of sphagnum moss found throughout the **Pennines**, especially in the Dark Peak of the **Peak National Park**, in Yorkshire, and also in the **Dartmoor National Park** (Foxtor Mires, near Whiteworks, is usually considered to be the 'Grimpen Mires' of Conan Doyle's *The Hound of the Baskervilles*). A featherbed is a bright green swamp which quakes when approached, is springy in nature, and into which the walker may sink to his knees. When disturbed they sometimes give off a foul smell, but although they are not usually dangerous, unless the walker should trip, they should be avoided where possible. 'Featherbed Moss' occasionally appears as a place name on **maps** published by the **Ordnance Survey**.

Federation of Rambling Clubs The Federation was formed in 1905 by delegates from several London rambling clubs, including **Walker Miles** of the **Forest Ramblers**, with the aim of maintaining and preserving ramblers' rights and privileges in the countryside. Other aims, which with hindsight were less important, were to persuade all railway companies to offer cheap fares to ramblers, to maintain a register of interesting places to visit, and to compile a list of suitable places of refreshment where ramblers were welcomed. **Lawrence Chubb** and **J. A. Southern** were appointed joint secretaries, and in 1913 the Federation published the first *Ramblers' Handbook* which was edited by Southern. The Federation proved to be the first of many such regional organisations that sprang up all over the country and led to the formation of the **National Council of Ramblers' Federations** in 1931, which changed its name to the **Ramblers' Association** in 1935. In the same year, the Federation became the Southern Federation of the Ramblers' Association.

Fell A term confined to the north of **England** and used to describe **mountains**, **moorland** and other upland areas of barren land. It is derived from the Old Norse *fiall*, a mountain and forms part of the name of several peaks as in Scafell, Bowfell and Crossfell, hence the term **fell walking**.

Fell and Rock Club The Club was founded in 1906 *'to encourage the pursuits of fell walking and rock climbing particularly in the English Lake District, to serve as a bond of union for its members and to enable them to meet together, to provide for them books,* **maps***, lantern slides and other equipment, information and advice, to protect the amenities of the District, and to guard and promote the general interests of* **mountaineers***.'* A London Section, which arranges monthly Sunday walks, weekend meets and winter lectures, was formed in 1920. The Club owns four **huts** in the **Lake District National Park**, and presented three thousand acres of land, which included Lingmell, Great End and Great Gable to the **National Trust** as a memorial to members who died in the First World War.

The library of the **Fell** and Rock Club, which contains the archives, an important collection of mountaineering books, and a valuable collection of photographic plates, is housed at the University of Lancaster. The Club also owns the valuable Abraham Collection of several hundred glass photographic negatives of mountaineering photographs made by the Abraham brothers between the years 1890-1934. This collection is deposited at the Abbot Hall Art Gallery and Museum, Kendal. The Club publishes a quarterly *Chronicle* and a biennial *Journal*. The Fell and Rock Club is unusual in that it has always included both walkers and climbers, and from its beginning membership was open to both sexes. *(For address see Appendix.)*

Fell walking An old-fashioned term used to describe the practice of walking on the **fells** or upland areas of Great Britain, especially the north of **England**. It has now been largely superseded by the modern term **hill walking**.

Fermor, Patrick Leigh (1915-) A distinguished travel writer who wrote two books *A Time of Gifts*, John Murray, 1977 and *Between Woods and Water*, John Murray, 1986 that describe a walk he made from the Hook of Holland to the Danube in 1933 when the author was eighteen. Although written long after the event, these evocations of a long, solitary walk through the troubled Europe of the nineteen thirties rank among the very best descriptions of a pedestrian journey ever written.

Fibrepile A synthetic material originally developed by Du Pont that looks somewhat like artificial fur and is warm to the touch, even when wet. It is often plagued by **pilling** and is used in **midwear** and as **insulation** for some types of **sleeping bag**.

FieldSensor A synthetic fabric manufactured by Toray Industries used for underwear and midwear. It **wicks** moisture away from the skin by capillary action (**vapour transmission**) leaving the body feeling dry and comfortable.

Finland Known as Suomi in Finnish, Finland is a large, thinly-populated Scandinavian country bordering on **Norway**, Sweden and the USSR. The total land area of Finland consists of 10% water (there are nearly 200,000 lakes), 65% forest and only 8% cultivated land. Much of the country is tableland between 120 and 200 metres in height, and the highest point in the country is Haltia Mountain in the north west which rises to 1324 metres. Finland has temperate summers and the advantage of very long days.

There are many **long-distance paths**, details of which can be obtained from the Hiking Department of the Finnish Travel Association (see below). In northern Finland there are **huts** beside the tracks in which walkers and skiers may spend the night. The Finnish Tourist Board has published an excellent booklet *Finland; Hiking Routes* which gives

much useful information and they can also provide information about guided walking tours.
Useful Addresses
The Finnish Tourist Board, 66 Haymarket, London SW1Y 4RF. Tel. 071-839-4048.
Ramblers' Organisation: Hiking Department, Finnish Travel Association, Mikonkatu 25, 00100 Helsinki.
National **Map** *Survey:* Map Centre of the National Board of Survey, Etelaesplanadi 4, PB 209, 00131, Helsinki. 1:2000, 1:25000 and 1:50000. All three series show **footpaths.**
Guide to Walking
Evans, Craig, *On Foot through Europe: a* **Trail** *Guide to Scandinavia*, Quill, 1982.

Firbank, Thomas A Canadian-born writer who purchased Dyffryn, a farm situated between Moel Siabod and the Glyders in what is now the **Snowdonia National Park.** In 1940, he published a book about the farm entitled *I Bought a* **Mountain** which contains some accounts of his walks including a detailed description of his record-breaking circuit of the **Welsh 3000s** made in 1938. He also wrote two **footpath guides** *The Welsh 3000s* and *The Snowdon Group* which were both published by St Catherine's Press in 1947.

Firsoff, V[aldemar] **A**[xel] A prolific scientific writer who wrote an account of his walks and exploration of the **Cairngorms** in *On Foot in the Cairngorms*, 1965.

First aid The term used to describe the practice of giving assistance to the sick and injured before the arrival of professional medical help. The conditions requiring first aid treatment most likely to be encountered by walkers include **blisters**, **exposure**, **frostbite**, cuts and abrasions caused by falls, twisted ankles, broken limbs, spinal injuries, and heart attacks. Shock is likely to be associated with some of these conditions.

The basic principles of first aid are to make the patient as warm and comfortable as possible (but *never* move anyone suspected of having spinal injuries unless they are in imminent danger of further injury), to prevent bleeding by the use of pressure points or staunching, to clear the airways of unconscious patients and put them into the recovery position, and at all times to remain cheerful and encouraging to assist in countering the effects of shock. Once the patient is comfortable, the next decision to be made is how to get assistance, which in upland areas usually means alerting the **mountain rescue** team.

First aid can be learned at classes run by the Red Cross and the St John's Ambulance Brigade, where the student will be taught the principles of mouth to mouth resuscitation and cardiac massage by practising on a dummy. All walkers who regularly lead groups in upland areas, especially those employed as guides and leaders by tour companies, should possess a current first aid certificate. An excellent book is *First Aid for* **Hill Walkers** by Jane Renouf and Stewart Hulse, Cicerone Press, 1982, and a more advanced treatise is *The Medical handbook for* **Mountaineers** by Peter Steele, Constable, 2nd Ed., 1988.

Fisher, Claude Journalist and editor of **The Ruc-Sac** who wrote a weekly series of horribly jocular articles about walking in the *Daily Mail*. Some of these pieces were later collected and published in *Hikecraft; an Illustrated Handbook of Ramblecraft and Lightweight Camping Hints from the Daily Mail*, 1931. In some ways Fisher's writings exemplified the worst traits of the **hiking** movement.

Fixed rope A **rope** permanently secured to a rock face or other difficult ascent to enable walkers to negotiate the obstacle safely. There are usually good footholds cut into the rock, and the main purpose of the fixed rope is to provide secure handholds. It is often helpful when carrying a heavy **rucksack** to climb without it, and then use a rope to recover it. Fixed ropes are mostly found in Alpine countries.

Flannel A soft woollen fabric that is sometimes used in heavy shirts and **breeches**, though its use is now much less common than once it was. Flannel made from a mixture of **wool** and **cotton** is known as union flannel. It can be made water repellent by coating with silicones, or by applying one of the proprietary waterproofing agents such as Technix.

Fleece A brushed woven **polyester** fabric with a warm, comfortable feel used in **salopettes** and other types of midwear **clothing**.

Fletcher, Colin (1922-) A Welsh-born journalist and writer, now living in the **United States**, and the author of three remarkable and perceptive books about walking, none of which appear to have been published in the United Kingdom. *The Complete Walker III*, Knopf, 3rd Ed., 1984 is an unusual manual of instruction for North American walkers leavened by the author's philosophy of walking.

The Thousand-mile Summer; in Desert and High Sierra, Knopf, 1968 is an account of a **trek** through California, and *The Man who Walked through Time*, Knopf, 1968 tells of his extraordinary walk through the length of the Grand Canyon which was the first time this feat is known to have been accomplished in one journey.

Food The purpose of eating is to provide energy to supply the body's needs. The amount of food required by walkers and **backpackers** depends on the quantity of energy they are using. This, in turn, depends on the size of the person, the strenuousness of the walk, the weight carried, and the temperature (the body expends energy to control temperature). As a rough and ready guide, an average-sized man carrying a day-pack in temperate conditions on an 18-kilometre walk will require about 3500 calories per day. An average-size woman will require about 2500 calories, and a teenager perhaps twice as much as a mature adult. In practice, these considerations are academic because experience and your stomach will let you know how much to eat. Walkers find that cheese sandwiches and fruit make suitable picnic lunches, with fruit cake or chocolate for snacks. Backpackers should be a little more careful in their choice of food, and bear in mind that carbohydrates contain about 4 calories to the gram, and provide instant energy; proteins also contain about 4 calories to the gram, but release the energy slowly; fats contain roughly 10 calories per gram, and also release the energy slowly.

Most backpackers rely as much as possible on accelerated freeze-dried food (AFD) because it cooks quickly, comes in a packet containing a complete meal, and is light in weight because all the water has been removed. Generally speaking, AFD meals are only available from outdoor shops, so backpackers sometimes mail packets to post offices along their route to be collected *poste-restante*.

Water, which is even more vital to support life than food, should normally be drawn from a reliable household supply. Backpackers sometimes have to rely on upland streams, but they should only take water for drinking purposes from near the source of the stream, and *always* use a proprietary water-purifying agent such as Puritabs. Water should *never* be drunk from lowland streams.

In upland areas it advisable to carry more than enough food and water for normal needs so that the walker has a supply to fall back on

in the event of an emergency.

Footbeds The name given to the detachable sole-lining found in walking **boots**. Sometimes they incorporate small pieces of **Sorbothane** that absorb shock.

Footloose An outdoor magazine, that first appeared bi-monthly and later monthly, which specialised in walking and related topics. It was published from June 1982 until October 1987, and was edited first by **Cameron McNeish** and subsequently by **Chris Townsend**.

Footpath The term footpath has several meanings and definitions. In its widest sense it means any **path**, public or private, used by pedestrians. Among the walking fraternity, it is usually understood to mean a public footpath which is one of the several kinds of path that form the **rights of way** network.

In **England** and **Wales** a public footpath is defined in the **Wildlife and Countryside Act, 1981** as '. . . a **highway** over which the public have the right of way on foot only, other than such a highway at the side of the road.'

In Scotland a public footpath is defined in the **Countryside Act (Scotland), 1967** and the Town and Country Planning (Scotland) Act, 1972 as 'A way over which the public have the following but not other rights of way, that is to say, a right of way on foot with or without a right of way on pedal cycles.'

Footpath guides The purpose of a footpath guide is to assist the walker to find his way about the countryside. A good footpath guide can be a useful supplement to the **maps** published by the **Ordnance Survey**, especially in enclosed countryside, because it should give some indication of the state of the **paths**, and information about **stiles**, gates etc. Most footpath guides cover a limited area (eg *Five Mile Walks in South-West Surrey* by George Hyde, Footpath Publications, 1983), others cover **long-distance paths**, and some cover the whole country, either by giving selected walks (eg *No Through Road*, Automobile Association, 1975), or by describing certain categories of walks (eg **Irvine Butterfield's** *The High Mountains* of Britain and Ireland, Diadem, 1986).

Until the coming of the motor car around the turn of the century, there was no ribbon development, most traffic travelled at little more than walking pace, and roads provided pleasant walking routes so there was no demand for footpath guides until the nineteen twenties. There are many accounts of walk-

ing tours dating as far back as the sixteenth century, but the first actual footpath guide seems to be *Tour of Picturesque Rides and Walks with Excursions by Water Thirty Miles around the Metropolis* by **John Hassell** which was published in two volumes 1817-8. Several more appeared but it was not until the eighteen-nineties that they became popular. **Walker Miles** was responsible for writing and publishing thirty-seven detailed footpath guides to the Home Counties which had a considerable vogue and spawned a number of imitators such as **J. A. Southern** and **Robert T. Voysey**. The guides of Walker Miles are characterised by very careful mapping, meticulous attention to detail, and precise instructions on how to follow the route. A considerable number of titles were published during the twenties and thirties, and it was common for both London and provincial newspapers to publish weekly walks which were often collected and published in book form. London Transport published a series of walks guides that were extremely popular but which, alas, were discontinued in 1980.

It was **A. Wainwright** who turned footpath guides into an art form. Before the publication of *A Guide to the Lakeland Fells* 7 vols., 1955-66, most footpath guides were little more than route descriptions supplemented by sketch maps or reproductions of maps published by the **Ordnance Survey**. Mr Wainwright changed this approach by re-drawing, and occasionally correcting, the 1:25000 **maps**, published by the **Ordnance Survey**. He also includes more detail by indicating whether field boundaries are hedges, walls or fences, and by marking the position of stiles, gates, **waymarks** and **signposts**. His methods have been adopted by many others, but only **Mark Richards** has achieved a comparable level of artistry.

From the seventies onwards, footpath guides appeared in ever-increasing numbers published by individuals, rambling clubs as well as by commercial publishers, some of whom now specialise in walking guides. The latest development is the publication of English-language footpath guides. Information on how to write and publish a footpath guide may be found on pp140-7 of *The Walker's Handbook* by **Hugh Westacott**, Oxford Illustrated Press, 1989.

Footpath Worker A duplicated newsheet, published by the **Ramblers' Association**, which was first issued in 1979 and is now published quarterly, that is of great interest to all those concerned in preserving **rights of way**. It gives detailed information about court cases, decisions of the Ombudsman, and parliamentary business involving public **paths**.

Forbes, James David (1809-68) Scientist and early Alpine explorer who went to the **Alps** on many occasions between 1839-50. His main purpose was to study **glaciers**, but he also enjoyed walking and climbing. In 1843 he published *Travels through the Alps* which was reissued in 1900.

Forest of Bowland An **area of outstanding natural beauty**, designated in 1963, covering 803 square kilometres of mostly open **moorland** between Carnforth, Settle and Clitheroe in the counties of North Yorkshire and Lancashire. This AONB links with the **Yorkshire Dales National Park** and is really part of the **Pennines**, but is separated from them by the Lune valley. Pendle Hill (557 metres) is famous because George Fox, the Quaker, climbed it in 1652 and described the event in his journal. It is even better known for its association with the Pendle witches who were tried and executed in 1612. (See figure 36 for a **map** showing the location of all AONBs in the United Kingdom.)
Maps
1:50000 **Landranger** sheets 102, 103.
1:25000 **Pathfinder** sheets P649 (SD56), P650 (SD66/76), P651 (SD86/96), P659 (SD45/55), P660 (SD65/75), P668 (SD44/54), P669 (SD64/74), P670 (SD84/94), P679 (SD43/53), P680 (SD63/73).
Footpath Guide
Lord, A. A., *Wandering in Bowland; a Walker's Guide to the* **Footpaths** *and Byways of Bowland*, Westmorland Gazette, New Ed., 1983.

Forest Ramblers This, the oldest and one of the most famous rambling clubs, was founded in 1884 by J. H. Porter in order to protect walkers' rights in Epping Forest when it was under threat from developers. It was, and still is, an all-male club as the founder expressed the belief in *A Note on Rambling Clubs* that he contributed to *Field-Path Rambles (Canterbury & Kent Coast Series)* by **Walker Miles** *'My experience is, that a rambling club is not likely to be successful if the two sexes are eligible for membership. Both should have organisations of their own, and special rambles can of course be arranged in which both may participate. In my Club about six days are set apart for ladies during the year.'* The chairman is known as the 'Ranger' because of the Club's

connection with Epping Forest. Its more noteworthy members include Walker Miles, **Sir Lawrence Chubb**, and the Foyle brothers of bookselling fame. (For address see Appendix.)

Forest Service for Northern Ireland The Forest Service of the Department of Agriculture is the authority responsible for state forestry in **Northern Ireland**. It publishes numerous guides of general interest about trees and forestry as well as **footpath guides** and nature **trails**. *(For address see Appendix.)*

Forester, Thomas The author of *Norway in 1848 and 1849; Containing* **Rambles** *among the Fjelds and Fjords of the Central and Western Districts and Including Remarks on its Political, Military, Ecclesiastical, and Social Organisation*, 1850 and *Rambles in the Islands of Corsica and Sardinia with Notices of their History, Antiquities, and Present Condition*, 1858 (2nd. Ed., 1861). These accounts of walking tours are full of interesting incident and illustrated with coloured engravings. In Norway, Forester travelled alone and did not hesitate to navigate by **compass** in dangerous, largely uninhabited terrain using **maps** of dubious accuracy. He was accompanied by a friend In Corsica and Sardinia, and they were much exercised by the very real dangers posed by bandits.

Forestry Commission The Commission was established by Act of Parliament in 1924 and has the general duty of promoting the interests of forestry, the development of afforestation, the production and supply of timber and the maintenance of reserves of growing trees in Great Britain. It is responsible for 900,000 hectares of woodland. The Commission operates camping and caravan sites, forest cabins and holiday homes, picnic areas, forest walks and nature **trails**, visitor centres and arboreta. It has been much criticised for the adverse effect that many of its conifer plantations have had on the upland areas of Great Britain.

The Commission publishes a *Catalogue of Publications*, available from Publications, Forest Research Station, Alice Holt Lodge, Wrecclesham, Farnham, Surrey GU10 4LH, which lists scientific and technical papers as well as handbooks and guides of interest to the non-specialist. *(For address see Appendix.)*

Foster, R[eginald] **Francis** (1896-1975) The author of *The Secret Places; Being a Chronicle of Vagabondage*, 1929, which is a collection of pieces that appeared originally in the [London]

Evening News. Foster describes his walks in Surrey, Sussex and Kent taken with his friend Longshanks to whom he addresses all his remarks. It is not a **footpath guide** but a series of essays about his walks.

4000s The name given to the eight peaks and thirteen additional tops over 4000 feet (1219.5 metres) in height that are of particular interest to those who enjoy **peak-bagging** (they are sometimes incorrectly called '4000ers', but this term should only be applied to those who climb the 4000s). They are all in **Scotland**, four in the **Cairngorms**, Ben Macdui 4296 feet (1309 metres), Braeriach 4248 feet (1296 metres), Cairn Toul 4241 feet (1293 metres), Cairn Gorm 4085 feet (1245 metres), and four in Lochaber, Ben Nevis 4406 feet (1344 metres), Aonach Beag 4060 feet (1234 metres), Carn Mor Dearg 4012 feet (1223 metres), and Aonach Mor 4005 feet (1221 metres). All have been climbed in one expedition that involves 158 kilometres of walking and more than 4000 metres of ascent.

Information on how to ascend all peaks exceeding 3000 feet in the British Isles can be found in *The High* **Mountains** *of Britain and Ireland; a Guide for Mountain Walkers*, by **Irvine Butterfield**, Diadem, 1986.

Fox, E[dward] **W**[illiam] (*c* 1860-1948?) A gentleman of leisure who lived for the latter part of his life in Harrogate, North Yorkshire. He was the author of *2000 Miles on Foot; Walks through Great Britain and* **France**, 1911 in which he describes a series of long, solitary walks. In 1903 he walked in France from Dieppe via Rouen and Paris and along part of what is now the N7, to Geneva in **Switzerland**. He walked from Harrogate to Land's End in 1905, and the following year went to Brittany. In 1909 he completed the **Land's End to John O'Groats** route by walking from Harrogate to John O' Groats visiting, on the way, Skibo Castle to call on Andrew Carnegie, the Scottish-American steel magnate and philanthropist. The book is simply written, but full of interesting anecdotes, and the author took great pride in his walking feats.

France A country with a great variety of scenery and regional differences ranging from the placid landscapes of Normandy and the Loire Valley to the magnificent high **mountain** ranges of the **Alps** and the **Pyrénées**. There is also splendid mountain walking in Corsica which has a strenuous **long-distance path**, the GR 20, that crosses the island.

Walking is extremely popular and very well organised with more than 40,000 kilometres of long-distance path (known in France as **sentiers de grande randonnée**), as well as an extensive local **path** network. The best source of information about walking in France is McCarta (see below) who are the official agents in Britain for the Institut Géographique National (IGN). They also have a wide selection of books and walking guides and have translated and published several of the famous Topoguides to French long-distance paths.

Useful Addresses

French Government Tourist Office, 178 Piccadilly, London W1V 0AL. Tel. 071-491-7622.

Ramblers' Organisation: Fédération Française de Randonnée Pédestre , 92 Rue de Clignancourt, 75883 Paris Cedex 18. At the same address is located the Comité National des Sentiers de Grande Randonnée which is responsible for long-distance paths.

National **Map** *Survey:* Institut Géographique National, 107 Rue La Boetie, 75008 Paris. (*UK agent:* McCarta, 122 King's Cross Road, London WC1X 9DS. Tel. 071-278-8276.)

Official Survey Maps: Carte de France 1:50000 and 1:25000. Both series show **footpaths**.

Other Maps: Didier Richard (once a separate imprint but now part of Institut Géographique National) publish a series of excellent 1:50000 and 1:25000 maps to the mountainous regions of France which show footpaths.

Guides to Walking

Evans, Craig, *On Foot through Europe: a* **Trail** *Guide to France and the Benelux Countries*, Quill, 1982.

Hunter, Rob, *Classic Walks in France*, Oxford Illustrated Press, 1985.

Hunter, Rob, *Walking in France*, Oxford Illustrated Press, 1982.

Nicolson, Adam, *The Elf Book of Long Walks in France*, Weidenfeld & Nicolson, 1983.

Footpath Guides

Battagel, Arthur, *Pyrénées, Andorra, Cerdagne*, Gastons-West Col, 1980.

Battagel, Arthur, *Pyrénées East*, Gastons-West Col, 1975.

Bishop, H., *The Way of St James; the GR 65*, Cicerone Press, 1990.

Caselli, G., and Sugden, K., *Ancient Pathways in the Alps*, George Philip, 1988.

Castle, Alan, *The Corsican High Level Route; Walking the GR20*, Cicerone Press 1987.

Castle, Alan, *The Pyrenean Trail; the GR10*, Cicerone Press, 1990.

Castle, Alan, *The Tour of the Queyras*, Cicerone Press, 1990.

Backpackers tackling the GR20 in Corsica (photo © Hugh Westacott).

Coastal Walks: Normandy & Brittany; a Guide to 900 Kilometres of Footpaths along the Dramatic Coastline of Brittany and Normandy, Robertson McCarta in association with the Fédération Française de Randonnée Pédestre 1989.

Collins, Martin, *Walking the French Alps; GR5 Lake Geneva to Nice*, Cicerone Press, 1984.

Collins, Martin, *Chamonix-Mont Blanc; a Walker's Guide*, Cicerone Press, 1989.

Collomb, Robin, G., *Mercantour Park*, West Col, 1985.

Harper, Andrew, *Tour of Mont Blanc*, Cicerone Press, 1982.

Harper, Andrew, *Tour of the Oisans; GR54; a Circular Walk round the Dauphiné Alps*, Cicerone Press, 1986.

Normandy and the Seine; a Guide to 799 Kilometres of Footpaths along the Seine from Paris to the Coast and through the Gentle Normandy Countryside, Robertson McCarta in association with Fédération Française Randonnée Pédestre, 1989.

Parker, Malcolm and Nicola, *Grande Traverse: the GR5*, Diadem, 1986.

Reynolds, Kev, *Classic Walks in the Pyrénées*, Oxford Illustrated Press, 1989.

Reynolds, Kev, *Walks and Climbs in the Pyrénées*, Cicerone Press, 2nd ed., 1983.

Spencer, Brian, *Walking in the Alps*, Moorland Publishing Co., 1983.

Spring, Ira, and Edwards, Harvey, *100 Hikes in the Alps*, Cordee, 1979.

Veron, Georges, *Pyrénées High Level Route*, Gastons-West Col, 1981.

Walking the Pyrénées; a Guide to 7000 kilometres of Footpaths along the Pyrénées, from the Mediterranean to the Atlantic (GR 10), Robertson McCarta in association with the Fédération Française de Randonnée Pédestre, 1989.

Walking through Brittany; a Guide to 1100 Kilometres of Footpaths through the Countryside and Villages of Brittany, Robertson McCarta in association with the Fédération Française de Randonnée Pédestre, 1989.

*Walks in Provence; a Guide to over 300 kilometres of Footpaths through the **Hills** of Provence and Down to the Sea*, Robertson McCarta in association with the Fédération Française de Randonnée Pédestre, 1989.

Walks in the Auvergne; a Guide to 400 Kilometres of Footpaths through the Spectacular Volcanic Landscape of France's Auvergne, Robertson McCarta in association with the Fédération Française de Randonnée Pédestre, 1989.

Frere, R[ichard Burchmore] The author of *Thoughts of a **Mountaineer***, 1952 which is a sensitive and evocative account of the author's walks and climbs in **Scotland**. It was reissued in a revised form under the title *In Symphony Austere* by Balmain Books in 1989.

Friends of the Earth One of the leading pressure groups and a major force behind today's growing green movement. Friends of the Earth campaigns for energy conservation, wildlife, the countryside, tropical rain forests, public transport, wildlife in general, and whales in particular, and against pollution and acid rain. It conducts research and publishes reports on environmental issues. There are 250 autonomous local groups that take their lead from the national organisation but also campaign on behalf of purely local interest. The organisation publishes a journal, *Friends of the Earth Supporters' Newspaper*, and a wide range of information sheets and reports. *(For address see Appendix.)*

Friends of the Earth (Scotland) A Scottish organisation that has similar aims to **Friends of the Earth**. It publishes a journal, *Issues*, and a range of leaflets on environmental matters. *(For address see Appendix.)*

Friends of the Lake District This organisation aims to promote an energetic and consistent application of unified planning policy for the Lake District as a whole under effective statutory powers created by legislation for **national parks**; to organise concerted action for protecting the landscape and natural beauty of the Lake District and the County of Cumbria as a whole; to co-operate with other bodies having similar objects or interests. The Friends represents the **Council for the Protection of Rural England** within the county of Cumbria. It publishes a journal, *Conserving Lakeland*, and a newsletter. *(For address see Appendix.)*

Friends of the Ridgeway An organisation that exists to ensure the preservation and conservation of the **Ridgeway Path** for quiet recreational use. It is particularly opposed to its use by motor vehicles and has pressed hard for a Traffic Regulation Order on those parts of the **path** which vehicles are legally entitled to use. It publishes a newsletter. *(For address see Appendix.)*

Frostbite A serious condition caused by extreme cold that can be aggravated by the lack of proper **clothing**, or restricted circulation (eg too tight **boots**), and can result in the loss of, or permanent damage to a limb. The tissues of the extremities of the body (fingers, toes, nose and ears) become frozen and **ice** crystals form in the cells. The first signs are known as frostnip where the victim loses feeling in the extremities, and the affected areas go white and waxy-looking. At this stage feeling can be restored by body warmth (but never rub or chafe the skin), and the danger of frostbite can be averted. If frostbite occurs the only course of action is to get the patient to hospital as quickly as possible. Never apply direct heat, rub with **snow** or chafe the skin of a frostbite victim.

P181/Walkers Encyclopedia/SP/G-section/44

G

Gaberdine The name given to a **cotton** weave that produces a smooth, fine cloth. It is used mainly for **breeches** and lightweight jackets although it is not so popular as once it was.

Gaiters Knee-length leggings made from **nylon**, **Cordura**, **cotton duck** and **Gore-Tex** that attach to the **boot** and are designed to protect the wearer from mud, **peat** and wet vegetation. The best gaiters, manufactured by Berghaus, completely enclose the boot and can keep the feet dry in the worst conditions.

Galton, Sir Francis (1822-1911) Meteorologist, explorer, psychologist, eugenicist, inventor of finger-printing, Fellow of the Royal Society and member of the **Alpine Club**. He edited *Vacation Tourists; Notes of Travel*, 1860-3 which aimed to be an annual collection of the best accounts of journeys, but only three volumes appeared and only the first contained a walking tour, which was made by **J. J. Cowell**. Galton also wrote an early expedition handbook entitled *The Art of Travel or, Shifts and Contrivances Available in Wild Countries*, 1855 which was so popular that it reached a sixth edition by 1876, and was reissued by David & Charles in 1971. He also designed a **sleeping bag**, much used in expedition work, which was based on a type used by shepherds in the **Pyrénées**.

A biography, *Francis Galton; the Life and Work of a Victorian Genius* by Derek W. Forrest, was published by Elek Books in 1974.

Galty Mountains (also spelled Galtee) This **mountain** range, situated in south west County Tipperary, **Eire** offers a good **ridge** walk from north of Mitchelstown to Galtymore, and has some fine rocky crags. The highest peak is Galtymore (905 metres).

Maps

Irish Ordnance Survey 1:63360 sheets 154, 155, 165, 166. 1:126720 sheets 18, 22

Footpath Guide

Martindale, Frank, *Irish Walks Guides South East: Tipperary and Waterford*, Gill & Macmillan, 1979.

Gemmell, Arthur (1915-) An architect and surveyor who has long been active in the promotion of walking, **rights of way**, and conservation. Before the war he wrote newspaper articles about walks in the Yorkshire Dales. In 1973 he was appointed by the Secretary of State for the Environment to be a member of the **Yorkshire Dales National Park** Committee, and served until 1982. He is the founder and partner of Stile Publications which specialises in publishing **maps** and **footpath guides**, mostly of the Yorkshire Dales National Park, that are updated regularly.

Publications about Walking

Three Peaks Walk Guide, Dalesman, 1974.

Arthur Gemmell, founder of Stile Publications (photo © Edward A. Winpenny).

Bradford Ringwalks (with P. Sheldon), Stile Publications, 1982.

Dales Way Route Guide (with **Colin Speakman**), Stile Publications, 1983.

Aysgarth Area Footpath Map, Stile Publications, 5th Rev. Ed., 1987.

Bolton Abbey Footpath Map, Stile Publications, 4th Rev. Ed., 1987.

Grassington and Area Footpath and Town Maps and Walking Guide, Stile Publications, 3rd Rev. Ed., 1987.

Malhamdale Footpath Map, Stile Publications, 7th Rev. Ed., 1988.

Upper Swaledale Footpath Maps and Guide, Stile Publications, 2nd Rev. Ed., 1987.

Wayfarer Walks in Upper Wharfedale, Stile Publications, 2nd Rev. Ed., 1988.

Easy Walks for the Disabled and Elderly in the Lower Dales, Stile Publications, 1989.

A Gentleman's Walking Tour of Dartmoor The title of a book by an unknown writer that was first published in 1864. It is a simple account of a four-day walking tour of what is now the **Dartmoor National Park**, undertaken with the author's friend 'Tom Steppitt', using **maps** published by the **Ordnance Survey**. There is a vivid description of convicts working in a chain gang. The book was edited by Simon Gray and reissued in 1986 by Devon Books.

Germany The Germans have always been keen walkers and have developed a large number of waymarked long-distance routes, as well as a dense local network of **paths**. Favourite walking areas are the Black Forest (where, it is claimed, the world's first **long-distance paths** were established) and the Bavarian **Alps**.

Useful Addresses:

German National Tourist Office, 61 Conduit Street, London W1R 0EN. Tel. 071-734-2600.

Ramblers' Organisation: Verband Deutscher Gebirgs und Wandervereine, Reichstrasse 4, 6600 Saarbrücken 3.

National **Map** *Survey*: There is no national map survey as each state in the Federal Republic is responsible for its own mapping.

Official Survey Maps: Topographische Karte official state surveys are available in four editions. The Wanderwegausgabe edition with scales of 1:50000 and 1:25000 show **footpaths**.

Other maps: Two series of Wanderkarte, published respectively by Reise-und-Verkehrsverlag, GmbH, Neumarkter Str 8, 8000 Munich 80, and Gleumes, D-5000, Cologne, 1 Hohenstaufenring 47-51. These cover, in various scales, the more popular walking areas and show footpaths.

Kompass 1:50000 cover selected areas and show footpaths.

Walking Guide

Evans, Craig, *On Foot through Europe: a* **Trail**

Guide to West Germany, Quill, 1982.

Footpath Guides

Caselli, G., and Sugden, K., *Ancient Pathways in the Alps*, George Philip, 1988.

Proctor, Alan, *The Kalkalpen Traverse; a Long Distance Walk in the Limestone Alps of* **Austria**, Cicerone Press, 1986.

Speakman, Fleur and Colin, *King Ludwig Way; a 120 Kilometre Long Distance Footpath through Bavaria from Lake Starnberg to Castle Neuschwanstein*, Cicerone Press, 1987.

Speakman, Fleur and **Colin**, *Walking in the Black Forest*, Cicerone Press, 1990.

Spring, Ira, and Edwards, Harvey, *100 Hikes in the Alps*, Cordee, 1979.

Gilbert, Richard [Frank] (1937-) Schoolmaster, expedition leader and writer about climbing and walking. He has led eight major school expeditions to **Iceland**, the High Atlas and Arctic **Norway**, and in 1977 was awarded a Winston Churchill Memorial Fellowship for leading the first schools expedition to the **Himalaya**. Since 1983 he has contributed a monthly column to **High**.

Publications

Hill Walking *in Scotland*, Thornhill Press, 1979.

Mountaineering for All, Batsford, 1981.

The Big Walks, (with Ken Wilson), Diadem, 1980.

Classic Walks, (with Ken Wilson), Diadem, 1982.

Richard Gilbert, a regular contributor to **High** *magazine.*

Memorable Munros, Diadem, 1983.
Wild Walks, (with Ken Wilson), Diadem, 1989.
Also contributed to
Expedition Planner's Handbook, Royal Geographical Society, 1984.
Smith, Roger, *The Great Outdoors* Book *of the Walking Year*, Thorsons, 1988.

Gill A term used in the north of **England** to describe a ravine, narrow valley or **glen** with precipitous banks, often rocky and wooded with a stream running through it. In the south it is sometimes known as a dingle. The pseudo-archaic 'ghyll' seems to have been invented by **William Wordsworth**.

Gilpin, William (1724-1804) A clergyman, writer and amateur draftsman who was the leading theorist of the **picturesque** which had a considerable influence on the development of walking. Gilpin wrote a series of very popular guides to 'picturesque' tours which instructed the tourist on where to stand to admire the best views, but he was not a walker.

The Gipsy Journal A penny magazine, issued monthly, devoted to rustic notes, **rambles**, protection of **rights of way** (including the reporting of court cases), natural history, sketches, stories, hints for cyclists and walkers, and the protection of wildlife that appeared during the 1890s. It seems not to have been very successful and had at least two changes of editorial board and publisher. By 1895 it had changed its title to *The Gipsy Journal and British Tourist*, was edited by Edith Carrington, A.G. Munro and **Walker Miles**, and was published by Robert Edmund Taylor & Son. **Miles** contributed several articles.

Glacier The study of glaciers is extremely complicated and the following information refers to valley glaciers which is the only type that walkers are likely to encounter. Although there are now no glaciers in Britain, it should be noted that the upland areas of **Wales**, **Scotland** and the northern half of **England** have been profoundly affected by glacial action.

Glaciers may be regarded as rivers of **ice** that are fed by the upper **snows**, and which flow imperceptibly under the influence of gravity. Sometimes this movement causes the brittle upper surface of the glacier to crack and form **crevasses**. Glaciers without snow cover are known as 'dry glaciers' and it is easy to see crevasses and avoid or jump over them. Walkers should exercise extreme caution on snow-covered glaciers, and should use a **rope** and know how to belay with an **ice axe**. The leader should constantly probe for crevasses with his ice axe. The existence of a **path** is no guarantee that crevasses do not lurk under the snow. Walkers should always anoint exposed flesh with glacier cream, and wear good quality sun-glasses or snow goggles as a protection against ultra-violet rays.

Glen A term used to describe valleys found especially in **Scotland** and Ireland. When used elsewhere, the term usually implies a particularly narrow valley. In Scotland, a wide valley is often known as a 'strath'.

Glen Tilt The scene of a famous confrontation between Professor John Hutton Balfour of the Edinburgh Association for the Protection of Public Rights of Roadways in **Scotland**, who was leading a party of botanists, and the sixth Duke of Athol in 1847. The Duke had closed this ancient Perthshire **drove road** and **right of way** and instructed his ghillies to prevent members of the public using the route. The Edinburgh Association decided to take their case to the Court of Session in 1849 seeking a declaration that the route was a public road. The Duke challenged the right of the Association to bring the case on the grounds that they had no local interest in the matter. The court ruled in favour of the Association but no decision was made on the legal status of the road. The Duke appealed to the House of Lords in 1852 and lost. This still left the legal position of the road in question, but the Duke abandoned his attempts to deny the public the use of the route, although as late as 1850 he had forcibly prevented two Cambridge undergraduates from walking through. They described the incident in a letter to *The Times* that provoked much public indignation, and the Duke was lampooned in *Punch*.

Glissading A method of descending hard-packed **snow** slopes by sliding on the soles of the **boots** using them as skis. It is best to learn and practise the technique on gentle slopes where it is easy to control the speed. Steep slopes are altogether more formidable and should only be attempted by experienced glissaders who know how to brake a fall with an **ice axe**. A crouch position should be adopted trailing the ice axe spike-down to act as a rudder and brake. Before glissading, always ensure that the bottom of the slope is visible, and is free from dangerous rocks.

Glory A phenomenon associated with **brocken spectres** in which the walker sees his greatly magnified shadow, surrounded by a coloured ring, cast on a bank of cloud or **mist**. It seems that each member of a party can only see his own glory.

Gloves Useful in cold weather to protect the hands and to avoid the loss of body heat, and essential in extreme conditions to prevent **frostbite**. Probably the most suitable combination to cope with all weathers is a pair of **silk**, **polypropylene**, **thermolactyl** or **wool** gloves worn under a pair of wind and rainproof **waxed cotton** or **Gore-Tex** overmitts, with a cuff sufficiently long to go inside the sleeve of a **cagoule**.

Goldsmith, Oliver (1731-74) Poet, dramatist and novelist, friend of Samuel Johnson and David Garrick, and the author of such famous works as *She Stoops to Conquer* and *The Vicar of Wakefield*. In 1754 he went to Leyden, in what is now the **Netherlands**, to study medicine. He left the university penniless and without a degree, and travelled on foot through Flanders, **France** and **Switzerland**, supporting himself by begging at convents, and by playing the flute. Later in life he gave his friends highly-coloured versions of his adventures, some of which, like his account of his meeting with Voltaire, are known to be untrue.

Gordon, Seton [Paul] (1886-1977) Naturalist, photographer and author of numerous books and articles about the natural world and walking in **Scotland**. *The Charm of the **Hills***, 1912, *The **Cairngorm** Hills of Scotland*, 1925, *The Charm of **Skye***, 1929, *Afoot in the Wild Places*, 1937, and *Afoot in the Hebrides*, 1950 contain accounts of some of his walks.

Gore-Tex The trade name of the first of the **poromeric fabrics**, and the world market leader in breathable waterproof materials. It was developed by W. L. Gore & Associates and uses a **polytetrafluoroethylene** (PTFE) membrane sandwiched between an inner and outer breathable fabric. It is widely used in shell **clothing**. All garments made of Gore-Tex have to be tested and approved by W. L. Gore & Associates before the manufacturer is permitted to market them. Approved garments carry a three-year Gore-Tex guarantee.

Gorge A steep-sided, narrow valley (in north America it is known as a canyon). The most famous and spectacular example in the United

Kingdom is Cheddar Gorge in the **Mendip Hills** AONB which is 150 metres deep and 6.5 kilometres long. It pales into insignificance when compared with the Grand Canyon in Arizona in the **United States** that is 450 kilometres long, and almost 2 kilometres deep.

Gosling Report More properly known as the *Report of the* **Footpaths** *Committee, 1968* it was the work of a committee under the chairmanship of Sir Arthur Gosling (1901-82) set up by Minister of Housing and Local Government. Its terms of reference were to *'To consider how far the present system of footpaths,* **bridleways** *and other comparable* **rights of way** *in* **England** *and* **Wales** *and the arrangements for recording, closure, diversion, creation and maintenance of such routes are suitable for present and potential needs in the countryside, and to make recommendations.'* Its work was largely pre-empted by the passing of the **Countryside Act, 1968**.

The Gower The first **area of outstanding natural beauty** to be designated (1956), the Gower is an area of 189 square kilometres on a peninsula to the west of Swansea in the county of West Glamorgan. It contains fine beaches, coves and sand dunes, and has no towns of any size. (See figure 36 for a **map** showing the location of all AONBs in the United Kingdom.)
Maps
1:50000 **Landranger** sheet 159.
1:25000 **Pathfinder** sheets P1126 (SS49/59), P1127 (SS69/79), P1145 (SS48/58/68).
Footpath Guide
Jones, Roger, *Thirty Walks in Gower,* published by the author at 45 Greyhound Lane, Stourbridge, West Midlands DY8 3AD, 1982.

Graham, Bob (ie Robert Graham 1889-1966) Gardener, hotelier, walker and **fell**-runner. In 1932, he ran over the summits of 42 major peaks in what is now the **Lake District National Park**, covering a distance of 116 kilometres with approximately 7200 metres of ascent in 23 hours and 39 minutes. He started from Keswick Moot Hall and was paced by four friends on a clockwise route that took him over Skiddaw (931 metres), Great Calva (691 metres), Blencathra (868 metres), Clough Head (726 metres), Great **Dodd** (856 metres), Watson's Dodd (788 metres), Stybarrow Dodd (840 metres), Raise (881 metres), White Side (863 metres), Helvellyn Lower Man (925 metres), Helvellyn (950 metres), Nethermost **Pike** (887 metres), Dollywaggon Pike (857 metres), Fairfield (873 metres), Seat Sandal

(736 metres), Steel **Fell** (552 metres), Calf Crag (537 metres), High Raise (762 metres), Sergeant Man (736 metres), Thunacar Knott (717 metres), Harrison Stickle (736 metres), Pike of Stickle (708 metres), Rossett Pike (651 metres), Bowfell (902 metres), Esk Pike (885 metres), Great End (910 metres), Ill Crag (922 metres), Broad Crag (930 metres), Scafell Pike (977 metres), Scafell (964 metres), Yewbarrow (627 metres), Red Pike (801 metres), Steeple (819 metres), Pillar (892 metres), Kirk Fell (802 metres), Great Gable (899 metres), Green Gable (801 metres), Brandreth (715 metres), Grey Knotts (697 metres), Dale Head (754 metres), Hindscarth (727 metres), and Robinson (737 metres).

Graham's record stood for 28 years until Alan Heaton achieved a time of 22 hours and 18 minutes. Since then, many others have completed the round (some have even included additional summits), and the **Bob Graham 24 Hour Club** has been formed to monitor and record successful rounds. Further information about Bob Graham may be found in *42 Peaks; the Story of the Bob Graham Round* by **Roger Smith** published by the Bob Graham 24 Hour Club in 1982.

Graham, Stephen (1884-1975) A writer who made a deliberate decision to become a professional tramp, and whose extraordinary walking feats have only been rivalled by **Thomas Coryate**, **William Lithgow**, **A. N. Cooper**, and in our own day by **John Merrill**. During his long life, Graham walked incessantly in many parts of the world. His first and favourite walking area was Russia, and in the years before that country was closed to him by the Revolution of 1917, he tramped through the Caucasus, the Urals, the Crimea, and the inhospitable wastes of the far north. In 1914 he walked through Turkestan, and in the following two years went to **Norway**, Egypt and the Balkans. From 1917 onwards he made a number of visits to the **United States**, and walked from New York to Chicago, through Georgia in 1919, and in 1921 walked with the poet **Vachel Lindsay** across the **Rocky Mountains** from Glacier **National Park**. He was in central America in 1922-3 and crossed the notorious Darien Gap, and the following year walked round the borders of Soviet Russia from Lake Ladoga to the Baltic, and in 1925 explored Dalmatia, the Balkans and the Carpathians. In 1929, 1930 and 1935 he was in the Balkans again, and in 1936 in **South Africa**.

Graham invented two novel kinds of walks. The first, for use in towns, was the zigzag walk, where the walker was advised to take the first turning on the right, the first on the left, the first on the right, and to continue repeating the pattern. He should then vary the process by taking the first turning on the left, the first on the right etc. The second was the trespasser's walk in which the walker follows a dead straight line, using a **compass** if necessary.

His journeyings resulted in the publication of numerous books which once had a considerable following but are now largely forgotten. His two best books are *A Tramp's Sketches,* 1912 and *The Gentle Art of Tramping,* 1927, and he also wrote *A Vagabond in the Caucasus, Tramping with the Poet* **Vachell Lindsay** *in the Rockies,* 1922, *In Quest of El Dorado,* 1924, *The Moving Tent; adventuring with a Tent in Southern Yugoslavia,* 1939. More details of his walks are given in his autobiography *Part of the Wonderful Scene,* Gollancz, 1964.

Grant, Johnson (1774-1844) Anglican priest who was sometime incumbent of Kentish Town, north London. Whilst an undergraduate at Oxford he set out on July 1st 1797, with three college friends, to tour Derbyshire and the Lake District. They travelled mostly by coach and on horseback but made a number of pedestrian excursions. They walked in Dovedale, and when they reached the Lakes they climbed Helvellyn, where one of the party **fell**, and they were almost benighted. They considered exploring Borrowdale but got no farther than the Bowder Stone, just south of Grange, because the beetling aspect of the **mountains** discouraged them. On their return journey to Oxford they climbed Ingleborough, in what is now the **Yorkshire Dales National Park**, which they believed to be 3987 feet (1215 metres) high (it is actually 2376 feet or 724 metres). An account of this tour, made interesting by seeing the countryside through the youthful eyes of the participants, may be found in *British Tourists* by **William Mavor**, 1809.

Grattan, Thomas Colley (1792-1864) Irish novelist and man of letters who lived in Europe from 1828-39, and was later appointed British consul to the state of Massachusetts. During the time he spent in Europe he walked extensively in **France** and Flanders. In his reminiscences *Beaten* **Paths** *and Those who have Trod Them,* 1862, there is a chapter entitled *A Three Days' Tour with* **Coleridge** *and* **Wordsworth**. This is an account of his meeting with

William Wordsworth, his daughter, Dora, and Samuel Taylor Coleridge, who were then on a walking tour of the Meuse and the Rhine, in which he walked with them for three days from 25th June, 1828, from Waterloo to Namur.

He also wrote pseudonymously three series of tales published under the title *Highways and Bye-ways; or Tales of the Roadside Picked up in the French Provinces* by A Walking Gentleman. The first appeared in 1823, the second series, in three volumes, in 1825, and the third series, also in three volumes, in 1827. These collections of stories use the age-old device employed in *The Arabian Nights* and *The Canterbury Tales* of linking a collection of unrelated tales by a common theme, in this case a walking tour undertaken with his dog, Ranger. They are well-written and entertaining bearing such titles as *The Bear Hunter, The Father's Curse, The Exile of Landes* etc.

Gray, Thomas (1716-1771) Poet and scholar whose most famous poem is *Elegy in a Country Churchyard*. Apart from his Grand Tour of **France**, **Switzerland** and **Italy**, made in a carriage when a young man with his friend Horace Walpole, he led a quiet, uneventful life, and his greatest pleasure was to visit friends in the country and do a little gentle walking. In 1769 he planned a walking tour of what is now the **Lake District National Park** with his friend Dr Wharton who, at the last moment, was unable to travel because of illness, and Gray went alone. We can bless Dr Wharton's attack of asthma because Gray kept a journal of the tour to give to his friend, and we now possess a delightful description made by an early visitor to the Lakes. It is very well written with some fine descriptions of scenery, and contains one of the few literary references to the use of a **Claude glass**. An account of the tour can be found in Gray's *Journal; Sketch of a Tour* published in 1769.

Greasy rock The term applied to rocks and boulders that are slippery. Greasy rock may be caused by water or lichen.

The Great Outdoors A monthly magazine founded in 1978, published by Holmes McDougall Ltd and edited from 1978-87 by **Roger Smith**. It covers a wide range of walking interests and appeals to both family amblers and experienced **hill-walkers**. It contains news items, tests equipment, and reviews books and **footpath guides**. *(For address see Appendix.)*

Greece The cradle of western civilisation and blessed with a wonderful cultural heritage, a magnificent coastline, as well as superb **mountains** rising to a height of 2917 metres. The country is made up of mainland Greece and numerous islands, some of which are uninhabited. In recent years the *hoi polloi* have flocked to Greece to sun themselves on the beaches, but walkers will leave the crowds behind when they explore the lovely countryside of the hinterland.

Large scale official Greek survey **maps** are difficult to obtain because they are published by the military and contain sensitive information. McCarta Ltd, 122 King's Cross Road, London WC1X 9DS (Tel. 071-278-8276) stock reproductions of the 1:50000 official survey maps, with sensitive material removed. These maps are published by a Greek mountaineering magazine and cover the Pindos Mountains and some other areas.

Useful Addresses
National Tourist Organisation of Greece, 195-197 Regent Street, London W1R 8DL. Tel. 071-734-5997.
Ramblers' *Organisation:* Hellenic Federation of Mountaineering Clubs, 7 Karageorgi Servias str., 105 63 Athens. (This organisation looks after the interests of walkers and **mountaineers** and has offices throughout the country.)
Guides to Walking
Evans, Craig, *On Foot through Europe: a* **Trail** *Guide to Central Southern and Eastern Europe*, Quill, 1979.

Footpath Guides
Caughey, Bruce and Naomi, *Crete off the Beaten Track*, Cicerone Press, 1989.
Dubin, Marc S., ***Backpacker's*** *Greece*, Bradt Enterprises, 1982.
Dubin, Marc S., *Greece on Foot;* **Mountain Treks***, Island* **Trails**, Cordee, 1986.
Salmon, Tim, *The Mountains of Greece; a Walker's Guide*, Cicerone Press, 1986.
Sfikas, George, *The Mountains of Greece*, Efstathiadis, 1982.

Green road There is no statutory definition of a green road. As its name implies, it is usually a grassy **track**, often enclosed between hedges or walls. Green roads are often ancient routes such as prehistoric **trackways**, Roman, Saxon and medieval roads, **drove roads**, pack roads or other routes that have now largely fallen into disuse except for recreational purposes. Often, they lost their original purpose

when new roads were built. In **England** and **Wales**, a green road may be classified as a **footpath**, a **bridleway**, a **byway open to all traffic** (the most common definition), or it may not even be a **right of way**. The best book on old roads is *Roads and Tracks of Britain* by Christopher Taylor, Dent, 1979, and a useful guide is *Walking Ancient Trackways* by Michael Dunn, David & Charles, 1986.

Greenfields, William Edward A doctor of medicine and the author of *Country Walks in Greater London; being the Circuit of the Metropolis by Lane,* **Footpath** *and Ferry*, 1909. This is an early example of a **footpath guide** to a **long-distance path**, and it gives detailed instructions for following a route around London at a radius of between thirteen and sixteen kilometres from the city centre. It was an early version of the London Countryway devised by **Keith Chesterton**, but it would now be impossible to walk the route and enjoy the experience.

Grid lines Lines running north-south and east-west at one kilometre intervals on all **maps** published by the **Ordnance Survey** with a minimum **scale** of 1:63360 which includes the **Landranger**, **Pathfinder**, **Outdoor Leisure Maps** and **Tourist Maps**. They form part of the **national grid** reference system and are used for identifying locations on the map by means of a **grid reference**, and for plotting **bearings** and making fixes with a **compass**.

Grid north When using **maps** published by the **Ordnance Survey**, the navigator ignores true north (the north pole) in favour of the north–south **grid lines** (hence grid north). As the grid lines run exactly parallel to each other, only one in the whole of Great Britain can point exactly to the true north, but the difference is infinitesimal and can be ignored for the purposes of **navigation**.

Grid reference The **national grid** system can be used for locating and identifying any feature, such as a **mountain**, **hill**, road junction etc., shown on **maps** published by the **Ordnance Survey**, precisely and uniquely. The reference can be used on any map, irrespective of scale, that has national grid lines printed on it. **Grid lines** run north-south and east-west at 1 kilometre intervals to form squares on the map.

To give a grid reference Find the kilometre square in which the feature to which a grid reference is to be calculated lies (see figure

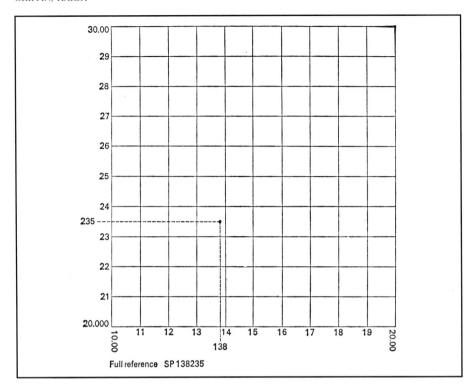

Figure 14: Grid references.

14). Identify the horizontal grid line immediately south of the feature, and from the western edge of the map, follow this line until it meets the vertical grid line immediately to the west of the feature. Follow this vertical grid line to the bottom or top of the map where a number will be found. Write this number down. Follow the grid line back to the feature and either measure with a **romer**, or estimate the number of tenths of a grid square along the horizontal line the feature lies. Write down this number. This forms the **easting** or half of the grid number, and the process has to be repeated on a vertical plane to establish the **northing**. This will result in a six figure grid reference which occurs every 100 kilometres. To make the figure unique throughout Great Britain, add the letters for the 100 kilometre square in which the map falls which can be found somewhere on the map. Most Ordnance Survey maps include an explanation of the national grid reference system.

Griffin, Harry (ie Arthur Harold Griffin 1911-) who also writes under the name A. Harry Griffin). Journalist, broadcaster and author of numerous books and articles on all aspects of walking, climbing, mountaineering

and skiing. Since 1946 he has had a regular column about **mountains** in the *Lancashire Evening Post*, and has contributed to *Country Diary* in the *Guardian* every fortnight since 1950. His particular speciality is the **Lake District National Park**, and he has probably written more about this subject than any other author.
Publications
Inside the Real Lakeland, Guardian Press, 1961.
In Mountain Lakeland, Guardian Press, 1963.
Pageant of Lakeland, Robert Hale, 1966.
The Roof of England, Robert Hale, 1968.
Still the Real Lakeland, Robert Hale, 1970.
Long Days in the Hills, Robert Hale, 1974.
A Lakeland Notebook, Robert Hale, 1975.
A Year on the Fells, Robert Hale, 1976.
Freeman of the Hills, Robert Hale, 1978.
*Adventuring in Lakeland; **Scrambling**, 'Geriatric' Rock Climbing, Gill-climbing, **Snow**-climbing and Ski Mountaineering*, Robert Hale, 1980.
Also contributed to
The 'Introduction' to **Baker, Ernest A.**, *The British Highlands with **Rope** and Rucksack*, 1973.
Wilson, Ken *and* **Gilbert, Richard**, Editors, *Classic Walks*, Diadem, 1982.

Grough A V-shaped channel, cutting or ravine caused by the action of water on **peat**.

Groughs are found particularly in the **Peak National Park**, especially on **Kinder Scout** where they are sometimes as much as three metres deep. In wet conditions the sides can be very slippery and awkward to climb. For a good description of a grough see the entry for **John Hutchinson**.

H

Hachures A system of showing relief on **maps** by a system of shading that gives a three-dimensional effect. The **Tourist Maps** published by the **Ordnance Survey** use hachures as well as **contours**.

Hag A **peat** bog, especially those found in the **Peak National Park** and the **Pennines**.

Hall, Richard W. The author of an excellent, sound and comprehensive manual *The Art of **Mountain** Tramping; a Practical Guide for both Walker and Scrambler among the British Peaks*, 1932. He also wrote *On Cumbrian **Fells***, 1932, and sometimes used the pseudonym 'Hobcarton' in his articles.

Hanging valley A small valley in a mountainside which lies above the main valley. The stream from a hanging valley usually reaches the main valley by a waterfall.

Hannon, Paul [Anthony] (1957-) Former civil servant and author of numerous **footpath guides** to areas in the north of **England**. In 1984 he founded his own imprint, Hillside Publications, which to date has only issued his own works which are all in the '**Wainwright**' style.
Publications
The Furness Way, Hillside Publications, 1984.
The Cumberland Way, Hillside Publications, 1985.
Walks in Nidderdale, Hillside Publications, 1985.
Walks in the Craven Dales, Hillside Publications, 1986.
The Westmorland Way, Hillside Publications, 2nd Ed., 1986.
***Cleveland Way** Companion*, Hillside Publications, 1986.
Walks in Wensleydale, Hillside Publications, 1987.
The North Bowland Traverse (with David Johnson), Hillside Publications, 1987.
Walks in the Western Dales, Hillside Publications, 1987.

Walks in Swaledale, Hillside Publications, 1987.
*Walks in the **Brontë** Country*, Hillside Publications, 1987.
Walks on the North York Moors, No. 1 Western, Hillside Publications, 1988.
Walks on the North York Moors, No. 2 Southern, Hillside Publications, 1988.
Walks on the North York Moors, No. 3 Northern, Hillside Publications, 1988.
Walks in Wharfedale, Hillside Publications, 2nd. Ed., 1988.
Dales Way Companion, Hillside Publications, 1988.
Walks in Calderdale, Hillside Publications, 1989.
80 Dales Walks, Cordee, 1989.

Harding, Mike [ie Michael Harding 1944-] Humourist, journalist, broadcaster, president of the **Ramblers' Association** 1985-7, and author of a number of books about walking.
Publications about Walking
Rambling On, Robson books, 1986.
Walking the Dales, Michael Joseph, Rev. Ed., 1989.
Footloose in the Himalayas, Michael Joseph, 1989.

Mike Harding, president of the Ramblers' Association 1985-7 (photo © Michael Joseph).

Harper, Andrew [James] (1930-) Outdoor journalist and author of guides to French **long-distance paths**.
Publications about Walking
Tour of Mont Blanc Walking Guide, Cicerone Press, 3rd. Ed., 1988.
Tour of the Oisans: GR 54 a Circular Walk round

the Dauphiné **Alps**, Cicerone Press, 1986.
Also contributed to:
Unsworth, Walt, *Classic Walks in Europe*, Oxford Illustrated Press, 1987.

Hardy, Thomas (1840-1928) Novelist, poet and dramatist who chronicled the lives of humble folk in his native **Dorset** in a series of profound novels that depict a way of life that has now disappeared. Throughout his life, Hardy was fond of walking especially in the countryside around his home in Dorchester, and there are many references to walking in his books. Several **footpath guides** describe walks associated with his life and literature including *In the Steps of Thomas Hardy*, Countryside Books, 1989 (this is the third edition of a title originally published as *Discovering Hardy's Wessex*); and two books by Rodney Legg: *Hardy Country Walks; 22 Walks of Moderate Length through the Heart of Thomas Hardy's Dorset*, Dorset Publishing Co., 1984, and *Walks in Dorset's Hardy Country*, Dorset Publishing Co., 1987.

Hassell, John (17--?-1825) The author of **Picturesque** *Rides and Walks with Excursions by Water Thirty Miles round the British Metropolis* published in two volumes in 1817-18. This interesting book. which is probably the first ever published that gives detailed instructions on how to follow **footpaths**, is a curious mixture of **footpath guide** and general topographical survey, and makes it very clear that early nineteenth century Londoners enjoyed walking expeditions into the surrounding countryside. Many of the places he describes as villages and hamlets are now completely urbanised.

Hatts, Leigh (1946-) Outdoor journalist, guide, and the author of a number of **footpath guides**. He prepared a feasibility study of the **Thames Path** for the **Countryside Commission**, and devised the 32-kilometre Bournemouth Coast **Path** that extends the **South West Coast Path** to Emsworth.
Publications about Walking
Country Walks around London, 1972-80. (These are annual publications issued by London Transport.)
Country Walks around the New Forest, Circle Publications, 1976.
Country Walks around London, David & Charles, 1983.
The Thames Walk; a Feasibility Study, **Countryside Commission**, 1984.

The Bournemouth Coast Path, Countryside Books, 1985.
*Middlesex **Rambles***, Countryside Books, 1990.
Walks along the Thames, Thorsons, 1990.
Also contributed to
Whatmore, John, Editor, *The Shell Book of British Walks*, David & Charles, 1987.

Haultain, [Theodore] **Arnold** (1857-1941) Canadian journalist, educationalist and author who was assistant librarian and secretary of Toronto Public Library 1887-91. He was the author of *Of Walks and Walking Tours; an Attempt to Find a Philosophy and a Creed*, 1914 which contains a series of essays, some of which had appeared originally in *The Nineteenth Century*, *Blackwoods Magazine* and *Atlantic Monthly*, with such titles as *English **Byways***, *The Mood for Walking*, *The Instinct for Walking* and *The Walking Tour*. In the essay *Great Walkers*, he lists Jesus of Nazareth, Mahomet, Enoch, Socrates, Virgil, Horace, Chaucer, Spenser, Shakespeare, Milton, **Oliver Goldsmith**, **Robert Louis Stevenson**, Matthew Arnold, Benjamin Jowett, **Thomas de Quincey**, William Cowper, **Henry Thoreau**, **John Burroughs**, **Richard Jefferies**, and **George Borrow** as having been walkers. He also wrote *Two Country Walks in **Canada***, 1903.

Hazards It is impossible to list all the hazards that have endangered walkers because some of them, such as what befell the elderly man walking in lowland country who was trapped for two days in a coil of barbed wire, or the unfortunate couple murdered whilst walking the **Pembrokeshire Coast Path**, are freak events that are unlikely to recur. Illness and accidental injury cannot be entirely prevented, but some walkers become victims of their own folly. For example, it is not unknown for foolish, macho unfit men to suffer heart attacks as a consequence of eating chip butties and drinking several pints of beer before starting a strenuous walk.

Some hazards such as **mist, exposure, lightning, avalanches, cornices** and **frostbite** are associated with the weather; others such as **river crossings**, walking in **snow** and **ice**, and **scrambling** are inherently dangerous; and a third group comprising **navigation** errors and **benightment** are usually caused by inexperience or carelessness. Providing that the walker does not attempt feats beyond his capabilities, is properly equipped, exercises a prudent degree of caution to avoid such possibilities as being injured by a **stonefall**, and follows the **Country Code**

59

and the **Mountain Code**, it is unlikely that he will come to any harm.

Hazlitt, William (1778-1830) Essayist, literary critic and one of the greatest of English prose stylists. The first time that we know he went walking was in January 1798 when he tramped the 18 kilometres from Wem to Shrewsbury to hear **Samuel Taylor Coleridge** preach. Later that year he walked to Llangollen to initiate himself into the mysteries of appreciating scenery, and then walked from Wem to Nether Stowey in Somerset to visit Coleridge. Together with a friend, they walked along the coast to Lynton and returned to Nether Stowey before Hazlitt set out on the long walk home to Wem.

In 1822, when he was trying to get a divorce in **Scotland**, he walked with his friend Sheridan Knowles along Loch Lomond, but was prevented by too much **snow** from climbing Ben Lomond. Immediately after his second marriage in 1824, he went with his new wife to **Italy** across **France** and **Switzerland**. Most of the journey was by coach, but they both did a certain amount of walking, including crossing the Col de Mont Cenis from Lanslebourg, and walking over the Col de Peaune from Martigny to Chamonix. The account of this journey was published in a series of articles for *The Morning Chronicle*, and reissued as a book entitled *Notes of a Journey through France and Italy*, 1826. Also in 1826, he walked with his friend Peter George Patmore (1786-1855), the father of the poet Coventry Patmore, in the countryside around Salisbury.

Hazlitt also wrote a famous essay about walking entitled *On Going on a Journey* in which he expresses his taste for solitary tramping, and describes his philosophy of walking. After he married and settled at Winterslow on Salisbury Plain, Hazlitt was often visited by **Charles** and **Mary Lamb**, and they would take long walks together.

Headland path A **path** that runs round the headland, ie the edge, of a field. In **England** and **Wales** the **ploughing** of headland **paths** is illegal unless a common law right to plough is recorded on the statement accompanying the **definitive map**.

Helenca A special weave of **nylon**, often used in **breeches**, that is warm and has two-way stretch. It will not absorb water, remains warm when wet, and dries very quickly.

Helm wind The name given to the strong north-easterly wind that sometimes blows across the summit of Crossfell (893 metres), the highest peak in the **Pennines**. It is caused by a combination of unusual meteorological conditions which often results in exceptionally severe weather.

Heritage Coasts A form of protection and management against development and over-use that can be applied to the coastal landscapes of **England** and **Wales**. The concept grew out of lobbying by the Coastal Preservation Committee during the thirties which drew attention to '*the moral duty of each generation to preserve the precious heritage of the coast*'. During the war, the government commissioned Professor J. A. Steers to assess the scenic quality of the undeveloped coastline of **England** and **Wales**. His report *Coastal Preservation and Planning* later formed the basis for selecting heritage coasts. In 1965, the **National Trust** launched Enterprise Neptune to buy threatened coastlines for the nation, and the government responded to public concern by ordering a review of the coastline of **England** and **Wales**. In 1970, the Countryside Commission published a report that recommended that '. . . *the most scenically outstanding stretches of undeveloped coast be defined and protected as heritage coasts*.' In 1972, the government gave the **Countryside Commission** the authority '*to recognise outstanding lengths of undeveloped coastline in* **England** *and* **Wales** *by definition as Heritage Coast and encourage good management of it*.'

There is no set pattern for the management of heritage coasts though it is nearly always administered by the local authority assisted by environmental groups. **England** and **Wales** have 4411 kilometres of coastline of which 1455 kilometres have been designated heritage coasts. (See page **XXX** for a **map** showing the approximate location of all heritage coasts in the United Kingdom.)

High A monthly magazine, first published in 1982 by **Geoff Birtles**, devoted to climbing and **hill walking** that also includes articles and news about skiing and caving. It contains news items, reviews books and equipment, and is now the official journal of the **British Mountaineering Council**. *(For address see Appendix.)*

High Weald An **area of outstanding natural beauty**, designated in 1983 by the Secretary of State for the Environment on the advice of the **Countryside Commission**, covering an area of 1450 square kilometres in the counties of Kent, East Sussex and West Sussex, and bounded by the towns of Tenterden, Hastings, Haywards Heath, Horsham, Crawley and Tonbridge. It includes some **downland** but it is mostly well-wooded, gently rolling low **hills**, and it contains many attractive towns and villages. (See figure 36 for a **map** showing the location of all AONBs in the United Kingdom.)

Maps

1:50000 **Landranger** sheets 187, 188, 198, 199.

1:25000 **Pathfinder** sheets P1228 (TQ44/54), P1229 (TQ64/74), P1247 (TQ23/33), P1248 (TQ43/53), P1249 (TQ63/73), P1250 (TQ83/93), P1268 (TQ22/32), P1269 (TQ42/52), P1270 (TQ62/72), P1271 (TQ82/92), P1289 TQ41/51), P1290 (TQ61/71), P1291 ((TQ81/91).

Footpath Guides

Martin, Sybil, *Walks in the High Weald*, Middleton Press, 1989.

On Foot in East Sussex; 24 **Rambles** *based on Brighton, Lewes, Eastbourne, Seaford, Hastings, Battle, Rye, Winchelsea, Wadhurst and Uckfield Areas*, compiled and published by the Society of Sussex Downsmen, 254 Victoria Drive, Eastbourne, East Sussex BN20 8QT, 1986.

Twenty Short Circular Walks around East Grinstead, compiled and published by the Ashdown Rambling Club, 98 Holtye Road, East Grinstead, West Sussex RH19 3EA.

Highway In common law a highway is a route over which the public have the right to pass and repass. When used without qualification a highway may be used by everyone from a pedestrian to an articulated lorry. Highways are normally classified as **footpaths**, **bridleways**, and carriageways (which may be used by vehicles). However, these common law classifications have been amended by statute and further definitions such as a **byway open to all traffic** and a **road used as a public path** have been introduced.

Hike, hiking A north American term, sometimes used in the United Kingdom, especially in the nineteen thirties, that is almost synonymous with the British '**ramble**' and 'rambling', and used to describe a country walk. The origin of the word is obscure but it may be connected with 'hitch'. 'Hiking' is a term now rarely used in the United Kingdom by walkers, and when it was first introduced into the country in the nineteen twenties there was much argument as to its suitability. There is some evidence that 'rambling' and 'hiking' were slightly different kinds of activities. The popular image of the hiker was of a person weighed down with a heavy **rucksack** who enjoyed walking in noisy groups that sang on the march. This is exemplified in the popular song of the time *I'm Happy when I'm Hiking*. The terms 'ramble' and 'rambling' are never used in north America, and 'walking' has come to mean exercise-walking for fitness, often done as being less strenuous and easier on the joints and muscles than running.

Hiker and Camper *'A compact monthly magazine for the rambler, hiker, camper, camping motorist, cyclist, and all lovers of the open air'* controlled by the Trades Union Congress and edited first by John E. Walsh, and from 1933 by **Tom Stephenson**. The *Hiker and Camper* first appeared in February 1931 and contained *'official notes and gossip of the* **Federation of Rambling Clubs** *and the Camping Club of Great Britain and Ireland'* (now the **Camping and Caravan Club**). It was an uneasy mixture of interests that sometimes had differing aims, and the magazine did not survive very long.

Hill Throughout the British Isles a hill is usually defined as an eminence or summit that does not exceed two thousand feet (610 metres). Summits above this height are usually considered to be **mountains** although many would not regard Yes Tor (2230 feet/680 metres) in the **Dartmoor National Park** or even **Kinder Scout** (2088 feet/636 metres) in the **Peak National Park** as mountains.

To add to the confusion, the term 'the hill' is also used colloquially in some contexts to denote mountainous areas eg 'When on the hill it is important to wear suitable clothing' or 'Are you going onto the hill today?'

Hill walking The term used to describe walking in the upland areas of the United Kingdom where the **mountain** and **moorland** terrain calls for expertise in **navigation** and the wearing of suitable **boots** and **clothing**, 'Hill walking' has largely superseded the old-fashioned term '**fell walking**'.

Hillaby, John [D] (1917-) Naturalist, traveller, broadcaster and one of the most distinguished and literate of contemporary writers about walking. He enjoys solitary walks, and has explored parts of the Congo, Rawenzori,

John Hillaby, one of the most literary contemporary writers about walking (photo © Constable & Co).

Sudan, Tanzania and Kenya on foot, and the Appalachian **Trail**, **Land's End to John O'Groats**, The Hague to Nice, Provence to Tuscany, Lake District to London, and Athens to Mount Olympus via the Pindos **Mountains**.

Publications about Walking
Journey to the Jade Sea, Constable, 1964.
Journey through Britain, Constable, 1968.
Journey through Europe, Constable, 1972.
Journey Through Love, Constable, 1976.
Journey Home, Constable, 1983.
Also contributed to
Hillaby, John, Editor, *Walking in Britain*, Collins, 1988.

Himalaya The highest **mountain** range in the world that extends for some 2500 kilometres between China and the Indian subcontinent, from the Bramaputra river in the east to the Indus in the west. The Himalaya, which means 'the abode of snow' from *hima* ('snow') and *alaya* ('abode'), lie in the countries of Bhutan, Sikkim, Nepal, India, Tibet (now occupied by China), Kashmir, and Pakistan. Everest (8848 metres) is the highest mountain in the world, and the Himalaya contains thirteen other summits that exceed 8000 metres.

None of the major summits is accessible to walkers, but there are a number of well-used

trails that enable the pedestrian to enjoy the magnificent scenery, and reach heights greater than anywhere else in the world. Most walkers visit the Himalaya under the auspices of one of the tour companies that specialise in the area because they employ experienced guides and sherpas, arrange for the transportation of kit and equipment, and plan routes that take into account the problems of **acclimatisation**. Tour companies specialising in the Himalaya include Classic Nepal Ltd., Exodus Expeditions, Karakorum Experience, Roama Travel, Sherpa Expeditions *(for addresses see Appendix)*, and the addresses of others may be found in the advertising pages of outdoor magazines and the quality Sunday newspapers. A series of 1:50000 and 1:25000 maps to the more popular walking routes in the Himalaya is available from Roger Lascelles *(for address see Appendix)*.
Guides to Walking
Armington, Stan, ***Trekking*** *in the Nepal Himalaya*, Lonely Planet, 1985. (Distributed in UK by Cordee.)
Bezruchka, Stephen, *Trekking in Nepal*, Cordee, 5th Rev. Ed., 1985.
Chabloz, Phillippe, ***Hiking*** *in Zanskar and Ladakh*, Editions Olizane, 1986. (Distributed in UK by Cordee.)
Hayes, John L., *Trekking North of Pokhara, the Thak Cola Canyon and the Annapurna Sanctuary*, Roger Lascelles, 1985.
Martin, Stephen, *Katmandu and the Everest Trek*, Roger Lascelles, 1987.
Weare, Garry, *Trekking in the Indian Himalayas*, Lonely Planet, 1986. (Distributed in UK by Roger Lascelles.)

Hobhouse Report More properly known as *The Report of the Sub-committee on* **Footpaths** *and* **Access** *to the Countryside, 1947* [Cmd 7207], this report was the result of deliberations of a sub-committee, chaired by Sir Arthur Hobhouse (1886-1965), of the **National Parks** Committee set up to consider the recommendations of the **Dower Report**. When it reported directly to the Minister of Town and Country Planning, it refined and endorsed the proposals in the Dower Report, and most of its recommendations, except the one dealing with access, were incorporated in the **National Parks and Access to the Countryside Act, 1949**.

Holland, John (1794-1872) A poet and miscellaneous writer who was sometime editor of the *Sheffield Mercury*. In 1836 he published a series of weekly anonymous articles in his newspaper describing a 'fluvial peregrination' along the banks of the river Don from its source to its confluence with the Ouse. In 1837 these articles were published in book form under the title *Tour of the Don; a Series of Extempore Sketches made during a Pedestrian* **Ramble** *along the Banks of that River and its Principal Tributaries*. It contains a detailed description of the topography, fauna, flora and manufactures found along the route but it is a pompous, verbose and tedious account as the following excerpt reveals. *'Thus we have arrived on the last day of the year 1836, at the termination of the twelve months' weekly rambles along the banks of the Yorkshire Don–having, in the interval, accompanied the river through all its deflections of interest and beauty from its fountain-source in the high moors above Penistone, to its confluence with the Ouse at Goole, as just described. Whatever readers may have thought of these papers, it would ill-become the writer to lay down his pen, at such a season as this, without the first recording a testimony of grateful acknowledgement to the goodness of that Divine Being who has spared him to bring his project to so auspicious a conclusion. Between the composition of the first paper of the series, at the beginning of the month of January, and the present one, which appears at the close of December, how many contingencies might have interposed themselves! Health and opportunities, through the recurrence of fifty-three consecutive weeks, were, at the least, conditions essential to the realization of my scheme, to say nothing about the intervention of those seasons of lassitude, or occasional dejection of spirits, against which most authors of my nervous constitution have to provide.'*

Hollofil A resilient synthetic fibre made by Du Pont. Each filament has a hole throughout its length that not only reduces weight but gives added insulation because of the air that is trapped. It will not absorb water, dries quickly, remains warm when wet, and is used as **insulation** in **sleeping bags** and **duvet clothing**. It requires some form of **quilting** to contain the material.

Holworthy, Sophia Matilda (18--?-?) The author of a most unusual book, published anonymously as *Alpine* **Scrambles** *and Classic* **Rambles**; *a Gipsy Tour in Search of Summer* **Snow** *and Winter Sun, a Pocket Companion for the Unprotected*, 1885 describing her solitary *'semi-pedestrian tour, taken in gipsy fashion'* of **Switzerland** made in an age when it was most unbecoming for a lady to travel alone. It is not very well-written, and there are only a few descriptions of her walks, but it is still a very interesting book. *'I will name a few things I found*

useful, a batch of polish to black your boots, as the foreign blacking cracks the leather, a good field-glass for distant views; for light portable refreshment, chocolate, raisins (which are Sir W Gull's wine), and a small glass of brandy, to put a few drops on a lump of sugar if you feel faint.'* [Sir William Withey Gull (1816-90) was a famous physician and advocate of temperance.]

Hooker, Richard (1554?-1600) An Anglican divine, theologian and author of *Treatise on the Laws of Ecclesiastical Polity*. Izaac Walton, in his *Life of Mr Richard Hooker*, 1665, describes, tongue in cheek, a delightful incident when Hooker was on one of his regular walks from his Oxford college to his home in Exeter. *'As soon as he was perfectly recovered from this sickness, he took a journey from Oxford to Exeter, to satisfy and see his good mother, being accompanied by a countryman and companion of his own college, and both on foot; which was then either more in fashion, or want of money, or their humility made it so: but on foot they went, and took Salisbury in their way, purposely to see the good bishop, who made Mr Hooker and his companion dine with him at his own table; which Mr Hooker boasted of with much joy and gratitude when he saw his mother and friends: and at the bishop's parting with him, the bishop gave him good counsel, and his benediction, but forgot to give him money; which when the bishop had considered, he sent a servant in all haste to call Richard back to him: and at Richard's return, the bishop said to him, "Richard, I sent for you back to lend you a horse which hath carried me many a mile, and, I thank God, with much ease;" and presently delivered into his hand a walking staff, with which he professed he had travelled through many parts of Germany. And he said "Richard, I do not give, but lend you my horse; be sure you be honest, and bring my horse back to me at your return this way to Oxford. And I do now give you ten groats to bear your charges to Exeter; and here is ten groats more, which I charge you to deliver to your mother, and tell her, I send her a bishop's benediction with it, and beg the continuance of her prayers for me. And if you bring my horse back to me, I will give you ten groats more, to carry you on foot to the college: and so God bless you, good Richard".*

'And this, you may believe, was performed by both partners. But, alas! the next news that followed Mr Hooker to Oxford was that his learned and charitable patron had changed this for a better life.'

Hoosier A crude, temporary gate in a fence (see figure 27). Two or three strands of barbed wire are attached to the fence post on one side of the gap, and then secured to a moveable post. This is then attached to the

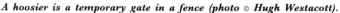

A hoosier is a temporary gate in a fence (photo © Hugh Westacott).

fence-post on the other side of the gap by a loop of wire. Thus it is possible to open the gap by pulling back the moveable post.

Horne, Thomas Hartwell (1780-1862) A bibliographer, biblical scholar and the author of *The Lakes of Lancashire, Westmorland, and Cumberland; Delineated in Forty-three Engravings, from Drawings by Joseph Farington, R.A. with Descriptions Historical, Topographical, and* **Picturesque**; *the Result of a Tour made in the Summer of the Year 1816*, 1816. This is a detailed itinerary, not especially for pedestrians but including routes suitable only for them. The author and his companion, the artist Joseph Farington, walked from Rosthwaite to Wast Water along the **bridleway** via Sty Head and Wasdale Head, and wondered how riders ever got over the **pass**. The book contains some excellent engravings.

Howardian Hills An **area of outstanding natural beauty**, designated by the Secretary of State for the Environment on the advice of the **Countryside Commission** in 1987, covering 205 square kilometres of countryside running north north west from Malton, North Yorkshire to join the **North York Moors National Park**. It contains delightful, unspoiled villages and there are beautiful views from the hilltops. (See figure 36 for a **map** showing the location of all AONBs in the United Kingdom.)
Maps
1:50000 **Landranger** sheet 100.
!:25000 **Pathfinder** sheets P642 (SE47/57), P643 (SE67/77), P655 (SE66/76) plus **Outdoor Leisure Map** 26 North York Moors (Western area).
Footpath Guide
White, Geoffrey, and Green, Geoffrey, *Walks North of York*, Dalesman, 1983.

Hucks, Joseph (1772-1800) A friend of **Samuel Taylor Coleridge** with whom he made a famous walking tour of **Wales** in 1794 when they were both undergraduates at Cambridge. Hucks appears to have been a rather solemn young man and records their adventures in considerable detail, gives sententious descriptions of the effect that scenery had upon him, but scarcely mentions his more famous friend. He wrote an account of their tour in *A Pedestrian Tour through North Wales, in a Series of Letters* in 1795. The best modern edition was published in 1979 by the University of Wales Press. Coleridge, too, has left a lively, if dis-

jointed, account of this expedition which may be traced through his letters.

Humble, B[enjamin] **H**[utchinson] The author of *Tramping in* **Skye**, originally published in 1933 which ran to a second edition in 1947, that contains accounts of his walks in the island. He also wrote *Wayfaring around* **Scotland**, 1936 which is an instructional book about **hill walking** based on articles originally published in the *Glasgow Evening Times*.

Hunter, Rob (ie Robin Hunter Neillands 1935-) A writer, journalist, military historian, novelist and the author of numerous books and articles about walking. He also writes under the names Robin Neillands and Neil Lands. In 1971 he founded Spurbooks which published numerous outdoor titles, many written by himself in collaboration with Terry Brown, in the *Spur* **Footpath Guides**, *Spur Venture Guides* and *Spur Master Guides* series, at a time when books on walking and camping were not treated very seriously by general publishers. The imprint was sold in 1980 and is no longer in existence, although a couple of titles are still in print.

He is a founder member of the **Outdoor Writers' Guild**, and vice-chairman of the Guild of British Travel Writers 1989-90. He has walked extensively in **France** and **Spain** and pioneered the **Robert Louis Stevenson**

Rob Hunter, founder of Spurbooks, writer and pioneer of the Robert Louis Stevenson trail.

Trail across the Cevennes which is now a **Sentier de Grande Randonnée**.
Publications about Walking
The Spur Book of **Map** *and* **Compass**, (with Terry Brown), Spurbooks, 1975.
The Spur Book of Winter Camping, (with Terry Brown), Spurbooks, 1977.
The Spur **Backpacking** *and Camping Cookbook*, Spurbooks, 1978.
The Spur Book of Walking, Spurbooks, 1978.
The Outdoor Companion, Constable, 1979.
The Spur Book of Walking, Spurbooks, 1978.
The Spur Book of Lightweight Camping, (with Terry Brown), Spurbooks, 2nd Ed., 1978.
Walking in France, Oxford Illustrated Press, 1982.
Winter Skills, Constable, 1982.
The Road to Compostella, Moorland Publishing Co., 1985.
Classic Walks in France, (with David Wickers), Oxford Illustrated Press, 1985.
Walking through France; from the Channel to the Camargue, Collins, 1988.
Walking through Spain; Biscay to Gibraltar, Queen Anne Press, 1990.

Hut A term used to describe a kind of **mountain** accommodation or refuge. In the British Isles, huts are usually situated in valleys and are invariably owned by climbing or walking clubs, and may only be used by members of that club, or by members of other clubs that have negotiated reciprocal rights. There is no resident guardian but facilities are provided for self catering. In Britain, there are also a number of remote **bothies** maintained by the **Mountain Bothies Association** which provide shelter, but no facilities, in remote upland areas.

Alpine and other huts in the mountainous areas of western Europe are altogether different. They were originally established to obviate the need for climbers to **bivouac**, and are mostly located high in the mountains. Most huts have resident guardians that either provide food and meals, or cook food brought by climbers and walkers. Some are quite large and more nearly resemble simple guesthouses. They are open to all, the tradition being that nobody is turned away, even if it means sleeping on floors or tables. Accommodation is usually in a dormitory shared by men and women alike, sleeping in large communal shelf-like bunks. Many huts are owned by clubs and universities, which make lower charges to their members, but some are family-owned.

Hutchinson, John (17--?-18--?) A bookseller

from Chapel-en-le-Frith and the author of *Hutchinson's Tour Through the High Peak of Derbyshire* which was published in 1809. He went with his son and a servant and covered much of the journey on horseback, but also did a considerable amount of walking. Some of the place-names he refers to are either changed, or he was mistaken, because a number of them no longer appear on **maps** published by the **Ordnance Survey**. He explored the Hope Woodlands, climbed Grindsbrook *'to the Font'* [the Nab?] and visited many of the dales and caverns giving quite vivid descriptions, and displaying a facetious wit. He was remarkably adventurous for his time. On one occasion in Longdendale, he hired a guide at Salterbrook to explore the howling wilderness south of Woodhead, which most modern walkers shun if they have any sense. *'Barrow Stones lay in a westerly direction, about three miles from Lady Cross* [they are actually south west], *which we reached without much difficulty. But Grinow Stones* [Grinah Stones?], *which appear by far the highest land in the country, was our principal aim. There was now a large flat boggy piece of ground, for at least two miles, to be passed over, before we could reach this object. The rain fell in torrents, so that it was necessary to take shelter, for some time, in the caves formed by Barrow Stones. As soon however as it was tolerably fair, we set out. Our difficulties were only beginning; for, from the quantity of rain which had fallen in the preceding night, and in the course of the day, the moors were extremely wet, and the* **groughs**, *as they are called, nearly impassable. The* **groughs**, *or deep channels, are innumerable, and in general, not above half a dozen yards from each other, intersecting the moor in serpentine directions, which are an entire* **peat** *moss, of the most spongy nature. As far as leaping would do, we proceeded tolerably, until we came to Grinow Stones, a few slips excepted.'* Then follows a long description of a thunderstorm, the **mist** came down, the guide got lost and they found themselves at the Barrow Stones again. Hutchinson then took charge and navigated by **compass** to Woodhead where the servant was waiting with the horses. It is probable that the 'Grinow Stones' were the Bleaklow Stones as the description of the route fits this eminence better. He also climbed onto **Kinder Scout** from Ollerset, and walked past the Kinder Downfall before returning to Hayfield.

Hutton, William (1723-1815) A self-made and self-educated Birmingham businessman and antiquarian who was passionately, and sometimes obstinately, fond of walking. Not only did he make pedestrian tours but he also walked long distances in the pursuit of his business activities. He had a delightful, gentle nature, appears to have been loved by all who came in contact with him, and his books are as pleasing as his character. Some of his lone walking exploits were truly prodigious. He made no less than sixteen tours in **Wales**, some by carriage but many on foot; at the age of seventy-six he climbed Snowdon; and two years later walked from Birmingham and back on a tour that included the whole length of Hadrian's Wall, often covering 32 kilometres in a day. He lived to be ninety-two, and on his ninetieth birthday he walked 16 kilometres. He described some of his walks in *Remarks upon North Wales; being the Result of Sixteen Tours through the Principality*, 1803, and *The History of the Roman Wall*, 1802.

Hydrophyllic fabrics A particular kind of breathable waterproof fabric that allows water vapour to escape, thus preventing the formation of **condensation** (the other kind of breathable waterproof fabrics are known as **poromeric fabrics**). The waterproof and **moisture vapour transmission** properties of hydrophyllic fabrics come from two entirely different, yet compatible, molecular chains. One chain is hydrophyllic (from the Greek meaning water-loving) and the other chain is hydrophobic (water-hating). Molecules of water vapour given off by the body are attracted to the hydrophyllic molecules in the fabric coating, and pass through to the outside. Rain striking the hydrophobic molecules on the outside of the fabric is repelled. Examples of hydrophyllic fabrics used in shell **clothing** are **Sympatex** and breathable **polyurethane** coatings.

Hypothermia The medical term, colloquially known as exposure, used to describe the loss of core body heat by the chilling of the skin. In extreme cases it can lead to the failure of the vital organs and death. The condition is caused by the surface of the body being cooled by the wind and the ambient temperature, known as **wind chill**. The reaction of the body is to send blood from the body core to warm the skin, the blood is then chilled and returns to the recesses of the body and unless the cycle is broken, the body temperature is gradually lowered. The condition can be exacerbated by hunger, fatigue, menstruation, and fear. The symptoms of hypothermia are frequent stumbling, accompanied by a sense of unreality, and difficulty in making rational decisions. Hypothermia can occur in unsuitably dressed walkers in conditions of strong wind and rain in comparatively mild temperatures. By wearing the proper combination of wind and waterproof shell **clothing**, suitable sweaters and thermal underclothes, supplemented by adequate supplies of high-energy **food**, the prudent walker should never be at risk from hypothermia.

The standard **first aid** treatment is to find shelter and impart warmth to the patient. Place him in a **tent**, **sleeping bag**, **survival bag**, or anywhere that is sheltered from the elements. If possible, warm him with body contact with another person, and administer hot drinks. *Never* give alcohol or other stimulants, rub the skin, or place a hot-water bottle near the patient. Hypothermia is a life-threatening condition, and if the patient cannot be warmed quickly, help must be obtained as soon as possible. A *warm* bath under medical supervision will quickly aid recovery.

A useful book is ***Mountain*** *Hypothermia*, compiled and published by the **British Mountaineering Council**, 1973.

I

Ice All ice is formed by water freezing, but the walker will find that there are several varieties of the substance. Unless properly equipped with an **ice axe** and **crampons**, ice that forms on a flat surface, let alone a slope, is extremely dangerous, and retreat is advised. Short stretches of ice covered in **snow** which is sufficiently soft to provide a foothold, may be traversed with caution, providing that the slope is not steep. One of the most dangerous forms of ice is **verglas**, a thin coating of ice that forms on **paths** and rocks in Britain in conditions of **mist** or drizzle. Even crampons are of little help in such conditions and the prudent walker will make for lower ground.

Ice axe A device carried by climbers and walkers in upland country in conditions of **snow** and **ice** (see figure 15). An ice axe has a head consisting of an adze and a pick attached to a shaft culminating in a spike. Ice axes come in various lengths and it is important to select one suitable for your height and use. A general-purpose model suitable for walkers should be sufficiently long for the tip of the spike to be two centimetres from the ground when the fingers grasp the head. An ice axe can be used for the following purposes:

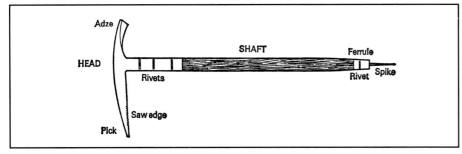

Figure 15: Ice axe.

As a walking stick: when crossing slopes the axe is held diagonally across the body with one hand grasping the head and the other about halfway along the shaft. The spike points towards the slope and is used to assist in maintaining balance. When climbing slopes, the head is held in one hand and the spike thrust into the snow and used to balance and support the walker while he kicks steps in the snow.

As a brake: In the event of a fall, the ice axe should be brought under the armpit, the pick thrust into the snow and pressure exerted until friction brings the slide under control. The feet have to be kept clear of the ground, especially if wearing crampons. This is a difficult technique to master and can only be learned under proper instruction. (See figure 16).

For cutting steps: On ice and hard snow, it is sometimes necessary to cut steps in order to climb a steep slope. There are two basic techniques. Slash-cutting is used when traversing or zigzagging up a slope where the pick is used to slash a groove wide enough to accommodate the side of a **boot**. When ascending a steep slope, the adze is used to chisel a purchase that slopes slightly inwards and is large enough to take at least half the boot; this is a much more tiring method than slash-cutting. The more widespread use of crampons has rendered the technique of step-cutting less important than once it was.

Ice axes are dangerous tools, can inflict nasty injuries and must be treated with respect. When in use they are usually attached to the wrist by a sling to prevent them being lost if accidentally dropped. When not in use, the head and spike must be covered with rubber protectors and carried on the **rucksack** using the loops provided. The shaft is usually passed spike-first through a loop at the bottom of the sack, and then turned upwards and secured by a strap above the loop. If the rucksack has no pockets, the axe is sometimes strapped spike down on the side of the sack. It can also be slid between the pocket and the main sack if the pockets are detachable.

Figure 16: Braking with an ice axe.

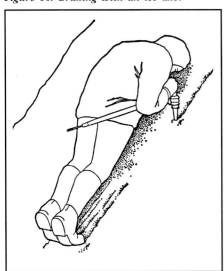

Iceland The second largest island in Europe lying just south of the Arctic Circle. It is a land of **mountains**, **glaciers**, volcanoes and geysers, and is a wonderful country in which to walk and **backpack** in rugged conditions. Despite its northerly latitude, Iceland has a remarkably temperate climate, and the short summers can be quite pleasant. Iceland is the most thinly populated European country with only a quarter of a million inhabitants. Ninety thousand of them live in the capital, Reykjavik, and most of the rest in small towns around the coast; the hinterland is virtually uninhabited. It is ideally suited for those who love remote places. The best British source for walking tours, books, **maps** etc is Dick Phillips Specialist Icelandic Travel Service (see below).
Useful Addresses
Icelandair/Iceland Tourist Information Bureau, 3rd Floor, 172 Tottenham Court Road. London W1P 9LG. Tel. 071-388-5346.
Dick Phillips Specialist Icelandic Travel Service, Whitehall House, Nenthead, Alston, Cumbria CA9 3PS. Tel. 0498-81440.
Útivist (Outdoor Life Tours), Grofinni 1, Reykjavik.
Ramblers' Organisation: Feröafélag Íslands, 3 Öldugata, Reykjavik.
National Map Survey: Landmailingar Íslands, 178 Laugavegur, Reykjavik.
Official Survey Maps: Atlas Blondin 1:100000, Fjordungsblondin 1:50000. Both series show tracks, cairned **paths** and indistinct paths.
Guides to Walking
Escritt, Tony, *Iceland: a Handbook for Expeditions*, Iceland Information Centre, 2nd Rev. Ed., 1986.
Evans, Craig, *On Foot through Europe: a* **Trail** *Guide to Scandinavia*, Quill, 1982.

Icknield Way Association This Association has been established to promote and publicise the use of the Icknield Way, a **long-distance path** that runs from the southern end of the **Peddars Way** to the **Ridgeway Path**, as a route for walkers. The Association urges the official adoption and completion of the Way as a **national trail**, and aims to promote a body of informed opinion that will improve the enjoyment and knowledge of the Way and its amenities. It publishes a newsletter and a **footpath guide** *The Icknield Way; a Walker's Guide*, 1988. (*For address see Appendix.*)

Inglis, **H**[enry] **D**[avid] (1795-1835) Traveller, novelist and miscellaneous writer who also used the pseudonym Derwent Conway. He enjoyed solitary walking tours and made a number of quite adventurous expeditions, including some in the less developed countries of Europe. The accounts of his tours had a considerable vogue and often ran to more than one edition. *Switzerland, the South of* *France, and the* *Pyrénées in 1830*, 2 Volumes, 1831, which was published under the pseudonym Derwent Conway, contains a great deal of walking, but the author also describes the countries and their peoples, customs, government etc. He visited the **Alps** again and recorded his adventures in *The Tyrol; with a Glance at Bavaria*, 3rd Ed., 1837. In *Ireland in 1834; a Journey throughout Ireland during the Spring, Summer and Autumn of 1834*, 2 Vols, 3rd Ed.,

1835, the author gives a detailed description of the condition of Ireland that proved very influential, but he only walked occasionally. *A Personal Narrative of a Journey through* **Norway**, *Part of* **Sweden** *and the Islands and States of* **Denmark**, 4th Ed., 1837 is a particularly adventurous journey in which he navigated across country, using a **compass**, at a time when Norway was under-developed and roads were few. *Solitary Walks through Many Lands*, 3rd Ed., 1843 includes walks in **England**, Hungary, France, **Italy**, Norway, Sweden, Denmark and the **Netherlands**.

Rambles in the Footsteps of Don Quixote, 1837 is a journey on mule-back following Cervantes' hero, and *Rambles in Spain*, 2nd Ed., 1839 is about a journey by diligence.

Innerleithen Alpine Club This organisation, founded in 1889 by local worthies, was not, as its name implies, a mountaineering club, but a Victorian improvement society whose members undertook long day excursions on foot '. . . *to the neighbouring* **hills** *and* **glens**, *to elucidate the botanical and geological features and the antiquarian lore of Peeblesshire.*' Detailed accounts of the early activities of the Club may be found in *Principal Excursions of the Innerleithen Alpine Club During the Years 1889-94, with a Memoir of the late Mr Robert Mathison, First President of the Club* published in 1895. Personal reminiscences of the Club and its members may also be found in *The Cleikum; Being Interesting Reminiscences of Old Innerleithen* by John A. Anderson, 1933. The Club's fortunes declined during the early years of this century and it was absorbed into the Tweeddale Society (*for address see Appendix*).

Insulating mat A length of lightweight closed-cell foam material that is slid underneath the **tent** groundsheet to prevent body heat from seeping into the ground when the **backpacker** is in his **sleeping bag**. Insulating mats are either carried coiled inside the **rucksack**, or strapped onto the outside. Some walkers carry a small section of insulating mat on which to sit during rests and **brew-ups**.

Insulation Materials that prevent the loss of body heat form the basis of insulation in **clothing** and **sleeping bags**. Insulation may be made from materials occurring naturally, such as **down** and **wool**, or synthetic, man-made materials such as **Hollofil**, **Isodry**, **Libond**, **Quallofil** and **Thinsulate** that are all derived from petrochemicals. They may further be divided into **waddings**, which can be incorporated into garments in the manner of

a lining, and loose materials such as **down** and **Hollofil** that require some form of **quilting** to contain them.

International mountain distress signal A distress signal used by **mountaineers** and **hill-walkers** that was first proposed by the **Alpine Club** in 1894, and is now in universal use. When in trouble give six blasts on a whistle (or six flashes with a torch), followed by a minute's silence and then repeat. The response is three whistle blasts (or lamp flashes) repeated at minute intervals. Should a whistle or torch not be available (although every hill-walker should always carry a whistle attached to his clothing), wave a brightly coloured garment six times.

Irish 3000s There are nine peaks in **Eire** that exceed 3000 feet, and they all lie south of a line drawn between Dublin and Limerick. They are Lugnaquillia, County Wicklow (3039 feet); Galtymore, County Tipperary (3018 feet); Cummeennapeasta (3062 feet), Cruach Mhor (3062 feet), Lackagarrin (3100 feet), Bearna Rua (3159 feet) and Cnoc an Chuilinn (3141 feet), Carrantoohil (3141 feet), Caher (3250 feet), and Beenkeragh (3314 feet). Information on how to ascend all peaks exceeding 3000 feet in the British Isles can be found in *The High* **Mountains** *of Britain and Ireland; a Guide for Mountain Walkers*, by **Irvine Butterfield**, Diadem, 1986, and in *Guide to Ireland's 3000-foot Mountains; the Irish Munros* by H. Mulholland, Mullholland-Wirrall, 1988.

Isle of Man This beautiful island covers an area of 585 square kilometres in the Irish Sea midway between **England** and Ireland. It has much attractive scenery including rough **moorland**, cliff-bound coasts and wooded **glens**.
Useful Address
Department of Tourism and Transport, 13 Victoria Street, Douglas, IOM. Tel. 0624-74323.
Maps
1:50000 Landranger sheet 95 (NB the **Pathfinder** series does not include the Isle of Man).
Footpath Guides
Evans, Aileen, *Isle of Man Coastal* **Path**; *"Raad ny Foillan"—The Way of the Gull; includes also the Millenium Way and the 'Byr ny Skeddan'—The Herring Way*, Cicerone Press, 1988.
Manx **Hill** *Walks*, compiled and published by the Manx Conservation Council (**Footpath** Group).

Isle of Wight An **area of outstanding natural beauty** of 189 square kilometres, which covers nearly two-thirds of the island, including some of the finest beaches, was designated in 1963. The scenery of the hinterland is rolling **downland** with charming villages nestling in the valleys. This is excellent walking country with many waymarked routes vigorously promoted by the County Council. (See figure 36 for a **map** showing the location of all AONBs in the United Kingdom.)
Maps
1:50000 **Landranger** sheet 196.
1:25000 **Outdoor Leisure Map** 29 Isle of Wight.
Footpath Guides
McInnes, R. G., *Isle of Wight Walks for Motorists*, Warne, 1982.
Spibey, Patricia, *Walking in the Isle of Wight*, Hale, 1988.
West Wight Ways, compiled and published by the West Wight Hotel and Catering Association, Sandford Lodge, Totland Bay, IOW PO39 0DN, 1984.

Isles of Scilly An **area of outstanding natural beauty** covering 16 square kilometres of this group of islands situated 45 kilometres south-west of Land's End. They are exceptionally beautiful, and are so mild that sub-tropical plants grow in profusion. Motor vehicles are banned, except on St Mary's, and although there are no long walks, there are numerous pleasant strolls on all the inhabited islands. (See figure 36 for a **map** showing the location of all AONBs in the United Kingdom.)
Maps
1:50000 **Landranger** sheet 203.
1:25000 **Outdoor Leisure Map** 12 Isles of Scilly.

Isodry Manufactured by Neidhart of **Switzerland**, Isodry is a thin insulating synthetic **wadding** that the manufacturers claim improves with washing.

ISPO The acronym for the International Trade Fair for Sports Equipment and Fashion, which is the largest and most important European trade show for sporting goods, is held twice a year in the spring and autumn in Munich, West Germany. It is usually reported in the outdoor press.

Italy A predominantly mountainous country with two significant **mountain** regions. The **Alps** in the north include the distinctive peaks of the Dolomites as well as the beautiful lakes

Italy boasts two significant mountain ranges—the Alps and the Apennines (photo © Italian Tourist Commission).

of Como, Maggiore, Garda and Lugano. The Appennines run for 1200 kilometres down the leg of Italy and are, in places, 200 kilometres wide. In the south there are several active volcanoes, and the country is renowned for its beautiful coastline. Add to this the innumerable beautiful cities, towns and villages and the incomparable architecture, and it is easy to see that Italy has a great deal to offer the discerning walker.

Useful Addresses
Italian State Tourist Office, 1 Princes Street, London W1R 8AY. Tel. 071-408-1254.
Ramblers' *Organisation:* Federazione Italiana Escursionismo Consiglio Nazionale, 1-10143 Turin, Via Cibrario 33.
National **Map** *Survey:* Instituto Geografico Militare, Florence 50100.
Official Survey Maps: Carta Topografica d'Italia 1:50000 and 1:25000. Both series show **footpaths**.
Other maps: Carta delle Zone Turistiche 1:50000 published by the Touring Club Italiano, Milan, cover such areas as the Alps and the Bay of Naples and show footpaths.

Kompass Wanderkarten 1:50000 maps cover selected areas and show footpaths.
Guides to Walking
Evans, Craig, *On Foot through Europe: a* **Trail** *Guide to Central Southern and Eastern Europe*, Quill, 1982.
Footpath Guides
Ardito, Stefano, **Backpacking** *and Walking in Italy; Long and Short Walks from the Alps to Sicily*, Bradt Publications 1987.
Caselli, G., and Sugden, K., *Ancient Pathways in the Alps*, George Philip, 1988.
Collins, Martin, *Alta Via; High Level Walks in the Dolomites*, Cicerone Press, 1986.
Harper, Andrew, *Tour of Mont Blanc*, Cicerone Press, 1982.
Sedge, Michael, *Walking Adventure Guide to Italy*, Moorland Publishing Co., 1988.
Höffler, Horst and Werner, Paul, *Via Ferrata; Scrambles in the Dolomites*, Cicerone Press, 2nd Ed., 1991.
Spencer, Brian, Walking in the Alps, Moorland Publishing Co., 1983.
Spring, Ira, and Edwards, Harvey, *100 Hikes in the Alps*, Cordee, 1979.

J

Jackson, W Holt- The author of a number of indifferent but hearty books on the outdoor life that advocated a regimented approach to camping, suggesting that he was connected with the scout movement. He recommends the appointment of a camp commandant whose duties include the maintenance of discipline, and a daily and minute inspection of the latrines. His books include *The Camper's Guide to the Ideal Holiday; Camping out for Men and Women, Boys and Girls*, 1924; *Handbook of Camping Out; a Manual for every Camper*, 1927; *The Camper's Guide*, 1930; *Camping and* **Hiking** *for All; a Book for Campers, Caravanners and* **Hikers**, 1931.

Jebb, Miles (1930-) The leader of walking tours for Serenissima Travel, and the author of several books about walking. *Walkers* gives some information about the history of walking. He has also devised a **long-distance path**, the Thames Valley Heritage Walk.

Publications about Walking
The Thames Valley Heritage Walk, Constable, 1980.
*A Guide to the **South Downs Way***, Constable, 1984.
Walkers, Constable, 1986.
*A Guide to the Thames **Path***, Constable, 1988.

Jefferies, Richard (1848-87) A naturalist and author. Jefferies was one of the outstanding writers about the English countryside and its wildlife, and many of his books are classics of their genre. He only occasionally mentions his walks in his writings, nevertheless much of his observation of nature was done on foot. He was especially devoted to the **downland** of southern **England**, particularly the area around his boyhood home in Wiltshire. When he was fifteen, he went to **France** with the intention of walking to Russia, but ignorance of foreign languages impelled him to return to England. His autobiography, *The Story of my Heart*, was published in 1883.

Jeffers, Le Roy (1878-1926) American author, lecturer, librarian, **mountaineer** and author of *The Call of the **Mountains**; Rambles among the Mountains and Canyons of the **United States** and **Canada***, 1923. This account of some of Jeffers walks and climbs in north America also contains an essay on **John Muir**.

Jennings, Louis J[ohn] (1833-94) Journalist, novelist, sometime editor of the *New York Times*, Member of Parliament for Stockport, and the author of two books about walking. *Field **Paths** and Green Lanes; being Country Walks Chiefly in Surrey and Sussex*, 1877 (5th Ed.,1907) was a deservedly popular, beautifully written discursive **footpath guide** giving a certain amount of historical background and accounts of encounters with local characters. It describes some walks which are now part of the **North Downs Way** and the **South Downs Way**. *Rambles among the **Hills** in the Peak of Derbyshire and the South Downs*, 1880 contains an interesting account of the problems of **trespass** on **Kinder Scout**.

Joad, C[yril] **E**[dwin] **M**[itchinson] (1891-1953) A university professor, famous broadcaster and member of the *Brains' Trust* team, polemicist, vice-president of the **Ramblers' Association**, populariser of philosophy, and author of numerous books and articles about walking and the countryside. Joad was an intellectual gadfly with a stinging

pen, and something of a mugwump, but he was passionately fond of the English countryside, especially what is now the **Lake District National Park**, and the wooded **hills** of Surrey, and fought strenuously to prevent its despoilation, and to protect **rights of way**. He liked to **trespass** and thoroughly enjoyed confrontations with gamekeepers, and would try to goad them into prosecuting him. His books about walking and the countryside include *A Charter for **Ramblers***, 1935, and *The Untutored Townsman's Invasion of the Country*, 1948 which still make entertaining reading.

Jock's Road A popular Scottish walking route along an old **track** that runs southeast from Braemar through **Glen** Callater and Glen Doll to Glen Clova. In 1885, it was the scene of a confrontation between the laird, Duncan Macpherson who wished to close the route, and members of the Scottish **Rights of Way** and Recreation Society (as the **Scottish Rights of Way Society** was then known). One of the members of the party was a notary public who proceeded to 'take instruments', an ancient Scottish legal procedure, and the laird allowed the party through. However, he continued to discourage use of the route and the Society raised an action against him in the Court of Session seeking to have the route declared a public road or **right of way** on foot and on horseback, and for driving cattle and sheep from Auchallater through the Glen of Doll to Braedownie in Glen Cova. The Society won the case which was upheld in an appeal to the House of Lords in 1887. It is sometimes known as the Glen Doll right of way case.

John Muir Trust An organisation named after **John Muir** who was born in **Scotland** and is world-renowned as the leader of the campaign that lead to the founding in the **United States** of the world's first **national park** system. He was also a leader of the conservation movement. The Trust aims to become the guardian of some of the wildest and most beautiful areas of Britain and to protect it from development and exploitation. (*For address see Appendix.*)

Jonson, Ben (1572-1637) The great dramatist and contemporary of William Shakespeare inexplicably, at the age of 45 and weighing '*twenty stones less two pounds*', walked from London to Edinburgh along what is now the Great North Road. It seems he intended to

write an account of his 'foot pilgrimage' to **Scotland**, but it was either never written, or the manuscript perished in the fire that destroyed his library in 1623. His walk coincided with that of **John Taylor** whom he accused of trying to upstage him when Taylor called on him at Leith. In 1618 Johnson edited *Coryate's Crudities* written by his friend **Thomas Coryate**.

K

Kanter A term, apparently invented by the **Long Distance Walkers' Association**, used to describe a walking event that involves following a route using **map-reading** and **navigation** skills to locate the checkpoints on the route. It is not competitive in the accepted sense, although the route has to be completed within a specified time. It could be described as a walking form of non-competitive **orienteering**, but there is no international governing body.

Kay, Ernie (1931-) and **Kathy** (1928-) A husband and wife team, both retired local government officers, who have been deeply involved for many years in the planning and development of **Offa's Dyke Path**. They are the authors of books and articles about this **national trail** as well as the editors of the **Offa's Dyke Association** *Newsletter*.
Publications about Walking
Offa's Wye Frontier, Offa's Dyke Association, 1981.
Walks along Offa's Dyke, Warne Gerrard, 1983.
Diocesan Way, Offa's Dyke Association, 1983.
***Path** Guide Notes; North–South* and *Path Guide Notes: South–North*, Offa's Dyke Association, 1985.
Walks round Knighton, Offa's Dyke Association, 2nd Ed., 1987.
Castles Alternative, Offa's Dyke Association, 2nd Ed., 1987.
Offa's Dyke Path (with **Mark Richards**), Aurum Press in association with the **Countryside Commission** and the **Ordnance Survey**, 1989.
*Offa's Dyke Path **Backpackers'** Camping List* published annually by Offa's Dyke Association.
Offa's Dyke Path Accommodation and Transport List published annually by Offa's Dyke Association.

Keats, John (1795-1821) One of the major poets of the **romantic movement** who, in the fashion of the time, went on a walking tour.

In June 1818, he walked with his friend **Charles Armitage Brown** in what is now the **Lake District National Park**, called on **William Wordsworth**, who was not at home, climbed Skiddaw and covered 183 kilometres by the time they reached Carlisle. Here they took the coach to Dumfries and then, while walking to Stranraer, Keats composed *Meg Merrilies*. They sailed from Stranraer to Ireland intending to visit the Giant's Causeway, but they did not care for the Irish, returned to **Scotland** and went via Ayr, Glasgow, Loch Lomond to Oban. Here they crossed to Kerrera and had a very tough walk to Mull, and an even harder one the next day. Keats had a sore throat and a feverish cold, but they crossed to Iona and visited Staffa before returning to Oban. By 1st August the two friends had reached Fort William, and the following day climbed Ben Nevis, and then pressed on to Inverness having covered 1033 kilometres on foot, and a further 650 by coach. Keats was now seriously ill and returned to London by boat, but he never really recovered from his exertions and died of tuberculosis in Rome three years later.

The story of this tour is recorded by Keats in letters to his family and friends. Brown also mentions the tour in a letter to his friend Charles Dilke, and then, many years after the event, wrote a series of articles published in the *Plymouth & Devonport Weekly Journal Nos 146-7* of 1st–22nd October, 1840.

An American, Nelson S. Bushnell, followed the route taken by Keats and Brown and published a well-written book *A Walk after John Keats* which was issued in the **United States** in 1936 (there does not seem to have been a British edition).

Kemp, William (15--?-1603?) Actor, dancer and associate of William Shakespeare. He was something of a buffoon, and in 1599 he laid odds of three to one that he could Morris Dance from London to Norwich. He set off on February 11th, 1600 accompanied by his servant and two friends, one of whom played the tabor, and arrived in Norwich on March 5th. Although the journey took 23 days he spent only 9 days dancing and 14 days recovering from his exertions. Kemp made a triumphal entry into Norwich and was met by the Lord Mayor who presented him with five pounds, and awarded him a pension of forty shillings for life. The Elizabethan balladmongers annoyed him by publishing false reports of his dance, so he wrote his own

account in *Kemp's Nine Day's Wonder, Performed in a Morrice from London to Norwich. Wherein every Day's Journey is Pleasantly Set Down, to Satisfy His Friends* [as to] *the Truth; against all Lying Ballad Makers: What he Did, How He Was Welcomed, and by Whom Entertained*. The original is exceedingly rare but it was reprinted in volume 7 of *An English Garner*, 1877 edited by Edward Arber.

Kennedy, Bart (1861-1930) A self-educated cotton-spinner and sailor who went to sea before the mast and later became an author, novelist and lecturer. He walked across **Spain** from Gibraltar to Andorra '*armed with a revolver, a passport, a* **knapsack**, *and no knowledge of the language*', and described his adventures in *A Tramp in Spain; from Andalusia to Andorra*, 1904. Kennedy also wrote a *A Tramp Camp*, 1906, which is an interesting account of his travels as a hobo in north America, but is not really about walking.

Kennovan, James (1812-18--?) An American exponent of **pedestrianism** who achieved a number of prodigious feats in California. In 1855, in San Francisco, he walked for 100 consecutive hours against the Englishman John Phillips, and won. In 1856, in Sacramento, he walked for 90 consecutive hours against the watch, and in the next few years performed a number of similar challenges of which the longest was in 1857 when he walked 106 hours and thirty minutes (ie 4 days 10 hours and 30 minutes of *continuous* walking) against the clock. Possibly his most famous and remarkable feat of endurance took place in 1859 when he was matched against a '**mountain** man', Moses Edwards (also known as Moses Rome) to walk with a regulation US army musket and a 30-lb **knapsack** 'until they dropped'. They were allowed one hour's rest in twenty-four. Edwards retired after 50 hours but Kennovan kept going for another 6 hours. These events are recorded in Woodson, J. A., *Fact and Fancy in the Life of a Pedestrian; Being a full History of the Champion Pedestrian James Kennovan*, San Francisco, 1863.

Kent Downs An **area of outstanding natural beauty**, designated in 1968, which covers 845 square kilometres, and runs from Orpington, where it joins the **Surrey Hills** AONB, to Dover. The Kent Downs AONB includes classic chalk **downland** scenery that makes for excellent walking country which is very popular with Londoners. (See figure 36 for a **map** showing the location of all AONBs in the United Kingdom.)

Maps
1:50000 **Landranger** sheets 178, 179, 187, 188.
1:25000 **Pathfinder** sheets P1192 (TQ46/56), P1193 (TQ 66/76) P1194 (TQ86/96), P1208 (TQ45/55), P1209 (TQ65/75), P1210 (TQ85/95), P1211 (TR05/15), P1212 (TR25/35), P1228 (TQ44/54), P1230 (TQ84/94), P1231 (TR04/14), P1232 (TR24/34), P1251 (TR03), P1252 (TR13/23).
Footpath Guides
Plascott, Roy, *Kent* **Rambles***; 10 Country Walks in Kent*, Countryside Books, 1987.
Reynolds, Kev, *Walking in Kent*, Cicerone Press 1988.
Spayne, Janet and Krynski Audrey, *Walks in the* **Hills** *of Kent*, Spurbooks, 1981.
Tidy, Brian, *Kentish Times Ramblers' Book*, Kentish Times, 1987.

Kephart, Horace (1862-1931) An American librarian and author of *The Book of Camping and Woodcraft*, 2nd Ed., 1909 which was later revised and expanded as *Camping and Woodcraft; a Handbook for Vacation Campers and for Travelers in the Wilderness*, 1917. These comprehensive manuals contain extremely detailed instructions on all aspects of surviving in the American wilderness, and cover such subjects as pack-carrying, fire-making and camp cooking, cabin-building, axemanship, **navigation**, **path**-finding and **trail**-blazing etc. They were issued in this country, where conditions are entirely different, and some of the more popular British outdoor writers continued to extol his methods until the nineteen fifties. Kephart is rightly acknowledged as an early and influential writer about wilderness travel and survival, with a sound knowledge of his subject, but his influence in Britain has not been beneficial.

Kerry and West Cork This is probably the finest walking and **scrambling** country in the whole of **Eire**. The region includes the **mountain** range of Macgillycuddy's Reeks which gives superb views over the peninsulas of Invereagh, Beare and Dingle.
Maps
Irish Ordnance Survey 1:63360 District Map of Killarney. 1:126720 sheets 20, 21, 24.
Footpath Guides
Mersey, Richard, *The* **Hills** *of Cork and Kerry*, Sutton, 1987.
O'Suilleabhain, Sean and **Lynam, Joss**, *Irish Walks Guides South West; Kerry and West Cork*, Gill and Macmillan, 1979.

Kerry Way A magnificent **long-distance path** in **Eire** that runs for 60 kilometres from Killarney **National Park** to Glenbeigh, and will ultimately be extended to provide a circuit of the Iveragh peninsula. The Kerry Way passes through the beautiful **mountains** and lakes of Killarney, and rises to a maximum elevation of 366 metres.

Maps
Irish Ordnance Survey 1:126720 sheet 20 and 1:63360 District Map of Killarney.
Leaflet: Irish Tourist Board Information Sheet 26c *The Kerry Way.*

Kett, Henry (1761-1825) Miscellaneous writer, scholar and clergyman, known to his contemporaries as 'Horse' from his long face. He made a pedestrian tour of what is now the **Lake District National Park** in 1798. Kett used West's guidebook which indicated the 'stations' from which the best views could be obtained. He did not climb any major summits in the Lake District because he believed that the most **picturesque** effects could be obtained only from a distance. On his way home he climbed Ingleborough, in what is now the **Yorkshire Dales National Park**, which, like **Johnson Grant**, he believed to be 3987 feet (1215 metres) high (it is actually 2376 feet or 724 metres), and higher than most **mountains** in the Lake District. An account of this tour may be found in *British Tourists* by **William Mavor**, 1809.

Kildare Way A 37-kilometre Irish **long-distance path** that runs along canal towpaths from Kildare to Edenderry, with a link to Rathangan. The Kildare Way links with a number of other designated routes so that it is possible to plan a longer itinerary that is suitable for casual walkers.
Maps Irish Ordnance Survey 1:126720 sheet 22.
Footpath guide The Kildare Sports Advisory Committee, VEC, Naas, Co Kildare publish *A Walker's Guide to Towpath* **Trails** *in Kildare* as well as leaflets and maps about the route.

Kilvert, [Robert] **Francis** (1840-79) Sometime curate of Clyro in what is now Powys, Chippenham in Wiltshire, and rector of St Harmon, also in present-day Powys. He is famous for his *Diary*, a minor classic, that vividly records his work and the everyday life of a parish on the Welsh Marches. Quite apart from the descriptions of the appalling poverty and brutishness of country life in the last quarter of the nineteenth century, the book is remarkable for the descriptions of his walks, taken both for pleasure and as part of his work in visiting remote areas of the parish.

Kinder Scout The highest summit (636 metres) in the **Peak National Park**, located at **grid reference** SK 087886, is a large, steep-sided plateau of quaking **peat** bog and **featherbed** moss broken by deep **groughs**. It is one of the most difficult sections of the **Pennine Way**.

Since the 1870s, large landowners have attempted to close many of the **rights of way** in the area of Kinder Scout in order to protect their shooting rights. Legal battles were fought over the route that runs from Hayfield via William **Clough** to the Snake Inn, and the ancient Doctor's Gate **path**. These paths were kept open, but there was no right of way over Kinder Scout itself, and trespassers were firmly evicted by gamekeepers. There was considerable pressure from the strong rambling organisations in Sheffield and Manchester to obtain **access** to Kinder Scout, and this culminated in the famous mass **trespass** of 24 April 1932, about which there is still much controversy. What seems indisputable is that the British Workers' Sports Federation, a communist front organisation, was responsible for the trespass led by its secretary, **Bennie Rothman**, and that neither the Sheffield Federation of Rambling Clubs, the Manchester Federation of Rambling Clubs nor the **National Federation of Rambling Clubs** would have anything to do with it, although some individual members of those organisations joined in. The result was a running fight between the trespassers and the police and gamekeepers, and Rothman and five others were arrested, and all except one who was acquitted, were ultimately imprisoned for riotous assembly and assault. Access to Kinder Scout was not finally obtained until the creation of the Peak National Park.

Accounts of the struggles for access to Kinder Scout may be found in *Forbidden Land; the Struggle for Access to* **Mountain** *and* **Moorland** by **Tom Stephenson**, Manchester University Press, 1989; *Freedom to Roam; the Struggle for Access to Britain's Moors and Mountains* by Howard Hill, Moorland Publishing Co., 1980; and *The Kinder Scout Trespass* by Bennie Rothman, Willow Publishing, 1982.

Kissing gate A small gate that is hung in a U or V-shaped enclosure that allows persons, but not animals, to pass. An old country tradition allows a man to claim a kiss from a lady when he operates the gate for her. Kissing gates are sometimes known as wicket gates.

Kitchiner, William (1775?-1827) A doctor of medicine, miscellaneous writer, and author of a most engaging book entitled *The Traveller's Oracle; or, Maxims for Locomotion: Containing Precepts for Promoting the Pleasures and Hints for Preserving the Health of Travellers*, published posthumously in 1827. This delightfully eccentric work gives much practical advice on subjects as diverse as travelling medicine chests, what to carry for personal protection (a brace of double-barrelled pistols with spring bayonets is recommended), how to use a pocket corkscrew-like fitting to secure your bedroom door if it has no bolt, how to choose well fitting footwear, and travelling in foreign countries. Although Kitchiner was an epicure, he was also abstemious and he recommends a good diet and plenty of exercise but for the wrong reasons. There is a chapter *Observations for Pedestrians*, in which he recommends the use of a **pedometer**, and the book is interspersed throughout with the words and music of patriotic songs that the traveller is urged to sing whilst on the road.

Knapsack An obsolete term for a **rucksack**. The word is derived from the German *knapp* meaning 'food', hence a sack to contain food. It was a bag or case of canvas or leather used by soldiers, and later by travellers, to contain changes of linen and other necessities.

Knight, E[dward] **F**[rederick] (1852-1925) Journalist, correspondent for *The Times* and the *Morning Post*, and small-boat sailor. As a boy, he spent much time in solitary wandering among the Somerset **hills**, and he also explored the neighbourhood of Honfleur when he went to live in **France** at the age of fourteen. He extended his tours to include much of Brittany and Normandy, usually sleeping rough and existing on very little money. In 1872, he walked well over 3000 kilometres across the **Alps** and into **Italy**, and the following year set out alone to cross the Sahara on foot. In 1879, he went with three friends and crossed what is now Yugoslavia on foot and on horseback, and described his adventures in *Albania and Montenegro*, 1880. After he became a war correspondent, he travelled thousands of kilometres on foot, horseback and camel in Africa, **Greece**, Cuba, Russia, Japan and Turkey. He described his walks and adventures in his autobiography *Reminiscences* which was published in 1923.

Knott The local name for outcrops of rock found in the **Lake District National Park**.

KS 100 A tough, highly-resistant **nylon** fabric, similar in appearance to **cotton duck**, that was developed for Karrimor, the well-known manufacturer of **rucksacks** and outdoor **clothing**. It comes in various weights, denoted by a suffix, and is used for rucksacks and **gaiters**. KS 100e Standard is a 500 denier fabric, KS 100e Heavyweight is a 1000 denier fabric, and KS 100t Granite has a very high tear strength with good abrasive resistance.

Kunst, David (1939-) From 1970-74 he was a self-styled 'world walker' raising funds for UNICEF (United Nations Children's Fund). He and his brother were attacked by bandits in Afghanistan, John was killed and David severely injured and left for dead. He had many exciting adventures, and his book, which reads as though it has been ghosted, could have made enthralling reading, but it is shapeless and badly written. Travel does not seem to have broadened his mind for he reprints the interview with his local newspaper in which he gave his opinion of foreigners *'I've never seen so many stupid people in my life. You can really appreciate our education system when you see people in some other countries. They're really stupid. Part of it's lack of education, but part of it's their cultural heritage. They need more self-confidence.'* These and similar pearls of wisdom may be found in his book *The Man who Walked Round the World*, Morrow, 1979.

L

Lagan Valley An **area of outstanding natural beauty** in **Northern Ireland** that lies in the green belt of the Belfast-Lisburn conurbation. It is much used by walkers from Belfast and was created to relieve the pressure for development. (See figure 36 for a **map** showing the location of all AONBs in the United Kingdom.)
Maps
1:50000 **Ordnance Survey of Northern Ireland** sheets 15, 20.

Lake District National Park This **national park** is the largest in Britain, covers an area of 2243 square kilometres and con-

tains the highest **mountains** in **England**. It is lozenge-shaped and is bordered by the towns of Penrith. Cockermouth, Millom and Kendal. The Lake District's unique beauty lies in the combination of numerous lakes nestling among steep-sided mountains. As the region is so near the sea, the mountains appear higher than they actually are because they rise dramatically from low ground. The beauty of the Lake District is enhanced by its pleasing, if humble, stone buildings. The larger towns, Keswick, Ambleside and Windermere, can be very crowded in high summer, but there are some quiet hamlets and villages, and providing the more popular walks are avoided, it is still possible to enjoy the mountains. (See figure 36 for a **map** showing the location of all national parks in the United Kingdom.)

The Lake District became a magnet for tourists, who were often referred to as 'lakers', from the late eighteenth century onwards after **William Wordsworth** and his fellow **Lake poets** had made it fashionable.
(For addresses of National Park Headquarters and Information Centres see Appendix.)
Official Guidebook
Wyatt, John, *Lake District*, Webb & Bower in association with Michael Joseph, 1987.
National Park Newspaper
The Lake District Guardian.
Maps
1:63360 **Tourist Map** of the Lake District.
1:50000 **Landranger** sheets 85, 89, 90, 96, 97.
1:25000 **Outdoor Leisure Maps** The English Lakes 4 (NW area), 5 (NE area), 6 (SW area), 7 (SW area).
Footpath Guides
Duerden, Frank, *Best Walks in the Lake District*, Constable, 1986.
Parker, J., *Walk the Lakes: 40 Easy Walks*, Bartholomew, 1983.
Parker, J., *Walk the Lakes Again: 38 Easy Walks*, Bartholomew, 1983.
Poucher, W. A., *The Lakeland Peaks*, Constable, 1984.
Wainwright, A, *A Pictorial Guide to the Lakeland Fells*, Westmorland Gazette, 7 vols. 1955-66. (NB this is the classic guide to walking in the Lake District but it is now very out of date and must be used with caution.)

Lake poets A term of derision applied by *The Edinburgh Review* to **William Wordsworth**, **Samuel Taylor Coleridge** and **Robert Southey** who resided in what is now the **Lake District National Park**, and sought

inspiration in the simplicity of nature. Others associated in the popular mind with the Lake Poets include **Charles Lamb**, **William Hazlitt** and **Thomas de Quincey**. All the Lake Poets and their friends were enthusiastic walkers which is often reflected in their writings. It should be noted that many of them also walked extensively in other parts of the country, and abroad. Once it was accepted that Wordsworth and his circle were important literary figures, the term lost its contemptuous connotation, although the name stuck as a convenient way of defining the school.

Lakeland Country of County Fermanagh An area of **Northern Ireland** that lies in the extreme south-west of the province, centred on Enniskillen, that offers some excellent walking. It contains a number of beautiful lakes dotted with islands, extensive state forests, and some nature reserves.
Maps
1:50000 **Ordnance Survey of Northern Ireland** sheets 17, 18, 26, 27.
Footpath Guide
Simms, P., and Foley, G., *Irish Walks Guides North West; Donegal, Sligo, Armagh, Derry, Tyrone and Fermanagh*, Gill and Macmillan, 1979.

Lamb, Charles (1775-1834) Essayist, poet, and author of *Tales from Shakespeare* and *Essays of Elia*. His name is ever associated with Mary (1764-1847), his poor deranged sister, who accompanied him on many of his walks. Lamb loved London life and could not be separated from the metropolis for long, but he also

Charles Lamb walked extensively in England (photo © National Portrait Gallery).

enjoyed the countryside and lived for some years at Enfield (now a London borough) and did a great deal of walking in Hertfordshire. 'Old China' and 'New Years Eve', found in his *Essays of Elia*, are two of his compositions that express his love of walking and the countryside.

In 1797, he visited **Samuel Taylor Coleridge** at Nether Stowey, and went walking with **William** and **Dorothy Wordsworth** while his host was confined to the garden by a slight accident. He visited Coleridge again in 1802, this time at Keswick in what is now the **Lake District National Park**, called at the Wordsworths' cottage (they were in **France** at the time), and climbed Helvellyn and Skiddaw which excited him greatly. In 1809, he visited **William Hazlitt** at Winterslow on Salisbury Plain and wrote enthusiastically *'We have had nothing but sunshiny days and daily walks from 8 to 20 miles a-day, have seen Wilton, Salisbury, Stonehenge etc.'* The following year he made another visit to Hazlitt at Winterslow. In 1816, he and Mary holidayed at Calne, Wiltshire and walked a great deal, and the following year they visited Brighton and walked in what is now the **Sussex Downs** area of outstanding natural beauty. Lamb wrote to Dorothy Wordsworth describing the Downs as *'almost as good as the Westmorland* **mountains***.'*

Landranger maps A series of metric **maps** published by the **Ordnance Survey** that replaced the Seventh Edition of the 1:63360 maps. The First Series was introduced in 1974 as an interim measure, and was based on the 1:63360 survey which was photographically enlarged. The current edition is the Second Series which cover Great Britain in 204 sheets each spanning an area measuring 40 km x 40 km on a **scale** of 1:50000. Most maps in this series are now completely metric, but until metrication is completed sometime in the 1990s, some sheets will show **contours** based on imperial contours of 50 feet converted to the nearest metre. On the great majority of Second Series maps, height is indicated by contours at 10 metre intervals, with metric spot heights. The Second Series is a considerable improvement on both the First Series and the old 1:63360 (1 inch to the mile). Minor revisions of significant changes, especially new roads and changes in the **path** network, are often incorporated whenever the map is reprinted. Every sheet is identified by a sequential number which starts at 1 for the northern

tip of the Shetland Isles, and ends at 204 at the Lizard in Cornwall. Note that **Northern Ireland** (which has its own **Ordnance Survey for Northern Ireland**) and the **Channel Islands** are not included in the Landranger series. The only significant feature essential for walking in lowland areas that is lacking are field boundaries, These maps are suitable for navigating in mountainous and **moorland** regions, and are useful for the initial planning of routes in lowland areas. **Pathfinder** maps are best for use in lowland areas.

Land's End to John O'Groats The concept of linking the two most distant parts of mainland Great Britain has long had a fascination for walkers (who sometimes refer to it as the 'End to End' walk), cyclists and motorists, and at both Land's End and John O'Groats records are kept of many of these attempts. **Patrick Moloney** and Dr **Barbara Moore** established walking records, and in 1960, Billy Butlin, of holiday camp fame, organised a walking race that attracted 700 starters. Competitors in these events followed roads.

Three post-war books give accounts of walking between Land's End and John O'Groats using **paths**. The best-written account, *Journey through Britain* by **John Hillaby**, published by Constable in 1968, is a classic of travel literature. In 1978, **John Merrill** wrote a mundane book *Turn Right at Land's End*, reissued by JNM Publications in 1989, that describes his 11,000 kilometre clockwise walk around the whole coastline of Britain, and in 1981, **Hamish M. Brown** wrote the excellent *Hamish's Groat's End Walk* published by Gollancz.

In theory, there is an infinite variety of routes to choose from, but in practice, it is easier, if less adventurous, to follow **long-distance paths** as much as possible, and to use **footpath guides**. An obvious route to the Scottish border, which neatly avoids the midland and northern conurbations, is to take the **South West Coast Path** to Minehead, the Somerset Way to Bath, the **Cotswold** Way to Chipping Campden, the Heart of **England** Way to Cannock Chase, the northern section of the Staffordshire Way to Rushton Spencer, the Gritstone Trail to Kettleshulme, the Cestrian Link Walk to Edale, and the **Pennine Way** to Kirk Yetholm (details of these routes that do not have main entries will be found under long-distance paths). **Scotland** has few long-distance paths, but the **West Highland**

Way is a useful route from the outskirts of Glasgow to Fort William.

Langmuir, Eric [Duncan Grant] (1931-) A **mountaineer** and conservationist specialising in outdoor education who was sometime Principal of Glenmore Lodge National Outdoor Pursuits Centre, and Natural Resources Officer of Lothian Regional Council. He helped form what is now the **Association of Heads of Outdoor Education Centres**, and the Scottish Avalanche Project, was the chairman of the **Mountain Rescue Committee of Scotland**, and is currently chairman of the Scottish **Mountain** Safety Group. He is the author of *Mountaincraft and Leadership; a Handbook for Mountaineers and* **Hillwalking** *Leaders in the British Isles* published jointly by the **Scottish Sports Council** and the **Mountainwalking Leader Training Board**, 1984 which is the official handbook of the Mountain Leader Training Boards of the United Kingdom. In 1985 he was awarded the MBE for his services to mountaineering.

Lapse rate The term used to describe the rate of change in temperature caused by increased altitude. In normal conditions, the air gets cooler as the walker ascends, but sometimes temperature inversion can occur and it is actually warmer on the tops than in the valley (the example with which walkers will be most familiar is when cold air is trapped in the valley forming a thick **mist** above which the sun is shining brightly). As a rule of thumb guide, temperature decreases by 2°C for every 300 metres of height gained.

Latocnaye, Jacques Louis de Bougrenet, Chevalier de (1767-18--?) A French royalist officer of cavalry who made two walking tours of the British Isles whilst in exile from the French Revolution. The first, *Promenade dans la Grande Bretagne* was published in Edinburgh in 1795, but does not seem to have been translated into English. The second was *Promenade d'un Français dans l'Irelande* which was published in Dublin in 1797. An English translation by John Stevenson was published in 1917 as *A Frenchman's Walk through Ireland*, and reissued by Blackstaff in 1984. This book is important for the light it sheds on the state of Ireland just prior to the rebellion of 1798. The author was a nobleman, and was furnished with letters of introduction to the local gentry, and was usually well entertained, although he sometimes stayed with peasants. He gives some perceptive opinions about the state of the country, but there is little description of his actual walking.

Le Messurier, Brian (1929-) A former bank official who has also worked for the **National Trust** and served as a ministerially appointed member of the **Dartmoor National Park** and is a guide, broadcaster, and author of books and articles about walking.
Publications about Walking
*The South Devon Coast **Path***, HMSO, 1980.
Dartmoor Walks for Motorists, Warne Gerrard/Penguin, 6th Ed., 1987.
The Visitor's Guide to Devon, Moorland Publishing Co., 2nd Ed., 1988.
The National Trust Guide to the Coast (with Tony Soper), Webb & Bower, 2nd Ed., 1986.
Great Walks on Dartmoor and Exmoor (with John Weir), Ward Lock, 1988.
*The **South West Coast Path**; Falmouth to Exmouth*, Aurum Press in association with the **Countryside Commission** and the **Ordnance Survey**, 1990.
Also 38 walks booklets for the Cornwall, Devon and Wessex Regions of the National Trust 1982-9.
Also contributed to
Le Messurier, Brian, Editor, ***Crossing's** Guide to Dartmoor*, David & Charles. 1965.
Gill, Crispin, Editor, *Dartmoor; a New Study*, David & Charles, 1970.
No Through Road, Automobile Association, 1975.
Lowther, Kenneth E., Editor, *Dartmoor*, Ward Lock, 1979.
The Coastlines of Devon, Devon County Council, 1980.
Mercer, Derrik, Editor, *Exploring Unspoilt Britain*, Octopus, 1985.
Cady, Michael, Editor, *Devon plus Exmoor*, Automobile Association in association with the Ordnance Survey, 1988.
Hillaby, John, Editor, *Walking in Britain*, Collins, 1988.

Lecale Coast An **area of outstanding natural beauty** in **Northern Ireland** that lies in County Down between the **Mourne** and **Strangford Lough** AONBs. It is a region of extensive low dunes and sands that is much used by the military. (See page figure 36 for a **map** showing the location of all AONBs in the United Kingdom.)
Map
1:50000 **Ordnance Survey of Northern Ireland** sheet 21.

Leonard, T[homas] **A**[rthur] (1864-1948) A Congregational minister, sometime president of

the **Ramblers' Association**, who is often described as 'the father of the outdoor movement'. In 1891, as part of his work as a minister at Colne in Lancashire, he persuaded a group of young men to go walking in Ambleside instead of taking a traditional working-class holiday in Blackpool. The experiment was such a success that he formed the Co-operative Holidays Association (later renamed as the Countrywide Holidays Association) which opened a number of country houses that organised inexpensive holidays. In 1913, he resigned to form the Holiday Fellowship which was in many ways a similar organisation, but was financed by members buying shares in the Fellowship. Both organisations are still flourishing. (*For addresses see Appendix.*)

Ley lines A theory first promulgated by Alfred Watkins, and elaborated in his book *The Old Straight **Track***, 1925. According to Watkins, the tracks that can be observed in some parts of the country running dead straight for many kilometres were laid out in prehistoric times by surveyors he called dod-men. He believed that these were ancient trading routes that could be identified by lining up at least five 'ley markers' such as tumuli, hill forts, standing stones, castles, prehistoric circles, pre-reformation churches etc. Watkins' theories have been considerably refined, and many modern ley hunters believe that the leys were only alignments implied by the positioning of sacred sites for purposes that we do not now understand. But ley hunters still look for twenty kilometre alignments of five supposed ley markers on **maps** published by the **Ordnance Survey**, draw a line through them, and then go out and try to find evidence of the links between them. Many ley-hunters associate ley lines with geomancy and unidentified flying objects. Few, if any, scholars or professional archaeologists of repute support the ley line theory, and most argue that although it is a harmless enough pursuit, it gives a distorted view of history, and devalues the very real cultural achievements of prehistoric peoples.

There are a few walking guides to ley lines including *East Anglia; Walking the Ley Lines and Ancient Tracks* by Shirley Toulson, Wildwood House, 1979. The handiest introduction to the subject is *Ley Guide; the Mystery of Aligned Ancient Sites* by Paul Devereux and Ian Thomson, Empress, 1988 (this is the second edition of *The Ley Hunter's Companion; Aligned Ancient Sites—a New Study with a Field Guide*).

Libond A low-**loft** synthetic fibre **wadding**

insulation with a soft feel used as an **insulation** for winter **clothing**.

Liddiard, William (1773-1841) Anglican clergyman, miscellaneous writer and author of the dull *A Three Months' Tour in **Switzerland** and **France**; with a Route to Chamouni* [Chamonix], *the Bernese **Alps** etc*, 1832. When in Switzerland he walked with guided parties which, he implies, was the usual thing to do. The guides provided mules for part of the journey, and the tourists took it in turns to ride. Liddiard gives the conventional tourist responses to **mountains** and seems more interested in food than scenery.

Lightning A **hazard** in the form of an electrical storm that will make **ice-axes** and **rucksack** pack frames hum, and the skin and hair to tingle. A flash of lightning is caused by electrical activity ionising the air, allowing electricity to arc to earth. Lightning takes the shortest route to earth and will usually strike the nearest prominent feature. A useful analogy to help appreciate the effects of lightning is to liken it to water dropped from a height. It will splash in all directions and then follow the line of least resistance through gullies, cracks and the surface of wet rock. If a human body offers the line of least resistance to the path of the current, then electricity will be attracted to it. A direct strike is the most dangerous, and is often fatal, but ground currents, which occur as the electricity is dispersing itself into the earth, can also be dangerous.

If caught in an electrical storm, the walker should try to find a prominent feature such as a large rock at least ten metres high. The area immediately around the rock, formed by a radius equivalent to the height of the rock, is an area of relative safety. Having protected yourself from the risk of a direct strike, it is now necessary to take precautions against injury from ground currents. Try to find a small boulder or stone to sit on well away from any cracks, crevices or gullies along which electricity might travel, insulate yourself as well as possible by placing a rucksack on the boulder and wait for the storm to pass. Avoid being caught on **ridges** and the summits of **mountains** and **hills** during an electrical storm. If in a forest, shelter under trees that are lower than their fellows. Do not shelter in caves or recesses in the rock as these are likely to attract a lightning strike.
For further information, consult ***Mountain Weather; a Practical Guide for **Hillwalkers** and Climbers in the British Isles*** by D. E. Pedgley,

73

Cicerone Press, 1979 and *Mountain Weather for Climbers* by D. J. Unwin, Cordee, 1978.

Limestone pavements Large flat areas of limestone, found particularly in the **Yorkshire Dales National Park**, that have been eroded by wind and rain. The surface or 'clint' is flat but traversed by numerous narrow grooves known as 'grikes'. There is a fine example at the top of Malham Cove (**grid reference** SD 896642) that is crossed by the **Pennine Way**.

Lincolnshire Wolds An **area of outstanding natural beauty** covering a series of chalk **hills** rising to some 170 metres which run from the north-east corner of Lincolnshire, parallel to the sea, but about 20 kilometres inland. Because much of the surrounding country is flat, they offer extensive views over coast and fen. This is very good walking country and well worth exploring. (See figure 36 for a **map** showing the location of all AONBs in the United Kingdom.)

Maps

1:50000 **Landranger** sheets 113, 121, 123. 1:25000 **Pathfinder** sheets P719 (TA00/10), P720 (TA20/30), P730 (TF09/19), P731 (TF29/39), P747 (TF08/18), P748 (TF28/38), P766 (TF27/37), P767 (TF47/57), P783 (TF26/36), P784 (TF46/56).

Footpath Guides

Tennyson **Trails***; Walks in the* **Lincolnshire Wolds**, compiled and published by the Boston Group of the **Ramblers' Association**, 79 Sydney Street, Boston, Lincs PE21 8NZ, 1985. *Walks in South Humberside and Lincs*, compiled and published by the Wanderlust Rambling Club, 5 Pelham Crescent, Keelby, Grimsby, Humberside DN37 8EW.

Lindsay, [Nicholas] **Vachell** (1879-1931) An American poet whose literary reputation has declined in recent years. In 1906, he went on a walking tour through some of the southern states of America repaying hospitality by donating a specially printed copy of his poem *The Tree of Laughing Bells*. He described this journey in a book entitled *A Handy Guide for Beggars. . . being sundry Explorations Made. . . in Florida, Georgia, North Carolina, Tennessee, Kentucky, New Jersey and Pennsylvania* which was published in 1916. In 1912, he set out to walk to the Pacific coast but found that ranchers lacked the tradition of hospitality that he found in the southern states, and he abandoned his tour in New Mexico. This expedition was described in his book *Adventures while Preaching the Gospel of Beauty* which appeared in 1914. Probably his

Top: Detail of the clints and grikes of a limestone pavement. Above: This limestone pavement can be seen on the Pennine Way near Malham Cove (photos © Hugh Westacott).

most famous walking tour was when he crossed the **Rocky Mountains** from Glacier **National Park** with **Stephen Graham** in 1921. Lindsay mentions this tour in his correspondence, and it is described in detail in Graham's book *Tramping with the Poet Vachell Lindsay in the Rockies*, 1922.

Linton, Mrs [Eliza] **Lynn** (1822-98) She was born Eliza Lynn and married the landscape artist William James Linton (1812-98), from whom she separated in 1867, and from 1858 onwards was known as Mrs Lynn Linton. She was a writer and journalist who lived at 'Brantwood' on the shores of Lake Coniston which later became the home of **John Ruskin**. In 1864, Mrs Linton published *The Lake Country*, illustrated by her husband, which is a well-written survey of what is now the **Lake District National Park**. It contains numerous descriptions of walks, and also a robust debunking of some of the romantic nonsense written by earlier authors. '*It is a long time since any book was written descriptive of the Lake Country. Green and West, and Mrs Radcliffe, and others of the* **Picturesque** *School, gave their absurdly exaggerated accounts of what they saw perilled in these 'inhospitable regions', as it was then the fashion to call them; but when the reaction set in, and people had learnt for themselves that the ascent of Blencathra could be made without a fit of apoplexy and the necessity of blood-letting midway—that Borrowdale had nothing maniacal in it, and that Newlands was rather lonesome but not in the least degree terrifying—then all this idealistic writing was at a discount, and only guidebooks containing useful road-side information were asked for.*'

Lithgow, William (1582-1650) A Scotsman who, in what he described as a series of 'pedestriall pilgrimages', walked 58,000 kilometres in nineteen years. In his first two journeys he covered most of Europe, Asia Minor, Syria, Palestine, Egypt and north Africa. On his third tour he intended to visit the mythical kingdom of Prester John in Ethiopia, but on reaching **Spain**, after crossing Ireland, he was arrested and imprisoned as an heretic and spy, and racked and tortured by the Inquisition. He was now a cripple, and was brought back to England by one of His Majesty's ships. Shortly after his return, he was imprisoned for assaulting the Spanish ambassador. He published a vivid and absorbing account of his journeys in *The Totall Discourse of the Rare Adventures and Painefull Peregrinations of Long Nineteene Years of Travayles* in 1632.

Lleyn An **area of outstanding natural beauty**, designated in 1957, situated on a peninsula in Gwynedd and running westwards towards the Irish Sea, and containing the towns of Pwllheli, Abersoch, Aberdaron, and Nevin. Most of the beautiful coastline is included in the 155 square kilometres of the designated area. This is an exceptionally beautiful and remote part of the country with narrow lanes running through gorse, bracken and rough pasture. There are white cottages, and **hills** giving extensive views across rocky headlands and tiny harbours and bays of the coast. (See figure 36 for a **map** showing the location of all AONBs in the United Kingdom.)
Maps
1:50000 **Landranger** sheet 123.
1:25000 **Pathfinder** sheets P785 (SH45/55), P801 (SH34/44), P821 (SH13/23), P822 (SH33/43), P843 (SH12/22/32).

Lloyd, John [David] (1947-) Freelance pho-

tographer and outdoor journalist. He was editor of *Practical Camper* 1978-86, editor-at-large of *Camper* 1986-7 and consultant and contributor to **Outdoor Action** since 1988. He also acts as consultant to gear manufacturers. He contributed to *Coastal Walks: Normandy and Brittany*, Robertson McCarta, 1989.

Lochan The Gaelic diminutive of 'loch' which is used in **Scotland** to denote a small lake.

Loft A property of **down**, which is used as a filling for **sleeping bags** and **duvet clothing**. Down gets its remarkable property of **insulation** by trapping tiny pockets of air in the soft material. When down is crushed (eg when thrusting a sleeping bag into a **stuff sack**), much of the air is expelled, and the next time the bag is required it will have lost much of its insulating qualities unless it is removed from the stuff sack before use. The natural spring, or loft, in the down will allow it to expand and trap more air and the sleeping bag will be ready for use. Sleeping bags and **clothing** containing other forms of insulation are not subject to lofting.

Lofthouse, Jessica (1916-88) Educator, journalist, lecturer, broadcaster, and author who wrote a series of popular books about the north of **England**. *The Rediscovery of the North; Exploration on Foot and by Car*, 1939, *Three Rivers; Being an Account of Many Wanderings in the Dales of Ribble, Hodder and Calder*, 1946, *Off to the Lakes; a Lakeland Walking Year*, 1949, *Lancashire and Westmorland* **Highway**; *with* **Byways** *and Footways for the Curious Traveller*, 1953, and *The Curious Traveller through Lakeland; Historic Ways North from Kendal and Cartmel to Keswick and Penrith*, 1954 all contain descriptions of walks.

Long-distance paths Known colloquially as an LDP, a long-distance **path** is usually defined in Britain as a route of at least 30 kilometres that has been given a distinctive name. Sometimes shorter routes are also referred to as long-distance paths, especially if they provide a link between two other long-distance paths.

It is likely that the Schwarzwaldverein (Black Forest Association), formed in **Germany** in 1864, was the first organisation to promote and develop long-distance paths. The first was the 280-kilometre West Way from Pforzheim to Basle, opened in 1900, which was followed in 1903 by the 233-kilometre Middle Way (Pforzheim—Waldshut), and 238-kilo-

metre East Way (Pforzheim—Schaffhausen). **Sweden** established the Kungsleden in Lapland before the First World War, and James Paddock Taylor founded the Green **Mountain** Club and began to carve out the 427-kilometre Long **Trail** from Massachusetts to the Canadian border in 1910. In 1921, Benton MacKaye first proposed the establishment of the 3400-kilometre Appalachian Trail down the eastern **United States** from Maine to Georgia which was completed in 1937. In **England**, **Tom Stephenson** first publicised the idea of establishing a long-distance path along the watershed of northern England in an article in the Daily Herald in June 1935. This led to the formation of the **Pennine Way** Association, but long-distance paths were not formally established until the implementation of the **National Parks and Access to the Countryside Act, 1949** which followed the publication of the **Hobhouse Report**. **Scotland** and **Northern Ireland** had to wait much longer for legislation, but Scottish and Irish walkers tend to regard long-distance paths as alien to their walking traditions. Long-distance paths have been established in most European countries as well as in other developed nations. There are now a number of **European international long-distance paths** that criss-cross western Europe, and it is likely that the political events of 1989 will ultimately lead to links with the long-distance routes in eastern Europe.

There are two kinds of long-distance path in Britain; official routes, now known in England and **Wales** as **national trails**, and unofficial routes. In England and Wales, official routes, which were first established under the provisions of the National Parks and Access to the Countryside Act, 1949 are now the responsibility of the **Countryside Commission** which oversees the **Cleveland Way**, the **North Downs Way**, Offa's Dyke Path, the **Peddar's Way and North Norfolk Coast Path**, the **Pembrokeshire Coast Path**, the Pennine Way, the **Ridgeway Path**, the **South Downs Way**, the **South West Coast Path**, the **Thames Path** (this route still awaits official designation but is included here as it is walkable throughout its length), and the **Wolds Way**. Provision for the creation of long-distance paths in **Scotland** was included in the **Countryside (Scotland) Act, 1967** which also established the **Countryside Commission for Scotland**, the body responsible for the **Southern Upland Way**, the **Speyside Way**, and the **West Highland**

75

Way. The **Ulster Way** is the only official long-distance path in Northern Ireland and is the responsibility of the **Sports Council for Northern Ireland**. (See figure 36 for a **map** showing the location of all national trails and official long-distance paths in the United Kingdom.)

Unofficial routes may be devised by local authorities, rambling clubs or individuals (in England and Wales, the Countryside Commission refers to them as 'regional routes'). The following list of 197 unofficial long-distance paths has been compiled from the register kept by the **Long Distance Paths Advisory Service** giving the length of the route and details of the start and finish including **grid references**. By February 1990, there were almost 400 long-distance paths on the register, but in a number of cases, details of the **footpath guides** were not available. The following list includes only those entries in the register that contain bibliographical details of the footpath guide or leaflet that describes the route. Where a guide appears under the imprint of an established publisher, no address is given because the book can be obtained by ordering it from a bookshop. The easiest way to obtain a guide where an address is given is to write requesting it and enclosing a signed cheque crossed 'not to exceed £5·00'. Leave the details of payee and the amount payable blank for the recipient to complete. Be sure to put your address on the top left-hand corner of the envelope so that the Post Office can return it if the person has moved.

Abbott's Hike
127 kilometres through the **Yorkshire Dales National Park** and **Pennines** from Ilkley (SE 117476), North Yorkshire to Pooley Bridge (NY 470247), Cumbria.
Footpath guide: Abbott, Peter, *Abbott's Hike*, published by the author at 6 Hillstone Close, Greenmount, Bury, Lancashire BL8 4EZ.

Allerdale Ramble
80 kilometres through the **Lake District National Park** from Seathwaite (NY 235119) to Grune Point (NY 145571).
Footpath guide: Appleyard, Harry, **The Allerdale Ramble**, 2nd Ed., The Tourism Officer, Allerdale District Council, Holmewood, Cockermouth, Cumbria CA13 0DW, 1985.

Angles Way
A 124-kilometre waymarked route from Great Yarmouth (TG 522081), Norfolk to Knettishall Heath (TM 944807), Suffolk.
Footpath guide: *The Angles Way*, compiled and published by the Norfolk & Suffolk Areas of

the **Ramblers' Association**, 150 Armes Street, Norwich NR2 4EG, 1989.

Anglesey Coast Path
A 202-kilometre circular route around the island from the Menai Bridge (SH 556716) following paths and roads.
Footpath guide: Rowlands, E., *Anglesey Guide to Walks*, Ynys Môn group of the Ramblers' Association, 6 Fayars Bay, Llanfaes, Beaumaris, Anglesey, Gwynedd LL58 8RE.

Around Norfolk Walk
A 357-kilometre waymarked circular route from Knettishall Heath (TM 944807), Suffolk comprising the **Peddar's Way** and **North Norfolk Coast Path**, the Weavers Way, and the Angles Way. Leaflet available from Norfolk County Council, County Hall, Martineau Lane, Norwich NR1 2DH.

Avon Walkway
A 50-kilometre waymarked route from Pill (ST525759), near Bristol to the Dundas Aqueduct (ST 785626), near Bath following rivers and canals.
Footpath guide: The Avon Walkway, 1984. A map of the route compiled and published by the Avon County Council, Planning Department, PO Box 46, Avon House North, St James Barton, Bristol BS99 7NF.

Bakewell Circular Walk
A 160-kilometre circular route through the best of the **Peak National Park** from Bakewell (SK 217685), Derbyshire.
Footpath guide: Hyde, George, *Circular walks around Bakewell; 100 miles in the Peak District*, Dalesman, 1984.

Bilsdale Circuit
A 50-kilometre circular waymarked **challenge walk** through the **North York Moors National Park** from Newgate Bank Top (SE 564890), near Helmsley, North Yorkshire.
Footpath guide: Teanby, Michael, *The Bilsdale Circuit; a 30-mile Challenge Walk across the North York Moors*, Dalesman, 1981.

Bob Graham *Round*
A 116-kilometre circular route through the Lake District National Park from Keswick Moot Hall (grid reference NY 266234) which includes 42 major peaks and involves approximately 7200 metres of ascent. It was devised as a challenge for super-fit fell-runners, but it also makes a grand walk.
Footpath guide: **Smith, Roger**, *42 Peaks; the Story of the Bob Graham Round*, Bob Graham **24 Hour Club**, 1982.

Bolton Boundary Walk
An 80-kilometre circular challenge walk around Bolton starting at Affetside Cross (SD 753158),

Greater Manchester.
Footpath guide: Cresswell, Michael, *The Bolton Boundary Walk*, 2nd Ed., Bolton Metropolitan Borough Council, Public Relations and Information Officer, Town Hall, Bolton, BL1 1RU.

Bounds of Ainsty
A 70-kilometre circular route from Tadcaster (SE 488434), North Yorkshire following the rivers Wharfe, Nidd and Ouse.
Footpath guide: Townson, Simon, *The Ainsty Bounds Walk; a 44-mile Circular Walk of the Vale of York*, Dalesman, 1984.

Bournemouth Coast Path
32 kilometres from the end of the **South West Coast Path** at Sandbanks (SZ 037871), Dorset along cliffs and promenades to Milford-on-Sea (SZ 292918), Hampshire.
Footpath guide: **Hatts, Leigh**, *The Bournemouth Coast Path: Swanage, Bournemouth Christchurch and Lymington*, Countryside Books, 1985.

Bradford Ring
A 51-kilometre circular route around the city of Bradford starting at Cottingley Bridge (SE 112380).
Footpath guide: Sheldon, Paul and **Gemmell, Arthur**, *Bradford Ringwalks*, Stile Publications, 1982.

Bradley 20
A 32-kilometre (20-mile) circular route through the **Lincolnshire Wolds** starting at Bradley Woods (TA 242059), south of Grimsby.
Footpath guide: The Bradley 20 and Walks on the Eastern Lincolnshire Wolds, compiled and published by Humberside County Council, Technical Services Department, County Hall, Beverley, North Humberside HU17 9XA.

Brindley Trail
97 kilometres from Buxton (SK 218686) to Stoke-on-Trent (SJ 872479) following a route associated with James Brindley, the canal engineer.
Footpath guide: Speakman, Lydia, The Brindley Trail, Scenesetters, Bircher Cottage, Little Stretton, Shropshire SY6 6RE, 1989.

Bristol Countryway
130 kilometres from the Slimbridge Wildfowl Trust nature reserve (SO 722048) in Gloucestershire to Weston-super-Mare (ST 317614), Avon.
Footpath guide: **Main, Laurence**, *A Bristol Countryway*, Thornhill Press, 1980.

Bristol to London Long Distance Path
277 kilometres from the Clifton Suspension Bridge (ST 565731), Avon to Westminster Bridge (TQ 305797), London mainly following rivers and canals.
Footpath guide: Critchley, Edward, *Face the Dawn;*

Above: The Camel estuary near Padstow on the Cornwall Coast Path (photo © Hugh Westacott).

Below: Walkers enjoying the view east from Devonshire Head towards Lyme Regis on the Devon Coast Path (photo © Hugh Westacott).

the Bristol to London Walk, The **Ramblers'
Association**, 1/5 Wandsworth Road, London
SW8 2XX, 1984.

Brontë Round

A 37-kilometre circular challenge walk through
the Brontë country from Hebden Bridge (SD
992272), West Yorkshire.

Leaflet available from Derek Magnall, 217
Booth Street, Tottington, Bury, Lancashire
BL8 3JD.

Calderdale Way

An 81-kilometre circular waymarked walk
around the Calder valley starting at Greetland
(SE 097214), West Yorkshire.

Footpath guide: The Calderdale Way, 2nd Ed., written and published by the Calderdale Way
Association and the West Yorkshire Metropolitan Council, Department of Recreation and
Arts, 1983. Available from the Tourist Information Centre, Piece Hall, Halifax HX1 1RS.

Cal-Der-Went Walk

A 48-kilometre challenge walk linking the rivers
Calder and Derwent from Horbury Bridge (SE
280179) near Wakefield, West Yorkshire to the
Ladybower reservoir (SK 205865) in the **Peak
National Park**.

Footpath guide: Carr, Geoffrey, *The Cal-Der-Went
Walk*, Dalesman, 1979.

Cambrian Way

427 kilometres from Cardiff (ST 180765) to
Conwy (SH 783775), Gwynedd following a
high-level route over some of the wildest and
toughest country in Britain. The **Countryside
Commission** wisely declined to designate it
a national trail.

Footpath guides: Drake, A. J., *The Cambrian Way;
the* **Mountain** *Connoisseur's Walk*, Cordee, 3rd
Ed., 1990.

Sale, Richard, *A Cambrian Way; a Personal
Guide to an Unofficial Route*, Constable, 1983.

Camuplodunum

A 40-kilometre circuit around Colchester (the
Roman Camulodunum—hence the appalling
pun) which starts at Colchester Hythe station
(TM 016248) and finishes at the Rising Sun
public house (TM 015248).

Footpath guide: Keeble, Derek, *The Camuplodunum;
a Pedestrian Route around Britain's Oldest Recorded
Town—Colchester*, Roy Tover Venture Routes,
9 Shelley Road, Colchester CO3 4JN, 2nd Ed.,
1982.

Castles Alternative

50 kilometres from Monmouth (SO 505129),
Gwent to Hay-on-Wye (SO 229425), Powys
devised as an unofficial alternative to part of
Offa's Dyke Path.

Footpath guides: **Kay, Kathy** and **Ernie**, *The*

Castles Alternative, Offa's Dyke Association, The
Old Primary School, West Street, Knighton,
Powys LD7 1EW, Rev. Ed., 1987.

Centenary Way

A 134-kilometre route, devised by North Yorkshire County Council to celebrate the 100th
anniversary of Yorkshire County Council, from
York Minster (TA 603522) to Filey Brigg (TA
131816).

Footpath guide

The Centenary Way compiled and published by
the North Yorkshire County Council, County
Hall, Northallerton, North Yorkshire DL7
8AD.

Cestrian Link Walk

180 kilometres from Edale (SK 125858) in the
Peak National Park across the Cheshire
plain to Prestatyn (SJ 081838) on the North
Wales coast.

Footpath guide: Davenport, John N., *A Cestrian
Link Walk; a Route Linking the* **Pennine Way** *to*
Offa's Dyke Path, Westmorland Gazette
1983.

Cheshire Ring Canal Walk

A 156-kilometre circular waymarked route
along towpaths starting at Marple (SJ 961887),
Greater Manchester.

Footpath guides: The Cheshire Ring, 11 booklets
compiled and published by Cheshire County
Council, Countryside and Recreation Department, Goldsmith House, Hamilton Place,
Chester CH1 1SE.

Merrill, John, *Canal Walks Vol 4; the Cheshire
Ring*, JNM Publications, 1989.

Clarendon Way

A 39-kilometre waymarked route from Salisbury (SU 143297), Wiltshire to Winchester (SU
483293), Hampshire.

Footpath guide: Shurlock, Barry, *The Test Way and
the Clarendon Way*, Hampshire County Council, Recreation Department, North Hill Close,
Andover Road, Winchester, Hants SO22 6AQ.

Cleveland Way *Missing Link*

An 81-kilometre route between Crook Ness
(TA 026936) , near Scarborough and Helmsley (SE 611839) that turns part of the
Cleveland Way into a 231-kilometre circular
walk.

Footpath guide: **Boyes, Malcolm**, *Walking the
Cleveland Way and the Missing Link*, Cicerone
Press, 1988.

Coast to Coast **Trek**

193 kilometres from Arnside (SD 456788),
Cumbria to Saltburn (NZ 668216), Cleveland.
(NB Despite the similar name this route is
entirely different from the *Coast to Coast Walk*
below).

Footpath guide: French, Richard, *A One Week Coast
to Coast Trek*, published by the author at Expedition North, Wilkinstile, Dowbiggin, Sedbergh,
Cumbria LA10 5LS.

Coast to Coast Walk

306 kilometres from St Bees Head (NX
959119), Cumbria and Robin Hood's Bay (NZ
953048), North Yorkshire.

Footpath guide: **Wainwright, A.**, *A Coast to Coast
Walk*, Westmorland Gazette, 1973. Accommodation list available from Mrs Doreen White-
head, East Stonesgate Farm, Keld, Richmond,
North Yorkshire DL11 6LJ.

Coed Morgannwg Way

A 50-kilometre waymarked route across **Forestry Commission** land from Cwmdare (SN
985025), Mid Glamorgan to Margam (SS
814852), South Glamorgan.

Footpath guide: The Coeg Morgannwg Way, written
and published by the Forestry Commission,
London Road, Neath, West Glamorgan SA1
3SG.

Cotswold *Way*

A 161-kilometre waymarked route from Bath
(ST 751647) along the Cotswold escarpment
to Chipping Campden (SP 153392), Gloucestershire. The Countryside Commission has
issued a consultation paper proposing that this
route should become a **national trail**.

Footpath guides: **Reynolds, Kev**, *The Cotswold
Way*, Cicerone Press, 1990.

Richards, Mark, *The Cotswold Way; the Complete Walker's Guide*, Penguin Books, 1984.

Sale, Richard, *A Guide to the Cotswold Way*,
Constable. 1980.

The Cotswold Way Handbook, compiled and published by the Gloucestershire Area of the
Ramblers' Association, 1/5 Wandsworth
Road, London SW8 2XX. (NB this is revised
biennially and gives essential information about
accommodation, public transport etc.)

Cumberland Way

131 kilometres across the Lake District
National Park from Ravenglass (SD 084963)
to Appleby (NY 683204).

Footpath guide: **Hannon, Paul**, *The Cumberland
Way*, Hillside Publications, 1988.

Cumbria Way

113 kilometres across the Lake District
National Park from Ulverston (SD 284785) to
Carlisle (NY 400554).

Footpath guide: **Trevelyan, John**, *The Cumbria
Way*, 3rd. Ed., Dalesman, 1987.

d'Arcy Dalton Way

A 104-kilometre waymarked route from
Wormleighton Reservoir (SP 448518), Warwickshire to Wayland's Smithy (SU 281853),

Oxfordshire on the **Ridgeway Path**.

Footpath guide: The d'Arcy Dalton Way, compiled and published by the Oxford Fieldpaths Society, High Bank, Wootton, Woodstock, Oxford OX7 1EH, 1987.

Dales Traverse

A 40-kilometre circular challenge walk in the **Yorkshire Dales National Park** commencing at Kilnsey (SD 974679), North Yorkshire.

Footpath guide: Townson, Simon, *The Dales Traverse: a 25-mile Circular Challenge Walk in Upper Wharfedale*, Dalesman, 1984.

Dales Way

A 130-kilometre waymarked route linking from Ilkley (SE 117476), West Yorkshire to Bowness-on-Windermere (SD 402968), Cumbria that links the Yorkshire Dales National Park with the Lake District National Park.

Footpath guide: **Gemmell, Arthur** and **Speakman, Colin**, *The Dales Way Route Guide: with Associated Walks: Specially Drawn* **Maps** *of Associated* **Footpaths**, Stile Publications, 1983. *The Dales Way Handbook*, compiled and published by the West Riding Area of the Ramblers' Association, 9 Church Avenue, Bilton, Harrogate HG1 4HE. (NB this is revised annually and gives details of accommodation, public transport etc.)

Delamere Way

A 35-kilometre waymarked route from Stockton Heath (SJ615858) near Warrington, Cheshire through Delamere Forest to Frodsham (SJ 519781), Cheshire.

Footpath guide: Waymarked walks in Central Cheshire compiled and published by the Mid-Cheshire **Footpath** Society, 72 Osborne Grove, Chavington, Crewe CW2 5BX.

Derbyshire Gritstone Way

90 kilometres from Derby (SK 353365) to Edale (SK 125858) in the Peak National Park where it links with the Pennine Way.

Footpath guide: Burton, Steve and others, *The Derbyshire Gritstone Way*, Thornhill Press, 1980.

Derwent Way

145 kilometres from Barmby-on-the-Marsh (SE 690285), Humberside following the river Derwent to its source at Lilla Howe (SE 889987) in the North York Moors National Park.

Footpath guide: Kenchington, Richard C., *The Derwent Way; an 80-mile Walk from North Humberside to the North York Moors via Malton*, Dalesman, 1978.

Diocesan Way

64 kilometres from Newchurch to Montgomery designed as an unofficial alternative to part of Offa's Dyke Path.

Footpath guide: Kay, Kathy and Kay, Ernie,

Diocesan Way, Offa's Dyke Association, The Old Primary School, West Street, Knighton, Powys LD7 1EW, 1982.

Dorset Downs Walk

76 kilometres from Blandford Forum (ST888067) to Bridport SY 466929).

Footpath guide: **Proctor, Alan**, *A* **Dorset** *Downs Walk*, Thornhill Press, 1982.

Dorset Walk

161 kilometres from Sherborne (ST 376164) to South Haven Point (SZ 036866) where it links with the **South West Coast Path**.

Footpath guide: Dacombe, Ron, and others, *The Dorset Walk; a Hundred Mile Walk, Staggered into Stages, across the Dorset Downs and Coast from Sherborne to Shell Bay*, Dorset Publishing Co., Knock-Ne-Cre, Milborne Port, Sherborne, Dorset DT9 5HJ, 1984.

Downs Link

A 48-kilometre waymarked **bridleway** that runs from St Martha's Hill (TQ 032483) near Guildford, Surrey to St Botolph's Church (TQ193094) south of Bramber, West Sussex, and links the **North Downs Way** to the **South Downs Way**.

Footpath guide: The Downs Link compiled and published by Waverley District Council, The Burys, Godalming, Surrey GU7 1HR. Reynolds, Kev, *The South Downs Way and the Downs Link*, Cicerone Press, 1989

Ebor Way

A 112-kilometre waymarked route through North Yorkshire from Helmsley (SE 611839) in the North York Moors National Park to Ilkley (SE 117476), West Yorkshire.

Footpath guide: **Piggin, J. K. E.**, *The Ebor Way; a 70-Mile Walk from Helmsley to Ilkley Passing the Ancient City of York*, Dalesman, 1978.

Eden Trail

A 55-kilometre challenge walk through the Vale of Eden from Brougham (NY 575288) near Penrith, Cumbria.

Footpath guide: Explore Eden, compiled and published by the Westmorland Visitor Centre, Brough School, Brough, Penrith, Cumbria CA10 2AE.

Eden Way

A 124-kilometre route following the course of the river Eden from its source in Mallerstang (SD 776970), Cumbria to Rockcliffe Marsh (NY 334620) on the Solway Firth.

Footpath guide: **Emett, Charlie**, *The Eden Way*, Cicerone Press, 1989.

Esk Valley Walk

50 kilometres through the North York Moors National Park from Blakey (SE 683989) to Whitby (NZ 900117).

Footpath guide: The Esk Valley Walk, compiled and published by the North York Moors National Park, The Old Vicarage, Bondgate, Helmsley, York YO6 5BP, 1982.

Eskdale Way

A 132-kilometre circular route from Whitby (NZ 900117) through the North York Moors National Park.

Footpath guide: Dale, Louis S., *The Eskdale Way; an 82-Mile Circular Walk in the North York Moors National Park*, Dalesman, 1983.

An accommodation list is available from the author at 10 Mulgrave View, Stainsacre, Whitby, North Yorkshire YO22 4NX.

Essex Clayway

A 120-kilometre waymarked route from Burnham-on-Crouch (TQ 948965) to Witham (TL 820151).

Footpath guide: Dowding, J., and others, *The Essex Clayway*, Matthews/Bitten Publications, 'Glen View', London Road, Abridge, Romford RM4 1UX.

Essex Way

A 130-kilometre waymarked route from Epping (TL 465012) to Harwich (TM 259329).

Footpath guide: **Matthews, Fred** and Bitten, Harry, *The Essex Way*, Matthews/Bitten Publications, 'Glen View', London Road, Abridge, Romford RM4 1UX. 1984.

Falklands Way

A 72-kilometre circular walk from Kirkby Stephen (NY 775085), Cumbria.

Footpath guide: The Falklands Way and the Mallerstang Horseshoe and Nine Standards Yomp, P. N. Denby Ltd., Kirkby Stephen, Cumbria.

Fells *Way*

A 394-kilometre route from Leek (SJ 989565), Staffordshire to Haltwhistle (NY 707638), Northumberland.

Footpath guide: St John, Ian, *The Fells Way*, Footpath Guides, PO Box 369, Addlestone, Surrey KT15 1LT, 1990.

Ffordd y Bryniau (sometimes known as the Ridgeway Walk)

A 32-kilometre waymarked route through Mid Glamorgan from Heol-y-Cyw (SS 969862) near Pencoed to Caerphilly (ST 155852).

Leaflet, published in 1980, available from Taff-Ely Borough Council, Planning Department, County Buildings, Mill Street, Pontypridd, Mid Glamorgan CF37 2TU.

Footpath *Touring*

A 134-kilometre waymarked route from Stratford-upon-Avon (SP 203549) to Cheltenham (SO 950225).

Footpath guide: **Ward, Ken**, *Footpath Touring; the Cotswolds*, Footpath Touring, 1988.

Forest Way

A 32-kilometre route that links Epping Forest (TQ 420995) with Hatfield Forest (TL 530187).

Footpath guide: The Forest Way, compiled and published by Essex County Council, County Planning Department, Globe House, New Street, Chelmsford, CM1 1LF.

Foss Walk

A 45-kilometre route from York (SE 603522) along the banks of the river Foss to Easingwold (SE 528698).

Footpath guide: The Foss Walk compiled and published by the River Foss Amenity Society, Millfield Lane, Nether Poppleton, York YO2 6NA.

Fountains Walk

60 kilometres from Malham (SD 901628), North Yorkshire through the Yorkshire Dales National Park to Fountains Abbey (SE 271683), near Ripon, North Yorkshire.

Footpath guide: The Fountains Walk compiled and published by the Yorkshire Dales Society, c/o the **National Trust**, Fountains Abbey, Fountains, Ripon, North Yorkshire HG4 3DZ.

Furness Boundary Walk

A 177-kilometre circular route around the Furness peninsula in Cumbria starting at Barrow-in-Furness (SD 190688).

Footpath guide: Dillon, Paddy, *The Furness Boundary Walk*, published by the author at 82 Arthur Street, Barrow-in-Furness, Cumbria LA14 1BH.

Furness Way

120 kilometres through the Lake District National Park from Arnside (SD 456788) to Ravenglass (SD 084963).

Footpath guide: **Hannon, Paul**, *The Furness Way*, Hillside Publications, 1982. *Glyndŵr's Way.*

A 193-kilometre waymarked route through central Wales from Knighton (SO 283724) to Welshpool (SJ 229071) linking with Offa's Dyke Path at each end. The Countryside Commission proposes to make this route a national trail.

Footpath guide: Sale, Richard, *Owain Glyndŵr's Way*, Hutchinson, 1985.

Grafton Way

A 20-kilometre waymarked route from Wolverton (SP 821415), Buckinghamshire to Green's Norton (SP 671490), Northamptonshire that links with the North Bucks Way and the Knightley Way to form an 87-kilometre waymarked route.

Footpath guide: The Grafton Way, compiled and published by Northamptonshire County Council, Leisure and Libraries Dept., 27 Guildhall, Northampton NN1 1EF, 1984.

Grassington Circuit Walk

A 36-kilometre near-circular route in the Yorkshire Dales National Park from Grassington (SD 999639) to Threshfield (SD 993639) 2 kilometres from Grassington.

Footpath guide: Belk, Les, and Hills, John, *The Grassington Circuit Walk*, published by the authors at 82 Northcote Crescent, Leeds LS11 6NN.

Greensand Way

An 89-kilometre waymarked route across Surrey from Haslemere (SU 898329) to Limpsfield (TQ 436522). There are plans for an extension through Kent.

Footpath guides: Adams, A., J., *Walk the North Downs Way and the Greensand Way*, published by the author at 2 Dryden Court, Lower Edgeborough Road, Guildford GU1 2EX.

McLennan, Jim, *The Greensand Way*, Gemplan Services Ltd., PO Box 185, Harrow, HA2 8UB.

The Greensand Way in Surrey compiled and published by Surrey County Council, County Engineer's Dept., **Rights of Way** Section, 21 Chessington Road, West Ewell, Epsom, Surrey KT17 1TT, 1989.

Gritstone Trail

A 29-kilometre waymarked route in Cheshire from Lyme Park (SJ 962823), southeast of Stockport, to Rushton Spencer (SJ 935625), Staffordshire where it joins the Staffordshire Way.

Footpath guide: The Gritstone Trail Walker's Guide, compiled and published by Cheshire County Council, Countryside and Recreation Department, Goldsmith House, Hamilton Place, Chester CH1 1SE, 1986.

Guildford Boundary Walk

A 32-kilometre circular challenge walk around Guildford, Surrey starting at St Catherine's Chapel (SU993483) on the North Downs Way.

Footpath guide: Blatchford, Alan and Barbara, *The Guildford Boundary Way and Other Walks*, Greenway Publications, 11 Thornbank, Guildford GU2 5PL, 1979.

Hadrian's Wall Walk

118 kilometres along Hadrian's Wall from Wallsend (NZ304660), Tyne & Wear to Bowness-on-Solway (NY 225628), Cumbria. The Countryside Commission has issued a consultation paper proposing that a national trail be created in the Hadrian's Wall area.

Footpath guide: Mizon, Graham, *Guide to Walking Hadrian's Wall*, Hendon Publishing Co., 1977.

Harcamlow Way

A 225-kilometre figure-of-eight walk commencing at Harlow (TL 445113), Essex and cross-

ing Hertfordshire and Cambridgeshire.

Footpath guide: Matthews, Fred, and Bitten, Harry, *The Harcamlow Way*, Matthews/Bitten Publications, 1980.

Harrogate Ringway

A 34-kilometre circular route around Harrogate, North Yorkshire commencing at Pannal (SE 307514).

Footpath guide: Further Walks around Harrogate, compiled and published by the Harrogate Group of the Ramblers' Association, 20 Pannal Ash Grove, Harrogate HG2 0HZ, 1984.

Haslemere Hundred

A 160-kilometre figure-of-eight route through Surrey and West Sussex commencing at Haslemere station (SU 898329).

Footpath guide: Hyde, George, *The Haslemere Hundred; Walking the Best of Surrey and Sussex; Two 50-mile Circular Routes Arranged in a Series of Easy Walks*, Footpath Publications, 69 South Hill, Godalming Surrey GU7 1JU, 1988.

Headland Walk

A 34-kilometre waymarked route around Flamborough Head from Bridlington (TA 176680), Humberside to Filey Brigg (TA 126817), North Yorkshire.

Leaflet available from Humberside County Council, Technical Services Department, County Hall, Beverley, North Humberside HU17 9XA.

*Heart of **England** Way*

A 131-kilometre route from Cannock Chase (SJ 990166), Staffordshire to Chipping Campden (SP 153392), Gloucestershire.

Footpath guides: Watts, J. T., Editor, *The Heart of England Way Walker's Guide*, compiled by the Heart of England Way Steering Committee, Thornhill Press, 1982.

Roberts, J. S., *Heart of England Way*, WALK-WAYS, 4 Gilldown Place, Birmingham B15 2LR, 2nd Ed., 1989.

Hereward Way

A 164-kilometre waymarked route from Oakham (SK 861088), Leicestershire to Harling Road station (TL 978879) near Thetford, Norfolk.

Footpath guide: Noyes, Trevor, *The Hereward Way* published by the author at 8 Welmore Road, Glinton, Peterborough PE6 7LU.

Heritage Way

A 113-kilometre waymarked circular route around Newcastle-upon-Tyne and Gateshead, focussing on industrial archaeology, that starts at Wylam (NZ 119647), Northumberland, west of Newcastle.

Footpath guide: The Heritage Way; 4 leaflets compiled and published by Tyne and Wear County

Above: Cradle Mountain and Dove Lake, Australia (photo © Australian Tourist Commission).

Left: Most of Austria is mountainous and offers exceptionally fine opportunities for walking (photo © Austria Tourist Office).

Above: Canada contains vast areas of wilderness for backpackers to explore (photo © Tourism Canada Photo).

Below: Walkers enjoying an easy stroll along the Brecon and Monmouth canal (photo © Hugh Westacott)

Above: Backpackers on the Robert Louis Stevenson trail in the Cevennes, France (photo © Hugh Westacott).

Below: Les Aiguilles in the French Alps offer spectacular walking (photo © Hugh Westacott).

Above: The hot springs in Iceland can be used as baths for tired walkers (photo © Hugh Westacott).

Left: Rural Italy at its best at Val Tournancho (photo © Italian Tourist Commission).

Above: Durdle Door on the Dorset Coast Path (photo © Hugh Westacott)

Below: Typical chalk path along open land on the Ridgeway long-distance path (photo © Ramblers Association)

Left: Dawn greets the backpackers at Canterbury in New Zealand (photo © New Zealand Tourist Commission).

Below: Norway is a paradise for walkers with numerous long-distance paths and tourist huts for overnight stops (photo © Norwegian Tourist Board).

Above: Spain offers excellent walking, especially in the Sierra Nevada and on the Balearic Islands (photo © Spanish National Tourist Office).

Right: Early summer in Glen Kinglass, Scotland (photo © Hugh Westacott).

Above: Spectacular scenery in the Grand Canyon National Park, USA, but the heat in summer can be oppressive (photo © Hugh Westacott).

Below: Malham Cove in the 1760-square-kilometre Yorkshire Dales National Park (photo © Hugh Westacott).

Council, Planning Department, Sandyford House, Newcastle-upon-Tyne NE2 1ED, 1985.

Herriot Way

An 89-kilometre circular route from Aysgarth (SE 012885), North Yorkshire through the Yorkshire Dales National Park.

Footpath guide: Scholes, Norman F., *The Herriot Way*, published by the author at YHA, 96 Main Street, Bingley, West Yorkshire BD16 2JH.

High Hunsley Circular

A 39-kilometre circular challenge walk in the Yorkshire Wolds which starts at Walkington (SE 999368), Humberside near Beverley.

Footpath guide: The High Hunsley Circular compiled and published by Humberside County Council, Technical Services, County Hall, Beverley, North Humberside HU17 9XA.

Holderness Way

A 34-kilometre route through Humberside from Kingston-upon-Hull (TA 097288) to Hornsea (TA 208479).

Footpath guide: Dresser, Roy, *The Holderness Way* published by the author at 128 Kirklands Road, Kingston-upon-Hull HU5 5AT.

Howden 20

A 32-kilometre (20-mile) circular route starting at Howden (SE 748283), north of Goole, Humberside.

Footpath guide: The Howden 20 compiled and published by Humberside County Council, Technical Services, County Hall, Beverley, North Humberside HU17 9XA.

Hull Countryway

An 83-kilometre waymarked semi-circular route through Humberside from Kingston-upon-Hull (TA 097288) to Hedon (TA 188287).

Footpath guide: Killick, Alan, *The Hull Countryway*, Lockington Publishing Co. Ltd.

Humber Bridge Link Walk

A 55-kilometre circular walk from Hessle (TA 035256), Kingston-upon-Hull with circuits on both sides of the Humber that are linked by the Humber Bridge.

Footpath guide: The Humber Bridge Link Walk compiled and published by Humberside County Council, Technical Services, County Hall, Beverley, North Humberside HU17 9XA.

Icknield Way

168 kilometres from Ivinghoe Beacon (SP 960168), near Tring, Hertfordshire to Knettishall Heath (TM 944807), near Thetford, Norfolk.

Footpath guide: The Icknield Way; a Walker's Guide, compiled and published by the **Icknield Way Association**, 19 Boundary Road, Bishops

Stortford, Herts CM23 5LF, 1988.

Inkpen Way

100 kilometres from Monk Sherborne (SU 609561), near Basingstoke, Hampshire to Salisbury (SU 143297).

Footpath guide: Ward, Ian, *The Inkpen Way*, Thornhill Press, 1979.

Isle of Man *Coastal Footpath*

A 145-kilometre circular route around the coast of the Isle of Man starting at Douglas (SC 379754). It is also known as Raad Ny Foillan (the Gull's Road).

Footpath guide: Evans, Aileen, *Isle of Man Coastal Path ; "Raad ny Foillan" -The Way of the Gull; includes also the Millenium Way and the "Bayr ny Skeddan"—The Herring Way*, Cicerone Press, 1988.

Isle of Wight *Coastal Path*

A 105-kilometre waymarked route encircling the island starting at Ryde (SZ 596919).

Footpath guides: Charles, Alan, *The Isle of Wight Coast Path*, Thornhill Press, 1986.

Merrill, John, *Isle of Wight Coastal Path*, JNM Publications, 1988.

A set of eight 1:25000 maps showing all rights of way on the island is available from the County Surveyor, County Hall, Newport, Isle of Wight P030 1UD.

Kettlewell Three Walk

A strenuous 53-kilometre circular challenge walk in the Yorkshire Dales National Park from Kettlewell (SD 968723).

Footpath guide: Belk, Les, and Hills, John, *The Kettlewell Three Walk*, published by the authors at 82 Northcote Crescent, Leeds LS11 6NN.

King Alfred's Way

174 kilometres from Portsmouth (SU 628006) to Oxford (SP 516060).

Footpath guide: Main, Laurence, *King Alfred's Way*, Thornhill Press, 1980.

Knightley Way

A 19-kilometre waymarked route in Northamptonshire from Greens Norton (SP 671490) to Badby (SP 560587). It links with the Grafton Way, which in turn joins the North Bucks Way, to form an 87-kilometre route.

Footpath guide: The Knightley Way compiled and published by Northants County Council, Leisure and Libraries Dept., 27 Guildhall, Northampton NN1 1EF, 1983.

Lakes Link

A 196-kilometre circular route through the Lake District National Park from Ambleside (NY 376045).

Footpath guide: Dixon, Michael, *The Lakes Link; a 128 Mile Circular Route from Ambleside Connecting all the Major Lakes*, Dalesman, 1984.

Lancashire ***Trail***

113 kilometres from St Helens (SJ 512956), Merseyside to Thornton-in-Craven (SD 906484), North Yorkshire, west of Skipton.

Footpath guide: The Lancashire Trail; a Series of Short Walks which Link Together to form a Long-distance Route Connecting St Helens, Wigan. Bolton, Blackburn and Burnley with the Pennines, 2nd Ed., compiled and published by the St Helens District CHA and Holiday Fellowship Rambling Club, 40 St Mary's Avenue, Birchley, Billinge, Wigan WN5 7QL, 1982.

Langbaurgh Loop

A 61-kilometre waymarked circular route from Saltburn-by-the-Sea (NZ 668216), Cleveland. Leaflet available from Langbaurgh Business Association, Jordans Guest House, 15 Pearl Street, Saltburn-by-the-Sea, Cleveland TS12 1DU.

Leeds Country Way

A 97-kilometre waymarked circular route around Leeds starting at Golden Acre Park (SE 267417). Leaflet available from Leeds Metropolitan Borough Council, Civic Hall LS1 1UR, 1981.

Leeds Dalesway

A 32-kilometre walk through West Yorkshire from Leeds (SE 293351) to Ilkley (SE 117476).

Footpath guide: Gemmell, Arthur and Speakman, Colin, *The Dales Way Route Guide: with Associated Walks: Specially Drawn Maps of Associated Footpaths*, Stile Publications, 1983.

Leeds to the Sea

145 kilometres from Roundhay (SE 336372), Leeds to Saltburn-by-the-Sea (NZ 668216), Cleveland. The guide mentioned below covers 71 kilometres of the route from Roundhay to the Kilburn White Horse (SE 514813) in the North York Moors National Park where it joins the **Cleveland Way**. From then on it is necessary to use a guide to this long-distance path.

Footpath guide: A Walk from Leeds to the Sea, compiled and published by the West Riding Area of the Ramblers' Association, 9 Church Avenue, Bilton, Harrogate HG1 4HE, 1983.

Leicestershire Round

A 161-kilometre circular waymarked route through the county from Burrough Hill Country Park (SK 766115), near Melton Mowbray.

Footpath guide: The Leicestershire Round, written and published in three sections by the Leicestershire Footpath Association and available from the Tourist Information Bureau, 12 Bishop Street, Leicester LE1 6AA.

Section 1: *Burrough Hill to Foxton Locks*, 1981.

Section 2: *Foxton Locks to Market Harborough*,

1983.

Section 3: *Market Harborough to Burrough Hill*, 1983.

Leland **Trail**

A 45-kilometre waymarked **path** through Somerset from Alfred's Tower (ST 746350), near Stourhead to Ham Hill (ST 481164), near Stoke-sub-Hamdon following the route traversed by John Leland during his survey of Britain made in the 1530s.

Footpath guide: The Leland Trail, compiled and published by South Somerset District Council, Brympton Way, Yeovil, Somerset BA20 1PU, 1990.

Limestone Way

A 42-kilometre waymarked route through the Peak National Park from Matlock (SK 298603) to Castleton (SK 150829).

Leaflet available from West Derbyshire District Council, Town Hall, Bank Road, Matlock, Derbyshire DE4 3NN.

Limey Way

64 kilometres from Castleton (SK 150829) through the Peak National Park to Thorpe ((SK 157054), north of Ashbourne.

Footpath guide: Merrill, John, *The Limey Way*, JNM Publications, 1989.

Lindsey Loop

A 161-kilometre figure-of-eight route from Market Rasen (TF 111897), Lincolnshire.

Footpath guide: Collier, Brett, *The Lindsey Loop*, Lincolnshire and South Humberside Group of the **Ramblers' Association**, Chloris House, 208 Nettleham Road, Lincoln LN2 4GH, 1986.

Lipchis Way

42 kilometres from Liphook (SU 842309), Hampshire to Chichester (SU 858043), West Sussex (hence the punning name).

Footpath guide: Clark, David, and Clark, Margaret, *The Lipchis Way*, published by the authors at 21 Chestnut Close, Liphook, Hants GU30 7JA, 1985.

Llwybr Bro Gwy

A 58-kilometre waymarked route through Powys from Hay-on-Wye (SO 229425) to Rhayader (SN 968679).

Leaflet available from Powys County Council, Shire Hall, Llandrindod Wells LD1 5LG.

London Countryway

A 330-kilometre circular route around London from Box Hill (TQ 173513), near Dorking, Surrey.

Footpath guide: **Chesterton, Keith**, *A London Countryway*, 2nd Ed., Constable, 1981.

Lyke Wake Walk

A 64-kilometre challenge walk across the North York Moors National Park from Beacon Hill (SE 459997), near Osmotherley to Ravenscar (NZ 980018) on the coast. Unfortunately, the route has received a great deal of publicity, encouraged by the antics of the organiser of the **Lyke Wake Club**, is now seriously eroded and should be avoided by all who care about the environment.

Footpath guide: Cowley, William, *The Lyke Wake Walk and the Lyke Wake Way; Forty Miles across the North York Moors in 24 hours or 50 Miles in a Day as Long as You Like!: with, in Addition, the Shepherd's Round, the Monk's Trod and the Rail Trail Thrown in for Good Measure*, Dalesman, 1988.

Maidstone Circular Walk

A 32-kilometre circular route around Maidstone, Kent starting at Sandling (TQ 755581).

Footpath guide: The Maidstone Circular Walk, compiled and published by the Maidstone Group of the Ramblers' Association, 18 Firs Close, Aylesford, Maidstone ME20 7LH.

Mallerstang Horseshoe and Nine Standards Yomp

A 37-kilometre circular challenge walk from Kirkby Stephen (NY 775087), Cumbria.

Footpath guide: The Falklands Way and the Mallerstang Horseshoe and Nine Standards Yomp, P. N. Denby Ltd., Kirkby Stephen, Cumbria.

Millenium Way

A 45-kilometre waymarked route across the Isle of Man from Sky Hill (SC 432945), Ramsey to Castletown (SC 265675).

Footpath guides: Evans, Aileen, *Isle of Man Coastal Path; 'Raad ny Foillan'—Way of the Gull; includes also the Millenium Way and the 'Bayr ny Skeddan'—The Herring Way*, Cicerone Press, 1988.

Millennium Way, compiled and published by the Isle of Man Tourist Board, 13 Victoria Street, Douglas, I. O. M.

Minster Way

An 81-kilometre waymarked route from Beverley (TA 038393), Humberside to York (SE 603522).

Footpath guide: Wallis, Ray, *The Minster Way*, Lockington Publishing Co. 1979.

Navigation *Way*

161 kilometres along canal towpaths from Birmingham (SP 064864) to Chasewater (SK 041073) near Brownhills, West Midlands.

Footpath guide: Groves, Peter, *The Navigation Way; a Hundred Mile Towpath Walk around Birmingham and the West Midlands*, Tetradon Publications, 40 Hadzor Road, Oldbury, Warley, West Midlands B68 9LA for the University of Aston in Birmingham, 1978.

Nene Way

A 108-kilometre waymarked route through the Nene valley from Badby (SP 560587), Northamptonshire to Wansford-in-**England** (TL 076993), Cambridgeshire.

Leaflets available from the Leisure & Libraries Dept., 27 Guildhall Road, Northampton NN1 1EF.

Nidderdale Way

An 85-kilometre waymarked circular route from Hampsthwaite (SE 259587), near Harrogate, North Yorkshire.

Footpath guide: **Piggin, J. K. E.**, *The Nidderdale Way; a 53-Mile Walk around the Valley of the River Nidd*, Dalesman, 1983.

North Bowland Traverse

A 52-kilometre route from Slaidburn (SD 712524), Lancashire to Stainforth (SD 822673), North Yorkshire.

Footpath guide: Johnson, David, *The North Bowland Traverse*, Hillside Publications, 1987.

North Buckinghamshire Way

50 kilometres from Chequers Knap (SP 830053), near Wendover to Wolverton (SP 821415), Milton Keynes.

Footpath guide: The North Buckinghamshire Way, compiled and published by the Buckinghamshire and West Middlesex Area of the Ramblers' Association and available from the Ramblers' Association, Southern Area, 1/5 Wandsworth Road, London SW8 2XX, 3rd Ed.

North Wolds Walk

A 32-kilometre circular walk from Millington Road End (SE 836567), 24 kilometres east of York.

Footpath guide: Watson, R. N., The *North Wolds Walk*, published by the author and available from him at the Library and Information Service, Reckitt & Colman Pharmaceutical Division, Kingston-upon-Hull HU8 7DS.

North Worcestershire Path

A 34-kilometre waymarked route through Hereford and Worcester from Forhill picnic site (SP 055755), south of Birmingham to Kingsford Country Park, north of Kidderminster.

Leaflet: *The North Worcestershire Path (Countryside Recreation Service Information Sheet no. 7)* compiled and published by Hereford and Worcester County Council, County Planning Department, Spetchley Road, Worcester WR5 2NP.

North York Moors Challenge Walk

A 40-kilometre circular challenge walk in the North York Moors National Park commencing at Goathland (NZ 838014).

Footpath guide: Merrill, John, *John Merrill's North York Moors Challenge Walk*, JNM Publications, 1986.

Northumberland Coast Walk
A 40-kilometre waymarked route from Alnmouth (NU 248108) to Budle (NU 155350).
Footpath guide: Hopkins, Tony, *Walks on the Northumberland Coast,* Northumberland County Council, 1983.

Offa's Wye Frontier
96 kilometres from Monmouth (SO 505129), Gwent to Kington (SO 298566), Hereford and Worcester designed as an unofficial alternative to part of **Offa's Dyke Path.**
Footpath guide: Kay, Kathy and Ernie, *Offa's Wye Frontier,* Offa's Dyke Association, The Old Primary School, West Street, Knighton, Powys LD7 1EW, 1987.

Oxfordshire Trek
A 103-kilometre circular route from Sir Winston Churchill's tomb at Bladon (SP 449149), near Woodstock.
Footpath guide: **Main, Laurence**, *Guide to the Oxfordshire Trek,* Kittiwake Press, 1989.

Oxfordshire Way
A 105-kilometre waymarked route from Bourton-on-the-Water (SP 170209), Gloucestershire to Henley-on-Thames (SU 757833), Oxfordshire.
Footpath guide: The Oxfordshire Way, compiled and published by Oxford County Council, Speedwell House, Speedwell Street, Oxford OX1 1SD.

Painters' Way
39 kilometres from Sudbury ((TL 877410), Suffolk to Manningtree (TM 094322), Essex through countryside associated with Turner and Gainsborough.
Footpath guide: Turner, Hugh R. P., *The Painters' Way,* Peddar Publications, Croft End Cottage, Bures, Suffolk CO8 5JN, 1982.

Peak District Challenge Walk
A 40-kilometre circular challenge walk through the Peak National Park from Bakewell (SK 217685).
Footpath guide: Merrill, John, *John Merrill's Peak District Challenge Walk,* JNM Publications, 1986.

Peak District High Level Route
A 145-kilometre circular challenge walk around the Peak National Park from Matlock (SK 298603).
Footpath guide: Merrill, John, *The Peak District High Level Route,* JNM Publications.

Peakland Way
A 155-kilometre circular challenge walk through the Peak National Park from Ashbourne (SK 178479).
Footpath guide: Merrill, John, *The Peakland Way Guide,* JNM Publications, 1989.

Peddars Way and North Norfolk Coast Path Extension

63 kilometres extending the national trail from Cromer (TG 215420) to Great Yarmouth (TG 522081) .
Footpath guide: Kennett, David H., *A Guide to the Norfolk Way,* Constable, 1982.

Peel Trail
A 56-kilometre circular route from Bury (SD 809123), Greater Manchester.
Footpath guide: Burton, Michael, *The Peel Trail,* published by the author at 6 Carrwood Hey, Ramsbottom, Lancashire BL0 9QT.

Pendle Way
A 72-kilometre waymarked circular route from Barrowford (SD 863398), Lancashire. Leaflet available from Pendle Borough Council, Bank House, Albert Road, Colne, Lancashire BB8 0AQ.

Pilgrims' Way
A 210-kilometre waymarked route from Winchester (SU 483293), Hampshire to Canterbury (TR 150579), Kent following the prehistoric trackway inaccurately associated in the popular mind with the route taken by mediaeval pilgrims travelling between the shrines of St Swithun and St Thomas à Beckett. Considerable sections run parallel to or concurrent with the North Downs Way which is now a national trail.
Footpath guide: **Wright, Christopher John**, *Guide to the Pilgrims' Way and the North Downs Way,* Constable, 1982.

Plogsland Round
A 72-kilometre circular route around Lincoln starting at Fiskerton (TF 058715).
Footpath guide: Collier, Brett, *The Plogsland Round,* published by the author at Chloris House, 208 Nettleham Road, Lincoln LN2 4DH, 1982.

Ramblers' Way
61 kilometres through the Peak National Park from Castleton (SK 150829) to Hathersage (SK 232815).
Footpath guide: Newton, Andrew, and Summers, Paul, *The Ramblers' Way* published by the authors and available from Mountain Peaks Climbing Club, 17 Humberston Road, Wollaton, Nottingham NG8 2SU.

Red Kite Trail
A 119-kilometre circular route from Llanwrtyd Wells (SN 879467), Powys. Leaflet available from Gordon Green, Neuadd Arms Hotel, Llanwrtyd Wells, Powys

Ribble Way
A 116-kilometre waymarked route from Longton (SD 458255), near Preston, Lancashire to near Horton-in-Ribblesdale (SD 813827), North Yorkshire following the river Ribble from its estuary to its source.

Footpath guide: **Sellers, Gladys**, *The Ribble Way,* Cicerone Press, 1985.

Ridge Walk
A 32-kilometre circuit around upper Nidderdale, North Yorkshire starting at Middlesmoor (SE 091741).
Footpath guide: Belk, Leslie, and Hills, John, *The Ridge Walk,* published by the authors at 82 Northcote Crescent, Leeds LS11 6NN.

Rivers Way
A 64-kilometre challenge walk across the Peak National Park, mainly following rivers, from Edale (SK 125858) to Ilam (SK 135508).
Footpath guide: Merrill, John, *The Rivers Way,* JNM Publications, 1987.

Robin Hood Way
A 142-kilometre waymarked route through Nottinghamshire from Nottingham Castle (SK 569392) to Edwinstowe Church (SK 626669) where Maid Marion is reputed to have married Robin Hood.
Footpath guide: The Robin Hood Way, compiled and published by the Nottingham Wayfarers Rambling Club, 22 The Hollows, Silverdale, Wilford, Nottingham NG11 7FJ, 1985.

Rossendale Way
A 72-kilometre circular route through Lancashire from Sharneyford (SD 889246) near Bacup.
Footpath guide: Goldthorpe, Ian, *The Rossendale Rambles including the Rossendale Way and Selected Town and Village Trails,* 2nd Ed., Rossendale Groundwork Trust and the Rossendale Borough Council, Planning Department, 6 St James' Square, Bacup, Lancashire OL13 9AA, 1985.

St Peter's Way
73 kilometres through Essex from Chipping Ongar (TL 551036) to Bradwell-on-Sea (TM 032082).
Footpath guide: **Matthews, Fred**, and Bitten, Harry, *The St Peter's Way; a Long-distance Route from Chipping Ongar to the Ancient Chapel of St Peter-on-the-Wall at Bradwell-on-Sea, Essex,* Matthews/Bitten Publications, 1978.

Saints Way
A 42-kilometre route across **Cornwall** from Padstow (SW 920754) on the north coast to Fowey (SX 127522) on the south coast.
Footpath guide: Gill, M., and Colwill, S., *The Saints Way,* Co-operative Retail Society, 29 Dantzic Street, Manchester M4 4BA, 1986.

Sandstone Trail
A 51-kilometre waymarked route through Cheshire from Frodsham (SJ 519781) to Grindley Brook (SJ 522433), Shropshire.
Footpath guide: The Sandstone Trail, compiled and

published by Cheshire County Council, Countryside and Recreation Department, Goldsmith House, Hamilton Place, Chester CH1 1SE, 1986.

Saxon Shore Way
A 225-kilometre waymarked route along the Kent coast from Gravesend (TQ 647744) to Rye (TQ 918205) in East Sussex.
Footpath guides: The Saxon Shore Way compiled by the Kent Area of the Ramblers' Association, 11 Thirlmere Drive, Barnehurst, Kent DA7 6PL.

Severn to Solent Walk
193 kilometres from Burnham-on-Sea (ST 302480), Somerset to the Hampshire coast near Lymington (SZ 364953).
Footpath guide: **Proctor, Alan**, A Severn to Solent Walk, Thornhill Press, 1981.

Sheffield Country Walk
An 85-kilometre waymarked circular route around Sheffield starting at Eckington (SK 434798), Derbyshire.
Footpath guide: The Sheffield Country Walk, compiled and published by the South Yorkshire County Council, Recreation Culture and Health Department, 70 Vernon Road, Worsborough Bridge, Barnsley S70 5LH.

Shepherd's Round
A 65-kilometre waymarked challenge walk across the North York Moors National Park commencing at Scarth Nick (SE 471994), near Osmotherley.
Footpath guide: Cowley, William, *The Lyke Wake Walk and the Lyke Wake Way; Forty Miles across the North York Moors in 24 hours or 50 Miles in a Day as Long as You Like!: with, in Addition, the Shepherd's Round, the Monk's Trod and the Rail Trail Thrown in for Good Measure,* Dalesman, 1988.

Sheriff's Way
44 kilometres through North Yorkshire from York ((SE 603522) to Malton (SE 786704).
Footpath guide: The Sheriff's Way, compiled and published by the Moor and Fell Club (Hon. Sec. Mrs B. Batty), Rowntree Mackintosh Ltd., The Cocoa Works, York YO1 1XY.

Shropshire Way
A 201-kilometre waymarked circular route from Wem (SJ 517289).
Footpath guide: Kirk, Robert, *The Shropshire Way; a Walker's Guide to the Route and Matters of Local Interest,* Thornhill Press, 1983.

Six Dales Hike
A 67-kilometre challenge walk through North Yorkshire from Settle (SD 820636) to Skipton (SD 990518).
Footpath guide: Burland, J. D., *The Six Dales Hike,* Dalesman, 1983.

Snowdonia Panoramic Walk
A 48-kilometre challenge walk through **Snowdonia National Park** from Aber (SH 662720), near Llanfairfechan, Gwynedd to Pant-glas (SH 473483), north of Criccieth, Gwynedd.
Leaflet available from E. Dalton, 'Mountain View', Fachell, Hermon, Bodorgan, Gwynedd LL62 5LL.

Solent Way
A 97-kilometre waymarked route through Hampshire from Milford-on-Sea (SZ 292918) to Emsworth (SU 753055).
Footpath guide: Shurlock, Barry, *The Solent Way; a Guide to the Hampshire Coast,* Hampshire County Council, Recreation Department, North Hill Close, Andover Road, Winchester, Hants SO22 6AQ, 1984.

Somerset Way
174 kilometres from Minehead (SS 972467) to Bath (ST 751647).
Footpath guide: Main, Laurence, *A Somerset Way,* Thornhill Press 1980.

South Cheshire Way
A 50-kilometre waymarked route from Grindley Brook (SJ 522433) to Mow Cop (SJ 856573).
Footpath guide: The South Cheshire Way, compiled and published by the Mid-Cheshire Footpath Society, 72 Osborne Grove, Chavington, Crewe CW2 5BX.

South Coast Way
130 kilometres from Dover Castle (TR 324419), Kent to Eastbourne Pier (TV 618989), East Sussex.
Footpath guide: Main. Laurence, *A South Coast Way,* Thornhill Press, 1980.

South Wessex Way
188 kilometres from Petersfield (SU 746233), Hampshire to Sandbanks (SZ 037871), Poole Harbour, Dorset that links the South Downs Way with the South West Coast Path.
Footpath guide: Main, Laurence, *A South Wessex Way,* Thornhill Press, 1980.

Staffordshire Way
A 148-kilometre waymarked route from Mow Cop (SJ 856573) to Kinver Edge (SO 829822).
Footpath guide: The Staffordshire Way, compiled and published by Staffordshire County Council, Planning and Development Department, Martin Street, Stafford ST16 2LE.
    Section 1: *Mow Cop to Rocester*
    Section 2: *Rocester to Cannock Chase*
    Section 3: *Cannock Chase to Kinver Edge*

Stockport Circular Walk
A 43-kilometre circular walk around Stockport (SJ 893903), Greater Manchester.

Footpath guide: Brammal, Geoffrey, *The Stockport Circular Walk,* The Old Vicarage Publications, Reades Lane, Congleton, Cheshire CW12 3LL, 1986.

Suffolk Coast Path
An 80-kilometre waymarked route from Felixstowe (TM 324364) to Lowestoft (TM 548926).
Footpath guide: The Suffolk Coast Path, compiled and published by Suffolk County Council, Planning Department, St Peter's House, Cutler Street, Ipswich IPI 1UR.

Sussex Border Path
242 kilometres from Emsworth (SU 753055), Hampshire to Rye (TQ 918205), East Sussex.
Footpath guide: Perkins, Ben, and Mackintosh, Aeneas, *The Sussex Border Path,* published by the authors at 11 Old London Road, Brighton BN1 8XR.

Swan Way
A 105-kilometre waymarked route from Goring and Streatley railway station (SU 602806), Berkshire to Salcey Forest (SP 802513), Northamptonshire between Milton Keynes and Northampton.
Leaflet available from the County Engineer, County Hall, Aylesbury, Buckinghamshire HP20 1BR.

Ten Reservoirs Walk
A 35-kilometre circular challenge walk from Binn Green (SE 018044), Greater Manchester.
Footpath guide: Tait, Bob, *Walks around Saddleworth,* published by the author at 6 Leefields Close, Uppermill, Oldham OL3 6LA, 1979.

Test Way
A 71-kilometre waymarked route along the Test valley from Totton (SU 360140), near Southampton to SU 369621 near Walbury Hill (popularly known as Inkpen Beacon), 7 kilometres south-east of Hungerford, Berkshire.
Footpath guide: Shurlock, Barry, *The Test Way and the Clarendon Way,* Hampshire County Council, Recreation Department, North Hill Close, Andover Road, Winchester, Hants SO22 6AQ, 1986.

Thames Valley Heritage Walk
172 kilometres from Whitehall (TQ 300801), central London to Woodstock (SP 447166), Oxfordshire.
Footpath guide: **Jebb, Miles**, *The Thames Valley Heritage Way,* Constable, 1980.

Thetford Forest Walk
A 37-kilometre waymarked route from High Ash Forest (TL 813967), Norfolk to West Stow (TL815715), Suffolk.
Footpath guide: The Thetford Forest Guide Map, compiled and published by the Forestry Commission, District Office, Santon Downham,

Above: The open vista of the South Down Way (photo © Hugh Westacott).

Below: Bracken, loch and mountain—typical scenery on the West Highland Way (photo © Ramblers' Association).

Brandon, Suffolk IP27 0TJ.

Three Forests Way

A 97-kilometre waymarked circular route from Harlow (TL 445113), Essex.

Footpath guide: **Matthews, Fred**, and Bitten, Harry, *The Three Forests Way; a Long-distance Circular Walk Linking the Three Essex Forests of Epping, Hatfield and Hainault*, Matthews/Bitten Publications, 'Glen View', London Road, Abridge, Romford RM4 1UX, 1977.

Three Reservoirs Challenge

A 40-kilometre circular challenge walk in the Peak National Park commencing at the Ladybower Reservoir (SK 205865).

Footpath guide: Newton, Andrew, and Summers, Paul, *The Three Reservoirs Challenge*, published by the authors at Mountain Peaks Climbing Club, 17 Humberstone Road, Wollaton, Nottingham NG8 2SU.

Three Towers Circuit

A 56-kilometre challenge walk commencing at Tottington (SD 776129), Lancashire. Leaflet available from Lancashire 217 Booth Street, Tottington, Bury, Lancashire BL8 3JD.

Trans-Pennine Walk

87 kilometres from Adlington (SD 610130), near Bolton, Lancashire to Haworth (SE 030372), near Keighley, West Yorkshire.

Footpath guide: Mackrory, Richard, *The Trans-Pennine Walk*, Dalesman, 1983.

Two Crosses Circuit

A 40-kilometre challenge walk commencing at Tottington (SD 776129), Greater Manchester. Leaflet available from Derek Magnall, 217 Booth Street, Tottington, Bury, Lancashire BL8 3JD.

Two Moors Way

A 166-kilometre partly waymarked route from Ivybridge (SX 636563), near Plymouth, south Devon to Lynmouth (SS724494), north Devon linking the **Dartmoor National Park** with the **Exmoor National Park**.

Footpath guide: Rowett, Helen, *The Two Moors Way*, Devon Area of the Ramblers' Association and available from the Ramblers' Association, 1/5 Wandsworth Road, London SW8 2XX.

Two Seasons Way

48 kilometres from Watton at Stone (TL 297193), near Stevenage, Hertfordshire to Good Easter (TL 629121), northwest of Chelmsford, Essex.

Footpath guide: Matthews, Fred, and Bitten, Harry, *The Two Seasons Way*, Matthews/Bitten Publications, 'Glen View', London Road, Abridge, Romford RM4 1UX, 1990.

Upper Lea Valley Through Walk

A 46-kilometre waymarked route from Luton (TL 061249), Bedfordshire to Ware (TL 359142), Hertfordshire.

Footpath guide: The Upper Lea Valley Through Walk, compiled and published by the Community Council for Hertfordshire, 2 Townsend Avenue, St Albans AL1 3SG.

Upper Nidderdale Way

A 37-kilometre route in North Yorkshire from Pateley Bridge (SE 157658) to Kettlewell (SD 968723) in the Yorkshire Dales National Park.

Footpath guide: Belk, Leslie, and Hills, John, *The Upper Nidderdale Way*, published by the authors at 82 Northcote Crescent, Leeds LS11 6NN.

Usk Valley Walk

A 40-kilometre waymarked route through Gwent from Caerleon (ST 342902) to Abergavenny (SO 292139).

Footpath guide: The Usk Valley Walk, compiled and published by Gwent County Council, Planning Department, County Hall, Cwmbran, Gwent NP44 2XH, 1983.

Vanguard Way

101 kilometres from Croydon (TQ 328657) to Seaford (TV 482992), East Sussex.

Footpath guides: The Vanguard Way, compiled and published by the Vanguard Rambling Club, 10 Selsdon Park Road, London Croydon CR2 8JJ, 2nd Ed., 1986.

Reynolds, Kev, *The Wealdway and the Vanguard Way*, Cicerone Press, 1987.

Vermuyden Way

A 32-kilometre circular route around the Isle of Axholme in south Humberside commencing at Haxey (SE770000).

Footpath guide: Walks South of the Humber, compiled and published by the Humberside County Council, Technical Services Department, County Hall, Beverley, North Humberside HU17 9XA.

Viking Way

A 225-kilometre waymarked route from the Humber Bridge (TA 028234) to Oakham (SK 861088), Leicestershire.

Footpath guides: Stead, John, *The Viking Way*, Cicerone Press, 1990. *The Viking Way*, compiled and published by Lincolnshire County Council, Recreational Services Department, County Offices, Newlands, Lincoln LN1 1YL, 1984. A Viking Way accommodation leaflet is available from Major Brett Collier, Chloris House, 208 Nettleham Road, Lincoln LN2 4DH.

WALKWAYS; Birmingham to Aberystwyth

A 220-kilometre route from Birmingham (SP 064864) to Aberystwyth (SN 580813), Dyfed.

Footpath guides: Roberts, John S., *WALKWAYS Series 2; Birmingham to Ludlow.*

Roberts, John S., *WALKWAYS Series 2; Ludlow to Aberystwyth.*

(Both titles published by WALKWAYS, 15 Gilldown Road, Birmingham B15 6JR.)

WALKWAYS; Llangollen to Snowdon

A 98-kilometre route from Llangollen (SJ 215420), Clwyd to Snowdon (SH 607546) in the Snowdonia National Park.

Footpath guides: Roberts, John S., *WALKWAYS Series 1; Llangollen to Bala.*

Roberts, John S., *WALKWAYS Series 1; Bala to Snowdon.*

(Both titles published by WALKWAYS, 15 Gilldown Road, Birmingham B15 6JR.)

Wayfarer's Walk

A 113-kilometre waymarked route across Hampshire from Emsworth, Hampshire to SU 369621 near Walbury Hill (popularly known as Inkpen Beacon), 7 kilometres south-east of Hungerford, Berkshire.

Footpath guide: Herbst, Linda, *The Wayfarer's Walk*, Hampshire County Council, Recreation Department, North Hill Close, Andover Road, Winchester, Hants SO22 6AQ, 2nd Ed.,1989.

Wealdway

A 131-kilometre waymarked route across Kent and Sussex from Gravesend (TQ 647744) to Eastbourne (TV 588991).

Footpath guides: The Wealdway compiled and published by the Wealdway Steering Group, 11 Old London Road, Brighton, BN1 8XR, 1981.

The Wealdway Accommodation and Transport Guide available from the above address.

Mason, John H. N., *A Guide to the Wealdway*, Constable, 1984.

Reynolds, Kev, *The Wealdway and the Vanguard Way*, Cicerone Press, 1987.

Wear Valley Way

A 74-kilometre route across County Durham and Tyne & Wear from Waskerley Reservoir (NZ 027430), to Willington (NZ 218345) between Wallsend and Tynemouth.

Footpath guide: Earnshaw, Alan, *The Wear Valley Way*, Discovery Guides, 1 Market Place, Middleton-in-Teesdale, Co. Durham DL12 0QG, 1983.

Weardale Way

126 kilometres from Monkwearmouth (NZ 408587), Tyne & Wear to the source of the river Wear near Cowshill (NY 855405), Cumbria.

Footpath guide: Piggin, J. K. E., *The Weardale Way; a 78 Mile Walk Following the River Wear from Monkwearmouth to Cowshill*, Dalesman, 1984.

Weaver Valley Way

A 32-kilometre route through Cheshire from Bottom Flash (SD 657655), near Winsford to Weaver Lock (SD 508798), Runcorn.

Leaflet available from Cheshire County Council, Countryside and Recreation Department, Goldsmith House, Hamilton Place, Chester

CH1 1SE.
Weavers' Way
A 90-kilometre waymarked route through Norfolk from Cromer (TG 215420) to Great Yarmouth (TG 522081).
Footpath guides: Walking the Peddars Way / Norfolk Coast Path and the Weaver's Way compiled and published by the **Peddars Way Association**, 150 Armes Street, Norwich NR2 4EG, 1987. *The Weavers' Way*, compiled and published by Norfolk County Council, Planning Department, County Hall, Martineau Lane, Norwich NR1 2DH.

    Section 1: *Blickling to Cromer*, 1982.
    Section 2: *Blickling to Stalham*, 1980.
    Section 3: *Stalham to Great Yarmouth*, 1984.

Wessex Way
166 kilometres from Overton Hill (SU 118681), west of Marlborough, Wiltshire to Swanage (SZ 034804), Dorset.
Footpath guide: **Proctor, Alan**, *The Wessex Way*, Thornhill Press, 1980.
West Mendip Way
A 48-kilometre waymarked route through Somerset from Wells (ST 549461) to Weston-super-Mare (ST 315585).
Footpath guide: Eddy, Andrew, *The West Mendip Way*, published by the Rotary Club of Weston-super-Mare and available from the Weston-super-Mare Civic Society, 3-6 Wadham Street, Weston-super-Mare, Avon BS23 1JY.
West Midland Way
A 261-kilometre circular route around Birmingham from Meriden (SP 238823), near Coventry.
Footpath guide: Leek, Ronald, and Jones, Eric, *A Guide to the West Midland Way*, Constable, 1979.
Westmorland Boundary Way
A 274-kilometre circular route around the Lake District National Park commencing at Kendal (SD 520931), Cumbria.
Footpath guide: Emett, Charlie, *In Search of the Westmorland Way*, Cicerone Press, 1985.
Westmorland Heritage Walk
An anti-clockwise near-circular route from Arnside (SD 456788) roughly based on the boundaries of the old county of Westmorland but making diversions to include the best walking country. The high level route is 320 kilometres and the alternative low level route is 290 kilometres.
Footpath guide: **Richards, Mark** and **Wright, Christopher**, *The Westmorland Heritage Walk*, Cicerone Press, 1988.
Westmorland Way
158 kilometres through the Lake District National Park from Appleby-in-Westmorland

(NY 683204), Cumbria to Arnside (SD 456788), Cumbria.
Footpath guide: Hannon, Paul, *The Westmorland Way*, Hillside Publications, 1983.
Wey-South Path
58 kilometres from Guildford (SU 994493), Surrey to Amberley (TQ 026118), near Arundel, West Sussex.
Footpath guide: Mackintosh, Aeneas, *The Wey-South Path; from Guildford to the South Downs*, Wey and Arun Canal Trust, 24 Griffiths Avenue, Lancing West Sussex BN15 0HW, 1987.
White Peak Way
A 129-kilometre circular route through the Peak National Park commencing at Bakewell (SK 217685).
Footpath guide: Haslam, Robert, *The White Peak Way; an 80 Mile Circular Walk within the Peak National Park*, 2nd Ed., Cicerone Press, 1990.
White Rose Walk
A 174-kilometre challenge walk across the North York Moors National Park from Newton under Roseberry (NZ 571128), Cleveland to the Kilburn White Horse (SE 514813) North Yorkshire.
Footpath guide: White, Geoffrey, *The White Rose Walk*, 2nd Ed., Dalesman, 1976.
Wight Heritage Trail
A 121-kilometre circular waymarked route commencing at Ryde (SZ 596919), Isle of Wight.
Footpath guide: The Wight Heritage Trail compiled and published by the Isle of Wight County Council, County Surveyor, County Hall, Newport, Isle of Wight P030 1UD.
Wiltshire Way
A 261-kilometre circular route from Salisbury (SU 143297).
Footpath guide: Main, Laurence, *A Wiltshire Way; a Walker's Guide*, Thornhill Press, 1980.
Witches Way
48 kilometres through Lancashire from Rawtenstall (SD 812232) to Slaidburn (SD 712524).
Footpath guide: Johnson, David and Ashton, James, *The Witches' Way; a 30 Mile Walk through Upland Lancashire*, Dalesman, 1984.
Worcestershire Way
A 58-kilometre waymarked route through the county of Hereford and Worcester from Kingsford (SO 836821) to North Malvern (SO 766477). Leaflet available from Hereford and Worcester County Council, County Hall, Spetchley Road, Worcester WR5 2NP.
Wychavon Way
A 64-kilometre waymarked route from Winchcombe, Gloucestershire ((SP 025283), near Cheltenham to Holt Fleet (SO 824633), near Worcester.
Footpath guide: Richards, Mark, *The Wychavon Way*,

Wychavon District Council, 37 High Street, Pershore, Worcester WR 10 1AH, 1982.
Wye Valley Walk
A 132-kilometre waymarked route from Chepstow (ST 529924), Gwent to Hereford (SO 509395). Leaflet available from Wye Valley AONB Joint Advisory Committee, County Planning Department, Gwent County Council, Cwmbran, Gwent NP44 2XF.
Yoredale Way
161 kilometres from York (SE 603522) to Kirkby Stephen (NY 775087), Cumbria following the river Ure to its source.
Footpath guide: Piggin, J. K. E., *The Yoredale Way*, Dalesman, 1980.
Yorkshire Dales Centurion Walk
A 161-kilometre circular challenge walk through the Yorkshire Dales National Park from Horton-in-Ribblesdale (SD 809725).
Footpath guide: Ginesi, Jonathan, *The Official Guidebook to the Yorkshire Dales Centurion Walk*, John Siddall Ltd., Horncastle Street, Cleckheaton, West Yorkshire BD19 3HJ.
Yorkshire Dales Challenge Walk
A 40-kilometre circular challenge walk through the Yorkshire Dales National Park commencing at Kettlewell (SD 968723).
Footpath guide: Merrill, John, *John Merrill's Yorkshire Dales Challenge Walk*, JNM Publications, 1986.
Yorkshire Pioneer Walk
A 106-kilometre circular route through the Yorkshire Dales National Park commencing at the former Dacre Banks Youth Hostel (SE 198618), northwest of Harrogate.
Footpath guide: Scholes, Norman F. *The Yorkshire Pioneer Walk*, published by the author and available from the YHA, 96 Main Street, Bingley, West Yorkshire BD16 2JH.

Long Distance Paths Advisory Service
This organisation was established by the **Long Distance Walkers' Association**, the **Ramblers' Association**, the **Countryside Commission** and ***The Great Outdoors*** (which has since withdrawn from the project) in an attempt to record all **long-distance paths**, and to prevent the duplication of routes which can result in erosion and other environmental damage. The register of long-distance paths is kept on a computer database, and the routes are recorded on **Landranger** maps. Anybody contemplating devising a long-distance path may consult the register and will be advised of the proximity of any other routes, and whether the area is subjected to heavy use. Note that the register acts primarily as an advisory service for authors, publishers, local authorities etc, but does provide details of routes and **footpath guides**,

to the general public. Since March 1990, the LDPAS has been funded on a contractual basis by the Countryside Commission. *(For address see Appendix.)*

Long Distance Walkers' Association This organisation exists to further the interests of those who enjoy long-distance walking. It is an association of people with the common interest of walking long and ultra long distances especially in rural, mountainous and **moorland** areas. It promotes organised **challenge walks**, pioneers new walking routes and receives and publishes information on all aspects of non-competitive walking. It is now recognised as the governing body for the activity of long-distance walking, and can arrange insurance. The LDWA caters for many kinds of walking including challenge walks; walks organised by local groups; walks along **long-distance paths** and routes designed by the Association; and **kanters** organised by local groups. It publishes a journal, *Strider*. *(For address see Appendix.)*

Loopstitch A method of knitting, widely used in walking **socks** and **stockings**. The inside of the garment has the appearance of terry-towelling that gives a pleasant cushioned feeling, and completely covers all seams which helps to obviate **blisters** and chafing.

Lotus A synthetic fabric with irregularly shaped microfibres that feels like **cotton** and is inherently water-repellent. It is used for jackets.

Luxembourg The Grand Duchy of Luxembourg is a tiny country of 2587 square kilometres lying at the southern tip of **Belgium**. Geographically it is divided into two; in the north lies the upland area of the Ardennes while in the south there is rolling farmland and woods bordered on the east by the beautiful Moselle valley. Luxembourg has a splendid network of well-maintained waymarked public **paths**. There are a number of **long-distance paths** based on the network of **youth hostels**, as well as more than 140 circular one-day walks from village centres. **Footpath guides** and **maps** are available from local bookshops.

Useful Addresses
Luxembourg National Tourist and Trade Office, 36/37 Piccadilly, London W1V 9PA. Tel. 071-434-2800.
Ramblers' Organisation: Luxembourg Youth Hostel Association, 18 Place d'Armes, L-2013, Luxembourg. (This organisation looks after the interests of walkers and can provide information about routes).
National Map Survey: Administration du Cadastre et Topographie, Service de la Topographie,

Cartographie, 54 Ave Gaston Diderich, L-1420, Luxembourg.
Official Survey Maps: 1:20000, 1:25000 and 1:30000 all show **footpaths**.

Lyke Wake Club The Club was formed to cater for those who have completed the Lyke Wake Walk, an unofficial **long-distance path** through the **North York Moors National Park** within twenty-four hours. It publishes a newssheet and *Lyke Wake Lamentations; the Lyke Wake Walkers' Bogside Book.* *(For address see Appendix.)*

Lynam, Joss (1929-) Irish **mountaineer** who has written numerous books and articles about walking and climbing and who plays a leading role in developing mountaineering activities in Ireland. He has been successively secretary, chairman and president of the Association for Adventure Sports, both the secretary and chairman of the Irish Mountain Training Board, the secretary of the Federation of Mountaineering Clubs of Ireland 1973-9, and since 1978 has been chairman of the Long Distance Walking Routes Committee of the Irish National Sports Council. He was editor of **Mountain** *Log* 1977-86, *Irish Mountain Log* from 1986 to date, and was general editor of *The Irish Walks Guides*, Gill & Macmillan, 6 vols, 1978-80.
Publications about Walking
The Twelve Bens, Federation of Mountaineering Clubs of Ireland, 1971.
Irish Walks Guides South West; Kerry and West Cork (with Sean O'Suilleabhain), Gill & Macmillan, 1979.
The Mountains of Connemara (with Tim Robinson and Justin May), Folding Landscapes, 1988.
Also contributed to
Wilson, Ken, and **Gilbert, Richard**, *The Big Walks; Challenging Mountain Walks and Scrambles in the British Isles*, Diadem, 1980.
Wilson, Ken, and Gilbert, Richard, *Classic Walks*, Diadem, 1981.
Lynam, Joss, Editor, *The Irish Peaks*, Constable, 1982.
Wilson, Ken, and Gilbert, Richard, *Wild Walks*, Diadem, 1989.
Reynolds, Kev, Editor, *The Mountains of Europe*, Oxford Illustrated Press, 1990.

M

MacCulloch, John (1773-1835) A doctor of medicine and Fellow of the Royal Society who has achieved lasting fame as one of the pioneers of geology. He was appointed mineralogical and geological surveyor to the trigonometrical survey

of 1814, and during the years 1811-21 visited the Highlands and islands north of the Clyde. Many of his travels were accomplished on foot, and in his delightful book *The Highlands and Western Isles of Scotland*, published in 4 volumes in 1824, in the form of letters to Sir **Walter Scott**, claimed to *'have ascended almost every principal mountain in Scotland.'* He described Rannoch Moor as *'an inconceivable solitude, a dreary and joyless land of bogs.'*

Macdonald, Hugh (1885-1958) A solicitor and publisher who wrote *On Foot; an Anthology*, Oxford University Press, 1942. The book is a collection of short extracts from fiction, poetry and accounts of walks. The link between walking and some of the material is often tenuous.

Mackintosh The name given to a waterproof material, originally invented and patented by Charles Mackintosh (1766-1843), consisting of layers of cloth cemented with india-rubber. Subsequently, the name was applied to all waterproof coats made from such materials. Before the invention of mackintosh, the only way that pedestrians could keep dry in inclement weather was by using an umbrella, or by wearing clothes made from oiled silk or thick, tightly woven materials. Mackintosh, like all impermeable fabrics, is subject to **condensation**, and some medical authorities regarded the dampness induced from this source as more injurious to health than a thorough wetting from rain! It is clear from numerous accounts of early walking tours that pedestrians expected to get wet.

McNeish, Cameron (1950-) Prolific author, journalist and broadcaster on walking, climbing, Nordic ski-touring and environmental matters. He was the first editor of **Footloose**, and since 1986 has edited **Climber and Hill Walker**. His most important book is The **Backpacker's** *Manual* which is the best book on **backpacking** yet published in Britain.
Publications about Walking:
The Spur Master Guide to **Snow** *Camping*, Spurbooks 1980.
Backpacker's **Scotland**, Hale, 1982.
The Backpacker's Manual, Oxford Illustrated Press, 1984.
Let's Walk There!: Northern Scotland, Javelin, 1987.
Classic Walks in Scotland (with **Roger Smith**), Oxford Illustrated Press, 1988.
Also contributed to
Smith, Roger, Editor, *The Winding Trail, a Selection of Articles and Essays for Walkers and Backpackers*, Paladin, 1986.
Smith, Roger, Editor, *Book of the Walking Year*,

Patrick Stephen, 1988.

Hillaby, John, Editor, *Walking in Britain*, Collins, 1988.

Macrow, Brenda [Grace] The author of *The Torridon Highlands* which first appeared in 1953 with a fourth edition published by Hale in 1983. It contains a detailed description of this region of **Scotland** as it was just after the war, as well as excellent descriptions of the scenery and the camping and walking opportunities.

Magnetic north True north (also known as **grid north**) lies at the north pole and is a fixed position. Magnetic north, created by the earth's magnetic field and to which the **compass** needle always points, is currently located in Canada to the north of Hudson Bay, and a considerable distance from the north pole. The position of magnetic north is constantly changing, but its movements can be predicted accurately by scientists. The difference between true north and magnetic north is known as **magnetic variation** and a proper understanding of it is vital for accurate **navigation**.

Magnetic variation The difference between magnetic north and true or **grid north** (see figure 17) which varies widely in different parts of the world, and is constantly changing. In Britain, magnetic north was about 5° west of grid north in 1990 (see figure 18). This means that 5° has to be *added* to the **bearing** when plotting routes from the **map** ('grid to mag—add' is the popular mnemonic), and *subtracted* when making a fix or **resection** ('mag to grid—get rid'). The difference between magnetic north and true north is given in the key on maps published by the **Ordnance Survey**. Magnetic variation is also known as declination, and the adjustable setting found on some of the more sophisticated compasses to compensate for magnetic variation is known as a declinometer (a strip of paper pasted underneath the base plate of the compass will serve just as well). Magnetic variation should not be confused with magnetic deviation which refers to needle-distortion of the **compass** caused by the attraction of ferrous objects.

Main, Laurence [Cyril] (1950-) Prolific author of articles, reviews, idiosyncratic **footpath guides**, including several long-distance routes he has devised himself, and from 1979-85 a full-time official of the Vegan Society.

Publications

The Thamesdown **Trail**, Thornhill Press, 1978.

A Wiltshire Way, Thornhill Press, 1979, 2nd Ed., 1980.

An Oxon **Trek**, Thornhill Press, 1979.

A Somerset Way, Thornhill Press, 1980.

A Bristol Countryway, Thornhill Press, 1980.

A South Wessex Way, Thornhill Press, 1980.

King Alfred's Way, Thornhill Press, 1980.

A South Coast Way, Thornhill Press, 1980.

Guide to the Dyfi Valley Way, Kittiwake Press in association with Bartholomew, 1988.

Walk Snowdonia and North **Wales**, Kittiwake Press in association with Bartholomew, 1988.

Family Walks in Mid Wales, Scarthin Books, 1989.

Walk South Wales and the **Wye Valley**, Kittiwake Press in association with Bartholomew, 1989.

Walk **Dorset** *and* **Hardy's** *Wessex*, Kittiwake Press in association with Bartholomew, 1989.

Arthur's Camlan, R. Street, Meirion Mill, Dinas Mawddwy, Machynlleth, Powys SY20 9LS, 1989.

Laurence Main, prolific author of idiosyncratic footpath guides (photo © Chantal Main).

Figure 17: Magnetic variation.

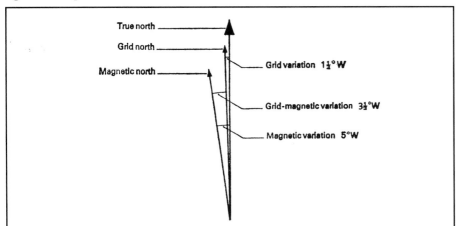

Figure 18: Correcting for magnetic variation.

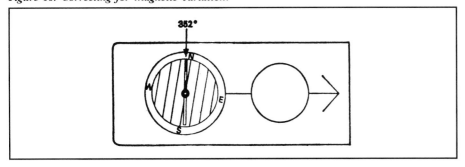

Elan Valley Day Walks, WALKWAYS, 15 Gilldown Road, Birmingham B15 6JR, 1989.

Rambles in Mid Wales, Thornhill Press, 1989.
Guide to the Oxfordshire Trek, Kittiwake Press in association with Bartholomew, 1989 (NB this is the 2nd Ed. of *An Oxon Trek).*
Walk Hertfordshire and Buckinghamshire, Kittiwake Press in association with Bartholomew, 1990.
Walk the South **Pennines**, Kittiwake Press in association with Bartholomew, 1990.
A Cambrian Coast Walk; Aberdyfi-Pwllheli, Kittiwake Press in association with Bartholomew, 1990.
A Guide to Walks along the **Ley-lines** *in Wales,* Kittiwake Press in association with Bartholomew, 1990.
Family Walks in Snowdonia, Scarthin Books, 1990.
The Mary Jones Trek; Tywyn-Bala, Gwasg Carreg Gwalch, 1990.
Daywalks; Tywyn & Aberdyfi, WALKWAYS, 15 Gilldown Road, Birmingham B15 6JR, 1990.
Daywalks; Tywyn & Fairbourne, WALKWAYS, 15 Gilldown Road, Birmingham B15 6JR, 1990.
Daywalks; Barmouth, WALKWAYS, 15 Gilldown Road, Birmingham B15 6JR, 1990.
Daywalks; Rhayader, WALKWAYS, 15 Gilldown Road, Birmingham B15 6JR, 1990.

Malvern Hills An **area of outstanding natural beauty**, designated in 1959, lying between Great Malvern and Ledbury, and covering 104 square kilometres in the counties of Gloucestershire, and Hereford and Worcester. There are a number of summits over 300 metres with magnificent views over the surrounding countryside. The many excellent **footpaths** make this fine walking country. (See figure 36 for a **map** showing the location of all AONBs in the United Kingdom.)
Maps
1:50000 **Landranger** sheet 150.
1:25000 **Pathfinder** sheets P995 (S065/75), P1018 (S064/74), P1041 (S063/73).
Footpath guides
Country Walks: East Malvern, compiled and published by Malvern Hills District **Footpath** Society, 8 Kingshill Close, Malvern, Worcs WR14 2BP, 1985.
Country Walks: West Malvern, compiled and published by Malvern Hills District Footpath Society, 8 Kingshill Close, Malvern, Worcs WR14 2BP, 1987.

Manchester Association for the Preservation of Ancient Footpaths This Association was founded in 1826 to prevent Ralph Wright, a Flixton landowner and magistrate, removing **paths** from his estate. A legal battle ensued and the case went to the King's Bench Division where Wright lost his case. In the following years the Association frequently took action to protect **rights of way** in the Manchester area, and gave advice to those with grievances in other parts of the country which often resulted in the establishment of other **footpath** protection societies. It seems that membership declined in the eighties, and after the establishment of the **Peak & Northern Footpath Society** in 1894, the Manchester Association wound itself up and transferred its funds to the new organisation.

Manchester Pedestrian Association A walking club, founded in 1903, whose *'object is the union of gentlemen in Manchester and district interested in the encouragement of healthy walking exercise by the organisation of periodical Country Walks and tours for the Club members'.* It is one of the few remaining walking clubs that only admit men to its membership, and is also unusual in that it awards a silver cup to the member who has covered the greatest distance on club outings during the year. In 1904 the Club made headline news throughout the country by organising a walk from Manchester to London, a distance of 303 kilometres which had to be completed in five days. Only six members finished the journey. In subsequent years, the Association organised several similar events both at home and abroad. The Association's archives are housed in the Manchester Central Reference Library, and there is a chapter about the Association in *The Gentle Art of Walking* by Geoffrey Murray, 1939. *(For address see Appendix.)*

Manks, Richard (1818-?) One of the leading exponents of **pedestrianism** who was known as the 'Warwickshire Antelope' and the 'Eastern Warwickshire Star'. Between 17th June and 29th July 1850 he walked 1000 miles in 1000 consecutive hours in Sheffield, and is said to have walked 1000 quarter miles in 1000 consecutive quarter hours finishing on 4 July 1851. It is known that he walked 1000 miles in 1000 consecutive half hours at the Kensington Oval from 10 October to 31 October 1851.

Map-reading The art of route-finding by the use of **maps**. It is an essential part of the wider skill of **navigation** that involves the use of a **compass** and specialised techniques. Those who confine their walking to lowland

A young map reader (photo © Hugh Westacott).

country have no need to progress beyond map-reading. The best books on general map-reading are: *Manual of Map Reading* compiled by the Ministry of Defence, HMSO, 1973, *Follow the Map; the* **Ordnance Survey** *Guide* by John G. Wilson published jointly by A. and C. Black and the Ordnance Survey, 1985, and *Land Navigation; Routefinding with Map and Compass,* by Wally Keay, Duke of Edinburgh Award, 1989. Also useful is *Plan Your Route; the New Approach to Map Reading* by Victor Selwyn, David & Charles, 1987.

Maps Cartographers have designed maps for many purposes, but the majority of walkers are only interested in topographical maps. A topographical map is a two-dimensional (length and width) depiction of an area of three-dimensional (length, width and height) countryside, and shows relief (ie heights) by means of **contours** or **hachures**, or a combination of both. The **scale** of the map determines the amount of detail that can be shown. The best maps for walkers are published by the **Ordnance Survey**.

Marriott, Mike (ie Michael Marriott 1928-) Prolific author and journalist contributing numerous articles to the outdoor press. He has walked in many parts of the world including the Sahara, Afghanistan and the outback of **Australia**. He was the originator and co-founder of the **Backpacker's Club** and

designed one of the first British ultra-lightweight backpacking **tents** for Black & Edgington.
Publications about Walking
*The Shell Book of the **Pennine Way**,* Queen Anne Press, 1968.
The Shell Book of the South West Peninsula Path, Queen Anne Press, 1970.
*Start **Backpacking**,* Stanley Paul, 1981.
*The **Footpaths** of Britain,* Queen Anne Press, 1981.
*The **Mountains** and **Hills** of Britain,* Willow Press in association with Collins, 1982.
Collins Concise Guide to the Uplands of Britain, Collins, 1983.
Collins Concise Guide to the Footpaths of Britain, Collins, 1983.
*Footpaths of **France**,* Crowood Press, 1990.

Matthews, [Harold] **Fred**[erick] (1923-) A retired civil servant who is the author of numerous **footpath guides**, many of which are published under his own imprint, Matthews/Bitten Publications *(for address see Appendix)*. He has contributed articles about walks for several Essex newspapers, has devised a number of **long-distance paths**, and is a tireless worker for the improvement of **footpaths** in Essex.
Publications about Walking
Walking with the West Essex, published by the author, 1972.
More Walks with the West Essex, published by the author, 1972.
The Three Forests Way, Matthews/Bitten Publications, 1972.
St Peter's Way, Matthews/Bitten Publications, 1978.
Epping Forest Centenary Walk, Conservators of Epping Forest, 1978.
Short Walks in London's Epping Forest, Matthews/Bitten Publications, 1979.
The Harcamlow Way, Matthews/Bitten Publications, 1980.
The Two Seasons Way, Matthews/Bitten Publications, 1990.
The Essex Clayway, Matthews/Bitten Publications, 1990.
Also contributed to
Campbell, Ian, Editor, *South East **England**; a Guide to Family Walks,* Croom Helm, 1975.
Sharp, David, Editor, *Ramblers' Ways,* David & Charles, 1980.
Bagley, William A., *Walks for Motorists in Essex,* Warne Gerrard, 1982.
Ramblers' Association, *Walks in the Countryside around London,* Foulsham, 1985.

Duncan, Andrew, Editor, *Walkers' Britain 2 ; the Complete Pocket Guide to over 160 more Walks and **Rambles**,* Pan Books in association with the **Ordnance Survey**, 1986.

Mattingly, Alan (1949-) A member of the National Executive Committee of the **Ramblers' Association** 1972-4, and director since 1974. He was also chairman of the **Council for National Parks** 1979-83.
Publications about Walking
Tackle Rambling, Stanley Paul, 1981.
*Walking in the **National Parks**,* David & Charles, 1982.

Alan Mattingly, director of the Ramblers' Association (photo © Ramblers' Association).

Maverick, Albert (1854-1947) A banker and realtor from a prominent family in San Antonio, Texas who, as a young man of twenty-two, came to **England** in 1876 and walked from London to Dover, and then explored parts of **France**. He kept an interesting diary of his adventures which was published as *A Maverick Abroad; Foot **Trails** in England and France* by the Principia Press of Trinity University, San Antonio in 1965.

Mavor, William Fordyce (1758-1837) The author and compilor of numerous educational and travel works including *British Tourists,* 6 Volumes, 1798 which is a collection of travels made in Britain, chiefly in **Wales**, **Scotland** and Derbyshire. Most of the individual works had already been published separately, and appear in abbreviated form (what the Reader's Digest would call a 'condensed book'), but

some of the accounts were commissioned and are found only in *British Tourists*. The compilation contains accounts of pedestrian tours by **Grant Johnson** and **Henry Kett**. The popularity of this work, which ran to three editions by 1809, is an indication of the interest in domestic travel at the beginning of the nineteenth century.

Mendip Hills An **area of outstanding natural beauty** stretching for 202 square kilometres from Weston-super-Mare to the cathedral city of Wells in the counties of Avon and Somerset. The Mendip has short turf, limestone walls and typical **mountain** limestone scenery. There are several **hills** over 300 metres high which give views over the Bristol Channel. Wookey Hole and Cheddar **Gorge** form part of a large cave system for which the area is famous. There are a number of **drove roads** suitable for walking. (See figure 36 for a **map** showing the location of all AONBs in the United Kingdom.)
Maps
1:50000 **Landranger** sheet 183.
1:25000 **Pathfinder** sheets P1182 (ST46/56), P1197 (ST25/35), P1198 (ST45/55), P1199 (ST65/75), P1218 (ST44/54).
Footpath guide
Wright, Peter, *Mendip Rambles,* Ex Libris, 1985.

Menmuir, W[illiam] **Henry** The author of a naive account of a walking tour on roads, undertaken with his wife, entitled *A Walking Tour of the Scottish Highlands* which was published in 1912. He laments the increase in motor traffic and the improvements being made to the major roads to accommodate it, and comments that walkers were not welcomed in the better hotels. *'Our walk has now come to an end. It has been very enjoyable in some respects, but the sparseness of the population, the few shops, the want of social feeling in some of the hotel people, and the uncertainty of lodgings after a very long walk, took away a great deal from the charm of our tramping. Yet, with hearty accommodation at convenient distances, and genial weather, a walking tour in the Highlands makes a glorious holiday.'*

Meredith, **George** (1828-1909) Poet and author of a series of outstanding novels, now, alas, rarely read, that contain penetrating analyses of human character as well as a richly comic vein. In his youth he was desperately poor and walked as much as possible in order to save money. Once he was established, he bought Flint Cottage on Box Hill near Dorking, Surrey and he explored much of the county on foot. He was a friend of Sir **Leslie Stephen**, and occasionally walked with the **Sunday Tramps**, although he was never a member, and entertained the club on several occasions at his home at the conclusion of some of their outings. Meredith was a strong walker with the gift of acute observation and love of nature that has been compared to that of **William Wordsworth** and **Percy Bysshe Shelley**. Shortly before his death he wrote '*when I ceased to walk briskly part of my life was ended.*'

Meriwether, Lee (1862-1966) A lawyer and **United States** special agent in Europe during the First World War. As a naive young man he travelled on foot through **Italy**, **France**, and much of eastern Europe and described his adventures in *A Tramp Trip*, 1887 which includes a chapter on *Hints for Pedestrians*. He also published *Yesteryears; an Autobiography* in 1942.

Merrill, John [N] (1948-) Long-distance walker, lecturer, publisher and prolific author of **footpath guides**. He is best known for his extraordinary walking achievements, and claims to have covered more than 160,000 kilometres on foot in the past fifteen years. His major walks include:
Land's End to John O'Groats (2589 kilometres); Hebridean journey (1515 kilometres); Northern Isles journey (1469 kilometres); Irish island journey (2541 kilometres); Parkland journey (3289 kilometres); the entire coastline of Britain (10987 kilometres); across Europe (3358 kilometres and more than 183,000 metres of ascent) in 107 days in 1982; Appalachian **Trail** (3542 kilometres); Mexico to **Canada** via the Pacific Crest Trail (4347 kilometres) in 118 days; and across America from Virginia Beach, Virginia to San Francisco, California (6804 kilometres) in 178 days.

Some of his books were originally published by Dalesman and Oxford Illustrated Press, but he has now issued them under his own imprint JNM Publications. *(For address see Appendix.)*
Publications about Walking
Walking in Derbyshire, Dalesman, 1969.
Peak District Walks No. 1; Short Walks for the Motorist, Dalesman, 1972.
Peak District Walks No. 2; Long Walks for the Rambler, Dalesman, 1974.
Walking in South Derbyshire, Dalesman, 1975.
Derbyshire Trails, Dalesman, 1976.
Emerald Coast Walk, JNM Publications, 1981.

John Merrill, long-distance walker, author and publisher (photo © Ron Duggins).

From Arran to Orkney, Spurbooks, 1981.
Striding with Merrill, JNM Publications, 1981.
Walks in the White Peak, Dalesman, 1981.
John Merrill's Favourite Walks, Dalesman, 1982.
Walks in the Dark Peak, Dalesman, 1982.
Circular Walks in Western Peakland, JNM Publications, 1983.
Hike to be Fit, JNM Publications, 1983.
Short Circular Walks in the Peak District, JNM Publications, 1983.
Short Circular Walks in the Dukeries, JNM Publications, 1984.
Walking my Way, Chatto & Windus, 1984.
John Merrill's Peak District **Challenge Walk**, JNM Publications, 1985.
John Merrill's Yorkshire Dales Challenge Walk, JNM Publications, 1985.
With Mustard on my Back, JNM Publications, 1985.
Canal Walks Vol. 1; Derbyshire and Nottinghamshire, JNM Publications, 1986.
Canal Walks Vol. 2; Cheshire and Staffordshire, JNM Publications, 1986.
Circular Walks in the Staffordshire **Moorlands**, JNM Publications, 1986.
John Merrill's North Yorkshire Moors Challenge Walk, JNM Publications, 1986.
John Merrill's Walks Record Book, JNM Publications, 1986.
Turn Right at Death Valley, JNM Publications, 1986.
Peak District End to End Walks, JNM Publications, 1987.
Peak District Marathons, JNM Publications, 1987.

Peak District; High Level Route, JNM Publications, 1987.
Short Circular Walks around Buxton, JNM Publications, 1987.
Short Circular Walks around Derby, JNM Publications, 1987.
Short Circular Walks around Matlock, JNM Publications, 1987.
Short Circular Walks in South Yorkshire, JNM Publications, 1987.
The Little John Challenge Walk, JNM Publications, 1987.
The Rivers Way, JNM Publications, 1987.
Canal Walks Vol. 3; Staffordshire, JNM Publications, 1988.
Isle of Wight Coast Path, JNM Publications, 1988.
John Merrill's Dark Peak Challenge Walk, JNM Publications, 1988.
John Merrill's Lakeland Challenge Walk, JNM Publications, 1988.
John Merrill's Staffordshire Moorlands Challenge Walk, JNM Publications, 1988.
John Merrill's White Peak Challenge Walk, JNM Publications, 1988.
Short Circular Walks around the Towns and Villages of the Peak District, JNM Publications, 1988.
Aosta Valley High Route, JNM Publications, 1989.
Canal Walks Vol 4; the Cheshire Ring, JNM Publications, 1989.
Canal Walks Vol. 7; the Trent & Mersey Canal, JNM Publications, 1989.
Long Circular Walks in the Peak District, JNM Publications, 1989.
Short Circular Walks in South Nottinghamshire, JNM Publications, 1989.
Short Circular Walks in Cheshire, JNM Publications, 1989.
Short Circular Walks in the Hope Valley, JNM Publications, 1989.
Short Circular Walks on the Northern Moors, JNM Publications, 1989.
The Limey Way, JNM Publications, 1989.
The Peakland Way, JNM Publications, 1989.
Turn Right at Land's End, JNM Publications, 1989.
The **Cleveland Way**, JNM Publications, 1990.
40 Short Circular Walks in the Peak District, JNM Publications, 1990.
Pembrokeshire Coast Path, JNM Publications, 1990.
The Rutland Challenge Walk, JNM Publications, 1990.

Metamorphosis The term used to describe the alterations in the structure and characteristics of snowflakes that are caused by changes in atmospheric condition. It is one of the main causes of **avalanches**, and all who walk in winter in upland areas should have some understanding of **snow** conditions.

Miles, Walker (1854-1908) The punning pseudonym of Edmund Seyfang Taylor known as the 'Chief Pathfinder' or 'Great Pathfinder' and sometimes even the 'Prince of Pathfinders, who wrote a series of very popular **footpath guides**, and was celebrated in a famous eponymous essay written by **A. H. Sidgwick**. He was a member of the **Forest Ramblers' Club** and the author of numerous articles about walking, and his pocket-sized footpath guides were deservedly popular for their carefully written and accurate descriptions of walks in Kent, Sussex and Surrey. He was the proprietor of the family printing business of Robert Edmund Taylor & Son which issued his footpath guides and also *The Rambler's Library* and *The Gipsy Journal and British Tourist* which Miles edited. In his book *The Complete Rambler*, published under the pseudonym 'Pathfinder', A. J. Simpson states that Miles used the Six Inch series of **maps** published by the **Ordnance Survey** as a basis for his guides (although when published they were scaled down to about 3/4 of an inch to the mile with no acknowledgement of their source), and goes on to write *'In consequence his forty or so footpath guides were marvels of exact description'*. So particular was he about accuracy that whenever a new title was published, or an old one reprinted, there would be included a list of corrections to all guides in the series, that could be cut out and pasted in the appropriate page. Miles was clearly a delightful character, beloved by all who met him, and he exuded a child-like innocence that manifested itself in the verses he wrote, and also in his love of puns. The photographs printed in the guides were supposedly taken by persons with such unlikely names as Phil Minerol (film in a roll), Plato Glass (plate of glass) and Kaye Merabois (camera boys). His obituary was published in the *Croydon Advertiser* on 25th April, 1908, and assessments in the *Rambler's Handbook*, the journal of the **Federation of Rambling Clubs**, in 1925 and 1928. In 1928, a viewpoint indicator was placed on top of the tower on Leith Hill, near Dorking, Surrey to commemorate Miles' contribution to walking. After her husband's death, Mrs Miles opened their home as the Walker Miles Tea-House and served light refreshments to rambling parties. She emigrated to California and was still

Walker Miles, the punning pseudonym of Edmund Seyfang Taylor, author of guides to Kent, Surrey and Sussex in the 19th century (photo courtesy Ramblers' Association).

alive in the late thirties.

Walker Miles is a bibliographer's nightmare. The guides appear to have been reprinted many times, sometimes with minor changes, but still bearing the original date of publication, and without any indication that they are reprints, although very occasionally the number of the edition is stated. To add to the confusion, although all the guides were printed by Miles' company Robert Edmund Taylor & Son, whose name appears prominently on the title-page, some editions have 'Now published by Cassell & Co' printed on a sticker gummed to the title-page, and others have the name E. J. Larby (who was a vice-president of the Federation of Rambling Clubs and whose company published a number of footpath guides and printed the *Rambler's Handbook*) printed on the cover. Some were also issued by the Homeland Association in the *Homeland Pocket Books* series. (The British Library catalogue and the *English Catalogue of Books* list only two works by Miles, *Field **Path** Rambles*, 1893, and *Off Your Bikes!* issued as Number 2 in the *Rambler's Library* in 1898). There is a fairly complete collection in the library of the **Ramblers' Association**, and the following list of Miles' books has been compiled from that source, supplemented by information

gleaned from advertisements in the books. It should be noted that the guides appeared in a number of series, classified by location, all with the same format. They were issued in parts, with continuous pagination, and when the last part was published, the separate parts were bound together and offered as an omnibus edition. The route maps for the series were sold separately, although they were included in the omnibus editions. Not all the walks were circular, as in those days practically all walkers travelled by train, so it was just as convenient to make a linear walk from station to station.

Field-Path Rambles—West Kent Series
1 *Round Bromley*, 2nd Ed., 1893.
2 *From Bromley to Gravesend*, 1893. (Cassell).
3 *From Bromley to Maidstone*, 1893.
4 *From Bromley to Tunbridge Wells*, 1893. (Cassell).
Collected as *Field-Path Rambles in West Kent; a Practical Handbook for Pedestrians Containing Minute and Carefully-Prepared Directions for Out-of-the-Way Walks through Parts of the Garden of **England***, 1893.
Field-Path Rambles—**Surrey Hills** Series
5 *Round Dorking, Box Hill, Leatherhead etc.*, 1894.
6 *Round Dorking, Leith Hill, Holmwood, Walton etc.*, 1894.
7 *Round Reigate & Redhill, Dorking, Headley, etc.*, 1894.
8 *Round Guildford, Clandon, Shere, Godalming etc.*, 1894.
Collected as *Field-Path Rambles Amongst the Surrey Hills; a Practical Handbook for Pedestrians*, 1895.
Field-Path Rambles—East Surrey Series
9 *Round Croydon, Whyteleafe, Coulsdon, Warlingham, Chipstead, Caterham, Chaldon etc* [no date].
10 *Round Epsom, Sutton, Leatherhead etc.*, 1896.
11 *Round Oxted, Caterham, Godstone etc.*, [no date].
12 (1st Division) *Round Lingfield, Horley, Cranleigh* etc
12 (2nd Division) *Across Surrey from Edenbridge & Lingfield to Cranleigh & Back*, 1902.
Collected as *Field-Path Rambles in East Surrey*.
NB The 1st & 2nd Divisions of no. 12 were also available in one volume.
Field-Path Rambles–Garden of England Series
13 *Down by the Darent from Dartford to Westerham*, 1896.
14 *Along the Medway between Groombridge & Tonbridge also Routes round Tunbridge Wells, Cowden, Penshurst etc.*, 1897.
19 *Round Maidstone, Wateringbury etc.*, 1900.
20 *Through Kentish Hoplands*, 1901. (Cassell).
21 *Round West Malling and over the Kentish Hills*, [no date].
Collected as *Field-Path Rambles in West Kent*, 1893.

Field-Path Rambles—Canterbury & Kent Coast Series

22 *Routes between Ramsgate & Margate & to Canterbury, Minster, Sandwich, Grove Ferry, Sarre, Ash, Broadstairs etc.*, 1901.

23 *Routes between Margate & Herne Bay & to Birchington, Minster, Reculver, Broomfield, Hoath, Chislet, Sarre etc.*, 1902.

24 *Routes between Whitstable & Herne Bay & Canterbury*, 1903. (Cassell).

25 *Routes round Canterbury*, 1903.

Collected as *Field-Path Rambles (Canterbury & Kent Coast Series)*, 1904.

Field-Path Rambles—Mid Surrey Series

27 *Round Dorking, Box Hill, Gomshall, Horsley, Ranmore, Abinger, Leatherhead etc.*, 1903.

28 *Round Reigate, Kingswood, Horsley, Bookham, Cobham, Byfleet, Shere, Ripley etc.*, 1904.

29 *Over Leith Hill & between Dorking & Horsham*, 1907.

35 *Round Gomshall, Holmbury Hill, Leith Hill, Peaslake, Clandon, Weybridge, Byfleet, Woking etc,* completed by Walker Miles Jr., 1910. (NB Walker Miles Jr may have been **J. A. Southern**.)

Collected as *Field-Path Rambles—Mid Surrey Series*

Field-Path Rambles–Eastbourne Series

30 *Field-Path Rambles (Eastbourne Series); First Part*, 1904. [Includes Beachy Head, Pevensey, Willingdon and Hailsham].

31 *Field-Path Rambles (Eastbourne Series); Second Part*, 1904. [Includes Hurstmonceux, Alfriston, Wilmington and Hellingly.]

Collected as *Field-Path Rambles—Eastbourne Series*. [This title also contains two short and two longer 'Rambling Tours'].

Field-Path Rambles–Seaford, Lewes & Brighton Series

32 *Field-Path Rambles (Seaford Series)*, 1906. (Cassell). [Includes Seaford, Eastbourne, Glynde, Hailsham and Firle Beacon.]

33 *Field-Path Rambles (Brighton Series)*, completed by Walker Miles Jr., 1909. (NB Walker Miles Jr may have been J. A. Southern.)

The following titles, although numbered, do not appear to be part of any particular series:

34 *New Routes in Kent & Surrey*, 1906.

37 *New Routes through* **Picturesque** *Surrey*, 1907.

Other titles in the series were written by J. A. Southern who used Miles' methods.

Most of the titles in the *Field-Path Rambles series* remained in print until 1939 and were revised from time-to-time by J. A. Southern and A. T. O. Sorrell. Miles was also the author of several other books including *Off Your Bikes!*, 1898, which is a footpath guide aimed at per-suading cyclists to become pedestrians, in much the same way that some modern footpath guides are written for motorists, and *Hey, for the Holidays!*, a collection of rhymes that includes instructions for a ramble written in verse. His printing company also published the anonymous *A Pathfinder's Pocketful of Jog-Trot Rhymes* which seems likely to be the work of Walker Miles.

Mist A generic term used to describe poor visibility caused by low cloud or fog that can be a serious **hazard** in the upland areas of the British Isles. Mist encountered on high ground is actually low cloud caused by a depression which is often accompanied by strong winds; it may last for several hours, or even for days. Mist can be thousands of metres thick and the walker may be unable to ascend above it. Fog that collects in valleys, is caused by temperature inversion, and seldom lasts for more than a few hours because it will disperse when exposed to sunshine or wind. It rarely extends above the summits of **hills**, and it is often possible to climb above it. As mist consists of tiny droplets of water suspended in the atmosphere, **clothing** will become wet as the water vapour condenses on it, and **verglas** will form if the temperature drops below freezing point.

Poor visibility is dangerous because perspective becomes distorted and small objects can appear to be much larger than they actually are. Good **navigation** and **map-reading** becomes of critical importance to obviate the risk of falling, getting lost, and **benightment**.

Mist can form very quickly and walkers should ensure that they know their exact position before it descends.

Moisture vapour transmission (MVT) The passing of water vapour given off by the human body through a waterproof material. The body controls its temperature by the emission of water vapour. If water vapour cannot escape into the atmosphere, **condensation** will form on the inside of the **clothing** that traps it. Until a few years ago, most waterproof fabrics were non-porous and could not 'breathe' (ie they were unable to allow water vapour to escape) so that active outdoor people often got almost as wet from condensation as they did from the rain. In recent years, a number of materials have appeared that are both waterproof and 'breathable'. Some (eg **Ventile**) are porous fabrics that swell when wet, others are **poromeric** (eg **Aquatex, Cyclone, Entrant** and **Gore-Tex**), and a third group (eg 'breathable' **polyurethane** and **Sympatex**) are **hydrophyllic**. Fabrics that, to a greater or lesser extent, allow water vapour to escape are said to encourage moisture vapour transmission. Note that the term moisture vapour transmission is applied to waterproof clothing and **vapour transmission** to underwear.

Moleskin A thick, heavy **cotton** fabric that will absorb a lot of water. It can be made water-repellent by treating with silicones or applying one of the proprietary waterproofing agents such as Technix. Moleskin was once popular for use in **breeches** but it has now been almost entirely superseded by more modern materials.

Moloney, Patrick (1925-) A professional soldier who established a number of long-distance walking records. In 1959 he walked from John O'Groats to Land's End (see **Land's End to John O'Groats**) in 18 days and 7 hours. He has also crossed the widest part of mainland Great Britain from St David's Head to Lowestoft in 5 days and 12 hours, walked from Edinburgh to London in 6 days and 9 hours (easily beating Dr **Barbara Moore's** record), and from one end of Ireland to the other (Londonderry to Cork) in 4 days and 9 hours. His most notable feat was to walk the 4882 kilometres from San Francisco to New York in 66 days and 4 hours. These and other events are recorded in his autobiography *I Never Walked Alone*, Merlin Books, 1987.

Monkhouse, Patrick [James] (1904-81) Journalist, sometime deputy editor of the *Manchester Guardian* and author of three excellent and influential books about walking, *On Foot in the Peak*, 1932, *On Foot in North* **Wales**, 1934, and *Walking in the* **Pennines** (with **Donald Boyd**), 1937. The first two titles were reissued in one volume by Diadem in 1989 as *On Foot in Wales and the Peak; Two Classic Walking Guides of the Thirties*.

Monro, Harold [Edward] (1879-1932) Author, poet, editor, publisher, bookseller, proprietor of the famous Poetry Bookshop, and enthusiastic walker all his life. He wrote only one book about walking, *The Chronicle of a Pilgrimage; Paris to Milan on Foot*, 1909. On his journey, in which he followed the N7 to Dijon, crossed the Jura **Mountains**, followed the Rhône Valley and then went over the Simplon Pass, he carried with him '*Shakespeare, one volume of Emerson, and my diary.*'

Montague, C[harles] **E**[dward] (1867-1928) Author, journalist and sometime deputy editor of the *Manchester Guardian*. Montague was a keen walker and **mountaineer** and wrote *The Right Place; a Book of Pleasures*, 1924. This contains a collection of his writings about travel, many of them expanded versions of articles that had been published originally in the *Manchester Guardian*. They are polished essays that, alas, are unlikely to appeal to present-day readers.

Moore, A[dolphus] **W**[arburton] (1841-87) A senior civil servant, sometime secretary to Lord Randolph Churchill, and one of the greatest of the Victorian **mountaineers**. He was an early explorer of the Alps, and in 1867 published for private circulation his journal, *The Alps in 1864*, which contains well-written and absorbing accounts of Alpine walks and climbs. The book was reissued commercially in 1902, and again in 1939 in *Blackwell's Mountaineering Library*.

Moore, Barbara (1904-77) A doctor of Russian origin who achieved some notoriety in the nineteen-fifties and sixties by her eccentricity and her long-distance walking achievements. She made good copy for the popular press because she attributed her remarkable fitness and stamina to her vegetarian diet, and was always willing to express an unconventional opinion. Among her many exploits was walking from John O'Groats to Land's End (see **Land's End to John O'Groats**) in 23 days in 1960, and later walking from San Francisco to New York in 85 days. Many of her records were considerably improved upon by the much younger **Patrick Moloney**.

Moore, John C[ecil] (1907-67) Novelist, journalist, and the author of several popular books about walking and the countryside. In *Tramping through **Wales** in Search of the Red Dragon*, 1931; *The **Cotswolds***, 1937; and *A Walk through Surrey*, 1939 he wrote interesting accounts of his long walks in which he explored the countryside and wrote discursive accounts of his adventures. Moore also wrote *The Life and Letters of **Edward Thomas***, 1939.

Moorland Wild, barren upland country beyond the limits of cultivation, often covered in **heather** and **peat**, that will support only deer, sheep and hardy cattle. Many moors are preserved for grouse-shooting, and over the years many landowners have been subjected to pressures to grant **access**.

The open moorlands of the Dartmoor National Park (photo © Hugh Westacott).

Moran, Benjamin (1820-86) A **United States** diplomat, diarist and bibliographer who spent much of his life in **England**. He was the author of *The **Footpath** and **Highway**; or Wanderings of an American in Great Britain in 1851 and '52* which was published in 1853. It gives a detailed account of his pedestrian journeys throughout Britain, together with comments on what he saw.

Moran, Martin (1955-) Writer and outdoor journalist. In 1985, he became the first person to achieve the extraordinary feat of completing all the **Munros** in one continuous expedition in winter. He described his adventures in *The Munros in Winter; 277 Summits in 83 Days*, David & Charles, 1986, which also gives an account of other expeditions encompassing all the Munros, as well as other record-breaking achievements in the Scottish **hills**. His second book, ***Scotland's** Winter **Mountains**; the Challenge and the Skills*, David & Charles, 1988, is a treatise on all aspects of winter mountaineering in Scotland and also contains accounts of some of his walks and climbs. The Appendix includes a useful historical review of the major milestones in Scottish walking and climbing in winter.

Moritz, Carl Philip (1756-93) German travel-writer, novelist and friend of Goethe. He visited **England** in 1782 and wrote a description of his walk from London to Derbyshire in *Reisen eines Deutschen in England im Jahr 1782*, 1783, and a second, superior version, in 1785. An English version appeared in 1795 entitled *Travels, Chiefly on Foot, Through Several Parts of England in 1782, Described in Letters to a Friend*. This edition was not an accurate translation and was subject to much editorial 'correction'. The best English edition is *Journeys of a German in England in 1782* translated and edited by Reginald Nettel, Cape, 1965. The book is interesting for its vivid description of scenery, inns, social customs and the hostile attitude adopted towards pedestrians.

Morton, G[eorge] **F**[letcher] (1883?-1975) Sometime headmaster of Leeds Modern School and the author of a series of articles in Yorkshire newspapers that later formed the basis of *Hike and Trek; Education in the School of Adventure*, 1928, and *Hike and Hero*, 1931. In these books, Morton tries to relate walking to character-building and education based on his experiences of taking schoolboys to **Spain**, the **Alps** and **Canada.** He appears to have invented the 'trike cart' which was a sort of lightweight folding wheelbarrow that could be carried on the back and was used for transporting heavy **rucksacks** in suitable terrain.

Mountain There is no precise definition of

a mountain that is applicable throughout the world. In the British Isles there seem to be two schools of thought on what constitutes a mountain. Both are agreed that the minimum height is two thousand feet (610 metres), but one definition regards *every* summit over this height as a mountain, and the other argues that a mountain must possess a distinct summit or peak. Thus, under the first definition **Kinder Scout** (636 metres), in the **Peak National Park**, would be classified as a mountain, but under the second definition, it would be considered a high plateau. But Pen-y-ghent (694 metres) in the **Yorkshire Dales National Park**, and on the **Pennine Way**, certainly is a mountain. It may even be necessary to add the qualification that a mountain must lie north of latitude 51° to take account of Yes Tor and High Willhays in the **Dartmoor National Park**. They both exceed two thousand feet, and have quite satisfactory rocky peaks, but are never described as mountains (although **William Crossing** did so by implication in his pretentiously titled *Amid Devonia's **Alps***). The **Ordnance Survey** does not have a definition of a mountain, and its policy is to reflect local nomenclature.

In **Scotland**, the situation is more straightforward. Summits above three thousand feet are described by walkers and climbers as **Munros**; those 2500-2599 feet as **Corbetts**; and in the Lowlands all heights exceeding two thousand feet are **Donalds**. Each of these classifications, which were made before metrication, has a reasonably exact definition that makes a distinction between the main summit and any subsidiary tops. All the main summits in these classifications are accepted as mountains.

A complete list of summits higher than two thousand feet in **England** and **Wales** may be found in *The Mountains of England and Wales; Tables of Mountains of Two Thousand Feet and more in Altitude* by Nick Wright, Gaston's Alpine Books/West Col Productions, 1973 and also in *The Mountains of England and Wales* by **John** and **Anne Nuttall**, *Part 1: Wales*, 1990, *Part 2: England*, 1991, published by Cicerone Press. A complete list of all Scottish mountains exceeding two thousand five hundred feet in height (Corbetts and Munros) together with a list of all mountains in the Lowlands exceeding two thousand feet (Donalds) may be found in *Munro's Tables of the 3000-feet Mountains of Scotland and other Tables of Lesser Heights* edited and revised by J. C. Donaldson and **Hamish M. Brown, Scottish Mountaineering Club**

District Guide Books, Scottish Mountaineering Trust, 1984. A brief description of the walking and climbing opportunities of the major mountain ranges of every country can be found in *Guide to the World's Mountains* by Michael Kelsey, 1984 (distributed in the UK by Cordee).

Mountain Bothies Association This Association, founded in 1965, is a voluntary body formed to maintain simple unlocked shelters in upland country for the use of walkers, climbers and other outdoor enthusiasts in remote places. Agreements are negotiated with the owners of the buildings to permit the Association to keep them in repair. Members are expected to give financial or physical assistance in maintaining the buildings in the care of the Association.

*The **Bothy** Code*

1   Whenever possible seek owner's permission to use a bothy, particularly if proposing to take a group of six or more, or to use it as a base over a period. Note that all use of bothies is at own risk.

2   Do not stray from recognised routes during stalking and game-shooting seasons (mainly mid-August to mid-October).

3   Leave bothies cleaner, tidier and in better condition as a result of your visit.

4   Burn all rubbish you can; take all tins and glass away with you.

5   Lay in a supply of fuel and kindling for the next user (don't cut live wood).

6   If you leave unused food, date perishables and leave safe from rodents.

7   Do not burn, deface or damage any part of the structure.

8   Guard against risk of fire and ensure that the fire is safely out before leaving.

9   Secure windows and doors on departure.

10   Safeguard the water supply. Do not use the neighbourhood of the bothy as a toilet.

11   Protect and preserve animal and plant life.

12   Respect the countryside, its occupants and the country way of life.

13   Reports on the state of bothies maintained by the Association will be welcomed by the Maintenance Organiser or the General Secretary.

The MBA publishes an annual journal and a newsletter. *(For address see Appendix.)*

Mountain Code This is the **British Mountaineering Council** guide to safe practice for those who walk in the upland areas of the British Isles:

Be Prepared

Do not tackle anything that is beyond your training and experience.

Ensure that your equipment is sound.

Know the rescue facilities available in the area you are in and the procedures in case of accidents.

*Know **first aid**.*

*Avoid going into the **mountains** alone unless you are very experienced.*

Leave word of your route and proposed time of return. Always report your return.

*Make sure your **map** and **compass** skills are well practised.*

Rely on your compass.

Consider Other People

Avoid game-shooting parties.

Lead only climbs and walks which you are competent to lead.

Enjoy the quiet of the countryside; loud voices and radios do disturb.

Do not throw stones and dislodge boulders.

Do not pollute water.

Choose a climb which will not interfere with others, or wait your turn.

Be Weather Wise

Know the local weather forecast.

*Weather conditions change rapidly. Do not hesitate to turn back. Know the conditions on the mountain; if there is **snow** or **ice** only go out when you have mastered the use of **ice axe** and **rope**.*

Respect the Land

*Keep to **footpaths** through farm and woodland. If in doubt, ask.*

Camp on official sites or obtain permission of the landowner.

Dig a hole to make a latrine and replace the turf.

Remember the danger of starting a fire.

Take all your litter home.

Avoid startling sheep and cattle.

Help Conserve Wild Life

Enjoy the plants, flowers and trees but never remove or damage them.

Avoid disturbing wild life.

Mountain rescue In the United Kingdom **mountain** rescue services, for which no charge is made, are coordinated by the police who are alerted by telephoning 999. In most countries very high charges are made to those who have to be rescued. The procedure to be followed in the event of an accident depends very much on the circumstances, but the first requirement is to render **first aid** and to make the patient as warm, safe and comfortable as possible using spare **clothing, sleeping bags** and **survival bags**. If necessary, build a rock shelter to act as a windbreak. Ideally, two people should stay with the patient and two should go for help, but the party may be too small to permit this. The worst possible incident is when the patient is on his own, in which case his only recourse is to use the **international distress signal** in the hope that somebody will hear and come to his aid. If there is only one person, other than the patient, then the uninjured walker will have to leave the victim to seek assistance. Food, water and spare clothing should be left with the patient, and he should be told approximately how long it will take to raise the alarm. It helps if something brightly coloured can be secured in a prominent position near the patient. If he is unconscious, leave a note explaining the situation. This will serve to reassure him if he recovers consciousness, and also inform anybody else who may find him. Remember that it takes a considerable time to assemble a mountain rescue team who are all volunteers and will have to come from their home or workplace. Before setting out, those going for help should *independently* write down the six figure **grid reference** that will locate the victim and a description of his injuries. Next, decide on how to reach the nearest telephone which may be at an *inhabited* farm or house or it may be quicker to make for a *through* road and flag down a passing motorist. The police will decide whether to call out the mountain rescue team or to use a helicopter. You may be asked to accompany the rescue team, but remember that they are fit and can move very fast.

The two best British texts on mountain rescue techniques are *International Mountain Rescue Handbook* by Hamish MacInnes, Constable, 1972 and *Mountain Rescue Training Handbook for Royal Air Force Mountain Rescue Teams* compiled by the Ministry of Defence, HMSO, 1979. There are also a number of narrative accounts of mountain rescue activities including *Helicopter Rescue*, by J. Chartres, Ian Allen, 1980; *Rangi, Highland Rescue Dog* by E. Dudley, Harvill Press, 1970; *Call-out* by Hamish MacInnes, Hodder & Stoughton, 1973; *High Drama; Mountain Rescue Stories from Four Continents* by Hamish MacInnes, Hodder & Stoughton, 1980; *Sweep Search* by Hamish MacInnes, Hodder & Stoughton, 1985 and *Two Star Red; a Book about RAF Mountain Rescue* by Gwen Moffat, Hodder & Stoughton, 1964.

Mountain Rescue Committee The MRC, which coordinates **mountain** rescue activities in **England** and **Wales**, had its origins in the Joint Stretcher Committee formed in 1933 by the **Rucksack Club** and the **Fell and Rock Club** to produce a stretcher specially adapted

for British conditions. The report was published in 1935 and it gave a specification of all material and equipment, including medical and **first aid** items that should be available for coping with mountain accidents, as well as specifications for the Thomas stretcher. The success of the report led to the setting up of the First Aid Committee of Mountaineering Clubs in 1936 which after the Second World War became the **Mountain Rescue** Committee.

The Mountain Rescue Committee is a charitable trust and voluntary body comprising organisations formed by official mountain rescue teams and representatives from the **Sports Council**, the police, the RAF rescue service and other interested bodies. It is the organisation through which the Department of Health and Social Security recognises the affiliated mountain rescue teams and approves the issue of morphia and equipment to them. The MRC organises and co-ordinates mountain rescue in England and Wales with the support and recognition of the Department; it assists and encourages the formation of mountain rescue teams and posts in England and Wales where the need exists, and assists the rescue teams in their work; it promotes the exchange of experience and information between teams and others engaged in mountain and cave rescue; it arranges for the supply of medical first aid equipment and other equipment through the Department of Health and Social Security to mountain rescue teams and posts; it encourages and arranges investigation and research into methods and apparatus involved in mountain rescue; and it makes representations on mountain rescue interests to other national, international or government bodies. The MRC publishes *Mountain and Cave Rescue with Lists of Official Rescue Teams and Posts; the Handbook of the Mountain Rescue Committee. (For address see Appendix.)*

Mountain safety Virtually all the **mountain** peaks in the British Isles are accessible to walkers, and none exceed 1400 metres in height. It is probably the ease of **access** to the wilder parts of the country, and the fickleness of our weather, that is the cause of so many accidents in our mountains and **moorlands**. In the summer of 1987, according to statistics issued by the **Mountain Rescue Committee, mountain rescue** teams were called out 197 times to assist a total of 223 fell-walkers (of whom 23 died) in **England** and **Wales** alone. The 'Report of

the Mountain Rescue Committee' which is contained in the *Mountain and Cave Rescue with Lists of Official Rescue Teams and Posts; the Handbook of the Mountain Rescue Committee*, commenting on climbers and fell-walkers states *'The most important lessons again shown in the 1987 incident report is the need both to treat our **hills** with respect and both learn and acquire, or be taught the basic safety rules — 238 people in 1987 were either incompetent, inexperienced, ignorant, or ignored the basics of **navigation**, or the proper **clothing** or equipment necessary for the conditions for the terrain.'* In addition, there must be many hundreds, perhaps even thousands, of unrecorded cases who require and receive assistance from fellow-walkers.

Some accidents are unavoidable and can happen to the most experienced of walkers (**A. Wainwright** once got trapped in a **peat** bog and was rescued by a **ranger**), but the great majority are due to inexperience, foolhardiness, and the failure to follow the elementary precautions laid down in the **Mountain Code** which is applicable to all areas of mountain and moorland in the British Isles. The most common risks encountered in the upland areas of Britain are **hypothermia**, getting lost, slipping due to unsuitable footwear, and heart attacks.

Mountain Walking Leader Training Board The Board was set up in 1964 to provide a scheme of training for leaders who take groups of young people into the **mountains**. The Board consists of representatives of the **British Mountaineering Council**, the **Association of Heads of Outdoor Education Centres**, the **Sports Council** and other interested bodies. The Board grants a number of awards including:
Mountain Leader Assessment
This is the basic award which aims at raising the standard of knowledge and competence of leaders in mountainous country. Minimum age: (a) for registration and training, 18 years; (b) for assessment, 20 years.

To obtain the award a candidate must:
1. Complete a training course of at least six days' duration at a training centre approved by the Board; this course is not a beginner's course but an introduction to the scheme. All candidates should be committed **hill-walkers** or climbers with a substantial recent history of mountainous country activities. *It is not suitable for novices.*
2. Following this, have at least one year's practical experience as an assistant leader or group member of expeditions during week-ends

and holidays, details of which must be recorded in a personal log book. This period is designed to allow candidates to prepare for assessment by putting into practice the techniques and theories acquired on the training courses; and to provide the assessor with the evidence needed to carry out a fair assessment.

3. Attend a final week's residential course at an approved centre for assessment.

4. Be conversant with the following books: *Mountaincraft and Leadership* by Eric Langmuir, *Safety on Mountains* by John Barry and Tim Jepson, *The Mountain Code*, *Mountain Rescue* and *Cave Rescue*

5. Produce a current certificate in **First Aid** of the St John's Ambulance Brigade or of the British Red Cross Society or a First Aid at Work Certificate.

All candidates must be registered with the MWLTB and possess a log book.

Exemption: Exemption from training and log book, but not assessment, may be applied for if the candidate is exceptionally experienced and fully conversant with the requirements of the syllabus. Unjustified exemptions can result in failure at assessment.

Mountaineering Instructor's Certificate
This certificate is a progression from the Mountain Walking Leader Training Scheme. Training and certification are designed to meet the needs of anyone instructing in rock or **ice**-climbing or general mountaineering in the UK, whether on a full or part time basis. *(For address see Appendix.)*

Mountaineer In its original sense, as used by **William Wordsworth**, the term was applied to anyone who dwelt among **mountains**, irrespective of whether they ever climbed them. During the 1860s the term came to be applied to those who climbed mountains. In the strictest sense of the word, even the strongest and hardiest mountain walkers are not mountaineers unless they possess rock-climbing skills.

Mountaineering Council of Scotland The MCS exists to promote mountaineering in **Scotland**. It is the governing body for the sport in Scotland and represents member clubs in all mountaineering matters at national level and co-operates closely with the **British Mountaineering Council**. It publishes a newsletter, a list of Scottish mountaineering clubs' **huts**, and *Heading for the **Hills**. (For address see Appendix.)*

Mourne An **area of outstanding natural beauty** in County Down on the south-east coast of **Northern Ireland**. It is one of the most beautiful areas in the Province, and offers excellent **hill-walking**. The highest peak is Slieve Donard (849 metres), and there are numerous other peaks over 600 metres high. The region has the best network of mountain **paths** in Northern Ireland, and on the lower slopes there are beautiful forests containing many waymarked **trails** and nature trails. (See figure 36 for a **map** showing the location of all AONBs in the United Kingdom.)

Maps
1:50000 **Ordnance Survey of Northern Ireland** sheets 20, 21, 29.

Footpath Guide
Rogers, R., *Irish Walks Guides North East; Down and Antrim*, Gill and Macmillan, 1980.

Muir, John (1838-1914) Scottish-born American naturalist, explorer and conservationist who was a passionate advocate for the preservation of the Sierra Nevada and the **Rocky Mountains** from development, and helped found the **Sierra Club**. He was largely responsible for influencing public opinion which impelled the Congress of the **United States** to establish the Yosemite **National Park** over the protests of the timber companies who wanted to exploit its natural wealth. The President was also given the power to create Forest Reserves which are now found all over the United States.

He was brought up on a farm in Wisconsin, but in 1868 he moved to California, bought a farm and devoted his life to wandering in the Sierra Nevada, the Rocky Mountains, and Alaska studying the geology, botany and **glaciers** of the region. He was a very strong walker and climber with quite remarkable powers of endurance, and did much of his exploration on foot. His name is recorded in the topography of the **United States** by the Muir Glacier in Alaska and the 338-kilometre John Muir **Trail** in California. In Britain, his work has inspired the founding of the **John Muir Trust**. Muir must be counted among the greatest prose stylists who have written about **mountains**, and when his ire was aroused in defence of the wilderness, his writings are suffused with the passion and power of an Old Testament prophet.

In his early manhood he walked extensively in Wisconsin, Iowa, Illinois and Indiana, as well as venturing into **Canada**. During these explorations he conceived his lifetime interest in botany. From 2nd September to

23rd October 1867, he walked from Louisville, Kentucky to Savannah, Georgia, took a boat to Fernandina, Florida and walked across the isthmus to Cedar Keys on the Gulf of Mexico. He kept a journal of this walk, during which his philosophy of the natural world began to take shape, which was published posthumously, like many of his books, as *A Thousand-mile Walk to the Gulf*, in 1916. During this walk he collected and described botanical specimens, had many fascinating adventures, and almost died from typhus.

His other works of interest to walkers include *The Mountains of California*, 1894, *Our National Parks*, 1901 (reissued in Britain by Madison, 1981), *Stickeen*, 1909, *My First Summer in the Sierra*, 1911 (reissued in Britain as *Summering in the Sierra* edited by Robert Engberg, Madison, 1984), *The Yosemite*, 1912, *The Story of my Boyhood and Youth*, 1913, *Travels in Alaska*, 1915, and *Steep Trails*, 1918 (reissued in 1970). His journal was edited by Linnie Marsh Wolfe and published as *John of the Mountains; the Unpublished Journals of John Muir* by Houghton, Mifflin in 1938 (reissued in Britain by Madison in 1979).

Mulcaster, Richard (1530-1611) Scholar, educationalist, champion of English over Latin, and the first Master of the Merchant Taylors' School. He was the author of *Positions wherin those Primitive Circumstances be Examined, which are Necessarie for the Training up of Children, either for Skill in their Booke, or Health in their Bodie*, 1581 (the best modern edition was edited by R. H. Quick and published in 1888). *Positions* is a treatise dealing with the education and training of the young, including a concern for their physical fitness which was unusual at that time. Chapter 20, entitled 'Walking', is interesting because the author gives the impression that walking for recreation was a popular pastime in the sixteenth century *'When the weather suffereth* [permits], *how emptie are the townes and streates, how full be the fieldes and meadowes, of all kinds of folkes which by flocking so abroad, protest themselves to be fauourers* [favourers] *of that they do, and delite in for their health.'* He classifies walking into moderate walking, swift and quick walking, slow walking and then goes on to describe the virtues of each. He believed that the ambience of the walk was important and described the effect on the humours of the body of walking by the sea, evening walks and morning walks. He declared that it is dangerous to walk under dewy trees, that it is better to walk in the shade than in the sun, that the most beneficial walks are those taken in the open air in a green place, because that colour is so good for the eyes, and even goes so far as to describe the effects of the direction of the wind on body humours.

Munro A Scottish peak more than 3000 feet (914 metres) high that is separated from another summit by a drop on all sides of at least 500 feet (152 metres), by a considerable distance, or by a natural obstacle. A Munro top must be over 3000 feet high and have a separate identity of its own. There are 276 Munros and a further 516 tops, and more than 300 persons, known as Munroists, have climbed them all. The first person to climb all the Munros was the Reverend **A. E. Robertson** who completed them in 1901, an achievement that was not repeated until 1923. The first woman to climb all the Munros was Mrs Hirst in 1947. In 1974, **Hamish M. Brown** became the first person to climb them all in one expedition; in 1982, Kathy Murgatroyd became the first female Munroist to complete the round in one itinerary; and in 1985 **Martin Moran** distinguished himself by climbing them all in the first winter expedition.

The original list of summits was compiled by **Sir Hugh Munro** in 1891, and since then his definitions have been refined and the list revised. Munros are one of the principal objectives of those who enjoy **peak-bagging**. A complete list of Munros, together with the names of those known to have climbed them all, together with a list of **Corbetts** and **Donalds** may be found in *Munro's Tables of the 3000-feet **Mountains** of **Scotland** and other Tables of Lesser Heights* edited and revised by J. C. Donaldson and Hamish M. Brown, **Scottish Mountaineering Club** District Guide Books, Scottish Mountaineering Trust, 1984. The official record of Munroists is kept by the editor of the *Journal* of the Scottish Mountaineering Club. Information on how to ascend the Munros, as well as all other peaks exceeding 3000 feet in the British Isles can be found in *The High Mountains of Britain and Ireland; a Guide for Mountain Walkers*, by **Irvine Butterfield**, Diadem, 1986.

Munro, Sir Hugh [Thomas] (1856-1919) A Scottish **mountaineer** and walker who compiled the first list of 3000-foot Scottish peaks (subsequently known colloquially as a **Munro**) which was published in 1891. Until then, it was widely believed that only about 30 Scottish peaks exceeded 3000 feet, but the latest list includes 276 Munros and 516 tops. Munro contributed numerous articles to the **Scottish**

Mountaineering Club *Journal*, including many on the topography of Scottish **mountains** in which he was considerably more knowledgeable than the **Ordnance Survey** which did not publish really accurate **maps** to some of the remote areas of **Scotland** until many years after his death. Munro never managed to climb all the summits in his list although he completed most of them.

A complete list of Munros, together with the names of those known to have climbed them all, together with a list of **Corbetts** and **Donalds** may be found in *Munro's Tables of the 3000-feet Mountains of Scotland and other Tables of Lesser Heights* edited and revised by J. C. Donaldson and **Hamish M. Brown**, Scottish Mountaineering Club District Guide Books, Scottish Mountaineering Trust, 1984.

Munster Way An 81-kilometre walk through County Waterford, **Eire** from The Vee to Carrick-on-Suir. It links with the **South Leinster Way**, which in turn joins the **Wicklow Way**, giving the **wayfarer** a total of 307 kilometres of waymarked **path** that will take him all the way to Dublin. Ultimately, it is planned that the Munster Way will extend westward to link with the **Kerry Way** at Killarney. The route is strenuous in places and rises to over 300 metres.

Maps
Irish Ordnance Survey 1:126720 sheet 22.
Leaflet: Irish Tourist Board Information Sheet 26J *The Munster Way (Stage One).*

Mursell, Walter Arnold (1870-19--?) The author of *Footnotes; a Pedestrian Journal*, 1926, which is an account of a walking tour around the coast of **Northern Ireland** by four Scots. They commenced their walk at Larne, and after making an excursion across the border into Donegal, returned to Londonderry where they took a ship to Glasgow. The work is clearly influenced by *The Four Men* by **Hilaire Belloc** (the participants are referred to as the Author, the Bard, the Babe and the Quartermaster), but is a worthless trifle when compared with its inspiration. The four hearties have a series of jolly (and often tasteless) japes involving dim policemen, pretty waitresses and half-witted yokels.

Naismith's rule A formula for calculating the time needed to complete a journey in

upland country, devised by the Scottish climber and Alpinist William W. Naismith (1856-1935), that is widely used by walkers. The rule assumes reasonable conditions and takes no account of meal breaks and other stops. It states that one should allow one hour to cover 5 kilometres (3 miles) plus 30 minutes for every 300 metres (1000 feet) of ascent (see figure 19). For most reasonably fit **hill-walkers** it is acceptably accurate except for short or very long days. Various refinements, known as **Tranter's variations**, have been made to take into account fitness, weather and weight carried, but these are so complicated that a chart is required.

National Council of Ramblers' Federations The first local **Federation of Rambling Clubs** had been formed in London in 1905, and federations with similar aims were gradually established throughout the country. There was a strong feeling that a national body was required to look after the interests of ramblers, and in 1931 a conference, under the chairmanship of **T. A. Leonard**, was held at Longshaw, in what is now the **Peak National Park**, which was attended by delegates from many Federations. By a unanimous vote, it was resolved to form the National Council of Ramblers' Federations and elect an executive committee. The National Council met once a year, and in 1933 started publishing its journal *Rambling*. In 1934 the National Council resolved to change its name to the **Ramblers' Association** as from the 1st January, 1935.

National grid A system of lines forming squares devised by the **Ordnance Survey** for mapping purposes. The United Kingdom has been divided into 100-kilometre squares and each square has been assigned two identifying letters (see figure 20). These are used as part of a numbering system for some series of **maps** published by the Ordnance Survey. Within each 100-kilometre square, numbered **grid lines** are placed at one-kilometre intervals which can be used for assisting in **navigation**, and also as a means of identifying a precise location on the map (known as a **grid reference**).

National parks The world's first national park was established at Yellowstone, Wyoming by the Congress of the **United States** in 1872 '. . . *as a pleasuring ground for the benefit and enjoyment of the people.*' National parks are usually created to protect and preserve areas of outstandingly beautiful natural scenery and have

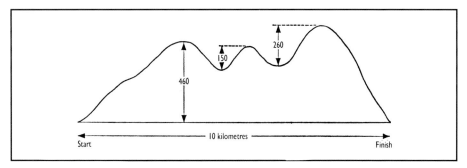

Figure 19: Naismith's Rule.

now been established in many countries.

Attempts were made in Britain to follow the example of America, and in 1945 the **Dower Report** recommended that national parks should be established. These proposals were largely implemented by the **National Parks and Access to the Countryside Act, 1949** when the **Brecon Beacons**, **Dartmoor**, **Exmoor**, **Lake District**, **North**

Figure 20: The national grid devised by the Ordnance Survey for mapping purposes.

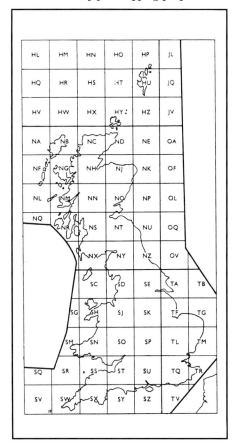

York Moors, **Northumberland**, **Peak District**, **Pembrokeshire Coast**, **Snowdonia**, and **Yorkshire Dales** national parks were established following the advice submitted by the **Hobhouse Committee**. In 1988, the **Broads** Act established the Broads Authority which, in effect, granted national park status to the Broads. Despite the recommendations of the **Ramsay Committee**, and the current pressure from some quarters to establish them, there are no national parks in **Scotland**. In **Northern Ireland**, under the provisions of the Amenity Lands Act, 1965 and the Nature Conservation and Amenity Lands Order (Northern Ireland), 1985, the legislation exists to designate national parks, but none have been created. (The location of all national parks in the United Kingdom is shown on the **map**, figure 36.)

In British national parks, unlike those in many countries in the New World, there is no change in the ownership of the land. The nation does not own its national parks so there is no general right of **access** for walkers, riders and others using them for recreation, unless local arrangements have been negotiated. British national parks are administered by boards or committees of county councils in which each park is situated. One third of the members of each board or committee are appointed by the government to reflect the national interest, and about seventy-five per cent of the running costs are met from central government funds. The **Countryside Commission** is the government agency with the responsibility for overseeing the work of national parks, and the **Council for National Parks** is the voluntary body which protects their interests.

National Parks and Access to the Countryside Act, 1949 This is the most important piece of legislation affecting walkers' interests in **England** and **Wales** yet enacted and implemented many of the proposals con-

tained in the recommendations of the **Scott Committee**, the **Dower Report** and the **Hobhouse Committee** report.

The Preamble to the Act describes it as *'An Act to make provision for **National Parks** and the establishment of a **National Parks Commission**; to confer on the **Nature Conservancy** and local authorities powers for the establishment and maintenance of nature reserves, and to make further provision for the recording, creation and improvement of public* **paths** *and for securing* **access** *to* **open country***, and to amend the law relating to* **rights of way***; to confer further powers for preserving and enhancing natural beauty; and for matters connected with the aforesaid.'* This Act established the framework for present-day legislation on rights of way, **long-distance paths**, national parks, **areas of outstanding natural beauty**, and **access agreements**. The only major disappointment for walkers in the Act was the failure to include provision for granting unrestricted access to open country. The legislation incorporated in this Act has been amended and expanded by later Acts including the **Countryside Act, 1968**, the **Highways Act, 1980**, and the **Wildlife and Countryside Act, 1981**.

National Parks Commission This Commission was established under the provisions of the **National Parks and Access to the Countryside Act, 1949**, and was charged with setting-up and overseeing the work of the **national parks**. Legislation embodied in the **Countryside Act, 1968** transferred its duties to the newly created **Countryside Commission** which was given wide responsibilities for the countryside generally.

National Scenic Areas In 1978, the **Countryside Commission for Scotland** published *Scotland's Scenic Heritage* after making a survey of Scottish scenery. The report identified 40 '. . . *areas of unsurpassed attractiveness which must be conserved as part of our national heritage.'* They were designated by the Secretary of State for Scotland in 1980, and the Countryside Commission for Scotland now has the statutory right to be consulted on matters of large-scale development. Most conservation bodies believe that the Commission's powers are not adequate to protect the NSAs properly. National Scenic Areas have been established at Assynt-Coigach; Ben Nevis & **Glen** Coe; the **Cairngorms**; Cuillin **Hills**; Deeside & Lochnagar; Dornoch Firth; East Stewartry Coast; Eildon and Leaderfoot; Fleet Valley; Glen

Great Gable from near Esk Hause in the Lake District National Park—a popular walking area (photo © Hugh Westacott).

Affric; Glen Strathfarrar; Hoy & West Mainland; Jura; Kintail; Knapdale; Knoydart; Kyle of Tongue; Kyles of Bute; Loch Lomond; Loch na Keal; Loch Rannoch & Glen Lyon; Loch Shiel; Loch Tummell; Lynn of Lorn; Morar, Moidart & Ardnamurchan; Nith Estuary; North Arran; North-west Sutherland; River Earn; River Tay; St Kilda; Scarba, Lunga and the Garvellachs; Shetland Islands; the Small Isles; South Uist Machair; South Lewis, Harris & North Uist; the Trossachs; Trotternish;

Upper Tweeddale; and Wester Ross. (See figure 36 for a **map** showing the location of all national scenic areas.)

National trails The term adopted by the **Countryside Commission** in 1988, which has been much criticised by walkers (for reasons see **trails**), to describe those **long-distance paths** in **England** and **Wales** for which it is responsible. These are the **Cleveland Way**, the **North Downs Way**,

Offa's Dyke Path, the **Peddars Way and Norfolk Coast Path**, the **Pembrokeshire Coast Path**, the **Pennine Way**, the **Ridgeway Path**, the **South Downs Way**, the **South West Coast Path**, the **Thames Path** (this proposed route has not yet been officially designated but is included here as it is walkable throughout its length), and the **Wolds Way**. (See figure 36 for a **map** showing the location of all **national trails** and official long-distance paths in the United Kingdom.)

The Countryside Commission aims to increase the number of national trails. In *Paths, Routes and Trails, Policies and Priorities* [CCP 266], published in 1989, it proposes that consideration should be given to establishing a **Pennine** Bridleway, a route in the area of Hadrian's Wall, and upgrading the existing Cotswold Way and Glynwr's Way to the status of national trails. At three-yearly intervals from 1992, the Commission intends to invite bids for additional routes to be accorded national trail status.

National Trust The Trust, whose full name is the National Trust for Places of Historic Interest or Natural Beauty, was founded in 1895 by Miss Octavia Hill, Sir Robert Hunter and Canon H. D. Rawnsley to halt the destruction of the countryside by the uncontrollable growth of industry. The first secretary was **Lawrence Chubb**. The Trust is now the largest private landowner and conservation society in Britain. It has branches throughout the United Kingdom, except **Scotland** which has its own organisation, the **National Trust for Scotland**. It aims to educate public opinion and to give people **access** to the countryside by acting as trustees to the nation by acquiring land and buildings worthy of permanent preservation. It publishes a journal, *The National Trust Magazine,* and numerous guides and handbooks on architecture and the countryside. *(For address see Appendix.)*

National Trust for Scotland The Trust, founded in 1931, aims to promote the permanent preservation for the benefit of the nation of lands, buildings, places and articles in **Scotland** of national architectural, artistic, antiquarian or historic interest, or lands of natural beauty, along with, where appropriate, their animal and plant life. Of equal importance is the stated purpose of the Trust to encourage and facilitate the **access** to and the enjoyment of such places and things by the public. It owns much wild land and has been criticised for encouraging too easy access to some popular **mountains** by providing car parks and other facilities. The Trust publishes a journal, *Heritage Scotland* and numerous guidebooks including **footpath guides** to Ben Lawers and Torridon. *(For address see Appendix.)*

Nature Conservancy Council The Council, established by statute in 1973, is the government body that promotes nature conservation in Great Britain. It gives advice on nature conservation to government and all those whose activities affect our wildlife and wild places. It also selects, establishes and manages a series of National Nature Reserves, and undertakes or commissions relevant research. It publishes a journal, *Earth Science Conservation,* several newsletters (*Urban Wildlife News, Topical Issues and Batchat*) and numerous handbooks, guides, reports, booklets, information sheets, wallcharts and posters. *(For address see Appendix.)*

Navigation The art of using **map** and **compass** to find one's way about the countryside. Navigation is an extension of **map-reading** involving techniques that do not normally have to be used in lowland countryside where, in most cases, simple map-reading skills will suffice for route-finding. To become a good navigator in upland country, the walker must acquire a detailed knowledge of the maps published by the **Ordnance Survey**, be competent in the use of a compass, and learn specialised techniques such as **aiming off**, attack points, and know how to conduct **spiral searches** and **sweep searches**. In lowland country, a compass is not essential, especially if using the **Pathfinder** or **Outdoor Leisure** series of maps, but it can still be very useful, especially in those areas where **paths** are not readily visible on the ground. The best books on the subject are *Mountain Navigation* by Peter Cliff, Cordee, Rev. Ed., 1986, *Mountain Navigation Techniques* by **Kevin Walker**, Constable, 1986, and *Land Navigation; Routefinding with Map and Compass,* by Wally Keay, Duke of Edinburgh Award, 1989.

Naylor, John (1844-1923) and **Robert** [Anderton] (1847-1908) Brothers who were timber merchants and partners in the family business of R. A. Naylor Ltd of Warrington. In 1870, Robert walked from Warrington to London where he was studying law, and the following year the brothers resolved to walk from John O'Groats to Land's End. They set out on September 7th intending to walk forty kilometres per day, except on Sundays which were set aside for attendance at Divine Service, and to stick to their temperance principles. They followed a meandering route via Inverness, Ballachullish, Stirling, Edinburgh, Hawick, Gretna Green, Windermere, York, Hathersage, Oxford, Salisbury, Lyme Regis, Exeter, Plymouth and Penzance, a distance they estimated to be 2195 kilometres. They walked on both roads and **paths**, and had many adventures including **benightment** near the Bridge of Orchy, and getting lost on the **fells** above Dunmail Raise.

Every night Robert wrote his diary in shorthand, and towards the end of his life began to transcribe it for publication. After his brother's death, John completed the work and it was published privately as *From John O'Groats to Land's End or 1372 Miles on Foot; a Book of Days and Chronicle of Adventures by Two Pedestrians on Tour* in 1916 in a large volume of 659 pages. There is a great deal of information about their itinerary, and some graphic descriptions of their adventures, but the book is unnecessarily inflated by the amount of historical and literary background material included.

Needle A tall sharp crag or rock found particularly in the **Lake District National Park**. Needles can normally only be ascended by climbers.

Nephins and North Mayo Highlands An isolated group of **mountains** in the far northwest of County Mayo in **Eire**. There are few roads and it is necessary to walk quite long distances to enjoy them properly. The highest peak is Nephin (806 metres).
Maps
Irish Ordnance Survey 1:63360 sheets 63, 64. 1:126720 sheet 6.
Footpath Guides
Whilde, T., *Irish Walks Guides West; Clare, Galway and Mayo,* Gill and Macmillan, 1979.

The Netherlands Holland, as the Netherlands is popularly known in the United Kingdom, is a small country that appears very flat to British eyes. Its charm lies in the neatness of its landscape, its flowers, and its beautiful towns. The Dutch have a tradition of marching festivals, which are long-distance events, often along roads, for which teams come from abroad to compete.

There are a number of **long-distance paths**, and most tourist offices, known universally as VVVs, are able to provide **maps** and walking routes. Some VVVs organise walking tours in which, for a fixed fee, a map, **footpath guide**, **rucksack** and accommodation are all provided. Enquiries should be addressed to VVV followed by the name of the town.
Useful Addresses
Netherlands Board of Tourism, 25-28

Buckingham Gate, London SW1E 6LD. Tel. 071-630-0451.

Ramblers' Organisation: Nederlandse Wandelsport Bond, Pieterskerhof 22, 3512 JS, Utrecht.

National Map Survey: Topographische Dienst, Westvest 11, 2611 AX, Delft.

Official Survey Maps: Topographische Kaart 1:50000 and 1:25000 (**footpaths** are shown on both scales).

New Zealand New Zealand is an extremely beautiful, mountainous country with a well-developed network of national and forest parks. Walking, often referred to as tramping, is a popular pastime and there are many long-distance routes. There is no local **footpath** network such as we have in Britain, but the government has established the New Zealand Walkway Commission which is responsible for the creation of a network of walkways throughout the country. On some of the long-distance routes a permit is required which can be obtained in advance from the New Zealand High Commission (see below) which can also provide information about travel companies specialising in walking tours.

A leaflet, *New Zealand* **National Parks** *Publications,* available from the Department of Conservation (see below), gives the addresses of national parks together with information about **footpath guides**.

Publishers of footpath guides include:

Government Printing Office, Mulgrave Street, Wellington.

Methuen (New Zealand), PO Box 4439, Auckland.

A.H. and A.W. Reed Ltd, Private Bag, Wellington.

Whitcoulls Ltd, Private Bag, Wellington.

Useful Addresses

New Zealand Travel Commissioner/New Zealand Government Tourist Bureau/New Zealand High Commission, New Zealand House, Haymarket, London SW1Y 4TQ. Tel. 071-930-8422.

The reference library, which is open to the public, contains a useful collection of books about the country as well as the New Zealand National Bibliography on microfiche from which details of up to date footpath guides can be found under the heading '**Trails**'.

Ramblers' Organisation: New Zealand Walkway Commission, c/o Department of Conservation, PO Box 10420, Wellington.

National **Map** *Survey:* Department of Survey and Land Information. Private Bag, Wellington.

Official Survey Maps: 1:63360 cover the whole

Walkers resting on the spectacular Milford Track, New Zealand (photo © New Zealand Tourist Commission).

country and show **footpaths**.

Guides to walking

Burton, R., *A Tramper's Guide to New Zealand's National Parks,* Read Methuen, 1987.

Cobb, John, *The Walking Tracks of New Zealand's National Parks,* Endeavour Press, 1985.

Footpath Guides

AA Guide to Walkways, Landsdowne Press, 1987. Vol 1: *North Island,* Vol 2: *South Island.*

Du Fresne, Jim, *Tramping in New Zealand,* Lonely Planet (distributed in the UK by Roger Lascelles).

Pickering, Mark, *101 Great Tramps in New Zealand,* Read Methuen, Rev. Ed., 1988.

Newby, [George] **Eric** (1919-) Travel writer and sometime seaman, fashion buyer and advertising executive. He is the author of *A Short Walk in the Hindu Kush,* Secker & Warburg, 1958, a classic of walking and travel-writing, that describes his unsuccessful attempt to climb Mir Samir (6059 metres) in Afghanistan.

Newell, R[obert] H[assell] (1778-1852) An amateur artist, author and sometime dean of St John's College, Cambridge, rector of Little Hormead, Hertfordshire, and curate of Little Hormead. He wrote an account of a walking tour undertaken for the purpose of **picturesque** sketching entitled *Letters on the Scenery of* **Wales**; *Including a Series of Subjects for the Pencil with their Stations Determined on a General Principle: and Instructions to Pedestrian Tourists,* 1821. One of the letters (which are all addressed to an

undergraduate contemplating taking a sketching tour of Wales), is given over to general advice on walking. '. . . *It should, in fact, be the first aim of a pedestrian to carry as little weight and incumbrance as possible. Let this then be your dress: jacket, waistcoat, trowsers, and* **gaiters** *of the stuff called Jean — light and strong.* **Shoes** *stout, broad, well-seasoned, made to each foot, and without nails — they are dangerous on rocky ground: top the whole with a straw, or rather a willow hat. Nor must an umbrella, by any means, be forgotten; it is a trusty, useful servant, choose it of silk, and of the largest size.*

Next for your luggage. Get made, of the brown-dressed calf-skin used by saddlers, a case about eleven inches and a half long, by seven wide, a trifle rounded at the bottom, lined with canvas, and having a flap and a button. This is to be slung over the shoulder with loops and button (not buckle); and this may easily be shifted to either side and adjusted to any height. A complete change of linen, shaving implements, **map**, *and the smaller drawing books, are all it need contain, and when filled, the whole will not weigh more than between three and four pounds . . . I can give you no rule for laying out your day; so much must depend upon your constitution, habit, weather, length of stages, and various accidental circumstances. If, to avoid the heat, you walk late in an evening, this plan can hardly be followed up by an early morning walk, and that has never succeeded with me . . . The plan I have found most eligible is, to begin my walk after as early a breakfast as I can procure, reach my destination in the afternoon, then taking another meal, give the evening to exploring and sketching . . .'*

Newell followed roads and gives his itinerary and mileages. He enjoyed walking, but the real purpose of the book was to give precise information on where to make the best sketches from vantage points he called 'stations' for which he devised elaborate mathematical formulae. His instructions for sketching Brecon read *'At the water's edge. Let the distant church tower be exactly* over *the right-hand arch . . .'*

Norfolk Coast An **area of outstanding natural beauty**, designated in 1968, which follows the coast from King's Lynn to Mundesley, and covers 450 square kilometres of beaches, mud flats and salt marsh. Not particularly good walking country, but it appeals greatly to those who love the peculiar atmosphere of flat coastal scenery. (See figure 36 for a **map** showing the location of all AONBs in the United Kingdom.)
Maps
1:50000 **Landranger** sheets 132, 133.
1:25000 **Pathfinder** sheets P818 (TF64/74), P819 (TF84/94), P820 (TG04/14), P838 (TF43/53), P839 (TF63/73), P840 (TF83/93), P841 (TG03/13), P842 (TG23/33), P858 (TF42/52), P859 (TF62/72).
Footpath Guide
Kennet, David, *Discovering Walks in Norfolk*, Shire Publications, 1985.

North Derry An **area of outstanding natural beauty** in **Northern Ireland** that includes the Foyle estuary, and contains some of Ireland's finest beaches including Magilligan Strand onto which are washed innumerable shells of all sizes and varieties. It is one of the best walking areas in the Province. (See figure 36 for a **map** showing the location of all AONBs in the United Kingdom.)
Map
1:50000 **Ordnance Survey of Northern Ireland** sheet 4.
Footpath Guides
Hamill, James, *North Ulster Walks Guide*, Appletree Press, 1988.
Simms, P., and Foley, G., *Irish Walks Guides North West; Donegal, Sligo, Armagh, Derry, Tyrone and Fermanagh*, Gill and Macmillan, 1979.

North Devon An **area of outstanding natural beauty** that covers the whole of the north Devon coast from the boundary with Cornwall to the **Exmoor National Park**. The 171 square kilometres of rugged coastline, high cliffs and beautiful seascapes contains much lovely scenery and charming old villages.

(See figure 36 for a **map** showing the location of all AONBs in the United Kingdom.)
Maps
1:50000 **Landranger** sheets 180, 190.
1:25000 **Pathfinder** sheets P1253 (SS22/32), P1273 (SS21/31), P1292 (SS20/30).
Footpath Guide
Coastal Rambles, compiled and published annually by North Devon Print, 5 Oxford Grove, Ilfracombe, Devon EX34 8HG.

North Downs Way A **national trail** designated by the **Countryside Commission** and opened in 1978. It runs for 227 kilometres over chalk **downland** from Farnham (**grid reference** SU 844468), in Surrey to Shakespeare Cliff (grid reference TR 308399), Dover in Kent. There is an alternative route from Boughton Lees (grid reference TR 029475) to Connaught Park (grid reference TR 316426), Dover that goes via Canterbury. A popular misconception exists that this **long-distance path** follows the line of the ancient **Pilgrims' Way**; it does in one or two places, but the route was chosen for its scenic qualities, not for its supposed historical associations. It is an easy route, and is so well served by public transport that it can be walked from London in a series of separate days. The North Downs Way is never far from large centres of population, and on many sections of the route the hum of distant traffic can always be heard. (See figure 36 for a **map** showing the location of all national trails and official long-distance paths in the United Kingdom.)
Youth Hostels
Tanner's Hatch, Kemsing, Canterbury, Dover.
Maps
1:50000 **Landranger** sheets 177, 178, 179, 186, 188, 189.
1:25000 **Pathfinder** sheets P1193 (TQ66/76), P1206 (SU81/91), P1207 ((TQ25/35), P1208 (TQ45/55), P1209 (TQ65/75), P1210 (TQ85/95), P1211 (TR05/15), P1212 (TR25/35), P1225 (SU84/94), P1226 (TQ04/14), P1230 (TQ84/94), P1231 (TR04/14), P1232 (TR24/34), P1252 (TR13/23).
Footpath Guides
Adams, A. J., *Walk the North Downs Way* and *The Greensand Way*, published by the author at 2 Dryden Court, Lower Edgeborough Road, Guildford GU1 2EX.
Herbstein, Denis, *The North Downs Way*, HMSO, 1982.
Wright, C. J., *A Guide to the Pilgrims' Way and the North Downs Way*, Constable, 1982.

North Pennines A large **area of outstanding natural beauty** located in North Yorkshire, County Durham, Cumbria and Northumberland, that was designated in 1989 by the Secretary of State for the Environment on the advice of the **Countryside Commission**. It stretches from the northern tip of the **Yorkshire Dales National Park** to the northern edge of the Tyne valley, and nearly connects with the **Northumberland National Park**. This AONB contains superb walking country and include Crossfell (893 metres), the highest summit in **England** outside the **Lake District National Park**. (See figure 36 for a **map** showing the location of all AONBs in the United Kingdom.)
Maps
1:50000 **Landranger** sheets 86, 87, 91, 92.
1:25000 **Pathfinder** sheets P546 (NY 66/76), P547 (NY 86/96), P558 (NY 45/55), P559 (NY 65/75), P560 (NY 85/95), P568 (NY 44/54), P569 (NY 64/74), P570 (NY 84/94), P571 (NZ 04/14), P578 (NY 63/73), P580 (NZ 05/15), P597 (NY 61/71), P598 (NY 81/91), P607 (NY 60/70), P608 (NY 80/90) plus **Outdoor Leisure Map** 31 *Teesdale*.
Footpath Guides
Watson, Keith, *Walking in Teesdale*, Dalesman, 1978.
Walking in the Northern Dales compiled by the North Yorkshire & South Durham Area of the **Ramblers' Association**, Dalesman, 1981.

North Wessex Downs A large **area of outstanding natural beauty**, designated in 1972 by the Secretary of State for the Environment on the advice of the **Countryside Commission**, that covers 1738 square kilometres in Hampshire, Wiltshire, Oxfordshire and Berkshire, bordered by the towns of Reading, Newbury, Andover, Devizes and Swindon. This area contains the largest and least-spoiled tract of chalk **downland** in southern **England**, and the northeast corner joins the **Chilterns** AONB. There are several **hills** over 300 metres high, and the area includes some of the most important prehistoric sites in the country. (See figure 36 for a **map** showing the location of all AONBs in the United Kingdom.)
Maps
1:50000 **Landranger** sheets 164, 173, 174.
1:25000 **Pathfinder** sheets P1136 (SU49/59), P1153 (SU08/18), P1154 (SU28/38), P1155 (SU48/58), P1169 (SU07/17), P1170 (SU27/37), P1171 (SU47/57), P1172

(SU67/77), P1184 (ST86/96), P1185 (SU06/16), P1186 (SU26/36), P1187 (SU46/56), P1201 (SU05/15), P1202 (SU25/35), P1203 (SU45/55), P1223 (SU44/54).

Footpath Guides
Channer, Nick, *North Hampshire Walks; 10 Country Rambles near Winchester, Alton, Andover and Basingstoke*, Countryside Books, 1981.

Parker, Brenda, *Walks in North Hampshire*, Paul Cave Publications, 1984.

North York Moors National Park This **national park** covers an area of 1432 square kilometres bordered by the towns of Saltburn, Scarborough, Helmsley and Northallerton. It contains the largest heather moor in England which makes a marvellous picture when in flower in August. Another feature of this national park is the magnificent cliff scenery that includes Robin Hood's Bay and the beautiful fishing village of Staithes. The moors are littered with reminders of prehistoric man, and there are a number of medieval crosses. By contrast, the huge, weird concrete domes of the early-warning radar system are situated on Fylingdales Moor. (See figure 36 for a **map** showing the location of all national parks in the United Kingdom.) *(For addresses of National Park Headquarters and Information Centres see Appendix.)*

Official Guidebook
Carstairs, Ian, *North York Moors*, Webb & Bower in association with Michael Joseph, 1987.

National Park Newspaper
North York Moors Visitor.

Maps
1:63360 **Tourist Map** of the North York Moors.
1:50000 **Landranger** sheets 93, 94, 99, 100, 101.
1:25000 **Outdoor Leisure Maps** North York Moors 26 (Western area), 27 (Eastern area).

Footpath Guides
Collins, Martin, *North York Moors; Walks in the National Park*, Cicerone Press, 1987.
Ramblers' Association, *Walking on the North York Moors*, Dalesman, 1987.

Northern Highlands An area of **Scotland** that includes Sutherland, the northern half of Ross-shire and the southwest corner of Caithness. It is defined by Dingwall, Garve, and Strath Ban to Achnasheen and westwards to Glen Carron and the western seaboard. There is some spectacular **mountain** scenery with a wild and largely uninhabited hinterland

crossed by a number of old **drove roads** that give excellent walking. (See figure 25 for **map** on showing the major scenic divisions of Scotland.)

Maps
1:50000 **Landranger** sheets 9, 10, 15, 16, 17, 19, 20, 21, 24, 25, 26.
1:25000 **Outdoor Leisure map** 8 of Cuillin and Torridon **Hills** covers part of the region.

Guidebook
Bennet, Donald and Strang, Tom, *The North West Highlands*, Scottish Mountaineering Trust, 1990.

Footpath Guides
Barton, Peter, *Torridon; a Walker's Guide*, Cicerone Press, 1989.
MacInnes, Hamish, *Highland Walks Vol 2: Skye to Cape Wrath*, Hodder and Stoughton, 1984.

Northern Ireland Most parts of the Province of Ulster are rural (Belfast is the only large city) and well worth exploring on foot to savour the strikingly beautiful countryside. The **Access** to the Countryside (Northern Ireland) Order, 1983 places responsibility on district councils to **map** and keep open **rights of way**, and to create new ones where necessary. It also gives district councils the power to close rights of way where they are no longer needed. Under common law, certain individuals, families and those engaged in a particular pursuit such as the extraction of timber or turf may have the right of passage in particular circumstances, but such considerations do not normally apply to the walker.

The walker, if he keeps away from the vicinity of large towns where, over the years, friction may have developed between 'townies' and **farmers**, is unlikely to encounter any difficulties using **paths** and tracks shown on maps published by the **Ordnance Survey for Northern Ireland**. There is a dense network of lanes and minor roads on which motor traffic is sparse, but comparatively few field or mountain paths except in **Mourne**. There are also more than fifty state forests and several country parks where walking is encouraged. The **Ulster Way** is an important **long-distance path**. Despite the 'troubles', it is not dangerous to walk in Ulster and the chances of being involved in an incident are remote.

There are no **national parks**, although under the provisions of the Amenity Lands Act, 1965, and the Nature Conservation and Amenity Lands Order, 1985, legislation exists to create them, but it is not the policy of the

government to implement it. The best walking areas are in the **areas of outstanding natural beauty** of the **Antrim Coast and Glens**, the **Causeway Coast**, **Lagan Valley**, the **Lecale Coast**, **Mourne**, **North Derry**, **South Armagh**, the **Sperrin** and **Strangford Lough**. Another popular walking area is the **Lakeland Country of County Fermanagh**. The Countryside and Wildlife branch of the Department of the Environment for Northern Ireland is the government body responsible for caring for the countryside *(for address see Appendix)*.

Northing The term used, along with **easting**, to describe one half of a **grid reference**.

Northumberland Coast An **area of outstanding natural beauty**, designated in 1958, that contains some marvellous scenery in its 129 square kilometres that stretch from Berwick-on-Tweed southwards to Amble. The cold exposed beaches discourage conventional holidaymakers so it is quite unspoiled. There are magnificent castles and charming fishing villages as well as Holy Island and the Farne Islands to explore. (See figure 36 for a **map** showing the location of all AONBs in the United Kingdom.)

Maps
1:50000 **Landranger** sheets 75, 81.
1:25000 **Pathfinder** sheets P452 (NU04/14), P465 (NU13/23), P477 (NU22), P489 (NU21/22), P501 (NU20).

Footpath Guide
Hopkins, Tony, *Walks on the Northumberland Coast*, Northumberland County Council, 1983.

Northumberland National Park This **national park** is long and narrow stretching from just west of Hexham to the Scottish border. In its 1031 square kilometres, it contains the Cheviot, rising to a height of 816 metres, and the best preserved section of Hadrian's Wall. Walkers exploring the park have numerous routes from which to choose, and traditionally, **access** to **open country** has been permitted providing game and livestock are not disturbed. (See figure 36 for a **map** showing the location of all national parks in the United Kingdom.) *(For addresses of National Park Headquarters and Information Centres see Appendix.)*

Official Guidebook
Hopkins, Tony, *Northumberland*, Webb & Bower in association with Michael Joseph, 1987.

Maps

1:50000 **Landranger** sheets 74, 75, 80, 81, 87.

1:25000 **Pathfinder** sheets P463 (NT83/93), P475 (NT82/92), P476 (NU02/12), P486 (NT61/71), P487 (NT81/91), P488 (NU01/11), P498 (NT60/70), P499 (NT80/90), P500 (NU00/10), P509 (NY69/79), P510 (NY89/99), P511 (NZ09/19), P521 (NY68/78), P522 (NY88/98), P533 (NY67/77), P534 (NY87/97), P546 (NY66/76), P547 (NY86/96).

Footpath Guides

Bleay, Janet, *Walks in the Hadrian's Wall Area*, Northumberland National Park, 1985.

Williams, J., *Walks in the Cheviot Hills*, Northumberland National Park, 1981.

Norway an exceptionally beautiful country, consisting largely of **mountains**, and having a long, deeply indented coastline. It is a paradise for walkers, with numerous **long-distance paths** and a large number of tourist **huts** within a day's march of each other. The Open Air Act, passed in 1957, grants the right to walk and camp anywhere except on enclosed land, which gives the walker the freedom of 96 per cent of the countryside.

A most helpful booklet, *Mountain Touring Holidays in Norway*, available from the Norwegian Tourist Board (see below), gives an account of the mountain ranges and offers much practical advice.

Useful Addresses

Norwegian Tourist Board, 20 Pall Mall, London SW1Y 5NE. Tel. 071-839-6255.

Ramblers' Organisation: Den Norske Turistforening, PO Box 1963 Vika, N-0125 Oslo 1.

*National **Map** Survey:* Statens Kartverk, N-3500 Honefoss.

Official Survey Maps: Topografiske Kart 1:50000 (shows **paths** and tourist shelters). Turistkart with various scales from 1:50000 to 1:200000 of main tourist areas (show **footpaths**).

Guide to Walking

Evans, Craig, *On Foot through Europe: a **Trail** Guide to Scandinavia*, Quill, 1982.

Nuttall, John (1939-) and **Anne** (1941-) A husband and wife team who write **footpath guides**. John is also an artist, lecturer and outdoor journalist.

Publications about Walking

Great Walks; Peak District, Ward Lock, 1987.

*The **Mountains** of **England** and **Wales**; a Guide to the 2000 Feet Peaks*, Cicerone Press.

Part 1 Wales, 1989.

Part 2 England, 1990.

Nylon The generic name given to a man-made material that was invented in the laboratories of the Du Pont Company, and first used commercially in 1939. Subsequently, various types of nylon have been developed, and it is now widely used in the manufacture of **clothing** and equipment for walkers.

The Observant Pedestrian, or Traits from the Heart in a Solitary Tour from Caernarvon to London, 1795. An anonymous work, by the author of *The Mystic Cottage*, which purports to be an account of his journey on foot with his spaniel, Trudge, from Caernarvon to London. It is a strange, voyeuristic work, slightly reminiscent of Laurence Sterne's *A Sentimental Journey*, that reads like a moral tale. The author is fond of drawing moral conclusions from incidents which read as though they were invented. He claims to be ugly and unattractive, and has the unpleasant habit of giving tips to young servant girls so that he can look down their cleavage when they curtsy their thanks. He also hides behind hedges to spy on unsuspecting women. The book contains so little information about the walk that it is probably largely the product of the author's imagination.

Obstruction Any kind of barrier, device or obstacle that prevents free passage along a **right of way**. In **England** and **Wales**, there is no statutory definition of an obstruction, but there are two useful judicial definitions. In *Seekings v Clarke* (1961) Lord Chief Justice Parker remarked '*It is perfectly clear that anything which substantially prevents the public from having free access over the whole of the highway which is not purely temporary in nature is an unlawful obstruction.*' Mr Justice Byles in R v Matthias (1861) stated '*A nuisance to a way is that which prevents the convenient use of the way by passengers.*' Highway authorities have a statutory duty to prevent obstructions. Under the **Highway Act, 1980** section 130 (1) they have a duty to protect and assert the rights of the public to the use and enjoyment of the highways for which they are the highway authority. Under section 130 (3) they must prevent the stopping up or obstruction of those highways. Highway authorities may enforce the law through the courts or, after serving notice and getting no response, they may do what is necessary themselves and recover the cost from the landowner. In certain circumstances walkers may remove obstacles from the line of the **path** providing they remove no more than is actually necessary, and also providing that they did not undertake the journey with specific

Walkers in Norway can walk and camp anywhere except on enclosed land (photo © Norway Tourist Board).

tion of dealing with the obstruction. Walkers are advised to use this right with great circumspection.

In **Scotland**, the common law does not permit obstructions on a right of way, and in theory the remedy is to remove as much of the obstruction as is necessary to allow free passage. The problem is knowing whether the highway is acknowledged as a right of way. Obstructions are also covered by statute, and under the provisions of the **Countryside (Scotland) Act, 1967** a duty is placed on local planning authorities '. . . *to assert, protect, and keep open and free from obstruction or encroachment any public right of way which is wholly or partly in their area.*'

Odyssey A monthly magazine, which was edited by **Chris Townsend** and first published in 1988, that was devoted to outdoor adventure including walking, **backpacking**, climbing, cross-country skiing, **mountain** biking, canoeing, and caving in all parts of the world. It ceased publication in February 1989.

Offa's Dyke Association This Association was formed in 1969 to promote the conservation, improvement and better knowledge of the Welsh border region along the **Offa's Dyke Path**. It publishes a newsletter and information about the route, as well as several guides which are listed in the Offa's Dyke Path bibliography. The ODA also publishes guides to three alternative unofficial **long-distance paths** to sections of Offa's Dyke Path, *Castles Alternative, Diocesan Way* and *Offa's Wye Frontier*, details of which may be found in the entry for long-distance paths. *(For address see Appendix.)*

Offa's Dyke Path A **national trail**, designated by the **Countryside Commission**, which was opened officially in 1971. It runs for 285 kilometres from Sedbury Cliffs (**grid reference** ST 552927), near the Severn Bridge, Gloucestershire to Prestatyn (grid reference SJ 081838), Clwyd in North **Wales**. For most of its route, it follows Offa's Dyke, an earthwork constructed by the King of Mercia in the eighth century to mark the boundary between his lands and those of the Welsh. On the whole, this is an easy walk, but the two high sections over the Black **Mountains** in the **Brecon Beacons National Park** and the **Clwydian Hills** must be treated with respect, especially in bad weather. The **Offa's Dyke Association** publishes some unofficial alternative routes to sections of the **path**.

(See figure 36 for a **map** showing the location of all national trails and official **long-distance paths** in the United Kingdom.) *Path Association*

Offa's Dyke Association
Youth Hostels
Chepstow, St Briavel's, Monmouth, Capel-y-ffin, Knighton, Clun Mill, Llangollen and Maeshafn.
Maps
1:50000 **Landranger** sheets 116, 117, 126, 137, 148, 161, 162, 172.
1:25000 **Pathfinder** sheets P737 (SJ08/18), P755 (SJ07/17), P772 (SJ06/16), P788 (SJ05/15), P789 (SJ25/35), P806 (SJ24/34), P827 (SJ23/33), P847 (SJ22/32), P868 (SJ21/31), P888 (SJ20/30), P909 (SO29/39), P930 (SO28/38), P950 (SO27/37), P971 (SO26/36), P993 (SO25/35), P1016 (SO24/34), P1039 (SO23/33), P1086 (SO21/31), P1087 (SO41/51), P1111 (SO40/50), P1131 (ST49/59) plus Outdoor Leisure Maps 13 Brecon Beacons (Eastern), 14 Wye Valley and Forest of Dean.
Footpath Guides
Kay, Ernie and **Kathy** and **Richards, Mark**, *Offa's Dyke Path*, Aurum Press in association with the **Countryside Commission** and the **Ordnance Survey**, 1989.
Kay, Kathy and **Ernie**, *Path Guide Notes; North–South* and *Path Guide Notes: South–North*. Both titles published by the Offa's Dyke Association, 1985.
Noble, Frank, *The Offa's Dyke Association Book of Offa's Dyke Path*, Offa's Dyke Association, 1981.
Offa's Dyke Path **Backpackers'** *Camping List* published annually by Offa's Dyke Association.
Offa's Dyke Path Accommodation and Transport List published annually by Offa's Dyke Association.
Richards, Mark, *Through Welsh Border Country Following Offa's Dyke*, Thornhill Press, 1985.
Wright, C. J., *A Guide to Offa's Dyke Path*, Constable, 1987.

Olmsted, Frederick Law (1822-1903) An influential American landscape architect from a farming background who designed Central Park, New York, the parks and parkways of Boston, Massachusetts, and open spaces in many parts of the **United States**. He was the author of *Walks and Talks of an American Farmer in England*, 1852 which is an account of a walking tour, undertaken with his brother and a friend to observe British farming practices, through Cheshire, north **Wales** and Shropshire, and illustrated with woodcuts

made from the author's sketches. Olmsted was an acute, intelligent observer with a keen eye for scenery who delighted in the beauty and freshness of the British countryside. '*There we were right in the midst of it! The country–and such country!–green, dripping, glistening, gorgeous! We stood dumb-stricken by its loveliness, as, from the bleak April and bare boughs we had left at home, broke upon us that English May–sunny, leafy, blooming May–in an English lane; with hedges, English hedges, hawthorn hedges, all in bloom; lovely old farm-houses, quaint stables, and haystacks; the old church spire over the distant trees; the mild sun beaming through the watery atmosphere, and all so quiet–the only sounds the hum of bees and the crisp, grass-tearing of a silken-skinned, real (unimported) Hereford cow over the hedge. No longer excited by daring to think we shall see it, as we discussed the scheme round the old home-fire; no longer cheering ourselves with it in the stupid, tedious ship; no more forgetful of it in the bewilderment of the busy town–but there we were; right in the midst of it; long-time silent, and then speaking softly, as it were enchantment indeed, we gazed upon it and breathed it–never to be forgotten!*'

Open country A term used to describe rough, uncultivated upland countryside beyond the limits of **enclosure**. There is no absolute right to wander at will in open country although in **Scotland** and Ireland, and in some parts of **England** and **Wales**, it is sanctioned by tradition subject to the interests of deer-stalking and grouse shooting. In England and Wales, some **access agreements** have been negotiated by such bodies as the **Countryside Commission** and **national parks**.

Open Spaces Society Formerly the **Commons**, Open Spaces and **Footpaths** Preservation Society, which was founded in 1865. The Society claims to be Britain's oldest national conservation body (the **Peak & Northern Footpaths Society** is more venerable but is a regional organisation) and campaigns for the protection of common land, town and village greens, and open spaces. In its early years, the Society prevented the **enclosure** of such important public spaces and commons as Epping Forest, Hampstead Heath and Wimbledon Common. In 1899 it absorbed the National Footpaths Preservation Society, and since that date has included the protection of **rights of way** within its remit. It also presses for **access** to all commons. Sir **Lawrence Chubb** was the secretary from 1896-1948. The Society publishes a journal *Open Space*. *(For address see Appendix.)*

Ordnance datum The term used to describe absolute sea level as used by the **Ordnance Survey**. The mean level of the sea was calculated at the Tidal Observatory, South Pier, Newlyn, Cornwall by an automatic tidal gauge from 1st May 1915 to 30th April 1921. All heights shown on **maps** issued by the Ordnance Survey, **triangulation stations**, and most **bench marks** are based on this calculation.

Ordnance Survey The government agency responsible for surveying Great Britain and producing official **maps**. Until 1921 it was also responsible for surveying the whole of Ireland, but there is now a separate organisation for Ulster, the **Ordnance Survey for Northern Ireland**. The Channel Islands are responsible for their own mapping. **Eire** assumed responsibility for its own maps when the Irish Free State was founded.

During the 1745 uprising, it was found that the Hanoverian troops were at a severe disadvantage because there were no reliable topographical maps of **Scotland**. After the defeat of the Highlanders, William Roy, a renowned surveyor, engineer and archaeologist, surveyed Scotland and produced a military map. The lack of suitable maps became apparent again during the Napoleonic era when Britain was threatened by invasion by **France**. In 1791 the Board of Ordnance, which was responsible for army engineering, surveyed part of the south coast and produced maps on an imperial **scale** of 1:63360 (1 inch to the mile). These proved so useful to the civilian authorities that the survey was gradually extended until, in 1841, the operation was put on a proper legal footing and civilian control by the passing of the Ordnance Survey Act. There was a great demand from the authorities responsible for roads, sewers etc for maps on a larger scale, and it was decided to introduce maps on an imperial scale of 1:10560 (6 inches to the mile), but this, too, proved inadequate. In 1863 it was decided to make the basic scales 1:500 (127 inches to the mile) for urban areas (this scale was effectively abandoned in 1893), 1:2500 (25 inches to the mile) for cultivated areas, and 1:10560 (6 inches to the mile) for **mountains** and **moorland**.

During the first part of this century, the Ordnance Survey was severely underfunded and unable to fulfil its proper functions. The Davidson Committee, set up to report on its future, produced a report in 1938 which was largely implemented in the post-war years.

These recommendations included the introduction of a metric **national grid**, a re-triangulation of the whole country (which resulted in the present **triangulation stations**), the introduction of a national projection rather than a county projection for the 1:2500 series, and most important of all for walkers, the introduction of a new medium scale map, the 1:25000 (2½ inches to the mile) which became the basis for the current **Pathfinder** and **Outdoor Leisure maps**. Subsequently the decision was taken for all maps to be totally metric. The old 1:63360 map series was withdrawn (although the **Tourist** series was retained), and replaced by the 1:50000 **Landranger** series. The Ordnance Survey now employs highly sophisticated mapping techniques including satellite and aerial surveys, and computers to store the survey data in digital form.

The Ordnance Survey (often affectionately and familiarly referred to as the OS) publishes a useful free catalogue and index of maps. *(For address see Appendix.)*

Bibliography
Harley, J. B.. *Ordnance Survey Maps; a Descriptive Manual*, Ordnance Survey, 1975.
Seymour, W. A., *A History of the Ordnance Survey*, Dawson, 1980.

Ordnance Survey for Northern Ireland
This is the government agency responsible for surveying and mapping Ulster. It was founded in 1921, when it separated from the **Ordnance Survey**, and it now has no connection with the British Ordnance Survey at Maybush, Southampton. The best **map** for walkers is the new 1:50000 series which covers **Northern Ireland** in eighteen sheets (although these maps show fewer tracks than the series they replace). Some of the third series' 1:63360 maps are still available but when stocks are exhausted they will not be reprinted. **Ordnance Survey for Northern Ireland** maps may be obtained from Edward Stanford Ltd. or in case of difficulty by post from the Belfast office. *(For addresses see Appendix.)*
Publications
1:63360, 1:50000, 1:25000 (part of Province only), 1:10560 and 1:10000 maps, together with various technical works.

Orienteering A sport combining running and **map-reading** skills developed in Sweden during the nineteen thirties, and now popular throughout the western world. Each contestant has to work out the quickest route from the

map, supplied by the organisers of the event, on which are located the checkpoints that have to be found. The skill lies in appreciating the nature of the terrain and deciding whether it is quicker to take the direct, probably difficult line, or use a longer, but easier and possibly faster route. Orienteering has had a considerable influence on the development of map-reading skills, and many of its concepts such as **aiming off** and **attack points** are now in everyday use by walkers.

Out O'Doors Fellowship A Manchester-based organisation that exemplified many of the attitudes found in the outdoor movement between the two World Wars. Its aims were *'To protect and preserve from ruthless destruction the wild flowers, trees and all wildlife; to prevent the desecration of ancient buildings; to keep the country free from litter; to discourage the erection of objectionable signs and hoardings in picturesque places; and to foster the spirit of good fellowship amongst all wayfarers.'* It published a journal, **Out O' Doors Magazine**, and claimed to have branches, that organised walks, potholing and mountaineering activities, in most large towns. The Fellowship ran a **map**-lending service and negotiated concessionary railway fares for walkers. The Fellowship seems to have been wound up in the late nineteen thirties.

Out of Doors Magazine A periodical that first appeared as *Out O' Doors* and was published from August 1927 as the journal of the **Out O' Doors Fellowship**. In July 1934, it merged with *Hiker and Camper*, but the title reappeared in 1945 as the *Out O' Doors Magazine* and was edited by **Tom Stephenson**. The post-war issues were mostly about walking and mountaineering, with excellent articles by famous contributors, but despite incorporating *The Countrygoer*, and making attempts to widen its appeal, it ceased publication in 1955.

Outdoor Action A monthly magazine published since its foundation in 1988 by Haymarket Publishing Ltd, covering many outdoor adventure activities but concentrating on walking and **backpacking**. It contains articles, news items, brief book reviews and tests equipment.

Outdoor Leisure maps These **Ordnance Survey** maps, which were introduced in 1972, cover the more popular walking areas of the country on a **scale** of 1:25000 in a much larger format than the **Pathfinder maps** on which they are based. Some sheets are totally metric, but a few are still using a survey based on imperial measures with **contours** at 25 feet intervals. They include tourist information such as the location of camping and caravan sites, information centres, viewpoints, golf courses, car parks, picnic sites, **youth hostels** and **mountain rescue** posts.

Outdoor Leisure **maps** are available for the following areas: OLM 1 The Peak District–Dark Peak area; OLM 2 Yorkshire Dales–Western area; OLM 3 Aviemore and the **Cairngorms**; OLM 4 The English Lakes–NW area; OLM 5 The English Lakes–NE area; OLM 6 The English Lakes–SW area; OLM 7 The English Lakes–SE area; OLM 8 The Cuillin and Torridon Hills; OLM 9 Brighton and Sussex Vale (now discontinued); OLM10 Yorkshire Dales–Southern area; OLM11 Brecon Beacons–Central area; OLM12 Brecon Beacons–Western area; OLM13 Brecon Beacons–Eastern area; OLM14 **Wye Valley** and the Forest of Dean; OLM15 Purbeck; OLM16 Snowdonia–Conwy Valley area; OLM17 Snowdonia–Snowdon area; OLM18 Snowdonia–Harlech and Bala areas; OLM20 **South Devon**; OLM21 South **Pennines**; OLM22 New Forest; OLM23 Snowdonia–Cadair Idris area; OLM24 The Peak District–White Peak area; OLM25 **Isles of Scilly**; OLM26 North York Moors–Western area; OLM27 North York Moors–Eastern area; OLM28 Dartmoor; OLM29 **Isle of Wight**; OLM30 Yorkshire Dales–Northern & Central; and OLM31 Teesdale; and OLM 32 Mountainmaster of Ben Nevis.

P

Pace counting A technique used in **navigation** for judging distance covered. Every serious walker should know how many paces (or, more conveniently, double-paces) it takes to cover 100 metres in different kinds of terrain and conditions. It is often used in conjunction with a **spiral search** or **sweep search** to locate a small object, such as a **tent**, in poor visibility.

Palmer, W[illiam] **T**[homas] A travel writer who also wrote about walking and camping. *The Art of Camping; Practical Hints for Pedestrian, Cyclist and Motorist on Equipment, Method, and Locality*, 1932 is a first class treatise on the sub-

ject and *The Complete **Hill Walker**, Rock Climber and Cave Explorer*, 1934 is a sound practical guide, and one of the best of its era.

Papoose carrier A device, similar to a **rucksack**, in which a small child may be carried. Papoose carriers should be of rugged construction, and the top of the frame, where the child's head may loll, should be well-padded. The best models are adjustable according to the size of the child, and have a head support. Small children of suitable temperament and old enough to support their heads, can be carried comfortably for several hours in a well-designed papoose carrier. They should be strapped in to prevent them falling out. Papoose carriers for town use are sold in chain stores, but anyone contemplating serious walking should purchase a model with a hip-belt marketed by a well-known gear-manufacturer such as Karrimor.

Papoose carrier—note the duffel bag strapped to the frame (photo © Hugh Westacott).

Pass Lower ground between two **mountains** that provides relatively easy passage from one valley to another. A pass is often called by its French name of 'col'.

Paterson, M. The author of *Mountaineering Below the Snow-line; or the Solitary Pedestrian in*

Snowdonia and Elsewhere, 1886 which is an account of his walks in **Scotland**, Norway and what is now the **Snowdonia National Park** and the **Lake District National Park**.

Path A generic term used to describe routes used by pedestrians and horse-riders that are not usually available to vehicular traffic. A path may be either private, permissive or public.

A *private path* is one which the general public do not have the right to use, although the landowner may grant permission for certain individuals or groups to use the route. Examples are the driveways of houses set in parkland that the owners expect postmen, tradesmen and anyone having business at the house to use, and private paths used by members of angling clubs to reach their fishing waters.

A *permissive path* is a route used by the general public with the permission of the landowner. Very often, the owner has no objection to anybody using the path and is only concerned to prevent it becoming a **right of way**. This he can do in **England** and **Wales** by erecting notices disclaiming its use as a right of way, or by closing the path on one day each year. In **Scotland**, it is probably necessary to close a permissive path more frequently to prevent it becoming a right of way.

A *public path* should more properly be referred to as a right of way, and is a route which the public may use for legitimate purposes without let or hindrance.

Pathfinder maps These superb **maps** published by the **Ordnance Survey** cover **England**, **Wales** and **Scotland** on a scale of 1:25000. They depict the countryside in great detail and are essential for walking in lowland, pastoral areas. Pathfinder maps have their origins in a 1:25000 series produced for military purposes. This was followed by the First Series (Provisional Edition), which was introduced in 1945 and completed in 1956, with revised sheets printed from 1950-65. In 1957, the First Series (Regular Edition) began to appear with sheets that covered an area measuring 10 kilometres by 10 kilometres. The Second Series was introduced in 1961, and these were renamed Pathfinder maps in 1982.

Each Pathfinder sheet covers an area measuring 20 kilometres by 10 kilometres, and shows **rights of way** (except in **Scotland**). The most important feature for navigating in lowland areas is the field boundary (hedge, wall or fence) which allows the walker to follow the true line of the **path** with great confidence, and to recognise immediately the field he or she is in. Oddly enough, there is no mention of field boundaries on the key to these maps. **Outdoor Leisure maps** are based on the Pathfinder series and cover popular walking areas in a much larger format.

Patten, Claudius B[uchanan] (1835-86) An American banker and the author of *England as Seen by an American Banker; Notes of a Pedestrian Tour*, 1885. This is a well-written account of his tour, full of acute observations, and also contains an essay on 'Walking as a Fine Art'.

Payn, James (1830-98) Journalist and prolific popular novelist whose first book *Leaves from Lakeland*, 1858 is a collection of stories about life in what is now the **Lake District National Park**. Three of the stories, 'Wastdale Head', 'Cragfast'; an 'Adventure in Langdale' and 'A Tremendous Ascent' (which describes a fictional walk over Fairfield and is a skit on some of the exploits of the early Alpine explorers) are about walking adventures. Payn also wrote *A Handbook to the English Lakes*, 1859 which could be used both by pedestrians as well as other tourists.

Peak and Northern Footpath Society The Society was founded in 1894 and took over the work of the **Manchester Association for the Preservation of Ancient Footpaths**, which had been founded in 1826, and thus claims to be the oldest extant conservation body in Britain. The Peak and Northern was established as a result of the threat to close the **right of way** along the Kinder Track from Hayfield to the Snake Inn. Other notable achievements include establishing the right of way up Grindsbrook from Edale to the Kinder plateau, and the re-opening of the Doctor's Gate and Alport - Westend **bridleways**, as well as preventing the closure of many other rights of way. The Society has erected and currently maintains 225 signposts, and regularly inspects rights of way within its area. *(For address see Appendix.)*

Peak-bagging The term used to describe the systematic collection of ascents of certain classes of **mountains**, **hills** and peaks which is a source of endless fascination to some walkers. The major categories are the **Munros**, **Corbetts**, **Donalds**, the **Four Thousands**, the **English Three Thousands**, the **Irish Three Thousands**, the **Welsh Three Thousands** and the **County Summits of the British Isles**. Note that all these categ-

ories, except the **County Summits of the British Isles** use imperial heights as they were devised long before the **Ordnance Survey** went metric. **Challenge walks** also have an element of competition. Information on how to ascend all peaks exceeding 3000 feet in the British Isles can be found in *The High Mountains of Britain and Ireland; a Guide for Mountain Walkers*, by **Irvine Butterfield**, Diadem, 1986.

Peak National Park The Peak **National Park** (formerly the Peak District National Park) was the first national park to be designated in Britain. It covers an area of 1404 square kilometres and is bordered by the towns of Huddersfield, Sheffield, Ashbourne and Stockport. The southern part of the park is largely limestone and known as the White Peak, whereas the northern section is millstone grit and referred to as the Dark Peak. The former is gentler, greener and more cultivated than the latter which is mountainous and contains a wilderness of **groughs** and **hags** which stretch for miles. **Kinder Scout** (637 metres) is the highest point and is a stern test for walkers. There are numerous caverns in the Castleton area which can be visited. Some villages still keep up the old custom of well-dressing, when the wells are decorated with flowers to illustrate a bible story. **Access agreements** have been negotiated with some landowners, although sections of these moors may be closed during the grouse-shooting season. Notices giving details of closures are posted. (See page figure 36 for a **map** showing the location of all national parks in United Kingdom.)

The growth of tourism and the interest in **picturesque** scenery that occurred at the end of the eighteenth century brought many visitors to the area which was, and is, often referred to as 'the Peak'. *(For addresses of National Park Headquarters and Information Centres see Appendix.)*

Official Guidebook
Smith, Roland, *The Peak*, Webb & Bower in association with Michael Joseph, 1987.
National Park Newspaper
The Peakland Post.
Maps
1:63360 **Tourist map** of the Peak District.
1:50000 **Landranger** sheets 109, 110, 118, 119.
1:25000 **Outdoor Leisure maps** of the Peak District 1 (Dark Peak), 24 (White Peak).
Footpath Guides

Duerden, Frank, *Best Walks in the Peak District*, Constable, 1988.
Hyde, George, *Circular Walks around Bakewell*, Dalesman, 1984.
Sanders, Norman, *A Walker's Guide to the Upper Derwent*, Peak National Park, 1984.
Richards, Mark, *High Peak Walks*, Cicerone Press, 1982.
Richards, Mark, *White Peak Walks*
    Vol 1: *Northern Dales*, Cicerone Press, 1985.
    Vol 2: *Southern Dales*, Cicerone Press, 1988.
Walks Around series compiled and published by the Peak National Park
    Six Walks around Tideswell Dale, 1984.
    Six Walks around Bakewell, 1986.
    Eight Walks around Edale, 1987.
    Walks around Longdendale, 1977.
    Six Walks around Hartington, 1987.
    Walks around Dovedale, 1987.

Peat A brownish-black material formed from vegetation decomposed by water. Peat is found mainly in the upland areas of Britain where it often forms very extensive bogs that will absorb vast quantities of water. When dried by the sun and wind, peat is powdery, springy underfoot and very pleasant to walk on, but when wet it is similar to very light mud, and is slippery and unpleasant. Peat can accumulate to a depth of several metres, but the bogs are never very deep, and despite Sir Arthur Conan Doyle's fictitious Grimpen Mires on what is now the **Dartmoor National Park**, are only dangerous in the event of a fall. In the deeper bogs it is possible for the feet to be trapped by a vacuum. Should this happen, the walker should calmly remove his **rucksack** and gently rock his feet until the vacuum is released. Resist the efforts of others to pull you free or you may lose your balance and end up with a broken leg. Peat, as it becomes fossilised, first forms lignite, and then coal.

Peddars Way and Norfolk Coast Path A **national trail** devised by the **Countryside Commission** and officially opened in 1986. It runs for 143 kilometres from Knettishall Heath (**grid reference** TM 944807), near Thetford through Norfolk to Holme-next-the-Sea, and then east along the coast to Cromer (grid reference TG 215420). There is also a south-west spur that leads from Holme-next-the-Sea to Hunstanton. The terrain is very flat, making for fast, easy walking through pleasant, atmospheric countryside following, for the first half of the route, a Roman road. This route makes an ideal introduction to the pleasures of long-distance walking. (See figure 36 for a map showing the location of all national trails and official **long-distance paths** in the United Kingdom.)

Path Association
The Peddar's Way Association.

Youth Hostels
Brandon, Castle Acre, Hunstanton and Sheringham.

Maps
1:50000 **Landranger** sheets 132, 133, 144.
1:25000 **Pathfinder** sheets P818 (TF64/74), P819 (TF84/94), P820 (TG04/14), P839 (TF63/73), P842 (TG23/33), P859 (TF62/72), P880 (TF61/71), P881 (TF81/91), P901 (TF80/90), P922 (TL89/99), P943 (TL88/99).

Footpath Guides
Kennett, David, *A Guide to the Norfolk Way*, Constable, 1983.
Robinson, Bruce, *The Peddars Way and Norfolk Coast Path*, HMSO, 1986.
The Peddars Way and Norfolk Coast Path; a Guide and Accommodation List for Walking the Peddars Way and Norfolk Coast Path with the Weavers' Way, compiled and published by the Peddars Way Association, 1988.

Peddars Way Association This Association was founded in 1981 to promote and publicise the **Peddars Way and Norfolk Coast Path**. The Association publishes a newssheet and a guide to the route *The Peddars Way and Norfolk Coast Path; a Guide and Accommodation List for Walking the Peddars Way and Norfolk Coast Path with the Weavers' Way*, 1988. *(For address see Appendix.)*

'Pedestres' The pseudonymous author of *A Pedestrian Tour of Thirteen Hundred and Forty-seven Miles through* **Wales** *and* **England** by 'Pedestres' and Sir Clavileno Woodenpeg, Knight of Snowdon, 1836. This extraordinary book purports to be the account of a walking tour from Sidmouth, Devon via Exeter, Bristol, around the Welsh coast to Liverpool, and on to Manchester and Bristol. The travellers mainly kept to roads but managed to climb Snowdon in bad weather. The work appears to be a pastiche of *Don Quixote* (eg Clavileno Woodenpeg was knighted when he saved his master in a drunken brawl in Snowdonia). The dedication gives a flavour of the book *'To all petty walkers in go-carts as well as mighty pedestrians on their own hind-legs, who are able to declare themselves such by having accomplished either a cockstride in the one case, or a seven-league pace of Peter Schlemihl in the other* [Peter Schlemihl was a character in Adalbert von Chamisso's ballad, written in 1814, who sold his shadow to the devil, and

the term is applied to anyone who makes a foolish bargain]; - *and with hearty wishes for the prosperity of St Crispin* [the patron saint of shoemakers], *and plenty of tough* **shoe**-*leather, this tour is respectfully dedicated by the author'*. 'Pedestres' carried in his **knapsack** a sketch book, *Romeo and Juliet*, - *'for whom would be so crazy as to think of roaming sentimentally among* **mountains**, *without a volume of Shakespeare?'* and a wry-necked flute *'to beguile the length of a solitary hour on some lofty crag . . .'*

It is possible that the author was Peter Orlando Hutchinson (1810-97), antiquarian artist, diarist and historian of Sidmouth, Devon, who is known to have undertaken a 1991-kilometre walking tour in 1833. Extracts from his journal describing this walk exist in manuscript at the Devon County Record Office.

'Pedestrian' The unimaginative pseudonym, sometimes 'A Pedestrian', sometimes 'The Pedestrian' adopted by the authors of several accounts of walking tours. **John Aiton** used the pseudonym 'The Pedestrian', and **Count Armand Bon-Louis Maudet de Penhouet** wrote under the sobriquet 'A Pedestrian Traveller'.

A Guide to the Lakes of Killarney and the South of Ireland by 'A Pedestrian', 1838. According to the author the tour took place in 1837. *'The plan I adopted was to sling a haversack on my back and cross the country at my leisure; and either foot it, or ride, as my inclination may prompt me'*. It is a prosaic account of things to be seen, and although he travelled much on foot, he does not mention whether he enjoyed it. To modern readers, though probably not to his contemporaries, the book will appear to be violently anti-catholic. The writer despises Irish peasants whom he regards as ignorant, dirty, lazy, and the authors of their own poverty and misfortunes, and seems to have no conception of the villainies inflicted on the country by successive British parliaments. Protestants, on the other hand, are thrifty, hard-working and wholly admirable. The best thing in the book is the description of his journey by canal boat from Shannon Harbour to Dublin.

The Highlands of **Scotland** by 'A Pedestrian', 1843 (the British Library copy of this work has 'C. S. Bell' written in manuscript on the title page, which suggests that this may be the name of the author). A second edition under the title *A Six Week's Tour in the Highlands of Scotland* was issued in 1851. This is an engaging account of a walk from Edinburgh

embracing much of the **Central Highlands**, **Southern Highlands** and **Western Highlands** (Inverness was the most northerly point reached). He climbed Ben Lomond, but bad weather prevented his ascending Ben Nevis. It seems that the Scots were, at that early date, deeply involved in the tourist industry, and the book gives the impression that there were many walkers and visitors to the Highlands. The author has a pointed pen and is frequently critical of the cupidity of some of those he met, especially the elderly lady who claimed to be a descendant of Rob Roy, and charged sixpence per head to view the musket he was alleged to have owned.

Hints to Pedestrians on how to Enjoy a Week's Ramble through North and South **Wales** *and along the Banks of the Wye* by 'A Pedestrian', 1837. The first section of the book gives instructions on how to set about a walking tour. The author recommends for a month or two's march *'a light* **knapsack**, *a valise with two or three shirts, about four pairs of* **stockings**, *the absolute necessities for the toilet, a little writing paper, a good* **map** *(Walker's is the best), and a small pocket* **compass**.' The pedestrian is advised to wear stout wellfitting cloth **boots**, to carry an oaken walking stick, *'and above all, to have a stock of affability and good nature.'* The feet should be bathed daily with rum and then candle-grease should be rubbed into the skin. He remarks that he does not regard himself as a good pedestrian and therefore restricts his walking to twenty-five miles (forty kilometres) per day for a week. Then follows a detailed description of his tour following roads together with a mileage chart, a list of interesting objects and details of coaches. He recommends engaging guides for the ascent of Snowdon at the Royal Victoria Hotel on the Pass of Llanberis.

A Peep at the **Pyrénées**; *being a Tourist's Notebook with a Map* by 'A Pedestrian', 1867. *'This little book is compiled from notes taken during a walk through some portions of the Pyrénées in the early part of last summer. . . but it is, as its title implies, merely a record of a short* **ramble** *through some of the prettier and more interesting spots in and around the Pyrenean district . . . I am a pedestrian in the fullest sense of the word. My knapsack, when full, weighs about 10 lbs, and my kit is composed as follows: an Oxford shooting coat, tweed trousers and vest, a light-coloured alpaca coat, a pair of flannel trousers, two flannel shirts, a night-shirt, two pairs of woollen* **socks**, *collars, a few small stores, and a light pair of* **shoes**, *besides my clumped boots. The knapsack is waterproof, and provided with a wicker frame to keep it well off the back . . . I do not carry a water-*

proof, as on a walking tour it is of very little service, and I always have some dry **clothing** *in my knapsack . . .*' The book is a pleasant mixture of detailed directions and accounts of his small adventures which includes an attempted crossing of the Breche, which was thwarted by deep snow and the reluctance of the guide to continue for fear of losing his guiding licence. The author often used **footpaths** although the small-scale map only depicts the roads he followed.

Rambles and *Remarks on the Borders of Surry and Kent*, by 'A Pedestrian', 1833. An early guide for walkers covering Southwark, Rotherhithe, Deptford, Greenwich, Blackheath and Shooter's Hill, much of which is now completely urbanised. '*It is a common complaint with persons residing in London, that the environs of the metropolis are now so built over, that it is a difficult matter to find a country-walk without being tired out previous to arriving at it. I am happy to have it in my power, in one instance at least, to point out a walk which is acknowledged to possess all the requisites that render a country-walk exhilarating, and that within the short distance of one mile and a half from the Surry side of London Bridge. I dare say some of my readers will smile, when I inform them that it is to be found in Bermondsey, a parish but little known to most persons, except for its taverns and glue makers; neverthelesss, there is a country walk, and that a delightful one for at least three parts of the year. . .*' A description of that route and several others follows.

Recollections of a Pedestrian by 'Pedestrian', 3 Vols, 1826. This unusual, well-written book reads like a cross between a three-decker picaresque novel and a travelogue. The author, an Englishman in straitened circumstances, walked from Toulon, via Lyons and Paris to Calais, where he took ship to Dover. On the way he had a series of extraordinary adventures, and had the happy knack of encountering characters who were prepared to relate their life-stories at length. One army officer he met at Lyons gave him a graphic and exciting account of the Revolution in Lyons in 1792, including a vivid and sickening description of a prisoner being broken on the wheel. I am inclined to believe that the author made the walk but that he embellished his adventures.

A Tour on the Banks of the Thames from London to Oxford by 'A Pedestrian', 1834 (the British Library copy has 'A. Walton' written in manuscript on the dedication page which suggests that this may be the name of the author). This is a walker's guidebook to the Thames towpath that describes the route in some detail giving instructions on which bridges to cross,

what ferries to use, as well as much information about the sights along the way (Fulham is described as a village!). This is an early version of the **Thames Path**.

Pedestrianism A curious byway in the history of walking, and the forerunner of the modern competitive sport of road-walking, that had a great vogue in the eighteenth and early nineteenth centuries. Pedestrianism took various forms ranging from city to city walks (eg London to York) or covering certain standard distances against the clock (eg 5 miles, 10 miles, 25 miles, 50 miles, 100 miles and 1000 miles) or such feats as walking 1000 miles in 1000 consecutive hours (ie the competitor had to walk only one mile in each and every hour and could rest for the remainder of that hour). It should be noted that 1000 hours is 41 days and 16 hours. The events were not races in the accepted sense because there was normally only one competitor, who usually undertook the task for a fee or wager, and the excitement for the public lay in betting on whether he could achieve his objective. The most famous 'peds', as they were popularly known, were **Foster Powell**, **Captain Barclay** and **Richard Manks**.

The best source of information about pedestrianism is William Thom's *Pedestrianism, or an Account of the Performances of Celebrated Pedestrians during the Past and Present Century; with a Full Narrative of Captain Barclay's Public and Private Matches; and an Essay on Training* published in 1813, which was written '*to encourage the nobility to make soldiers fitter*'. It also contains brief details of other walking exploits but without citing authorities for the information.

The sport was also popular in the **United States** where the challenges sometimes took a slightly different form which usually involved walking specific distances against the clock. One of the best-known exponents was **James Kennovan**.

Pedometer An instrument for measuring the distance covered by walkers and runners. Pedometers are usually attached to the belt or strapped to the ankle, and a bob-weight inside counts the number of strides which are then converted mechanically or electronically onto a dial, scale or display that gives an indication of the distance covered. For maximum accuracy, it is important for the user to know the exact length of his stride which should be calculated by counting the number of paces (or double-paces divided by two) over a measured distance of several kilometres in undulating

country. It should be noted that the length of an individual's stride varies according to speed, slope, terrain and conditions underfoot, and to use a pedometer properly, accurate records of number of paces and distance covered in differing kinds of country must be kept. Most pedometers are not reliable over short distances, but when used by an expert they can give an acceptably accurate result over several kilometres.

Pedometers date from the eighteenth century. Early examples had the bob-weight operated by a cord attached to the foot. The first British patent was taken out by William Payne in 1831.

Pembrokeshire Coast National Park The Pembrokeshire Coast **National Park** is the smallest in Britain covering an area of only 583 square kilometres. It is quite different in character from the other national parks in that it has only one small tract of **moorland**, in the Preseli Hills. Its chief glory and attraction is its large area of magnificent, unspoiled coastal scenery. There are many prehistoric remains in the park and a surprisingly large number of medieval castles. (See figure 36 for a **map** showing the location of all national parks in the United Kingdom.) *(For Addresses of National Park Headquarters and Information Centres see Appendix.)*
Official Guidebook
Williams, Herbert, *Pembrokeshire Coast*, Webb & Bower in association with Michael Joseph, 1987.
National Park Newspaper
Coast to Coast.
Maps
1:50000 **Landranger** sheets 145, 157, 158.
1:25000 **Pathfinder** sheets P1010 (SN04/14), P1032 (SM83/93), P1033 (SN03/13), P1055 (SM62/72), P1057 (SN02/12), P1079 (SM81/91), P1080 (SN01/11), P1102 (SM70), P1103 (SM80/90), P1104 (SN00/10), P1124 (SR89/99), P1125 (SS09/19).
Footpath Guides
Thomas, Roger, *Great Walks; Brecon Beacons and Pembrokeshire Coast*, Ward Lock, 1989.
Walks leaflets compiled and published by the National Park
Carew Jubilee Walk.
Deer Park and Marloes.
Ffos y Mynach.
Goodwick-Carreg Wasted
Gwaun Valley Woodland Walk.
St David's to Caerfai.
Stackpole Lakes.

Upton Castle Grounds.
Walk around Carew.
Walk around St David's Head.

Pembrokeshire Coast Path A **national trail** developed by the **Countryside Commission** and officially opened in 1970. It runs for 292 kilometres from Amroth (**grid reference** SS 168071) through Dyfed along cliffs, beaches and dunes to St Dogmaels (grid reference SN 163469). The scenery is very beautiful and largely unspoiled, but it is quite strenuous walking in parts. Accommodation is plentiful, but likely to be full at peak holiday times, so booking is essential. There are plenty of camp sites, and there should be no difficulty in obtaining water. During the summer, there is a special Coast **Path** bus service which links all the coastal car parks from Dale to Newgale. The Countryside Commission has issued a consultation paper proposing that the route should be extended by 97 kilometres to include the Daugleddau estuary around Milford Haven. (See figure 36 for a **map** showing the location of all national trails and official **long-distance paths** in the United Kingdom.)

Youth Hostels
Poppit Sands, Pwll Deri, Trevine and St David's. Broad Haven, Marloes Sands, Manorbier, Pentlepoir.

Maps
1:50000 **Landranger** sheets 145, 157, 158.
1:25000 **Pathfinder** sheets P1010 (SN04/14), P1032 (SM83/93), P1033 (SN03/13), P1055 (SM62/72), P1056 (SM82/92), P1079 (SM81/91), P1102 (SM70), P1103 (SM80/90), P1104 (SN00/10), P1124 (SR89/99), P1125 (SS09/19).

Footpath Guides
John, Brian, *Pembrokeshire Coast Path*, Aurum Press in association with the Countryside Commission and the **Ordnance Survey**, 1989.
Merrill, John, *Pembrokeshire Coast Path*, JNM Publications, 1990.
Accommodation list available from the Pembrokeshire Coast **National Park** Office *(for address see Appendix)*.

Penhouet, Count Armand Bon-Louis Maudet de (1764-1839) French naval officer, archaeologist, and author of the psuedonymous *Letters Describing a Tour through Part of South Wales; with Views Designed and Etched by the Author* by 'A Pedestrian Traveller', 1797. The tour took place from 4th to 27th June 1797 during the year he spent in Britain trying to muster support for the French royalist cause. The letters are addressed to a lady, probably

his wife as he was newly married. The tour was undertaken as a sketching holiday to satisfy the author's antiquarian interest in castles, but it can also be read as a fascinating account of the towns and scenery of south Wales before the beautiful scenery of the Rhondda was ruined by coal-mining and iron and steel-making.

Pennell, Elizabeth (1855-1936) and **Joseph** (1857-1926) An American couple who spent much of their lives in **England**, and were on intimate terms with George Bernard Shaw and other literary and artistic figures. Joseph was an artist, and Elizabeth a writer and biographer of James McNeill Whistler. They were enthusiastic walkers and cyclists and wrote an account of a walking tour in **Scotland** entitled *Our Journey to the Hebrides*, 1889. Elizabeth also wrote the biography of her husband *The Life and Letters of Joseph Pennell*, 1929.

Pennine Way A **national trail** developed by the **Countryside Commission** and officially opened in 1965. The Pennine Way was conceived and promoted by **Tom Stephenson**, and is unquestionably the most famous of the British **long-distance paths**. It is also one of the roughest and toughest, and is suitable only for experienced **fell-walkers**, as the weather is frequently atrocious and there are extensive **peat** bogs. It runs for 402 kilometres from Edale (**grid reference** SK 125858), in the **Peak National Park** to Kirk Yetholm (grid reference NT 827282), just over the border in **Scotland**, along the top of the **Pennines** through some of the wildest scenery in **England**. One of the fascinations of the Pennine Way is the numerous evidence of old mine workings, **drove roads** and Roman roads. There are magnificent waterfalls, huge limestone cliffs, and for the naturalist, sub-alpine flora.

There is a fair amount of bed and breakfast accommodation along the Pennine Way but also some long stretches with no towns or villages. Probably the most satisfactory method is to camp, because there is never any shortage of drinking water, and there are many suitable camp sites on the **fells**.

Trans Pennine Transport *(for address see Appendix)* run a daily summer minibus service for Pennine **wayfarers**, and will transport walkers and collect and deliver unaccompanied luggage between **youth hostels**, bed and breakfast accommodation, and camp sites. (See figure 36 for a **map** showing the location of all national trails and official long-distance

paths in the United Kingdom.)
Path Association
Pennine Way Council.
Youth Hostels
Edale, Crowden, Mankinholes, Haworth, Earby, Malham, Stainforth, Dentdale, Hawes, Keld, Baldersdale, Langdon Beck, Dufton, Alston, Greenhead, Once Brewed, Bellingham, Byrness, and Kirk Yetholm.
Maps
1:50000 **Landranger** sheets 74, 75, 80, 86, 97, 91, 92, 98, 103, 109, 110.
1:25000 **Pathfinder** sheets P486 (NT61/71), P487 (NT81/91), P475 (NT82/92), P498 (NT60/70), P509 (NY69/79), P510 (NY89/99), P522 (NY88/98), P533 (NY67/77), P534 (NY87/97), P546 (NY66/76), P559 (NY65/75), P569 (NY64/74), P661 (SD85/95), P670 (SD84/94), P701 (SD81/91), P702 (SE01/11), P714 (SE00/10) plus **Outdoor Leisure maps** 1 The Peak District (Dark Peak), 2 Yorkshire Dales (Western area), 10 Yorkshire Dales (Southern area), 30 Yorkshire Dales (Northern & Central), 31 Teesdale.
Footpath Guides
Hardy, Graeme, *North to South along the Pennine Way*, Warne Gerrard, 1983.
Hopkins, Tony, *Pennine Way North*, Aurum Press in association with the Countryside Commission and the **Ordnance Survey**, 1989.
Hopkins, Tony, *Pennine Way South*, Aurum Press in association with the Countryside Commission and the Ordnance Survey, 1989.
The Pennine Way: Map and Guide, 2 vols, Footprint, 1988.
Vol. 1: *Edale to Teesdale*.
Vol. 2: *Teesdale to Kirk Yetholm*.
Wainwright, A., *The Pennine Way Companion*, Westmorland Gazette, 1968. (NB this is the classic guide to the route but it is now very out of date and must be used with caution.)
Wright, C. J., *A Guide to the Pennine Way*, Constable, 1983.

Pennine Way Council The Council was founded in 1970 and exists to secure the protection of the **Pennine Way**; to provide information about the Way to the public; to educate users of the Way and its environs in a proper respect for the countryside; to assist in the organisation of voluntary efforts directed at the maintenance of the Way and to provide a forum in which different interests connected with the Way and its use can discuss problems of mutual concern. The Council publishes a newsletter and *The Pennine Way Accommodation and Camping Guide. (For address see Appendix.)*

113

Pennines A range of carboniferous limestone and millstone grit **moorland** hills that run from the northern tip of the midland plain to the Tyne gap. Many summits exceed 600 metres in height, and the Pennines are often described as 'the backbone of **England**'.

The name 'Pennines' has a curious history. Attempts have been made to associate it with the Celtic 'pen' meaning '**hill**', but this cannot be correct because the name is not recorded before the middle of the eighteenth century. Charles Julius Bertram (1723-65), who was Professor of English at Copenhagen University, claimed to have discovered a medieval chronicle entitled *De Statu Britanniae*, supposedly written by a monk named Richard of Cirencester, describing Britain in Roman times and stating that Britain was divided into two by the 'Alps Penina'. Before the manuscript was proved to be a forgery, two early geologists, William Conybeare and William Phillips, quoted from the spurious document and used the term 'Penine Chain' in *Outlines of the Geology of England and **Wales*** published in 1822. It was useful for such an important range to be identified, and the name stuck with addition of another 'n'.

The **Pennine Way** takes its name from the range which it follows for part of its route between Edale and Lambley.

Permissive path A **path** that is not a public **right of way** but one that the public may use. In **England** and **Wales**, the use of permissive paths is usually negotiated between landowners, local authorities and **national parks**. Permissive paths may be closed at the discretion of the landowner to suit his convenience, but sometimes it is only done symbolically on one day each year to demonstrate that the path is not dedicated to public use.

Pern, Stephen (1950-) The author of two well-written and unusually perceptive accounts of long walks through Africa. *Another Island, Another Sea* is the story of his 600-kilometre circuit of Lake Rudolph in Kenya in which he carried his gear on pack animals. *The Beach of Morning; a Walk in West Africa*, Hodder & Stoughton, 1983 is an account of his walk from the Sahara to the Atlantic which was cut short by serious illness. He also wrote *The Great Divide*, Phoenix House, 1987 which is an account of his walk along the Continental Divide of the **United States**, although he did not follow the **long-distance path** of that name. He contributed an essay to *Walking in Britain* by **John Hillaby**, Collins, 1988.

Pertex A closely woven, non-waterproof **nylon** material manufactured by ICI which disperses water by capillary action. It is used for lightweight towels, clothing, **sleeping bag** covers and lining fabrics.

Petulengro, Gypsy [Xavier] He claimed to be the grandson of the Gypsy Petulengro immortalised by **George Borrow**. He wrote *Romany Hints for **Hikers***, 1936 which is a silly manual, supposedly based on Romany lore, but in reality cashing in on some of the slightly spurious attitudes of the open air movement of the thirties.

Philpott, Don (1946-) Journalist, writer about food and drink, correspondent and contributor to several outdoor magazines, and co-founder and contributing editor to ***Footloose***. He was also the co-founder and Chairman of the **Outdoor Writers' Guild**.
Publications about Walking
*The Visitor's Guide to **Iceland***, Moorland Publishing Co., 2nd Ed., 1989.
*Off the Beaten Track; **France***, Moorland Publishing Co., 1988.

The Picturesque A theory of landscape appreciation, both of scenery and in paintings, that was popular in the late eighteenth and early nineteenth centuries. According to **William Gilpin**, who was its leading exponent, a landscape was picturesque if it contained ruins, curious details and interesting textures.

Picturesque scenes were to be preferred over the merely beautiful (ie serene) and the sublime (ie awe-inspiring and on a vast scale). It became the rage for pedestrian travellers and other tourists to seek out picturesque scenes, and William Gilpin wrote a series of influential and popular guidebooks describing picturesque tours that had many imitators. Some writers even went so far as to describe in detail the viewpoint, called a 'station', from which the picturesque scene could best be observed. The theory of the picturesque had a considerable influence on the **romantic movement** in English literature, and on travel generally.

Piggin, [James] **Ken**[neth Edward] (1923-) A retired British Rail engineer, sometime proprietor of Milestone Walking Holidays, and now proprietor of Leisure Books *(for address see Appendix)*, a company based in York specialising in the sale of **maps** and guides. He is best known for his **footpath guides**, and especially for the number of **long-distance paths** that he has devised in northern **England**.
Publications about Walking
The Ebor Way, Dalesman, 1978.
The Yoredale Way, Dalesman, 1980.
Countryside Walks around York, Dalesman, 1982.
The Nidderdale Way, Dalesman, 1983.
The Weardale Way, Dalesman, 1984.
Drive and Walk; Swaledale and Wensleydale, Jarrold, 1987.

A 'picturesque' view of the Lake District.

Walking in 'Pie Country'; 10 Walks around Denby Dale plus a 50 mile Walk - the Denby Way, Leisure Books, 1989.

Pike A term used especially in Lancashire and the **Lake District National Park** to describe a **mountain** or peak with a pronounced pointed summit. Well-known examples are Scafell Pike, Dollywagon Pike, Pike of Blisco, Pike of Stickle, and Stoodley Pike.

Pilgrims' Way A prehistoric **trackway** that runs from Canterbury in Kent to Guildford in Surrey, where it joins the Harroway and continues to Stonehenge in Wiltshire. It gets its name from the popular theory that it was the route used by medieval pilgrims travelling between the shrines of St Swithin, Winchester and St Thomas à Becket in Canterbury. The theory was promulgated by the Very Reverend Arthur Penrhyn Stanley (1815-81), the famous Dean of Westminster, and later by Julia Cartwright (Mrs Henry Ady c 1860-1924) who published a description of the route in *The Pilgrims' Way*, 1893. That incurable romantic **Hilaire Belloc** walked the route and published *The Old Road* (1904) which further popularised the theory, and in 1905 Frank C[harles] Elliston-Erwood wrote *The Pilgrims' Road; a Practical Guide for Pedestrians on the Ancient Way from Winchester to Canterbury* which was the first **footpath guide** to the route.

There is little firm evidence that the route was used to any great extent by pilgrims. The name 'Pilgrims' Way' first occurs in the eighteenth century, and as C. G. Crump argued in an article in Volume XXI of *History*, it is more likely that most travellers either took the slightly longer route via London, which afforded better roads and gave them the opportunity of seeing the capital, or went by sea from Southampton to Dover. Quite long sections of the Pilgrims' Way are incorporated into the **North Downs Way**.

Pilling A condition that afflicts some **fibre-pile** clothing in which the 'fur' contracts into little balls.

Platten, David [George Martin] (1947-) Outdoor pursuits instructor, director of Bivvybug Designs *(for address see Appendix)* which manufactures and markets innovative **backpacking** equipment, and outdoor journalist.
Publications about Walking
Outdoor Survival Handbook; for Campers, Hikers and **Backpackers**, David & Charles, 1979.

Making Camping and Outdoor Gear; a Practical Guide to Design and Construction, David & Charles, 1981.

Ploughing The practice of turning the soil before sowing by making deep furrows. One of the greatest difficulties faced by walkers using **rights of way** is caused by **paths** being ploughed. It is usually illegal to plough a right of way without restoring the surface of the path. In **England** and **Wales**, under section 134 of the **Highways Act, 1980** as amended by section 61 of the **Wildlife and Countryside Act, 1981** a **farmer** may, in the interests of good husbandry, plough **footpaths** and **bridleways** (except most **headland paths**), but not paths with vehicular rights over them. The surface must be made good within two weeks of ploughing or, if the weather makes that impossible, as soon as practicable. In certain circumstances, farmers may have a common law right to plough headland paths, but if this is not recorded in the statement accompanying the **definitive map**, then the onus of proof of that right lies with the farmer. **Highway** authorities, district and local councils have the right to prosecute farmers who fail to restore the surface of the path, or do the job themselves and charge the cost to the offender.

The law on ploughing and **obstruction** has been strengthened by the passing of the Rights of Way Act, 1990. This requires the surface of any path that has been disturbed (eg by ploughing or harrowing) to be made good for the reasonable convenience of users. Cross-field footpaths must be at least 1 metre wide: cross-field bridleways must bge at least 2 metres wide: headland footpaths must be at least 1.5 metres wide: and headland bridleways at least 3 metres wide. Crops, with the exception of grass, must be prevented from growing or falling over the line of the path. Local authorities have ghe right to restore the line of the path after giving the landowner 24 hours notice and to charge him for any costs incurred. Prosecutions against offenders may be instigated by local authorities and by members of the public.

In **Scotland**, section 43 of the **Countryside (Scotland) Act, 1967** permits a landowner to plough a right of way for agricultural purposes, providing that he gives notice to the planning authority beforehand, and reinstates the surface of the path. The common law allows the public to continue to use a right of way that has been ploughed.

Poland Walking is very popular in Poland, especially among young people, and there are 36000 kilometres of public **paths**. Main routes are waymarked in red and connecting routes in black, and there are notices at the beginning of each route describing the degree of difficulty. 524 kilometres of the 2717-kilometre International Friendship Route which runs from Eisenbach, East Germany to Budapest, Hungary passes through Poland. The best walking areas are the Tatra **Mountains** in the south and the Carpathian Mountains.
Useful Addresses
Polorbis Travel Ltd, 82 Mortimer Street, Regent Street, London W1N 7DE. Tel. 071-636-2217.
Ramblers' Organisation: PTTK (Polish Tourist and Country-lovers' Association), Śenatorska str., Warszawa 11.

(NB this organisation deals with tourism in general, including walking, and maintains mountain refuges and hostels). The section dealing with visitors from overseas, and which also organises walking tours, is PTTK (Foreign Tourist Office), Świeçtokrzyska 36, 00-116 Warszawa.
National **Map** *Survey:* PPWK (State Office of Cartography) publishes maps showing **footpaths** on **scales** varying from 1:37500 to 1:75000. These are readily available in local bookshops and have the key printed in Polish, Russian, German and English.

Polycotton A mixture of **polyester** and **cotton**, used in varying proportions, woven to make a material that has the pleasant feel of cotton, but which absorbs less water and dries more quickly. Polycotton can be made water repellent by coating with silicones, or by applying one of the proprietary waterproofing agents such as Technix. It is used for jackets, shirts, shorts and lightweight **breeches**.

Polypropylene A synthetic fibre, used in underwear and midwear, that **wicks** water away from the skin (**vapour transmission**). It needs frequent washing to prevent it becoming smelly and contaminated by body salts.

Polytechnic Rambling Club Second only to the **Forest Ramblers** in age, this venerable club was founded in 1885 by W. K. Davis under the auspices of the Christian Workers' Union. Members are restricted to those who also belong to the Polytechnic Institute, Regent Street, London. For many years membership was confined to men with **rambles** conducted on a Saturday afternoon. In 1910, the Polytechnic Ladies' Cycling Club was formed which arranged rambles as well as cycle rides. This organisation changed its name to the Polytechnic Cycling and Rambling Club, and later to the Ladies' Rambling Club. During the Second World War, the ladies section took over the running of both clubs until, in 1946, the men's section was re-formed, but it was not until 1955 that the two clubs amalgamated. The Polytechnic Rambling club was one of the founder members of the **Federation of Rambling Clubs**. *(For address see Appendix.)*

Polyurethane A waterproof coating which can be applied to **nylon** for use in shell **clothing**. It comes in two versions **hydrophyllic** and non-breathable. The latter type prevents **moisture vapour transmission** which makes **condensation** inevitable.

Poromeric fabrics Also known as microporous fabrics, poromeric fabrics are waterproof materials (eg **Aquatex**, **Cyclone**, **Entrant** and **Gore-Tex**) that prevent or reduce **condensation** by applying the principle that a molecule of *liquid water* is twenty thousand times larger than a molecule of *water vapour*. Water vapour given off by the body passes through tiny pores in the material that are too small to allow rain to penetrate. Poromeric fabrics must be kept clean to prevent the tiny pores becoming clogged.

Portugal Although part of the Iberian peninsula, Portugal is quite distinct, both culturally and scenically, from its larger neighbour, **Spain**. The backbone of the country is formed by the Beira Alta which form the divide between the two major valleys of the Douro and the Tagus. The landscape is well-wooded with lush green valleys.
Useful Addresses
Portuguese Tourist Office, New Bond Street House, 1 New Bond Street, London W1Y 0NP. Tel. 071-493-3873.
*National **Map** Survey:* Instito Geografico e Cadastral, Lisbon.
Official Survey Maps: Carta Corografica de Portugal 1:50000 (covers the whole country and shows **footpaths**).

Poucher, W[illiam] **A**[rthur] (1891-1988) Known to his intimates as Walter, Poucher was a climber, hill-walker, **mountaineer**, landscape photographer, and author of numerous articles and guidebooks. He walked and climbed extensively in the British Isles, the **Alps**, the **Rocky Mountains**, and the

William Poucher, photographer and author of numerous articles and guidebooks (photo © Constable & Co).

western states of the **United States**. He is best-known in walking circles for his series of guidebooks, published by Constable, in which he shows **mountain** routes by superimposing the line of the **path** on a photograph. Like many Constable guides his books use 100000 Bartholomew **maps** that are sometimes enlarged.
Publications about Walking
The Lakeland Peaks; a Pictorial Guide to Walking in the Region and to the Safe Ascent of its Principal Mountain Peaks, Constable, 8th Ed., 1981.
*The Peak and **Pennines**; a Pictorial Guide to Walking in the Region and to the Safe Ascent of its **Hills** and Moors*, Constable, 5th Ed., 1981.
The Welsh Peaks; a Pictorial Guide to Walking in the District and to the Safe Ascent of its Principal Mountain Groups, Constable, 8th Ed., 1983.
The Scottish Peaks: a Pictorial Guide to Walking in the District and to the Safe Ascent of its most Spectacular Mountains, Constable, 5th Ed., 1979.

Powell, Foster (1734-93) An attorney's clerk who was one of the most famous exponents of **pedestrianism**. His first recorded effort was to walk 50 miles (80 kilometres) on the Bath Road in 7 hours, covering 16 kilometres in the first hour. In 1773, he first achieved fame by walking from London to York and back again, a distance of 647 kilometres in 5 days and $15\frac{1}{4}$ hours, a feat that he repeated twice more. In 1786, he walked 100 miles (160

kilometres) in $23\frac{1}{4}$ hours on the Bath Road, and the following year he walked the 179 kilometres from London Bridge to Canterbury and back in 24 hours. An account of his exploits may be found in *Short Sketch of the Life of Mr Foster Powell*, 1793.

Proctor, Alan (1931-) Climber, walker and author of several guides to **long-distance paths** for which he devised some of the routes himself. He works with the disabled, underprivileged and with the probation service to introduce youngsters to outdoor pursuits, and leads walking parties in the Austrian **Alps**.
Publications about Walking
The Wessex Way, Thornhill Press, 1980.
A Severn to Solent Walk, Thornhill Press, 1981.
*A **Dorset** Downs Walk*, Thornhill Press, 1982.
A Visitor's Guide to Somerset and Dorset, Moorland Publishing Co., 1983.
A Visitor's Guide to the Tyrol, Moorland Publishing Co., 1984.
The Kalkalpen Traverse, Cicerone Press, 1986.
*Let's Walk There! South West **England***, Javelin Books, 1987.
The Wessex Ridgeway, The Ramblers, 1988.
Also contributed to
Smith, Roger, Editor, *Weekend Walking*, Oxford Illustrated Press, 1982.

Progressive Rambling Club A London-based rambling club founded by Philip Poole in 1937. It held numerous dances and socials in aid of causes (eg Basque children) dear to the heart of its predominantly left-wing membership, and also campaigned vigorously on behalf on the **Access to the Mountains Act**. The Club's journal was *The Progressive Rambler* which proclaimed itself as *'a forum for the outdoor movement'*. It started as a cyclostyled newsheet in 1937 and later became a cyclostyled magazine, and appears to have been published monthly until sometime in 1943 when it became a quarterly. The first and most influential editor was Philip Poole who was succeeded in March 1941 by Rose King. The editorial matter was lukewarm about the war effort until the USSR was attacked by **Germany** in June 1941 which overnight transformed the conflict into a just war.

The library of the **Ramblers' Association** has most issues from March 1940 until Easter 1945 when it seems to have ceased publication.

Pugh, Edward (1761?-1813) A painter of miniatures and landscapes. One of his most important works is *Cambria Depicta; a Tour through North **Wales** Illustrated with **Picturesque** Views by a Native Artist*, 1816. This handsome quarto work, beautifully printed, and illustrated with his own coloured aquatints, took ten years to complete. He spent each of those summers walking and sketching *'I shall feel amply recompensed for the fatigue which I experienced for many months, in travelling as a pedestrian between two and three thousand miles, over one of the roughest districts of Great Britain.'* The book contains good descriptions of scenery, numerous historical and literary notes, and Pugh describes some of his walks in detail. He climbed many **mountains** but was disappointed that the weather prevented him from reaching the summit of Snowdon.

Pyrénées A **mountain** range that runs for 400 kilometres from the Mediterranean to the Atlantic and straddles the border between **France** and **Spain**. The Pyrénées are generally lower than the **Alps**, with the highest summit Pic de Néthou reaching 3405 metres, and are characterised by numerous waterfalls and magnificent **cirques**. There is a good network of **paths** as well as two **sentiers de grand randonnée**, the comparatively low-level GR 10 and the extremely arduous Haute Randonnée Pyrénéenne. Early pedestrian explorers include **Hilaire Belloc**, **H. D. Inglis**, and the pseudonymous **'A Pedestrian'**.

Footpath Guides

Battagel, Arthur, *Pyrénées, Andorra, Cerdagne*, Gastons-West Col, 1980.

Battagel, Arthur, *Pyrénées East*, Gastons-West Col, 1975.

Castle, Alan, *The Pyrenean Trail; GR10, Cicerone Press, 1990.*

Reynolds, Kev, *Classic Walks in the Pyrénées*, Oxford Illustrated Press, 1989.

Reynolds, Kev, *Walks and Climbs in the Pyrénées*, Cicerone Press, 2nd Ed., 1983.

Veron, Georges, *Pyrénées High Level Route*, Gastons-West Col, 1981.

*Walking the Pyrénées; a Guide to 7000 kilometres of **Footpaths** along the Pyrénées, from the Mediterranean to the Atlantic (GR 10)*, Robertson McCarta in association with the Fédération Française de Randonnée Pédestre, 1989.

Quallofil A synthetic fibre made by Du Pont and similar to **Hollofil**, except that it has four holes in each individual filament, thus increas-

ing the **insulation**. It remains warm when wet, requires some form of **quilting** to contain it, and is used as insulation in **sleeping bags** and **duvet clothing**.

Quantock Hills An **area of outstanding natural beauty**, designated in 1957, that covers a range of **hills** in Somerset that run from just north of Taunton to Watchet on the coast. 99 square kilometres have now been designated, and the area includes wooded **combes**, bracken-clad hills and picturesque villages. (See figure 36 for a **map** showing the location of all AONBs in the United Kingdom.)
Maps
1:50000 **Landranger** sheets 181, 182.
1:25000 **Pathfinder** sheets P1216 (ST04/14), P1236 (ST03/13), P1237 (ST23/33), P1257 (ST02/12), P1258 (ST22/32).

Footpath Guides

Rivers, Lyn, **Walk Exmoor and the Quantocks**, Bartholomew, 1990.

Walks on the Quantocks, compiled by the Friends of the Quantocks, Merlin Press, 1987.

R

Railway Ramblers An organisation, founded in 1978, to promote the preservation of disused railway lines as public **paths**. It encourages the purchase of old railway lines for use by the public, organises walks along disused lines, and assists those interested in **railway walking**. The association publishes a quarterly journal *Railway Ramblings*. (For address see Appendix.)

Railway walking A term used to describe the exploration on foot of *disused* railway lines (it is not only illegal, but exceedingly dangerous to walk along the permanent way of routes that are still operational). Thousands of kilometres of track have been abandoned in this century, most notably in the 1960s when the notorious Dr Beeching wielded his infamous axe.

Several fates can befall abandoned lines. Sometimes the land is sold to **farmers** who then incorporate the line into their field system and often destroy it by **ploughing**, or erect fences across the route. If the land is sold for housing or industrial development, the line of the route is lost. Occasionally, the line may be purchased by a local authority or **national park** and converted for the use of pedestrians, cyclists and horse-riders, sometimes by **Sustrans Ltd** who specialise in such work. There

are many examples but probably the best-known are the several old lines purchased by the **Peak National Park**, and by Durham County Council.

Exploring old railways has a particular fascination for some walkers who go to considerable lengths to pursue their hobby, and delight in discovering mouldering relics of industrial archaeology. Old railways are usually marked on current **maps** published by the **Ordnance Survey**, and more may be discovered by referring to earlier editions of the 1:63360 map that are normally kept in the local history department of the public library.

The **Railway Ramblers** is the organisation that looks after the interests of those who like to explore old railway lines.

Bibliography

Appleton, J. H., *Disused Railways in the Countryside of **England** and **Wales***, HMSO for the **Countryside Commission**, 1970.

Burton, Anthony, *Walking the Line*, Blandford Press, 1985.

Cockman, F. R., *Discovering Lost Railways*, Shire Publications, 3rd Ed., 1980.

Davies, Hunter, *A Walk along the Tracks*, Weidenfeld & Nicolson, 1982.

Ellison, M. H., *Scottish Railway Walks*, Cicerone Press, 1989.

Emett, Charlie, *Walking Northern Railways; East*, Cicerone Press, 1986.

Emett, Charlie, *Walking Northern Railways; West*, Cicerone Press, 1989.

Grimshaw, John, *A Study of Disused Railways in England and Wales*, HMSO, 1982.

Hemery, Eric, *Walking the Dartmoor Railroads*, David & Charles, 1983.

Jones, Gareth Lovett, *Railway Walks; Exploring Disused Railways*, David & Charles, 2nd Ed., 1983.

Rhys ab Ellis, *Railway **Rights of Way***, Branch Line Society, 1986. *First Supplement*, 1987. *Second Supplement*, 1989. (Available from Mike Ellison, 5 North Crescent, North End, Durham DH1 4NE.)

Searle, Muriel V., *Lost Lines*, New Cavendish, 1982.

Somerville, Christopher, *Walking Old Railways*, David & Charles, 1979.

Somerville, Christopher, *Walking West Country Railways*, David & Charles, 1982.

Vinter, Jeff, *Railway Walks; GWR and SR*, Alan Sutton, 1990.

Vinter, Jeff, *Railway Walks; LMS*, Alan Sutton, 1990.

Vinter, Jeff, *Railway Walks; LNER*, Alan Sutton, 1990.

Ramble The *Oxford English Dictionary* defines a ramble as *'An act of rambling; a walk (formerly any excursion or journey) without definite route or other aim than recreation or pleasure.'* Thus Boswell records on 21 March 1776 that he and Dr Johnson *'set out in a post-chaise to pursue our ramble.'* The first recorded use of the modern sense, meaning 'to walk', occurs in George Crabbe's poem *The Borough* in 1810:

'These walks were made
Not a sweet ramble, but a slow parade'.

It was not tautologous for an eighteenth century author to write of 'a pedestrian ramble'. The terms 'ramble' and 'rambling' are never used in North America where '**hike**' and '**hiking**' are universal. 'Ramble' was in almost universal use in Britain from about 1820 until the nineteen twenties when 'hike' became popular. Some modern walkers dislike being described as 'ramblers' because it connotes aimlessness.

The Rambler The official quarterly journal of the **Ramblers' Association**. It first appeared in 1986 as the successor to *Rucksack*. It contains a comprehensive news section covering all matters relating to **paths** and the countryside, together with well-informed comments on the **Ordnance Survey** and the amenity and conservation scene in general. There are articles about walking, and brief notices of books and **footpath guides**. *(For address see Appendix.)*

Ramblers' Association The national organisation that looks after the interests of walkers. In 1905, a number of London-based rambling clubs met and established the first local **Federation of Rambling Clubs**. During the nineteen twenties, a number of other regional federations were founded, and it became clear that a national organisation was required. In 1931, a conference, chaired by **T. A. Leonard**, was held at Longshaw, in what is now the **Peak National Park**, where delegates from the rambling federations voted unanimously to form a **National Council of Ramblers' Federations**. The Council met once a year, elected an executive committee and published a journal *Rambling*. Since January 1935 it has been known as the Ramblers' Association.

In 1946, the commercial travel arm, Ramblers' Association Services, was founded and the profits contributed substantially to the revenues of the Ramblers' Association. **Tom Stephenson** was appointed the first full-time

Top: The modern Ramblers' Association logo which replaced the old one (bottom)

secretary in 1948, and membership rose in two years from 4000 to 8600. This was a period of intense lobbying by Stephenson and the RA of the first post-war Labour government which contained more members sympathetic to the RA's cause than any before or since. Considering the size of the Ramblers' Association, its achievements were remarkable.

Chris Hall became secretary in 1969 after the retirement of Tom Stephenson. He was a much younger man, and tried with some success to introduce a new generation into positions of power, increase the membership, give the organisation a more modern image, and to become more militant by using the courts to protect **rights of way**.

In 1974 **Alan Mattingly** became secretary, an appointment that coincided with the explosion of walking and recreation in the countryside generally. Under his leadership, membership has continued to increase, and the headquarters' staff has been expanded considerably giving the RA a much more professional image.

What the Ramblers' Association has achieved with a relatively small membership and a tiny budget is quite remarkable, but in the opinion of some, it would have been even more effective had it shed its cloth cap and hob-nailed **boot** image earlier, and made determined efforts to engage the sympathies of the mass of middle-class walkers. 18 million people regularly walk in the countryside, yet at the end of September, 1989, the RA had only 73,000 members. This is but a tiny fraction of the membership of the **National**

Trust (nearly 2 million), and the Royal Society for the Protection of Birds (nearly 700,000). With more business acumen, the RA could have cornered the market in **footpath guides** and exploited the profitable potential of publications about the countryside.

Accounts of the history of the RA may be found in *Making Tracks; a Celebration of Fifty Years of the Ramblers' Association* edited by Ann Holt and published by the Ramblers' Association, 1985, and also in *Forbidden Land; the Struggle for **Access** to **Mountain** and **Moorland*** by Tom Stephenson and edited by Ann Holt, Manchester University Press, 1989.

The aims of the Ramblers' Association are:

1 To help all persons, especially those of limited means, to a greater love, knowledge and care of the countryside.

2 To work for and assist in

   i The provision of and the prevention of **obstruction** to public rights of way over **footpaths** and other ways used mainly for footpaths.

   ii The preservation and enhancement for the benefit of the public of the beauty of the countryside.

   iii The provision and preservation of public access to **open country**.

   iv With the object of improving the conditions of life for the persons for whom the facilities are intended, namely the public at large, and in the interests of social welfare to encourage the provision of facilities for and the organising of healthy open-air recreational activities in the countryside and in particular **rambling** and mountaineering.

3 To do all such other lawful things as are incidental or conducive to the attainment of the above objects and which may be lawfully done by a body established for charitable purposes only.

Journals: The Ramblers' Association has had a number of journals. *Rambling* was the magazine of the National Council of Ramblers Federations from June 1933. In 1935, issue no. 4 became the first journal of the newly-formed Ramblers' Association and continued until issue no. 6 of June 1936. In 1937, the name was changed to the *Ramblers' Association Gazette* which was published irregularly until issue no. 6 of June 1939 when it was superseded by a broadsheet, *Ramblers' Association News*, which continued until 1949. Issue no. 1 of *Ramblers' News* appeared in the summer of 1949 and ran until the Winter 1959-60, issue no. 34, when it was replaced by the first issue of *Rucksack* which continued to volume 12 no. 6 of January 1986. The first issue of the clumsily titled *Rucksack Rambler* came out in April 1986, and *Rucksack* was dropped from its title in the October 1986 issue. **Rambler** and **Footpath Worker** appear quarterly. The several journals of the Ramblers' Association are important sources of information about the world of walking, rights of way and conservation.

Publications: The Ramblers' Yearbook. Making Tracks; a Celebration of Fifty Years of the Ramblers' Association, 1985. *Rights of Way; a Guide to Law and Practice*, 2nd Ed., 1989. Computer print-outs for every county listing footpath guides, and various guides, reports etc.

The Association's library and archives, which contain much important material relating to the rambling movement, and a collection of early footpath guides, are housed at its headquarters and is gradually being catalogued. A guide to material housed in the library is contained in *List of the Records of the Ramblers' Association* by Philippa Bassett, Centre for Urban and Regional Studies, University of Birmingham and Institute of Agricultural History, University of Reading, 1980 (since this was published the Association's archives have been augmented by the library and papers of Tom Stephenson and a collection of Ramblers' Association leaflets presented by **Walter Tysoe**).

The Ramblers' Library Subtitled *for Hedgeside, Seaside, Fireside*, the *Ramblers' Library* was a series of paperback titles published by Robert Edmund Taylor and Son, 19 Old Street, Aldersgate, London E, price one shilling each, written for those who enjoyed the outdoors. Only three titles seem to have appeared:

No. 1 *Nature-chat* by Edward A. Martin, 1897. This is a series of short entries about diverse nature subjects in no obvious order. Topics can be traced by using the index.

No. 2 *Off Your Bikes!* by **Walker Miles**, 1898. An appeal to cyclists, who, before the age of the motor car, invaded the countryside in hordes at weekends and bank holidays, to leave the roads behind and walk the **footpaths**. It also describes in considerable detail a number of walks on both the North and South Downs, and deals with such subjects, familiar to modern walkers, as dodging the **bull**, how fieldpaths are lost, 'byeway robbery', the apathy of local authorities, etc. It is similar in intention to a modern **footpath guide** written for motorists.

No. 3 *Ianthe of 'The Devil's Jumps'; a Story of Hind Head in the Old Smuggling Days* by Thomas Wright, 1900. This is a novelette.

Rambling Notes of a Rambling Tour through some of the English Lake Scenery This short account of a walking tour through what is now the **Lake District National Park** was undertaken in 1859 by 'A Volunteer Rifleman', and published in 1861. The author went by train from Newcastle to Windermere, and then walked through Coniston, Eskdale, Wastdale Head, Buttermere, Keswick, Penrith, and Alston to Hexham. He does not seem to have climbed any **mountains**, but includes a description of an ascent of 'Scawfell' that he made in 1851.

Ramsey Committee Two separate government committees were chaired by Sir J. Douglas Ramsey in the nineteen forties to consider the subject of **national parks** in **Scotland**. The first was an informal committee set up by the Department of Health for Scotland *'To advise upon the areas in Scotland which might be suitable for national parks, and to supervise an actual survey of potential areas by one of the Planning Officers of the Department of Health for Scotland.'* The report, *National Parks; a Scottish Survey. Report by the Scottish National Parks Survey Committee* [Cmd 6631],1944, defined a national park and recommended that they be established for Loch Lomond—Trossachs; Glen Affric—Glen Cannich—Strath Farrar; Ben Nevis—Glen Coe—Black Mount; the **Cairngorms**; and Loch Torridon—Loch Maree—Little Loch Broom. The committee also published a reserve list which recommended Moidart—Morar—Knoydart; Ben Lawers—Glen Lyon—Schiehallion; and St Mary's Loch as second choices.

The second and more important committee, and the one usually meant when the 'Ramsey Committee' or 'Ramsey Report' is referred to, had the same chairman and some of the same members as the earlier report. Its findings were published as *National Parks and the Conservation of Nature in Scotland. Report by the Scottish National Parks Committee and the Scottish Wild Life Conservation Committee* [Cmd 7235], 1947. This report makes no mention of the work of the 1944 committee, but recommended the same areas for national parks except those on the reserve list. It also recommended the establishment of a national parks authority, and that the land designated as a national park should be bought outright using compulsory purchase powers if necessary.

Scotland had to wait another thirty years for any major legislation affecting the countryside, and when the **Countryside (Scotland) Act, 1967** was finally passed, it contained no measures for establishing national parks.

Ranger A term, introduced from north America that has now largely superseded the more British 'warden', used to describe an official or volunteer who patrols the countryside, especially **national parks**, to offer help and advice to the public. Some local authorities have even changed the name of the traditional urban park-keeper to ranger and fitted them out in bush hats and jungle-green uniforms. The **Association of Countryside Rangers** is the professional body that looks after the interests of rangers *(for address see Appendix)*.

Red Rope The official name of the Socialist Walking and Climbing Club which exists to promote access to the countryside for socialist walkers and climbers. It encompasses all kinds of walking and climbing from gentle strolls to winter mountaineering. The Club publishes a monthly information sheet and a quarterly bulletin. *(For address see Appendix.)*

Resections Also known as 'backbearings' or 'cocked hats'. This is the most accurate way of pin-pointing a position when traversing pathless country. Take a **bearing** on at least two, and preferably three, known physical objects that can be identified on the **map**. Convert these to the map and draw intersecting lines. It is difficult to be sufficiently accurate to get the three lines to intersect at one point and the result will be a 'cocked hat'. The most accurate fix is the centre of the 'cocked hat' (see figure 21). In practice, this technique is rarely used because it presupposes fine weather, and in those conditions, if two or three landmarks can be identified, the position is known.

Retreat A term, originally coined by the climbing fraternity, and sometimes used by walkers to describe the termination or aborting of a walk usually due to a **hazard** such as injury or inclement weather. It is a most unfortunate expression as it connotes failure, whereas in the majority of cases it is merely the application of common sense; a person who has no hesitation in retreating is a mature and safe walker, and is unlikely ever to come to harm.

Reynolds, Kev (ie Keith Ronald Reynolds 1943-) Former **youth hostel** warden in **Switzerland** and Kent, outdoor journalist,

119

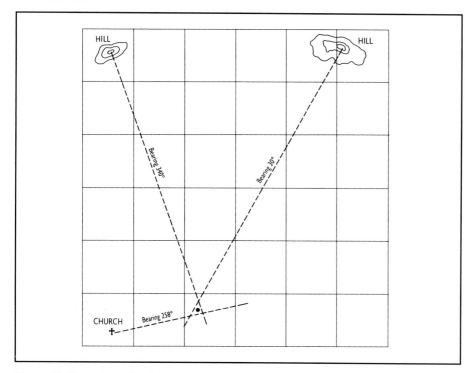

Figure 21: Resections showing position in centre of 'cocked hat'.

Richards, Mark [Brunskill] (1949-) Erstwhile Cotswold **farmer** and prolific author of **footpath guides** distinguished by their exquisite cartography, calligraphy and line drawings. His acknowledged inspiration is **A. Wainwright**, who encouraged his early efforts, and in the opinion of many, the pupil has eclipsed his master in both artistry and technical skill. He contributes articles and reviews to the outdoor press, is co-founder of the **Long Distance Paths Advisory Service**, and publishes footpath guides to the **Cotswolds** under his own imprint, Walx Publications *(for address see Appendix)*.

The Cotswold Way, Thornhill Press, 1973.
Walking the North **Cornwall** *Coastal* **Footpath**, Thornhill Press, 1974.
Through Welsh Border Country Following **Offa's Dyke Path**, Thornhill Press, 1976.
The Wychavon Way, Wychavon District Council, 1982.
The Devon South Coast Path (with **Hugh Westacott**), Penguin Books, 1982.
The Dorset Coast Path (with Hugh Westacott), Penguin Books, 1982.
The **Ridgeway Path** (with Hugh Westacott), Penguin Books, 1982.
High Peak Walks, Cicerone Press, 1982.
The **Brecon Beacons National Park** (with Hugh Westacott), Penguin Books, 1983.
Dartmoor for Walkers and Riders (with Hugh Westacott), Penguin Books, 1983.
The **North Downs Way** (with Hugh Westacott) Penguin Books,1983.

reviewer, lecturer and author specialising in countryside and **mountain** topics. He is the author of numerous walking guides to southern **England**, the **Alps** and the **Pyrénées**.

Publications

Walks and Climbs in the Pyrénées, Cicerone Press, 2nd Ed., 1983.
The Wealdway and the Vanguard Way, Cicerone Press, 1987.
Walks in the Engadine **Switzerland**, Cicerone Press, 1988.
Walking in Kent, Cicerone Press, 1988.
The Jura: Walking the Jura High Route, Cicerone Press, 1988.
The **South Downs Way** *and the Downs Link*, Cicerone Press, 1989.
The Valais Switzerland: a Walking Guide, Cicerone Press, 1989.
Classic Walks in the Pyrénées, Oxford Illustrated Press, 1989.
Classic Walks in Southern England, Oxford Illustrated Press, 1990.
The **Cotswold** *Way*, Cicerone Press, 1990.
Also contributed to
Smith, Roger, Editor, The Winding *Trail: a Selection of Articles and Essays for Walkers and* **Backpackers**, Paladin, 1986.
Unsworth, Walt, Editor, *Classic Walks of the World*, Oxford Illustrated Press, 1985.

Unsworth, Walt, Editor, *Classic Walks in Europe*, Oxford Illustrated Press, 1987.
Smith, Roger, Editor, *The* **Great Outdoors** *Book of the Walking Year*, Patrick Stephens, 1988.
Cleare, John, Editor, **Trekking**: *Great Walks of the World*, Unwin Hyman, 1988.

Kev Reynolds specialises in writing on England, the Alps and Pyrénées (photo © Linda Reynolds).

Mark Richards, author and illustrator of footpath guides.

The Somerset and North Devon Coast Path (with Hugh Westacott), Penguin Books, 1983.

The Cotswold Way; the Complete Walker's Guide, Penguin books, 1984.

A Guide to the Isle of Purbeck (with Chris Jesty) Dovecote Press, 1984.

White Peak Walks; the Northern Dales, Cicerone Press, 1985.

The Westmorland Heritage Walk (with **Christopher Wright**), Cicerone Press, 1987.

White Peak Walks; the Southern Dales, Cicerone Press, 1988.

Country Walks around Stow-on-the-Wold, Walx Publications, 1988.

Country Walks around Chipping Norton, Walx Publications, 1988.

Country Walks around Burford, Walx Publications, 1989.

Offa's Dyke Path (with **Ernie** and **Kathy Kay**), Aurum Press in association with the **Countryside Commission** and the **Ordnance Survey**, 1989.

Also contributed to

Sharp, David, Editor, *Rambler's Ways,* David & Charles, 1980.

Smith, Roger, Editor, *Weekend Walking,* Oxford Illustrated Press, 1982.

Hillaby, John, Editor, *Walking in Britain,* Collins, 1988.

Ridge A term used to describe a long narrow crest on a **mountain** or **hill**. A mountainous ridge that has very steep sides and a particularly narrow crest is often referred to as an **arête**.

Ridgeway Path A **national trail** designated by the **Countryside Commission** and officially opened in 1973. It runs for 137 kilometres from Overton Hill (**grid reference SU 118681**), near Avebury in Wiltshire to Ivinghoe Beacon (grid reference SP 960168), near Ivinghoe in Buckinghamshire. Its name causes some confusion, as the Great Ridgeway is a prehistoric route which ran from the Wash to Axmouth in Devon. The line of the national trail coincides with the Great Ridgeway between Streatley on the Thames, and Overton Hill, but the last 66 kilometres uses ancient routes only occasionally where it follows the Icknield Way. The first half is all **bridleway** and thus of interest to riders and cyclists. It is an easy walk made particularly interesting by the extensive prehistoric remains that lie on or near the route. The Countryside Commission has issued a consultation paper proposing that the route should be extended by 160

kilometres to link with the **South West Coast Path** at Lyme Regis. (See figure 36 for a **map** showing the location of all national trails and official **long-distance paths** in the United Kingdom.)
Path Association
Friends of the Ridgeway
Youth Hostels
The Ridgeway, Streatley, Bradenham, Ivinghoe.
Maps
1:50000 **Landranger** sheets 164, 165, 173, 174, 175.
1:25000 **Pathfinder** sheets P1094 (SP81/91), P1117 (SP60/70), P1118 (SP80/90), P1137 (SU69/79), P1154 (SU28/38), P1155 (SU48/58), P1156 (SU68/78), P1169 (SU07/17), P1170 (SU27/37), P1185 (SU06/16).

Footpath Guides
Burden, Vera, *Discovering the Ridgeway,* Shire Publications, 1985.
Charles, Alan, *Exploring the Ridgeway,* Countryside Books, 1988.
Curtis, Neil, *The Ridgeway,* Aurum Press in association with the Countryside Commission and the **Ordnance Survey**, 1989.
Ridgeway Information and Accommodation Guide compiled and published by Oxfordshire County Council and available from the Ridgeway Officer, Speedwell House, Speedwell Street, Oxford OX1 1SD.

Right of way The term used to describe any **highway** over which the public have the right of passage. Legally, it includes roads, but when used by walkers the term is synonymous with **path** and is usually intended to denote a **footpath**, **bridleway**, **road used as a public path**, or a **byway open to all traffic**. According to the **Countryside Commission's** estimates, there are approximately 217,000 kilometres of rights of way in **England** and **Wales** alone. All rights of way have legal protection, but the legislation in **Scotland** and **Northern Ireland** differs from that in England and Wales. The law covers such matters as **diversions and extinguishments**, **bulls**, **ploughing** and **obstructions**.
Bibliography
Clayden, Paul, and **Trevelyan, John**, *Rights of Way: a Guide to Law and Practice,* published jointly by the **Open Spaces Society** and the **Ramblers' Association**, 2nd Ed., 1989.
Garner, J. F., *Garner's Rights of Way,* Oyez Longmans, 5th Rev. Ed., 1989.

Garner, J. F., and Jones, B. L., *Countryside Law,* Shaw and Sons, 1987.

Ripstop nylon A fabric made from a special weave of **nylon** that is highly resistant to tearing and is used extensively in the manufacture of **tents**, **rucksacks** and shell **clothing**. It can be rendered waterproof by coating with **polyurethane**.

River crossing In the United Kingdom, **rights of way** are usually carried over rivers and streams by footbridges, stepping stones, or ferries, and it is rare for the walker to have to wade (a notable exception to this generalisation is the **South West Coast Path** where it is sometimes necessary to ford the tidal estuaries of the Gannel at Newquay, Gillan Harbour in south **Cornwall**, and the Erme and Avon in south Devon). But the walker who chooses to navigate across **open country** may, perforce, have to wade across rivers. Before attempting to cross, you should check that the river is not in spate, and that you have chosen a point well away from bends and rapids. It is often worth making a detour to a point where the **map** shows the river to have divided into channels, as each one will carry less water than the main stream, or to find a section that is wider, and therefore shallower, and the current correspondingly less strong.

Once you are satisfied that the crossing is feasible, take off your **socks** and **breeches** and cross in your **boots** and underwear (this is where ladies who wear old-fashioned gym-knickers for walking have an advantage). Close your **rucksack** tightly to trap as much air as possible, undo your hip belt and loosen your shoulder straps so that you can slip it off if swept away, and use it as an aid to buoyancy. A solo crossing should be made by taking short shuffling steps, facing the current diagonally, and supporting yourself with a stick or **tent** pole. Three people can cross in a huddle with their heads together, linking arms and keeping their feet apart. The heaviest person faces the current, and each walker takes one step at a time in turn without crossing the legs. (These techniques are illustrated in figure 22). In the event of being swept away, slip off the rucksack and try to place it under your chest to assist buoyancy. Let the current take you, and try to gently direct yourself to the bank.

Road used as a public path A type of **right of way**, known colloquially as a 'RUPP', found in **England** and **Wales** that was defined under the **National Parks and**

Figure 22: Methods of crossing rivers.

Access to the Countryside Act, 1949 as '. . . a **highway**, other than a public **path**, used by the public mainly for the purposes for which **footpaths** and **bridleways** are so used.' Under the **Wildlife and Countryside Act, 1981** every RUPP must be reclassified either as a **byway open to all traffic**, or as a bridleway, or as a **footpath**.

Robertson, A[rchibald] **E**[neas] (1870-1958) A Scottish clergyman, sometime chairman of the **Scottish Rights of Way Society**, and **mountaineer** who was the first person to climb all the **Munros**, a feat that took him ten years and which he completed in 1901. There were then no modern roads, cars or public transport, other than railways, and he had to walk much of the way, although he sometimes used boats and a pony and trap. Robertson revised the 1908 edition of **Baddeley's Scotland**.

Robinson, Henry Crabb (1775-1867) Diarist, gossip, and sometime correspondent and foreign editor of *The Times*. He knew everybody in the nineteenth century literary world, and was a close friend, and sometimes a walking companion, of the **Wordsworths**, the **Lambs**, **Samuel Taylor Coleridge**, **Robert Southey**, **Thomas de Quincey**, and **Sir Thomas Noon Talfourd**. Robinson was an enthusiastic walker all his life, but unfortunately, the published selections from his voluminous diary and letters reveal few details. In 1799, he made a pedestrian tour of **Wales** and visited Stonehenge and Bath, and in 1801 he made a walking tour of **Germany** and climbed the Brocken. In his diary for 23 December 1809, he records that he walked sixty kilometres from London to Royston in Hertfordshire, and in 1814 walked from Cambridge to Bury St Edmunds. On the 10th September 1816 he walked to Cockermouth from Keswick accompanied by William Wordsworth, who was on horseback, and continued towards Ravenglass on the 13th. They got caught in foul weather on Cold Fell, and Wordsworth was so fatigued that they stayed the night at 'The Fleece' at Calder Bridge. During this holiday he walked with Wordsworth and **De Quincey** on the Lake District **fells**. In 1820, he accompanied the Wordsworths to **Switzerland**, and made a tour of **Scotland** in 1821. He went to Scotland again in 1833 with the Wordsworths, and left them for a time to make a solitary walking tour of the 'Perth Highlands'. As late as 1846, when he was seventy-one, he made a tour of Switzerland and northern **Italy**, and walked in both countries.

Robinson's letters and diary, amounting to some 40 volumes, are deposited in Dr Williams' Library in London. Selections were edited by Thomas Sadler and published as *Diary, Reminiscences and Correspondence*, 2 Vols, 1869.

Rocky Mountains The principal division of a huge **mountain** range that extends for 7500 kilometres from northern Mexico to Alaska on the western side of the north American continent. The Rockies run for about half this distance from the Mexican border with the **United States** to the Yukon in **Canada**. The associated mountains of the Pacific border range which include the Sierra Madre Occidental, the Sierra Nevada, the Cascades, the Coast Mountains, the Alaskan Range, the Mackenzie Mountains, and the Brooks Range, are not considered to be part of the Rocky Mountains. Mount Elbert (4400 metres) in Colorado is the highest summit in the Rocky Mountains proper, and there are more than 200 peaks that exceed 4000 metres in height. The Continental Divide **Trail** is an arduous **long-distance path** that winds its way through the Rocky Mountains.

Walking in the Rockies usually involves visiting one of the numerous **national parks** situated in the range. Further information may be obtained by consulting the entries for Canada and the United States.

Romantic movement The term used to describe the literary and artistic outpouring at the end of the eighteenth century that emphasised the primacy of emotion over reason. In Britain, the leaders of the movement were **William Wordsworth** and **Samuel Taylor Coleridge**, and the cause was enthusiastically taken up by **Keats**, **Shelley** and **Sir Walter Scott**. It was largely due to the romantic movement that the beauties of **mountain** scenery came to be appreciated, and it became fashionable to take tours, including pedestrian tours, to the mountainous areas of Britain and Europe.

Romer A handy device for measuring distances on **maps** (see figure 23). It consists of a piece of plastic or card on which is engraved or printed the most popular map **scales** (eg 1:50000, 1:63360 and 1:25000) which the navigator can use for reckoning distances and **grid references**. The more sophisticated versions contain protractors for calculating **bearings**.

Rope Most people associate ropes with climbing, but the serious walker may occasionally use a rope, and properly handled, it can extend his skills considerably. A walker may use a rope in any situation where additional security is required, eg when walking on **glaciers**, when **scrambling**, when negotiating **fixed ropes** etc. Ropework cannot be learned from a book, and walkers who have reached the stage where they feel knowledge of these techniques will be

| FROM : Conies Down Water | Grid.ref : 592787 | Dep : 10.00 |
| TO : Batworthy | Grid ref : 662867 | ETA : 13.00 |

STEP	INSTRUCTION	DISTANCE (metres)	TOTAL ASCENT (m)	EST. TIME (mins)
1	Path E. to West Dart river	1175	—	20
2	Bearing 76° to wall	1300	60	16
3	Follow wall N & NW to East Dart	3400	120	40
4	N to boulders & across river	800	—	9
5	Bearing 56° to path	500	—	6
6	N through 2 walls to Forest	2600	50	30
7	Leave path & follow forest boundary to 2nd wall	1400	—	16
8	Bearing 38° to wall	1500	—	17
9	TR & follow wall to Batworthy	600	—	7
	TOTAL		230	161

Figure 24: Route card.

useful, should contact their local climbing club for help and advice, or attend one of the many courses on elementary climbing advertised in the outdoor press.

Rothman, Benny [ie Bernard Rothman] (1911-) Writer, broadcaster and political activist on behalf of **access**. In 1932, when secretary of the Lancashire branch of the British Workers' Sports Federation, he organised the mass **trespass** on **Kinder Scout** which is still the subject of much controversy. He was convicted of incitement to cause a riotous assembly and sentenced to four months' imprisonment. He described his experiences in *The 1932 Kinder Trespass*, Willow Publishing, 1982.

Route card A series of navigational instructions and compass **bearings** derived from a **map**, and written on a card for easy reference. The preparation of a route card concentrates the mind, helps to find the most suitable route, is a useful discipline against sloppy **map-reading**, and often saves time by obviating the need to examine the map frequently (see figure 24).

The Ruc-Sac A periodical, published by the *Daily Mail* and edited by **Claude Fisher**, that first appeared in July 1931 and seems to have ceased publication in January 1932. It was popular in style as the following extract from the first issue under the caption 'Editorial Sunbeams' illustrates: *'The Ruc-Sac is open! From today it unfolds its treasures for your delectation and to serve the great Brotherhood and Sisterhood of the Open Air in their Quest for Health and Happiness.'* Every issue contained an uplifting thought under the heading 'The Silver Lining', and one contained the following memorable verse:
'Be kind to little animals wherever they may be,
And give a stranded jellyfish a shove into the sea.'

Figure 23: Romer.

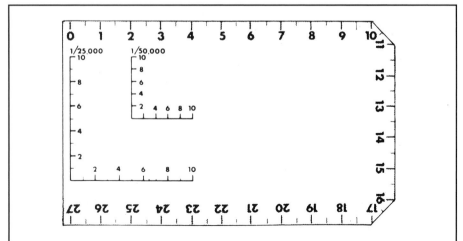

The woman's page was conducted by 'Jill of the Jaunt'.

Rucksack From the German *rucken* meaning 'back' and 'sack', hence 'back-sack'. The term 'rucksack' is still widely used in the UK but never 'rucksacking' or 'rucksacker' (unless referring to a member of the **Rucksack Club**)—the verb in universal use is **'backpacking'** and the noun is **'backpacker'**. The American word 'backpack' is now entering our vocabulary ('rucksack' is never used in north America).

A rucksack is a device consisting of a sack, into which the load is placed, that is carried on the back suspended from the shoulders by adjustable carrying straps. Rucksacks come in a variety of sizes and designs. Capacity is measured in litres (eg a 50-litre rucksack will hold, including all pockets, 50 litres of water). It is generally reckoned that a day-sack or day-pack (ie a rucksack large enough to carry the essentials required for a walk encompassing only one day—it seems the term 'day rucksack' is never used) range in size from 20-40 litres, with the larger size capable of carrying the needs of a whole family. 40-60-litre rucksacks are suitable for use on a tour where the walker uses hostels or bed and breakfast accommodation. 60-80 litre rucksacks are used for backpacking with the largest size suitable for expedition work. All rucksacks are liable to leak at the seams, and both the main compartment and the pockets should be lined with strong plastic bags.

The principles of packing a rucksack are the same irrespective of the size; light items go at the bottom and away from the spine, while heavy objects go at the top and as close to the spine as possible. Keep items that are in frequent use, such as waterproofs and water bottles, where they are readily available. Most backpackers try to arrange things so that they do not have to open the main compartment between camp sites.

Before purchasing a rucksack, draw up an ideal specification based on your requirements. You should decide the size, the number of pockets you require, and whether you want fittings for **crampons**, **ice axes**, and cross-country skis. Smaller rucksacks should have a non-load-bearing waist-strap, which gives improved stability by restricting any tendency for the sack to swing. Rucksacks are made from **nylon**, **Cordura** or **KS100**.

Rucksacks suitable for backpacking come in a bewildering variety of styles and many kinds of ingenious load-bearing systems. There are two basic classifications; *internal frame and external frame*. The internal frame is now the more popular as it hugs the body more closely and gives greater stability, but the external frame is widely used by expeditions because the sack can be removed and awkward loads strapped directly onto the strong tubular frame. Every rucksack designed for backpacking should have a padded hip-belt that can be tightened allowing about 75 per cent of the weight to be supported by the pelvic girdle. Some rucksacks are adjustable for fit and one size will accommodate persons of different height; others come in a range of sizes based the length of the trunk. Manufacturers are now introducing rucksacks specially designed for women. As the correct fitting of a rucksack is critical, it is important that it should be purchased from a reputable, specialised outdoor shop with a properly trained staff.

The easiest way to hoist a heavy rucksack onto the shoulders is to place it on a convenient wall or boulder, and then to slip your arms through the straps. If this is not possible, extend one leg, bend the knee and lift the rucksack onto it. From this position it is relatively easy to slip one arm through a shoulder-strap and to swing it onto the back. It is also possible to sit on the ground immediately in front of the rucksack and slip your arms through the straps. Unfortunately, this clumsy method often results in an undignified scramble to get onto your feet.

Rucksack Club An influential all-male walking and mountaineering club founded in Manchester in 1902 (the London Section was formed in 1937). In 1933, the **Rucksack** Club and the **Fell and Rock Club** set up a Joint Stretcher Committee to produce a suitable **mountain rescue** stretcher. The report was published in 1935. It gave a list of all material and equipment, including medical and **first aid** items, that should be available for coping with **mountain** accidents, and also gave specifications for the Thomas stretcher. From this report sprang the First Aid Committee of Mountaineering Clubs, and ultimately the **Mountain Rescue Committee**.

The Club opened the first British **hut** in 1912, currently owns two huts, and has a programme of climbs, walks, dinners and lectures. Some members are enthusiastic competitors in **challenge walks** (Mike Cudahy was the first person to complete the **Pennine Way** in less than three days). The objects of the Club are to *'facilitate walking tours, cave explorations and mountaineering in the British Isles and elsewhere, and bring into fellowship men who are interested in these pursuits, and to do whatever shall be deemed by the Committee from time to time to be conducive to the foregoing.'* The Club publishes an excellent *Journal* and *Handbook* which are issued annually, and its library is housed in the care of Manchester City Library. *(For address see Appendix.)*

Ruskin, John (1819-1900) Writer, artist, critic, and social reformer who had a profound influence on the taste of the Victorians, and was a doughty champion of gothic architecture, J.M.W. Turner, and the Pre-Raphaelites. Ruskin was a keen walker all his life. He was particularly fond of the Swiss **Alps** and what is now the **Lake District National Park**, and retired to the latter region when he bought his house 'Brantwood', which is now open to the public, on the shores of Lake Coniston.

Although he mentions his walks briefly in his autobiography *Praeterita*, it is his descriptions of **mountain** scenery that are so remarkable. In his monumental work *Modern Painters*, 1843-59, he delivers two disquisitions on the subjects of *Mountain Gloom* and *Mountain Glory* in which he writes very movingly about the

John Ruskin wrote remarkable descriptions of mountain scenery (photo © National Portrait Gallery).

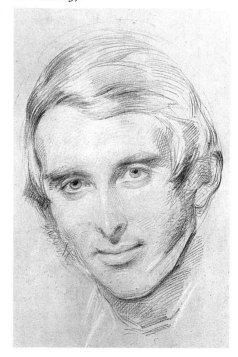

beauty of mountain scenery, and its effect on the human soul, religious beliefs, and art. Charlotte **Brontë** wrote of these essays *'I feel now as if I had been walking blindfold; the book seems to give me eyes.'* Ruskin was one of the greatest of English prose writers, but his intricate literary style, and subtlety of thought and argument, make his writings appear prolix and difficult to understand to those educated in an age that demands instant comprehension.

S

Saddle A broad dip between two areas of higher ground in mountainous country. The term is derived from equestrianism as it resembles that part of a horse's back on which the saddle is placed. It differs from a **pass** in that it does not provide a route across a **mountain** range. This may be because the flanks of the saddle do not provide suitable terrain for a **path**, or because it does not offer a suitable or useful route.

Sale, Richard [Geoffrey] (1946-) A research physicist, author and journalist (who also writes as Dick Sale) who came to walking through climbing. He has written a number of guides to **long distance paths**, and collaborated on a useful book about walking in Europe.

Publications about Walking

A Guide to the Cotswold Way, Rev Ed., 1988. A Visitor's Guide to the Cotswolds, Moorland Publishing Co., 4th Ed., 1989.
A Walker's Guide to Europe (with Arthur Howcroft), Wildwood House, 1983.
A Cambrian Way; a Personal Guide to an Unofficial Route, Constable, 1983.
Owain Glyndwr's Way, Hutchinson, 1985.
The Ancient Ways of Lakeland; a Circular Route for Walkers, Andre Deutsch, 1986.
A Guide to the Cleveland Way, Constable, 1988.

Also contributed to
Smith, Roger, Editor, *The Winding Trail*, Paladin, 1986.
Duncan, Andrew, Editor, *Walker's Britain; the Complete Pocket Guide to over 240 Walks and Rambles*, Pan Books in association with the **Ordnance Survey**, 1982.

Salopettes A French word meaning overalls or dungarees. Salopettes are items of midwear **clothing**, similar in design to bib and brace overalls, that are worn by skiers and climbers,

and sometimes by walkers, in winter conditions. Salopettes provide warmth to the legs and trunk, and eliminate the uncomfortable overlap between sweaters, shirts and **breeches**. They are usually made from one of the proprietary **fleece** materials.

Scale The term used to describe the special relationship between a map and the area of ground that it covers. The easiest way of grasping the concept of **map** scale is to appreciate that it is expressed as a proportion. In the example 1:50000, the first figure represents the unit on the map, and the figures after the colon represent the number of units on the ground. The smaller the number of units on the ground, the larger is the scale of the map, and the greater the detail that can be depicted. Most maps published by the **Ordnance Survey** are now metric so it is useful to express the scale of the 1:50000 map as 1 centimetre to 50000 centimetres (which is 500 metres) or, to make it even more convenient, 2 centimetres to 1 kilometre. (Note that imperial measure *can* be used, but 1 inch on the map is 50000 inches on the ground which converts to 0.7891413 miles, which is not a convenient fraction!) Note that the larger the map scale the more accurate the map will be. Even the 1:25000 map contains some distortions in the interests of clarity. For example, the width of roads shown on these and smaller scale maps is considerably exaggerated to make them clearly visible.

Metric scales in current use by the Ordnance Survey are:
1:50000 (2 centimetres to the kilometre);
1:25000 (4 centimetres to the kilometre);
1:10000 (10 centimetres to the kilometre);
1:2500 (40 centimetres to the kilometre);
1:1250 (80 centimetres to the kilometre).
Imperial scales in current use are 1:63360 (1 inch to the mile) for **Tourist Maps**; and 1:10560 (6 inches to the mile) which is currently being phased out in favour of the metric 1:10000. The Ordnance Survey gives the following popular map series, all of which are suitable for walkers, distinctive titles like **Landranger Maps** (scale 1:50000); **Tourist Maps** (various scales 1:258545, 1:126720, 1:63360 and 1:50000); **Pathfinder Maps** (scale 1:25000); and **Outdoor Leisure Maps** (scale 1:25000).

Scar A bluff precipice of carboniferous limestone found in upland country, especially in the **Yorkshire Dales National Park**, that has

often been formed by a geological fault. A striking example is Gordale Scar (**grid reference** SD 915640) near Malham, North Yorkshire.

Scotland Walking in Scotland is a memorable experience for the hill-walker as the country is so empty and remote, and contains far more wild and unspoiled countryside than **England** and **Wales** put together. The country may be divided into three main geographical areas. In the extreme south lie the **Southern Uplands**, further north is the Glasgow-Edinburgh industrial belt where most of the country's 5 million inhabitants live, further north still are the Highlands which are mountainous and remote with few towns of any size. Scotland has no **national parks**, although there is pressure for some to be established, but has 40 **national scenic areas** and 4 Regional Parks (Pentland Hills, Loch Lomond, Clyde-Muirshie, and Fife).

The wilder parts of the country are not for novice walkers because of the rugged terrain and the likelihood of severe weather, even in summer. Route-finding is more critical and it is essential to be expert in the use of **map** and **compass**.

The legal basis of **rights of way** differs from that of England and Wales. By custom and tradition, the walker may usually use any **path** shown on **maps** published by the **Ordnance Survey** and wander anywhere in **open country,** providing that he respects sporting interests and avoids areas in the hunting season where grouse-shooting (12th August—31st October) and deer-stalking (August to February) is taking place. Information on where shooting and stalking is taking place may be obtained locally from the factor's (estate manager's) office, post offices, police stations, public houses, hotels and **youth hostels**. The addresses and telephone numbers of landowners, factors and keepers in the Highlands may be obtained from *Heading for the Scottish Hills*, compiled by the **Mountaineering Council of Scotland** and the Scottish Landowners' Federation, **Scottish Mountaineering Club**, 1988.

Against considerable opposition from Scottish walkers, who feel they are alien to the country's walking tradition, the **Southern Upland Way**, the **Speyside Way** and the **West Highland Way long-distance paths** have been established by the **Countryside Commission for Scotland**. There are also plans for a **long-distance path** through the

Walking in Scotland is memorable for the empty and remote countryside. Above: Loch Etive (photo © Hugh Westacott).

Below: Ben Alder from Culra Lodge Bothy (photo © Hugh Westacott).

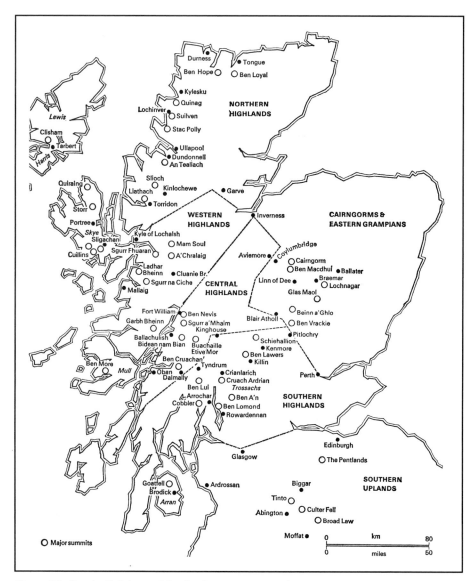

Figure 25: Scenic divisions of Scotland.

Great Glen from Fort William to Inverness (much of the route can be walked now).

Footpath guides are listed under the main scenic divisions (see figure 25), Cairngorms, **Central Highlands**, **Northern Highlands**, **Skye**, **Southern Highlands**, **Southern Uplands**, and **Western Highlands**, but guides covering more than one region are listed below.

General Guidebooks and Footpath Guides

Butterfield, Irvine, *The High Mountains of Britain and Ireland; a Guide for Mountain Walkers*, Diadem, 1986.

Butterfield, Irvine, *The High Mountains Companion*, Diadem, 1987.

Bennet, Donald, *The **Munros,*** Scottish Mountaineering Club, 1985.

Inglis, Harry, *Hill **Path** Contours of the Chief Mountain **Passes** in Scotland*, Gall and Inglis, 1976.

Innes, Athol, *Let's Walk There!; Southern Scotland*, Javelin, 1987.

McNeish, Cameron, *Let's Walk There! Northern Scotland*, Javelin, 1987.

Moir, D. G., *Scottish Hill Tracks*, 2 Vols, Bartholomew, 1975. Vol. 1 *Southern Scotland*. Vol. 2 *Northern Scotland*.

Murray, W. H., *Scotland's Mountains: Scottish*

Mountaineering Club Guide, Scottish Mountaineering Trust, 1987.

Poucher, W. A., *Scottish Peaks: a Pictorial Guide to Walking in this Region and the Safe Ascent of its Most Spectacular Mountains*, Constable, 6th Rev. Ed., 1982.

*Scotland: **Hill Walking**, Scottish Tourist Board*, Rev. Ed., 1985.

Storer, Ralph, *100 Best Routes on Scottish Mountains*, David and Charles, 1987.

*Walks and **Trails** in Scotland*, Scottish Tourist Board, 1984.

Scott, J[ohn] **M**[aurice] (1906-86) Writer, explorer, and the author of two interesting and well-written accounts of walking tours. In *A Walk along the Apennines*, Geoffrey Bles, 1973 he describes his route from Montenotta on the Franco-Italian border to Reggio de Calabria on the toe of **Italy**. During this walk, he revisited the location of some of his wartime exploits. In *From Sea to Ocean*, Geoffrey Bles, 1969, he walked along the length of the **Pyrénées** from the Mediterranean to the Atlantic.

Scott Report This important report of a committee, chaired by Lord Justice Leslie Frederic Scott (1869-1950), a member of the **Alpine Club**, is more properly known as *Land Utilization in Rural Areas* (Cmd 6378), and was published in 1942. It was set up by the government during the war to enquire into '. . .*the factors affecting the location of industry, having regard to economic operation, part-time and seasonal employment, the well-being of rural communities and the preservation of rural amenities.*' It recommended a five-year plan to be initiated after the war in **England** and **Wales** during which there would be a compulsory ascertainment and signposting of **rights of way**, local authorities would be made responsible for rights of way, a survey of **commons** would be made, and **national parks** and **long-distance paths** would be established.

The Scott Report was considered by the **Hobhouse Committee**, and many of its recommendations were endorsed and reached the statute book with the passing of the **National Parks and Access to the Countryside Act, 1949**.

Scott, Sir Walter (1771-1832) Scottish literary lion, poet and novelist. Although he was lame in one leg as a result of a childhood illness, Scott was a powerful man, and in his youth thought nothing of walking between 30 and 50 kilometres in a day to visit some of the places that later featured in his novels. When he lived in Edinburgh, he used to wander over Arthur's Seat with his friend John Irving, composing romantic ballads. It seems that he gave up pedestrian travel after he married.

Scottish Mountain Leader Training Board The SML~~TB~~ is the body that administers the Scottish **Mountain** Leader Award (Summer) and the Winter Mountain Leader Scheme which are designed to provide training and assessment in the technical and leading skills required by those who wish to lead groups into the mountains and **moorlands** of the British Isles.

Scottish Mountain Leader Award (Summer)
The purpose of the Scottish Mountain Leader Training Scheme is to encourage the safe enjoyment of the **hills** by all who go there. It provides training and assessment in the technical and leading skills required by those who wish to lead groups of young people into the mountains and moorlands of the British Isles. It is not a mountaineering or educational qualification. Entrants are strongly advised to attend an approved course and before assessment must be 20 years old, to have completed at least 40 quality mountain days and obtained a valid **first aid** certificate. The candidate will submit a log-book of his mountain experience and will be assessed at a centre approved by the Board.

Winter Mountain Leadership Scheme
This scheme provides training and assessment in the special skills and techniques required when leading parties on the hills and mountains of the United Kingdom in winter conditions. Candidates have to provide evidence of substantial winter experience before they are accepted for registration, training and assessment. They then have to take a rigorous training course at an approved centre and are required to possess an approved **first aid** certificate, and to have completed at least 40 quality mountain winter days, including at least 10 Grade 1 winter climbs. *(For address see Appendix.)*

Scottish Mountaineering Club The SMC, founded in 1889, is **Scotland's** premier mountaineering club. Although membership is restricted to experienced male climbers, the Club is of interest to walkers and **backpackers** because the editor of the SMC *Journal*, founded in 1890 and published annually, keeps the register of those who have completed all the **Munros**. Also, the Scottish Mountaineering Trust, which is the publishing arm of the Scottish Mountaineering Club, publishes

Munro's Tables and a series of *District Guide Books* to the **Cairngorms**, the **Central Highlands**, the **Northern Highlands**, the **Scottish Highlands**, and the *Islands of Scotland* that contain much useful information for walkers. Titles published by the Scottish Mountaineering Trust are distributed by Cordee. The Club has an extensive library of mountaineering literature which is housed at Edinburgh Central Library, and may be consulted by the public. *(For addresses of the Scottish Mountaineering Club and Cordee see Appendix.)*

Scottish Rights of Way Society Ltd The Society is the successor to the Scottish **Rights of Way** and Recreation Society formed in 1845. It exists for *'the preservation, defence and acquisition of public rights of way in **Scotland**; the doing of such acts as may be necessary to preserve or restore such rights of way as may be in danger of being lost; the erection, restoration and repair of bridges, guideposts, notice or direction boards and plates, fences, **stiles**, gates and resting places in connection with such rights of way; and also the repairing of the roads and pathways themselves; the defence and prosecution, directly or indirectly, of suits or actions for the preservation or recovery of such rights of way; and the doing of such other lawful things as are incident or conducive to the above objects.'* The Society publishes *Rights of Way: a Guide to the Law in Scotland*, 1986. *(For address see Appendix.)*

Scottish Sports Council The Council was established to foster the knowledge and practice of sport and physical recreation in **Scotland**. It allocates government grants for sports facilities, and helps finance **mountain rescue** teams and the National Outdoor Training Centre at Glenmore Lodge, Aviemore. *(For address see Appendix.)*

Scottish Tourist Board The STB was established under the Development of Tourism Act, 1969. The Board is responsible for promoting **Scotland** within Britain, and administering the hotel incentives scheme. It gives fundamental assistance to other tourist information services, carries out research and works with the British Tourist Authority in publicising Scotland overseas. The STB publishes *Where to Stay in Scotland, Scotland: Hill Walking* and various ***maps***, guides and lists of accommodation. *(For address see Appendix.)*

Scottish Wild Land Group The Group exists to promote the conservation of wild land and its flora and fauna by increasing public awareness of the problems facing wild land in **Scotland**. By helping to co-ordinate the efforts

of like-minded groups and individuals to create a strong voice through which the case for conservation can be expressed. By pressing for the adoption of planning policies which recognise conservation as a relevant factor in the national economy, compatible with appropriate development, the provision of long-term employment, and the tourist industry, to which the landscape and its particular qualities are vital. It publishes a journal, *Wild Land News*. *(For address see Appendix.)*

Scottish Youth Hostels Association The SYHA exists *'to help all, but especially young people of limited means living and working in industrial and other areas to know, use, and appreciate the Scottish countryside and places of historic and cultural interest in **Scotland**, and to promote their health, recreation and education, particularly by providing simple hostel accommodation for them on their travels.'* The SYHA has 81 hostels, most of which are self-catering (though some serve meals), and they provide facilities for members to cook their own **food**. Prices are kept low because members have to do a few household chores before departing. Accommodation is in single-sex dormitories although some hostels have family rooms. SYHA organises tours and adventure holidays, and a current membership card entitles the holder to use **youth hostels** throughout the world. It publishes a journal, *The Scottish Hosteller. (For address see Appendix.)*

Scrambling The terms 'scramble' and 'scrambling' were originally used by early **mountaineers** as a synonym for 'climbing'. Nowadays it is used only to describe the action of negotiating rocks where handholds are required, but where it is not sufficiently steep or dangerous to require the use of a **rope**.

The essence of good scrambling is to keep as upright a stance as possible so that the centre of gravity runs through the feet. This requires the scrambler to overcome the natural instinct to hug the rock, and may mean holding the body away from the rock-face by the hands. It is essential that at all times the body is supported by three contact points (either two feet and one hand, or one foot and two hands), and that all movements are made slowly and deliberately, testing each new hold for security before committing the body's full weight on it (the knees should not be used). The weight should be taken on the feet, and the hands used only for steadying. The scrambler should not lunge for handholds, nor place the hands above shoulder-height. Never feel for footholds, but look down to see where to place the feet. Shout *'below'* immediately if loose stones are dislodged to warn those lower down. Most walkers find descending more difficult than ascending.

Scree The term used to describe areas of loose stones, which may range in size from quite large boulders to pebbles, sometimes found on mountainsides. Boulder scree can be very dangerous to cross, climb or ascend because of the risk of starting a rock-slide. Pebble-sized scree is fatiguing to climb because, for every step forward, the walker takes half a step back, but it is very fast and exhilarating to descend. The technique, known as scree-running, is similar to running down steep shingle on a beach. The stones move beneath the feet and balance is controlled by flailing the arms. It is very bad for the **boots**.

Scroggie, [W.] Sydney (1919-) Author, broadcaster, poet, and walker. He was a lieutenant in the Lovat Scouts and was blown up in **Italy** in 1945 losing his eyesight and a leg. Despite his severe handicaps, he gradually resumed **hill walking**, encouraged by his wife, Margaret, his constant companion, and has walked thousands of kilometres over some of the roughest country in **Scotland**. In 1971, he was made *Nationwide* 'Man of the Year' and 'Disabled Sportsman of the Year', and he was featured in *This is Your Life* in 1964.
Publications about Walking
Give Me the Hills; Verse by Syd Scroggie selected and arranged by David Phillips, David Winter, 1978.
The Cairngorms Scene and Unseen, Scottish Mountaineering Trust, 1989.
Also contributed to
Smith, Roger, Editor, *Walking in Scotland*, Spurbooks, 1982.
Brown, Hamish M., Editor, *Poems of the Scottish Hills*, Aberdeen University Press, 1982.
Brown, Hamish M., and Berry, Martyn, Editors, *Speak to the Hills*, Aberdeen University Press, 1985.
A Century of Scottish Mountaineering, Scottish Mountaineering Trust, 1988.

Sellers, Gladys A retired industrial chemist and the author of several excellent **footpath guides** to northern **England**. She also contributes semi-technical articles to the outdoor press, and reviews equipment.
Publications about Walking
The Yorkshire Dales; a Walker's Guide to the National Park, Cicerone Press, 1984.
The Ribble Way, Cicerone Press, 1985.

Walks on the West Pennine Moors, Cicerone Press, 2nd Ed., 1988.
The Douglas Valley Way, Cicerone Press, 1990.

Sentier de Grande Randonnée The name given in **France** and **Belgium** to a **long-distance path**.

Serac A term used by **mountaineers** to describe large columns or pinnacles of **ice** found at the foot of ice-falls, and at the edge of ice-cliffs formed by the intersection of **crevasses**. They are often unstable and should be given a wide berth as they can be very dangerous. The word is derived from the name of a white cheese.

Sharp, Arthur The author of *The Rucksack Way; How to Enjoy the Countryside on Foot*, 1934 which is one of the better and more literate walking manuals of the period.

Shelley, Mary [Wollstonecraft] (1797-1851) Writer, author of *Frankenstein*, and second wife of **Percy Bysshe Shelley** with whom she eloped to **France** at the age of 16 accompanied by her step-sister, Claire Clairemont. By the time they reached Paris, they were very short of money, and so determined to walk to **Switzerland** with their luggage carried on the back of a donkey. They covered 193 kilometres and got as far as Troyes where they decided to complete the journey by voiture. Even so, Mary and Shelley still walked for sections of the journey, sending their conveyance ahead. The Shelleys lived most of their married life in **Italy**, and Mary's journals make constant references to the walks that she took, sometimes accompanied by her husband. After his death in 1822, there are no more references to walking in her journal. The best edition of the *Journal* was edited by F. L. Jones and published in the **United States** in 1947.

Shelley, Percy Bysshe (1792-1822) One of the outstanding poets of the **romantic movement**, and throughout his short life an enthusiastic walker. Whilst at Oxford, he took many walks in the surrounding countryside, and after being sent down, he walked to **Wales** to stay with his uncle and explored the neighbourhood. He honeymooned with his first wife, Harriet, in what is now the **Lake District National Park**, and walked a great deal. Whilst living in Marlow, Buckinghamshire, he often walked the 52 kilometres to London with his friend Thomas Love Peacock

covering much of the journey on **footpaths**. His most famous walking exploit was his elopement with Mary Wollstonecraft which is described in the entry for **Mary Shelley**.

Shelton, Harold The author, who described himself as 'late classical scholar of University College, Oxford', of a number of articles about walking, and a book entitled *Upland Rambles in Surrey and Sussex*, 1932. This is a fairly detailed walks guide containing sketch **maps** and a lot of descriptions of views. The Appendix gives suggested routes for a week's walking on the North Downs, a week's walking on the South Downs, and a fortnight's walking in Surrey and Sussex.

Shoes According to conventional wisdom, **boots** are to be preferred for serious walking, but the only advantage that they have over good quality walking shoes is that the higher cuff offers more protection from mud and surface water, and protects the sensitive anklebone from painful knocks. A number of companies market what they are pleased to call 'walking shoes', but most experienced walkers find them insufficiently stiff and supportive. Probably the best walking shoe is the 'veltschōoen' style manufactured from highly water-resistant Zug leather. The term veltschōoen (from the Cape Dutch meaning 'shoes for wearing on the veldt') is applied to the most expensive and refined form of shoe construction in which the upper is lasted separately from the sole and is then turned outward (as opposed to inward in the conventional shoe) and sewn onto the inner sole, which in turn is sewn or cemented onto the outer sole. This design effectively prevents the ingress of water at the welt, and results in a stiffer shoe that gives adequate support to the foot. Until a few years ago, veltschōoen were readily available from the better High Street shops, but they are now difficult to find although A.T. Hogg (Fife) Ltd will supply them by mail order *(for address see Appendix)*.

Gaiters can be worn with shoes, but they do not fit very well. There is no reason why shoes, or even rubber boots, providing that they do not have a smooth sole, may not be worn in all but the most rugged terrain, and some experienced hill walkers regularly wear good quality running shoes in all but the most extreme conditions. Until he has gained some experience, the novice hill walker will be well-advised to wear conventional walking boots.

Shropshire Hills An irregularly shaped **area of outstanding natural beauty**, designated in 1972, which lies to the south of Shrewsbury and includes the towns of Wellington, Church Stretton, and Craven Arms. In its 777 square kilometres will be found fine walking in the **hills**, that rise in places to over 500 metres, giving some splendid views. (See figure 36 for a **map** showing the location of all AONBs in the United Kingdom.)

Maps
1:50000 **Landranger** sheet 126, 137.
1:25000 **Pathfinder** sheets P870 (SJ61/71), P888 (SJ20/30), P889 (SJ40/50), P890 (SJ60/70), P909 (SO29/39), P910 (SO49/59), P911 (SO69/79), P929 (SO08/18), P930 (SO28/38), P931 (SO48/58), P932 (SO68/78), P949 (SO07/17), P950 (SO27/37), P951 (SO47/57), P952 (SO67/77).

Footpath Guide
Smart, Robert, *Church Stretton and South Shropshire* **Rambles**, published by the author at 'Brackendale', Longhills Road, Church Stretton, Salop SY6 6DS.

Sidgwick, A[rthur] **H**[ugh] (1882-1917) A civil servant at the Board of Education who wrote *Walking Essays*, 1912. This collection of belles-lettres, of a kind much admired in Victorian and Edwardian Britain, contains essays on 'Walking in Literature', 'Walking and Music' and the eponymous '**Walker Miles**'. He also wrote *Jones's Wedding ; a Tale in Rhymed Prose*, published posthumously in 1918 after he died of wounds on the western front, which contains some descriptions in verse of walking in what is now the **Lake District National Park** (the general tone is out of keeping with our times and is unlikely to appeal to feminists). Sidgwick got himself fit for military service by undertaking a series of 32-kilometre walks in which he completely encircled London in 8 days between April and July 1916. Had he published a guide to his route we should have had an early version of the London Country-way **long-distance path**.

Sierra Club One of the most influential and powerful environmental pressure groups in the **United States**. It was founded in 1892 by **John Muir**, who was its first president, and Robert Underwood Johnson, the publisher of *Century*, to counter the threats from developers in the most beautiful areas of the country. The Sierra Club has chapters in every state, and branches in most large cities, and organises local walks and other outdoor activities. It has a current membership in excess of half a million. *(For address see Appendix.)*

Signpost A signpost is a metal or wooden arm, usually attached to a free-standing post that indicates the direction of the **right of way**, Signposts on public **paths**, often colloquially, but sometimes inaccurately referred to as '**footpath signs**', were erected as early as the nineteenth century by the **Peak and Northern Footpath Society** and the **Scottish Rights of Way Society Ltd**. In **England** and **Wales**, **highway** authorities have a statutory duty to erect signposts wherever a right of way leaves a public road. They are only absolved from this liability if the parish council (or chairman of the parish meeting if there is no council) agrees that signposts are not necessary. If the parish council insists on signposting then the highway authority must acquiesce. Signposts must indicate whether the right of way is a footpath, **bridleway** or byway. Highway authorities may also erect signposts at points along the right of way if it deems them necessary. Signposts are often complemented by **waymarks**.

Silk The warmest, strongest, most absorbent, lightest and most expensive of all natural fibres. It can absorb moisture up to 30 per cent of its own weight and still feel warm and dry to the touch. It is used in underwear and **glove** linings.

Simpson, A. L. A prolific writer of **footpath guides** to the countryside around London. He is the author of *Afoot around London*, 1912; *Wayfarings around London*, 1915; *The* **Footpath** *Way Round London; Fieldpath and Woodland* **Rambles** *with Directions and* **Maps**, 1922; and the posthumous *Rambles in Essex*, 1950 (published by the Railway Executive). All these titles were published under the pseudonym 'Pathfinder'. Simpson was also 'The Star Rambler', and wrote a series of weekly articles for the [London] *Star* newspaper. They were collected and published by the newspaper as a series of pocket-sized footpath guides which had a foreword signed with the initials A. L. S. *The Star Rambles around London*, 1922; *The Star Rambles*, 4 vols, 1926; *Star Rambles for Hikers*, 2 Vols., 1931; *The Star Rambles (New Series); North of the Thames Vol. I.* 1937; and *The Star Rambles (New Series); South of the Thames Vol. II.* 1937. He also wrote *The Complete Rambler; a Book for Lovers of the Open Air and the Complete Joys of the Countryside*, 1930.

Skye A large mountainous island, about 80 kilometres long, off the west coast of **Scotland**. For the really tough **hill-walker**, Skye probably offers the finest walking in the whole of the United Kingdom. No part of the island is more than 8 kilometres from the sea, and the coastline is heavily indented by sea lochs. There are many peaks over 900 metres offering wonderful vistas of **mountains** and seascape. Many of the peaks are only accessible to rock-climbers, and walkers must expect some **scrambling**. The Black Cuillin, probably the finest ridge in Scotland, cannot be walked throughout its length without some rock-climbing. (See figure 25 for map showing the major scenic divisions of Scotland.)

Maps
1:50000 **Landranger** sheets 23,24, 32, 33.
1:25000 **Outdoor Leisure Map** 8 of the Cuillin and Torridon Hills covers part of the island.

Guidebook
Slesser, Malcolm, *The Islands of Scotland, including Skye*, **Scottish Mountaineering Club**, 1990.

Footpath Guides
MacInnes, Hamish, *Highland Walks Vol 2: Skye to Cape Wrath*, Hodder and Stoughton, 1984.
Parker, J. Wilson, *Scrambles in Skye, Guide to Walks and Scrambles in the Black Cuillin*, Cicerone Press, 1983.

Sleeping bags A sleeping bag is an insulated sack used by **backpackers** instead of conventional bedding. Sleeping bags are classified according to their seasonal suitability in British conditions. Thus a one-season bag is for summer use only, a three-season bag is for spring, summer and autumn use, and a four-season bag is designed for winter use. Some sleeping bags come in matching sets so that a one-season bag can be used with a three-season bag for winter use.

The efficiency of sleeping bags is affected by their design, construction and filling (see figure 26). The simplest form of bag is the so-called 'happy camper' which is oblong in shape, very inefficient at conserving heat, and useless for **backpacking**. Next comes the simple tapered bag which is a considerable improvement, but still not suitable for backpacking, except in mild conditions. The designs that conserve heat best are the body-hugging tulip and mummy-shaped bags. These have a boxed foot to accommodate the feet comfortably, and a hood which can be secured with a draw-string that traps as much body heat as possible, thus economising on the amount of filling required, and saving weight.

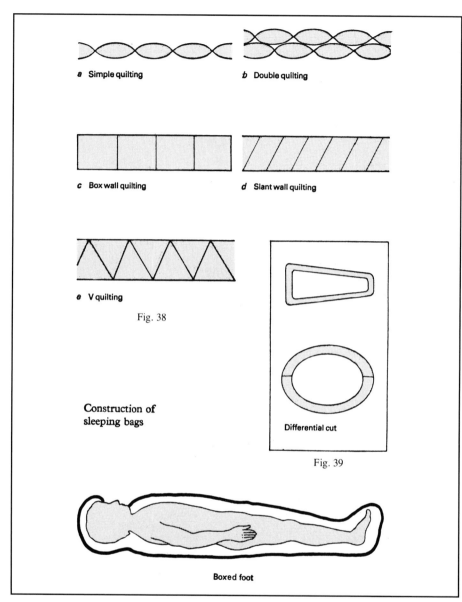

a Simple quilting

b Double quilting

c Box wall quilting

d Slant wall quilting

e V quilting

Fig. 38

Construction of
sleeping bags

Differential cut

Fig. 39

Boxed foot

Figure 26: Construction of sleeping bags.

bag of superb quality can weigh as little as 1 kilogram; a three-season synthetic bag weighs about 1.5 kilograms; and a four-season bag is correspondingly heavier ranging from 1.5 kilograms to 2.5 kilograms. Sleeping bags should be used with an **insulating mat**.

Sli Chorcha Dhuibhne (Dingle way) This **long-distance path** traverses almost the entire length of the Dingle peninsula, County Kerry, **Eire**, from Tralee to Dingle, giving delightful views of the sea. It is an easy itinerary running for 50 kilometres along **boreens**, country roads and mountain **tracks** that are suitable for casual walkers.
Maps
Irish Ordnance survey 1:126720 sheet 20.
Leaflet: Irish Tourist Board Information Sheet 26G *Sli Chorcha Dhuibhne.*

Slieve Bloom Way A circular **long-distance path** of 50 kilometres through the Slieve Bloom **mountains** in the counties of Offaly and Laoise, **Eire**. The itinerary includes forest roads, firebreaks, mountain **tracks** and riverside **paths**.
Maps
Irish Ordnance Survey 1:126720 sheet 15.
Leaflet: Irish Tourist Board Information Sheet 26F *The Slieve Bloom Way.*

Sligo and Leitrim A high plateau of limestone in the west of **Eire**. The region is characterised by vertical cliffs that have fractured into sheer rock spires. The poet W. B. Yeats wrote about the many legends associated with the area, and he is buried at the foot of Ben Bulben.
Maps
Irish Ordnance Survey 1:63360 sheets 43, 44, 55, 56. 1:126720 sheet 7.
Footpath Guide
Simms, P., and Foley, G., *Irish Walks Guides North West; Donegal, Sligo, Armagh, Derry, Tyrone and Fermanagh,* Gill & Macmillan, 1979.

Smith, Albert [Richard] (1816-60) One of the first Englishmen to climb Mont Blanc, and an engaging self-publicist who made a great deal of money by lecturing about his exploits. As a result of a lecture given before the Royal Family at Osborne, he was chosen to guide the future **Edward VII** over the Glacier des Boissons in 1857.

Smith, B[aker] **P**[eter] (1800-88) A London barrister who wrote two flowery, portentously

Most sleeping bags use a loose filling to provide **insulation**. The lightest, and most expensive is **down**, but the most popular fillings are now **Hollofil** and **Quallofil Fibrepile**, which is not a filling but an insulating material from which the sleeping bag is constructed, is also used. Bags that rely on a loose material for their **insulation** need to be constructed so that the filling does not shift in use (see figure 26). *Simple quilting* is the cheapest and least efficient as it allows the cold to enter wherever the bag is stitched. *Double quilting* is two layers of simple quilting sewn together which eliminates the cold spots. *Box-wall quilting* is an improvement on simple quilting, but the upright dividing sections allow the filling to fall away from the dividing sections. *Slant-wall quilting* has the sections cut on the slant so that the filling cannot fall away. *V-quilting* is the most expensive and efficient design to hold the filling in place.

An ultra-lightweight three-season down

literary, and tedious accounts of walking tours. The first, *Journal of an Excursion round the South-eastern Coast of England*, privately published in 1834, describes his journey by steamer to the Isle of Thanet, and his walk from there, via the Cinque Ports, to Brighton, from where he returned to London by stagecoach. The second, *A Trip to the Far West*, 1840, records a voyage by steamer to Falmouth from where he made three walking excursions and visited some tin mines.

Smith, Roger [William] (1938-) Journalist, author, and from 1978-87 the editor of ***The Great Outdoors***. He is deeply involved in the conservation movement in **Scotland**, was co-founder and first chairman of the **Scottish Wild Land Group**, and a member of the council of the **National Trust for Scotland** since 1982.
Publications about Walking
*42 Peaks; the Story of the **Bob Graham** Round*, **Bob Graham Club**, 1982.
A Visitor's Guide to the Scottish Borders, Moorland Publishing Co., 1984.
Weekend Walking, Oxford Illustrated Press, 1985
Classic Walks in Scotland (with **Cameron McNeish**), Oxford Illustrated Press, 1988.
Also contributed to
Smith, Roger, Editor, *The Winding **Trail***, Diadem, 1986.
Smith, Roger, Editor, *Walking in **Scotland***, Spurbooks, 1982.
Unsworth, Walt, Editor, *Classic Walks in Europe*, Oxford Illustrated Press, 1987.
Smith, Roger, Editor, *The Great Outdoors Book*

Roger Smith, editor of **The Great Outdoors**, *1978-87.*

of the Walking Year, Thorsons, 1988.

Smith, Roland [Samuel George] (1944-) Head of Information Services for the **Peak National Park**, editor of *Peakland Post* and *Peak Park News*, and author of several books about **national parks**. His early career was in journalism, and he still writes for the *Birmingham Post* and outdoor magazines.
Publications about Walking
First and Last; the Peak National Park in Words and Pictures, Peak National Park, 3rd Ed., 1980.
Wildest Britain; a Visitor's Guide to the National Parks, Blandford Press, 1983.
The Peak National Park: a Pictorial Guide, Peak National Park in association with Jarrold, 1985.
The Peak, Webb & Bower in association with Michael Joseph, 1987.
The Peak; a Park for all Seasons, Constable, 1989.
Walking; the Great Views (with **John Cleare**), David & Charles, 1991.
Also contributed to
Ordnance Survey *Leisure Guide; the Peak District*, Ordnance Survey in association with the Automobile Association, 1987.
Hillaby, John, Editor, *Walking in Britain*, Collins, 1988.

Roland Smith, editor of **Peakland Post** *and* **Peak Park News.**

Snow When water vapour is frozen it forms crystals known as snow. There are many different kinds of snow, ranging from the relatively dry powder snow, beloved by skiers, to very large wet flakes. Snow can change its character when lying on the ground, and it is this property that is often responsible for **avalanches**. In the eyes of many walkers, the countryside is never more beautiful than when covered in a mantle of snow which transforms quite ordinary scenes into landscapes of astonishing beauty. In lowland country, there are few **hazards** associated with snow providing that the walker is well shod and has plenty of warm waterproof **clothing**. In upland areas the situation is quite different, and snow must be treated with extreme caution. Because of the strong winds found in higher altitudes, snow drifts much more, and dangerous **cornices** may form in exposed areas. **Navigation** tends to be more difficult because familiar landmarks may be altered or obscured, and **paths** may not be visible. Not only will plenty of warm garments and good quality shell clothing be required, but the prudent walker will take an **ice axe** and **crampons**. If the weather deteriorates, it is essential to seek lower ground as soon as possible to avoid being caught in a **white-out** or blizzard.

Snow blindness An extremely painful form of temporary blindness caused by ultra-violet rays reflected off **snow**. It is most common in high altitudes, but it can occur almost anywhere, even in cloudy conditions, when snow is lying on the ground. The symptoms usually appear after the damage has been done, but the condition can be avoided by always wearing good quality sun-glasses or snow goggles.

Snow bridge A covering of **snow** that forms over a **crevasse** or stream. Snow bridges are often unstable and not readily identifiable, and when walking on wet **glaciers** it is essential for the leader to be attached to a **rope**, and to probe constantly with his **ice axe**. Snow bridges over streams are also unstable, but it is usually possible to hear the water bubbling below the surface and to take suitable precautions.

Snow, Sebastian (1935-) Author and long-distance walker. In 1973, he set out to walk from Tierra del Fuego, on the extreme tip of south America, to walk to Alaska. The walk proved tougher than even he expected, he became ill in Panama and gave up after covering 14,000 kilometres. He had a number of extraordinary adventures and suffered many hardships which he described in his entertaining book *The **Rucksack** Man*, Hodder & Stoughton, 1976.

Snow shelters In the event of **benightment** or other emergency in **snow**, it is essential to find shelter. All Esquimos know that safe and secure shelters can be made from snow, but it takes an expert several hours to construct one in good conditions, and it can be impossible in a strong wind. It is usually better to find a boulder or tree trunk where the wind may have formed an area free of snow that can be used as a natural shelter. To build a classic snow hole, a bank of snow at least three metres deep is required. The hole should be excavated using an **ice axe**, a cooking canteen or some other improvised tool, and should be made just sufficiently large to accommodate the number of people sheltering in it as this will conserve energy and warmth. When completed, the entrance should slope down from the sleeping platform and the size of the

Figure 27: Snow shelters.

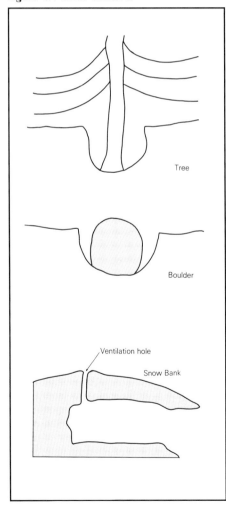

Tree

Boulder

Ventilation hole

Snow Bank

entrance reduced by packing it with snow so that it can be blocked with a **rucksack**. Ventilation should be provided by poking a hole through the roof with an ice axe, an action which should be repeated at regular intervals to prevent the hole being sealed by snow (see figure 27).

Snowdonia National Park The second largest British **national park** covering an area of 2171 square kilometres. It includes the coastline of Wales from Aberdovey to just north of Harlech, and is then bounded by the towns of Conway, Bala and Machynlleth. Snowdon (1085 metres) is the highest **mountain** in Britain outside **Scotland**, and the Snowdon range contains some of the wildest country in Britain, with numerous lakes to enhance the beauty of the mountains. Over the years, much slate has been quarried, and this national park is under constant threat from industry. (See figure 36 for a **map** showing the location of all national parks in the United Kingdom.) *(For addresses of National Park Headquarters and Information Centres see Appendix.)*
Official Guidebook
Styles, Showell, *Snowdonia*, Webb & Bower in association with Michael Joseph, 1987.
National Park Newspaper
The Snowdonia Star.
Maps
1:126720 ½ in. to the mile) **Tourist Map** of Snowdonia.
1:50000 **Landranger** sheets 115, 116, 124, 125, 135.
1:25000 **Outdoor Leisure Maps** of Snowdonia 16 (Conwy Valley area), 17 (Snowdon area), 18 (Harlech and Bala areas), 23 (Cadair Idris area).
Footpath Guides
Walks leaflets and maps compiled and published by Snowdonia National Park:
Footpaths on Cader Idris:
  *Minffordd **Path***
  Pony Path from Ty Nant
  Pony Path from Llanfihangel y Pennant
Footpaths on Snowdon:
  Llanberis Path
  *Miners' **Track***
  Rhyd Ddu Path
  Snowdon Ranger
  Watkin Path
  Branwen's Walk (Harlech)
  Bridges and Rivers (Betws-y-Coed)
  Cwmorthin
  Glyn Aran (Dolgellau)
  Precipice Walk (Dolgellau)

  Torrent Walk (Dolgellau)
  Walks around Maentwrog
Contour Maps:
  Llanberis Path
  Miners' Track and Pyg Path
  Snowdon Ranger and Rhyd Ddu
  Watkin Path
Ashton, Steve, *Classic Walks in Wales*, Oxford Illustrated Press, 1990.
Ashton, Steve, **Hill Walking** in *Snowdonia*, Cicerone Press, 1989.
Maddern, Ralph, *Walk in the Beautiful Conwy Valley*, Focus Publications, 5th Rev. Ed., 1986.
Maddern, Ralph, *Walk in Magnificent Snowdonia*, Focus Publications, 3rd Rev. Ed., 1986.
Maddern, Ralph, *Walk in the Vale of Ffestiniog*, Focus Publications, 1986.
Poucher, W. A., *The Welsh Peaks*, Constable, 9th Rev. Ed., 1987.
Rowland, E. G., *The Ascent of Snowdon*, Cicerone Press, 5th Rev. Ed., 1975.
Rowland, E. G., *Hill Walking in Snowdonia*, Cicerone Press, 4th Rev. Ed., 1975.
Sale, Richard, *Best Walks in North **Wales***, Constable, 1989.

Socks The only difference between a sock and a **stocking** is that the former comes up only as far as the mid-calf whilst the latter is knee-length. Socks are normally worn only with shorts, but may be used with **breeches** on mild days. Most walkers favour woollen **loopstitch** socks rather than the old-fashioned Norwegian raggsocks. It is now possible to buy socks made from non-woollen materials.

Solway Coast An **area of outstanding natural beauty** that stretches from the Scottish border to Maryport in Cumbria, and covers an area of 107 square kilometres overlooking the Solway Firth to **Scotland**. *The area is flat and contains several fine sandy beaches, and there are splendid views across to the Scottish* **hills**. (See figure 36 for a **map** showing the location of all AONBs in the United Kingdom.)
Maps
1:50000 **Landranger** sheets 85, 89.
1:25000 **Pathfinder** sheets P543 (NY06/16), P544 (NY26/36), P556 (NY05/15), P557 (NY25/35), P566 (04/14), P575 (03/13).

Somerville, Christopher [James Fownes] (1948-) Author and broadcaster who specialises in thematic walks such as disused railways, literary walks, river walks etc.
Publications about Walking
Walking Old Railways, David & Charles, 1979.

Walking West Country Railways, David & Charles, 1982.
Twelve Literary Walks, W. H. Allen, 1985.
*Coastal Walks in **England** and **Wales***, Grafton Books, 1988.
Fifty Best River Walks of Britain, Webb & Bower in association with Michael Joseph, 1988.

Sorbothane An exceptionally dense material that feels like very heavy rubber and can absorb shock without immediately rebounding, thus dispersing the energy slowly. It is used in **footbeds** to cushion the shock transmitted from the sole striking hard surfaces.

Sotheby, William (1757-1833) A man of letters, and sometime army officer, who was highly regarded in his day but is now quite forgotten. He is the author of a literary curiosity *A Tour through Parts of **Wales**, Sonnets, Odes and other Poems with Engravings from Drawings Taken on the Spot*, 1794. This is an account of a walking tour taken with his brother written entirely in uninspiring blank verse. The book is interesting more for its beautiful typography than for its literary merit.

South Africa South Africa is the most prosperous country in southern Africa, has a wealth of beautiful scenery, and probably offers better walking and **backpacking** opportunities than any other in the continent. All **hiking** facilities are integrated.

The National Hiking Way Board is in the process of developing a **long-distance path** that will run for hundreds of kilometres in a huge horseshoe through the most mountainous areas of the country from the Soutpans range in the north, to the Cedarberg Wilderness Area in Cape Province. Parts of this **trail** are now waymarked and open with **huts** and refuges along the route. Permits, for which a small charge is made, are required to walk the trail. A brochure, *Follow the Footprints* is available from the South African Tourism Board (see below). More information and guides are available from the National Hiking Way Board.
Useful Addresses
South African Tourism Board, Regency House, 1/4 Warwick Street, London W1R 5WB. Tel. 071-439-9661.
Ramblers' Organisation: Federation of Hiking and Rambling Clubs. (No permanent address as each rambling club in turn takes on the duties for a year. The National Hiking Way Board can supply the current address.)
National Hiking Way Board, Private Bag X447, Pretoria 0001 is the government depart-

ment responsible for long-distance paths.
*National **Map** Survey:* The Government Printer, Private Bag X85, Pretoria 0001.
Official Maps: the whole country is covered by 1:50000 maps on which **footpaths** are marked.
Footpath Guides: a number are published by the National Hiking Way Board (see above), the Department of Forestry, Private Bag X313, Pretoria 0001, and the **National Parks** Board, PO Box 787, Pretoria 0001.
The most detailed guide to walking in South Africa is Levy, Jaynee, *Complete Guide to Walks and Trails in Southern Africa*, Struik, 1988 (distributed in the United Kingdom by New Holland Publishers).

South Armagh An **area of outstanding natural beauty** in **Northern Ireland**, centred on Slieve Gullion **Mountain** to the east of Newry, which is rich in archaeological remains. It joins the **Mourne** AONB, which in turn links with the **Lecale Coast** and **Strangford Lough** AONBs. (See figure 36) for a **map** showing the location of all AONBs in the United Kingdom.)
Maps
1:50000 **Ordnance Survey of Northern Ireland** sheets 28, 29.
Footpath Guide
Simms, P., and Foley, G., *Irish Walks Guides North West; Donegal, Sligo, Armagh, Derry, Tyrone and Fermanagh*, Gill & Macmillan, 1979.

South Devon This **area of outstanding natural beauty**, designated in 1960, runs from Torbay to Plymouth, includes most of the South Hams, and covers 332 square kilometres. The region is famous for its fine beaches, cliff scenery and the beautiful estuaries and inlets that stretch for miles inland. (See figure 36 for a **map** showing the location of all AONBs in the United Kingdom.)
Maps
1:50000 **Landranger** sheets 201, 202.
1:25000 **Pathfinder** sheets P1356 (SX45/55), P1357 (SX65/75), P1362 (SX54/64) plus **Outdoor Leisure Map** 20 South Devon.
Footpath Guides
15 Walks in the Kingsbridge Area, compiled and published by the South Hams Group of the **Ramblers' Association**, 'St Malo', Stentiford, Fore Street, Kingsbridge, Devon TQ7 1AX, 1986.
16 Walks around Salcombe, compiled and published by the South Hams Group of the Ramblers' Association, 'St Malo', Stentiford, Fore Street, Kingsbridge, Devon TQ7 1AX, 1986.

South Downs Way This **national trail**, designated by the **Countryside Commission** and officially opened in 1972, runs for some 60 kilometres from Eastbourne (**grid reference** TV 600972) in Sussex to Winchester (grid reference Z 482293), in Hampshire. It is an easy walk on **tracks** and **downland** turf with only an occasional stiff climb, so no special kit or equipment is required. There is an excellent rail network which crosses the **path** at several points. It is quite practicable, with some planning, to walk this path in a series of separate day outings from London. Camping is not recommended because of the lack of water, but there is plenty of accommodation en route. (See figure 36 for a map showing the location of all national trails and official **long-distance paths** in the United Kingdom.)
Youth Hostels
Beachy Head, Alfriston, Telscombe, Truleigh Hill and Arundel.
Maps
1:50000 **Landranger** sheets 197, 198, 199.
1:25000 **Pathfinder** sheets P1285 (SU61/71), P1286 (SU81/91), P1287 (TQ01/11), P1288 (TQ21/31), P1306 (TQ00/10), P1307 (TQ20/30), P1308 (TQ40/50), P1324 (TV49/59/69).
Footpath Guides
Comber, Harry, *Along the South Downs Way*, Society of Sussex Downsmen, 254 Victoria Drive, Eastbourne, Sussex, BN20 8QR. 1985.
Jebb, Miles, *A Guide to the South Downs Way*, Constable, 1984.
Millmore, Paul, *South Downs Way*, Aurum Press in association with the Countryside Commission and the **Ordnance Survey**, 1990.

South Hampshire Coast An **area of outstanding natural beauty**, designated in 1967, that, like **Chichester Harbour** AONB, is a famous sailing centre. It covers 78 square kilometres from just east of Beaulieu to west of Lymington with the northern edge bordered by the New Forest. (See figure 36 for a map showing the location of all AONBs in the United Kingdom.)
Maps
1:50000 **Landranger** sheet 196.
1:25000 **Outdoor Leisure Map** 22 New Forest.

South Leinster Way A **long-distance path** that runs for 94 kilometres from the end of the **Munster Way** at Carrick-on-Suir, County Kilkenny, **Eire** to the beginning of the

Wicklow Way at Kildavin, County Carlow, making a total route of 307 kilometres. The scenery is an interesting combination of forest **tracks**, mountain **trails** rising to 450 metres, and riverside **paths**.
Maps: Irish Ordnance Survey 1:126720 sheets 19, 22 & 23.
Leaflet: Irish Tourist Board Information Sheet 26D *The South Leinster Way.*

South West Coast Path A **national trail** formerly known as the South West Peninsula Coast Path, that runs for approximately 956 kilometres following, as far as possible, the very edge of the coast from Minehead (**grid reference** SS 972467), Somerset to South Haven Point (grid reference SZ 036866), near Poole, **Dorset** through some of the finest coastal scenery in **England**. For much of the route it follows the **path**, patrolled daily by the coastguard until 1913, which was described by **Walter White**, Sir **Leslie Stephen** and **G. M. Trevelyan**. It is a strenuous route with many steep climbs from beach to cliff-top, and a number of **river crossings** have to be made. Walkers are advised to obtain a copy of *The South West Way; the Complete Guide to Great Britain's Longest* **Footpath** compiled by the South West Way Association and published annually by Devon Books. Despite its title, this is not a **footpath guide**, but an invaluable source of information giving details of ferry crossings, tide-tables for **river crossings**, landslips, accommodation, and the latest information about the state of the route.
The path is divided into the following sections:
1 The Somerset and **North Devon** Coast Path (140 kilometres).
2 The **Cornwall** Coast Path (440 kilometres).
3 The **South Devon** Coast Path (243 kilometres).
4 The **Dorset** Coast Path (130 kilometres). (See figure 36 for a map showing the location of all national trails and official **long-distance paths** in the United Kingdom.)
Path Association
The South West Way Association.

1. Somerset and North Devon Coast Path
Youth Hostels
Minehead, Lynton, Ilfracombe, Instow, Hartland.
Maps
1:50000 **Landranger** sheets 180, 181, 190.
1:25000 **Pathfinder** sheets P1213 (SS44/54), P1214 ((SS64/74), P1215 (SS84/94), P1233 (SS43/53), P1253 (SS22/32), P1254 (SS42/52), P1273 (SS21/31).

Footpath Guides
Collings, A. G., *Along the South West Way; Part 1 Minehead to Bude*, Tabb House, 1985.
Collins, Martin, *The South West Way; a Walker's guide to the Coast Path, Vol. 1: Minehead to Penzance*, Cicerone Press, 1989.
Tarr, Roland, *South West Coast Path; Minehead to Padstow*, Aurum Press in association with the **Countryside Commission** and the **Ordnance Survey**, 1989.

2. Cornwall Coast Path
Youth Hostels
Boscastle, Tintagel, Treyarnon Bay, Newquay, Perranporth, Penzance, Coverack, Pendennis, Boswinger, Golant.
Maps
1:50000 Landranger sheets 190, 200, 201, 203, 204.
1:25000 Pathfinder sheets P1273 (SS21/31), P1292 (SS20/30), P1310 (SX19), P1325 (SX08/18), P1337 (SW87/97), P1346 (SW86/96), P1352 (SW75), P1354 (SX05/15), P1355 (SX25/35), P1356 (SX45/55), P1359 (SW54/64), P1361 (SW94/SX04), P1364 (SW33/43/53/), P1365 (SW63/53/73), P1366 (SW83/73/93), P1368 (SW32/42), P1369 (SW52/62/72), P1370 (SW72/82), P1372 (SW61/71).
Footpath Guides
Collins, Martin, *The South West Way; a Walker's guide to the Coast Path, Vol. 1: Minehead to Penzance*, Cicerone Press, 1989.
Collins, Martin, *The South West Way; a Walker's guide to the Coast Path, Vol. 2: Penzance to Poole*, Cicerone Press, 1989.
Tarr, Roland, *South West Coast Path; Minehead to Padstow*, Aurum Press in association with the Countryside Commission and the Ordnance Survey, 1989.
Macadam, John, *South West Coast Path; Padstow to Falmouth*, Aurum Press in association with the Countryside Commission and the Ordnance Survey, 1990.

3. South Devon Coast Path
Youth Hostels
Plymouth, Salcombe, Start Bay, Maypool, Exeter, Beer.
Maps
1:50000 Landranger sheets 192, 193, 201, 202
1:25000 Pathfinder sheets P1316 (SY29/39), P1330 (SY08/18), P1342 (SX87/97), P1351 (SX86/96), P1356 (SX45/55), P1362 (SX54/64), P1367 (SX73/63/83) plus **Outdoor Leisure Map** 20 South Devon.
Footpath Guides
Collins, Martin, *The South West Way; a Walker's*

guide to the Coast Path, Vol. 2: Penzance to Poole, Cicerone Press, 1989.
Gant, Roland, *A Guide to the South Devon and Dorset Coast Path*, Constable, 1982.
Le Messurier, Brian, *South West Coast Path; Falmouth to Exmouth*, Aurum Press in association with the Countryside Commission and the Ordnance Survey, 1990.
Tarr, Roland, *South West Coast Path; Exmouth to Poole*, Aurum Press in association with the Countryside Commission and the Ordnance Survey, 1989.

4. Dorset Coast Path
Youth Hostels
Bridport, Litton Cheney, Lulworth, Swanage.
Maps
1:50000 Landranger sheets 193, 194, 195.
1:25000 Pathfinder sheets P1316 (SY29/39), P1317 (SY49/59), P1331 (SY58), P1332 (SY68/78), P1343 (SY67/77), P1344 (SY87/97/SZ07) plus Outdoor Leisure Map 15 Purbeck.
Footpath Guides
Collins, Martin, *The South West Way; a Walker's Guide to the Coast Path, Vol. 2: Penzance to Poole*, Cicerone Press, 1989.
Gant, Roland, *A Guide to the South Devon and Dorset Coast Path*, Constable, 1982.
Tarr, Roland, *South West Coast Path; Exmouth to Poole*, Aurum Press in association with the Countryside Commission and the Ordnance Survey, 1989.

South West Way Association The Association, founded in 1973, exists to promote the interests of users of the **South West Coast Path**. The South West Way brings pressure to bear on the appropriate authorities to improve the **path** and to provide a coastal route where none exists at present. The Association compiles *The South West Way; the Complete Guide to Great Britain's Longest* **Footpath** published annually by Devon Books which, although no substitute for **maps** or **footpath guides** to the route, provides essential information about tides, ferries, **river crossings**, changes of route etc., and contains an accommodation list. The Association publishes a newsletter, leaflets and maps to various sections of the path. *(For address see Appendix.)*

Southern Highlands This area of **Scotland** is bounded in the north by the rivers Orchy and Tummel which form the boundary with the **Central Highlands** and run down

SOUTHERN, J. A.

almost to the Glasgow—Edinburgh axis. The Southern Highlands are mountainous in character, and include Loch Lomond and the Trossachs. As this area lies so close to Scotland's industrial belt, it is the country's most popular walking area, and its most famous **mountains** include Ben Lomond, The Cobbler and Ben Lawers. (See figure 25 for **map** showing the major scenic divisions of Scotland.)
Maps
1:50000 **Landranger** sheets 49-52 inclusive and 55-58 inclusive.
1:63360 **Tourist Map** of the Trossachs.
Guidebook
Bennet, D. J., *The Southern Highlands*, Scottish Mountaineering Trust, 2nd Rev. Ed., 1985.
Footpath Guide
MacInnes, Hamish, *Highland Walks Vol 1: Ben Lui to the Falls of Glomach*, Hodder and Stoughton, 1984.
Summers, Gilbert, *Walk Loch Lomond and the Trossachs*, Bartholomew, 1986.

Southern, J. A. (18--?-19--?) A member of the Highbury United Rambling Club, the St Mary Magdalene Rambling Club, and one of the founders and joint honorary secretary (with **Lawrence Chubb**) of the **Federation of Rambling Clubs**. He was the author of several **footpath guides** in the style and manner of his friend **Walker Miles**, whose guides he revised and edited after the master's death. He wrote guides under his own name, and also under the punning pseudonyms Alf Holliday (Half Holiday) and Noah Weston (Nor' Western). All the titles in the following list of Southern's guides were published before the death of Walker Miles in 1908 in the *Rustic Rambles* series issued by Miles' printing company Robert Edmund Taylor & Sons:
Northern Heights Series
    15   *Over Northern Heights* by Alf Holliday, 1896. [Includes Harrow, Barnet, Highgate, Enfield, Finchley and Edgware.]
    16   *Over Northern Heights* by Alf Holliday, [Includes Burnham Beeches, Uxbridge, Windsor, Eton and Taplow.]
    36   *Home Counties* **Rambles**; *Part 1 Comprising New Routes in Middlesex and Hertfordshire* by Noah Weston, 1907. [Includes Southgate, Edgware, Enfield, Barnet etc.]
    38   *Home Counties Rambles; Part 2 Comprising New Routes in Middlesex and Hertfordshire* by Noah Weston, 1910. [Includes Potter's Bar, Hatfield, South Mimms, Stanmore etc.]
West Herts Series
    17   [Includes St Alban's, Hatfield, Edg-

ware, Elstree, Shenley and Smallford]
    18   [Round Watford, King's Langley, Chipperfield, and Aldenham]
The following guides appeared under under Southern's own name:
Rustic Rambles through Kentish Orchards
    Part I   The Neighbourhood of Bromley.
    Part II   The Neighbourhood of Bromley, Second Series.
Rustic Rambles among the Bucks Beeches
    Part 1 The Neighbourhood of Wendover (the **Chiltern Hills***) with routes to Princes Risborough, Hampden, Tring, Aylesbury etc.*
Rustic Rambles through Middlesex Pastures (The 'Northern Heights')
    Part I   The Enfield Chase with Routes to Enfield, Barnet, Cuffley, Cheshunt etc.
    Part II   The Neighbourhood of Barnet with routes to Potter's Bar, Ridge, Elstree, Edgware etc.
    Part III   The Neighbourhood of Harrow with Routes to Edgware, Stanmore, Pinner, Ruislip etc.
Rustic Rambles in the Surrey Uplands
    Part I   The Neighbourhood of Croydon with Routes to Sanderstead, Addington Hills, Warlingham, etc.
    Part II   Round Coulsdon, with Routes to Banstead, Chipstead, Merstham, Chaldon etc.
Rustic Rambles through Hertfordshire Meadows
    Part 1   The Neighbourhood of St Albans with routes to Hatfield, King's Langley, Wheathampstead etc.
Rambles in Epping Forest and Rural Essex, 1916 was published as *'official guide of the Great Eastern Railway.'*
NB *Rustic Rambles to Beauty Spots round London with Routes to the* **Surrey Hills***, Kentish Commons, the Northern Heights, the Chiltern Hills, the Hindhead etc.* has no author on the title-page but appears to be based on other titles in the series.
    Most of the above titles were published with no date on the title-page, but according to the catalogue of the British Library they were issued between 1916-9. They were all bound with reproductions of 1:63360 **map**s published by the **Ordnance Survey**.

Southern Upland Way A **long-distance path**, created by the **Countryside Commission for Scotland**, which runs for 340 kilometres through southern **Scotland** from Portpatrick (**grid reference** NW 998542) near Stranraer, Dumfries & Galloway on the west coast, to Cockburnspath (grid reference NT 774709) near Dunbar on the Berwickshire coast. This is probably the most strenuous and demanding of the long-distance paths, and should only be undertaken by fit **fell-walkers**.

Accommodation in some sections is very sparse, and as there are considerable stretches where none is available, **backpacking** is to be preferred. **Thomas Carlyle** described a small section of the route. (See figure 36 for a **map** showing the location of all **national** trails and official long-distance paths in the United Kingdom.)
Youth Hostels
Minnigaff, Kendoon, Wanlockhead, Broadmeadows, Melrose, Coldingham.
Maps
1:50000 **Landranger** sheets 67, 71, 74, 76, 77, 78, 79, 82.
1:25000 **Pathfinder** sheets P409 (NT67/77), P422 (NT66/76), P435 (NT45/55), P436 (NY65/75), P449 (NT44/54), P460 (NT23/33), P472 (NT22/32), P481 (NS61/71), P482 (NS81/91), P483 (NT01/11), P484 (NT21/31), P493 (NS60/70), P494 (NS80/90), P495 (NT00/10), P461 (NT43/53), P504 (NX69/79), P515 (NX48/58), P516 (NX68/78), P526 (NX27/37), P527 (NX47/57), P537 (NW95/96/97), P538 (NX06/16), P539 (NX26/36), P551 (NX05/15).

Footpath Guides
Andrew, Ken, *The Southern Upland Way; Eastern Section*, HMSO, 1984.
Andrew, Ken, *The Southern Upland Way; Western Section*, HMSO, 1984.
Williams, David, *A Guide to the Southern Upland Way*, Constable, 1989.

Southern Uplands Also known as the Lowlands, this area comprises that section of **Scotland** lying south of the Glasgow—Edinburgh axis, and runs down to the border with **England**. Although the term 'Lowlands' is something of a misnomer as they contain **mountains** almost as high as any in England, this region lacks the rugged quality normally associated with Scottish scenery. The A74 road divides the region into two. On the eastern side lies the Border country formed by the river Tweed and its tributaries, where the **hills** are smooth in outline and covered in grass. On the western side, the hills tend to be more rugged, and generally have a more mountainous appearance. This is fine walking country more akin to the **Lake District National Park** and the **Pennines** than the more truly mountainous regions of Scotland. (See figure 25 for **map** showing the major scenic divisions of Scotland.)
Maps
1:50000 **Landranger** sheets 63-67 inclusive

136

and 70-87 inclusive.

Guidebooks

Andrew, K. M., and Thrippleton, A. A., *The Southern Uplands*, Scottish Mountaineering Trust, West Col, 1972.

Footpath Guides

Hallewall, Richard, *Walk Lothian, the Borders and Fife*, Bartholomew, 1988.

Hallewall, Richard, *Walk South West Scotland*, Bartholomew, 1989.

Moir, D. G., *Scottish Hill Tracks: Old **Highways** and **Drove Roads**, Southern Scotland*, Bartholomew, 1975.

Walton, Robert D., *Dumfries and Galloway Highways and **Byways**: Guide to 200 Walks and Climbs*, T. C. Farries, 1985.

Walton, Robert D., *Seventy Walks in Arran*, published by the author at 27 Castle Douglas Road, Dumfries DG2 7PA, 1987.

Southey, Robert (1774-1843) Poet Laureate, biographer of Horatio Nelson, and friend and associate of **Samuel Taylor Coleridge**, **William Wordsworth** and other **Lake poets**. He was an indefatigable walker all his life, and made a number of pedestrian excursions. In August, 1794 he walked with Coleridge from Bath to Huntspill, and on to Nether Stowey. In 1795, he walked with his friend Robert Lovell from Bristol to Marlborough to meet Coleridge off the London coach, but he failed to arrive, and the two men repeated the excursion several times in the next few days. He walked to **Wales** in 1794, and his letters reveal excellent descriptions of scenery, and in 1799 he walked in Devonshire. The Southeys removed to Greta Hall, in what is now the **Lake District National Park** in 1803, and lived there until Robert's death.

Spain Spain is a predominantly mountainous country with the highest peak being Mulhacen (3478 metres) in the Sierra Nevada. The Meseta is a 600-metre high plateau in the centre of the country which is surrounded by a series of **mountain** ranges. The evocative landscape, combined with the Moorish influence and its own peculiar form of Catholicism, makes it a fascinating country. There is also excellent walking in the Balearic Islands of Majorca, Minorca and Ibiza.

Useful Addresses

Spanish National Tourist Office, 57-58 St James's Street, London SW1A 1LD. Tel. 071-499-0901.

Ramblers' Organisation: Federacion Espanola de Montanismo, Alberto Aguilera 3, Madrid 15.

*Official Survey **Maps**:* Servicio Geografico del Ejercito 1:50000 (shows **footpaths**).

The pleasant countryside of Gerona, Spain (photo © Spanish Tourist Office).

Other Maps: Editorial Alpina maps with **scales** of 1:80000, 1:40000 and 1:25000 cover some of the best walking areas and show footpaths and mountain refuges.

Guide to Walking

Evans, Craig, *On Foot through Europe: a **Trail** Guide to Spain and **Portugal***, Quill, 1982.

Footpath Guides

Collomb, Robin G., *Gredos Mountains and Sierra Nevada*, West Col, 1987.

Parker, June, *Walking in Mallorca*, Cicerone Press, 1986.

Reynolds, Kev, *Walks and Climbs in the **Pyrénées***, Cicerone Press, 2nd Ed., 1983.

Walker, Robin, *Walks and Climbs in the Picos de Europa*, Cicerone Press, 1990.

Speakman, Colin (1941-) Freelance consultant to the **Countryside Commission** and local authorities on countryside, walking and transport matters, and author of numerous **footpath guides** and books about walking. He was Hon. Secretary of the West Riding Area of the **Ramblers' Association** (1969-74); member of the National Executive Committee of the Ramblers' Association (1971-5); officer of the **Yorkshire Dales National Park** (1975-81); founder and Secretary of the Yorkshire Dales Society (1981-) and editor of its journal *Yorkshire Dales Review;*

founder and managing director of Transport for Leisure which promotes green tourism and walking in the countryside.

Publications about Walking

Walking in the Craven Dales, Dalesman, 4th Ed., 1979.

*The Dales Way; from Ilkley to Windermere by Riverside **Path***, Dalesman, 6th Ed., 1987.

Walking in Historic Yorkshire, Dalesman, 1971.

*Wayfarer Walks in the South **Pennines***, Dalesman, 1982.

Walking in the Three Peaks, Dalesman, 1983.

Walking in the Yorkshire Dales, Hale, 2nd Ed., 1986.

Malhamdale; Walks from your Car, Dalesman, 1985.

*Let's Walk There!; Yorkshire and North West **England***, Javelin, 1987.

Twenty Great Walks from British Rail (with Les Lumsden), Sigma Press, 1987.

Great Walks from Welsh Railways (with Les Lumsden) Sigma Press, 1989.

King Ludwig Way (with Fleur Speakman), Cicerone Press, 1987.

Walking in the Salzkammergat (with Fleur Speakman), Cicerone Press, 1989.

Also contributed to

No Through Road; the AA Book of Country Walks, Drive Publications, 1975.

Duncan, Andrew, Editor, *Walkers' Britain 1; the Complete Pocket Guide to over 240 Walks and **Rambles***, Pan Books in association with the **Ordnance Survey**, 1981.

Gilbert, Richard and Wilson, Ken, Editors, *Classic Walks*, Diadem, 1985.

Duncan, Andrew, Editor, *Walkers' Britain 2 ; the Complete Pocket Guide to over 160 more Walks and Rambles*, Pan Books in association with the Ordnance Survey, 1986.

Unsworth, Walt, Editor, *Classic Walks of Europe*, Oxford Illustrated Press, 1987.

Smith, Roger, Editor, *The **Great Outdoors** Book of the Walking Year,* Thorsons 1988.

Speed lacing The system of hinged eyelets and hooks on walking **boots** through which laces are threaded. It is possible, by experiment, to vary the pressure on different parts of the foot by missing out the appropriate eyelet or hook, or having the lace slack at one point and tight at another. This technique is not only helpful in reducing pressures on **blisters**, but, as most boots are made only in one width per size, can be used to accommodate those with wide feet.

Spencer, Brian (1931-) The author of numerous walking guides, outdoor journalist

and leader of **treks** for tour companies in the **Pyrénées**, Lapland, the Black Forest, the High Atlas, Egypt, **Canada** and the **Himalaya**. He is a member of the Buxton **mountain rescue** team.

Publications about Walking

The Dove and Manifold Valleys (with Lindsey Porter), Moorland Publishing Co., 1972.

The Derbyshire Wye and Lathkill Dale (with John Robey), Moorland Publishing Co., 1973.

Matlock and the Upper Derwent Valley (with John Robey), Moorland Publishing Co., 1975.

*Walking in the **Alps***, Moorland Publishing Co., 1983.

*Walking in **Switzerland***, Moorland Publishing Co., 1986.

Walk the North York Moors, Bartholomew, 1986.

Walk the Peak District, Bartholomew, 1986.

Walk the Dales, Bartholomew, 1988.

*Walking in **Austria***, Moorland Publishing Co., 1988.

*North-East **England**; Northumberland, Co. Durham, Cleveland and Tyne & Wear*, Michael Joseph, 1988.

Also contributed to

Duncan, Andrew, Editor, *Walkers' Britain; the Complete Pocket Guide to over 240 Walks and **Rambles***, Pan Books in association with the **Ordnance Survey**, 1986.

Sperrin An **area of outstanding natural beauty** in County Londonderry, **Northern Ireland**, that includes Ulster's most extensive **mountain** range. It contains the highest peaks outside the **Mourne** AONB, including Sawel Mountain (683 metres), and is one of the Province's most attractive walking areas. Sperrin contains a large number of prehistoric archaeological sites. (See figure 36 for a **map** showing the location of all AONBs in the United Kingdom.)

Maps

1:50000 **Ordnance Survey of Northern Ireland** sheets 7, 8, 13, 18, 19.

Footpath Guides

Hamill, James, *North Ulster Walks Guide*, Appletree Press, 1988.

Simms, P., and Foley, G., *Irish Walks Guides North West; Donegal, Sligo, Armagh, Derry, Tyrone and Fermanagh*, Gill & Macmillan, 1979.

Speyside Way A **long-distance path** established by the **Countryside Commission for Scotland.** When complete, it will run for 97 kilometres from Spey Bay (**grid reference** NJ 350653), Grampians via Bridge of Avon, Nethybridge and Abernethy Forest to Glen-

more Lodge (grid reference NH 987095) near Aviemore. At the time of writing only the first 55 kilometres from Spey Bay (grid reference NJ 350653) to Bridge of Avon (grid reference NJ 183359) is open. This section is an easy, very beautiful walk following, for much of the way, a disused railway line.

Although not part of the official route, the District Council in co-operation with local landowners has opened a route from Bridge of Avon (grid reference NJ 183359) to Tomintoul (grid reference NJ 168186). (See figure 36 for a **map** showing the location of all **national trails** and official long-distance paths in the United Kingdom.)

Youth Hostels

Tomintoul.

Maps

1:50000 **Landranger** sheet 28.

1:25000 **Pathfinder** sheets P147 (NJ36/46), P163 (NJ25/35), P179 (NJ04/14), P180 (NJ24/34), P195 (NJ03/13).

Spiral search A skill used in solo **navigation** to find a small object, such as a **tent**, in poor visibility. Using a combination of techniques such as compass **bearings**, **aiming off**, **attack points** and **pace counting** an expert navigator can arrive close to his objective, but still be unable to see it. A spiral search ensures success. Using the **compass** walk north for 10 paces, east for 10 paces, south for 20 paces, west for 20 paces, north for 30 paces and so on until the object is found (see figure 28). A party of walkers would conduct a **sweep search**.

SPOGA The acronym for Sports und Gartenausstellung (Sports and Garden Exhibition) which is an international trade show for sporting goods that is held annually in Cologne, **West Germany**. It is second in importance only to **ISPO**.

Sports Council for Northern Ireland The Council exists to foster the development of sport in **Northern Ireland**. It has established a committee for the development of the **Ulster Way** and other **long-distance footpaths** in the Province. *(For address see Appendix.)*

Spur A subsidiary height or ridge that projects from a mountain.

Stanley, Bernard The author of *The Hiker's Companion*, 1932. This dreadful little book gives advice and instruction on walking techniques, how to identify wildlife, and contains a collection of songs for hikers, and a section on

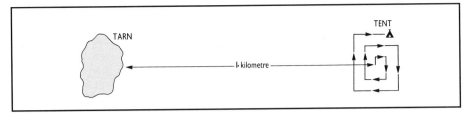

Figure 28: Spiral search.

Tom Stephenson, Secretary of the Ramblers' Association 1948-68 (photo © Ramblers' Association).

exciting and hilarious post-**hike** games such as passing a matchbox cover from nose to nose.

Starkie, Walter [Fitzwilliam] (1894-1976) A scholar who was sometime professor of Spanish at Dublin University and Director of the British Institute in Madrid. He was interested in gypsies, and walked extensively in **Spain**, Hungary and **Italy**, studying romanies and keeping himself by playing the fiddle. His adventures are described in a number of well-written books which, almost uniquely in accounts of long walks, have a strong theme of eroticism running through them. Starkie describes his walks in *Raggle-taggle*, 1933 (reissued in 1964); *Spanish Raggle-taggle*, 1934; *Don Gypsy*, 1936; *The Waveless Plain*, 1938; and *Scholars and Gypsies*, 1963. *The Road to Santiago*, 1957 is a discursive account of his walk to Santiago enlivened by much historical information about pilgrimages.

Stephen, Sir **Leslie** (1833-1904) Critic, essayist, biographer, editor of the *Dictionary of National Biography*, father of Virginia Woolf, and a keen walker and climber. He was a member of the **Alpine Club** and editor of *Alpine Journal* 1868-72. Ill-health made him give up climbing in favour of walking, and he helped found the **Sunday Tramps**.

Few have written better about scenery and walking, and his celebrated essay 'In Praise of Walking', which first appeared in the *Monthly Review* of August 1901 and was reprinted in *Studies of a Biographer; Second Series* Volume 3, 1902, is justly famous. 'In Praise of Walking' is an early attempt to explore the relationship between walking and literature, but it gives the impression that Stephen was relying on a lifetime of wide reading rather than undertaking any serious research. It contains at least one serious error; he states that Jonathan Swift writes in the *Journals to Stella* that he walked from London to Holyhead. He did not; he rode (but Swift does record, in passing, that he walked from Moor Park, Hertfordshire, to London).

The following extract describes what is now the modern **South West Coast Path**:

'*Of all the walks that I have made, I can remember none more delightful than those round the south-western promontory. I have followed the coast at different times from the mouth of the Bristol Avon by the Land's End to the* **Isle of Wight***, and I am only puzzled to decide which bay or cove is the most delightful. I only know that the most delightful was the more enjoyable when placed in its proper setting by a long walk. When you have made an early start, followed the coastguard* **track** *on the slopes above the cliffs, struggled through the gold and purple carpeting of gorse and heather on the moors, dipped down into quaint little coves with a primitive fishing village, followed the blinding whiteness of the sands round a lonely bay, and at last emerged upon a headland where you can settle into a nook of the rocks, look down on the glorious blue of the Atlantic waves breaking into foam on the granite, and see the distant sea-levels glimmering away till they blend imperceptibly into cloudland; then you can consume your modest sandwiches, light your pipe, and feel more virtuous and thoroughly at peace with the universe than it is easy to conceive yourself elsewhere. I have fancied myself on such occasions to be a felicitous blend of poet and saint which is an agreeable sensation.*'

Much of Stephens' work appeared in literary magazines and the *Alpine Journal*, sometimes anonymously. The following books contain most of his essays about walking and **mountains** *Men, Books and Mountains; Essays by Leslie Stephen*, collected and edited by S.O.A. Ullman, Hogarth Press, 1956 and *The Playground of Europe*, 1871. His friend and fellow Sunday Tramp, F. W. Maitland, wrote his biography, *Life and Letters of Sir Leslie Stephen*, 1906, and there is an affectionate and revealing portrait of him by another Sunday Tramp, James Sully, in the *Atlantic Monthly* Vol. 95 No. 3 of March 1905 pp. 347-56.

Stephenson, Tom (1893-1987) Pacifist, sometime civil servant, journalist, campaigner for the countryside, secretary of the **Ramblers' Association** 1948-68, and a greatly revered figure in the rambling movement. In his youth, Stephenson worked as a printer and then became a full-time official at Transport House, the Labour Party headquarters. On the suggestion of Ernest Bevin, he became a journalist on the Labour newspaper, the now defunct *Daily Herald*, and also edited the ***Hiker and Camper*** which was owned by the Trades Union Congress. Stephenson became increasingly interested in the outdoor movement, and in 1935 wrote an article in the *Daily Herald* advocating a **long-distance path** along the length of the **Pennines**. It was many years before he saw the **Pennine Way** actually opened, and it is fitting that he should have written the first official **footpath guide** to the route. In 1943, he became the press officer at the Ministry of Town and Country Planning and worked closely with **John Dower** in promoting the concept of **national parks**.

Stephenson became the Ramblers' Association first full-time secretary in 1948. Here, working with a tiny staff of volunteers, he was able to use the parliamentary contacts he had built up as a result of his political activities and from his employment at Transport House and the Ministry of Town and Country Planning, and was able to exert an influence on countryside legislation out of all proportion to the strength of the Ramblers' Association. He edited the ***Out of Doors Magazine***, as well as various in-house publications, wrote numerous articles and was a popular lecturer. His library and papers are now in the care of the Ramblers' Association.

Stephenson had a delightful personality and nursed a passionate love of the British countryside. He was extremely knowledgeable about the history of **rights of way** and the origins of the rambling movement, but his writings reveal that he had little understanding of the early history of walking for pleasure. He was the author of *The **Pennine Way***, HMSO, 1969, and *Forbidden Land; the Struggle for Access to **Mountain** and **Moorland*** edited by Ann Holt and published posthumously by Manchester University Press in 1989. The latter title contains much information about Stephenson's life.

Stevenson, Robert Louis (1850-94) Novelist, poet, essayist and traveller. Despite his wretched health, Stevenson thoroughly enjoyed walking. His collection *Essays of Travel*, published in 1905, contains some essays about walking including 'An Autumn Effect' (1875) which describes a **footpath** walk from High Wycombe, Buckinghamshire to Tring, Hertfordshire along a section of what is now the **Ridgeway Path**; 'A Winter Walk in Galloway' is an unfinished fragment written in 1871 describing a walk from Kyle, via Dunure and Culzean, to Girvan; and 'Roads' (1873) is an essay on the pleasures of roads and **paths**. His philosophy of walking is given in an essay entitled 'Walking Tours' which was included in *Virginibus Puerisque* originally published in 1881. But his most interesting book about walking is *Travels with a Donkey*, 1879, in which he described his walk across the Cevennes in **France** from Le Monastier to Florac. He carried his gear, which included a **sleeping bag** he designed himself, on the back of a donkey that he christened Modestine. At the suggestion of **Rob Hunter**, this route is now a **sentier de grande randonnée**.

Stiles A stile is a stock-proof structure, usually incorporating a step, which allows human access through, or over, a fence, hedge, wall or footbridge. Stiles are of ancient origin and often, like **kissing gates**, associated in country lore with courting. They come in all shapes and sizes but may be classified into several main groups (see photographs). The *standard stile* comprises one or two wooden steps, set either parallel or at an angle to each other, that allows the pedestrian to climb up and cross the wooden barrier that forms part of the struc-

A standard stile (photo © Hugh Westacott).

A step stile (photo © Hugh Westacott).

ture. This type now has a British Standard specification, and some modern versions have a vertical sliding shutter to allow **dogs** to pass through. The *step stile* is a way of crossing walls by climbing a few steps embedded in the wall in the manner of mounting a staircase. A *ladder stile* is a wooden structure, similar in design to a household ladder, that straddles a wall, and are often found in **national parks** where they are used to prevent damage to walls. *Squeeze stiles* are narrow openings, tapering to the bottom, that are sufficiently wide to allow the pedestrian of average build to pass through sideways. Squeeze stiles are sometimes found on top of step stiles. Most stiles are found on **rights of way**, but **farmers** and landowners occasionally erect them for their own private use to facilitate movement across their land. In **England** and **Wales**, landowners have a statutory duty to maintain stiles crossed by rights of way, and may claim 25 per cent of the cost of repairing them from the county council.

Stockings A walking stocking is a knee-length **sock** usually made of wool with nylon-reinforced toes and heels (non-woollen stockings are also available). Most walkers find that the most comfortable socks and stockings are made of **loopstitch**, although some still prefer the Norwegian-style raggsocks. It is common

practice to wear a pair of stockings over a pair of socks to provide additional comfort.

Stokes, Frederick A[bbot] (1857-1939) An American publisher who made a walking tour of **England** with some college friends in the eighteen seventies and recorded their adventures in *College Tramps*, 1880.

Stonefall Stones which fall from **mountains** due to the effects of erosion, the sun, or by the careless action of walkers and climbers. Stonefall is not much of a problem in the British Isles, but it is a considerable **hazard** in some Alpine areas. It is particularly dangerous when the falling stones follow a natural chute, gully or **couloir**, and care should be taken to avoid resting in the neighbourhood of an area likely to be affected by stonefall.

Storer, Ralph [John] (1947-) A lecturer in computer studies at Napier College, Edinburgh, **mountaineer**, caver, **mountain** biker and the author of three excellent books on walking in **Scotland**.
Publications about Walking
100 Best Routes on Scottish Mountains, David & Charles, 1987.
*Skye; Walking, **Scrambling** and Exploring*, David & Charles, 1989.

A ladder stile (photo © Hugh Westacott).

A squeeze stile (photo © Hugh Westacott).

A step stile next to a ladder stile (photo © Hugh Westacott).

Exploring Scottish Hill **Tracks**, David & Charles, 1991.

Stormbeta A waterproof, 'breathable' **poly-cotton** fabric that encourages **moisture vapour transmission**. It was developed by Berghaus for use in shell **clothing** and jackets.

Stoves Portable cooking stoves (see illustration on page 14) are used by **backpackers**, and sometimes by other walkers who like to '**brew-up**' a hot drink. A good stove should be light in weight, strong, safe, have a valve for heat regulation, and be capable of raising water to boiling point quickly. Stoves are classified according to the type of fuel burned:
Solid fuel stoves burn specially-prepared tablets, but the heat cannot be regulated, the fuel is difficult to obtain, and they are only suitable for emergency use.
Methylated spirit stoves are popular, especially the Trangia which has a built-in canteen. These stoves tend to be bulky, on some models the heat cannot be regulated, and fuel is sometimes difficult to obtain in remote areas.
Paraffin (also known as kerosene) *stoves* are much less popular than once they were. The fuel has an unpleasant, oily quality, and if spilled, it is difficult to remove the resulting contamination. These stoves tend to be heavy, usually have to be primed with solid fuel or methylated

spirit, and are not so clean-burning as other liquid fuel stoves. Paraffin is not always readily obtainable, but it is less volatile than most liquid fuels.
Petrol stoves are popular, very efficient, and economical on fuel, and it is usually possible to persuade country garages to sell a small quantity, or buy some from a friendly motorist re-fuelling his car at a filling station. Some models have to be primed with methylated spirit.
Gas stoves are probably the most popular, and range from picnic stoves to sophisticated ultralightweight stoves ideal for **backpacking**. The fuel is either butane or propane, or sometimes a mixture of both, comes in lightweight sealed cylinders and is widely available, even in remote areas. Butane will not gasify below freezing point, and so is not suitable for use in winter, or at high altitudes unless the stove is fitted with a pre-heating device. The amount of fuel left in a cylinder can only be estimated by experience, and as the container is disposable it has, when empty, to be carried until a litter-bin is found.

The MSR, manufactured by Edelrid, is an ingenious stove that will run on any liquid fuel except unleaded petrol, but it is heavy and expensive and more suited to expedition work than backpacking.

Stoves and fuel containers should be left outside the **tent** to prevent the risk of harm-

ful, even lethal, fumes collecting inside. Tents are highly inflammable and stoves should be lit outside lest flaring should occur when they are first lit. It is very dangerous to use a stove inside a tent.

Strangford Lough An **area of outstanding natural beauty** in County Down, **Northern Ireland** lying between Bangor and Downpatrick. It links with the **Mourne** and the **Lecale Coast** AONBs. This is a low-lying area of drumlins that have been flooded by the rising sea level leaving the tips as islands. (See **map** showing the location of all AONBs in the United Kingdom.)
Map
1:50000 **Ordnance Survey of Northern Ireland** sheet 21.
Footpath Guide
Rogers, R., *Irish Walks Guides North East; Down and Antrim*, Gill & Macmillan, 1980.

Stuff sack A lightweight **nylon** bag that can be closed with a drawstring which is used for containing **sleeping bags**, clothes etc. when in the **rucksack**. Stuff sacks are manufactured in various sizes. Many **backpackers** use them for containing sleeping bags because the drawstring assists in compression, but find that ordinary household plastic bags serve just as well for other items.

141

Styles, [Frank] **Showell** (1908-) Outdoor journalist, walker, **mountaineer**, and since 1946, a professional writer and author of 119 books, including novels about the Royal Navy in the Napoleonic era. He led expeditions to Lyngen, in arctic Norway, in 1952 and 1953, and to the **Himalaya** in 1954. He was a pioneer **backpacker** in the **mountains** of Europe, and wrote one of the few reliable walking and **backpacking** manuals published in the 1950s.

Publications about Walking
The Tramper's and Camper's Weekend Book, Seeley Service, 1956.
*Blue Remembered **Hills***, Faber, 1965.
*The Mountains of North **Wales***, Faber, 1973.
The Snowdon Range, West Col, 1973.
The Glyder Range, West Col, 1974.
Backpacking, Macmillan, 1976.
*Backpacking in the **Alps** and **Pyrénées***, Gollancz, 1976.
Backpacking in Wales, Hale, 1977.
Welsh Walks and Legends, John Jones, 1979.
Walks in Gwynedd, John Jones, 1985.
Also contributed to
Wilson, Ken, and **Gilbert, Richard**, Editors, *The Big Walks*, Diadem, 1980.
Wilson, Ken, and Gilbert, Richard, Editors, *Classic Walks*, Diadem, 1982.
Hillaby, John, Editor, *Walking in Britain*, Collins, 1988.

Suffolk Coast and Heaths An **area of outstanding natural beauty**, designated in 1978 by the Secretary of State for the Environment on the advice of the **Countryside Commission**. It covers an area of 391 square kilometres of coast running from Ipswich and the Orwell estuary almost to Lowestoft. The region is very flat and contains some beautifully wooded estuaries and many creeks that are the haunt of wildfowl. (See **map** showing the location of all AONBs in the United Kingdom.)
Maps
1:50000 **Landranger** sheets 134, 156.
1:25000 **Pathfinder** sheets P946 (TM48/58), P966 (TM47/57), P987 (TM46), P1008 (TM25/35), P1009 (TM44/45), P1031 (TM24/34), P1054 (TM23/33).
Footpath Guides
Barrett, Elizabeth, *Exploring **Bridleways***, published by the author at 'Pip's Peace', Kenton, Stowmarket, Suffolk IP14 6JS.
Country Walks; No. 3 Suffolk Coast between the Deben and the Alde, 1983; *No. 4 Suffolk Coast between the Alde and the Blythe*, 1984, compiled and published by Suffolk Coastal District Council, Council Offices, Melton Hill, Woodbridge, Suffolk IP12 1AU.

Sunday Tramps A famous all-male London walking club founded in 1879 by Sir **Leslie Stephen**, George Croom Robertson, editor of *Mind*, and Sir Frederick Pollock. It had no constitution or subscription and was really an informal association of like-minded literati, intellectuals, doctors and lawyers who enjoyed walking. Stephen, known to the other members as the 'Chief', was the driving force, and both organised and led most of the walks which were held every other Sunday for about eight months of the year. Stephen resigned as organiser in 1891 because of failing health. Members would receive a postcard from him giving details of the next walk which would start and finish at a railway station. They would walk anything up to thirty-two kilometres, have their lunch in a pub, and would occasionally be invited to dine after their walk by a notable such as Charles Darwin, John Tyndall, **George Meredith** and Frederic Harrison. The total membership of the tramps was 61, plus one corresponding member, Professor Vinogradoff of Moscow, but it was rare for a walk to attract more than a dozen members. Each member was allotted a number by Stephen who kept records of the membership and the walks in a pocket book. After Stephen's resignation, Sir Frederick Pollock, R. G. Marsden and Douglas Freshfield organised the club until the 252nd and last walk took place in March 1885.

It is doubtful whether any other walking club could rival the Sunday Tramps in exclusiveness, or could claim such a distinguished membership (of the 61 members no less than 47 appeared in *Who's Who?*). The records indicate that they often indulged in high-minded conversations and discussions during their walks, but that there was also a high-spirited, almost schoolboyish delight in escaping from the ties of work and family. A. J. Butler composed a few verses in praise of the Tramps. A complete list of members, together with their membership number, may be found in Maitland's biography noted below. A number of other famous persons, including George Meredith, walked with the Tramps occasionally, but were not actually members.

Accounts of the Sunday Tramps exist in *Life and Letters of Sir Leslie Stephen* by F. W. Maitland, 1906, and there is an affectionate and revealing portrait of Stephen by another Tramp, James Sully, in the *Atlantic Monthly* Vol. 95 No. 3 of March 1905, pp347-56.

Surrey Hills An **area of outstanding natural beauty**, designated in 1958, that is a popular walking area for Londoners. It contains 414 square kilometres of chalk **downland** and greensand that stretches from Farnham and Haslemere eastwards to the Kent boundary, and links with both the **Sussex Downs** and **Kent Downs** AONBs. The Greensand **Hills** run to the south of the chalk downs and offer contrasting vegetation of bracken and silver birches, and splendid views across the Weald to the South Downs, and even to the sea from one or two places. (See page **XXX** for a **map** showing the location of all AONBs in the United Kingdom.)
Maps
1:50000 **Landranger** sheets 186, 187.
1:25000 **Pathfinder** sheets P1206 (TQ05/15), P1207 (TQ25/35), P1208 (TQ45/55), P1225 (SU84/94), P1226 (TQ04/14), P1227 (TQ24/34), P1228 (TQ44/54), P1245 (SU83/93).
Footpath Guides
Adams, A. L., *Walk the Charming Footpaths of South West Surrey*, published by the author at 2 Dryden Court, Lower Edgeborough Road, Guildford, Surrey GU1 2EX, 1983.
Adams, A. L., *Walk the Charming Country around Dorking*, published by the author at 2 Dryden Court, Lower Edgeborough Road, Guildford, Surrey GU1 2EX, 1984.
Bagley, William A., *Surrey Walks for Motorists; 30 Circular Walks*, Warne Gerrard, 2nd. Ed., 1982.
Haine, Angela, and Owen, Susan, *Discovering Walks in Surrey*, Shire Publications, 1981.
Hyde, George, *Five-mile Walks in South-west Surrey*, **Footpath** Publications, 69 South Park, Godalming, Surrey GU7 1SU, 1986.
Hyde, George, *More Five-mile Walks in South-west Surrey*, Footpath Publications, 69 South Park, Godalming, Surrey GU7 1SU, 1988.
Palmer, Derek, *Surrey **Rambles**; 10 Country Walks around Surrey*, Countryside Books, 1987.

Surveying The term used to describe the method of determining the position of features on the surface of the earth from which **maps** of the area can be made. Topographical surveying involves establishing a framework of large triangles, formed by markers known as **triangulation stations** or trig points, several kilometres apart. The principle of spherical trigonometry, upon which topographical surveying is based, is that if the length of one side and all the angles of one triangle are known, it is possible to calculate the lengths of the other two sides, and from these calculations to compute relative heights which can be plotted on a map. As all the triangles erected for the survey have at least one side in common, the length of the sides of all the other triangles can be calculated by merely measuring the angles at each triangulation station (it is much easier and less time-consuming to measure angles with a theodolite than to measure length using tapes or chains). These principles were in use for hundreds of years, but have now been superseded by taking measurements electronically, and also by aerial and satellite surveys.

Survival bag A large heavyweight plastic bag carried by prudent walkers in upland country to protect them from the elements and to prevent **exposure** in the event of **benightment** or accidental injury. Any suitably large heavyweight plastic bag may be used, or they may be purchased inexpensively at most outdoor shops. There are also lightweight 'space blankets' made of foil which are waterproof and reflect back the heat of the body, and very expensive **bivouac** bags, known colloquially as 'bivvy bags', usually made from **Gore-Tex**, which are used mainly by climbers.

Sussex Downs An **area of outstanding natural beauty** which was designated in 1966. The main feature of its 981 square kilometres is a series of whaleback chalk hills that run from Petersfield in West Sussex, where they link with both the **East Hampshire** and **Surrey Hills** AONBs, to Eastbourne in East Sussex. This is fine walking country with extensive views northwards across the Weald, and southwards to the coast. Near Eastbourne, the Downs reach the sea and form cliffs over 150 metres high. The **South Downs Way** traverses part of this AONB. (See **map** showing the location of all AONBs in the United Kingdom.)
Maps
1:50000 **Landranger** sheets 197, 198, 199.
1:25000 **Pathfinder** sheets P1245 (SU83/93), P1265 (SU62/72), P1266 (SU82/92), P1267 (TQ02/12), P1285 (SU61/71), P1286 (SU81/91), P1287 (TQ01/11), P1288 (TQ21/31), P1289 (TQ41/51), P1304 (SU60/70), P1305 (SU80/90), P1306 (TQ00/10), P1307 (TQ20/30), P1308 (TQ40/50), P1324 (TV49/59/69).

Footpath Guides
Perkins, Ben, *South Downs Walks for Motorists*, Warne, 1986.
*On Foot in East Sussex; 24 **Rambles** based on Brighton, Lewes, Eastbourne, Seaford, Hastings, Battle, Rye, Winchelsea, Wadhurst, and Uckfield Areas*, Society of Sussex Downsmen, 254 Victoria Drive, Eastbourne, East Sussex BN20 8QT, 1986.
Ulph, Colin, *Southdown Walks; 32 Downland Rambles from Brighton, Worthing and Surrounding District*, published by the author at 281 Upper Shoreham Road, Shoreham-by-Sea, West Sussex BN4 6BB, 2nd Rev. Ed., 1986.

Sustrans Ltd A planning and development company (the name is formed from 'Sustainable Transport'), founded by John Grimshaw, that specialises in reclaiming abandoned railway lines and converting them for use by walkers, cyclists, and horse-riders. **Railway walking** owes a great deal to Mr Grimshaw. In 1982, his monumental *A Study of Disused Railway Lines in **England** and **Wales*** was published by HMSO. This work showed in detail how a large number of abandoned lines could be converted for recreational use, and such was his faith in his proposals, that he formed Sustrans Ltd to carry out the necessary work. Normally, Sustrans is engaged by a local authority to survey and report on the possibilities of

conversion, and then often carries out the necessary work. Examples of railway lines converted to **paths** include routes from Chiseldon to Marlborough, York to Selby, Consett to Sunderland, and the Liverpool Loop Line from Halewood to Southport. The company is currently working on a Trans-Pennine **Trail** that utilises a number of routes radiating from Barnsley to York, Sheffield, Leeds and Liverpool, and a London to Bristol route. *(For address see Appendix.)*

Swale, Rosie (c 1950-) Journalist, single-handed transatlantic sailor, and adventuress who made a **backpacking** trip around **Wales** with the intention ' . . . *to learn about Wales by walking clockwise over a thousand miles round the country in winter, living in a **tent**, carrying survival equipment.*' She recorded her adventures in a lively, well-written book entitled *Winter Wales*, Golden Grove, 1988.

Sweden A northern European country that has numerous **mountains**, lakes, and **long-distance paths**. The north of the country, which includes part of Lapland, has been described as the last wilderness in Europe. Sweden caters well for walkers and has a law, Allemansratten (Everyman's Right), that allows the walker to wander at will and to camp

Backpackers on the Kingstrail, Lappland, Sweden (photo © Swedish National Tourist Office).

anywhere for one night without permission, except in private gardens.

Useful Addresses

Swedish National Tourist Office, 3 Cork Street, London W1X 1HA. Tel. 071-437-5816.

Ramblers' Organisation: Svenska Turistforeningen, Box 25, S 101 20, Stockholm. Personal callers: Vasagartan 48, Stockholm.

*National **Map** Survey:* National Land Survey of Sweden, 801 82 Gavle.

Official Survey Maps: Topografiska Kartan 1:50000 and 1:25000 (both scales show **footpaths**).

Other Maps: Fjallkartan, with scales of 1:100000 and 1:50000, are based on the official survey and cover some of the best **mountain** areas. They show footpaths and mountain **huts**.

Guide to Walking

Evans, Craig, *On Foot through Europe: a **Trail** Guide to Scandinavia,* Quill, 1982.

Sweep search A method used by a party of walkers to locate a small object, such as a **tent**, in poor visibility. Using a combination of techniques such as compass **bearings**, **aiming off**, **attack points** and **pace counting** the party should arrive close to their objective. For a sweep search they should spread out and walk parallel to each other, just within the limit of visibility, until the objective is found (see figure 29). A solo navigator would use a **spiral search**.

Switzerland A central European country famous for its beautiful **mountain** scenery and dense and splendidly waymarked network of **paths**. The **Alps** form the dominant range, offering walking at all levels of difficulty, but there is also good walking on the limestone in the Jura Mountains. All kinds of walkers can explore and enjoy Switzerland as the paths are graded according to difficulty, and there are many lowland paths that pass through meadows allowing the walker to enjoy distant prospects of the mountains. In the mountainous areas there are numerous Alpine **huts**

Walkers of any ability can enjoy the breathtaking scenery in Switzerland as all the paths are graded according to difficulty (photo © Swiss National Tourist Office).

that offer simple shelter. The Swiss National Tourist Office (see below) can usually supply booklets giving information about walking tours.

Useful Addresses

Swiss National Tourist Office, Swiss Centre, New Coventry Street, London W1V 8EE. Tel. 071-734-1921.

Ramblers' Organisation: Schweizerische Arbeits-gemeinschaft fuer Wanderwege (SAW), Im Hirshalm 49, CH 4125 Riehen.

*National **Map** Survey:* Eidgenoessische Land-estopographie, Seftigenstrasse 264, 3084 Wabern.

Official Survey Maps: Maps which cover the whole country and which show **footpaths** are available in **scales** of 1:100000, 1:50000 and 1:25000.

Other Maps: Kummerley and Frey, Hallerstrasse 6-10, CH-3001 Berne publish maps in scales from 1:150000 to 1:20000 which show footpaths, and walker's guides (in French and German only).

Kompass Wanderkarten 1:50000 cover selected areas and show footpaths.

Guide to Walking

Evans, Craig, *On Foot through Europe: a **Trail** Guide to **Austria**, Switzerland and **Leichtenstein**,* Quill, 1982.

Figure 29: Sweep search.

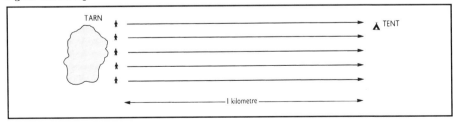

Footpath Guides

Caselli, G., and Sugden, K., *Ancient Pathways in the Alps*, George Philip, 1988.

Harper, Andrew, *Tour of Mont Blanc*, Cicerone Press, 1982.

Hurdle, Jonathan, *The Alpine **Pass** Route*, Dark Peak, 1983.

Lieberman, Marcia, *Walking Switzerland the Swiss Way*, Cordee, 1987.

Reynolds, Kev, *Walks in the Engadine, Switzerland*, Cicerone Press, 1988.

Reynolds, Kev, *Walks in the Valais, Switzerland*, Cicerone Press, 1989.

Reynolds, Kev, and Evans, R. Brian, *The Jura; Walking the Jura High Route and Winter Ski Traverses*, Cicerone Press, 1989.

Spencer, Brian, *Walking in the Alps*, Moorland Press, 1983.

Spencer, Brian, *Walking in Switzerland*, Moorland Press, 1986.

Spring, Ira, and Edwards, Harvey, *100 Hikes in the Alps*, Cordee, 1979.

'Sylvanus' The pseudonym of Robert Colton who was the author of *Pedestrian and other Reminiscences at Home and Abroad; with Sketches of Country Life*, 1846. The book consists of letters to a friend describing a walking tour he made through **France** from May to December, 1845. The author conveys very well his love of walking *'In a genuine love for the **footpaths**, or a little errantry "à pied", I yield to no man. The very thought of a long country walk, when the dew is on the ground, or the hoar frost glistens in the clear sharp wintry day, sets the blood rioting in my veins. What a glow comes over you as you briskly tread the crisp and spangled mead! What a glorious breeze sweeps the world! How light, how joyous, how well you feel as you leave the town far behind, and inhale the pure and invigorating gale. There are truly, few things that I remember under the name of real unalloyed enjoyment in my past life, that can equal the relish I always felt on a pedestrian excursion, or in its most pleasing recollection.'* He then goes on to describe his walking gear *'In the toilette I adopt for a "walking gentleman", I wear a short, loose, grey frock coat, sufficiently decent to take my seat at a table d'hôte, being also stout, and easy enough for all weathers. I particularly inculcate strong **shoes** and **gaiters**, Scotch shepherd's plaid trousers, and a good beaver [hat] on which the storm may beat and come again, whereat your **silk** chapeaux are soon disconcerted. In my **knapsack** (a Swiss one covered with the skin of a chamois),—I have three shirts, as many pairs of **stockings**, several items in collars, cravats and pocket handkerchiefs, with an extra pair of light shoes, fit for slippers or a light stroll, after I have found my quarters*

for the night. I have a large silk umbrella in a case, that I sling over my shoulder as a precautionary friend, and what does a man want more? with his proper baggage forwarded from time to time if he chooses to remain where it is needful.' Colton gives detailed descriptions of the landscape, towns, customs etc. and is particularly interested in the turf. Indeed, the last few letters are all about horse-racing in England, and he also comments on the British political scene. The frontispiece of the book shows the author in full walking gear.

'Sylvanus' who walked through France in 1845 (photo © British Library).

Jules Bonnasse del.   H. C. Maguire lith.

Sympatex The trade name of an **hydrophyllic** fabric, developed by Akzo, that is now the European market leader in breathable waterproof **clothing**. All garments made of Sympatex have to be tested and approved by Akzo before the manufacturer is permitted to market them. Approved garments carry a three-year Akzo guarantee.

Symonds, H[enry] **H**[erbert] (1885-1958) Schoolmaster, clergyman and sometime drafting secretary of the Standing Committee on **National Parks**, member of the Lake District Planning Board and the National Parks

Commission, and vice-president of the **Ramblers' Association**. He was the author of *Walking in the Lake District*, 1933, which is one of the best guides to the region, which contains no **maps** but gives suggested routes to the main peaks. There is a chapter on the geology of the Lake District and an Appendix that gives sound, pithy advice about walking. Symonds also wrote *Afforestation in the Lake District*, 1937, numerous magazine articles, and he edited the first few issues of *Rambling*, which was then the official journal of the Ramblers' Association.

T

Talfourd, Sir **Thomas Noon** (1795-1854) A High Court judge, man of letters, and friend of **Charles Lamb**, **William Wordsworth**, **Samuel Taylor Coleridge** and **William Hazlitt**. He spent several holidays in the **Alps** with his family where they occasionally went walking, and he describes these holidays in *Recollections of a First Visit to the **Alps***, 1842; *Vacation **Rambles** Comprising the Recollections of Three Continental Tours in the Vacations of 1841, 1842 and 1843*, 1845 (3rd Ed., 1851); and *Supplement to Vacation Rambles Consisting of Recollections of a Tour through **France** to **Italy**, and Homeward by **Switzerland***, in the Vacation of 1846, 1854. (It should be noted that Talfourd uses 'vacation' in its legal sense meaning that the law courts are not sitting, and 'rambles' in the old-fashioned sense meaning journeys undertaken for pleasure.)

Tarn The name for a small lake found in the upland areas of the north of **England**. Well-known examples are Malham Tarn in the **Yorkshire Dales National Park**, and Easedale Tarn, Sprinkle Tarn and Styhead Tarn in the **Lake District National Park**.

Taylor, Bayard (1825-78) American traveller and man of letters whose travel books were immensely popular. In his youth he was an enthusiastic walker and wrote several books which included much walking. He was an acute observer and his books contain well-written descriptions of scenery and the countryside. His first book *Views a-foot; or Europe Seen with **Knapsack** and Staff*, is an account, written when he was 19, of his wanderings through Britain, **Belgium**, Germany, **Switzerland**, **Austria**-Hungary, **Italy** and **France**. In the chapter *Advice and Information for Pedestrians* he writes:

'It is the best plan to take no more **clothing** than is absolutely required, as the traveller will not desire to carry more than fifteen pounds on his back, knapsack included. A single suit of good dark cloth, with a supply of linen, will be amply sufficient. The strong linen blouse confined by a leather belt will protect it from the dust; and when this is thrown aside on entering a city, the traveller makes a very respectable appearance. The slouched hat of finely-woven felt is a delightful covering to the head, serving at the same time as umbrella or night-cap, travelling dress or visiting costume. No one should neglect a good cane, which, besides its feeling of companionship, is equal to from three to five miles a day, and may serve as a defence against banditti, or wild Bohemian **dogs**. In the **Alps** the tall staves pointed with iron and topped with curved chamois-horn can be bought for a franc apiece, and are of great assistance in crossing **ice**-fields, or sustaining the weight of the body in descending steep and difficult **passes**. An umbrella is inconvenient, unless it is short and may be strapped on the knapsack, but even then an ample cape of oiled **silk** or India-rubber cloth is far preferable. The pedestrian need not be particular in this respect: he will soon grow accustomed to an occasional drenching, I am not sure that men, like plants, do not thrive on it when they have outgrown the hot-house nature of civilization in a life under an open heaven. A portfolio capable of hard service, with a guide-book or two, pocket **compass** and spyglass, complete the contents of the knapsack, though if there is still a small corner to spare, I would recommend that it be filled with pocket editions of one or two of the good old English classics. It is a rare delight to sit down in the gloomy fastnesses of the Hartz **mountains** or in the breezy villages of Styria and read the majestic measures of our glorious Saxon bards. Milton is first fully appreciated when you look up from his page to the snowy ramparts of the Alps which shut out all but the heaven of whose beauty he sang, and all times and all places are fitting for the universal Shakespeare. Childe Harolde bears such a glowing impress of the scenery on which Byron's eye has dwelt that it spoke to me like the answering heart of friend from the crag of Drachenfels, in the rushing arrowy Rhône and beside the breathtaking marbles of the Vatican and the Capitol.'

His other books that include accounts of walks are *At Home and Abroad*, 1862, *At Home and Abroad; Second Series*, 1862, and *Byeways of Europe* 2 vols, 1869.

Taylor, George Ledwell (1788-1873) A distinguished architect who helped lay out some of the best squares in Mayfair. In 1816, he walked with his friend Edward Cresy throughout **England** measuring and drawing plans of cathedrals, and in the following three years they extended their researches to the principal monuments of **France**, **Italy**, and **Greece**. It has been calculated that their journeys covered about 11,600 kilometres, of which about 6500 kilometres were on foot. Taylor described their adventures, sixty-five years after the events, in his book *The Autobiography of an Octogenarian Architect*, 2 Vols, 1870-72. It is not a real autobiography as the author is concerned only with the journeys described above, and most of the book is taken up with his architectural plans. It is clear that the two friends thoroughly enjoyed their walks, and on one occasion walked 92 kilometres from Marseilles to Fréjus in one day to win a wager that they could beat the coach.

Taylor, John (1580-1653) An eccentric self-publicist, known as 'the water poet' because he was a Thames waterman, who wrote doggerel verse and often ridiculed his contemporary **Thomas Coryate** with whom he had a literary feud. In *The Penniless Pilgrimage, or The Monylesse Perambulation, of John Taylor, Alias the King's Majestie's Water-poet*, published in 1618, he wrote the first known account of a walking tour in Britain. He describes, partly in prose and partly in execrable verse, his journey on foot from London to Aberdeen in which he called on **Ben Jonson** in Leith. In 1649, when 'a youth of three score and ten' he made a tour on 'footback' from London to Land's End and back, which he described in *Wanderings to See the Wonders of the West*, 1649.

'Six hundred miles, I (very neere) have footed,
And all that time was neither sho'd or booted;
But in light buskins I perform'd this travell
O're hill and dale, through dust, dirt, flint, or gravell.'

His work is interesting because of the vivid account of the small adventures he experienced, and because he admired **mountains** which, at the time, were generally considered barren, barbarous places.

Tent A lightweight portable shelter made from cloth that can be dismantled and erected as required. Tents have been used for thousands of years as dwellings, but the first person known to have used one for recreational purposes was **Thomas de Quincey**.

Backpackers require tents that are stable, stormproof and light in weight. Tents may be double-skinned or single-skinned. Double-skinned tents are more popular and have a large flysheet made from **polyurethane**-coated **ripstop nylon**. An inner-tent, made from lightweight porous **nylon** made waterproof by silicone treatment, and with a built-in waterproof groundsheet, is suspended from the flysheet. Expelled breath and body heat will pass through the porous inner tent and condense into water droplets on the underside of the flysheet. Should any of the **condensation** fall onto the inner tent it will roll harmlessly down the sides. Single-skin tents are usually made from **Gore-Tex** but have yet to prove their popularity. In practice, all tents suffer from some degree of condensation in very damp conditions.

Tents come in a variety of sizes and shapes (see page 14). The traditional tent was based on the triangle, but the development of flexible fibre-glass poles has encouraged the use of unorthodox designs. One of the most successful is the dome tent which is exceptionally stable, sheds rain and **snow** very efficiently, and is ideal for use in extreme conditions. Modern tents have such refinements as nesting aluminium poles to reduce bulk and save space, sectional poles secured by shock cord for neatness and to prevent loss, and lightweight aluminium or plastic pegs. Tents for summer use by solo backpackers can weigh as little as 1.4 kilograms, while a three-man dome tent with snow-valances and suitable for winter use weighs about 4 kilograms.

Thames Path A route along the banks of the Thames that the **Countryside Commission** recommends should be designated a **national trail**. When complete, it will run for 290 kilometres from Thames Head (**grid reference** ST 981991) near Kemble, Gloucestershire to the Thames Barrier (grid reference TQ 415794), Woolwich in east London. It has not yet been officially opened, but in practice is walkable along the towpath from Putney Bridge (grid reference TQ 241757) westwards, although a few diversions along roads are necessary here and there. (See figure 36 for a **map** showing the location of all national trails and official **long-distance paths** in the United Kingdom.)

Youth Hostels
London, Windsor, Henley-on-Thames, Streatley, Oxford, and Inglesham.

Maps
1:50000 **Landranger** sheets 163, 164, 174, 175,176.
1:25000 **Pathfinder** sheets P1115 (SP 20/30), P1116 (SP 40/50), P1133 (ST 89/99), P1134 (SU 09/19), P1135 (SU 29/39), P1136 (SU 49/59), P1137 (SU 69/79), P1151 (ST 68/78), P1152 (ST 88/98), P1155 (SU 48/58), P1156

(SU 68/78), P1157 (SU 88/98), P1159 (TQ 28/38).P1171 (SU 47/57), P1172 (SU 67/77), P1173 (SU 87/97), P1174 (TQ 07/17), P1175 (TQ 27/37), P1190 (TQ 06/16).

Footpath Guides

Jebb, Miles, *A Guide to the Thames* **Path**, Constable, 1988.

Perrott, David, Editor, **The Ordnance Survey** *Guide to the River Thames and River Wey*, Robert Nicholson Publications, 2nd Ed., 1989. (Covers the navigable part of the river as far as Cricklade which is 20 kilometres from the source at Thames Head.)

Sharp, David, *The Thames Walk*, **Ramblers' Association**, 2nd Ed., 1990.

Theroux, Paul (1941-) A distinguished American travel writer, journalist and broadcaster, and the author of *The Kingdom by the Sea; a Journey Round the Coast of Great Britain*, Hamish Hamilton, 1983. In this book he recounts his adventures and reflections whilst walking round Britain.

Thinsulate A synthetic microfibre **wadding** manufactured by 3M that is used as **insulation** in winter **clothing**.

Thomas, [Philip] **Edward** (1878-1917) A critic and naturalist who is now recognised as being one of the outstanding poets of the First World War. For much of his life, Thomas was desperately poor and made a living by writing books commissioned by publishers for a guinea per thousand words. He worked at a furious pace, often completing several titles each year, and almost destroyed his health. Walking was very important to him as a way of keeping in touch with the natural world and preserving his sanity. His wife, Helen (1877-1967), mentions some of his tramps in southern **England** and the Welsh Marches in her intimate and revealing portrait *As it Was* which was published in 1932 and reissued as *As it Was & World without End* by Faber in 1972. Thomas wrote only one book about walking, *The Icknield Way*, 1913 (reissued by Wildwood House in 1980) which is an interesting account of his journey along what is now an unofficial **long-distance path**.

Thompson, George The author of *A Sentimental Tour Collected from a Variety of Occurrencies, from Newbiggin, near Penrith, Cumberland, to London, by Way of Cambridge; and from London to Newbiggin by Way of Oxford etc.*, 1798. The book seems to have been inspired by *A Sentimental Journey*, although it is neither well-written nor particularly interesting, and cannot be com-

pared with Lawrence Sterne's classic. The book commences with a eulogy of **England**, followed by a panegyric addressed to his wife, and then describes his adventures. He appears to have lodged in cheap accommodation, and like **Carl Moritz**, to have experienced hostility towards pedestrians.

Thoreau, Henry D[avid] (1817-62) American naturalist, man of letters and outstanding prose stylist who lived for much of his life in Concord, Massachusetts. His most famous work is *Walden*, published in 1854, which describes the two years two months and two days that he spent in a cabin he built near Walden Pond outside Concord. Here he lived alone in the woods and studied nature. He went walking every day to discover and record the life of the woods, and invented what he called the 'fluvial walk' which involved wading naked along streams and rivers watching for wildlife. From 1837, he kept a detailed journal which ran to fourteen volumes and abounds in references to the pleasure he got from walking. The best edition is *The Journal of Henry D. Thoreau* edited by Bradford Torrey and Francis H. Allen, 2 Vols, New York, Dover Publications, 1962. He also wrote *The Maine Woods*, 1864, which gives an account of several expeditions to Maine which he explored mostly by canoe with Indian guides. He also did some walking, and there is a chapter devoted to his ascent of Mount Katahdin (1606 metres), the highest peak in Maine and the second highest in New England.

Thorpe, James The author of *Come for a Walk; a Book for Motorists and Others*, 1940 which is a well-written book about walking containing some practical advice, an essay on the joys of walking, and 150 pages of logs of walks.

Tog rating The term used to describe the unit that measures the thermal resistance of fabric, thus giving an indication of its relative warmth. A tog is one tenth of the metric unit used for measuring thermal resistance in metals, building insulation materials etc., and may be expressed as the temperature difference in degrees centigrade, in steady state conditions, between the two faces of a material when the flow of heat through it is one watt per square metre. Thus 1 tog = $0.1°Cm^2 \div W$. To give an indication of tog values, a man's suit is about 1 tog, and a domestic duvet is about 10 togs. The unit of thermal resistance in the United States is the 'clo' which equals 1.55 togs. Thermal resistance can be measured

in a test, British Standard 4745, by an instrument known as the 'Shirley Togmeter'. It should be noted that tog ratings are applied to *fabrics* not *garments*, and the distinction is important because the design of the finished product has a significant effect on its warmth. For example, a well-designed body-hugging **sleeping bag** with an integral hood is very much warmer than an oblong 'happy camper' bag made from material with the same tog rating.

Tor A term, used mainly in the **Dartmoor National Park**, the **Peak National Park** and **Cornwall**, which has two meanings. In one sense it means a rocky **moorland** summit or eminence, but it can also refer to the granite outcrop that is a feature of these summits. Tors are eroded by the action of wind, **ice** and rain, and the resulting detritus that falls around the base is known as 'clitter'.

Torbuck, John (1668-1741) The author of a literary curiosity *A Collection of Welsh Travels and Memoirs of* **Wales**, 1738. This early account of a walking tour is remarkable for its scatological content, and for the loathing the author expresses for all things Welsh.

Tourist Maps These **Ordnance Survey** maps, based on the old imperial **scale**, cover some of the most popular walking areas of the country, but vary somewhat in style and scale from **map** to map, though the majority are 1:63360 (1 inch to the mile). Unlike **Landranger** and **Pathfinder** maps, they are tailored to cover a specific area, and it is usually more satisfactory, and cheaper, to buy one Tourist map of, say, the **Lake District National Park**, rather than the several Landranger maps that cover the same area. Maps numbered T1 Dartmoor; T2 North York Moors; T3 Lake District; T4 Peak District; T5 Exmoor; T6 New Forest; T7 Ben Nevis and Glen Coe; T8 **Cotswold**; and T9 Loch Lomond are based on the old seventh series 1:63360 (1 inch to the mile) survey but are updated regularly for major changes and tourist information. Relief is indicated by **contours** at 50 feet intervals, and also by **hachures**. **Rights of way** are shown and updated from time to time, and camp sites, car parks, viewpoints and other tourist information are included. All these maps are suitable for walking purposes except T8 Cotswold, and T11 **The Broads**, which cover enclosed country where the lack of field boundaries on the map make route finding difficult, making them suitable only for route-planning. T10 Snowdonia is a useful map for route-planning as it shows rights of way, but the small scale 1:126720 (1/2 inch to the mile) does not give sufficient detail for **navigation**.

The West Country map has no number, and as it has a scale of 1:208545 (approximately 3 miles to the inch), it cannot be used for navigation purposes by walkers.

Townsend, Chris (1949-) Author, journalist, photographer, lecturer and long-distance wilderness walker. He was editor of *Footloose* and *Odyssey*. He has walked and written about several of the North American long-distance **trails** including the Pacific Crest Trail, the Continental Divide Trail, and made the first-ever walk along the 2600-kilometre length of the **Rocky Mountains** in **Canada**.

Chris Townsend, long-distance wilderness walker (photo © Denise Thorn).

Publications

*The Great **Backpacking** Adventure*, Oxford Illustrated Press, 1987.

High Summer; Backpacking the Canadian Rockies, Oxford Illustrated Press, 1989.

The Backpacker's Handbook, Oxford Illustrated Press, 1990.

*Adventure **Treks** in Western North America*, Crowood Press, 1990.

Also contributed to

Unsworth, Walt, Editor, *Classic Walks of the World*, Oxford Illustrated Press, 1985.

Track, trackway A track may be defined as a **path** sufficiently wide to be used by farm vehicles. It has no statutory or legal definition, nor are all tracks **rights of way**. If it is a right of way then it may be classified as a **footpath**, **bridleway**, or **byway open to all traffic**.

The distinction between a track and a trackway is subtle. A trackway is likely to be enclosed by hedges or walls, to have a sunken or hollow nature (in the south of **England** they are often known as holloways), and are often of ancient, even prehistoric, origin. There are numerous examples of trackways on the chalk **downland** of southern England.

Trail According to the latest edition of the Oxford English Dictionary, the term 'trail', meaning a **path** is used chiefly in north America, **Australia** and **New Zealand**. It has been used only occasionally in the British Isles as in 'nature trail' and 'farm trail', and appears in the name of only a handful of the 400 or so British unofficial **long-distance paths** recorded by the **Long Distance Paths Advisory Service**. The adoption by the **Countryside Commission**, which has responsibilities in **England** and **Wales** only, in 1988 of the term '**national trail**' to replace the clumsy 'official long-distance path' has been criticised on the grounds of arrogance and ignorance. Arrogant because the term does not extend to **Scotland** or **Northern Ireland**, and ignorant because 'trail' is an unnecessary transatlantic introduction that has virtually no literary warrant in the United Kingdom. The terms 'English national path' and 'Welsh national path' would probably be more acceptable to most walkers until such time as the **Countryside Commission for Scotland** and the **Sports Council for Northern Ireland** could agree with the Countryside Commission on a common name (eg 'national path' or 'British path') that could be applied to all long-distance paths for which these bodies are responsible.

The Tramp; an Open-air Magazine A monthly periodical which was published from September 1910 until March 1911. It contained many articles about walking and the outdoors, as well as short stories and poems. The earlier issues had a distinguished list of contributors including **E. A. Baker**, **Edward Thomas**, Eden Phillpotts, Wyndham Lewis, **W. H. Davies**, John Drinkwater, Ford Madox Ford (who was still using the name Ford Madox Hueffer), James Elroy Flecker, Jack

London, and Arthur Ransome, but the later issues could not maintain the same standard. The February 1911 issue contains a letter suggesting a 'Tramp's League' which would vet accommodation and arrange walks and walking tours.

Tranter's variations A method of refining **Naismith's rule**, formulated by Philip Tranter, to take into account those variable factors such as fitness, weather conditions and heavy **rucksacks**, which Naismith ignored. To use the table (see figure 30), it is first necessary to establish your fitness level or, in the case of a group, the fitness level of the weakest member of the party. This is done by calculating the time taken to climb 300 metres (1000 feet) in 800 metres (900 yards) when fresh, with no rests and at a normal pace. If this takes 25 minutes then your fitness level is 25.

Example: a walk of 12 kilometres with a total height gain of 800 metres will, according to Naismith's formula, take 4 hours and 6 minutes. Applying Tranter's variation to our fitness level of 30 we get an estimated time of 5 hours.

Tranter's variation can be applied in other ways:

weight of rucksack: drop one fitness line for every 13 kilograms

weather: drop one fitness line for poor visibility or strong winds

conditions underfoot: drop one fitness line for waterlogged or slippery conditions, and up to four fitness lines for **snow**.

Trek, trekking 'Trek' is a Cape Dutch word meaning to draw, pull, or march. It was originally applied to a journey by ox-wagon, and later to a migration or expedition by ox-wagon. When used in the context of modern travel, it has come to mean a long and arduous journey on foot in a foreign country. It is applied particularly, but not exclusively, to walking in Third World countries.

Trespass In the context of walking, trespass means to pass illegally and without permission onto another's property. In **England and Wales**, trespass is not a criminal offence (notices stating that trespassers will be prosecuted are a meaningless bluff) but a civil tort, and the injured party can either obtain an injunction against the offender, or sue for damages, even though no provable harm has been done. Landowners and tenants can require trespassers to leave their property or

FITNESS LEVEL	TIME TAKEN IN MINUTES ACCORDING TO NAISMITH'S RULE									
	60	120	180	240	300	360	420	480	540	600
15	30	60	90	120	165	210	270	330	405	465
20	40	75	135	195	270	330	390	465	525	600
25	50	90	180	255	330	420	510	600	690	795
30	60	120	210	300	405	510	630	750	870	
35	70	145	230	320	425	540	660			
40	80	165	255	345	450	570	690			
45	90	180	270	365	480					
50	100	195	285	390	510					

TOO MUCH TO BE ATTEMPTED

Figure 30: Tranter's variations to Naismith's rule.

return to the **right of way**, and may use reasonable force to compel them to do so. In practice, it is most unlikely that an action would result from unintentional trespass because of the cost involved. Providing that the walker keeps to the **right of way**, he cannot be held to be trespassing.

In **Scotland**, too, trespassing is not usually a criminal offence, but the law is quite different. An aggrieved party cannot sue for trespass unless it can be proved that damage has been done, that the trespass was in the pursuit of game, or that some other offence was committed. If none of these conditions apply, the only remedy open is to require the trespasser to leave the property or return to the right of way. Thus it can be seen that the considerate walker has nothing to fear from trespassing in Scotland, which is one of the main reasons why it is usually possible to walk any **path** shown on the **map**, and why in open country there is a tradition of **access**.

Trevelyan, G[eorge] **M**[acaulay] (1876-1962) Sometime Regius Professor of Modern History at Cambridge, first President of the **Youth** Hostels Association 1930-48, and keen walker. He was particularly fond of walking in **Italy**, especially Umbria, Tuscany and the Marches, and in what is now the **Lake District National Park**. He gave several Lake District farms to the **National Trust**, and in 1965 Side House Farm in Langdale was bought as a memorial to him.

In 1913 he published his famous essay 'Walking' in a book entitled *Clio, a Muse and other Essays Literary and Pedestrian* that describes his passion for walking which will strike a resonance with many a modern walker's footstep. He states that he has two doctors, his right leg and his left leg, and mentions his walks along what is now part of the **South West Coast Path** *'I have walked twice at least round the coast of Devon and **Cornwall** following for the most part the white stones that mark the coastguard **track** along the cliffs'.*

Trevelyan, John (1951-) Deputy director of the **Ramblers' Association** with special responsibility for financial services, financial management, policy, research, **rights of way** publications and the analysis of **path** orders.

He is a specialist on rights of way and parliamentary matters, and the author of two **footpath guides**. He is also the author, with Paul Clayden, of the best book on the legal aspects of rights of way in **England** and **Wales** yet published.
Publications
*The **North Downs Way**,* (with Tom Doggett), the Ramblers' Association, 1978.
The Cumbria Way, Dalesman, 1987.
Rights of Way; a Guide to Law and Practice (with Paul Clayden), Ramblers' Association in association with the **Open Spaces Society**, 2nd Ed., 1989.

Trevelyan, Katharine [Gotsch-] (1909-) A member of the Trevelyan family (**G. M. Trevelyan** was her uncle, and her father, Sir Charles Trevelyan Bt, 1870-1958, was a prominent politician and Minister of Education in the first two Labour governments, an enthusiastic walker and a vice-president of the **Ramblers' Association**) who had a privileged upbringing. In 1930 she walked alone across **Canada** with a **tent** and a revolver, and described her adventures in a well-written book *Unharboured Heaths,* 1934. She caught the public imagination and became something of a celebrity on both sides of the Atlantic. Mostly, she walked on roads, and often accepted lifts for considerable distances, and was entertained by the Governor-General and in humbler homes along the route. In her autobiography *A Fool in Love,* published by Gollancz in 1962, she mentions that she enjoys walking, but dismisses her Canadian adventure in a single paragraph.

Triangulation The system of topographical **surveying** that breaks down the country, or other area to be surveyed, into a series of triangles. With instruments capable of measuring angles and lengths it is possible, by using the principles of trigonometry, to make extremely accurate **maps**. The original **Ordnance Survey** triangulation was done by dedicated men tramping over the countryside in wellington boots and waterproofs carrying theodolites and measuring tapes, but these methods have been superseded by electronic instruments that can measure angles and distances with extraordinary accuracy.

Triangulation stations The term used by the **Ordnance Survey** to describe permanent markers, whose exact height above **Ordnance**

datum has been established by triangulation, and which are used for surveying purposes by the Ordnance Survey. The station marks of the Principal Triangulation completed in the nineteenth century were buried and had to be found by a probing tool known as a searcher. Following the recommendations of the Davidson Report, published in 1938, an entirely new triangulation was commenced using five kinds of stations.

Triangulation pillars are 1.2 metre-high hollow concrete pillars (see figure 31), familiarly known as 'trig points', and date from the period 1938-62. They are cast in situ and have a brass fitting, known as a spider, on the top into which the tribrach of a theodolite can be fitted.

Figure 31: Triangulation pillar.   150

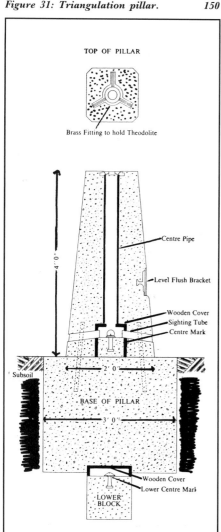

The plug in the centre of the spider can be removed with a special tool to allow a heliograph or an electric beacon to be fitted. The lower centre mark is beneath, and independent of, the foundations to provide a means of locating the station should it be destroyed. On the side of the pillar is a type of **bench mark**, called a flush bracket, on which is recorded the station number. The tip of the arrow represents the published height of the station. Other types of triangulation station are:

Surface marks which are normally brass bolts or rivets set into rock or concrete.

Buried marks which have a brass bolt or rod set in a concrete block 60 centimetres below ground-level.

Roof stations which are sited on flat roofs using a brass bolt or rivet.

Intersected stations which are located on church spires, chimneys, masts etc.

All triangulation stations, except surface and buried marks, are shown on **maps** published by the Ordnance Survey with a **scale** of 1:10560 and larger; triangulation pillars only are shown on maps with scales between 1:25000 -1:126720. A list of stations with their **grid reference**, number and height is available from the Ordnance Survey.

Tully, Clive [Vernon] (1953-) Writer and outdoor journalist specialising in the testing and reviewing of outdoor equipment. In addition to writing for walking magazines, he reviews equipment for *Geographical Magazine* and *The Adventurers*, and contributes adventure travel features to the national press. He leads walking and photographic holidays, and is a director of Writer's Block.

Publications about Walking
The A to Z Guide for Lightweight Travellers, Writer's Block, 1988.
Also contributed to
*The **Ordnance Survey** Leisure Guide to East Anglia*, Ordnance Survey in association with the Automobile Association, 1989.

Tweed A tough, hard-wearing material woven from **wool** that derives its name from the river Tweed where it was first made. Tweed comes in a variety of weights and degrees of softness, and can be made water-repellent by the application of silicones or one of the proprietary waterproofing agents such as Technix. The fibres of thornproof tweeds will not break or tear if snagged by vegetation. Derby tweed is a mixture of **cotton** and **wool**. Tweed is used mainly for breeches.

Tyndall, John (1820-93) An outstanding scientist and **mountaineer** who made an extensive study of Alpine **glaciers** which contributed much to our understanding of this phenomenon. He was sometime vice-president of the **Alpine Club** and associated with, but never a member of, the **Sunday Tramps**. His books *Glaciers of the **Alps***, 1860 and *Hours of Exercise in the **Alps***, 1871 contain accounts of long **mountain** walks and climbs with beautiful descriptions of scenery and cloud effects.

Tysoe, Walter S. (1911-89) A founder-member and one of the most influential members of the **Ramblers' Association**. He became a member of the Executive Council in 1936, Chairman 1954-7 and 1969-72, and President 1978-81. He wrote occasional articles about the history of walking for the official journal of the Ramblers' Association, and presented an important collection of leaflets to the Association's library.

Ulster Federation of Rambling Clubs This organisation aims to promote walking and the use of footpaths in **Northern Ireland**. *(For address see Appendix.)*

Ulster Society for the Preservation of the Countryside The Society was founded in 1937 and is the oldest conservation body in **Northern Ireland**. It is an independent body of people who recognise the need to cherish and maintain the natural environment and work for the preservation, conservation and improvement of the Northern Ireland countryside. The Society includes within its remit, **rights of way**, protection of trees, afforestation policy, water extraction, mining and quarrying, the siting of motorways and legislation dealing with the preservation of natural amenities. It publishes a journal, *Countryside Recorder*. *(For address see Appendix.)*

Ulster Way The longest **long-distance path** in **Northern Ireland**, created by the **Sports Council for Northern Ireland**, that encircles the Province passing through some of its finest scenery. Not all of the Way is officially open, but nearly 500 kilometres of it have been waymarked, and in practice it is walkable throughout its length of 725 kilometres.

A number of major link **paths** are being created which will lead to the Way from large centres of population. There are also a number of alternative paths that allow the walker to make a series of day excursions along the Ulster Way. (See figure 36 for a **map** showing the location of all **national trails** and official **long-distance paths** in the United Kingdom.)

Youth Hostels

Belfast, Ballygally, Cushendall, Ballycastle, Whitepark Bay, Castle Archdale, Newcastle.

Maps

Ordnance Survey of Northern Ireland 1:50000 sheets 4, 5, 7, 12, 15, 17, 18, 19, 21, 26, 27, 28.

Footpath Guides

The Ulster Way, compiled and published by the Sports Council of Northern Ireland, 1988.

  South East Section.

  North West Section.

  South West Section.

Warner, Alan, *On Foot in Ulster; a Journal of the Ulster Way*, Appletree Press, 1983.

Ultimate Challenge An unusual non-competitive **challenge walk**, devised by **Hamish M. Brown**, sponsored by Ultimate Equipment, and organised by **The Great Outdoors**. The event takes place in May, and participants have to walk from one of several starting points on the west coast of **Scotland** selecting their own route to reach Montrose on the east coast within 14 days. Some walkers choose high-level routes and endeavour to include as many **Munros** as possible, others prefer to take a lowland route, and others try to cover the route as quickly as possible. One of the main attractions of the event is the delightful sense of camaraderie.

United States The United States is the fourth largest country in the world (Texas alone is two and a half times the size of the United Kingdom) with enormous variations in climate and landscape. Britons will find the western states of California, Arizona, Colorado, Utah, Nevada, Wyoming, Montana, Idaho, Oregon, Washington and Alaska, the most scenic, but good walking can also be found in the Appalachian **Mountains** in the states of Vermont, Maine, New Hampshire, Massachusetts, New York, Virginia, Kentucky, Tennessee and the Carolinas, as well as in New Mexico. There is little to attract the British walker in the rolling prairies of the midwestern states.

There is no local **footpath** network, so walking in the United States usually involves

As there is no local footpath network in the USA, walking is usually in a State or National Park such as Big Bend, Texas, above (photo © Hugh Westacott).

visiting one of the **national parks**, which are quite different in character from British national parks, or a state park. The federal government actually owns the national parks, and in many cases makes a small admission charge. Many parks, especially in the west, are closed to visitors during the winter months.

Visitors have to observe the park's rules and regulations, and a permit, obtainable from the park office, is usually required for 'back country' (off-**trail**) **backpacking**. Descriptions of America's national parks can be found in the following books distributed in the United Kingdom:

Guide to the National Park Areas, Choke Pequot Press,

> *Eastern States*, 1988.
> *Western States, 1988.*

Frome, M., Editor, *National Park Guide*, Rand McNally, 1988.

Further information can be obtained from the Regional Offices of the National Park Service listed below.

The Congress has established a number of National Scenic and Historical Trails. Among the most famous of these **long-distance paths** are the Appalachian Trail that runs for over 3200 kilometres from Maine to Georgia; the Pacific Crest Trail that runs for 4122 kilometres from the Mexican border through the **Rocky Mountains** in the states of California, Oregon and Washington to the Canadian border; and the 5000-kilometre Continental Divide Trail which starts near the Mexican border in New Mexico and follows the Rocky Mountains and the watershed of the Continental Divide to the Canadian border in **Glacier** National Park. Guide books to national parks can be found under the heading 'National Parks' and to long-distance paths under the heading 'Trails' in *The Subject Guide to American Books in Print* which may be consulted in most British reference libraries.

Generally speaking, topographical **maps** are not readily available through retail outlets in the United States although some outdoor shops and map specialists stock them for their own area.

Useful Addresses

The United States does not have a tourist office in Britain and assistance can only be obtained from travel agents specialising in American tourism. The American Embassy, Grosvenor Square, London W1A 1AE (tel. 071-499-9000) has an excellent reference library which may be consulted by appointment and at the discretion of the librarian. The library staff will answer enquiries by post and telephone.

Ramblers' Organisations: American **Hiking** Society, 1015 31st Street NW, Washington DC 20007.

Sierra Club, 730 Polk Street, San Francisco, CA 94109.

National Map Survey: United States Geological Survey, 507 National Center, Reston VA 22092 (the office to which enquiries for information should be made) and the Distribution Branch, Geological Survey, Federal Center, Building 41, Box 25286, Denver, CO 80225 (the office from which maps may be pur-

chased).

Official Survey Maps: 1:250000, 1:125000 (certain areas only), 1:62500 (certain areas only), 1:24000 (certain areas only).

Regional Offices of the National Park Service
Alaska: 2525 Gambell Street, Anchorage, AK 99593.

Mid Atlantic: 143 South Third Street, Philadelphia, PA19106 (for the states of Delaware, Maryland, Pennsylvania, Virginia, West Virginia).

Mid West: 1709 Jackson Street, Omaha, NB 68102 (for the states of Illinois, Indiana, Iowa, Kansas, Michigan, Minnesota, Missouri, Nebraska, Ohio, Wisconsin).

North Atlantic: 15 State Street, Boston, MA 02109 (for the states of Connecticut, Maine, New Hampshire, Massachusetts, New Jersey, New York, Rhode Island, Vermont).

Pacific North West: 83 S King Street, Suite 212, Seattle, WA 98104 (for the states of Idaho, Oregon, Washington).

Rocky Mountain: PO Box 25287, Denver CO 80225 (for the states of Colorado, Montana, North Dakota, South Dakota, Utah, Wyoming).

South East: Federal Building, 75 Spring Street SW, Atlanta, GA 30303 (for the states of Alabama, Florida, Georgia, Kentucky, Mississippi, North Carolina, Puerto Rico, South Carolina, Tennessee, Virgin Islands).

South West: Old Santa Fe Trail, Box 728, Santa Fe, NM 87504 (for the states of Arkansas, Louisiana, New Mexico, Oklahoma, Texas).

Western: Box 36063, 450 Golden Gate Avenue, San Francisco, CA 94102 (for the states of Arizona, California, Guam, Hawaii, Nevada, Northern Mariana Islands).

Guide to Walking

Bradt, George and **Hilary**, *Backpacking in North America; the Great Outdoors*, Bradt Enterprises, 1979.

Footpath Guide

Penati, F, and Martegani, V., *Trekking in the USA*, Automobile Association, 1990.

Unsworth, Walt (1928-) Well known walker, climber, **mountaineer** and author of numerous books and articles. In 1969, he and R. B. Evans founded the Cicerone Press which has established itself as one of the most distinguished publishers of specialised climbing and walking guides. From 1974-86, he was editor of *Climber & Rambler* (now **Climber & Hill Walker**), he served until 1986 on the Management and Executive Committees of the British Mountaineering Council, and is cur-

Walt Unsworth, author and founder of Cicerone Press (photo © Duncan Unsworth).

rently President of the **Outdoor Writers' Guild**. Although not about walking in particular, mention must be made of his scholarly and well-written books *Everest*, Oxford Illustrated Press, 2nd Ed., 1989 and *Encyclopaedia of Mountaineering*, Oxford Illustrated Press, 2nd Ed., 1990.

Publications about Walking

The Young Mountaineer, Hutchinson, 1959.

*The High **Fells** of Lakeland*, Hale, 1972.

Walking and Climbing for Young People, Routledge, 1977.

Classic Walks of the World, Oxford Illustrated Press, 1985.

Classic Walks of Europe, Oxford Illustrated Press, 1987.

Classic Walks in the Lake District, Oxford Illustrated Press, 1988.

Classic Walks in the Yorkshire Dales, Oxford Illustrated Press, 1989.

Also contributed to

Reynolds, Kev, Editor, *The **Mountains** of Europe*, Oxford Illustrated Press, 1989.

Smith, Roger, Editor, *The Winding **Trail**; a*

Selection of Articles and Essays for Walkers and **Backpackers**, Paladin, 1986.
Smith, Roger, Editor, *Book of the Walking Year*, Patrick Stephen, 1988.

V

Vapour transmission A property of certain synthetic materials (eg **chlorofibre**, **Dunova**, **Fieldsensor** and **polypropylene**) that are capable of **wicking** moisture away from the skin keeping the body dry and free from the unpleasant, clammy feeling associated with conventional **cotton** clothing. Note that the term vapour transmission, known colloquially as VT, is applied to underwear and midwear, and **moisture vapour transmission** to waterproof **clothing**.

Ventile A high-quality material woven from Egyptian **cotton** by Thomas Ashton Ltd. It was developed during the war and supplied to airmen to protect them from exposure when ditched in the sea. The individual fibres in Ventile swell when wet, making it both windproof and waterproof, but still 'breathable', thus preventing **condensation** forming. It is heavier than most other fabrics used in shell **clothing** because it absorbs a great deal of water, and it takes a long time to dry.

Verglas A French word used to describe the thin coating of **ice** found on rocks and **paths** in the **mountains** which is formed by **mist** condensing and freezing. Verglas is extremely slippery and dangerous, and unless unusually thick, even **crampons** will not provide a satisfactory grip. The prudent walker **retreats** when confronted with verglas.

Vibram The proprietary name of the first of the hard-moulded rubber soles which appeared in 1935 and which are manufactured by Vibram S.p.A. in Italy. Vibrams were introduced into Britain after the Second World War, and within a short time they had completely superseded nailed soles for walking. There are now other makes of hard-moulded rubber soles, and they are sometimes, incorrectly, referred to generically as 'vibrams', in the same way that vacuum cleaners are sometimes called 'hoovers'.

Victoria (1819-1901) Queen of Great Britain and Ireland and Empress of India. Unlikely as it may seem, Queen Victoria enjoyed walking, although she failed to pass on her enthusiasm to her son, the future King **Edward VII**. After she and Prince Albert purchased Balmoral on the banks of the river Dee, beneath the shadow of the **Cairngorms**, they both enjoyed walking and riding in the **mountains**, and made a number of ascents. Queen Victoria continued to walk in **Scotland** after Albert's death, and would occasionally call unannounced at a crofter's cottage and request a glass of milk. On one occasion, in 1872, she joined a search party to look for a missing child, and was greatly distressed when it was found dead two days later. Several of the **hills** around Balmoral have **cairns** constructed to record events in the life of the Royal Family. From the age of 13, and throughout her long life, Queen Victoria kept a diary, and published extracts in *Leaves from the Journal of our Life in the Highlands*, 1867, and a subsequent volume *More Leaves from the Journal of a Life in the Highlands*, 1884. The best modern edition is *Queen Victoria's Highland Journals*, edited by David Duff, Webb & Bower 1980. This work contains accounts of her numerous journeys in Scotland, and is illustrated with some of the Queen's sketches.

Volunteer Centre UK The aim of this organisation is to provide information, training and support to people who work with volunteers, including those who work with volunteers in the countryside. The Centre publishes a journal, *Involve*, and a newsletter. *(For address see Appendix.)*

Voysey, Robert T. The author and publisher of a series of four **footpath guides** to Surrey in the style of **Walker Miles**. All the titles include a Bartholomew's 1/2 inch to the mile map.
1 *Rural* **Rambles** *Comprising Routes Round Dorking, Reigate, Gomshall, Holmbury, Ockley, Newdigate, Bletchworth, Friday Street, Leith Hill, Leigh*, 5th Ed., 1932.
2 *Rural* **Rambles** *Round Ashtead, Bletchingley, Caterham, Coulsdon, Dorking, Epsom, Headley, Leatherhead, Merstham, Nutfield, Redhill, Reigate, Woodmansterne*.
3 *Voysey's Rural* **Rambles** *Comprising Routes Round Guildford, Godalming, Horsley, Merrow, Chilworth, Gomshall, Peaslake, Shamley Green, Shackleford*, 1921.
4 *Rural* **Rambles** *Comprising routes round Blackheath, Chilworth, Dorking, Guildford, Holmbury, Hurt Wood, Peaslake, Pitch Hill, Shere, Winterfold Heath*. These titles were reprinted several times and were still appearing as late as 1939.

Wadding Any loose, fibrous material used for stuffing, quilting, padding etc. Wadding used in good quality walking kit and equipment should be a proprietary brand such as **Isodry**, **Libond**, or **Thinsulate** which have good insulating qualities.

Wainwright, A[lfred] (1907-) A former local government officer who was sometime Borough Treasurer of Kendal, and is now best known as an author, artist and broadcaster. From his early, impoverished youth, he conceived a passionate love of what is now the **Lake District National Park**, and he has made the exploration, study, and above all the sketching and description of the area his life's work. Mr Wainwright's classic **footpath guides** for walkers broke entirely new ground, and he pioneered the practice of re-drawing and amending the 1:25000 **maps** published by the **Ordnance Survey** to indicate whether a field boundary was a wall, hedge or fence, and to show the location of **stiles**, gates, **waymark**, **footpath** signs etc. His guides are embellished with exquisite drawings, and the combination of careful and intelligent cartography with the artistry of his sketches and the quality of his writing, produces a standard of guidebook that far surpasses all his contemporaries except **Mark Richards**, whom Mr Wainwright encouraged in his early efforts. His most important work is his monumental

Wainwright, best known for his footpath guides to the Lakes (photo © Michael Joseph).

A Pictorial Guide to the Lakeland **Fells** in seven volumes in which he describes and illustrates every **mountain** in the Lake District National Park. He has also written the classic guide to the **Pennine Way**. Many authors of guidebooks now use his methods which are often described as 'Wainwright-style' guides. Mr Wainwright seems reluctant to update his guides, and even though they are still classics of their genre, some are now very inaccurate, and must be used with caution. He has also been criticised for comments made about his first wife in his autobiography *Ex-Fell Wanderer*.
Publications about Walking
A Pictorial Guide to the Lakeland Fells, 7 Vols, Westmorland Gazette, 1955-66.
A Pennine Way Companion; a Pictorial Guide, Westmorland Gazette, 1966.
Fell Wanderer; the Story Behind the Guidebooks, Westmorland Gazette, 1966.
Walks on the Howgill Fells, Westmorland Gazette, 1972.
Walks in Limestone Country; Whernside, Ingleborough and Penyghent, Westmorland Gazette, 1973.
A Coast to Coast Walk; St Bee's Head to Robin Hood's Bay, Westmorland Gazette, 1973.
Outlying Fells of Lakeland, Westmorland Gazette, 1974.
Fell Walking with Wainwright; 18 of the Author's Favourite Walks, Michael Joseph, 1984
Old Roads of Eastern Lakeland, Westmorland Gazette, 1985.
Pennine *Journey; the Story of a Long Walk in 1938*, Michael Joseph, 1986.
Ex-Fell Wanderer, Westmorland Gazette, 1987. Also numerous sketchbooks of **Wales**, **Scotland**, the **Peak National Park**, and the Lake District National Park.

Waite, John (1953-) The author of a well-written account of a 4500-kilometre walk from Lagos, **Portugal** to Brindisi, **Italy**. He had intended to continue to Istanbul but suffered a back injury when shouldering his **rucksack** and had to return to **England**. His adventures are described in *Mean Feat; a 3000-Mile Walk through* **Portugal**, **Spain**, **France**, **Switzerland** and Italy, Oxford Illustrated Press, 1985.

Wales There is much excellent walking in this mountainous country on a good network of public **rights of way**. All the large cities and conurbations are sited along the south coast, so much of the rest of the country is rural. There is good walking in almost every part of Wales with the best in the **national parks**, the **areas of outstanding natural beauty**, and in central Wales and the Marches. **Offa's**

Dyke Path (partly in **England**) and the **Pembrokeshire Coast Path** are the only two **national trails**, but there are a number of other **long-distance paths**.

Wales Tourist Board The Board was established to give assistance to tourist projects in **Wales**, provide tourist information services and generally promote tourism in Wales. It is responsible for tourism in the counties of Clwyd, Dyfed, Gwent, Gwynedd, Mid Glamorgan, Powys, West Glamorgan and the **areas of outstanding natural beauty** of Anglesey, Clwydian Hills, Gower, Lleyn, and the **Wye Valley**. It publishes *Where to Stay in Wales*, *Wales Walking* and other tourist publications. *(For address see Appendix.)*

Walker, A[dam] (1731?-1821) Inventor and lecturer on experimental and natural philosophy. In 1791, he went by coach to Windermere and then walked mostly on roads, although he climbed Skiddaw, making the conventional tour of what is now the **Lake District National Park**. This is more of a guidebook than an account of a walking tour.

Walker, Kevin [Robert] (1952-) The author of numerous books, **footpath guides**, articles and reviews about **mountain** walking and the mountain environment. His books on mountain **navigation** and the **hazards** of mountains are among the best yet written. He is the proprietor of Kevin Walker Mountain Activities *(for address see Appendix)*, which provides instruction and guiding in all forms of mountain activity, and of the publishing house Heritage Guides. He provides original material and technical advice for radio and television programmes.
Publications about Walking
Mountain Walking in the Crickhowell Area, Heritage Guides, 1986.
Mountain Walking in the Brecon Beacons, Heritage Guides, 1986.
Family Walking in the Crickhowell Area, Heritage Guides, 1986.
The Ascent of Table Mountain, Heritage Guides, 1986.
Mountain Navigation Techniques, Constable, 1988.
Mountain Hazards, Constable, 1988.
Wild Country Camping, Constable, 1989.
The Complete Walker, Ashford Press, 1990.
Also contributed to
Smith, Roger, Editor, *The Great Outdoors Book of the Walking Year*, PSL, 1988.

Walking with children Children are

remarkably tough and will enjoy walking and scenery from an early age if introduced to it by their parents. Walking with a young family can be very enjoyable if the children's needs are considered carefully. Even children as young as 5 can cover 16 kilometres in fine weather in suitable terrain providing the day is broken up with plenty of rest periods, and a 10 year-old is likely to be able to tackle anything that their parents can. Many rambling clubs welcome children and often plan family walks.

Wallington, Mark (19--? -) Journalist and writer, and the author of *500-mile Walkies; One Man and His Dog Versus the South West Peninsula* **Path**, Hutchinson, 1986. This entertaining book is one of the few genuinely amusing accounts of a walking expedition, and describes his adventures on what the **Countryside Commission** now prefers to call the **South West Coast Path**.

Walsh, John E Journalist and sometime editor of **Hiker and Camper** and *The Tramper and Cyclist*. He was the author of *On the Hike; being Notes by the Wayside on the Greatest Movement in Modern Times*, 1932 which is not a 'how to' book, but a panegyric on various aspects of **hiking**. He also wrote *Tramping in* **Denmark**, 1934 which is an account of leading a group of hearty young people on a **youth hostel** tour.

Ward, Edward (1667-1751) Writer, publisher, humorist, recorder of low-life, and author of *The London Spy*. He wrote a series of scatological verses including *A Walk to Islington* published anonymously in 1699. This literary curiosity purports to be an account of a walk from London to Islington, which in those days was a village, but is actually a journey taken for the express purpose of whoremongering.

Ward, G[eorge] **H**[erbert] **B**[ridges] (1877-1957) Sometime a Labour election agent, trade union official, and civil servant. 'Bert' Ward founded the **Sheffield Clarion Ramblers** in 1900, the Hallamshire **Footpath** Preservation Society in 1912, and was a founder member of both the Sheffield **Federation of Rambling Clubs**, whose *Handbook* he edited for 50 years, and the **National Council of Ramblers' Federation**. He had a considerable influence on the movement to achieve **access** to the **moorland** between Sheffield and Manchester where his profound knowledge of local history proved to be invaluable. On numerous occasions he cheerfully trespassed on the Derbyshire grouse moors, had many an argument with gamekeepers, and was for 10 years under a court injunction not to **trespass** on **Kinder Scout**. In 1923, he was elected a Fellow of the Royal Geographical Society, and in 1945, Lose Hill in the **Peak District National Park** was purchased by his friends and admirers as a mark of respect for his life and work. Ward then presented it to the **National Trust**, and the summit was renamed 'Ward's Piece'. An account of his life may be found in *G. H. B. Ward 1876-1957; his Lifelong Campaign for* **Access** *to the Countryside,* by Ann Holt, The **Ramblers' Association**, 1985.

Ward, Ken[neth] (1926-) Outdoor journalist, author of several guidebooks, and appointed president of the **Backpackers' Club** in 1970. In 1979, he founded Lord Winston's Walking Tours which specialises in bringing visitors from overseas on walking tours of Britain, and in 1985, he was sent by the British Tourist Authority on a media tour of **Canada** to promote walking in Britain.

Publications about Walking
The South-west Peninsula Coast **Path** (with John H. M. Mason) 3 vols, Charles Letts & Co., 2nd Ed., 1980.
Discovering **Backpacking**, Shire Publications, 1980.
Footpath *Touring; an Introduction to Do-it-yourself Walking Holidays*, Jarrold, 1985.
Footpath Touring; Land's End and the Lizard, Jarrold, 1985.
Footpath Touring; Exmoor and Lorna Doone, Jarrold, 1985.
Footpath Touring; the Best of Lakeland, Jarrold, 1985.
Footpath Touring; the Cotswolds, Jarrold, 1988.
Footpath Touring; North York Moors, Jarrold, 1989.

Warner, Richard (1763-1857) A prolific author on antiquarian and religious subjects, and sometime a curate in Bath and of Boldre, Hampshire (1791-4) after the incumbent, **William Gilpin**, contracted the dropsy. He wrote a series of early and interesting topographical accounts of pedestrian explorations in the form of letters to friends. He normally followed roads, but did not hesitate to use **footpaths** if he could find somebody to guide him.

A Walk through **Wales** *in August 1797* was first published in 1798, and such was its popularity, that, much to the author's surprise and gratification, it had reached a fourth edition by 1801. There are sketch-**maps** of the route at the beginning of every chapter, and an itinerary and mileage chart at the front. He climbed Cadair Idris, and Snowdon from Caernarvon, which must have been a strenuous day. He was very practical as the following passage reveals: *In preparing for a pedestrian tour, few arrangements are requisite; a single change of raiment, and some other little articles for the comfort of the person, form all the necessary baggage for a foot-traveller. To convey these, however, light as they may be, in the most easy and convenient manner, is an object of importance, and requires some previous consideration. C__ [one of his companions] conceiving it might best be effected by the assistance of side-pockets, he has two receptacles of this kind, of considerable dimensions, added to his coat. My plan is a different one; a neglected Spencer (a short double-breasted overcoat without tails) which, though somewhat threadbare and rusty, may still make a respectable figure in North Wales, has, by the taylor's skill, been fitted up with a sportsman's pocket, that sweeps from one side to the other, and allows room for all the articles necessary to be carried. Accoutred in this manner, and provided with maps and a* **compass**, *which we understand are indispensably requisite among the* **mountains** *of Merioneth and Caernarvonshire, we left Bath this morning as the clock was striking five.*

Experience has since convinced us that both these modes of carrying necessaries are exceptionable, and by no means so commodious a method we observed to be adopted by a pedestrian party which we encountered in Cardiganshire. Each of the gentlemen (for there were three of them) carried a handsome leather bag, covered with neat net-work, which, being suspended from the right shoulder by a strap, hung under the left arm in the manner of a shooting-bag. This was occasionally shifted from one shoulder to the other, and at the same time that it proved a most convenient conveyance for linen etc, was no inelegant addition to the person; at least it gave the wearer much less the appearance of a pedlar than attached to us, from the capacious side-pockets of my companion, and my own swoln Spencer. It is proper to note also, that in addition to our stock of necessaries, we each found it convenient to provide ourselves with a small drinking-horn; for although we had no difficulty in procuring milk, and other sorts of beverage, yet the vessels from which we quaffed these potations were not always so clean as we were accustomed to use.

A Second Walk through Wales followed in 1800 in which he took a different route and called upon Thomas Pennant at Downing in present-day Clwyd. He explored the waterfall country between Pontneddfechan and Ystradfellte in the Brecon Beacons, south Wales, and between Aberystwyth and Machynlleth took a route recommended by a local which necessitated using a compass. *Examining occasionally the map, and looking at the compass, we kept a straight forward course, reckless of* **paths**, *descending into the vallies, and climbing the mountains as they respectively occurred.*

A Walk Through some of the Western Counties of England, published in 1800, is an account of a walking tour from Bath through Somerset, Devon and east **Cornwall** which he commenced on 2nd September 1799. One passage depicts the very real terror that a journey across Dartmoor entailed, which Warner avoided by travelling via Okehampton. Although he crossed the present **national park** from Whiddon Down to Moretonhampstead and Bovey Tracey, that was not then part of Dartmoor.

In his topographical works, Warner exhibits a lively interest in beautiful scenery, antiquities, husbandry and rural economy, factories and mines. He also describes the condition of the poor illustrated with suitably affecting examples, and his books are a joy to read.

Note that his *Excursions from Bath*, 1800, *Tour of the Northern Counties of* **England** *and the Borders of* **Scotland**, 1802 and *A Tour through Cornwall in the Autumn of 1808*, 1809 are not accounts of pedestrian tours.

Watson, G[eorge Bott] **C**[hurchill] (died c 1870) A doctor of medicine who lived for some time in Chester, and was the author of *Hints to Pedestrians; Practical and Medical* published in 1842, which proved so popular that it had reached a third edition by 1862. It is one of the few nineteenth-century books that gives practical advice for walkers. Dr Watson recommends dispensing with a **knapsack**, and wearing instead a tweed shooting-jacket with numerous pockets into which items of **clothing etc.** can be carried. He advocates wearing a tall hat because there is room for items to be carried under the crown. There is detailed advice on how to care for the feet, but some of his medical advice is just plain silly. For example, he claims that it is dangerous to drink water during the day in hot weather, and recommends, quoting the advice of Sir **Francis Galton**, eating a lot of butter for breakfast as this reduces thirst. He advises against wearing a **mackintosh** as **condensation** is dangerous, and favours instead a large lightweight cape of oiled **silk**.

Waxed cotton A hard-wearing windproof and waterproof material made from **cotton**

impregnated with wax suitable for use in shell **clothing** and **gloves**. Any tears can be repaired with needle and thread, and garments can be reproofed by applying more wax. Its main disadvantage is that it is **non-porous** and subject to **condensation**, and is heavier than other materials used in shell clothing. The most famous name associated with waxed cotton garments is Barbour.

Wayfarer The term used to describe one who walks a **long-distance path**; hence Pennine wayfarer (**Pennine Way**), **North Downs** wayfarer (**North Downs Way**) etc.

Waymark A symbol that assists walkers to follow **rights of way** (see figure 32). A waymark complements a **signpost**, which is normally only placed where the right of way leaves a road, or at a junction of **paths**. Waymarks may either be directional (eg an arrow pointing the way), or a symbol, such as the acorn used by the **Countryside Commission** on **national trails** (see figure 33) and the thistle used by the **Countryside Commission**

Figure 32: Directional waymarks.

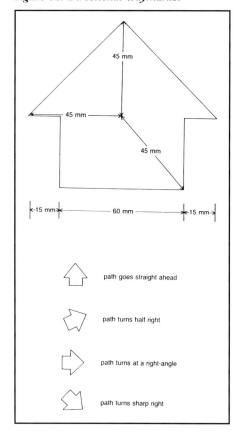

Figure 33 (left): Non-directional waymark used on national trails in England & Wales. Figure 34 (right): Non-directional waymark used on official long-distance paths in Scotland.

for Scotland on its **long-distance paths** (see figure 34), which merely confirms that the walker is still following the route. In **England** and **Wales**, much waymarking is done by volunteers, but before such work is undertaken, the permission of both the landowner and the **highway** authority is required. The Countryside Commission has issued recommended specifications for waymarks. Waymarking is contrary to the Scottish tradition of walking and is rarely used except on long-distance paths.

Weatherhead, G[eorge] **Hume** (1790?-1853) A Doctor of Medicine, medical writer and author of *A Pedestrian Tour through France and Italy*, 1834. This is a well-written account of a long walking tour designed '. . . *to give a lengthy guide book such as might be useful for the generality of tourists . . .*' Thus, he gives detailed descriptions of all the main tourist sights, and a room-by-room catalogue of the chief works of art in the Louvre. In the Appendix there is a catalogue of paintings and sculptures in the main palaces and churches. The author, who spoke fluent French and translated a number of French medical treatises into English, had numerous small adventures, and gives a horrifyingly vivid description of the public guillotining of a murderer which he witnessed in the Place de Grève in Paris from a seat on the balcony of a house overlooking the square.

Webb, Daniel Carless (17?-18?) The author of *Observations and Remarks During Four Excursions Made to Various Parts of Great Britain in the Years 1810 and 1811: I. From London to the Land's End in Cornwall; II. From London to Lancaster; III. From London to Edinburgh; and IV. From London to Swansea. Performed by Land, by Sea, by Various Modes of Conveyance, and Partly in the Pedestrian Style*, 1812. Webb walked quite extensively and

wrote lively, interesting accounts of his travels. He obviously enjoyed walking, but was something of a worrier and makes many comments about the relative standards of cleanliness of 'the lower classes'. '*Having travelled by land and by sea, on board of a packet and a man of war, in waggons, stage-coaches, mails, post-chaises, gigs, and by canal-boats, as well as on foot; I may be permitted to point out, what I found to be the best mode of proceeding on a tour, with a view to gain information.*

'*Walking appears to me to be attended with the greatest advantage; as by this method, the country comes more immediately under inspection, and the traveller is not so likely to pass objects, for want of information, which is always more readily obtained by pedestrians. I therefore throw in a few observations to those, who may choose to adopt this mode of travelling.*

'*The carriage of baggage may justly be considered an inconvenience, it is therefore proper to take as few things as possible; these carried in a light green bag, (I would on no account recommend a blue one, as that might occasion you to be mistaken for a lawyer) gives you a decent appearance, as if on business, and prevents you from meeting with the disagreeables, incidental to pedestrians, by a rough reception from ignorant waiters and surly innkeepers. I shall here enumerate such things, as I suppose you will want, viz. one shirt, one pair of* **stockings***, two neckcloths, two pocket handkerchiefs, a pocket* **compass***,* **map***, drinking horn, paper and implements for writing.*'

On seeing a snake in **South Devon** he manages to convince himself that it is probably an escaped rattlesnake brought over by a sailor from America. He walked along the coast from Exeter to Plymouth, took a boat to Mevagissey, and then continued along the coast, often using cliff **paths**, to Penzance. From here he crossed to St Ives and returned to Penzance via Land's End. He then walked to Exeter via Launceston and Okehampton. On another occasion he walked from London to Oxford, took the coach to Birmingham, walked to Wolverhampton and boarded a coach which '*flew at 10 miles per hour*', and then walked through part of Lancashire and took a canal boat. On his Scottish journey he went by man-of-war to Edinburgh, and back to Portsmouth, and then walked to London. On his final trip he took a coach to Oxford and walked to south **Wales** via Wilton, Stonehenge, Warminster, Bath, Bristol, and the **Wye Valley** to Abergavenny, where he climbed the Sugar Loaf. He double-backed to Brecon, found a guide who refused to take him to the summit of Pen-y-Fan because of the weather, so he climbed it alone taking compass **bearings** in case he got lost.

Weeton, Ellen (1776-18--?) A pedestrian who was remarkable for preferring to walk alone in an age when it was considered improper for ladies to travel unaccompanied. She led a miserable existence having contracted a disastrous marriage, and after she left her husband she was forbidden to see her only child, except for three visits a year. She sought solace by undertaking long walks, and in 1810, when a governess in what is now the **Lake District National Park**, climbed Fairfield, the Langdale Pikes and several other **mountains**. In 1812, she climbed Snaefell in the **Isle of Man**, and in 1825, reached the summit of Snowdon. Accounts of her walks may be found in *Journal of a Governess* which was first published by the Oxford University Press in two volumes in 1936 and 1939, and reissued by David & Charles as *Miss Weeton's Journal of a Governess* in 1969.

Weir, Tom (ie Thomas Weir 1914-) Scottish author, journalist and broadcaster who has written chatty books and articles about walking and climbing in **Scotland** and the **Himalaya**, as well as general books about Scotland.
Publications about Walking
Highland Days, 1948 (reissued by Gordon Wright in 1984).
The Ultimate **Mountains**; *an Account of Four Months Mountain Exploring in the Central Himalaya*, Cassell,1953
The **Western Highlands**, Batsford, 1973.
Weir's Ways, Gordon Wright, 1981.

Welsh 3000s The name given to the 14 summits in Snowdonia that exceed 3000 feet in height, and which are of particular interest to those who enjoy **peak-bagging** (they are sometimes incorrectly called 'Welsh 3000ers', but this term should only be applied to those who climb the Welsh 3000s). The first person known to have climbed them all within 24 hours was Eustace Thomas in 1919, who took $22\frac{1}{2}$ hours to cover the 30 miles (48 kilometres) of walking and 12000 feet (3700 metres) of ascent. His record was beaten in 1938 by **Thomas Firbank**, and by many people since.

The favoured route is to start at Pen-y-Pass, finish at Aber, and climb them in the following order: Crib Goch 3023 feet (922 metres), Crib-y-ddysig 3493 feet (1065 metres), Snowdon 3560 feet (1085 metres), Elidir Fawr 3029 feet (923 metres), Y Garn 3104 feet (946 metres), Glyder Fawr 3279 feet (1000 metres), Glyder Fach 3262 feet (995 metres), Tryfan

3010 feet (918 metres), Pen-yr-ole-wen 3210 feet (979 metres), Carnedd Dafydd 3246 feet (1045 metres), Carnedd Llewelyn 3484 feet (1062 metres), Yr Elen 3152 feet (961 metres), Foel Grach 3195 feet (974 metres), and Foel Fras 3091 feet (942 metres).

Information on how to ascend all peaks exceeding 3000 feet in the British Isles can be found in *The High* **Mountains** *of Britain and Ireland; a Guide for Mountain Walkers*, by **Irvine Butterfield**, Diadem, 1986.

West, Thomas The author of an exceptionally popular guidebook for tourists, *A Guide to the Lakes*, that was first published in 1778 and which reached an eleventh edition by 1821. It was written for artists, lovers of the **picturesque**, and those who wished to view the scenery from the best 'stations'. It contains little about walking, although **footpaths** that lead to particular 'stations' are described.

West Highland Way A **long-distance path**, established by the **Countryside Commission for Scotland**, that runs for 153 kilometres from Milngavie (**grid reference** NS 555745) north of Glasgow, to Fort William (grid reference NN 104732). The route follows the banks of Loch Lomond, climbs Glen Falloch to Crianlarich, takes a low-level route to Tyndrum and Bridge of Orchy before climbing over Rannoch Moor and the Devil's Staircase to Kinlochleven. Then it follows an old military road to Glen Nevis and Fort William. In general, it is well waymarked, and the only strenuous sections are over Rannoch Moor, and a short stretch near Glen Nevis. (See figure 36 for a **map** showing the location of all **national trails** and official long-distance paths in the United Kingdom.)
Youth Hostels
Glasgow, Rowardennan, Crianlarich and Glen Nevis.
Maps
1:50000 **Landranger** sheets 41, 50, 56, 57, 64.
1:25000 **Pathfinder** sheets P277 (NN07/17), P290 (NN06/16), P291 (NN26/36), P306 (NN25/35), P320 (NN24/34), P333 (NN23/33), P346 (NN22/32), P357 (NN21/31), P368 (NN20/30), P380 (NS29/39), P381 (NS49/59), P391 (NS48/59), P403 (NS47/57).
Footpath Guides
Hunter, Tom, *A Guide to the West Highland Way*, Constable, 2nd Rev. Ed., 1984.
The West Highland Way; a Complete Map-Guide

Giving Lots of Information for Walkers, Footprint, 1988.

Westacott, Hugh (ie Hugh Douglas Dyer-Westacott 1932 -) Prolific author of **footpath guides**, articles, reviews, and books about walking who also writes under the name H. D. Westacott (he combined his surname with that of his second wife to demonstrate the equality of the sexes). Until 1980 he was a librarian, but left the profession to become a full-time writer following the publication of *The Walker's Handbook*, now in its third edition and widely recognised as the standard work on the subject. He has also made original contributions to the history and bibliography of walking for pleasure. His business activities include the proprietorship of **Footpath** Publications, which specialises in publishing walking guides to the less popular regions, and **Rucksack** Holidays which brings Americans on walking holidays to Britain.

Hugh Westacott, author and proprietor of Footpath Publications (photo Survival Aids).

Publications about Walking
Footpaths *and* **Bridleways** *in Buckinghamshire No.1: Winslow Area*, Footpath Publications, 1974.
Footpaths and Bridleways in Buckinghamshire No.2: Buckingham Area, Footpath Publications, 1975.
Walks around Buckingham and Winslow, Footpath Publications, 1976.
A Practical Guide to Walking the Devon South Coast **Path**, Footpath Publications, 1976.

Walks and Rides on Dartmoor, Footpath Publications, 1977.

*A Practical Guide to Walking the **Ridgeway Path***, Footpath Publications, 4th Ed., 1978.

Discovering Walking, Shire Publications, 1979.

*A Practical Guide to Walking the **Dorset** Coast Path*, Footpath Publications, 1982.

The Devon South Coast Path (with **Mark Richards**), Penguin Books, 1982.

*The **Dorset** Coast Path* (with Mark Richards), Penguin Books, 1982.

The Ridgeway Path (with Mark Richards), Penguin Books, 1982.

*The **Brecon Beacons National Park*** (with Mark Richards), Penguin Books, 1983.

Dartmoor for Walkers and Riders (with Mark Richards), Penguin Books, 1983.

*The **North Downs Way*** (with Mark Richards) Penguin Books, 1983.

The Somerset and North Devon Coast Path (with Mark Richards), Penguin Books, 1983.

The Walker's Handbook, Oxford Illustrated Press, 3rd Ed., 1989.

Walking; an Annotated Bibliography from the Earliest times to 1950, Footpath Publications, 1989.

*The Illustrated Encyclopaedia of Walking and **Backpacking**: Places, People & Techniques*, Oxford Illustrated Press, 1990.

Also contributed to

Smith, Roger, Editor, *The Winding **Trail**; a Selection of Articles and Essays for Walkers and **Backpackers***, Paladin, 1986.

Hillaby, John, Editor, *Walking in Britain*, Collins, 1988.

Western Highlands An area of **Scotland** that includes part of the western seaboard and runs north from Loch Linnhe and the Great **Glen** to a line drawn from the Cromarty Firth along the valleys of the rivers Conon, Bran, and Carron to Loch Carron. The area measures approximately 140 kilometres form north to south, and about 50 kilometres from west to east, and includes Ardnamurchan, the most westerly point on the mainland of Great Britain.

The whole area, which includes Glen Affric, Glen Cannich and Glen Strathfarrer, which are generally acknowledged to be the three most beautiful glens in Scotland, is mountainous and there are a number of ranges that attain a height of nearly 1200 metres. The Western Highlands has few roads and these follow the coast and glens. For the experienced hill-walker, there is a splendid network of **paths** that reach into every part of the area. Unfortunately, this region is one of the wet-test areas of Scotland. and the walker must expect many days when it will be impossible to venture into the **mountains**. (See figure 25 for a map of the major scenic divisions of Scotland.)

Maps

1:50000 **Landranger** sheets 24, 25, 26, 33, 34, 40, 47, 49.

Guidebook

Bennet, D. J. and Strang, Tom. *The Northwest Highlands*, Scottish Mountaineering Trust, 1990.

Footpath Guides

Brown, Hamish M., *The Island of Rhum; a Guide for Walkers*, Cicerone Press, 1988.

Hallewall, Richard, *Walk Loch Ness and the River Spey*, Bartholomew 1987.

MacInnes, Hamish, *Highland Walks Vol 1: Ben Lui to the Falls of Glomach*, Hodder and Stoughton, 1984.

MacInnes, Hamish, *Highland Walks Vol 2: **Skye** to Cape Wrath*, Hodder and Stoughton, 1984.

Weston, Edward Payson (1839-1929) American journalist, lecturer on athletics, and professional pedestrian. Payson first excited the popular imagination by walking the 709 kilometres from Boston to the city of Washington in 208 hours in order to attend the inauguration of President Lincoln. Thereafter his career was launched, and his most famous exploits include walking from Portland, Maine to Chicago (2135 kilometres in 26 days) in 1867 (he repeated this feat in 1907 and beat his previous time by 29 hours); in 1909, at the age of 70, he covered the 6271 kilometres from New York to San Francisco in 104 days and 7 hours; in 1910, he returned to New York from San Francisco in 76 days, 23 hours and 10 minutes; and in 1913, he walked from New York to Minneapolis (2489 kilometres in 51 days) to lay the corner-stone of the headquarters of the Athletic Club. He came to Britain in 1883 under the auspices of the Church of **England**, walked 8000 kilometres, and gave a lecture on temperance every evening.

Wherry, George (1852-1928) Sometime surgeon at Addenbrookes Hospital, Cambridge, University Lecturer in Surgery, and member of the **Alpine Club**. In 1909, he published *Notes from a **Knapsack*** which is a curious collection of essays including some on climbing and walking, and others with such diverse titles as 'Tongue-swallowing', 'The Horns of Animals', and 'The Rising Posture of Ungulate Animals'. He reports that he managed to clamber onto the lintels of Stonehenge, but the Dean refused him permission to climb the spire of Salisbury Cathedral.

White, Richard Grant (1821-85) Influential American critic, essayist, and man of letters who contributed articles about **England** to the *Atlantic Monthly* which were collected and issued posthumously as *England Without and Within*, 1894. He travelled a great deal on foot, but did not describe his walks in any detail as his main interest was in English manners and attitudes.

White, Walter (1811-1893) Sometime Assistant Secretary and Librarian of the Royal Society, a friend of Alfred, Lord Tennyson, with whom he sometimes took short strolls, and an acquaintance of Charles Darwin and other famous people. White was a keen walker and author of numerous accounts of walking tours, some of which were sufficiently popular to run to several editions. He walked from Southampton to Land's End, and back to Taunton in the summer of 1854, and wrote a lively and fascinating account of his journey in *A Londoner's Walk to the Land's End and a Trip to the **Scilly Isles***, 1855 (2nd Ed., 1861). It is particularly interesting because he followed the route patrolled on foot by the coastguard from Charmouth in **Dorset** to Par in **Cornwall** which now forms part of the **South West Coast Path**. His other works are *To Mont Blanc and Back Again*, 1854; *On Foot through the Tyrol in the Summer of 1855*, 1856 (2nd Ed., 1863); *A July Holiday in Saxony, Bohemia and Silesia*, 1857 (2nd Ed., 1863); *A Month in Yorkshire*, 1858 (4th Ed., 1861); *Notes from the **Netherlands*** (*Chambers Journal* 1858 vol XV); *Northumberland and the Border*, 1859 (2nd Ed., 1863); *All Around the Wrekin*, 1860 (2nd Ed., 1860); *Eastern England from the Thames to the Humber*, 1865; *Holidays in the Tyrol, Kufstein, Klobenstein and Paneveggio*, 1876; and *Obladis; a Tyrolean Sour Spring*, 1881. *The Journals of Walter White*, which scarcely mention his walking tours, were published posthumously in 1898. He wrote vivid descriptions of scenery and the life of humble, country people, and related many anecdotes.

White-out A serious **hazard** caused by falling **snow**, or **mist** on snow-covered **mountains** and **moorland** that makes it impossible to distinguish the horizon. The earth and the sky seem to merge, visibility is very poor, and the walker feels disorientated making **navigation** very difficult.

Whymper, Edward (1840-1911) A wood-engraver and climber, one of the best-known names in mountaineering, and the first man to climb to the summit of the Matterhorn. His book *Scrambles Amongst the **Alps** in the Years 1860-9* published in 1875 is one of the great classics of mountaineering literature, and includes a number of descriptions of long Alpine walks.

Wick, wicking The popular term for **vapour transmission**.

Wicklow Mountains An extensive mountainous region of **Eire** that extends southwards from Dublin. The range lacks **ridges**, and its most notable feature is the characteristic rounded domes and deep **glens** which tend to be boggy underfoot. The highest peak is Lugnaquillia (912 metres).

Maps
Irish Ordnance Survey 1:63360 District Map of Wicklow. 1:126720 sheet 16.

Footpath Guides
Herman, David, **Hill Walker's** Wicklow, *Shanksmare Publications* (distributed in the UK by Cordee), 1989.

Herman, David, *Irish Walks Guides East; Dublin and Wicklow*, Gill and Macmillan, 1979.

Moriatry, Christopher, *On Foot in Dublin and Wicklow*, Wolfhound Press, 1989.

Wicklow Way A **long-distance path** in **Eire** that runs for 132 kilometres from its junction with the **South Leinster Way** at Clonegal, County Carlow to Dublin forming the final section of a 307-kilometre **path** from Clogheen, County Waterford. The scenery ranges from quiet field paths to **glens** and rugged **mountain** scenery. The maximum elevation reached is 661 metres.

Maps
Irish Ordnance Survey 1:126720 sheets 16 & 19.

Footpath Guides
Fewer, Michael, *The Wicklow Way from Marley to Glenmalure*, Gill & Macmillan, 1988.

Irish Tourist Board Information Sheet 26B *The Wicklow Way*. (Leaflet.)

Malone, J. B., *The Complete Wicklow Way*, O'Brien Press, 1988.

The Wicklow Way compiled and published by the Irish Ordnance Survey.

Wilderness An outdoor magazine, edited by **Chris Townsend**, devoted to such outdoor pursuits as walking, **trekking, backpacking**, nordic skiing, rafting and **fell**-running. It first appeared as a bi-monthly in March 1989, and was published monthly from March 1990. *(For address see Appendix.)*

Wildlife and Countryside Act, 1981 An important Act affecting **England** and **Wales** that amended and revised some of the provisions of the **National Parks and Access to the Countryside Act, 1948**, the **Countryside Act, 1968** and the **Highways Act, 1980**. Its main provisions were to require surveying authorities to keep the **definitive map** under continuous review, and to reclassify **roads used as public paths** as **byways open to all traffic**, **bridleways** or **footpaths**.

Wilkinson, Thomas A traveller who undertook a series of tours on horseback made with the intention of climbing **mountains** on foot. Among his more notable ascents were the Langdale Pikes, Coniston Old Man, Helvellyn, Crossfell and Ben Nevis. He was very fond of female company, and sometimes persuaded ladies to climb with him to the summit. He describes his adventures in *Tours to the British Mountains with the Descriptive Poems of Lowther and Emont Vale*, 1824.

Wills, Sir Alfred (1828-1932) A High Court judge and an early Alpine climber and explorer. He wrote two books that contain accounts of walking in the **Alps**, *Wanderings among the High Alps*, published in 1856 and reissued as No. 3 in *Blackwell's Mountaineering Library* in 1937, and *The Eagle's Nest in the Valley of the Sixt; a Summer Home among the Alps together with some Excursions among the Great **Glaciers***, 1860. He was President of the **Alpine Club** 1864-5.

Wilson, John (1785-1854) Scottish poet, critic and essayist. He lived in what is now the **Lake District National Park** for a time and frequently went walking with the **Wordsworths**, **Samuel Taylor Coleridge** and **Thomas de Quincey**. He undertook a walking tour of **Scotland** with his wife in 1815, and there is an account of this unusual tour, in which the couple seem to have slept in a **tent** for part of the time, in the author's pseudonymous memoirs entitled *Recreations of Christopher North*, which was published in three volumes in 1842.

Wind chill The technical term used to describe the effect that the wind speed has in cooling the human body that is of one of the most significant factors in **hypothermia**. The strength of the wind, as well as the actual ambient temperature, has a marked effect on the rate that the body will cool, and is known as the wind chill factor. The cooling effect of the strength of the wind can be dramatically demonstrated by figure 35 where it can be seen

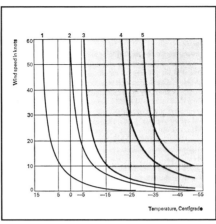

Figure 35: Wind-chill scale.

that a person exposed to a 30-knot wind when the temperature is 10°C (50°F) is subject to the same loss of temperature as if he were standing in still air at –25°C (–13°F).

Line 1 indicates when the temperature feels cold

Line 2 indicates when the temperature feels bitterly cold

Line 3 indicates when exposed flesh is likely to freeze

Line 4 indicates when exposed flesh is likely to freeze in one minute

Line 5 indicates when exposed flesh is likely to freeze in thirty seconds

The shaded area indicates when conditions are dangerous to survival.

Winstanley, William The author of *Poor Robin's Perambulation from Saffron Walden to London* which was published anonymously in 1678. It is a literary and pedestrian curiosity in the form of a long 'poem' in execrable doggerel verse, interspersed with passages of prose, that gives an account of a walk from Saffron Walden, Suffolk to London in 1678. The subject matter is unimaginative and mostly consists of accounts of inns on the route, and his drinking bouts with friends and others he met along the way.

Wolds Way A **national trail**, designated by the **Countryside Commission** and opened in 1982, that runs for 127 kilometres from Hessle (**grid reference** TA 035256), Humberside to Filey (grid reference TA 107826), on the Yorkshire coast where it links with the **Cleveland Way**. The route follows the northern and eastern edges of the Wolds, a range of chalk hills giving commanding views over the surrounding countryside. This is a very easy walk through cultivated farmland and many charming villages. (See figure 36 for a **map** showing the location of all national trails and official **long-distance paths** in the United Kingdom.)

Youth Hostels

Thixendale, Beverley.

Maps

1:50000 **Landranger** sheets 100, 101, 106. 1:25000 **Pathfinder** sheets P624 (TA08/09/18), P644 (SE87/97), P645 (TA07/17), P656 (SE86/96), P666 (SE85/95), P675 (SE84/94), P686 (SE83/93), P695 (SE82/92), P696 (TA02/12)

Footpath Guides

Ratcliffe, Roger, *The Wolds Way*, HMSO, 1982. Rubenstein, David, *The Wolds Way*, Dalesman, 1979.

Wool A natural fibre obtained from sheep that can be spun into a yarn and woven or knitted into a great variety of cloths such as **flannel** and **tweed**. Wool has the remarkable property of being able to absorb large quantities of water and still retain its warmth, but it takes a long time to dry. It can be made water-repellent by coating with silicones or one of the proprietary waterproofing agents such as Technix. Very fine knitted woollens, such as lambswool, are used in winter-weight underwear and for light-weight sweaters. The coarser, heavier woollens are used for sweaters. Some walkers favour wearing oiled-wool sweaters under shell **clothing** as these woollens will not absorb so much **condensation**.

Wordsworth, Dorothy (1771-1855) The sister of **William Wordsworth** whose fame has been unfairly overshadowed by that of her brother. She is a considerable literary figure in her own right, and like her brother, she, too, was an enthusiastic and strong walker. In 1799 she records that she and William walked *'10 miles over a* **mountain** *road with a strong wind behind them in two and a half hours 'by the watch'.'* After a 15-minute rest, they walked another 7 miles in 1 hour and 35 minutes, which is a total of 17 miles in 4 hours and 5 minutes. Her *Journals* frequently mention her almost daily walks, and she accompanied William on many of his tours, although on some of them she went by carriage. But she walked with William and **Samuel Taylor Coleridge** from Watchet to Lynton in 1797, and with William on his tour of the **Wye Valley** in 1798. In 1818, she climbed Scafell, the highest **mountain** in **England** in what is now the **Lake District National Park**, with her friend Miss

Barker and a shepherd who acted as a guide.

The best edition of her *Journals*, which include her account of the tours of **Scotland** in 1801 and 1803, is *The Journals of Dorothy Wordsworth* edited by Ernest De Selincourt, Macmillan, 2 Vols, 1941.

Wordsworth, William (1770-1850) Poet laureate and indefatigable walker throughout his long life. **Thomas De Quincey** calculated that he had walked between 175,000 and 180,000 miles (281,750 - 289,800 kilometres) by the time he was 65. Wordsworth's poetry is characterised by his love of nature and landscape, that amounted almost to worship, which expressed itself in poetry of peculiar intensity and passion. It was on their famous walk in 1797 from Watchet to Lynton, along what is now part of the **South West Coast Path**, that he and **Samuel Taylor Coleridge** composed many of the poems that appeared in *Lyrical Ballads* published in 1798. This seminal work broke away from the prevailing classical style, allowing the expression of genuine and personal emotion, and is usually regarded as the book that marked the start of the **romantic movement** in English literature. We know from **Dorothy Wordsworth's** *Journal* that her brother often composed poems whilst walking, which he later wrote down at home. At his home, which is now open to the public, at Rydal Mount near Windermere in the **Lake District National Park**, he would often compose while pacing up and down the garden in all weathers, and there seems little doubt that he found the physical rhythm of walking an aid to composition.

Wordsworth was born in Cockermouth and went to school at Hawkshead in the heart of the Lake District. It was here, when he was only 9 years old, that he commenced his 'starlight walks' when he would roam along country roads at night. He often completed the 8-kilometre circuit of Esthwaite before the start of morning school. In 1789, he walked from Dovedale to Penrith, and the following year walked with his fellow Cambridge undergraduate, Robert Jones, through **France**, **Switzerland** and **Germany** during the Long Vacation, sometimes covering as much as 64 kilometres in a day. In 1791, he and Jones walked extensively in north **Wales**, and in 1793, he walked from Salisbury via Bath and Bristol and up the **Wye Valley** to north Wales. 1798 saw him in the Wye Valley again, walking this time with Dorothy and his publisher Joseph Cottle, and it was on this tour

that he composed the last 20 lines of the celebrated poem *Tintern Abbey* as he walked down the hill from Clifton into Bristol. He walked with Coleridge and his brother John Wordsworth, from Sockburn, north Yorkshire to Grasmere to view Dove Cottage in 1799, and made two tours of **Scotland** in 1801 and 1803. The Scottish tours are described by Dorothy Wordsworth in *Recollections of a Tour Made in Scotland*. Wordsworth went to Scotland again in 1814, and in 1820 spent four months in Switzerland with his wife, Mary, and sister, and visited **Belgium** with Mary in 1823. In 1828 he walked up the Rhine from Belgium with his daughter, Dora, and Coleridge, and met **Thomas Gratton** at Namur, in present-day Belgium, and **Julian Charles Young** at Bonn in **Germany**. He visited Ireland in 1829, went to Scotland in 1831 to see **Sir Walter Scott**, and in 1833 he made a tour of the **Isle of Man** and Scotland. It should be noted that many of these excursions were carriage tours undertaken with his family and friends, but Wordsworth often preferred to walk beside the conveyance, and took every opportunity to explore on his own. His last tour was in 1837 to Italy with his friend **Henry Crabb Robinson**, but it appears from Robinson's account not to have involved any walking. Wordsworth lived at different times in the Lake District, Somerset and Yorkshire, and in all these places he walked frequently and far.

Many of his journeys are described in the long autobiographical poem *The Prelude*, in the various *Journals* of Dorothy Wordsworth, and in Christopher Wordsworth's *Memoirs of William Wordsworth* published in 1851. He wrote a guidebook to the Lake District, *A Description of the Scenery of the Lakes in the North of* **England**, first published in 1835, and still in print.

Wright, Christopher John (1943-) Hill-walker, mountaineer, guide, naturalist, photographer and the author of numerous articles, who also writes under the names Christopher Wright and Chris Wright. He is best known for the series of guides, published by Constable, to British **long-distance paths** using 1:100000 Bartholomew **maps**. Since 1986, he has edited the *Journal of the* **Fell & Rock Club**.

Publications

A Guide to the **Pennine Way**, Constable, 4th Ed., Constable, 1987.

A Guide to the **Pilgrims' Way & North Downs Way**, 3rd Ed., Constable, 1981.

*A Guide to **Offa's Dyke Path***, Constable, 3rd Ed., 1989.

*A Guide to the **Pembrokeshire Coast Path***, Constable, 2nd Ed., 1989.

The Westmorland Way Heritage Walk (with **Mark Richards**), Cicerone Press, 1988.

Also contributed to

No Through Road; the AA Book of Country Walks, Drive Publications, 1975.

Wilson, Ken and **Gilbert, Richard** *Classic Walks*, Diadem, 1982.

Wye Valley An **area of outstanding natural beauty**, designated in 1971, which covers 325 square kilometres of the Wye Valley. It stretches from Chepstow northwards almost as far as Hereford and lies in the counties of Gwent, Hereford and Worcester, and Gloucestershire. It contains some superb river scenery including, in the lower half, cliffs and gorges. (See figure 36 for a **map** showing the location of all AONBs in the United Kingdom.)

Maps

1:50000 **Landranger** sheets 149, 162.

1:25000 **Outdoor Leisure Map** 14 Wye Valley and the Forest of Dean.

Footpath Guides

Hurley, Heather, *Wyedean Walks*, Forest Bookshop, 8 St John Street, Coleford, Glos GL16 8AR, 1986.

Hurley, Heather, and John, **Paths** and *Pubs of the Wye Valley*, Thornhill Press, 1986.

Jones, Roger, *Exploring the Wye Valley and Forest of Dean*, published by the author at 45 Greyhound Lane, Stourbridge, West Midlands DY8 3AD.

Yorkshire Dales National Park This is Britain's third largest **national park** and covers an area of 1760 square kilometres bounded by the towns of Skipton, Settle, Sedbergh and Richmond. The Dales themselves, with their enchanting villages, are long, narrow valleys which cut into the **Pennines**. This is wonderful country for the walker, and except for one or two places such as Malham and Kettlewell, relatively uncrowded. One of the features of the Dales is the **scars** where the rocks have slipped, because of a geological fault, leaving the limestone as a huge cliff, as at Malham Cove and Gordale Scar. (See figure 36 for a **map** showing the location of all **national parks** in the United Kingdom.) *(For addresses of National Park Headquarters and Information Centres see Appendix.)*

Janet's Foss in the Yorkshire Dales' National Park (photo © Hugh Westacott).

Official Guidebook

Waltham, Tony, *Yorkshire Dales*, Webb & Bower in association with Michael Joseph, 1988.

National Park Newspaper

The Visitor

Maps

1:50000 **Landranger** sheets 91, 92, 97, 98, 99, 103, 104.

1:25000 **Outdoor Leisure Maps** 2 Yorkshire Dales (Western area), 10 Yorkshire Dales (Southern area), 30 Yorkshire Dales (Northern and Central).

Footpath Guides

Gemmell, Arthur, *Aysgarth Area Footpath Map*, Stile Publications, 5th. Rev. Ed., 1987.

Gemmell, Arthur, *Bolton Abbey Footpath Map*, Stile Publications, 4th. Rev. Ed., 1987.

Gemmell, Arthur, *Grassington and Area Footpath and*

161

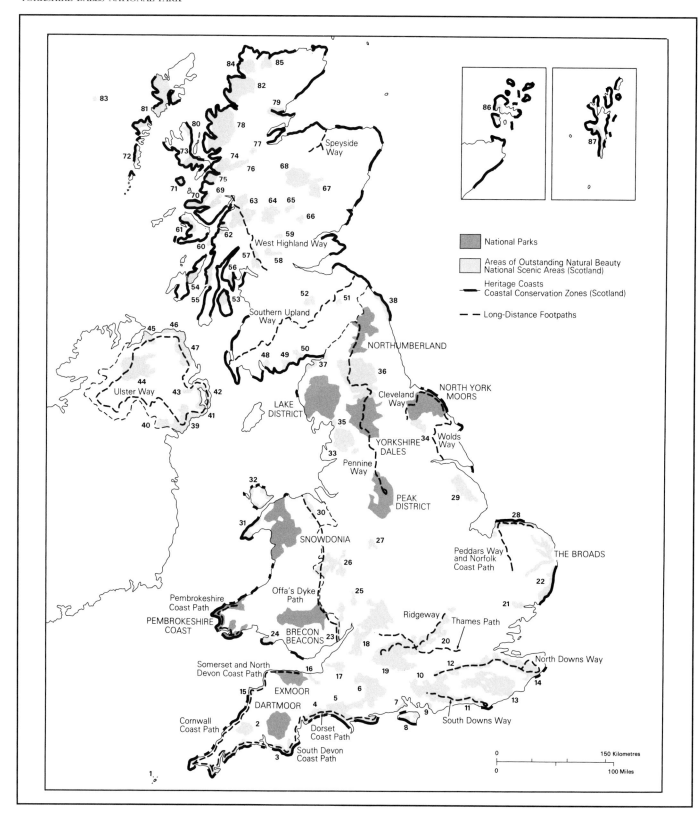

Speyside Way

West Highland Way

Southern Upland Way

Ulster Way

NORTHUMBERLAND

NORTH YORK MOORS

Cleveland Way

LAKE DISTRICT

YORKSHIRE DALES

Wolds Way

Pennine Way

PEAK DISTRICT

SNOWDONIA

THE BROADS

Peddars Way and Norfolk Coast Path

Offa's Dyke Path

Ridgeway

Thames Path

Pembrokeshire Coast Path

PEMBROKESHIRE COAST

BRECON BEACONS

North Downs Way

Somerset and North Devon Coast Path

EXMOOR

DARTMOOR

South Downs Way

Cornwall Coast Path

Dorset Coast Path

South Devon Coast Path

National Parks

Areas of Outstanding Natural Beauty
National Scenic Areas (Scotland)

Heritage Coasts
Coastal Conservation Zones (Scotland)

Long-Distance Footpaths

0   150 Kilometres

0   100 Miles

Areas of outstanding natural beauty

1	Isles of Scilly	59	River Earn
2	Cornwall	60	Scarba, Lunga and the Garvellachs
3	South Devon	61	Loch na Keal
4	East Devon	62	Lynn of Lorn
5	Dorset	63	Ben Nevis & Glen Coe
6	Cranborne Chase & West Wiltshire Downs	64	Loch Rannoch & Glen Lyon
7	South Hampshire Coast	65	Loch Tummell
8	Isle of Wight	66	River Tay
9	Chichester Harbour	67	Deeside & Lochnagar
10	East Hampshire	68	Cairngorms
11	Sussex Downs	69	Loch Shiel
12	Surrey Hills	70	Morrar, Moidart & Ardnamurchan
13	High Weald	71	Small Isles
14	Kent Downs	72	South Uist Machair
15	North Devon	73	Cuillin Hills
16	Quantock Hills	74	Kintail
17	Mendip Hills	75	Knoydart
18	Cotswolds	76	Glen Affric
19	North Wessex Downs	77	Glen Strathfarrar
20	Chilterns	78	Wester Ross
21	Dedham Vale	79	Dornoch Firth
22	Suffolk Coast and Heaths	80	Trotternish
23	Wye Valley	81	South Lewis, Harris & North Uist
24	Gower	82	Assynt-Coigach
25	Malvern Hills	83	St Kilda
26	Shropshire Hills	84	North-west Sutherland
27	Cannock Chase	85	Kyle of Tongue
28	Norfolk Coast	86	Hoy & West Mainland
29	Lincolnshire Wolds	87	Shetland Islands
30	Clwydian Range		
31	Lleyn, Wales		
32	Anglesey		
33	Forest of Bowland		
34	Howardian Hills		
35	Arnside and Silverdale		
36	North Pennines		
37	Solway Coast		
38	Northumberland Coast		
39	Mourne		
40	South Armagh		
41	Lecale Coast		
42	Strangford Lough		
43	Lagan Valley		
44	Sperrin		
45	North Derry		
46	Causeway Coast		
47	Antrim Coast and Glens		
48	Fleet Valley		
49	East Stewartry Coast		
50	Nith Estuary		
51	Eildon and Leaderfoot		
52	Upper Tweeddale		
53	North Arran		
54	Jura		
55	Knapdale		
56	Kyles of Bute		
57	Loch Lomond		
58	Trossachs		

Figure 36: Map showing the approximate location of national parks, areas of outstanding natural beauty, national scenic areas, heritage coasts, conservation zones, national trails and other long-distance paths in the UK.

Town Maps and Walking Guide, Stile Publications, 3rd. Rev. Ed., 1987.

Gemmell, Arthur, *Malhamdale Footpath Map*, Stile Publications, 7th. Rev. Ed., 1988.

Gemmell, Arthur, *Upper Swaledale Footpath Maps and Guide*, Stile Publications, 2nd. Rev. Ed., 1987.

Gemmell, Arthur, *Wayfarer Walks in Upper Wharfedale*, Stile Publications, 2nd. Rev. Ed., 1988.

Hannon, Paul, *80 Dales Walks; a Comprehensive Walking Guide to the Yorkshire Dales*, Cordee, 1988. Keighley, J., *Walks in the Yorkshire Dales*, Cicerone Press, 1990.

Sellers, Gladys, *The Yorkshire Dales; a Walker's Guide to the National Park*, Cicerone Press, 1984.

Young, Julian Charles (1806-1873) The son of the actor Charles Mayne Young. In his book *Last Leaves from the Journal of JY.* edited by E.A.G.Y[oung], published posthumously in 1875, he records walking in the neighbourhood of Bonn, in what is now **West Germany**, with **Samuel Taylor Coleridge**, **William Wordsworth** and his daughter Dora when the trio were on their walking tour of the Rhine in 1828. He gives a very detailed description of the poets and describes Coleridge as a poor walker. Young and Wordsworth spent one day walking together, and he comments that Wordsworth conversed unceasingly about the landscape.

Youth Hostels An international movement founded to provide simple, inexpensive accommodation to assist all, and especially the young, to explore the countryside. The youth hostel movement has its origins in **Sweden** where the Swedish Touring Club provided low-cost accommodation in simple shelters, but the person usually credited with being the founder of the movement was a German teacher, Richard Schirrman (*c* 1864-?). In 1907, he put straw palliasses in his classroom so that children on school expeditions had somewhere to sleep. His example was followed by other German teachers, and in 1910 these informal arrangements became more permanent when an organisation was formed, and the first youth hostel was opened. The movement spread quickly throughout Europe, but did not reach the United Kingdom until 1931. An account of the movement may be found in *Youth Hostel Story* by Oliver Coburn and published by the National Council for Social Service in 1950.

Many countries now have youth hostel associations. The type of accommodation and the conditions of use vary from country to country. Most hostels have a warden, some provide meals, and hostellers usually have to do some

Tanners Hatch Youth Hostel, one of 260 in England and Wales (photo © YHA).

housework so that prices can be kept low. The popularity of youth hostelling has declined recently in the western world because of rising affluence. There are three associations in the UK, the **Youth Hostels Association (England and Wales)**, the **Scottish Youth Hostels Association**, and the **Youth Hostels Association of Northern Ireland**. Membership of one Association gives the entitlement to use any youth hostel anywhere in the world.

Youth Hostels Association (England and Wales) The Association exists to help all, especially young people of limited means, to a greater knowledge, love and care of the countryside particularly by providing hostels or other simple accommodation for them in their travels, and thus to promote their health, rest and education. The YHA has 260 hostels in **England** and **Wales** (**Scotland** and **Northern Ireland** have their own organisations - the **Scottish Youth Hostels Association** and the **Youth Hostels Association of Northern Ireland**). Inexpensive meals are available at most hostels, and there are usually facilities for members to cook their own meals. Prices are kept low because members have to do a few household chores before departing. Accommodation is in single-sex dormitories, although a few hostels have family rooms. The YHA offers tours and travel services to its members, and a current membership card entitles the holder to use **youth hostels** throughout the world. The journal of the YHA is *The Hosteller. (For address see Appendix.)*

Youth Hostels Association of Northern Ireland This organisation aims to help all, especially young people of limited means, to a greater knowledge, love and care of the countryside particularly by providing hostels or other simple accommodation for them in their travels, and thus to promote their health, rest and education. There are 7 hostels mostly situated in the eastern half of the Province (there are separate organisations for **Scotland** and **England** and **Wales** - see the **Scottish Youth Hostels Association** and the **Youth Hostels Association**). Most hostels are self-catering (though some provide meals and snacks), and there are facilities for members to cook their own meals. Prices are kept low because members have to do a few household chores before departing. Accommodation is in single-sex dormitories, although some hostels have family rooms. A current membership card entitles the holder to use **youth hostels** throughout the world. *(For address see Appendix.)*

Appendix

Addresses of organisations, companies, magazines, societies etc. mentioned in the alphabetical section as they existed on 31 January 1991.

Organisations marked with asterisks do not have a permanent address. Correspondents should put their address on the envelope so that the Post Office can return the letter if the organisation has moved. The current address of organisations marked * may be obtained from the **Ramblers' Association**, and those marked ** from the **British Mountaineering Council.**

Adventure and Environmental Awareness Group
Hon. Secretary: Geoff Cooper, Low Bank Ground, Coniston, Cumbria LA21 8AA. Tel. 05394-41314.

Alpine Club
118 Eaton Square, London SW1W 9AF. Tel. 071-259-5591.

Association for the Protection of Rural Scotland
14a Napier Road, Edinburgh EH10 5AY. Tel. 031-229-1898.

Association of Countryside Rangers
Hon. Secretary: Mrs Sue Clark, 100 Station Road, Puckeridge, Herts SG11 1TF. Tel. 0920-822600.

Association of Heads of Outdoor Centres
Hon. Secretary: David Shearman, Aberglaslyn Hall, Beddgelert, Caernarfon, Gwynedd LL55 4YF. Tel. 076686-233.

**Association of National Park Officers
Hon. Secretary: Donald Connolly, Lake District National Park Special Planning Board, Busher Walk, Kendal, Cumbria LA9 4RH. Tel. 0539-7724555.

*Backpackers' Club
PO Box 381, 7-10 Friar Street, Reading RG3 4RL. Tel. 04917-739.

Bivvybug Designs
'Boscarhyn', Syra Close, St Kew Highway, Bodmin, Cornwall PL30 3ED. Tel. 0208-84649.

**Bob Graham 24 Hour Club
Chairman: Fred Rogerson, Tethers End, Lindeth, Windermere, Cumbria LA23 2NH. Tel. 09662-4586.

Brecon Beacons National Park
7 Glamorgan Street, Brecon, Powys LD3 7DP. Tel. 0874-4437.

British Activity Holiday Association
Rock Park, Llandrindod Wells, Powys LD1 6AE. Tel. 0597-823902.

**British Association of Mountain Guides
c/o British Mountaineering Council, Crawford House, Precinct Centre, Booth Street East, Manchester MR13 9RZ. Tel. 061-273-5835.

British Mountaineering Council
Crawford House, Precinct Centre, Booth Street East, Manchester M13 9RZ. Tel. 061-273-5835.

British Textile Technology Group
Wira House, West Park Ring Road, Leeds LS16 6QL. Tel. 0532-781381.

British Trust for Conservation Volunteers
36 St Mary's Street, Wallingford, Oxon OX10 0EU. Tel. 0491-39766.

The Broads
Thomas Harvey House, 18 Colegate, Norwich NR3 1BQ. Tel. 0603-610734.

*Byways and Bridleway Trust
The Granary, Charlcutt, Calne, Wilts SN11 9NL. Tel. 024973-273.

Cairngorm Club
Hon. Secretary: R.C. Shirreffs, 18 Bon-Accord Square, Aberdeen AB1 2DJ. Tel. 0224-315505.

Camping & Caravanning Club
Greenfields House, Westwood Way, Coventry CV4 8JH. Tel. 0203-694995.

Camping and Outdoor Leisure Association
Morritt House, 58 Station Approach, South Ruislip, Middlesex HA4 6SA. Tel. 081-842-1111/1292.

Camping & Walking
Link House, Dingwall Avenue, Croydon CR9 2TA. Tel. 081-686-2599.

Classic Nepal
33 Metro Avenue, Newton, Derbyshire DE55 5UF. Tel. 0773-873497.

Climber & Hill Walker
Outram Magazines, Plaza Tower, The Plaza, East Kilbride, Glasgow G74 1LW. Tel. 0355-246444.

Cordee
3a De Montford Street, Leicester LE1 7HD. Tel. 0533-543579.

Council for National Parks
45 Shelton Street, London WC2H 9HJ. Tel. 071-240-3603.

Council for the Protection of Rural England
Warwick House, 25 Buckingham Palace Road, London SW1W 0PP. Tel. 071-235-9481.

Council for the Protection of Rural Wales (Cymdethas Diogelu Cymru Wledig)
Ty Gwyn, 31 High Street, Welshpool, Powys SY21 7JP. Tel. 0938-552525.

Country Walking
EMAP Pursuit Publishing, Bretton Court, Bretton, Peterborough PE3 8DZ. Tel. 0733-264666.

Countryside Commission
John Dower House, Crescent Place, Cheltenham, Glos GL50 3RA. Tel. 0242-521381.

Countryside Commission for Scotland
Battleby, Redgorton, Perth PH1 3EW. Tel. 0738-27921.

Countrywide Holidays Association
Birch Heys, 52 Cromwell Range, Manchester M14 6HW. Tel. 061-225-1000.

Dartmoor Expedition Centre
Rowden Farm, Widecombe-in-the-Moor, Newton Abbot, Devon TQ13 7TX. Tel. 03642-249.

Dartmoor National Park
'Parke', Haytor Road, Bovey Tracey, Devon TQ13 9JQ. Tel. 0626-832093.

Department of the Environment for Northern Ireland
Countryside and Wildlife Branch, Calvert House, 23 Castle Place, Belfast BT1 1FY. Tel. 0232-230560.

Edward Stanford Ltd
12 Long Acre, London WC2E 9LP. Tel. 071-836-1321.

EMAP Pursuit Publishing
Bretton Court, Bretton, Peterborough PE3 8DZ. Tel. 0733-264666.

English Tourist Board
Thames Tower, Black's Road, London W6 9EL. Tel. 081-846-9000.

REGIONAL TOURIST BOARDS
Cumbria Tourist Board, Ashleigh, Holly Road, Windermere, Cumbria LA23 2AQ. Tel. 09662-4444.
Counties: Cumbria.
AONBs: **Arnside and Silverdale**, **Solway Coast**.

East Anglia Tourist Board, Toppesfield Hall, Hadleigh, Suffolk IP7 5DN.
Tel. 0473-822922.
Counties: Cambridgeshire, Essex, Norfolk, Suffolk.
AONBs: **Dedham Vale**, **Norfolk Coast**, **Suffolk Coast and Heaths**.

East Midlands Tourist Board, Exchequergate, Lincoln LN2 1PZ. Tel. 0522-531521.
Counties: Derbyshire, Leicestershire, Lincolnshire, Northamptonshire, Nottinghamshire.
AONBs: **Lincolnshire Wolds**.

Heart of England Tourist Board, Woodside, Larkhill, Worcester WR5 2EQ.
Tel. 0905-763436.
Counties: Gloucestershire, Hereford and Worcester, Shropshire, Staffordshire, Warwickshire, West Midlands.
AONBs: **Cannock Chase**, **Cotswolds**, **Malvern Hills**, **Shropshire Hills**, **Wye Valley**.

North West Tourist Board, The Last Drop Village, Bromley Cross, Bolton, Lancs BL7 9PZ. Tel. 0204-591511.
Counties: Cheshire, Greater Manchester, Lancashire, Merseyside.
AONBs: **Arnside and Silverdale**, **Forest of Bowland**.

Northumbria Tourist Board, Aykley Heads, Durham DH1 5UX. Tel. 091-386-2160.
Counties: Cleveland, Durham, Northumberland, Tyne and Wear.
AONBs: **North Pennines**, **Northumberland Coast**.

South East Tourist Board, The Old Brewhouse, Warwick Park, Tunbridge Wells, Kent TN2 5TU. Tel. 0892-540766.
Counties: East Sussex, Kent, Surrey, West Sussex.
AONBs: **Chichester Harbour**, **High Weald**, **Kent Downs**, **Surrey Hills**, **Sussex Downs**.

Southern Tourist Board, 40 Chamberlayne Road, Eastleigh, Hampshire SO5 5JH.
Tel. 0703-620006.
Counties: Dorset (East), Hampshire.
AONBs: **Chichester Harbour**, **Dorset**, **East Hampshire**, **Isle of Wight**, **North Wessex Downs**, **South Hampshire Coast**.

Thames and **Chilterns** Tourist Board, The Mount House, Church Green, Witney, Oxon OX8 5DZ. Tel. 0993-778800.
Counties: Bedfordshire, Berkshire, Buckinghamshire, Hertfordshire, Oxfordshire.
AONBs: **Chilterns**, **North Wessex Downs**.

West Country Tourist Board, Trinity Court, 27 Southernhay East, Exeter EX1 1QS.
Tel. 0392-76351.
Counties: Avon, Cornwall, Devon, Dorset (West), Somerset, Wiltshire.
AONBs: **Blackdown Hills**, **Cornwall**, **Cotswolds**, **Cranborne Chase and West Wiltshire Downs**, **Dorset**, **East Devon**, **Isles of Scilly**, **Mendip Hills**, **North Devon**, **North Wessex Downs**, **Quantock Hills**, **South Devon**.

Yorkshire and Humberside Tourist Board, 312 Tadcaster Road, York YO2 2HF.
Tel. 0904-707961.
Counties: Humberside, North Yorkshire, South Yorkshire, West Yorkshire.
AONBs: **Howardian Hills**, **Lincolnshire Wolds**.

*European Ramblers' Association
Europäische Wandervereinigung e. V., Reichstrasse 4, Postfach 401, D-6600 Saarbrücken, **Germany**.

Exmoor National Park
Exmoor House, Dulverton, Somerset TA22 9HL. Tel. 0398-23665.

Exodus Expeditions
9 Weir Road, London SW12 0LT.
Tel. 081-675-5550.

Explore Worldwide
1 Frederick Street, Aldershot, Hants GU11 1LQ. Tel. 0252-344161.

*Fell and Rock Club
Secretary: D. Staton Esq., 32 Warrenside Close, Blackburn BB1 9PF. Tel. 0254-249562.

Footpath Publications
86 Burford Gardens, London N13 4LP.
Tel. 081-886-1957.

Footpath Worker
The Ramblers' Association, 1–5 Wandsworth Road, London SW8 2XX. Tel. 071-582-6878.

*Forest Ramblers' Club
Hon. Secretary: H.L. Mitchell, 24 Oaklands, Constance Road, Whitton, Middlesex TW2 7JQ. Tel. 081-898-0873.
Forest Service for Northern Ireland
Dundonald House, Upper Newtownards Road, Belfast BT4 3SB. Tel. 0232-650111.

Forestry Commission
231 Corstorphine Road, Edinburgh EH12 7AT. Tel. 031-334-0303.

Friends of the Earth
26–28 Underwood Street, London N1 7JQ.
Tel. 071-490-1555.

Friends of the Earth (Scotland)
Bonnington Mill, 72 Newhaven Road, Edinburgh EH6 5QG. Tel. 031-554-9977.

*Friends of the Lake District
Secretary: J.M. Houston, No. 3 Yard 77, Highgate, Kendal, Cumbria LA9 4ED.
Tel. 0539-720788.

*Friends of the Ridgeway
Hon. Secretary: Nigel Forward, 90 South Hill Park, London NW3 2SN.
Tel. 071-794-2105.

The Great Outdoors
Outram Magazines, Plaza Tower, The Plaza, East Kilbride, Glasgow G74 1LW.
Tel. 0355-246444.

Hebden Cord Company
17–23 Oldgate, Hebden Bridge, West Yorkshire HX7 6EW. Tel. 0422-843152.

High
High Magazine Ltd, 164 Barkley Road, Leicester LE4 7LF. Tel. 0533-460722. (Editorial Office, 336 Abbey Lane, Sheffield S8 0BY. Tel. 0742-369296).

A.T. Hogg (Fife) Ltd
Strathmiglo, Fife KY14 7QB. Tel. 03376-202.

Holiday Fellowship Ltd
Imperial House, Edgeware Road, London NW9 5AL. Tel. 081-905-9956.

*Icknield Way Association
Hon. Secretary: Ken Payne, 65 London Road, Hitchin, Herts SG4 7NE.
Tel. 0462-450089.

Irish Tourist Board
150 New Bond Street, London W1Y 0AQ.
Tel. 071-493-3201.

JNM Publications
Winster, Matlock, Derbyshire DE4 2DQ.
Tel. 062988-454.

John Muir Trust
Director: Dr Terry Isles, Gardenhurst, Newbigging, Broughty Ferry, Dundee DD5 3RH. Tel. 082623-315.

Karakorum Experience
32 Lake Road, Keswick, Cumbria CA12 5DQ. Tel. 07687-73966.

Kevin Walker Mountain Activities
Laurel Cottage, James Street, Llangynidr, Crickhowell, Powys NP8 1NN.
Tel. 0874-730554.

Lake District National Park
National Park Visitor Centre, Brockhole, Windermere, Cumbria LA23 1LJ.
Tel. 09662-6601.

Leisure Books
53 Gillygate, York Y03 7EQ.
Tel. 0904-652410.

Long Distance Paths Advisory Service
Administrator: Gerald Cole, The Barn, Holme Lyon, Burneside, Kendal, Cumbria LA9 6QX. Tel. 0539-727837.

Long Distance Walkers' Association
Hon. Secretary: Alan Castle, Wayfarers, 9 Tainters Brook, Uckfield, East Sussex TN22 1UQ. Tel. 0825-761803.

Lord Winston's Walking Tours
The Manor, Moreton Pinckney, Daventry, Northants NN11 6SJ. Tel. 029576-342.

Lyke Wake Club
Chief Dirger: Goulton Grange, Swainby, Northallerton, North Yorkshire DL6 3HP.

Manchester Pedestrian Association
Hon. Secretary: E. Baker, 1 Nudger Close, Dobcross, Oldham OL3 5AP.
Tel. 0457-874780.

Mountain Bothies Association
General Secretary: Ted Butcher, 26 Rycroft Avenue, Deeping St James, Peterborough PE6 8NT. Tel. 0778-345062.

Mountain Camera
Hill Cottage, Fonthill Gifford, Salisbury SP3 6QW. Tel. 0747-89320.

Mountain Rescue Committee
Hon. Secretary: R.J. Davis, 18 Tarnside Fold, Simmondley, Glossop, Derbys SK13 9ND. Tel. 04574-3095.

Mountain Rescue Committee of Scotland
Hon. Secretary: Malcolm Duckworth, 5 Westfield Terrace, Aberdeen AB2 4RU. Tel. 0224-646995.

Mountain Walking Leader Training Board
Crawford House, Precinct Centre, Booth Street East, Manchester M13 9RZ.
Tel. 061-273-5835.

Mountaineering Council of Scotland
National Officer: Kevin Howett, 71 King Street, Crieff, Perthshire PH7 3HB.
Tel. 0764-4962.

National Trust
36 Queen Anne's Gate, London SW1H 9AS. Tel. 071-222-9251.

National Trust for Scotland
5 Charlotte Square, Edinburgh EH2 4DU. Tel. 031-226-5922.

Nature Conservancy Council
Northminster House, Peterborough PE1 1UA. Tel. 0733-340345.

North Yorks Moors National Park
The Old Vicarage, Bondgate, Helmsley, York YO6 5BP. Tel. 0439-70657.

Northumberland National Park
Eastburn, South Park, Hexham, Northumberland NE46 1BS.
Tel. 0434-605555.

Offa's Dyke Association
Old Primary School, West Street, Knighton, Powys LD7 1BW. Tel. 0547-528753.

Open Spaces Society
25a Bell Street, Henley-on-Thames, Oxon RG9 2BA. Tel. 0491-573535.

Ordnance Survey
Romsey Road, Maybush, Southampton SO9 4DH. Tel. 0703-792000.

Ordnance Survey of Northern Ireland
Colby House, Stranmillis Court, Belfast BT9 5BJ. Tel. 0232-661244.

Outdoor Action
Hawker Consumer Publications Ltd., 13 Park House, 140 Battersea Park Road, London SW11 4NB. Tel. 071-720-2108.

Outdoor Writers' Guild
Hon. Secretary: Hugh Westacott, 86 Burford Gardens, London N13 4LP.
Tel. 081-886-1957.

Outram Magazines
Plaza Tower, The Plaza, East Kilbride, Glasgow G74 1LW. Tel. 03552-46444.

Peak & Northern Footpath Society
Hon. General Secretary: Derek Taylor, 15 Parkfield Drive, Tyldesley, Manchester M29 8NR. Tel. 061-790-4383.

Peak National Park
Aldern House, Baslow Road, Bakewell, Derbyshire DE4 1AE. Tel. 062-981-4321.

Peddars Way Association
Hon. Secretary, George Le Surf, 150 Armes Street, Norwich NR2 4EG.
Tel. 0603-623070.

Pembrokeshire Coast National Park
County Offices, Haverfordwest, Dyfed SA61 1QZ. Tel. 0437-764591.

Pennine Way Council
Hon. Secretary: Chris Sainty, 29 Springfield Park Avenue, Chelmsford CM2 6EL.
Tel. 0245-256772.

Polytechnic Rambling Club
Hon. Secretary: Martin Sweet, 64 Thorpe Road, London E7 9EB. Tel. 081-555-4997.

Railway Ramblers
Hon. Secretary: Robin Wade, 7 Palmers Lane, Alconbury, Huntingdon, Cambs PE17 5HE. Tel. 0480-890748.

Ramblers' Association
1–5 Wandsworth Road, London SW8 2XX. Tel. 071-582-6878.

Red Rope
National Secretary: Jerzy Wieckorek, 3 Barnet Street, Oxford OX4 3AN. Tel 0865-250180.

Roama Travel
Larks Rise, Shroton, Blandford, Dorset DT11 8QW. Tel. 0258-860298.

Roger Lascelles
47 York Road, Brentford, Middlesex TW8
0QP. Tel. 081-847-0935.

Rucksack Club
Hon. Secretary: J.B. Rhodes, 33 Oakfield
Road, Poynton, Stockport SK12 1AS.
Tel. 0625-875159. London Section Hon.
Secretary: John C. Long, 'Copthorne', St
Nicholas Hill, Leatherhead, Surrey KT22
8NE. Tel. 0372-374801.

**Scottish Mountain Leader Training
Board**
Caledonia House, South Gyle, Edinburgh
EH12 9DQ. Tel. 031-317-7200.

Scottish Mountaineering Club
Hon. Secretary: John R.R. Fowler, 4 Doune
Terrace, Edinburgh EH3 6DY.
Tel. 031-226-4055.

*Scottish Rights of Way Society Ltd
Unit 2, John Cotton Business Centre, 10/2
Sunnyside, Edinburgh EH7 5RA.
Tel. 031-652-2937.

Scottish Sports Council
Caledonia House, South Gyle, Edinburgh
EH12 9DQ. Tel. 031-317-7200.

Scottish Tourist Board
23 Ravelston Terrace, Edinburgh EH4 3EU.
Tel. 031-332-2433.

Scottish Wild Land Group
Co-ordinator: Lionel Griffiths, 1/3
Kilgraston Court, Kilgraston Road,
Edinburgh EH9 2ES. Tel. 031-447-0853.

Scottish Youth Hostels Association
7 Glebe Crescent, Stirling FK8 2JA.
Tel. 0786-51181.

Sherpa Expeditions
131a Heston Road, Hounslow, Middlesex.
Tel. 081-577-2717.

Sierra Club
730 Polk Street, San Francisco, CA 94109,
USA.

Snowdonia National Park
Penrhyndeudraeth, Gwynedd LL48 6LS. Tel
0766-770274.

*South West Way Association
Membership Secretary: Mrs M. Macleod, 1
Orchard Drive, Kingskerswell, Newton
Abbot, Devon TQ12 5DG. Tel. 0803-873061.

Sports Council for Northern Ireland
House of Sport, Upper Malone Road,
Belfast
BT9 5LA. Tel. 0232-381222.

Sustrans Ltd
35 King Street, Bristol BS1 4DZ.
Tel. 0272-268893.

Transport for Leisure
67 Grove Road, Ilkley, West Yorkshire LS29
9PQ. Tel. 0943-607868.

Tweeddale Society
Hon. Secretary: P.S. Dell, 54 Edderston
Road, Peebles EH45 9DT.

*Ulster Federation of Rambling Clubs
Hon Secretary: Mary Doyle, 27 Slievegallion
Drive, Belfast BT11 8JN. Tel. 0232-624289.

**Ulster Society for the Preservation of
the Countryside**
Peskett Centre, 2a Windsor Road, Belfast
BT9 7FQ. Tel. 0232-381304.

Volunteer Centre UK
29 Lower King's Road, Berkhamsted, Herts
HP4 2AB. Tel. 0442-873311.

Wales Tourist Board
Brunel House, 2 Fitzalan Road, Cardiff CF2
1UY. Tel. 0222-499909.

Wilderness (has now ceased publication).

Yorkshire Dales National Park
Colvend, Hebden Road, Grassington,
Skipton, North Yorkshire BD23 5LB.
Tel. 0756-752748.

Youth Hostels Association
Trevelyan House, 8 St Stephen's Hill, St
Alban's, Herts AL1 2DY. Tel. 0727-55215.

**Youth Hostels Association of Northern
Ireland**
56 Bradbury Place, Belfast BT7 1RU.
Tel. 0232-324733.

Index

The page number of main entries is given in **bold type** and that of illustrations in *italic type*. The column is designated by the letters a b c. Index entries for colour illustrations are indicated by col. The following categories have not been indexed: a) place names given only passing mention in the text b) authors of modern books except where the writer is the subject of a main entry c) all book titles except those works published anonymously or under a pseudonym

Abbot's Hike **76a**
Abraham Collection 48c
accelerated freeze-dried food 50a
Access to the Countryside (Northern Ireland) Order, 1983 105b
Access to the Mountains Act, 1939 **7a**, 28b, 116c
Access to the Mountains Bill 23a
access **7a**, 16a, 18c, 42c, 95a, 97b, 100b, 102a, 123b, 149a, 154c
access agreements **7a**, 27a, 100c, 107c, 110b
accidents 97b
acclimatisation **7b**
Adventure & Environmental Awareness Group **7b**
Ady, Mrs Henry *see* Cartwright, Julia
Agassiz, Louis **7b**
Aikin, Arthur **7c**
aiming off **7c**, *8*, 102b, 108c, 144a
Aiton, John **8a**, 111b
Albert, *Prince Consort*, 43c
Alderney 27c
Algeria 11a
Allardyce, Robert Barclay *see* Barclay, Captain
Allemanstratten 143c
Allerdale Ramble **76a**
Allison, Lincoln **8b**
Alpine Club **8b**, 34a, 66b, 150c, 158b, 159b
Alpine Journal 8b, 139a, 139b
Alps **8c**, col
altitude sickness *see* mountain sickness
Amenity Lands Act, 1965 10b, 100b, 105b
Andes **8c**
Angles Way **76a**
Anglesey AONB **9a**
Anglesey Coast Path **76b**
Animals Act, 1971 42a
anorak **9a**, 24a
anthologies of walking **9a**
Antrim Coast & Glens AONB **9b**
Aonach Eagach 10b
AONB *see* area of outstanding natural beauty
Appalachian Trail 75c
Aquatex **9c**, 94b, 116a
areas of outstanding natural beauty *9*, **9c**, 100c
arête **10b**, 21c, 34c, 121a
Argentina 8c
Arnfield, Tom 19a
Arnold, Matthew 59c
Arnside & Silverdale AONB **10c**
Around Norfolk Walk **76b**
Ashton, Steve **10c**
Association for Adventure Sports 88b
Association for the Protection of Rural Scotland **10c**
Association of British Mountain Guides *see* British Association of Mountain Guides
Association of Countryside Rangers **11a**, 119c

Association of Heads of Outdoor Centres **11a**, 72c, 97c
Association of Mountaineering Instructors **11a**
Association of National Park Officers **11a**
Athol, *Duke of* 55b
Atlas Mountains **11a**
attack point *11*, **11b**, 102b, 108c, 144a
Austen, Jane **11c**
Austin, Alexander Berry **11c**
Australia **11c**, *12*, col
Australian National Trail 11c
Austria **12c**, *13*, col
avalanches **13b**, 34c, 35c, 93a, 132c
Avon Walkway **76b**
Ayton, Richard **13c**, 38b
backbearings *see* resections
backpack *see* rucksack
backpacker **13c**, 40c
Backpackers' Club **13c**, 90c, 155a
backpacking **14c**, 40c, 50a, 130c
Baddeley, M.J.B. **15c**, 122b
Baines, Edward **15c**
Baker, Ernest A. 9b, **16a**, 148b
Bakewell Circular Walk **76b**
balaclava **16a**
Balfour, John Hutton 55b
Barclay, Captain *16*, **16a**, 112b
Barker, Miss 160b
Barry, William Whittaker **16b**
bearings 8a, 123c
beck **16c**
Belgium **16c**
Belloc, Hilaire 9b, **16c**, *17*, 99b, 115a, 117c
belvedere **17b**
Ben Nevis 10b, 27b
bench mark *17*, **17b**, 108a, 150b
benightment **17b**, 18b, 59c, 94b, 133a, 143a
Bennett, G.J. **17c**
bergschrund **17c**
Berry, Geoffrey **17c**
Bertram, Charles Julius 114a
Berwyn Mountains 10b
Bevin, Ernest 139c
bicycles 21a
Bilsdale Circuit **76b**
Bingley, William 17c, **18b**
Bingley, W.R. 18b
Birtles, Geoff **18b**, 60b
bivouac **18b**
bivouac bags 143a
Black Forest Association 75b
Blackdown Hill AONB **10b**
Blenkinsop, Arthur **18c**
blisters **18c**, 88a, 138c
blizzard 132c
Board of Ordnance 108a
Bob Graham Round **76b**
Bob Graham 24 Hour Club **18c**, 56b
bog-trotting **19a**
Bolivia 8c
Bolton Boundary Walk **76b**
Booth, Derrick **19a**
boots 18c, **19a**, 50b, 129c, 138a
borecns **19b**

Borrow, George **19b**, 114b
Boswell, James 118a
Bothy Code 96b
bothy **19c**, 63c, *126*
Bounds of Ainsty **76c**
Bournemouth Coast Path **76c**
box-wall quilting *131*, 131b
Boyd, Donald **19c**, 94c
Boyes, Malcolm **20a**
Bradford Ring **76c**
Bradley 20, **76c**
Bradt, Hilary *20*, **20a**
braking with ice axe *65*, 65a
Brandling, Henry C. 30c
Brecon Beacons National Park **20b**, col
breeches **20c**, 94c, 115c
brew-up **20c**
Bridges, George Wilson **20c**
bridleway **21a**, 57c, 115b, 121b, 122a, 148b, 159b
Brindley Trail **76c**
Bristol to London Long Distance Path **76c**
British Activity Holiday Association **21c**
British Association of Mountain Guides **21a**
British Guides' Carnet 21b
British Mountaineering Council 11a, 18b, **21b**, 29a, 60b, 96b, 97c, 98a, 152b
British Textile Technology Group **21b**
British Tourist Authority 128b
British Trust for Conservation Volunteers **21b**
British Waterways 26a
British Workers' Sports Federation 70b, 123b
Broads Act 100b
Broads Authority 100b
Broads, The **21c**
Brocken spectre **21c**, 55c
Brontë Round **78a**
Brontë sisters *22*, **22a**
Brontë, Ann *22*, **22a**
Brontë, Charlotte *22*, **22a**, 125a
Brontë, Emily *22*, **22a**
Brown, Alfred J. **22a**
Brown, Alice **22a**
Brown, Charles Armitage **22a**, 69a
Brown, Hamish 11b, *22*, **22c**, 72b, 99a, 99b, 151a
Brown, Terry 63b
Bryce, Annan 7a
Bryce, James 7a, **23a**
Budworth, Joseph **23a**
bulls **23b**
Bunyan, John **23b**
burn **23c**
Burritt, Elihu **23c**
Burroughs, John **23c**
Burton, J.F. 19a
Bushnell, Nelson S. 69a
bushwalking 11c
Butler, A.J. 142b
Butlin, Billy 72b
Butterfield, Irvine **23c**
byway open to all traffic **24a**, 57c, 60c,

121b, 122a, 148b, 159b
Byways and Bridleway Trust **24a**
Cadogan, George 43c
cagoule 9a, **24a**
cairn **24b**
Cairngorm Club **24b**
Cairngorms **24b**
Calderdale Way **78a**
Cal-Der-Went Walk **78a**
Cambrian Way **78a**
Camping and Caravanning Club **24c**, 61a
Camping & Outdoor Leisure Association **24c**
Camping & Walking **25a**
Camping Club *see* Camping & Caravanning Club
Camping Trade Association of Great Britain Ltd *see* Camping & Outdoor Leisure Association
Camuplodunum **78a**
Canada *25*, **25a**, col
canal walking *26*, **26a**, col
Cannock Chase AONB **27a**
canyon 55c
Capper, Jack 19a
Captain Cook Memorial Walk 20a
Carlyle, Thomas **27a**, 29c
Carn Mor Dearg 10b
carriageway 60c
Carrington, Edith 55a
Cartwright, Julia 115a
Castles Alternative **78a**
Causeway Coast AONB **27b**
Cavendish, Colonel 43c
Centenary Way **78b**
Central Highlands **27b**, *126*
cerebral oedema 7b
Cestrian Link Walk 72b, **78b**
Channel Islands **27c**
challenge walks 19a, **27c**, 88a, 110b, 124b
Chaucer, Geoffrey 59c
Cheshire Ring Canal Walk **78b**
Chesterton, Keith **27c**, 57c
Chichester Harbour **28a**
children, walking with *see* walking with children
Chile 8c
Chilterns **28a**
Chlorofibre **28b**, 153b
Christian Workers' Union 115c
Chubb, Lawrence **28b**, 48c, 51b, 102a, 107c, 136a
cirque **28b**
Clairmont, Claire 129b
Clarendon Way **78b**
Claude glass **28b**, 57a
Clayden, Paul 149c
Cleare, John *28*, **28c**
Cleveland Way **29a**, 75c
Cleveland Way Missing Link 29a
Climaguard **29a**
Climber & Hill Walker **29a**
clints *74*, 74a
clitter 147c
clo 147b
clothing 14c, **29a**, 43a, 66a, 94b, 96c, 106c,

169

Index

114b, 145b, 153a, 157a
clothing, shell, *see* shell clothing
clough **29a**
Clwydian Hills AONB **29b**
Co-operative Holidays Association 73b
Coast & Glens of County Antrim
Coast to Coast Trek **78b**
Coast to Coast Walk **78c**
Coastal Preservation Committee 60b
Cochrane, John Dundas **29b**
Coed Morgannwg Way **78c**
col *see* pass
COLA *see* Camping & Outdoor Leisure Association
Coleridge, Samuel Taylor **29c**, *30c*, 57c, 60a, 63a, 71b, 72a, 122b, 123a, 137a, 145c, 159b, 160a, 160b, 160c, 163c
Collett, Anthony **30b**
Collins, Martin *30*, **30b**
Collins, Wilkie **30c**
Colne to Buxton Walk 19a
Colne to Rowsley Walk 19a
Colton, Robert *see* 'Sylvanus'
Columbia 8c
combe **30c**
Comeraghs **30c**
common **30c**, 44b, 127c
Commons Registration Act, 1965 31a
Commons, Open Spaces & Footpaths Preservation Society *see* Open Spaces Society
compass *31*, **31a**
Compton, Thomas **32a**
condensation **32b**, 64b, 88c, 94b, 116a, 146c, 153a, 156a
Connemara Mountains **32c**
Continental Divide Trail 122c, 148a
contour lines **32c**, *33*
contouring **33c**
contours **33c**, 35c, 58c, 109a
Conway, Derwent *see* Inglis, H.D.
Conway, William Martin **34a**
Conybeare, William 114a
Cooper, Arthur Nevile **34a**
Corbett 22b, **34b**, 96a, 99a, 99b, 110a
Corbett, J. Rooke 34b
Cordura 19b, **34b**, 124a
corduroy 20c, **34c**
cornice *34*, 34c, 59c, 132c
Cornwall AONB **34c**
Cornwall Coast Path *77*, 135a, 135b
Corps of Military Surveyors & Draftsmen 32a
corrie 28b, 34c, **35a**
Corsica *52*
Coryate, Thomas **35a**, 68c, 146b
Cotswold Way 72b, 102a, **78c**
Cotswolds AONB **35a**
Cottle, Joseph 160b
cotton **35b**, 94c, 115c, 153a
cotton duck **35c**
couloir 140c
Council for National Parks **35c**, 91b, 100b
Council for the Protection of Rural England **35c**, 53b
Council for the Protection of Rural Wales **36a**
Country & Travel **36a**
Country Code **36a**, 59c
Country Walking **36b**
Countrygoer Books **36b**
Countryside (Scotland) Act, 1967 7a, 21a,

23b, **37a**, 50b, 75c, 107a, 115b, 119c
Countryside Act, 1968 21a, **36c**, 56a, 100c, 159b
Countryside Commission 10a, 36a, **36c**, 42b, 60b, 75c, 87a, 100b, 100c, 101b, 102a
Countryside Commission for Scotland **37a**, 75c, 100c, 125c
Countrywide Holidays Association 73b
county projection 108b
county summits of the British Isles 22b, **37a**, 110a
Cowell, J.J. **38a**
Cowper, William 59c
Cox, Jack **38a**
Coxe, William *38*, **38a**
Crabbe, George 118a
crag-fast *38*, **38c**
crampons *38*, 38b, **38c**, 64c, 124a, 132c, 153a
Cranborne Chase and West Wiltshire Downs AONB **39a**
crevasse **39a**, 55a, 129b, 132c
Crib Goch 10b
Crossfell 60b
Crossing, William **39b**
Cudahy, Mike 124b
Cuillins 10b, 130c
Cumberland Way **78c**
Cumbria Way **78c**
cwm 28a, **39b**
Cyclone **39b**, 94b, 116a
Cymdethas Diogelu Cymru Wledig *see* Council for the Preservation of Rural Wales
d'Arcy Dalton Way **78c**
Dales Traverse **79a**
Dales Way **79a**
Daniell, William 13c, **39b**
Dartmoor letterboxes 40a
Dartmoor National Park **39c**
Darwin, Charles 142b
David-Neel, Alexandra **40a**
Davidson Committee 108a
Davidson Report 150a
Davies, Hunter *40*, **40b**
Davies, W.H. **40b**, 148b
Davies, W.K. 115c
Dawson, Cecil 19a
day pack *see* rucksack
De Quincey, Thomas **40c**, 71c, 122b, 122c, 146b, 159b, 160b
de Bougrenet, J.L. *see* Latocnaye, J.L. de Bougrenet
declination *see* magnetic variation
Dedham Vale AONB **40c**
deer stalking 125c
definitive maps **41a**, 60a, 115b, 159b
Delamere Way **79a**
Denmark **41a**
Department of Health & Social Services 97b
Department of Health for Scotland 119b
Department of the Environment 36c
Department of the Environment for Northern Ireland 105c
Derby tweed 150b
Derbyshire Gritstone Way **79a**
Derry, John **41b**
Derwent Way **79a**
deviation, magnetic *see* magnetic deviation
Dickens, Charles **41b**
Dilke, Charles 69a
Dingle Way *see* Sli Chorcha Dhuibhne

Diocesan Way **79a**
dip 46c
distress signal, international mountain *see* international mountain distress signal
diversions **41c**
dod-man 73b
dodd **41c**
dogs **41c**, 42a, 140b
Donald 22b, **42a**, 96a, 99a, 99b, 110a
Donald, Percy 42a
Donegal **42a**
Dorset AONB **42a**
Dorset Coast Path 135a, 135c, col
Dorset Downs Walk **79b**
Dorset Walk **79b**
double quilting *131*, 131b
Dower Report **42c**, 61a, 100a, 100c
Dower, John *42*, **42b**, 42c, 139c
down 43a, 75b, 131a
downland **42c**
Downs Link **79b**
driftway 42c
Drinkwater, John 148b
drove road **42c**, 46a, 57b, 105b
droving 42c
Duerden, Frank *43*, **43a**
Dunova **43a**, 153a
duvet clothing **43a**, 62a, 75b, 117b
Earle, John **43b**
East Devon AONB **43b**
East Hampshire AONB **43b**
East Way 75
easting **43c**, 58a, 105c
Ebor Way **79b**
Ecuador 8c
Eden Trail **79b**
Eden Way **79b**
edge **43c**
edging **43c**
Edinburgh Association for the Protection of Public Rights of Roadways in Scotland 55b
Edward VII **43c**, 131b, 153b
Edwards, Moses 69b
Eire **44a**
electric storm *see* lightning
elitism **44b**
Elliston-Erwood, Frank C. 115a
Elmslie, W.T. 45a
Enclosure Acts 31a, 44b
enclosure **44b**, 107c
End to End Walk *see* Land's End to John O'Groats
Engberg, Robert 98c
England **44c**
English 2000s **45a**
English 3000s **44c**, 110c
English Tourist Board **44c**
Enoch 7b
Enterprise Neptune 60b
Entrant **45a**, 94b, 116a
erosion of paths *45*, **45a**
escarpment **46b**
Esk Valley Walk **79b**
Eskdale Way **79c**
Essex Clayway **79c**
Essex Way **79c**
estovers 31a
Europäische Fernwanderwege 47b
European international long-distance paths *46*, **46c**, 75c
European Ramblers' Association 47a, **47b**
Evans, John (17??–1812) **47b**
Evans, John (1814–76) **47c**

Evans, R.B. 152b
Evans, Thomas **47c**
Everyman's Right 143c
Exmoor National Park **47c**
exposure *see* hypothermia
extinguishments **41c**
fabric testing 21b
Falcon Flyer 20a
Falklands Way **79c**
Farington, Joseph 63a
farm trail 148b
farmers 42a, **48a**, 117b, 140b
Fearon, Henry **48b**
featherbed **48b**, 70b
Federation of Mountaineering Clubs of Ireland 88b
Federation of Rambling Clubs 28b, **48b**, 61a, 93a, 99c, 118a, 136a
Fell & Rock Club **48c**, 97a, 124b
fell **48c**
fell walking **49a**, 97b
Fells Way **79c**
Fermor, Patrick Leigh **49a**
Ffordd y Bryniau **79c**
fibrepile **49a**, 115a, 131a
field *see* enclosure
'Fieldfare' *see* Fearon, Henry
FieldSensor **49a**, 153a
Finland **49a**
Firbank, Thomas **49b**, 157a
Firsoff, V.A. **49b**
First Aid Committee of Mountaineering Clubs 97b, 124b
first aid **49a**, 64c, 96c, 97b, 124b
Fisher, Claude **49c**, 123c
Fitzgerald, A.E. 34a
fix, making a *31*, *32*
fixed rope **49c**, 123a
flannel **49c**, 160a
Flecker, James Elroy 148b
fleece **49c**
Fletcher, Colin **49c**
flush bracket 150b
fluvial walk 147b
food **50a**, 64c
footbeds 19b, **50b**, 134a
Footloose **50b**, 114b, 148b
Footpath Touring **79c**
Footpath Worker **50c**, 119a
footpath **50b**, 57c, 60c, 115b, 121b, 122a, 148b, 159b
footpath guides **50b**
Forbes, James David **51a**
Ford, Ford Madox 148b
Forest of Bowland AONB **51a**
Forest Ramblers 28b, 48b, **51a**, 93a
Forest Service for Northern Ireland **51a**
Forest Way **80a**
Forester, Thomas **51b**
Forestry Commission 37a, **51b**
Forrester, Mac 19a
Foss Walk **80a**
Foster, R. Francis **51b**
Fountains Walk **80a**
Four Thousands **51c**, 110a
Fox, E.W. **51c**
Foyle brothers 51b
France **51c**, *52*, col
Frere, R. **53a**
Freshfield, Douglas 142b
Friends of the Earth (Scotland) **53b**
Friends of the Earth **53b**
Friends of the Lake District 17c, **53b**
Friends of the National Parks 35c

Friends of the Ridgeway **53b**
Frost, Thomas 41b
frostbite **53b**, 55c, 59c
frostnip 53c
fuel for stoves 140a
Furness Boundary Walk **80a**
Furness Way **80a**
gaberdine **53c**
gaiters **53c**, 129c
Galtee Mountains *see* Galty Mountains
Galton, Francis **53c**, 155c
Galty Mountains **53c**
Garrard, H. 19a
Gemmell, Arthur *54*, **54a**
Gentleman's Walking Tour of Dartmoor, A **54b**
Germany **54b**
ghyll *see* gill
Gibbs, Frederick 43c
Gilbert, Richard *54*, **54c**
gill **55a**
Gilpin, William **55a**, 114b, 155a
Gipsy Journal **55a**
glacial action 55a
glacier 35a, **55a**, 123a, 132c, 150c
Gladstone, William Henry 43c
Glen Tilt **55b**
glen **55b**
Glenmore Lodge National Outdoor Pursuits Centre 72c
glissading **55b**
glory 21c, **55c**
gloves **55c**, 130b, 156a
Glyndwyr's Way **80a**, 102a
Goldsmith, Oliver **55c**
Gordon, Seton **55c**
Gore-Tex 19b, **55c**, 94b, 116a, 143a, 146c
gorge **55c**
Gosling Report **56a**
Gosling, Arthur 56a
Gower AONB **56a**
GR20 *52*
Grafton Way **80a**
Graham, Bob 18c, **56a**
Graham, Stephen **56b**, 74b
Grant, Johnson **56c**
Grassington Circuit Walk **80a**
Grattan, Thomas Colley **56c**, 160c
Gray, Thomas 28c, **57a**
greasy rock **57a**
Great North Walk 11c
Great Outdoors **57c**, 87c, 132a, 151a
Greece **57b**
Green Mountain Club 75c
green road 42c, **57b**
Greenfields, William Edward **57c**
Greensand Way **80b**
grid lines **57c**, 99c
grid north **57c**
grid reference **57c**, 58, 99c, 123a
Griffin, Harry 16a, **58a**
grikes *74*, 74a
Grimpen Mires 38c, 48b
Grimshaw, John 143b
Gritstone Trail 72b, **80b**
grough 19a, **58b**, 63a, 70b, 110b
grouse shooting 125c
Guernsey 27c
Guild of British Travel Writers 63b
Guildford Boundary Walk **80b**
Gurney, Eric 13c
hachures **58c**, 147c
Hadrian's Wall Walk **80b**
hag 19a, **58c**, 110b

Hall, Chris 118b
Hall, Richard W. **58c**
Hallamshire Footpath Preservation Society 154c
Hambleton Drove Road 42c
hanging valley 35a, 39b, **58c**
Hannon, Paul 58c
Harcamlow Way **80b**
Harding, Mike *59*, **59a**
Hardy, Thomas **59b**
Harper, Andrew **59a**
Harrison, Frederic 142b
Harrogate Ringway **80c**
Haslemere Hundred **80c**
Hassell, John 50c, **59b**
Hatts, Leigh **59b**
Haultain, Arnold **59c**
Haute Randonée Pyrénéene 117a
hazards **59c**, 64c, 94b, 132c, 140c, 158c
Hazlitt, William 29c, **60a**, 71c, 72a, 145c
Headland Walk **80c**
headland path **60a**, 115b
Heardman, Fred 19a
Heart of England Way 72b, **80c**
heart attacks 97c
heather 95a
Helanca 20c, **60a**
Helm Wind **60b**
Hereward Way **80c**
Heritage Way **80c**
heritage coasts **60b**
Herriot Way **81a**
High 18b, 21b, 53c, **60b**
High Hunsley Circular **81a**
High Weald AONB **60b**
Highbury United Rambling Club 136a
highway **60c**, 121b, 122a
Highways Act, 1980 100c, 106c, 115b, 159b
hike **60c**, 118a
Hiker & Camper **61a**, 108c, 139c, 154c
hiking 49c, **60c**, 118a
hill **61a**
hill walking **61a**
Hill, Octavia 102a
Hillaby, John *61*, **61a**, 72b
Himalaya **61b**
hip belt 124b
Hirst, Mrs 99a
'Hobcarton' *see* Hall, Richard W.
Hobhouse Committee 42c, 100c, 127c
Hobhouse Report **61c**, 75c
Hobhouse, Arthur 61c
Holderness Way **81a**
Holiday Fellowship 73b
Holland *see* Netherlands
Holland, John **61c**
Holliday, Alf *see* Southern, J.A.
Hollofil 43a, **62a**, 131a
holloway 148b
Holworthy, Sophia Matilda **62a**
Hooker, Richard **62b**
hoosier *62*, **62c**
Horace 59c
Horne, Thomas Hartwell **63a**
horse-riders 21a
Howardian Hills AONB **63a**
Howden 20 **81a**
Hucks, Joseph 29c, **63a**
Hueffer, Ford Madox 148b
Hull Countryway **81a**
Humber Bridge Link Walk **81a**
Humble, B.H. **63b**
Hume & Hovel Track 11c

Hunter, Rob *63*, **63b**, 140a
Hunter, Robert 102a
hut **63c**, 98a, 124b
Hutchinson, John 58c, **63c**
Hutchinson, Peter Orlando 111b
Hutton, William **64a**
hydrophobic molecules 64a
hydrophyllic fabrics **64b**, 94c, 116a, 145b
hypothermia 59c, **64b**, 97c, 143a, 159b
ice 59c, **64c**, 153a
ice axe 55b, 64c, **64c**, *65*, 65a, 124a, 132c, 133a
Iceland **65b**, col
Icknield Way 65c, **81a**
Icknield Way Association **65c**
Inca Trail 8c
Ingleborough 56c, 70a
Inglis, H.D. **65c**, 117a
injuries 49b
Inkpen Way **81b**
Innerleithen Alpine Club **66a**
insulating mat **66a**, 131c
insulation 43a, 62a, **66a**, 73c, 75b, 117b, 131a, 147a
International Guide's Carnet 21b
international mountain distress signal **66b**, 97a
Ireland, Republic of *see* Eire
Irish 3000s **66b**, 110a
Irish Mountain Training Board 88b
Irish National Sports Council 88b
Irving, Edward 27c
Irving, John 128a
Isle of Man 19c, **66b**
Isle of Man Coastal Path **81b**
Isle of Wight AONB **66c**
Isle of Wight Coastal Path **81b**
Isles of Scilly AONB **66c**
Isodry **66c**, 153c
ISPO **66c**, 138c
Italy **66c**, *67*, col
Jackson, W. Holt– **67c**
Jebb, Miles **67c**
Jefferies, Richard **68a**
Jeffers, Le Roy **68a**
Jennings, Louis J. **68a**
Jersey 27c
Jesus of Nazareth 59c
Joad, C.E.M. 36b, **68a**
Jock's Road **68b**
John Muir Trail 98b
John Muir Trust **68b**, 98b
John O'Groats to Land's End 94c, 95a, 102b
Johnson, Robert Underwood 130a
Johnson, Samuel 118a
Joint Stretcher Committee 97a, 124b
Jones, Robert 160b
Jonson, Ben 35a, **68b**, 146b
Jowett, Benjamin 59c
kanter **68c**, 88a
Kay, Ernie **68c**
Kay, Kathie **68c**
Keats, John 22a **68c**, 123a
Kemp, William **69a**
Kennedy, Bart **69b**
Kennovan, James **69b**, 112b
Kent Downs AONB **69b**
Kephart, Horace **69c**
Kerry & West Cork **69c**
Kerry Way **70a**
Kett, Henry **70a**
Kettlewell Three Walk **81b**
Kildare Way **70a**

Kilvert, Francis **70a**
Kinder Scout 58c, 68a, 70b, 123b, 155a
King Alfred's Way **81b**
King, Rose, 116c
Kingstrail *143*
Kircher, Father 38c
kissing gate **70b**, 140a
Kitchiner, William **70c**
knapsack **70c**
Knight, E.F. **70c**
Knightley Way **81b**
knott **71a**
Knowles, Sheridan 60a
KS 100 **71a**, 124a
Kungsleden 75c
Kunst, David **71a**
ladder stile 140b, *141*
Ladies' Rambling Club 116a
Lagan Valley AONB **71a**
Lake District Defence Society 15c
Lake District National Park 30a, **71a**
Lake District Planning Board 145b
Lake Poets **71b**, 137a
Lakeland Country of County Fermanagh **71c**
Lakes Link **81b**
Lamb, Charles 40c, 60a, *71*, **71c**, 71c, 145c
Lamb, Mary 40c, 60a, 71c
Lancashire Trail **81c**
Land's End to John O'Groats 22b, 61b, **72b**, 92a, 94c, 95a
Landranger maps **72a**, 125b, 147c
Langbaurgh Loop **81c**
Langmuir, Eric **72c**, 98a
Lappland *143*
lapse rate 13c, **72c**
Larby, E.J. 93b
Latocnaye, Jacques Louis de Bougrenet **72c**
Laverack, Julian *see* Brown, A.J.
Le Messurier, Brian **73a**
Lecale Coast AONB **73a**
Leeds Countryway **81c**
Leeds Dalesway **81c**
Leeds to the Sea **81c**
Lees, Harry 19a
Leicestershire Round **81c**
Leland Trail **82a**
Leonard, T.A. **73a**, 99c, 118a
letterboxes 40a
Lewis, Wyndham 148b
ley lines **73b**
Libond **73b**, 153c
Liddiard, William **73c**
lightning 59c, **73c**
Limestone Way **82a**
limestone pavements *74*, **74a**
Limey Way **82a**
Lincolnshire Wolds AONB **74a**
Lindsay, Vachell **74a**
Lindsey Loop **82a**
Linton, Mrs Lynn **74b**
Linton, William James 74b
Lipchis Way **82a**
Lithgow, William **75a**
Lleyn AONB **75a**
Lloyd, John **75a**
LLwybr Bro Gwy **82a**
lochan **75b**
loft **75b**
Lofthouse, Jessica **75b**
London Countryway 28a, 57c, **82a**, 130c
London Transport 50c

Index

London, Jack 148c
Long Distance Walkers' Association 27c, 28a, 68c, 87c, **88a**
Long Distance Walking Routes Committee 88b
Long Trail 75c
Long-distance Paths Advisory Service 76a, **87c**, 120c
long-distance path 42c, 75b, **75b**, *77*, 100c, 125c, 127c
loopstitch **88b**, 133c, 140b
Lotus **88a**
Lowell, Robert 137a
Luxembourg **88b**
Lyke Wake Club **88b**
Lyke Wake Walk **82a**
Lynam, Joss **88b**
MacCulloch, John **88b**
Macdonald, Hugh 9b, **88c**
MacKaye, Benton 75c
mackintosh **88c**
Mackintosh, Charles 88c
Macpherson, Duncan 68b
Macrae case 7a
Macrow, Brenda **89a**
magnetic deviation 88b
magnetic north 89, **89a**
magnetic variation 89, **89a**
Mahomet 59c
Maidstone Circular Walk **82b**
Main, Laurence *89*, **89b**
Mallerstang Horseshoe & Nine Standards Yomp **82b**
Malvern Hills AONB *9*, **90a**
Manchester Association for the Preservation of Ancient Footpaths **90a**, 110a
Manchester Pedestrian Association 90b
Manks, Richard **90b**, 112b
map-reading *90*, **90b**, 94b, 102b, 123c
maps **90c**, 123a, 142c, 149c
Marriott, Mike **90c**
Marsden to Edale Walk 19a
Marsden, R.G. 142b
Mastiles Lane 42c, 46a
Matthews, Fred **91a**
Mattingly, Alan **91b**, 118b
Maverick, Albert **91b**
Mavor, William Fordyce 56c, 70a, **91b**
McNeish, Cameron 29a, 50b, **88c**
'Member of the University of Oxford, A' *see* Bridges, E.W.
Mendip Hills AONB **91c**
Menmuir, W. Henry 91c
Meredith, George **91c**, 142b
Meriwether, Lee **92a**
Merrill, John 72b, **92a**
metamorphism 13c, **92c**
Middle Way 75b
midwear 29b, 125a
Miles, Walker 48b, 50c, 51b, 55a, *93*, **93a**, 119a, 130a, 136a, 153b
Millennium Way **82b**
Milton, John 59c
Miners' Track 46a
Ministry of Town & Country Planning 139c
Minster Way **82b**
mist 59c, 64c, 72c, **94b**, 153a, 158c
moisture vapour transmission 64b, **94b**, 116a
moleskin **94c**
Moloney, Patrick 72b, **94c**, 95a
Monkhouse, Patrick **94c**

Monmouthshire & Brecon Canal 20b, col
Monro, Harold **94c**
Montague, C.E. **95a**
Moore, A.W. **95a**
Moore, Barbara 72b, 94c, **95a**
Moore, Cyril 36b
Moore, John C. **95a**
moorland **95a**
Moran, Benjamin **95b**
Moran, Martin **95b**, 99a
Moritz, Carl Philip **95b**, 147b
Morocco 11a
Morton, G.F. **95c**
Mountain Bothies' Association 19c, 63c, **96b**
Mountain Camera 28c
Mountain Code 60a, **96b**, 97c, 98a
Mountain Leader Assessment 97c
Mountain Rescue Committee 97a, 97b, 124b
Mountain Rescue Committee of Scotland 72c
Mountain Walking Leader Training Board **97c**
mountain **95c**
mountain distress signal *see* international mountain distress signal
mountain rescue **96c**
mountain rescue teams 128b
mountain safety **97b**
mountain sickness 7b
mountaineer **98a**
Mountaineering Council of Scotland 21b, **98a**
Mountaineering Instructor's Certificate 11a, 98a
mountains, calculating height of 38c
Mourne AONB **98a**
Muir, John 23c, 68a, 68b, **98b**, 130c
Mulcaster, Richard **98c**
Munro 22b, 95b, 96a, **99a**, 110a, 122a, 128c
Munro's Tables 42a, 96a, 99a, 99b
Munro, A.G. 55a
Munro, Hugh **99a**
Munster Way **99b**
Murgatroyd, Kathy 99a
Mursell, Walter Arnold **99b**
Naismith's rule **99b**, *100*, 148c
Naismith, William W. 99c
National Council of Ramblers' Federations **99c**, 118a, 118c, 154c
National Federation of Rambling Clubs 70b
National Footpaths Preservation Society *see* Open Spaces Society
National Outdoor Training Centre 128b
National Parks & Access to the Countryside Act, 1949 7a, 7b, 9c, 36a, 41a, 42c, 61c, 75c, 100a, **100b**, 100c, 121c, 127c, 159b
National Parks Commission 36b, **100c**, 145b
National Trust 28b, 60b, **102a**, 118c
National Trust for Scotland **102a**
national grid 99c, *100*
national nature reserves 102b
national parks 42c, **99c**, *101*, 100c, 105b, 109b, 119c, 125c, 127c, 139c
national projection 108b
national scenic areas 10b, **100c**, 125c
national trails 75c, **101b**
Nature Conservancy Council **102a**

Nature Conservation & Amenity Lands (Northern Ireland) Order, 1985 10b, 100b, 105b
nature trail 148b
Navigation Way **82b**
navigation 7c, 11b, 31, 31a, *32*, *32*, 89a, 90b, 94b, 97c, **102c**, 109a, 132c, 138c, 158c
Naylor, John **102b**
Naylor, Joss 18c
Naylor, Robert **102b**
needle **102c**
needlecord 20c, 34c
Neillands, Robin *see* Hunter, Rob
Nene Way **82b**
Nephins & North Mayo Highlands **102c**
Netherlands **102c**
New Zealand *103*, **103c**, col
Newby, Eric **103b**
Newell, R.H. **103b**
Nidderdale Moors AONB 10b
Nidderdale Way **82c**
Nikwax 19b
Norfolk Coast AONB **104a**
North Bowland Traverse **82c**
North Buckinghamshire Way **82c**
North Derry AONB **104a**
North Devon AONB **104a**
North Downs Way 75c, **103b**, 115a
North Pennines AONB **103c**
North Wessex Downs AONB **104c**
North Wolds Walk **82c**
North Worcestershire Path **82c**
North York Moors Challenge Walk **82c**
North York Moors National Park **105c**
North, Christopher *see* Wilson, John
Northern Highlands **105a**
Northern Ireland **105b**
northing 58a, **105c**
Northumberland Coast AONB **105c**
Northumberland Coast Walk **83a**
Northumberland National Park **105c**
Norway *106*, **106a**, col
Nuttall, Anne 45a, **106b**
Nuttall, John 45a, **106b**
nylon **106b**, 116a, 121c, 124a, 141c, 146b
'Observant Pedestrian' **106c**
obstruction **106c**, 115b, 118c
Odyssey **107a**, 148a
Offa's Dyke Association 68c, **107a**
Offa's Dyke Path 68c, 75c, **107a**
Offa's Wye Frontier **83a**
Olmstead, Frederick Law **107b**
Open Air Act 106a
Open Spaces Society 28b, 31a, **107c**
open country 7a, 42c, **107c**, 118c, 159b
Ordnance Survey 10a, 17b, 58a, 72a, 99b, 99c, 108a, **108a**, 109c, 125c, 147c, 149c
Ordnance Survey Act 108a
Ordnance Survey for Northern Ireland **108b**
ordnance datum **108a**, 149c
orienteering 7c, 11b, 68c, **108b**
Out O'Doors Fellowship **108c**
Out of Doors Magazine **108c**, 139c
Outdoor Action 75b, **108c**
Outdoor Leisure maps 102b, 108b, **108c**, 110a, 125b
Outdoor Writers' Guild 63b, 114b, 152c
outerwear 29b
Oxfordshire Trek **83a**
Oxfordshire Way **83a**
pane counting 11c, **109a**, 144a

Pacific Crest Trail 148a
Painters' Way **83a**
Palmer, Joseph *see* Budworth, Joseph
Palmer, W.T. **109a**
pannage 31a
papoose carrier *109*, **109b**
parka 9a
pass **109b**, 125a
pasture 31a
Paterson, M **109b**
path 50b, **109c**, 45a
'Pathfinder' *see* Simpson, A.L.
Pathfinder maps 102b, 108b, 109a, **109c**, 125b, 147c
Patmore, Peter George 60a
Patten, Claudius B. **110a**
Payn, James **110a**
Payne, William 112c
Peacock, Thomas Love 129b
Peak & Northern Footpath Society 90b, 107c, **110a**, 130b
Peak District Challenge Walk **83a**
Peak District High Level Route **83a**
Peak National Park **110b**
peak-bagging 27c, 99a, **110a**, 157a
Peakland Way **83a**
peat 31a, 58b, 70b, 95a, 97c, **110c**
Peddars Way & Norfolk Coast Path 65c, 75c, **110c**
Peddars Way & Norfolk Coast Path Extension **83a**
Peddars Way Association **11a**
'Pedestres' **11a**
'Pedestrian' **111b**
'Pedestrian, A' **111b**, 117a
'Pedestrian, The' *see* Aiton, John
'Pedestrian Traveller, A' *see* Penhouet, Armand Bon-Louis Maudet de
pedestrianism 16a, 69b, 90b, **112b**, 116b
pedometer **112b**
Peel Trail **83b**
Pembrokeshire Coast National Park **112c**
Pembrokeshire Coast Path 75c, **113a**
Pendle Way **83b**
Penhouet, Armand Bon-Louis Maudet de 111b, **113a**
Pennant, Thomas 17c, 47b, 155b
Pennell, Elizabeth **113b**
Pennell, Joseph **113b**
Pennine Bridleway 102a
Pennine Way 72b, **113b**, 124b, 139c
Pennine Way Association 75c
Pennine Way Council **113c**
Pennines **114a**
permissive path 7a, 109c, **114a**
Pern, Stephen **114a**
Pertex **114b**
Petulengro, Gypsy **114b**
Phillips, John 69b
Phillips, William 114a
Phillpotts, Eden 148b
Philpott, Don **114b**
picturesque, The 55a, 75a, 103b, *114*, **114b**, 157b
Piggin, Ken **114c**
pike **115a**
Pilgrims' Way 17a, 103b, **83b**, 115a
pilling 49a, **115a**
piscary 31a
Platten, David **115a**
Plogsland Round **83b**
plotting a course 31a, *32*
ploughing 60a, **115b**, 117b
Poland **115c**

Pollock, Frederick 142b
polycotton **115c**, 141a
polyester 49c, 115c
polypropylene **115c**, 153c
Polytechnic Cycling & Rambling Club 116a
Polytechnic Institute 115c
Polytechnic Ladies Cycling Club 116a
Polytechnic Rambling Club **115c**
polytetrafluoroethylene 55c
polyurethane 94c, **116a**, 121c, 146b
polyurethane coatings 64b
Poole, Philip 116c
poromeric fabrics 9c, 55c, 94b, **116a**
Porter, J.H. 51a
Portugal **116a**
Poucher, W.A. *116*, **116a**
Powell, Foster 112b, **116b**
Practical Camper 75b
principal triangulation 150a
private path 109c
Proctor, Alan 13b, **116c**
Progressive Rambler 116c
Progressive Rambling Club **116c**
Pugh, Edward **116c**
pulmonary oedema 7b
Pyrénées **117a**
Quallofil 43a, **117a**, 131a
Quantock Hills AONB **117b**
quilting 62a, 66b, 117b
R v Matthias 42a, 106c
raggsocks 133c, 140b
Railway Ramblers **117b**, 117c
railway walking **117b**, 143b
ramble 60c, **118a**
'Rambler, A' *see* Budworth, Joseph
Rambler, The 118a, 119a
Ramblers' Association 18c, 28b, 36a, 42b, 48c, 50c, 59a, 68a, 73b, 87c, 91b, 99c, *118*, **118a**, 118c, 139b, 139c, 140a, 145c, 149b, 149c, 150c
Ramblers' Association Gazette 118c
Ramblers' Association News 118c
Ramblers' Association Services 36a, 118a
Ramblers' Handbook 48c, 93a
Ramblers' Library 93a, **119a**
Ramblers' News 44a, 118c
Ramblers' Way **83b**
Rambling 99c, 118a, 118c, 145c
Rambling Notes of a Rambling Tour **119b**
rambling 60c, 18a
Ramsay Committee 100b, **119b**
Ramsay, J. Douglas 119b
ranger 97c, **119c**
Ransome, Arthur 148c
Rawnsley, H.D. 102a
Red Kite Trail **83b**
Red Rope **119c**
refuge 63c
regional routes 76a
Renfrew, *Baron* 43c
resections **119c**, *120*
retreat **119c**, 153a
Reynolds, Kev **119c**, *120*
Ribble Way **83b**
Richard of Cirencester 114a
Richards, Mark 50c, *120*, **120c**, 153c
Ridge Walk **83c**
ridge 34c, **121a**
Ridgeway Path 65c, 75c, **121a**, 140a, col
Ridgeway Walk *see* Ffordd y Bryniau
right of way 7a, 23b, 37c, 41a, 41c, 42a, 48a, 50b, 51a, 57c, 68b, 70b, 105b, 106c, 109c, 114a, 115b, 118b, **121b**,

125c, 127c, 128b, 130b, 140a, 140b, 147c, 148b, 149a, 150c, 156a
ripstop nylon **121c**, 146b
Ritchie, Francis 36b
river crossing 59c, **121c**, *122*
Rivers Way **82c**
roads used as a public path 24a, 60c, 121b, **121c**, 159b
Robert Louis Stevenson Trail 63b, col
Roberts, David *see* Cox, Jack
Robertson, A.E. 99a, **122a**
Robertson, George Croom 142b
Robin Hood Way **83c**
Robinson, Henry Crabb **122b**, 160c
Rocky Mountains 98b, **122c**
romantic movement 114c, **123a**, 129b, 160b
Rome, Moses 69b
romer 58a, *123*, **123a**
rope 49c, **123a**, 128c, 132c
Rossendale Way **83c**
Rothman, Benny 70b, **123b**
route card *123*, **123c**
routefinding *see* navigation
Roy, William 108a
Royal Air Force rescue services 97b
Ruc-Sac 49c, **123c**
Rucksack 65b, 70c, 121c, **124a**
Rucksack 118c
Rucksack Club 16a, 97a, **124b**
Rucksack Rambler 119a
Ruskin, John **124c**
saddle **125a**
Saints Way **83c**
Sale, Richard **125a**
salopettes 49c, **125a**
Sandstone Trail **83c**
Sark 27c
Saxon Shore Way **84a**
scale 123a, **125b**
scar **125b**
scarp 46c
Schirmann, Richard 163c
Schuckborough, George 38b
Schwarzwaldverein 75b
Scotland **125c**, *126*, 127, col
Scott Committee 100c
Scott Report **127b**
Scott, J.M. **127c**
Scott, Leslie Frederic 127c
Scott, Walter 88c, 123a, **127c**, 160c
Scottish Avalanche Project 72c
Scottish Development Department 37a
Scottish Mountain Leader Award 128a
Scottish Mountain Leader Training Board 11a, **128b**
Scottish Mountain Safety Group 72c
Scottish Mountaineering Club **128a**
Scottish Mountaineering Trust 128a
Scottish Rights of Way & Recreation Society *see* Scottish Rights of Way Society Ltd
Scottish Rights of Way Society Ltd 68b, 122a, **128b**, 130b
Scottish Sports Council **128b**
Scottish Tourist Board **128b**
Scottish Wild Land Group **128b**, 132a
Scottish Youth Hostels Association **128c**
scrambling 38c, 59c, 123a, **128c**
scree **129a**
Scroggie, Sydney **129a**
Seekings v Clarke 106c
Sellers, Gladys **129a**
sentier de grande randonnée **129b**

serac **129b**
Severn to Solent Walk **84a**
Shakespeare, William 59c
Sharp, Arthur **129b**
Shaw, George Bernard 113b
Sheffield Clarion Ramblers 143c
Sheffield Country Walk **84a**
Sheffield Federation of Rambling Clubs 70b, 145c
Shell clothing 9a, 9c, 24a, 29b, 35c, 45a, 55c, 64b, 64c, 116a, 121c, 140a, 153a, 156a
Shelley, Mary **129b**
Shelley, Percy Bysshe 123a, **129b**
Shelton, Harold **129c**
Shepherd's Round **84a**
Sheriff's Way **84a**
Shirley togmeter 147c
shoes 19a, **129c**
shooting 125c
Shropshire Hills AONB **130a**
Shropshire Way **84a**
Sidgwick, A.H. 93a, **130a**
Sierra Club 98b, **130a**, 152a
signposts **130b**, 156a
silk **130b**
simple quilting *131*, 131b
Simpson, A.L. 93a, **130b**
Six Dales Hike **84a**
Skye 10b, **130b**
slant wall quilting *131*, 131b
sleeping bags 49a, 53c, 62a, 66a, 75b, 96c, 114b, 117b, **130c**, *131*, 140a, 141c
Sli Chorcha Dhuibhne **131c**
Slieve Bloom Way **131c**
Sligo & Leitrim **131c**
Smith, Albert **131c**
Smith, B.P. **131c**
Smith, Roger 18c, *132*, **132a**
Smith, Roland *132*, **132b**
snow 59c, 93a, **132b**, 132c, 158c
snow blindness **132c**
snow bridge **132c**
snow goggles 132c
snow shelters *133*, **133a**
Snow, Sebastian **132c**
Snowdonia National Park **133b**
Snowdonia Panoramic Walk **84b**
Socialist Walking & Climbing Club *see* Red Rope
socks 18c, 19b, 88a, **133c**, 140b
Socrates 59c
Solent Way **84b**
Solway Coast AONB **133c**
Somerset & North Devon Coast Path 135a
Somerset Way **84b**
Somerville, Christopher **133c**
Sorbothane 19b, 50b, **134a**
Sorrell, A.T.O. 94a
Sotheby, William **134a**
South Africa **134a**
South Armagh AONB **134b**
South Cheshire Way **84b**
South Coast Way **84b**
South Devon AONB **134b**
South Devon Coast Path *77*, 135a, 135b
South Downs Way 75c, *85*, **134c**, 143a
South Hampshire Coast AONB **134c**
South Leinster Way **134c**
South Wessex Way **84b**
South West Coast Path 30a, 75c, *77*, **135a**, 139b, 149c, 158c, 160b, col

South West Penninsula Coast Path *see* South West Coast Path
South West Way Association 135a, **135c**
Southeby, William **134a**
Southern Federation of the Ramblers' Association 48c
Southern Highlands **135c**
Southern Upland Way 75c, 125c, **136b**
Southern Uplands **135c**
Southern, J.A. 48c, 50c, 94a, **136a**
Southey, Robert 71b, 122b, **137a**
space blanket 143a
Spain 19b, *137*, **137a**, col
Speakman, Colin **137c**
speed lacing 19b, **138a**
Spence, Joan 36b
Spencer, Brian **138a**
Spenser, Edmund 59c
Sperrin AONB **138b**
Speyside Way 75c, 125c, **138b**
sprial search 11c, 102b, 109a, **138c**, *139*, 144a
SPOGA **138c**
Sports Council 97b, 97c
Sports Council for Northern Ireland 76a, **138a**, 150c
spur **138c**
Spurbooks 63b
squeeze stiles 140b, *141*
St Mary Magdalene Rambling Club 136a
St Peter's Way **83c**
Staffordshire Way 72b, **84b**
stalking 125c
standard stile *140*, 140a
Standing Committee on National Parks 145b
Stanley, Arthur *Dean* 115a
Stanley, Bernard **138c**
Stanley, Frederick 43c
'Star Rambler' *see* Simpson, A.L.
Starkie, Walter **139a**
staying on course *31*, 31a
Steers, J.A. 60b
step cutting 65a
step stile *140*, 140b
Stephen, Leslie 92a, 135a, **139a**, 142b
Stephenson, Tom 7b, 28b, 36a, 61a, 70b, 75c, 108c, 113b, 118a, *139*, **139a**
Sterne, Laurence 106a, 147b
Stevenson, Robert Louis **140a**
stiles *140*, **140a**, *141*
stockings 88a, 133c, **140b**
Stockport Circular Walk **84b**
Stokes, Frederick A. **140c**
stonefall 35c, 59c, **140c**
Storer, Ralph **140c**
Stormbeta **141a**
stoves *14*, **140a**
Strangford Lough AONB **141c**
strath 55b
Striding Edge 10b
stuff sack **141c**
Styles, Showell **142a**
Suffolk Coast & Heaths AONB **142a**
Suffolk Coast Path **84c**
Sully, James 139b, 142b
Sunday Tramps 34a, 92a, 139a, **142b**, 150c
Surrey Hills AONB **142c**
surveying **142**, 149c
survival bag 18b, 96c, **143a**
Sussex Border Path **84c**
Sussex Downs AONB **143a**

Index

Sustrans Ltd 117b, **143b**
Sutton, Geoffrey 19a
Swale, Rosie **143c**
Swan Way **84c**
Sweden, *143*, **143c**
sweep search 102b, 109a, *144*, **144a**
Swift, Jonathan 139a
Swithin, St 115a
Switzerland *144*, **144a**
'Sylvanus' *145*, **145a**
Symonds, H.H. **145b**
Sympatex 19b, 64c, 94c, **145b**
Talfourd, Thomas Noon 122b, **145c**
Tamar & Tavy Valley AONB 10b
Tan Hill to Cat & Fiddle Walk 19a
tarn **145c**
Taylor, Bayard **145c**
Taylor, Edward Seyfang *see* Miles, Walker
Taylor, George Ledwell **146a**
Taylor, James Paddock 75c
Taylor, John 68c, **146b**
temperature inversion 72c
Ten Reservoirs Walk **84c**
tents *14*, 40c, 66a, 121c, **146b**
Test Way **84c**
Thames Path 59b, 75c, **146c**
Thames Valley Heritage Walk 67c, **84c**
Theroux, Paul **147a**
Thetford Forest Walk **84c**
Thinsulate **147a**, 153c
Thom, William 112b
Thomas à Becket, St 115a
Thomas stretcher 97b, 124b
Thomas, Edward **147a**, 148b
Thomas, Eustace 157a
Thomas, Helen 147a
Thompson, George **147a**
Thoreau, Henry David **147a**
Thornber, Billy 19a
Thorpe, James **147b**
Three Forests Way **86a**
Three Reservoirs Challenge **86a**
Three Towers Circuit **86a**
tog 147b
tog rating **147b**
tor **147c**
Torbuck, John **147c**
Toubkal Trail 11b
Tourist maps 108b, 125b, **147c**
Town & Country Planning (Scotland)
    Act, 1972 21a, 50b
towpaths 26a
track **57b**, 148b
trackway **57b**, 148b
trail **148b**
Tramp & Cyclist 154c
Tramp **148b**
tramp camper 13c
tramp camping 14c

Tramp's League 148c
Trans-Pennine Walk **86a**, 143c
Tranter's variations 99c, **148c**, *149*
Tranter, Philip 148c
trek **148c**
trekking **148c**
trespass 68b, 70b, 123b, **148c**, 155a
Trevelyan, Charles 149c
Trevelyan, G.M. 135a, **149a**, 149c
Trevelyan, John **149b**
Trevelyan, Katharine **149c**
triangulation 108b, **149c**
triangulation pillars *150*, 150a
triangulation stations 108a, 108b, 142c,
    149c, *150*
Tully, Clive **150b**
Tunisia 11a
turbary 31a
tweed **150b**, 160a
Tweeddale Society 66a
Two Crosses Circuit **86a**
Two Moors Way **86a**
Two Seasons Way **86a**
Tyndall, John 142b, **150c**
Tysoe, Walter 44a, 119a, **150c**
Ullman, S.O.A. 139b
Ulster Federation of Rambling Clubs
    150c
Ulster Society for the Preservation of the
    Countryside **150c**
Ulster Way 76a, 138c, **150c**
Ultimate Challenge **151a**
underwear 29b, 35c, 130b
union flannel 49c
United States *151*, **151a**, col
Unsworth, Walt 29a, *152*, **152b**
Upper Lea Valley Through Walk **86a**
Upper Nidderdale Way **86b**
Usk Valley Walk **86b**
V-quilting *131*, 131b
Vanguard Way **86b**
vapour transmission 94c, **153a**, 159a
veltschöen 129c
Venezuela 8c
Ventile 94b, **153a**
verglas 64c, 94b, **153a**
Vermuyden Way **86b**
Vibram 19b, **153a**
Victoria, *Queen* 43c, **153a**
Viking Way **86b**
Vinogradoff, *Professor* 142b
Virgil 59c
Volunteer Centre UK **153b**
'Volunteer Rifleman, A' 119b
Voysey, Robert T. 50c, **153b**
wadding 66a, 147a, **153b**
Wainwright, A. 50c, 97c, 120c, *153*, **153c**
waist strap 124a
Waite, John **154a**
Wales **154a**

Wales Tourist Board **154b**
Walker, A. **154b**
Walker, Kevin **154b**
'Walking Gentleman, A' *see* Grattan,
    Thomas Colley
walking stick 27
walking with children 109b, **154b**
WALKWAYS: Birmingham to
    Aberystwyth **86b**
WALKWAYS: Llangollen to Snowdon
    86c
Wallington, Mark **154c**
Walpole, Horace 57a
Walsh, John E 61a, **154c**
Ward, C.S. 15c
Ward, Edward **154c**
Ward, G.H.B. **154c**
Ward, Ken **155a**
Warner, Richard 18a, **155a**
water 50a
Watkins, Alfred 73b
Watson, G.C. **155c**
waxed cotton **155c**
wayfarer **156a**
Wayfarer's Walk **86c**
waymark 130b, *156*, **156a**
Wealdway **86c**
Wear Valley Way **86c**
Weardale Way **86c**
Weatherhead, G. Hume **156b**
Weaver Valley Way **86c**
Weaver's Way **87a**
Webb, Daniel Carless **156b**
Weeton, Ellen **157a**
Weir, Tom **157a**
Welsh 3000s 49b, 110a, **157a**
Wessex Way **87a**
West Highland Way 72b, 75c, *85*, 125c,
    157b
West Mendip Way **87a**
West Midland Way **87a**
West Way 75b
West, Thomas **157b**
Westacott, Hugh *157*, **157c**
Western Highlands **158a**, col
Westmorland Boundary Way **87a**
Westmorland Heritage Walk **87a**
Westmorland Way **87a**
Weston, Edward Payson **158b**
Weston, Noah *see* Southern, J.A.
Wey-South Path **87b**
Wharton, *Doctor* 57a
Wherry, George **158b**
White Peak Way **87b**
White Rose Walk **87b**
White, Richard Grant **158c**
White, Walter 135a, **158c**
white-out 132c, **158c**
Whymper, Edward **158c**
wick 153a, **159a**

wicket gate *see* kissing gate wicking 153a,
    159a
Wicklow Mountains **159a**
Wicklow Way **159a**
Wight Heritage Trail **87b**
Wilderness **159a**
Wildlife & Countryside Act, 1981 7a, 21a,
    23b, 24a, 50b, 100c, 115b, 122a,
    159b
Wilkinson, Thomas **159b**
Wills, Sir Alfred **159b**
Wilson, John 40c, **159b**
Wiltshire Way **87b**
wind chill 64b, *159*, **159b**
Winstanley, William **159c**
Winter Mountain Leader Scheme 128a
WIRA *see* British Textile Technology
    Group
Witches Way **87b**
Wolds Way 75c, **159c**
Wollstonecraft, Mary *see* Shelley, Mary
Wood, Charles 43c
Woodenpeg, Clavileno 111a
wool 140b, 150b, **160a**
Worcestershire Way **87b**
Wordsworth, Dora 30b, 57a, 160c, 163c
Wordsworth, Dorothy 30a, 72a, 122b,
    159b, **160a**, 160b
Wordsworth, John 30a, 160c
Wordsworth, Mary 160c
Wordsworth, William 29c, 55a, 57a, 69b,
    71b, 72a, 98a, 122b, 122c, 123a,
    137a, 145a, 159a, 160a, **160b**, 163c
Wright, Christopher John **160c**
Wright, Ralph 90b
Wychavon Way **87b**
Wye Valley AONB **161a**
Wye Valley Walk **87c**
Yoredale Way **87c**
Yorkshire Dales Centurion Walk **87c**
Yorkshire Dales Challenge Walk **87c**
Yorkshire Dales National Park *161*, **161a**,
    col
Yorkshire Pioneer Walk **87c**
Young, Julian Charles 160c, **163c**
Youth Hostels Association (England &
    Wales) 36a, 149b, **164a**
Youth Hostels Association of Northern
    Ireland **164b**
youth hostels 163c, *164*
zigzag walk 56c
Zug leather 129c